The Mar

D1363132

e of the most comprehensive

keting and sales available

from the

Published by Butterworth-Heinemann on behalf of the Chartered Institute of Marketing, the series is divided into three distinct groups: *Student* (fulfilling the needs of those taking the Institute's certificate and diploma qualifications); *Professional Development* (for those on formal or self-study training programmes); and *Practitioner* (presented in a more informal, motivating and highly practical manner for personal use).

Formed in 1911, the Chartered Institute of Marketing is now the largest professional marketing management body in Europe with over 22,000 members and 25,000 students located worldwide. Its primary objectives are focused on the development of awareness and understanding of marketing throughout UK industry and commerce and on the raising of standards of professionalism in the education, training and practice of this key business discipline.

Other titles in the series

The Marketing Book

Second Edition

Edited by
MICHAEL J. BAKER

Published on behalf of the
Chartered Institute of Marketing

Butterworth-Heinemann Ltd
Linacre House, Jordan Hill, Oxford OX2 8DP

 PART OF REED INTERNATIONAL BOOKS

OXFORD   LONDON   BOSTON
MUNICH   NEW DELHI   SINGAPORE   SYDNEY
TOKYO   TORONTO   WELLINGTON

First published 1987
Reprinted 1987, 1990 (twice)
Second edition 1991
Reprinted 1992

British Library Cataloguing in Publication Data
The Marketing Book–2nd ed.
  1. Marketing
  I. Baker, Michael J. (Michael John) *1935*–II. Chartered
Institute of Marketing III. Series
658.8

ISBN 0 7506 0023 3

Printed and bound in Great Britain by
Butler & Tanner Ltd, Frome and London

Contents

Illustrations

Tables

Contributors

Michael J. Baker, TD, BA, Bsc. (Econ), Cert. ITP, DBA, Dip.M, FCIM, F.CAM, FRSA, has been Professor of Marketing at the University of Strathclyde since its inception in 1971. After serving as Dean of the School of Business Administration/Strathclyde Business School, 1978–84, he was appointed Deputy Principal in 1984. He has been a Chairman of SCOTBEC (Scottish Business Education Council), Chairman of the Chartered Institute of Marketing, and Governor of the CAM Foundation.

After graduation (BA Durham) and military service, he spent six years in the steel industry selling flat-rolled products, followed by four years in further education as a lecturer in marketing. He attended Harvard Business School as a Foundation for Management Education Fellow 1968–71 and was awarded the Certificate of the International Teachers Programme and a Doctorate in Business Administration for research on industrial innovation (published as *Marketing New Industrial Products*, Macmillan, 1975). At Harvard he held an appointment as a research associate and taught the Creative Marketing Strategy Course, and he also held a research appointment at the Marketing Science Institute.

Winner of the Chartered Institute of Marketing's Gold Medal and designated Author of the Year 1978 for a paper entitled *Export Myopia*.

He is also the author/editor of fifteen books including *Marketing* 4th ed. (Macmillan, 1985), the most widely used UK text on the subject; *Marketing New Industrial Products* (Macmillan, 1975); *Offshore Inspection and Maintenance* (with S. T. Parkinson and M. A. Saren) (*The Financial Times*, 1978); *Industrial Innovation* (ed.) (Macmillan, 1979); *Market Development* (Penguin, 1983); *Marketing: Theory and Practice* 2nd ed. (Macmillan 1983); *Dictionary of Advertising and Marketing* (Macmillan, 2nd ed., 1990); *Marketing Strategy and Management* (Macmillan, 1985); *Organizational Buying Behaviour* (with S. T. Parkinson) (Macmillan, 1986); *The Role of Design in International Competitiveness* (with D. O. Ughanwa) (Routledge, 1989); *Marketing and Competitive Success* (with S. Hart) (Philip Allan, 1989); and he is the Editor of the *Journal of Marketing Management*.

David F. Birks, BA, MSc., Ph.D, is a lecturer in marketing at the University of Bath. Prior to this post, from 1985 to 1989, he administered and taught market research to the undergraduate and postgraduate classes in the Department of Marketing at Strathclyde University. His industrial experience was gained in the construction and housing industries where he was marketing manager of a housing association in the South of England. His doctoral research was based on the housing association movement, examining the problems of decision makers in expressing their information requirements.

Keith Blois, BA, Ph.D, is Fellow in Industrial Marketing at Templeton College, Oxford. His interests include the marketing of services as well as industrial marketing and he is currently researching into the effects of the advanced manufacturing technologies on marketing strategy and also the problems of increasing productivity in service firms. He has contributed to European and American journals on a variety of topics including economic theory, industrial marketing, industrial economics, the marketing of services and social responsibility. Prior to his current appointment he was Reader in Marketing at Loughborough University of Technology.

Douglas Brownlie a graduate in technology and business studies of the University of Strathclyde, worked in management services in the British Steel Corporation before joining the university to hold research and teaching posts in the Department of Marketing. During this period he launched research and consultancy interests in problems relating to the formulation of industrial marketing strategy. The major thrust of his research efforts was directed towards the diffusion of industrial innovation, and in particular the forecasting of long-term technical progress in offshore engineering.

In 1985 he joined the Department of Management Studies of the University of Glasgow where he now teaches marketing and marketing strategy to part-time MBA students. His current research efforts are devoted to the completion of a doctoral study of marketing strategy and competitiveness. He has published widely in the areas of industrial marketing, technological forecasting and strategic marketing planning.

James R. Bureau, a graduate in social studies from Durham University, began his career with five years' experience of market research for several large clients of a prominent London advertising agency. He became market research manager and then group brand manager for shaving and writing products at Gillette Industries and then Marketing Director of the Health and Chemical Products Division of Cadbury-Schweppes. Now teaches the Marketing III element of the BA degree course and administers the student counselling scheme for the University of Strathclyde Business School. He is the author of *Brand Management: Planning and Control*, (Macmillan, 1981).

Tom Cannon is Director of the Manchester Business School.

He has held previous teaching posts at Warwick University, Middlesex Polytechnic, Durham University Business School and Stirling University prior to taking up his present post in 1989. Besides this he has had industrial appointments in market research, export management and consumer marketing with large and small companies. He has extensive experience in small business management, education and training and has been actively involved in the development of such programmes as EXPORTS, Graduate Enterprise and Gateway Overseas as well as being Founding Director of the Scottish Enterprise Foundation.

He writes regularly for newspapers, magazines and journals, and makes regular contributions to TV and radio and he has written a number of books and numerous academic and professional papers largely in the fields of marketing, enterprise development and innovation. He holds several directorships besides being a member of a number of public bodies.

Peter M. Chisnall, MA, MSc., Ph.D, has had extensive business experience in many industries, including print, packaging, food and ceramic tableware, and he has written several standard marketing textbooks including *Marketing – A Behavioural Analysis* (McGraw-Hill), which won the 1976 Book Prize awarded by the European Association of Marketing Consultants.

Professor Chisnall is Dean of the Dublin Business School at Dublin City University. He acts as External Examiner at several academic institutions, is an assessor of the Market Research Society, and a Member of the Postgraduate Management Board of the Council for National Academic Awards (CNAA). He is a member of the Chartered Institute of Marketing and also of the Market Research Society, and is a Fellow of the Royal Society of Arts.

He contributed the marketing research section of the marketing handbook for PICKUP – a government programme to meet professional, industrial and commercial updating and training needs, and his research interests have included the influence of design on marketing strategies, and the contribution of market research to the development of health and social welfare policies.

In addition to academic work, Peter Chisnall is actively engaged in professional consultancy and marketing research projects. He is an industrial consultant researcher for the 'Open Door' research scheme organized by the Economic and Social Sciences Research Council.

Martin Christopher is Professor of Marketing and Logistics at Cranfield School of Management. He is the author of several books including *Strategy of Distribution Management* (Heinemann, 1986) and the editor of the *International Journal of Physical Distribution and Materials Management*. As a consultant he is actively involved with current problems in marketing and logistics in this country and overseas.

Donald W. Cowell, BA, MSc., Ph.D, FCIM. A graduate of the University of Leeds, he worked in the electrical engineering industry for eight years before going on to do a master's degree in management studies and a doctorate in marketing at the University of Loughborough where he was senior lecturer in marketing before moving on to a chair at Plymouth Business School.

Professor Cowell's current research interests are in the management of marketing, the effectiveness of marketing education and the marketing of services. He is author of a number of books, monographs and articles. His book, *The Marketing of Services* (Heinemann, 1984), is the major UK marketing text on this topic.

Keith Crosier, BSc., MSc., Dip. CAM, is a graduate in earth sciences, but spent most of his business career in advertising management with Olivetti in London and New York. He began lecturing at Teesside Polytechnic after a master's degree in management studies at the Durham University Business School and went to Strathclyde as a Foundation for Management Education Research Fellow, studying 'consumerism' in the UK, but stayed to take up a lectureship in marketing communications.

He is the author of many articles and conference papers and is Vice Chairman of the Marketing Education Group, Chartered Institute of Marketing Senior Examiner in Marketing Communications and an Associate Member of the History of Advertising Trust.

Peter Doyle is Professor of Marketing and Strategic Management at the University of Warwick. Previously he has taught at the London Business School, INSEAD, and Bradford University. He has also been Visiting Professor at Stanford, University of Hawaii and the University of South Carolina.

He graduated with a first in economics from Manchester University and took a Ph.D in industrial administration from Carnegie-Mellon University, USA. His research interests are in marketing modelling and strategic planning. Publications include five books and numerous articles in leading journals, including *Journal of Marketing Research, Management Science, Journal of Business, Journal of Marketing, Journal of the Operational Research Society* and the *Economic Journal*.

He is on the editorial boards of the *European Journal of Marketing, Journal of Business Research, International Journal of Advertising, International Journal of Research in Marketing* and the *Journal of Marketing Management* and he is a member of the Industry and Employment and International Activities Committees of the ESRC. He also acts as a consultant on international marketing and strategy with a number of companies including IBM, Shell, ICI, Unilever, 3M, Hewlett Packard, British Telecom and Marks and Spencer.

Keith Fletcher, MA, Ph.D, has recently been appointed a chair in the Graduate Business School at the University of Strathclyde. He has worked in insurance and linen hire and studied business and marketing at Leicester and Kingston Polytechnic, and marketing education at Lancaster University. He taught marketing at Brighton Polytechnic before moving to Strathclyde in 1980. He has published widely in the areas of consumer behaviour and the impact of information technology on marketing. He is author of *Marketing Management and IT* (Prentice Hall, 1990). He has recently received a research grant to investigate the diffusion of database marketing.

Gordon R. Foxall, BSc., MSc., Ph.D, FCIM, is a Professor of Marketing at the University of Birmingham. Since graduating in social science and undertaking applied research into the pricing of manufactured products, he has gained wide experience of teaching, research and consultancy. He took a Ph.D in consumer psychology at the University of Birmingham and has held lectureships in marketing and business policy at the Universities of Newcastle upon Tyne and Birmingham. Subsequently he was Reader in Marketing at Cranfield School of Management, where he taught managers at all levels and initiated new short courses in the development of new industrial products, and then Professor of Marketing at Strathclyde University.

He is author/co-author of nine books on marketing, including the bestselling *Consumer Behaviour* (Croom Helm, 1980), and he has also written over sixty academic papers on consumer choice, industrial innovation and related themes. His principal research interest is the innovative role of buyers in new product development.

He is currently conducting empirical investigations of buyer innovativeness in manufacturing industry (as part of the ESRC's Competitiveness of British Industry Initiative) and psychometric studies of consumers' cognitive styles and new product purchasing.

John Lidstone retired recently as Deputy Managing Director of Marketing Improvements Limited; Chairman of Management Consultancies Association, 1986–87; a Non-Executive Director of Kalamazoo plc; and a member of the National Executive Committee of the Chartered Institute of Marketing. Internationally recognized for his marketing consultancy lecturing, he began his career as an English master at Repton School. From 1952 to 1962 he held selling, marketing and management appointments with Shell-Mex and BP group and, before joining Marketing Improvements in 1965, he was sales manager and Deputy Managing Director of Vicon Agricultural Machinery Limited. The author of seven books on marketing, sales management and selling, *Training Salesmen on the Job* (Gower Press, 1986 and *Negotiating Profitable Sales* (Gower Press, 1981) were made into widely acclaimed, award-winning films by Rank and Video Arts. In 1981 John Lidstone was elected a Member of the British Academy of Film and Television Arts. He has recently rejoined the academic world at Surrey University.

Simon Majaro is Professor of Marketing at the Cranfield School of Management. He is Director of Strategic Management Learning and also Managing Director of a firm of international management consultants that bears his name, with offices in London and New York.

He is a graduate in law of the University of London, Barrister at Law, a graduate in business administration of the IMI, the Geneva-based business school, a Fellow of the Chartered Institute of Marketing, a Fellow of the Institute of Management Consultants and also a Fellow of the Royal Society of Arts.

After university he joined the plastics and chemical industries where he progressed through marketing responsibilities to become the Managing Director of an EEC-based Unilever Company. He left industry in order to return to the academic world, and for four years headed the Marketing Department at the IMI, where he was a full member of its faculty. For eight years he was a senior partner with Urwick Orr & Partners, and as visiting faculty member of a number of business schools and training centres in various parts of the world.

Simon Majaro is the author of *International Marketing – A Strategic Approach to World Markets* (Allen & Unwin, 1986) and *Marketing in Perspective* (Allen & Unwin, 1984). He is co-author of *Strategy Search* (Gower Publishing), and he has had many papers in the field of marketing and corporate planning published.

Malcolm McDonald is Professor of Marketing Planning and Director of the Distance Education Centre at the Cranfield School of Management and a Director of a number of companies. He is a graduate in English language and literature from Oxford University, in business studies from Bradford University Management Centre, and has a Ph.D from the Cranfield Institute of Technology. He has extensive industrial experience, including a number of years as Marketing Director of Canada Dry. During the past ten years he has run a series of successful seminars and workshops on marketing planning in the UK, Europe, the Far East, Australasia and the USA. He has written ten books on marketing and many of his papers have been published. He is editor of *International Marketing Review*.

Arthur Meidan is Professor of Marketing at the School of Management and Economic Studies at the University of Sheffield and Director of the MBA Programme. He has spent over eighteen years in management teaching, instructing, consulting and researching. He is the author of many articles, monographs and textbooks including *The Appraisal of Managerial Performance* (American Marketing Association, 1981); *Marketing Applications of Operational Research Techniques* (MCB University Press, 1981); *Bank Marketing Management* (Macmillan, 1984); and *Industrial Salesforce Management* (Croom Helm, 1986).

Stan Paliwoda, BA, MSc., Ph.D, MIEx, began his career in sales. He was lecturer in marketing and international business at the Manchester School of Management, UMIST and is currently Professor of Marketing at the University of Calgary, Canada. He is the author of five books including the popular text *International Marketing* (Heinemann, 1986); *Advances in International Marketing* (Routledge, 1990); and, with Peter Turnbull, *Research in International Marketing* (Croom-Helm, 1986). He is consultant editor of *MBA Review* and on the Editorial Board of the *Journal of Global Marketing* and *Journal of Teaching in International Business*. Research interests include East-West trade. He has taught marketing in many of the previously centrally-planned economies of Eastern Europe and Africa which have moved towards political and economic liberalization.

Stephen T. Parkinson is Professor of Marketing in the University of Bradford Management Centre. He is a Director of two companies specialising in industrial marketing consultancy and management training and development. He has published widely in the area of industrial marketing and more recently the use of computers in marketing. He is the author of *New Product Development in the Engineering Industry* (CUP, 1984), *Organizational Buying Behaviour* (with M. J. Baker) (Macmillan, 1986); *Using the Microcomputer* (with Lynn K. Parkinson) (McGraw-Hill, 1987). He has recently received a research grant from the Economic and Social Research Council to investigate the impact of the diffusion of EPOS scanning systems on the relationship between retailers and their suppliers.

Nigel Piercy Professor in Marketing and Business Policy and Head of Marketing and Strategy at Cardiff Business School, in the University of Wales. He has published widely on marketing and management and was the UK Marketing Author of the Year in 1980, 1981 and 1982. His books include *Export Strategy: Markets and Competition* (Allen & Unwin, 1982); *Managing Marketing Information* (joint-author) (Croom Helm, 1983); *The Management Implications of New Information Technology* (ed.) (Croom Helm, 1984). *Marketing Organization* (Allen & Unwin, 1985), *Marketing Budgeting* (Croom Helm, 1986), and *Management Information Systems: The Technology Challenge* (ed.) (Croom Helm, 1986).

John Saunders National Westminster Bank Professor of Marketing at the University of Technology, Loughborough. Previously he has worked for Bradford University Management Centre, the University of Warwick, the Pacific-Asian Management Institute (Hawaii) and the Hawker Siddeley Group.

He has a first degree in Aeronautical Engineering from Loughborough University, an MBA from Cranfield Institute of Technology and a doctorate from Bradford University. His research interests are marketing strategy, South-East Asia, computer and model-assisted marketing and his publications include several books, business games and over fifty articles in leading professional journals.

As a senior consultant he has worked with many companies and institutions. These include Unilever, ICI, TI, THF, Dixons, Woolworth, British Standards Institute, the Asian Development Bank and the Singapore Government.

Peter Spillard is a senior lecturer of Marketing at the University of Lancaster. He gained a BSc. (Econ) from the LSE and has spent a couple of extended periods as a Visiting Fellow at the University of Washington, Seattle and CIT Melbourne.

Author of *Sales Promotion : its Place in Marketing Strategy* 2nd ed. (Business Publications, 1977) and *Organization and Marketing* (Croom Helm, 1985), his work has also appeared from time to time in UK marketing journals.

With seven years practical marketing experience in industry and many marketing assignments both at home and overseas now behind him, his main research and consultancy activities concern the problems posed by the complex yet strategically important relationships between a firm's strategy and its structure.

Michael J. Thomas, BSc. MBA, FRSA, FCIM, having worked for the Metal Box Company in the 1950s, emigrated to the United States where he spent eleven years teaching on post-graduate courses in the School of Management, Syracuse University. He joined the Department of Marketing at Lancaster University in 1972 and was appointed Professor of Marketing at Strathclyde University in January, 1987. He is on the National Council of the Chartered Institute of Marketing, Chairman of the Marketing Education Group, a frequent visitor to overseas markets including Nigeria, Poland and, of course, North America. He is particularly interested in the management of new product development, brand management problems, and export marketing. He is the author of the *Pocket Guide to Marketing* (Economist/Basil Blackwell, 1986) and of *The Marketing Handbook* 3rd ed. (Gower, 1989).

Peter W. Turnbull is Professor of Marketing and a member of the marketing faculty in the Department of Management Sciences of Manchester Institute of Science and Technology. He is a well-known researcher and writer in the field of industrial and international marketing. His books include *International Marketing and Purchasing* (Macmillan, 1981); *Strategies for International Industrial Marketing* (John Wiley, 1986); and *Research in International Marketing*.

Additionally, he has written numerous articles for scholarly management journals. He has lectured widely in Western Europe and North America and has acted as consultant to a number of national and international companies.

Robin Wensley is Professor of Strategic Management and Marketing and Dean of the School of Industrial and Business Studies, University of Warwick. He was previously with RHM Foods, Tube Investments and the London Business School and a visiting professor at UCLA and University of Florida. He acts as consultant for many major companies including British Telecom, Philips NV, ICL, IBM, Glaxo, and the Ellerman Group. His research and consultancy interests include marketing strategy and planning, investment decision making and qualitative market research. He has co-authored a book and a number of articles in these areas and works closely with other academics and practitioners both in Europe and the USA.

John Winkler is well-known in this country for his knowledge of pricing techniques and has established an international reputation for his seminars for senior executives which have been held around the world in twenty-two countries. From IBM in New Zealand, to BASF and ICI in Australia, to Johnson & Johnson in South Africa and SKF in Sweden, Esso, BP, the Post Office, Mobil and many more blue chip clients in this country, to Libbey Owens Ford, Lady Seymour, and Dairylea among many others in the USA, he has taught their top people those techniques made famous in his bestselling book *Pricing for Results* (Heinemann, 1984) which has gone into eight languages, including Japanese. He has won the prestigious award of the Communauté Européene des Conseils en Marketing et Animateurs de Vente in Geneva. He was a Marketing Director at J Lyons and Co. and was also the Marketing Correspondent for *The Times*.

Editor's preface to the First Edition

The *New Collins Concise English Dictionary* offers thirteen distinct definitions of the word 'the', of which the ninth is 'the best, only, or most remarkable'. Certainly, this is not the only book on marketing, which means that, as editor, I must consider it the best and/or the most remarkable book on the subject. In fact, I consider it to be both in terms of the kind of book it is and the quality of the contributions it contains. A brief review of the origins and nature of the project may help explain why.

The origin of the proposal to compile a definitive handbook on marketing was a suggestion made by Malcolm McDonald to the Publications Committee of the Chartered Institute of Marketing. This committee, in conjunction with Heinemann the publisher, has been responsible for the very successful series of specialist texts on virtually all aspects of marketing. What was seen to be lacking, however, was an authoritative overview of the marketing function and its practice which would serve as a first point of reference for experienced practitioners and managers from other functions, and as an introduction to those embarking on a career in marketing. In short, the kind of book which every member of the Institute would find relevant and useful.

The Institute and Heinemann invited me to assume responsibility for the venture and suggested

(in June 1986!) that if I could produce a manuscript by the beginning of 1987 then it would be possible to publish the book in the summer and thereby celebrate the first appointment of a marketing educator to the Chair of the Institute. In discussion with Norman Waite of the Chartered Institute of Marketing, and Douglas Fox of Heinemann, I developed a 'product specification' and on 16 July 1986 I wrote to twenty-two unsuspecting individuals inviting them to join me in the venture.

> To produce an authoritative handbook setting out the scope and nature of the marketing function, its managerial applications and its contribution to corporate success.

Of the twenty-two, two were unable to accept the invitation to contribute a chapter in the time available but alternative experts were quickly found meeting the requirement that they be specialists in their field and able to write clearly, effectively and with authority. As the contents list shows, the authors of Chapters 2 to 23 inclusive meet these criteria with many of them enjoying international reputations as the authors of definitive textbooks on their subjects. As for the book itself, it falls into four main parts:

Organizing and planning for marketing (Chapters 1–5)

The framework of marketing   (Chapters 6–11)
Managing the marketing function   (Chapters 12–18)
The application of marketing   (Chapters 19–24)

In the first part we seek to establish what marketing is and, equally important, what it is not.

Chapter 1, for which I accept full responsibility, explores the nature and boundaries of marketing and seeks to explain why an activity which has been practised since the first commercial transaction was concluded should have only come to prominence in the last forty years. Although one of my distinguished former students frequently chides me for posing the question 'What is marketing?', I remain unrepentant. In defining anything it is as important to understand clearly what is to be *excluded* as it is to know what is to be *included*. Even more important, one must distinguish the counterfeit from the real for there are many activities passed off as marketing which have little or nothing to do with the practice enshrined in the marketing concept.

In *Chapter 2*, which covers marketing and competitive success, Professor John Saunders draws heavily upon military analogy in exploring the nature of competition and the strategic alternatives open to business firms as they struggle for survival and success. The ideas of Sun Tzu and his more recent disciple Clausewitz pervade the chapter and provide a robust framework for the commercial and economic analyses developed by Michael Porter and others.

The chapter itself falls into three main parts. The first comprises Porter's seminal works on *Competitive Strategy* and *Competitive Advantage* and the dominant strategic positions that are available and how they can be achieved are discussed. The second part follows the military analogy, as extolled by Kotler and others, to explain the dynamics of achieving tactical advantage over competition. Lastly, the research by Doyle *et al.* is used to show why many British firms have failed when facing Japanese competition.

I found this chapter an excellent summary and review of current thinking on the strategic options open to the firm with its emphasis upon the fact that business is *not* a game and that winning is everything. To win, however, it is necessary not only to know what options are available but to have the

experience and judgement to know which is most appropriate in a 'game' with a minimum of two players. It is also important to recognize the benefits of alternative interpretations and the opportunities created by innovative new solutions. Even the most convincing arguments should not necessarily be accepted at face value – there is always an alternative hypothesis. For example, are the differences reported in Doyle *et al.*'s study between UK and Japanese firms/managers competing in the UK market due to the fact that UK managers are defending and the Japanese attacking?

In *Chapter 3*, Professor Robin Wensley of Warwick University develops many of the themes introduced in John Saunders' analysis of the contribution of marketing to competitive success. In Wensley's view, business appears to be obsessed with strategy to the extent that *all* business decisions now seem to be strategic. To address the questions of whether strategic marketing decisions are really different from other marketing decisions, and just what is marketing strategy, this chapter first provides a definition, then examines a marketing strategy statement and an explicit statement of strategic marketing decisions. These concepts are illustrated in the context of Honda's decision to enter the US motorcycle market. Finally, the author considers both the role and forms of analysis in marketing strategy and some future issues.

Wensley is undoubtedly at the forefront of thinkers and writers on the subject of marketing strategy and the reader is invited to pay particular attention to his comments on 'facts, lies and doubts' – PIMS and Porter may never be the same again!

In *Chapter 4*, Peter Spillard of Lancaster University addresses directly the issue only touched on in the preceding chapter, namely, that strategy and planning are executed in an organizational context by people. Until comparatively recently, however, very little attention has been given to organizational issues in marketing and the 'people factor', save for the inevitable reference to motivating the sales force. As the author of a definitive text, *Organization and Marketing* (Croom Helm, 1985), Spillard is best qualified to remedy this deficiency and show how the structure of an organization may affect its strategy and vice versa. More so his analysis is specific to the nature of marketing and its tasks and provides clear guidance on the development, positioning and integration of a marketing function within an organization.

In that the idea for this book was originally conceived by Malcolm McDonald, it is only just that he should be required to make a substantial contribution to it. As the author of the bestselling British text, *Marketing Plans* (Heinemann, 1984), Malcolm was the logical choice for *Chapter 5*.

The chapter is in three sections. The first describes the widespread ignorance about strategic marketing planning and confusion about the difference between strategic marketing planning and sales forecasting and budgeting, which encourages business people to perpetuate an essentially parochial and short-term view of business. It also describes the resulting commonality of operating problems, which centre around declining organizational effectiveness and confusion over what to do about it.

The second section describes the marketing planning process itself and concentrates on the key steps – the marketing audit and the setting of marketing objectives and strategies.

The third section concludes the chapter by describing the necessary ingredients for success in the design and implementation of marketing planning systems.

Clear, succinct and above all else practical, this is essential reading for anyone charged with a responsibility for marketing planning.

Douglas Brownlie of Glasgow University is the author of *Chapter 6*, which covers environmental analysis, a topic in which he has undertaken extensive research and has considerable experience – and introduces the second part of the text which is concerned with the conceptual underpinnings of marketing practice. In Douglas's own words his chapter 'constructs an argument in favour of the view that formal environmental scanning provides a general methodological framework within which the tasks of environmental analysis and forecasting can be conducted.'

As became clear in the preceding chapter by Malcolm McDonald, environmental analysis is a vital input to the whole process of strategic planning. This chapter explains why it is so vital, what needs to be done and how to set about it. The discussion is comprehensive and amounts to a state of the art review of issues in and approaches to scanning the environment to provide early warning of the threats and opportunities the firm is likely to encounter. The treatment is thorough and tends to the academic in style and presentation, but practitioners will find considerable food for thought and welcome the helpful figures and tables which will serve as excellent aide-mémoires for implementation.

When invited to contribute a chapter on consumer behaviour to this book, Gordon Foxall was based at Cranfield – I am delighted to say he is now Professor of Marketing at Strathclyde. An international and widely published authority on his subject, Dr Foxall has avoided duplicating the widely available findings of his research into various aspects of consumer behaviour by delineating carefully the scope of the research findings he discusses. The themes covered in *Chapter 7* embrace the broad components of consumer research – individual consumer decision making, patterns of aggregate buying behaviour over time, and personal determinants of choice and style of decision taking. Further, the topics which illustrate these themes have been chosen deliberately to exemplify the current status of consumer research as a subdiscipline of marketing and emphasize its relevance to the practice.

Clearly written, easy to follow but academically rigorous, this chapter underlines that ultimately successful marketing is about satisfying consumers and that to do so we must first understand what makes them behave the way they do.

Chapter 8 shifts the emphasis from the consumer as an individual to the individual as a member of an organization. Organizational buying behaviour has become the subject of considerable interest and attention in the past two decades and Peter Turnbull of UMIST provides a comprehensive review of the seminal contributions to the literature over this period. As he comments in his opening paragraph:

An understanding of the organizational buying process is fundamental to the development of appropriate industrial marketing strategy. The organizational buyer is influenced by a wide variety of factors both from outside and within the organization. Understanding these factors and their interrelationships is critical to the competitive positioning of the business, to the development of appropriate market and product development plans, and to the management of the whole marketing task of the business.

Quite so, and this chapter provides the basis for

developing such an understanding.

It was Lord Kelvin who observed that if you cannot measure something then you know nothing about it. Few marketers would go so far and qualitative research methods enjoy a significant place in the marketers repertoire of techniques for improving their understanding of the markets they are seeking to serve. That said, quantitative methods also have a vital role to play in enabling the marketer to describe and analyse customers and markets and in this chapter, Dr Arthur Meidan, of Sheffield University, reviews some of the more appropriate and widely used techniques.

Opening *Chapter 9* with a review of factors which have delayed the take up of quantitative techniques in marketing – such as the complexity of marketing phenomena and the instability of marketing relationships – Arthur Meidan suggests that the development of computer software has significantly improved both access to and application of quantitative techniques to marketing problems. The chapter itself consists of a synoptic overview of such techniques classified into seven categories: multivariate methods; regression and forecasting techniques; simulation; statistical decision theory (stochastic methods); deterministic operational research methods; hybrid techniques; and network programming. For those unfamiliar with these methods, this chapter provides an excellent summary of what is available and when and how to use the particular techniques while the experienced analyst will find this a valuable guide and aide-mémoire.

The themes of information for marketing decision making are continued in *Chapter 10* by Dr Stephen Parkinson of Henley. Like quantitative methods, computers tend to 'scare off' many managers who see them more as a threat than a benefit. This chapter should do much to dispel this fear as it presents a clear overview of the contribution which computers can make to improving marketing decision making. It also provides a summary of the main stages in auditing the requirement for computer applications and developing a strategy to introduce the computer effectively.

Chapter 11 is by Dr Nigel Piercy of UWIST and is concerned with that management process in marketing which involves coping with diverse sources of marketing information and intelligence. As a starting point, information management is shown to be central to marketing's boundary-spanning role in the organization, in terms of exploiting information as a resource for supporting decision-making processes, and also as a 'marketing asset' providing a potential source of competitive advantage. In all this, however, it is important not to raise unrealistic expectations about such phenomena as the miracles of new information technology and the automation of decision making through information systems, but to stay within the bounds of what can usefully be achieved in a practical marketing setting. For this reason it is important to recognize various constraints and problem areas. It is possible then to provide a framework for tackling the problem of developing a marketing information system, and to put this framework into the context of the implications of new information technology and the organizational requirements for effective information processing. The chapter concludes by highlighting the need for an information strategy in marketing.

The third part of the book opens with an evaluation of the marketing mix and its constituent elements each of which is then examined in some detail.

Chapter 12 is by Peter Doyle, Professor of Marketing at Warwick University, and sets the scene for a discussion of the four Ps (product, price, promotion, and place).

Two key decisions are seen as central to marketing management – the selection of target markets which determine where the firm will compete and the design of the marketing mix which will determine its success in these markets. To this end, Doyle reviews target marketing, the differential advantage and the key analyses for developing the marketing mix. As he observes: 'In today's rapidly changing and highly competitive international environment a business can only be successful if its offer matches the wants of buyers at least as effectively as its best competitors. Marketing management is the task of planning this match.' And this chapter provides both guidance and advice on how to do so.

As Michael Thomas notes in his introduction to *Chapter 13*, product development and management are central to the marketing function. We are reminded that, while many observers consider marketing largely to be about selling and promotion, it is the product which is the heart of the process and that attention to it must permeate all marketing activity. Such an emphasis is welcome for it reflects a maturing of marketing thought and a distancing from the early and essentially misconceived criticism of the so-called production orientation.

Given that the product lies at the core of all marketing, and is thus addressed explicitly or implicitly in every chapter. Professor Thomas has chosen an eclectic approach and selected six topics for discussion – product development, strategic management of the product mix, the product life cycle, portfolio management, productivity analysis and the future of brand/product management. The treatment presumes a certain degree of prior knowledge, much of which is to be found elsewhere in this book, but some reference to the recommended readings may also be necessary to put these specific topics into context.

Like several other authors who have contributed to this book, John Winkler has written a definitive textbook on a subject which he has now been asked to encapsulate within the scope of *Chapter 14*. While many of the contributions have a slight academic flavour to them Winkler's approach is unashamedly practitioner biased. Few would disagree with his observation that 'The most critical factor in business, in its effect upon profits in the short term, is price. Put simply, pricing decisions are often arbitrary, usually hurried, sometimes a mess and seldom tested'. This deficiency he sets out to remedy with a clear and comprehensive analysis of how to set prices, price negotiation, price presentation, price bargaining and pricing management. Master this chapter and you should never be guilty of mishandling the price decision again.

Chapter 15 is written by the author of a bestseller on the subject of selling – John Lidstone. As noted in my introductory chapter, in the first flush of evangelical enthusiasm for marketing there was a distinct danger of dismissing the sales function as obsolescent if not dead. As Lidstone points out, all other business activities are worthless until a sale is made and, fortunately, this is reflected in a resurgence of interest in a professional selling function. If justification were needed, this chapter provides it but, equally important, the committed and experienced sales person will find much of interest and value here too.

As Keith Crosier explains in the introduction to

Chapter 16 on promotion, this is the collective noun for a wide spectrum of activities which are probably the most visible (and audible) manifestations of marketing and frequently mistaken by its critics as the totality of the subject. Having defined the specialist activities subsumed within the catchall of 'promotion', Crosier focuses upon advertising as 'the most complex and sophisticated to plan, implement, control and evaluate'. While largely descriptive of the institutions and practices of advertising the chapter contains a number of very helpful checklists and summaries which together give the reader a good feel for an activity which is often shrouded in mystery due to its 'creative' associations.

'Distribution and customer service' is the title of *Chapter 17* contributed by Professor Martin Christopher of Cranfield School of Management. About thirty years ago Peter Drucker described distribution as marketing's 'dark continent' and so it largely remains today despite the pioneering efforts of explorers like Christopher. As he explains with both force and clarity, a major reason for this may well be that traditionally, distribution has been seen as a function which only adds costs when in reality it also has the potential to add significant value. You only have to consider the frequently cited reason of 'poor delivery' as a justification for not buying British to realize that this chapter's emphasis contains a vital message for marketers struggling to develop a competitive advantage.

Chapter 18 is contributed by my colleague at Strathclyde, Jack Bureau. Although it is over ten years since Jack left a very successful career in product and brand management for the groves of academe I know he will regard it as a compliment when I say that this chapter is distinctly practitioner orientated. The need for effective control of marketing rests on six propositions:

1 Most marketing recommendations are based on speculation not facts.
2 Because of the speculative nature of marketing decision making, failure is normal.
3 Good marketing is expensive.
4 Marketing activity has high public visibility.
5 Marketing mistakes are difficult to reverse.
6 Marketing is cross-functional.

and results in three sets of routine which have to be

clearly identified and understood: corporate control systems; marketing department control systems; and external control systems.

Like distribution this is a neglected subject and Bureau provides a valuable service in his comprehensive overview of the issues involved.

The final section of the book contains five chapters which look at the application of marketing in a variety of contexts – industrial, international, services, small business and NPOs – all of which are emerging as distinctive subfields of the general discipline. The first of these is by Dr Peter Chisnall of Manchester Business School, another author of a definitive textbook on his topic – industrial marketing. Building upon the arguments presented by Turnbull in his chapter on organizational buying behaviour, Chisnall points to the size and importance of industrial markets and the need to develop a professional approach to selling and negotiation if one is to succeed in an increasingly competitive marketplace. As he points out in *Chapter 19*, 'To become efficient in marketing is not to debase in any way the qualities of technical efficiency of industrial products. Marketing has a role to play which should be viewed as strengthening and extending the technical attraction of products by targeting them at industrial firms where they are most likely to be successful . Required reading for those who still cling to a production orientation.

Another enormous subject in its own right is international marketing and this topic is addressed by Professor Simon Majaro, author of the bestselling *International Marketing* (Allen & Unwin, 1986). *Chapter 20* opens with a discussion on the similarities and differences between domestic and international marketing and it is emphasized that while the skills required for carrying out marketing tasks may be more or less the same, the knowledge and attitudinal factors usually vary significantly. This leads naturally into a discussion of the benefits of international marketing, organizational issues and three key issues which face any individual or organization thinking of 'going international': researching world markets; identifying the best markets for development; and standardizing the marketing mix – myth or reality? Checklists and diagrams provide an excellent foundation for getting to grips with this subject. Overall a very practical chapter which emphasizes its own central message – international marketing is something you *do*.

Chapter 21 by Professor Don Cowell, Dean of the Plymouth Business School, looks generally at the emerging topic of marketing services. The service sector is now the largest in terms of employment and is a major contributor to national output and 'invisible' earnings yet has been relatively neglected by marketing scholars. The chapter touches on two areas of concern. First, the problems of defining what is a service to delimit the boundaries of service marketing. It concludes that differences between services and goods are not fundamental. Services are a special kind of product. Second, adaptations to general marketing principles and practices may be required. Some general examples are given where further work is required to illustrate the scope there is for substantial further development of this topic.

In *Chapter 22*, Professor Tom Cannon of the University of Stirling addresses the subject of marketing for small businesses, a subject on which he is a major authority and of which he has considerable practical experience, particularly with the establishment of the Scottish Enterprise Foundation. As he points out in his introduction, there has been growing recognition in recent years of the major contribution made to the overall growth and health of economies by the small business sector. That said, it is also true that the overall growth in the number of small firms is relatively low in that the 'deaths' almost equal the births. Given this situation considerable attention has been addressed to improving the performance of small firms not least in the area of marketing. The dilemma, as Cannon points out, is whether marketing thinkers should be exploring ways in which ideas and practices developed in larger organizations may be adapted to fit with the need of smaller enterprises or whether smaller enterprises should be encouraged to modify their *modus operandi* to embrace practices and techniques used by larger and successful firms.

From a review of these broad alternatives, Tom Cannon concludes that a combination of both these approaches is required. He asserts 'the small business sector is too large and important to be ignored by marketing thinkers, while key features of marketing need to be appreciated by entrepreneurs if their enterprises are to prosper'. To achieve this he proposes a contingency model of marketing, together with much practical and useful advice.

Keith Blois, Fellow of Templeton College Oxford, is the author of *Chapter 23* which examines marketing for non-profit organizations. While marketing academics have long accepted the potential for transferring ideas and practices developed in a commercial environment to non-profit organizations it is only comparatively recently that such organizations have demonstrated any willingness to consider such a proposition. As Blois notes 'members of non-profit organizations often have a core product which is unchangeable because of their beliefs, convictions, training or the law. Often their commitment to supply their product is based upon a genuine desire to service the public. However, without marketing, two things can and do happen which lessen the value of what they do. First, their preoccupation with their core product (and its importance to them) can blinker them to the overall needs of their customers and ways in which their product can be augmented to increase consumer satisfaction. Second, when additions and alterations are made they sometimes, over time, become rigidly associated with the core product even though they are not essential to the achievement of the organization's prime goal. The consequence of this being both the deflection of resources from the achievement of the prime goal and consumer dissatisfaction, if the preoccupation with the extended product distracts from considering consumers' current needs'.

This chapter is required reading for anyone who doubts that marketing can make a significant contribution to furthering the objectives of non-profit organizations.

Finally, *Chapter 24* is an indulgence of the editor. Faced with the question of writing an 'end piece' it was clear that there was no way in which I could hope to summarize or add to the contributions of such a distinguished group of authors. However, a recurring theme selected independently by many of the authors is that marketing is essentially dynamic and future orientated. Accordingly, my indulgence is to conclude with a speculative forward look of my own which suggests that the turbulence of the 1970s and early 1980s heralded a significant change from a materialist, industrialized society with an emphasis upon quantity to a less materialistic, post-industrial society concerned with quality. Either way, marketing will have a continuing and important role to play.

In conclusion, it must be recognized that the authors and editor are only partially responsible for this finished product. Behind the scenes a great deal of effort has been put into the translation of a manuscript into a finished book. The credit for this belongs to the editorial staff at Heinemann and particularly to my personal assistant, Margaret Potts.

Michael J. Baker
University of Strathclyde 1987

Preface to the Second Edition

The Marketing Book was first published in August 1987 and was an immediate success with the first print run selling out within a month. Clearly the perceived need for 'an authoritative overview of the marketing function and its practice' was a real one and the book was seen as meeting this. Given the continuing interest in the book and the demand for further imprints the opportunity has now been taken to produce a second, revised edition.

The structure and approach of the book remain largely as described in the original *Preface* and will not be repeated here. Indeed the majority of the authors contributing to the first edition have decided not to modify their chapters on the grounds that their emphasis upon key issues, concepts and techniques has left their material unaffected by the comparatively minor developments in theory and practice since the publication of the first edition. The exceptions where the authors have taken the opportunity to 'tidy up' their input are:

Chapter 4   Organization for marketing by Peter Spillard
Chapter 6   Environmental analysis by Douglas Brownlie
Chapter 19   Promotion by Keith Crosier
Chapter 25   Marketing services by Donald Cowell
Chapter 27   Non-profit organizations and marketing by Keith Blois

Thus the main change compared with the first edition is the inclusion of the four additional chapters, namely:

Chapter 9   Market research by David Birks
Chapter 11   Information technology in marketing and sales by Keith Fletcher
Chapter 18   Branding by Peter Doyle
Chapter 24   International marketing – getting started by Stan Paliwoda

The omission of a chapter on market research in the first edition was clearly a major oversight on the editor's part. It has now been rectified by a contribution from David Birks of the University of Bath. In common with other contributors, Dr Birks seeks to provide an overview of the nature and contribution of market research from a non-technical, general practitioner's point of view. Commencing with an assessment of the *purpose* of market research the chapter emphasizes the importance of problem recognition and definition as a basis for effective research into marketing problems. In addressing such problems the choice between the use of qualitative and/or quantitative approaches is a key issue for the user/practitioner and is discussed at some length as are the attributes of researchers and the ways in which marketer and market researcher can work together most effectively.

Since the government launched its campaign to increase awareness of information technology (IT) in 1982 many firms have gained benefits from adopting IT, while others have made costly mistakes. In the new *Chapter 11*, Dr Keith Fletcher of Strathclyde University explains first the nature of IT and its importance. Attention is then focused on the impact of IT on marketing and two areas of particular importance to marketing managers – data base marketing and marketing information systems – are explored. Using a three level analysis of industry, firm and strategy the way in which IT is affecting exchange relationships and the nature of competition is explained and the strategic responses outlined.

Since the publication of the first edition there has been a considerable upsurge of interest in brands and branding as elements of the marketing mix. To reflect this interest a new *Chapter 18* has been included. Entitled *Branding*, this piece by Peter Doyle first appeared in the summer 1989 issue of the *Journal of Marketing Management* and is reproduced here with the Editor's permission. The debate on whether to include brands on the balance sheet has created much of the new interest in branding strategies, particularly as successful brands clearly generate higher returns on sales and on investment. In an analysis of the factors underlying successful brand development quality and service are shown to be more important than advertising. Doyle then explores the comparative advantages of buying brands versus building and developing them internally as well as the logic and economics behind brand extension strategies.

With the approach of 1992 in Europe and the continuing growth of international competition the opportunity has been taken to add to Simon Majaro's review of international marketing by including a new chapter focused on getting started in international marketing. *Chapter 24* is contributed by Dr Stan Paliwoda of the Manchester School of Management at UMIST where he is senior lecturer in international marketing and the author of numerous articles and a text book on the subject. Opening with a reprise of the issue addressed by Majaro – is international marketing different? – Paliwoda argues that it is significantly different from selling in foreign markets and requires a long-term commitment by the seller to meeting the needs of new customer groupings. Based upon a review of the benefits of 'going abroad' the author stresses the importance of indepth marketing research and provides detailed guidance on how to undertake this and assess both the risks and opportunities involved. Practical advice is also offered on overcoming psychic or psychological distance, segmentation, modes of market entry and dealing with competitive response. The chapter concludes with an examination of the implications of 1992 and the single European market as well as changes in Eastern Europe and their implications for East-West trade. A useful section on documentation on foreign markets is also provided.

As with the first edition the authors and editor would welcome feedback and suggestions as to how this handbook may be improved and extended to meet the needs of marketing practitioners. Meanwhile we sincerely hope you find the book a useful addition to your ready-reference library.

Michael J. Baker
University of Strathclyde 1990

PART ONE

Organizing and planning for marketing

1
One more time – what is marketing?

MICHAEL J. BAKER

The enigma of marketing is that it is one of man's oldest activities and yet it is regarded as the most recent of the business disciplines.
Michael J. Baker, *Marketing: Theory and Practice*, 1st Ed., Macmillan 1976

Introduction

As a discipline, marketing is in the process of transition from an art which is practised to a profession with strong theoretical foundations. In doing so it is following closely the precedents set by professions such as medicine, architecture and engineering, all of which have also been practised for thousands of years and have built up a wealth of descriptive information concerning the art which has both chronicled, and advanced its evolution. At some juncture, however, continued progress demands a transition from description to analysis, such as that initiated by Harvey's discovery of the circulation of the blood. If marketing is to develop it, too, must make the transition from art to applied science and develop sound theoretical foundations, mastery of which should become an essential qualification for practice.

Adoption of this proposition is as threatening to many of today's marketers as the establishment of the British Medical Association was to the surgeon–barber. But, today, you would not dream of going to a barber for medical advice.

Of course, first aid will still be practised, books on healthy living will feature on the bestsellers list and harmless potions will be bought over the counter in drug stores and pharmacies. This is an amateur activity akin to much of what passes for marketing in British industry. While there is no threat of the cancer of competition it may suffice, but, once the Japanese, West Germans and others invade your markets you are going to need much stronger medicine if you are to survive. To do so you must have the courage to face up to the reality that aggressive competition can prove fatal, quickly; have the necessary determination to resist rather than succumb, and seek the best possible professional advice and treatment to assist you. Unfortunately many people are unwilling to face up to reality. Even more unfortunate, many of the best minds and abilities are concentrated in activities which support the essential functions of an economy, by which we all survive, but have come to believe that these can exist by themselves independent of the manufacturing heart. Bankers, financiers, politicians and civil servants all fall into this category. As John Harvey-Jones pointed out so eloquently in the 1986 David Dimbleby lecture, over two-thirds of our wealth is created by manufacturing industry and much of the output of service industries is dependent upon manufactured products for its continued existence. To assume service industries can replace manufacturing as the heart and engine of economic growth is naive to say the least as shown by the example that it would require a doubling of tourist traffic from 6 to 12 million to generate £2 billion profit, which is what ICI achieved in 1985.

But, merely to increase the size of manufacturing .

industry will not solve any of our current problems. Indeed the contraction and decline of our manufacturing industry is not directly attributable to government and the city – it is largely due to the incompetence of industry itself. Those that survive will undoubtedly be the fittest and *all* will testify to the importance of marketing as an essential requirement for continued success.

However, none of this preamble addresses the central question 'What is marketing?' save perhaps to suggest that it is a newly emerging discipline inextricably linked with manufacturing. But, this latter link is of extreme importance because in the evangelical excess of its original statement, marketing and production were caricatured as antithetically opposed to one another. A quarter of a century later most marketers have developed sufficient self-confidence not to feel it necessary to 'knock' another function to emphasize the importance and relevance of their own. So, what is marketing?

Marketing is both a managerial orientation – some would claim a business philosophy – and a business function. To understand marketing it is essential to distinguish clearly between the two.

Marketing as a managerial orientation

> Management . . . the technique, practice, or science of managing or controlling; the skilful or resourceful use of materials, time, etc. *Collins Concise English Dictionary*

Ever since people have lived and worked together in groups there have been managers concerned with solving the central economic problem of maximizing satisfaction through the utilization of scarce resources. And, if we trace the course of economic development we find that periods of rapid growth have followed changes in the manner in which work is organized, usually accompanied by changes in technology. Thus from simple collecting and nomadic communities we have progressed to hybrid agricultural and collecting communities accompanied by the concept of the division of labour. The division of labour increases output and creates a need for exchange and enhances the standard of living. Improved standards of living result in more people and further increases in output accompanied

by simple mechanization which culminates in a breakthrough when the potential of the division of labour is enhanced through task specialization. Task specialization leads to the development of teams of workers and to more sophisticated and efficient mechanical devices and, with the discovery of steam power, results in an industrial revolution. A major feature of our own industrial revolution (and that of most which emulated it in the nineteenth century) is that production becomes increasingly concentrated in areas of natural advantage, that larger production units develop and that specialization increases as the potential for economies in scale and efficiency are exploited.

At least two consequences deserve special mention. First, economic growth fuels itself as improvements in living standards result in population growth which increases demand and lends impetus to increases in output and productivity. Second, concentration and specialization result in producer and consumer becoming increasingly distant from one another (both physically and psychologically) and requires the development of new channels of distribution and communication to bridge this gap.

And what of the managers responsible for the direction and control of this enormous diversity of human effort? By and large, it seems safe to assume that they were (and are) motivated essentially by (and occasionally enlightened) self-interest. Given the enormity and self evident nature of unsatisfied demand and the distribution of purchasing power, it is unsurprising that most managers concentrated on making more for less and that to do so they pursued vigorously policies of standardization and mass production. Thus the first half of this century is characterized in the advanced industrialized economies of the west by mass production and mass consumption – usually described as a production orientation and a consumer society. But changes were occurring in both.

On the supply side the enormous concentration of wealth and power in super-corporations had led to legislation to limit the influence of cartels and monopolies. An obvious consequence of this was to encourage diversification. Second, the accelerating pace of technological and organizational innovation began to catch up with and even overtake the natural growth in demand due to population increases. Faced with stagnant markets and the spectre of price competition, producers sought to stimulate demand through increased selling efforts. To succeed, however, one must be able to offer some tangible benefit which will distinguish one supplier's product from another's. If all products are perceived as being the same then price becomes the distinguishing feature and the supplier becomes a price taker thus having to relinquish the important managerial function of exercising control. Faced with such an impasse the real manager recognizes that salvation (and control) will be achieved through a policy of *product differentiation*. Preferably this will be achieved through the manufacture of a product which is physically different in some objective way from competitive offerings but, if this is not possible, then subjective benefits must be created through service, advertising and promotional efforts.

With the growth of product differentiation and promotional activity social commentators began to complain about the materialistic nature of society and question its value. Perhaps the earliest manifestation of the consumerist movement of the 1950s and 1960s is to be found in Edwin Chamberlin and Joan Robinson's articulation of the concept of imperfect competition in the 1930s. Hitherto, economists had argued that economic welfare would be maximized through perfect competition in which supply and demand would be brought into equilibrium through the price mechanism. Clearly, as producers struggled to avoid becoming virtually passive pawns of market forces they declined to accept the 'rules' of perfect competition and it was this behaviour which was described by Chamberlain and Robinson under the perjorative title of 'imperfect' competition. Shades of the 'hidden persuaders' and 'waste makers' to come.

The outbreak of war and the reconstruction which followed delayed the first clear statement of the managerial approach which was to displace the production orientation. It was not to be selling and a sales orientation for these can only be a temporary and transitional strategy in which one buys time in which to disengage from past practices, reform and regroup and then move on to the offensive again. The Americans appreciated this in the 1950s, the West Germans and Japanese in the 1960s, the British, belatedly in the late 1970s (up until the mid-1970s nearly all our commercial heroes were sales

people, not marketers – hence their problems – Stokes, Bloom, Laker). The real solution is marketing.

Marketing myopia – a watershed

If one had to pick a single event which marked the watershed between the production/sales approach to business and the emergence of a marketing orientation then most marketing scholars would probably pick the publication of Theodore Levitt's article entitled 'Marketing Myopia' in the July–August 1960 issue of the *Harvard Business Review*.

Building upon the trenchant statement 'The history of every dead and dying "growth" industry shows a self-deceiving cycle of bountiful expansion and undetected decay', Levitt proposed the thesis that declining or defunct industries got into such a state because they were product orientated rather than customer orientated. As a result, the concept of their business was defined too narrowly. Thus the railroads failed to perceive that they were and are in the *transportation* business, and so allowed new forms of transport to woo their customers away from them. Similarly, the Hollywood movie moguls ignored the threat of television until it was almost too late because they saw themselves as being in the cinema industry rather than the *entertainment* business.

Levitt proposes four factors which make such a cycle inevitable:

1 A belief in growth as a natural consequence of an expanding and increasingly affluent population.
2 A belief that there is no competitive substitute for the industry's major product.
3 A pursuit of the economies of scale through mass production in the belief that lower unit cost will automatically lead to higher consumption and bigger overall profits.
4 Preoccupation with the potential of research and development (R & D) to the neglect of market needs (i.e. a technology push rather than market pull approach).

Belief number two has never been true but, until very recently, there was good reason to subscribe to the other three propositions. Despite Malthus' gloomy prognostications in the eighteenth century the world's population has continued to grow exponentially; most of the world's most successful corporations see the pursuit of market share as their primary goal, and most radical innovations are the result of basic R & D rather than product engineering to meet consumer needs. Certainly the dead and dying industries which Levitt referred to in his analysis were entitled to consider these three factors as reasonable assumptions on which to develop a strategy.

In this then, Levitt was anticipating rather than analysing but, in doing so, he was building upon perhaps the most widely known, yet most misunderstood theoretical construct in marketing – the concept of the product life cycle (PLC).

The PLC concept draws an analogy between biological life cycles and the pattern of sales growth exhibited by successful products. In doing so it distinguishes four basic stages in the life of the product: introduction; growth; maturity; and decline (see Figure 1.1).

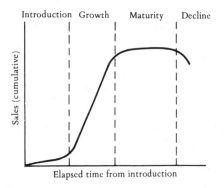

Figure 1.1   *The product life cycle*

Thus at birth or first introduction to the market a new product initially makes slow progress as people have to be made aware of its existence and only the bold and innovative will seek to try it as a substitute for the established product which the new one is seeking to improve on or displace. Clearly, there will be a strong relationship between how much better the new product is, and how easy it is for users to accept this and the speed at which it will be taken up. But, as a generalization, progress is slow.

However, as people take up the new product they will talk about it and make it more visible to non-

users and reduce the perceived risk seen in any innovation. As a consequence a contagion or bandwagon effect will be initiated as consumers seek to obtain supplies of the new product and producers, recognizing the trend, switch over to making the new product in place of the old. The result is exponential growth.

Ultimately, however, all markets are finite and sales will level off as the market becomes saturated. Thereafter sales will settle down at a level which reflects new entrants to the market plus replacement/repeat purchase sales which constitutes the mature phase of the PLC. It is this phase which Levitt rightly characterizes as self-deceiving. Following the pangs of birth and introduction and the frenetic competitive struggle when demand took off, is it surprising that producers relax and perhaps become complacent when they are the established leaders in mature and profitable markets? But consumers, like producers, are motivated by self-interest rather than loyalty and will be quite willing to switch their allegiance if another new product comes along which offers advantages not present in the existing offering. Recognition of this represents a market opportunity for other innovators and entrepreneurs which they will seek to exploit by introducing their own new product and so initiating another new PLC while bringing to an end that of the product to be displaced.

The import of the PLC is quite simple, but frequently forgotten – *change is inevitable*. Its misunderstanding and misuse arise from the fact that people try and use it as a specific predictive device. Clearly this is as misconceived as trying to guess the identity of a biological organism from the representation of a life cycle curve which applies equally to gnats and elephants.

Life cycles and evolution

As noted earlier the PLC concept is based upon biological life cycles and this raises the question as to whether one can further extend the analogy from the specific level of the growth of organisms and products to the general case of the evolution of species and economies. At a conceptual level this seems both possible and worthwhile.

Consider the case of a very simple organism which reproduces by cell division placed into a bounded environment – a sealed test tube containing nutrients necessary for the cell's existence. As the cell divides the population will grow exponentially, even allowing for the fact that some cells will die for whatever reason, up to the point when the colony reaches a ceiling to further growth imposed by its bounded environment. What happens next closely parallels what happens in product life cycles, industry life cycles and overall economic cycles – a strong reaction sets in. Discussing this in a biological context, Derek de Solla Price cites a number of ways in which an exponentially growing phenomenon will seek to avoid a reduction in growth as it nears its ceiling. Two of these, 'escalation', and 'loss of definition', seem particularly relevant in an economic context.

In the case of escalation, modification of the original takes place at or near the point of inflection and '. . . a new logistic curve rises phoenix-like on the ashes of the old'. In other words, the cell modifies itself so that it can prosper and survive despite the constraints which had impeded its immediate predecessor. In marketing such a phenomenon is apparent in a strategy of product rejuvenation in which either new uses or new customers are found to revitalize demand.

In many cases, however, it is not possible to 'raise the ceiling' through modification and the cell, or whatever, will begin to oscillate wildly in an attempt to avoid the inevitable (the 'hausse' in the economic cycle which precedes crisis and depression). As a result of these oscillations the phenomenon may become so changed as to be unrecognizable, i.e. it mutates or diversifies and recommences life in an entirely new guise. Alternatively, the phenomenon may accept the inevitable, smoothing out the oscillations and settling in equilibrium at a stable limit or, under different circumstances, slowly decline to nothing.

Over time, therefore, civilizations (and economies) rise and fall but the overall progression is upwards and characterized by periods of rapid development and/or stability when conditions are favourable and of decline when they are not. Observation would also seem to suggest that not only is change inevitable but that its pace is accelerating.

While it is often difficult to analyse the major causes and likely effect of major structural change

when one is living in the midst of it, it seems likely that future historians will regard the 1960s and 1970s as a period of hausse in our economic and social evolution. Certainly economic forecasters are inclined in this direction through their interest in 'the long wave' or Kondratieff cycle in economic development. Similarly, management writers of the standing of Drucker talk of 'turbulence' while Toffler speaks of the third wave which will bring about Galbraith's post-industrial society.

And what has this to do with marketing? Quite simply, everything. For the past two hundred years the advanced industrial economies have prospered because the nature of demand has been basic and obvious and entrepreneurs have been able to devote their energies to producing as much as possible for as little as possible. But, in a materialistic society, basic demand for standardized and undifferentiated products has become saturated and the ability to off-load surpluses on Third World developing economies is limited by their inability to pay for these surpluses. Product differentiation and an emphasis upon selling provide temporary respite from the imbalance but the accelerating pace of technological change rapidly outruns these. Indeed, in the short-run the substitution of technology for unskilled and semi-skilled labour has resulted in a rich working population, with much higher discretionary purchasing power than ever before, and a poor, unemployed and aging sector with limited or no discretionary purchasing power at all.

All the indications would seem to point to the fact that we are in an age of transition from one order to another. In terms of personal aspirations many people are growing out of materialism and want, in Maslow's terminology, to 'self-actualize' or 'do their own thing'. As a consequence we are moving towards a post-industrial, post-mass consumption society which is concerned with quality not quantity and the individual rather than the mass. To cope with this we need a complete rethink of our attitudes to production, distribution and consumption and it is this which marketing offers.

Marketing starts with the market and the consumer. It recognizes that in a consumer democracy money votes are cast daily and that to win those votes you need to offer either a better product at the same price or the same product at a lower price than your competitors. Price is objective and tangible but what is 'a better product'? Only one person can tell you – the consumer. It follows, therefore, that a marketing orientation starts and ends with consumers and requires one to make what one can sell rather than struggle to sell what one can make. But, marketing is not a philanthropic exercise in which producers give away their goods. Indeed the long run interest of the consumer requires that they do not, for otherwise as with eating the seed corn, we will eventually finish up with nothing at all. Producers are entitled to profits and the more value they add and the greater the satisfaction they deliver the more the customer will be prepared to pay for this greater satisfaction. Marketing therefore is all about mutually satisfying exchange relationships for which the catalyst is the producer's attempt to define and satisfy the customer's need better.

Marketing misunderstood

The emphasis thus far, and of the chapter as a whole, has been upon the need for a new approach to managing production and distribution in response to major environmental changes. The solution proposed is the adoption of a marketing orientation which puts the customer at the beginning rather than the end of the production–consumption cycle. To do so requires a fundamental shift of attitude on the part of all those concerned with production and consumption. Unfortunately, while this concept seems both simple and obvious to those who have subscribed to it there is ample evidence that it is widely misunderstood and hence misapplied.

In 1970, Charles Ames drew attention to this in an article in the *Harvard Business Review* entitled 'Trappings vs. Substance in Industrial Marketing'. The thesis of this was that industrial companies that complained marketing was not working for them as it appeared to do so for the consumer good companies had only themselves to blame as they had not understood the substance of the marketing concept but had merely adopted some of its superficial trappings. At worst they had merely changed the name of their personnel from 'sales' to 'marketing'.

More recently in the *Journal of Marketing Management* (1985), Stephen King diagnosed at least four different misinterpretations of marketing in the UK as follows:

1   *Thrust marketing* – this occurs when the sales managers change their name to marketing managers. But the emphasis is still upon selling what we can make with an emphasis upon price and cost cutting but little attention to fitness for purpose, quality and value for money. In other words, it ignores what the customer really wants.
2   *Marketing department marketing* – indicated by the establishment of a bolt-on specialized department intended to remedy the lack of customer understanding. Some improvement followed in markets where change was slow and gradual but it did not address the critical areas where radical innovation was called for. A sort of 'fine tuning' of the customer service function but based on existing products and customers.
3   *Accountants marketing* – prevalent where chief executive officers have no direct experience of selling or marketing and concentrate upon short-term returns to the neglect of long-run survival. This approach was pungently criticized by Hayes and Abernathy in their 1980 *Harvard Business Review* article 'Managing our way to Economic Decline', which has been echoed many times since. Accountants marketing neglects investment in R & D, manufacturing and marketing and leads to a vicious downward spiral.
4   *Formula marketing* – in which control is seen as more important than innovation. This emphasizes sticking to the tried and true and reflects a risk-averse strategy. It appears professional (many MBAs) and concentrates on managing facts and information but its consumer research bias tends to tell you more about the past than the future.

Failure of these approaches suggests that *real* marketing has four essential features:

1   Start with the customer.
2   A long-run perspective.
3   Full use of *all* the company's resources.
4   Innovation.

The marketing function

From the foregoing it is clear that without commitment to the concept there is little likelihood that the marketing *function* will be executed effectively. It is also clear that the size and nature of the marketing function will vary enormously according to the nature of the company or organization and the markets which it serves.

Basically, the marketing function is responsible for the management of the marketing mix which, at its simplest, is summarized by the four Ps of product, price, place and promotion. While much more elaborate formulations containing a dozen or more elements are to be found in the marketing textbooks such fine distinctions are not central to the present inquiry into the nature of marketing. As a function marketing has as many quirks and mysteries as research and development, finance and production but the important point to establish here is that the adoption of a marketing orientation does not mean nor require that the marketing function should be seen as the largest or the most important. In fact, in a truly marketing orientated organization the need for a specialized marketing function is probably far less than it is in a sales or production dominated company. Appreciation of this fact would do much to disarm the resistance of other functional specialists who equate the adoption of a marketing orientation with a diminution in their own organizational status and influence.

Ideally, of course, such functional divisions would not exist. Perhaps, if everyone were marketing orientated they would disappear to our continuing competitive advantage? Unfortunately, there is no evidence to suggest that this will occur in the near future despite the growing attention given to both the philosophy and function of marketing. Much remains to be done and this book represents a contribution to that process in that it is a compilation of insights and ideas from acknowledged experts on issues and activities central to professional marketing practice. While each chapter is a self-contained exposition of its subject matter, taken together they represent a definitive review and analysis of the present state of the art in marketing. Thus, while this chapter may not have answered completely the question it posed itself – what is marketing? – the book as a whole certainly does, a theme to which we return in the final chapter.

References

Ames, Charles, 'Trappings versus substance in industrial marketing', *Harvard Business Review*, July-August 1970, pp.93–103.

Hayes, R. and Abernathy W., 'Managing our way to economic decline', *Harvard Business Review*, July-August 1980, pp.67–77.

King, Stephen, 'Has marketing failed or was it never really tried?', *Journal of Marketing Management*, vol. 1(1), Summer 1985, pp.1–19.

Levitt, Theodore, 'Marketing Myopia', *Harvard Business Review*, July-August, 1960, pp.45–60.

2
Marketing and competitive success

JOHN SAUNDERS

Potter is potter's enemy, and craftsman is craftsman's rival; tramp is jealous of tramp, and singer of singer. Hesiod, *Works and Days*, eighth century BC.

Introduction

Neglect of competition is one of the major reasons why marketing plans fail. But, until recently, there was little written that could guide the analysis of competitive strategy. This has now changed; although marketing definitions still have difficulty in accommodating this most basic of business activities.

This chapter examines the strategy, tactics, and reality of competition. Borrowing from Porter's seminal works on competition, it first looks at the forces which shape strategy and the major strategic alternatives. It then uses the military analogy to examine the tactics of competition for the market lead, the strong number two, the follower and the nicher. Next, it seeks lessons from the observation of Japanese and British competition in the UK. It concludes by redrawing the competitive domain to show how the competitive options are reduced by British institutes and poor management training.

Competition, war and playing the game

If Wellington were right, and Waterloo was won on the playing fields of Eton, the battle was unique in modern warfare and offers us little which will help us understand modern competition. It is important to draw the distinction between competition in play and competition in war or business because the clubiness in sport, which was often extended to British business, hinders the facing of the new competition. The thoughts of the two great strategists, Carl von Clausewitz, a nineteenth-century Prussian, and Sun Tzu, a Chinese general from the fourth century BC, help us understand the difference. In good sport, well-matched teams or individuals meet in order to compete at a prearranged time and in a predetermined way. The process is as important as the end, and in Britain there is still the myth that participation is more important than winning. Compare this with Sun Tzu's statement that 'The supreme act of war is to subdue the enemy without fighting'. This is like a world champion boxer retaining his title by avoiding matches. Clausewitz comments upon what to do if conflict is unavoidable. The utmost exertion of powers should be used 'either to totally destroy the enemy . . . or else to ascribe peace terms to him'. In war there is no second prize for the runner up. In war and business, winning is everything; participating or surviving is nothing.

This discussion of marketing and competitive success will draw upon three major sources. The first are Porter's seminal works on *Competitive Strategy* (1980) and *Competitive Advantage* (1985). These works discuss the dominant strategic positions that are available and how they can be achieved. The second follows the military analogy, as extolled by Kotler and others, to explain the dynamics of achieving a tactical advantage over competition. Lastly, the research by Doyle *et al.* (1986) is used to show why many British firms have failed when facing Japanese competition.

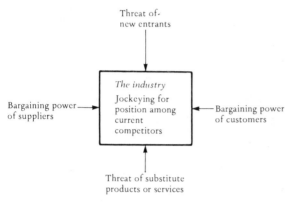

Figure 2.1 *Forces governing competition in an industry*
Source: M.E. Porter, 'How Competitive Forces Shape Strategy', *Harvard Business Review*, 47, March-April 1979, pp.137–45.

The competitive domain

A horse never runs so fast as when he has other horses to catch up and outpace. Ovid, *The Art of Love*, AD8.

Porter shows competitors within the industry jockeying for positions within a domain dictated by external powers (Figure 2.1). Two of the powers, suppliers and customers, are in the value chain which runs from raw materials to final consumption. A powerful supplier can reduce an industry's profitability by raising prices or reducing the quality of purchased goods and services. This power is highest when the supplier has a monopoly, for example British Telecom in the UK who has no competition in the supply of social telephone services. The power is weakened if there are many suppliers or substitutes. In the long term seemingly strong cartels of suppliers become weak if they ignore market forces, for example, OPEC and the tin cartel. Unless an industry has unique capability the bargaining power of customers can severely restrict the room to manoeuvre. This is particularly true if buying power is concentrated in a few hands.

Along the whole value chain the profitability of any link is limited by the danger of it being bypassed by either suppliers or customers. This became particularly apparent in the 1960s and 1970s when many large companies, such as General Motors and British Leyland, chose vertical integration as a means of controlling supplies and obtaining a larger share of value added. Recent events have shown this not to be a wise move. In a rapidly changing environment vertically integrated companies can end up being both higher cost manufacturers and less flexible than their slimmer and more agile competitors. A vertically integrated company can be at a competitive disadvantage because it finds it more difficult to control its own monopoly suppliers of labour than it would component manufacturers forced to compete for business. At the same time the vertically integrated company lacks flexibility because its capital investment in established methods forms a barrier to exit if technologies change. Many of Japan's leading companies have realized this and so concentrate upon what Peter Drucker sees as the only two functions of business: marketing and innovation. In the most agile of companies, such as Casio and the British Amstrad, manufacturing becomes a largely subcontracted operation.

The two other dimensions that Porter identifies as limiting the competitive domain are the threat of substitute products or services and the threat of new entrants. These are the reasons why, in the long run, the power of OPEC was limited. Initially, users of oil were forced to absorb the large increases in price that were imposed. Then, the high margins attracted high cost sources of oil to be exploited such as the North Sea and Alaska. Simultaneously there was a great incentive for Western nations to exploit coal and atomic energy as alternative sources of power. Add to this the incentive for energy saving and it can be seen why the bargaining power of OPEC was severely reduced.

Despite most attention being concentrated on the competitive strategy of firms within an industry, evidence suggests that it is the external threat that companies are least able to counter. Cooper and Schendel's (1976) study of seven industries facing a threat from substitute products or services, found that it was rare for even dominant incumbent firms to survive the onslaught. This often occurred despite the incumbent's early involvement and even

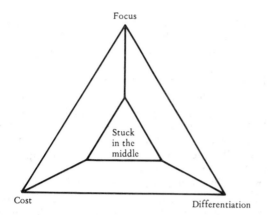

Figure 2.2 *Three generic strategies*
Source: M.E. Porter, *Competitive Strategy: Techniques for analysing industries and competitors*, Free Press, 1980.

success in the new technology. One result of this has been the use of radical new venture structures to incubate innovations. It seems as though after nearly three thousand years Hesiod has been proved wrong; the chief enemy of the Greek potter was not other Greek potters but imports from low cost countries and innovative manufacturers using metal, glass or plastic.

Jockeying for position

Competition brings out the best in products and the worst in people, David Sarnoff, American businessman, *Esquire* 1964

According to Porter there are three ways in which a company can achieve success in an industry (Figure 2.2). A company can aim to be:

1 A low cost producer of products or services, as the airline People's Express has done; or
2 A high cost but differentiated or unique producer as Mercedes is in cars; or
3 A focused company with a unique product or service in a market niche too small to attract bigger companies, as is Rolls-Royce Cars.

Since industries may offer more than one means of differentiation and several market niches, there are opportunities for numerous firms to be successful within the same industry. There are, however, pitfalls of being a follower in any one of the strategic

alternatives or just being stuck in the middle.

Each of the three successful competitive strategies is achieved through specific actions which depend on an appropriate corporate style being adopted. This dependence means it is not easy to switch from one strategy to the other. Although, as will be seen, some firms have become highly successful by following two generic strategies simultaneously.

Cost leadership

Cost leadership should not be confused with low price. Some cost leaders, such as Amstrad, may use a low price to achieve rapid market penetration, but many operate at the market price or demand a price premium. Boeing, IBM and Toyota are typical of cost leaders who use their low manufacturing costs to generate a high contribution so allowing a large investment in marketing, R & D and new plant. Cost leaders can, therefore, use their high contribution to fund investments which help maintain their dominant market positions.

In marketing the cumulative experience accruing from a high market share is the most frequently cited means of achieving low costs. Once a company has the advantage it can use the liberated funds to spend more on marketing or R & D in order to maintain or increase its dominance. Evidence in support of the relationship between experience and cost is strong but the pattern reflects association rather than causality. Making more products does not mean they will become cheaper; it just provides the opportunity to learn how technology, management techniques and labour can be better used. In fact, there are many cases in the engineering industry where the work force has gained experience at manipulating bonus systems so fast that manufacturing costs have increased with time. Experience curves also depend upon the company's commitment and ability to take advantage of the cost cutting opportunities that are available. Companies and countries have different rates of benefiting from experience. In particular American companies seem to gain experience faster than European ones, and Japanese companies even faster than the Americans.

Given the limitations of the experience curve, how can a firm become a cost leader? Several opportunities depend on large-scale manufacturing. In the steel industry the Japanese and developing countries have been able to undercut the far more experienced Western manufacturers by investing in large-scale modern plant. The globalization of businesses can also help. By marketing global brands companies are able to obtain economies of scale unachievable by multinational companies who allow regional autonomy. Global manufacturing also allows companies to concentrate manufacturing in larger plants in low cost countries. In reality the expected trend towards offshore manufacturing has not been as great as was expected since developments in manufacturing technology have allowed some countries with high labour costs to keep their manufacturing costs down.

The rapid price declines in the electronics industry have shown how improved designs using the latest technology can be produced less expensively than the generation they replaced. The same is true of less dynamic industries where new designs can incorporate new materials, electronic rather than electromechanical control systems can be used and new designs use fewer components. Here again economies are conferred to large-scale manufacturers; they can spend more on perfecting each design and replace products more frequently than their smaller competitors.

Final sources of economy are labour and low overheads. Labour can be relatively easily made more efficient by investing in more productive plant. The labour effectiveness which comes from cooperation, flexibility and commitment of the work force is not so mechanistically achieved. Neither are the lower overheads that should come from scale and the investment in office automation. A recent American study has shown that, although blue collar workers' productivity has improved significantly over the last ten years, the productivity of white collar workers has actually declined. It would be surprising if the same were not true of the UK.

To achieve cost leadership a company must focus upon the tight control of costs. Some of this can be achieved by scale and appropriate manufacturing. It also needs a structured organization so that costs can be clearly allocated and controlled and a lean organization motivated by strict quantitative incentives. Experiences curves are only a small part of the story.

Differentiation

Success through differentiation demands skills which differ completely from those needed for cost leadership. The differentiator wins by offering a product or service which is unique or superior to competitors'. In the early days of the microcomputer market competition was based on who could provide the most sophisticated machine with the most facilities. This changed suddenly with the arrival of the IBM PC which became a dominant design. Immediately differentiators, such as Hewlett Packard and Sinclair, suffered as differentiation became a disadvantage. The new game became low cost and high power but with as little differentiation as possible. It certainly does not follow that differentiation becomes an unsuccessful strategy once markets mature. Until recently 35 mm single lens reflex cameras had become almost standardized, then the electronic cameras launched by Minolta, Canon and others stimulated new differentiation and market growth. In other mature markets design can be used to differentiate products. This approach has been exploited by Bang and Olufsen in hi-fi and by Conran's Habitat chain.

A brand image can be used to differentiate products which are physically indistinguishable. These can be distinguished by the prominence of the packaging and the manufacturers' labels. Many experiments have shown that in blind tests even loyal consumers are unable to identify their favourite brand of cigarette, soft drink or beer. Without the benefit of the packaging most also find it difficult to distinguish between such seemingly different products as whisky and brandy. The importance of the label and brand image is particularly important among prestige and designer products. Brand names that used to be hidden inside the jacket, back of a collar of a shirt, or on the sole of a shoe, are now displayed prominently.

Seemingly identical products can also be differentiated by distribution. For instance, Rington Teas' house to house distribution of tea and coffee, Avon Cosmetics system of agents, and the distribution of some women's magazines through supermarkets or play groups. Perhaps one of the most difficult differentiation tasks is faced by the airlines who, because of bilateral agreements, are all forced to fly the same aeroplanes, to the same destinations and superficially charge the same prices. But, as any international traveller will know, there is wide divergence in the services offered by the airlines. Singapore Airlines, Thai Airlines and Japanese Airlines have all gained their high reputation on the basis of the inflight services they provide. Some of these are on the basis of better food with more choice, free movies, many accessories freely available to passengers, and slightly more modern aircraft, but it largely depends upon the attentiveness and professionalism of their cabin crews. The power of quality as a differentiating tool extends beyond services. In Britain, Sainsbury, and Marks and Spencer maintain a differential advantage by offering high quality products and good customer service which, although more expensive than competitors', are perceived as being good value for money.

Sir Clive Sinclair's early successes were due to his use of innovation as a means of differentiation. It also caused his fall. A more successful example is Sony, claimed to be world leader in the innovation of new consumer electronics. But even Sony has had to face the reality that innovation is risky. Its Betamax videorecorders were the first ones on the market but were eventually pushed out by JVC's VHS format. Sony's L-cassette audio format sank without trace. However, it remains the innovator. Rather than bow to the dominant VHS video technology Sony has introduced its own 8 mm system which is ideally suited for videophotography.

The differentiating company clearly needs different skills to the cost leader. Creative people are needed rather than cost controllers. These days 'me too's' follow quickly. So a differentiator has got to move quickly in order to stay ahead of the crowd. This needs close functional coordination, and broadly defined performance measures and incentives that encourage innovation.

Focus

Many small companies prosper by pursuing a focus strategy. Without size or resources to achieve cost leadership or overall superiority in a market, they concentrate on providing a product or service tailored to the needs of a well-defined group of customers.

After many British retailers failed by trying to follow Marks and Spencer, initial success came to Mothercare and Next, who concentrated on providing for distinct market segments. Amstrad, a late entrant into the microcomputer market, was able to gain market share quickly by concentrating on two benefit segments: first, the market for non-computer literates who wanted a basic machine with all the necessary facilities that they could just plug in and use; and then, the word processor for people with a very specific application in mind but who also needed cheap and easy-to-use equipment. In many ways these two successful Amstrad products were inferior to other micros on the market, but for the target market segments they had clear differential advantages.

To succeed, focused companies have to keep close to the customer, and develop the marketing and design skills necessary to serve their particular needs. Also, since the target market is well defined, focused companies often find it beneficial to provide related products that serve the same market, Richard Branson's Virgin Company is a good example of this. Lastly, because survival in the long term depends on the identification and exploitation of emerging segments, the focused company needs to be entrepreneurial and retain the spirit of the small firm. They need to follow the dictum, 'think small, stay small'; in style if not in size.

It is apparent from the examples given that some leading companies have not succeeded by being exclusively cost leaders, differentiators or focused. Many top companies are both cost leaders and differentiators. The buying power and expertise of Marks and Spencer makes it a low cost company but it trades on quality, service and its brand name; IBM is a cost leader which also trades on customer service and Boeing has lower costs than any other aeroplane manufacturer but the 747, its most profitable product, is unique. Many of the successful low volume manufacturers complement differentiation with a clear focus. For example, Jaguar, Landrover and Morgan in the automobile industry, and J. C. Bamford in earthmoving. Lastly, Amstrad's success needs explaining in terms of both cost leadership and focus. Its success in the hi-fi market was based on integrated systems at the bottom end of the market which the major Japanese manufacturers were neglecting. Equally, although Amstrad were cost leaders, it was its identification of segment needs which enabled it to become a major supplier with the audacity to challenge IBM.

The military analogy

I don't meet competition, I crush it.
Charles Revson, American businessman

Kotler and others (1980, 1985) have explored how the idea of the military strategists – such as Carl von Clausewitz, Sun Tzu and Liddell-Hart – can be used to explain the tactical alternatives available to gain competitive advantage. Taking military and commercial parallels is not a new idea, Clausewitz (1968) himself sees war as a social activity similar to others:

> War is a clash between major interests that is solved by bloodshed – that is the only way in which it differs from other conflicts. Rather than comparing it to an art we could more accurately compare it to commerce, which is also a conflict of human interests and activities; and it is still closer to politics which in turn may be considered as a kind of commerce on a large scale.

In this discussion four positions are explored. That of the defender trying to hold on to its existing markets, the challenger attempting to take market share, the follower and the nicher.

Defensive strategies

Clausewitz begins by making two points about defence. First, although its object is negative, it is a stronger form of war than attack: it is easier to hold ground than to take it, to preserve than to acquire. A weaker force, unless desperate, should not attack a stronger one; but stay on the defensive and make up for its weakness by maximizing the advantage of a defensive position. *Beatae sunt possidentes*, said Clausewitz; *blessed are those in possession* in war as in law.

But defence could not be purely passive. Clausewitz's second point was that defence essentially consists of two phases; waiting for a blow and parrying it. An army takes up a defensive position in order to fight for it. A defensive position consists in finding the right balance between these two elements, waiting and parrying, of choosing the right time and place to unleash that flashing sword of vengeance which Clausewitz describes as the greatest moment for the defender. There is a whole range of possibilities open, from immediate counter-attack, the moment the aggressor starts (minimum waiting, immediate riposte) to a long defensive withdrawal, delaying until the last possible moment before launching the counter-attack. All depends whether one wants to destroy the enemy by one's own force or by its own exertions. The various defensive alternatives will be explored.

Position defence: the fortress

Whether in warfare or business there are plenty of examples to show the futility of defence behind supposedly impregnable fixed positions. A static defence is one of the riskiest in military theory. In the twentieth century, we have the French Maginot line and the German Siegfried line as examples of failure of a position defence. Very rarely do enemies make a frontal attack. But they often attempt to undermine the defender in indirect manoeuvres. For example, Rover saw its big, expensive vehicles as invincible and did very little to move its front in line with product and market evolution. But Subaru and Toyota did not attempt to compete head-on with Landrover in the market for large vehicles, instead it undermined them by introducing 'fun' and cheap four-wheel drive vehicles.

A company attempting a fortress defence will find itself retreating from line after line of fortification into shrinking product markets. The stationary company will end up with outdated products and lost markets, undermined by competitors who find superiority in new positions in the market place. Even a dominant market leader cannot afford to maintain a static defence. It must continually engage in product improvement, line extensions and product proliferations. For instance, giants like Unilever spread their front into related household products; and Coca-Cola, despite having over 50 per cent of the world soft drinks market, has moved aggressively into marketing wines and has diversified into desalination equipment and plastics. These companies defend their territory by breaking it down into units and entrenching in each.

Mobile defence: defence in depth

A defence in depth follows Theodore Levitt's ideas advanced in 'Marketing Myopia' (1960). To defend itself a firm moves into new product market positions and establishes superiority. This requires, not so much normal brand proliferation and product line extension, but innovative activity resulting in market broadening and market diversification. Levitt argues that a company must shift its focus from the current product to the underlying generic need and get involved in R & D across the whole technology range associated with the need. It requires management to redefine the business its company is in. A cycle manufacturer, for example, might see itself in the business of leisure and health rather than providing a cheap means of transport. A mobile defence thus involves shifting to those product market opportunities that improve the firm's foothold in the broader market place.

A mobile defence aims to guard against failure when technology, the market or customer needs change. Certainly, since the mid-1970s, the Japanese giants in the electronics industry have moved into industries where they are now in the forefront of technology and market development. And in these territories they are generating strategic depths to enable them to weather attacks and to launch retaliatory attacks. Computers, semiconductors, various segments of machine tools, telecommunications, robotics, biotechnology, ceramics, carbon fibres and optical fibres are all good examples of Japan's mobile defence with technology providing the propelling force.

Leaders in product markets relying on a static defence and failing to redefine their business often lose out to competition. For example, the leaders in silicon chips are not the big valve companies of yesterday; the leaders in white bread did not become the leaders in high-fibre bread of today; and the leaders in fertilizers today did not start as manure farms!

Pre-emptive defence

A pre-emptive strike depends on a defender gathering intelligence which warns of a coming attack. It then strikes before the enemy does so. This requires the firm to identify strengths within the current product markets and build on them. It also involves identifying current competitive advantage and/or developing new ones. The rationale behind the pre-emptive behaviour is to close windows of opportunity for the enemy or to make it more difficult for them to exploit potential strategic windows.

Pre-emptive defence can be used in different ways. Casio defended its position in the electronic calculator market by having a very wide and dynamic product range, and by diversification into electronic watches. Marks and Spencer is moving out of town and also establishing speciality chains in order to counter developments in the retailing market.

Clausewitz explains the aggressive behaviour of many leading companies:

> If the enemy is thrown off balance he must not be given time to recover. Blow after blow must be struck.

For example, although it is the market leader, Procter and Gamble continues to saturate segments it is operating in with a broad range of products thus making it very difficult for competitors to get a foothold. Many leading Japanese companies follow the same strategy. They do not rest after achieving market domination but continue to have a wide range of innovative products which are replaced frequently. The aggressor is, therefore, faced with a moving front which is difficult to penetrate.

Often the threat of violent retaliation alone is sufficient to deter aggressors. A powerful company can let its strength be known and psychologically intimidate the aggressors until the latter is dissuaded from waging any defensive attack. In the pharmaceutical industry many firms have dominant products in particular segments, they also know that, unless the segment comes under attack by a competitor, their share of the market and the market size will change little. Rather than defend the segment continually, they hold a large strategic reserve and pre-prepare defensive strategies and let it be known that they would use the reserves if attacked. This is akin to Field Marshall Montgomery's statement that he knows the battle is won, not when he commits his crack regiments but, when he can withdraw one.

Dominant companies have also been observed to employ FUD marketing – that is spreading 'fear, uncertainty and despair' among the competitors by broadcasting what they intend to do in the future. IBM did this in the microcomputer market by widely broadcasting the launch of its Peanut Personal Computer prior to Christmas. Although the product was a failure in the market when it was eventually launched, the threat was enough to severely damage competitors' sales during the peak Christmas season. It has been argued that Boeing is currently using a similar strategy in broadcasting its long-term development of new technology airliners in order to damage the prospects of European Airbus.

Flank position defence

The flank is the part of an army which is most vulnerable to attack. It is also true of business that competitors will attack the unprotected flank of the dominant firm. A flank position defence therefore requires the firm to fortify its flanks to discourage attack. This means developing and holding secondary markets which could be cultivated by competitors to give them a springboard into the defender's core business.

Distillers provides an example of a market failure resulting from poor defence of its flanks. As whisky makers it lost its dominance in the spirits market by being excessively dependent upon the blended whisky. It dominated its core business with the major whisky brands such as Johnnie Walker, Dewars and White Horse, but did not develop the adjacent markets of malt whisky and white spirits which have become strong. Its position became very weak, because blended whisky demand is declining while that for malt whisky and white spirits is increasing. So weakened did Distillers become that it lost some of its share of blended whisky sales.

Counter-offensive defence

Counter-offensive manoeuvres can take three forms: meet the attack head on, attack the flank of the attacker, or launch a pincer movement to sever the attack formation at the base of its operation. Defenders have to mobilize their resources and counter-attack the aggressors.

For example, TWA and British Airways counter-attacked Laker's bid on the North Atlantic by lowering prices to match Laker's until the attacker was forced into bankruptcy. A counter-offensive flank attack describes the Japanese defensive of the RAM chip market. While American firms were concentrating on producing technically sophisticated and elegant designs that would incorporate the most advanced circuitry, the Japanese acquired over 40 per cent of the American 64k RAM market by concentrating on standard chips. Having gained the foothold the Japanese defended their position in a pincer-like fashion by dramatically reducing prices to a level which would force American firms to sell below costs. As a result many of the American companies left the market.

Contraction defence: the hedgehog

This is sometimes contemplated by market leaders who are weak and whose resources are spread too thinly. The logic is that a firm need not defend all its segments in its current position. The defendant retreats to unattacked positions when its segment is lost. This is seen as narrowing the front in order that resources can be concentrated in a strong defensive position. In military terms this has proved appropriate if defenders have room to manoeuvre in retreat and attackers are forced to over-extend their lines. Russia has used it twice: to defend against Napoleon and Hitler. This strategy would be clearly less effective for a small country like Britain whose size does not allow for a contracted defence. This explains why Montgomery intended using a mobile defence to defend British shores if they were attacked in the Second World War.

The British motorcycle industry provides an example of a contracting defence that failed. When the Japanese attacked the moped market, and particularly the markets in South-East Asia, the British retreated and convinced themselves that the Japanese development of the sector would, in the long term, stimulate demand for larger British bikes. The retreat continued through 125 cc bikes, to 250 cc and 350 cc bikes, until eventualy the only British manufacturers remaining were the superbike manufacturers – Norton and Triumph. By the time Honda launched its own super-bikes these two, now small, British manufacturers were in no position to defend against the now much larger Honda.

So common have these retreats become in Britain that the rest of the world now calls it 'the British method'. Faced with unprofitable businesses firms like British Leyland, British Steel Corporation, British Shipbuilding and the National Coal Board attempted to cut back to the few profitable centres. With what effect?

Defensive strategies concluded

Three important points can be made about defensive strategies.

1 Do not sleep behind walls, however high, they are not high enough.
2 Let your strength be known, and what you will defend.
3 Do not let the ease of defence cultivate a garrison army which is incapable of offence.

As Sun Tzu (1981) said:

> Weakness comes from having to prepare against possible attacks . . . strength, from compelling our adversary to make these preparations against us.

Market challenger: confrontation strategies

The challenger is the non-market leader who has decided to make an aggressive bid for more market share. The two fundamental military principles apply: the principle of the objective (pursue a clearly defined and decisive attainable objective) and the principle of mass (concentrate strength at the enemy's weakness). 'The best strategy is always to be very strong; first in general, and then at the decisive point' (Clausewitz 1968).

Who to attack?

Unlike war, where the enemy is given, the business firm is usually able to choose its opponent and a time for action. Who should it attack? It can choose to make an assault on the market leader, although this is a high risk (for example Freddie Laker against the world!) but sometimes a high return strategy. There are many examples of market leaders being successfully attacked when technologies change: Xerox attacked and captured the copy market from 3M by developing a better copying process. Stephenson, with his railways, defeated the established canal transport system. BOAC and TWA took on Cunard, and Next challenged Marks and Spencer in fashionwear.

The challenger can attack firms of the same size as itself. The example is the battle between Flymo and Qualcast in the domestic lawnmower market. Flymo introduced the innovative hover mower and dominated the hover sector. Qualcast hit back with a similar hover machine and an aggressive advertising campaign sparking off the so-called mower war of recent years. It is worth noting that one effect of this has been increasing lawnmower sales. Within this

market Black and Decker has survived as the third force, not because of its strength in the British lawnmower market, but because of its American base and the breadth of its market base in DIY generally.

Aggressors can also attack 'small fries'. For example, the large Japanese audio hi-fi manfucturers, Sony, National Panasonic Matsushita, Sanyo, attacked and destroyed the smaller British producers such as Wharfedale and Alba in the UK market.

Having defined its strategic objectives and amassed its forces the firm has to plan its attack. Five alternative strategies are available.

Frontal attack

This is a head-on attack on to a well-defended fortress. The firm can use a pure frontal attack by matching its competitor product for product, price for price, advertising for advertising, and so on. Alternatively, it could adopt a limited frontal attack by tempting away select customers from competitors. The Japanese semiconductor producers, for instance, beat their American rivals by offering very favourable price deals to important customers and committing themselves to close after-sales relationships. The frontal attack can also be price based, the challenger basically matching its competitors on other counts but beating it on price. Alternatively, the aggressor can invest heavily in R & D: investing in process R & D to achieve lower production costs and facilitate price based attacks, or product R & D leading to higher value features which differentiate its product from those of the competition.

Since defence is the stronger position, pure frontal attack is very difficult to justify unless the attacker has a three to one advantage in combat fire power. As Sun Tzu says, '. . . the worst policy of all is to besiege walled cities'. Laker airlines attempted a frontal attack on the major routes of the transatlantic carriers and failed. The major Japanese electronics firms failed in their head-on attack of the microcomputer market with their launch of the MSX microcomputers in 1984. In America, Britain and Japan sales of these machines never took off. In the early 1970s, General Electric, RCA and Xerox committed themselves to frontal attacks on the mainframe computer market which IBM dominated. All aimed to become a strong number two in the market, they all failed and lost millions of dollars in the process. At the same time, ITT were employing people to ensure that it did not make the same mistake of entering the mainframe computer market.

The overriding risk of frontal attacking strategies is that they will awaken 'sleeping giants', provoking intensive retaliation. Unless the aggressors have a sustainable differential advantage they run the risk of substantial losses. Sun Tzu (1981) tells how the military strategist overcomes the problem:

> In battle, there are not more than two methods of attack – the direct and the indirect . . . in all fighting, the direct method may be used for joining battle, but indirect methods will be needed in order to secure victory.

He adds that:

> Indirect tactics, efficiently applied, are as inexhaustible as heaven and earth, unending as the flow of rivers and streams; like the sun and the moon they end but begin again: like the four seasons . . .

Direct attacks are so hard as to be nearly impossible but there are numerous indirect alternatives.

Flanking attack

Flanking is a broad indirect attack where assailants pit their strength against the defender's weakness. Liddell-Hart (1967) found that in military history this indirect approach has overwhelming support as the most effective and economical strategic option.

In business, flanking can be geographical – attacking defenders in regions where their defences are non-existent or very weak. This is what the Japanese motorcycle manufacturers did starting in Asia and then rolling out to America and Europe. There is also segmental flanking, revolving around identification of niches or market needs neglected by competitors. In business the flanks of a defender are not static. Technological or market changes can create a flanking opportunity not recognized by the defender. Hewlett Packard, through the development of the minicomputer, outflanked IBM who neglected the small and less profitable end of the mainframe market. In a similar move Apple introduced microcomputers to become a new force facing both IBM and Hewlett Packard.

A flanking strategy should only be pursued if a distinct, and potentially profitable market segment is emerging and the attacking firm has the resources to defend itself should the defending firm retaliate. Apple had little difficulty countering Hewlett Packard, who showed little understanding of the microcomputer market. It equally had little difficulty combating IBM's attempt to enter the home computer market but it was unable to counter IBM's entry into the business PC market.

Encirclement

Whereas flanking attack aims at a weak point in the competitor's defence encirclement involves a multipronged onslaught which dilutes the defender's ability to retaliate in strength. Over time, the result of such an attack is a more fluid front line or market place that can be more easily pierced at several points and potentially developed into new markets. The aggressor can encircle competitors by producing enormous variety of types, styles and sizes of products including cheaper and more expensive models. By overwhelming them the defender's retaliatory options are reduced. Japan's attacks upon the audio hi-fi and motorcycle industry started as flanking moves but became encirclements as their strengths grew. The attacker's radical new product innovations, accelerated product life cycles and wide product range made it very difficult for the defenders to form in order to make any counter moves. This destabilization is what Sun Tzu encourages:

> For should the enemy strengthen his van, he will weaken his rear; should he strengthen his rear, he will weaken his van; should he strengthen his left he will weaken his right; . . . if he sends reinforcements everywhere, he will everywhere be weak.

There are two forms of encirclement attack. Product encirclement consists of launching products in a multitude of quality, models and features in order to swamp the opponent's product line. Honda clearly encircled competitors in the motorcycle industry by model proliferation – launching a new model of motorcycle every two weeks! Seiko, too, attacked the watch market by encirclement strategy. In the UK it has 400 models out of 2300 it markets world wide!

The second form of encirclement consists of expanding the firm's offerings into almost every adjacent market segment or into various distribution outlets. Again Seiko did this by distributing its watches through every possible channel, channel conflict being avoided by having several ranges. Not being satisfied with entering every possible distribution channel it also sought to absorb as much shelf space in each as possible. McDonalds provide another example of market encirclement. When it enters a regional market it seeks to saturate the market quickly – several outlets are positioned in close proximity to each other. In America, McDonalds is impossible to beat geographically.

Encirclement is feasible when the attacker has superior resources, is willing to commit those resources for a long time to achieve market dominance, has access to distribution channels and product development capacity. It involves a long-term commitment of resources and requires an organization to commit itself to making short-term losses in order to win critical terrain.

Bypass attack

Bypassing aggressors skip the defender's flank markets to build strength where the defendant has none. The essence is to develop new products to satisfy needs that are unserved by the competition. The firm could diversify into non-related products or into new geographical markets. The rapid move of Japanese consumer electronics firms into videorecorders and compact discs and the European and American markets is a product type of bypass attack where the traditional, and less lucrative audio visual markets were neglected in order to concentrate on the new ones. This can mean neglecting established markets; as the Japanese have done in allowing British manufacturers to gain a larger share of the mature TV market, while they concentrated on the rapidly developing videorecorder opportunities.

The bypass attack is akin to technological leapfrogging. This was forced upon the British telecommunications industry when its major buyer, now British Telecom, retained mechanical switchgear while other countries were using electromechanical systems. Having missed a stage in the development of switchgear the industry was forced to leapfrog from mechanical to the highly sophisticated electronic System-X. They found this difficult. To succeed the successful bypasser has to have some established

presence in the market, a springboard from which to bypass competition. This could be a strong R & D and technical capabilities to develop new products, exceptional marketing capabilities, or strength in geographically dispersed markets. The British telecommunications industry's dependence upon the state monopoly meant it had developed none of these skills. By the time British Telecom had been privatized the British telecommunications industry had declined from being the world leader to being a weakened domestic supplier. A bypass attack was the only strategy open given its inability in the intermediate technology, but it was not a leap on to firm foundations.

Guerilla warfare

Frontal, flanking, encirclement and bypass attacks are extensive, broad-based and continual attacks upon competitors. They tend to be large-scale and prolonged. Guerilla strategy, on the other hand, consists of waging small, intermittent attacks on different, especially weakly defended, positions. The overriding aim is to harrass, demoralize, and keep the competitors off-balance. The enemy is destabilized by 'pricks rather than blows' (Liddell-Hart 1967).

The challenger can target guerilla attacks directly at competitors in the market, that is market focused attacks. For example, the aggressor can run special promotions, reduce prices in selected outlets or geographical regions, or even threaten withdrawal of franchise with particular retail outlets, or putting pressure on specific distribution channels in order to secure more shelf space or other preferences. However, the essence is to keep the attacks sporadic, unpredictable and diverse. Guerilla warfare can be particularly effective if the attacker, since it intends to remain small, does not draw the full fire of the defendant. Laker was overaggressive and challenged the major transatlantic carriers while he had no major differential advantage. In contrast, People's Express and Virgin Airlines' attacks on the route are probably annoying to the large international airlines, but both of the radical new airlines have declared their intention of keeping their operations small.

Challengers can also harrass their opponents by non-market focused attacks. By using legislation to destabilize the opponent. The large-scale commercial operation of Concorde was severely damaged by flight restrictions in America which would probably not have been imposed if America's supersonic transport programme had not been ditched. More directly Singapore Airline's operation of Concorde was rendered impossible when Malaysia, who did not operate Concorde, banned supersonic flights over its territory. Non-domestic manufacturers have accused the British government of similar action favouring British drug manufacturers in its selection of products on the limited list that can be prescribed within the National Health Service. Other forms of guerilla attack involve public relations activity, support of pressure groups who can damage opponents and political manipulation. Several charismatic business leaders have become particularly good in using the mass media to promote their businesses' activities. For example, Harvey-Jones for ICI, Branson for Virgin, Edwards during his time at British Leyland and, in America, Chrysler's Iacocca.

Oddly, in war, guerilla warfare is often seen as unacceptable behaviour perpetrated by the other side. During the Second World War, although allied soldiers were usually treated well when they were captured by the Axis forces, partisans and commandos were killed. Businesses often make a similar ethical distinction, and the discussion of guerilla tactics quickly degenerates into consideration of illegal behaviour. One suspects that businesses, like governments, have no difficulty at looking at perpetrators of the same behaviour and calling one set guerillas and the others freedom fighters. Clausewitz (1968) provides one insight into the value of questionable guerilla tactics, '. . . any nation that uses it intelligently will, as a rule, gain superiority over those who disdain its use'.

Conclusions on challenging

Attackers are competitors who intitiate new competition in consolidating their hold on their current markets and extending their activities to new ones. The five attacking strategies discussed are not, of course, mutually exclusive. An aggressive firm would choose among them and probably use more than one at a time. Choice of strategies depends upon one's knowledge of oneself and the enemy.

If you know your enemy and know yourself, you need not fear the result of a hundred battles. If you know yourself but not the enemy, for every victory gained you will also suffer a defeat. If you know neither the enemy nor yourself, you will succumb in every battle.

So says Sun Tzu (1981):

To remain in ignorance of the enemy's condition simply because one grudges the outlay of a few hundred ounces of silver in honours and emoluments, is the height of inhumanity.

How true this is also of business.

Market followers

Followers are companies who have neither the resources, the market position, technical capabilities or the organizational commitment to challenge the market leaders in their industries. They succeed in industries where opportunities for product and large image differentiation are low, price sensitivity is high and where competitors are offering comparable services inadequately, for example in the steel, bulk chemicals and fertilizer industries. By following IBM and producing a perfectly IBM compatible microcomputer Compacq became the fastest growing company ever to appear in the Fortune 500. It did this partly by charging lower prices than IBM but also by exploiting the distribution channels left available while IBM were losing interest in its own distributors. Now Amstrad is making a success of following by severe price cutting made possible by its low cost operations and using mass distribution channels, such as Dixons, previously not used for the sale of professional personal business computers.

Several studies have shown how low market share businesses have succeeded. Common success strategies are:

1 Careful market segmentation, competing only in areas where their particular strengths were highly valued.
2 Efficient use of limited R & D budgets – they seldom won R & D battles but channelled their R & D spending into areas that were most likely to generate the greatest financial payoff, in terms of return on R & D expenditure. Where R & D capabilities were available, they concentrated on truly innovative products.

3 They thought small and stayed small. They tended to emphasize profitability rather than sales growth and market share, concentrating on specialization rather than diversification, high value added rather than mass products, quality rather than quantity.
4 The companies were willing to challenge conventional wisdom – their leaders were often strong willed, committed and involved in almost all aspects of their companies' operations.

Market nichers

To understand the importance of niching to small companies it is valuable to shift from the war analogy to the study of ecology. This tells us that two species cannot occupy the same ecological niche at the same time in the same geographical area. If two species are very close in terms of the habitat they require they will not exist side by side but one will drive out the other. In Britain observe the retreat of the indigenous red squirrel when in competition with the introduced American grey squirrel. Where species are very similar they often do not live side by side but in concentrations where they have a slight marginal advantage. In Britain one often finds areas with large numbers of sparrows, or areas with large numbers of greenfinches – rarely areas with both. This has implications for any company which tries to model itself upon the markets and organizations of another. While a company is different, it may be able to find a niche in which it is uniquely able to survive. However, if it follows the leader into markets and tries to be as much like the leader as possible, its chances of survival are diminished.

Many companies, however, avoid clashes with major competitors by occupying niches in the outer environment. Niching means occupying a market segment that is safe and profitable by offering products or services that meet the specific needs of customers in that segment.

The nicher must not allow itself to become oblivious to environmental variations including changes in customers' tastes and needs. When niches are inhabited, and the major competitors in the wider market environment become aware of the profitability of these niches, there will be an increasing probability of invasion by the major firms. To survive in the long term the nicher must develop strength in more than one niche. Also, success can be achieved by:

1 Product standardization; limiting frills and extra services (i.e. more efficient use of skills to cut costs).
2 Specific focus (i.e., specialize rather than generalize).
3 Emphasizing quality or good value for money products.
4 Effective deployment of 'cost drivers', a narrow product line, restricted expenditure on R & D and new product launches, promotional and sales service support.

The ends of competitive warfare

The once neglected area of competitive strategy has come to the fore because of necessity rather than desire. Its study was stimulated by new and aggressive competitors, particularly from Japan, who were winning victory after victory in the marketplace. Companies which once perceived themselves as strong were being beaten so it was no longer enough just to look at one's strengths, it became necessary to understand the strengths of the competitor and how limited resources could best be allocated to the defence or attack of markets. It has been shown in industry after industry that this was not a fight for market share points but for survival. Often the losers did not even survive. Take, for example, the British shipbuilding industry, the motorcycle industry or the American consumer electronics industry. But, perhaps, even more disturbing than these old industries destroyed is the ability of the new competition to grasp new markets as they arrive.

The military analogy does not provide a complete answer to understanding competitive strategy but it does provide some means of exploring the alternatives available. It also provides a moving and appropriate parallel because now, more than ever before, industries are not fighting for minor marketing gains but for the survival of their nation as an industrial power.

British and Japanese competitive strategies in the UK

Success is the old ABC – ability, breaks and courage.
Charles Luckman, American architect, *New York Mirror*, 1955
If A is success in life, then A = X + Y + Z. Work is X, Y is play, and Z is keeping your mouth shut.
Albert Einstein, *The Observer*, 1950

Between 1951 and 1984, Japan enjoyed the fastest rate of economic growth in the world, averaging almost 8 per cent annually. During that same period, Japanese GNP *per capita* grew from below 25 per cent of the British level to 25 per cent above it. The explanations offered for this phenomenon are many and interrelated – including those sociocultural features of Japan which support a strong competitive drive; government industrial policies; Japanese manufacturing skills and high industrial efficiency; the strength of domestic competition; the supportive financial system, and so on. But how the Japanese have used marketing to gain competitive success has attracted rather less attention.

Lack of attention to marketing is partly explained by the difficulty of making generalizations. While Japan's production efficiency is fairly constant, objective and measurable, marketing policies are normally affected by the special idiosyncracies of customers, competitors and distribution systems in different countries. A VCR unit or a CNC machine tool is marketed quite differently in Japan, Saudi Arabia, the US and the UK. Each of these markets may well demand different product specifications, advertising, promotion, channels of distribution and price positioning.

A consequence of this need to adapt to local conditions is that, unlike finance or production decisions, marketing ones tend to be decentralized, with local subsidaries enjoying considerable autonomy. By the same token, Japanese subsidaries operating in the UK are very largely managed by local personnel, who do not differ markedly in age, experience or background from those of British companies with which they compete.

Yet plenty of anecdotal evidence suggests that marketing has been a significant factor in the success of the Japanese overseas. And a number of common assumptions about Japanese – as opposed to Western – marketing methods can be tested in practice: like the common observation that, while the marketing of Western companies is orientated towards profitability, that of the Japanese attached greater importance to market share. (This is said to derive from the nature of the Japanese financial system, and from the need for Japanese business to provide long-term security of employment.) Again, Japanese companies seem more adept at exploiting 'strategic windows': i.e., opportunities created by

new market segments, changes in technology or new distribution channels.

Such marketing precision is apparently encouraged by MITI, and energetically adopted by many Japanese companies. Unlike many famous Western business names, Japanese companies have not had a reputation as technological pioneers. Indeed, Japanese culture has been described as risk-averse. For many companies, like Matsushita, avoidance of technological risk appears to be a deliberate policy: redesign, upgrading and the rapid commercialization of innovations made elsewhere are the preferred product strategies.

Japanese companies are everywhere credited with adopting aggressive marketing tactics. Indeed, the presumed priority for market share would tend to dictate low prices, a concern for rapid product-line extensions and high expenditure on advertising, promotion and dealer incentives. The organization of Japanese business, too, must have an effect on marketing; structures are said to emphasize market focus rather than functions; it is also noted that Japanese managements make great efforts to draw personnel into shared company-based value systems, and that their organization, planning and control procedures are less formal than those in the West. Japanese companies are also credited with a greater commitment to training, especially on-the-job development, and with possessing a strong belief in the importance of experimentation and entrepreneurship.

To test the accuracy of these assumptions – and particularly how far they might account for Japanese marketing success abroad – Doyle *et al.* (1986) obtained interviews with the top marketing decision-makers of fifteen leading Japanese companies operating within the UK; also, for the sake of comparison, with their counterparts in fifteen major British competitors. Both the Japanese and UK companies were chosen with an eye to their membership of particular industrial sectors, notably audio equipment and machine tools (CNC lathes and machining centres), but also plain paper copiers, microwave ovens and industrial bearings.

The industries, in turn, were selected for their importance in terms of size or growth. All were among the ten 'sensitive product areas' identified in the 1983–4 EEC–Tokyo trade discussions, and among the top twenty UK imports from Japan. The

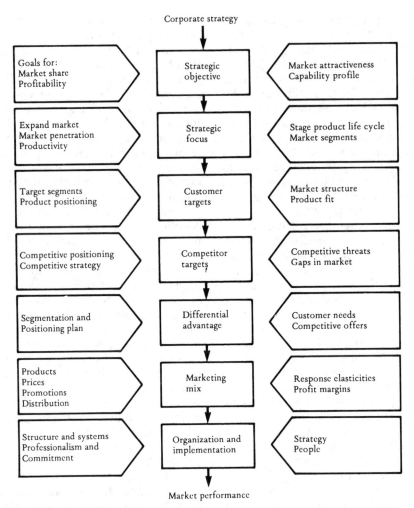

Figure 2.3 *Components of marketing strategy*
Source: P. Doyle, J. Saunders and V. Wong, 'Japanese Marketing Strategies in the UK: A comparative study', *Journal of International Business Studies*, 17, 1, Spring 1986.

Japanese share of the UK audio/hi-fi market in 1984 (when the interviews took place) was approximately 60 per cent and of the machine tool market 55 per cent (in the categories studied). In the case of plain paper copiers and microwave ovens, the figures were 60 per cent and 55 per cent respectively. The components of marketing strategy (Figure 2.3) were used to both guide the interviews and analyse the results.

Strategic objectives

There was a striking contrast between these two national groups in the clarity of their strategic thinking, and in their determination to achieve the objectives that they set themselves. Indeed, only one-third of the British (compared with two-thirds of the Japanese) even believed themselves to be good at sales and marketing. When entering a new market, the British usually arrived late, and few had a strong commitment to it. Two-thirds of UK companies gave defensive reasons for entry: 'we had to in order to survive'. Several admitted that they 'had never really thought it out'. In contrast, the Japanese were much more professional: over 70 per cent said that their moves were 'part of a planned global expansion', or related to the 'potential of the UK market'.

Once in the market, the British lack of commitment to beating the competition was again striking. Some 87 per cent of the Japanese gave 'aggressive growth' or 'market domination' as their goal, but only 20 per cent of the British thought these targets applied to them. Maintenance of the status quo or the prevention of decline were the most typical British objectives. Short-term profit was also much more important to the UK companies (93 per cent) than to the Japanese (40 per cent). The British were willing to allow their market position to be eroded in order to bolster short-term profitability.

Strategic focus

A company can improve profitability by raising volume or by cutting costs and improving productivity. An ambitious company would be expected to concentrate on the former, a defensive one on the latter. The Japanese overwhelmingly chose volume: 73 per cent were out to stimulate primary demand (47 per cent of the British); 67 per cent thought that 'entering newly emerging market segments' was a good description of what they were up to (versus 27 per cent); and 87 per cent aimed to build up market share by weaning customers away from their competitors (53 per cent). The British, by contrast, tended to focus on cost-cutting, range-reduction and rationalization as ways of preventing margin erosion. The fact that a lower market share usually results in a higher unit cost of manufacture (and marketing) did not concern the average British firm.

Customer targets

Market segmentation and positioning are at the heart of modern marketing. Successful companies are generally those which divide up the market into relatively uniform groups of customers, and then target their offerings at the groups with the greatest size or potential. It is therefore alarming to find that 47 per cent of British companies (13 per cent of Japanese) were unclear about the principal categories of customers, and their special needs.

The following comment by the marketing director of a British consumer durables company was typical:

> We have not broken the customers down. We have always held the opinion that the market is wide . . . and the product has wide appeal, therefore why break the market down at all?

The sales director of a British engineering company remarked in similar vein:

> We do not see the market as being made up of specific segments. Our market is made up of the whole industry.

So while the Japanese concentrate their marketing efforts on particular high-potential segments, the British tend to spread theirs thinly across the entire field. Where UK companies did employ market segmentation, it emerged that they tended to be positioned at the lower, cheaper end of the market. This was true whether they were manufacturers of consumer goods or of industrial products. Customers of machine tools and hi-fi equipment increasingly perceive the Japanese, rather than the British product as offering quality and status. Thus, 40 per cent of Japanese firms categorized their customers as up-market, compared with only 13 per cent of the British.

Competitor targets

It is always vital for a company to consider the position and relative strength of its main competitors. Only 20 per cent of Japanese companies in the sample regarded Europeans as their major rivals; the rest saw their main competition in the UK coming from other Japanese groups. Of the British, 60 per cent saw their major rival as Japanese, 40 per cent as British. When looking ahead, the Japanese were most concerned about new products and quality levels being developed by their competitors; the British worried more about price competition. These findings support the view that Japanese companies are as much competitors in export markets as at home. Also, the Japanese tend to position themselves in the quality, high added value sector of the market, while the British allow themselves to be positioned by their competitors – at the price-sensitive commodity end.

Differential advantage

In the absence of a deliberate positioning strategy, it was naturally difficult for British companies to apply the principle of differential advantage. The marketing director of one faltering British company confessed lamely:

> I don't know if we segment the market, or how we really position ourselves against the competition. I expect our advertising agency knows . . . I think we are probably up-market, because we advertise in some very posh magazines.

But the majority of British companies admitted being poor at differentiating themselves from the competition.

Identifying their own perceived advantages, 87 per cent of the Japanese cited 'superior quality and reliability' as a key characteristic (47 per cent of the British made the same claim). Twice as many Japanese as British companies thought that they enjoyed a real competitive advantage in the area of customer service. The most frequently mentioned advantages which the British saw themselves possessing were low prices, a 'traditional brand name' and 'being British'. The sales director of an industrial company observed with satisfaction that:

> . . . there is still a strong buy-British attitude in this country. Our customers know that we are an established British company. British-made is the benefit we are offering them.

The British companies considered themselves weaker at R & D, design, volume manufacturing, production engineering and in their capacity for cost reduction. If the sample companies are at all representative, it is hardly surprising that their performance in overseas markets should so often be disappointing.

Marketing mix

The marketing mix employed by the Japanese companies appears to be as well thought out as their strategic thrust. Their product policy focused on quality and range extensions, to broaden the market appeal. The vast majority of Japanese companies (87 per cent) believed their products to be superior in quality to the competition; only 34 per cent of the British shared this conviction. Cost-cutting and rationalization measures had left most of the British companies with fewer products on offer than their competitors, anyway.

The two groups seemed to attach very similar importance to advertising. However, the Japanese tended to spend more on promotions, and the British more on personal selling. (This could be explained in terms of the more ambitious objectives of the Japanese: personal selling is more efficient for small numbers of customers.) No significant differences emerged in distribution strategies, but the Japanese gave a much higher rating to dealer support.

Organization and implementation

All the Japanese subsidiaries considered that they enjoyed complete (or virtually complete) autonomy in marketing matters – over the choice of products for sale, pricing, promotion and distribution. Nevertheless, their performance was very closely monitored by their head offices in Japan. Control was not achieved by the formal methods favoured by Western multinationals – planning systems and international product management and marketing committees, etc. – but rather by continuous informal monitoring. In 80 per cent of the subsidiaries, a Japanese national acted as managing director and was obviously the key person in the reporting process. All the subsidiaries indicated that reporting was a 'daily' or 'constant' process. Head offices were extremely well-informed about activities, problems and progress.

While virtually all the British companies had traditional, functional structures, two-thirds of the Japanese were organized along product-division lines. The weakness of the functional approach is that few managers feel totally dedicated to the performance of key products. The sales or marketing director would supervise sales of a whole portfolio of products, but would not have the knowledge, incentive or time to champion an individual line.

Further, British companies did not possess budgeting or information systems which showed up performance at the market or product line level. Systems were often designed to show results by factory rather than by product or market. By contrast, organization, responsibilities and systems in the Japanese subsidiaries generally centred around the product or market. The usual explanation was that 'the parent company in Japan is set up this way – every division is a profit centre'.

Teamwork and informality were both more

characteristic in the Japanese companies than in the UK. Two-thirds of the senior managers in the Japanese subsidiaries were consciously concerned about promoting group responsibility and teamwork, compared with only 27 per cent of the British. The latter frequently appeared to have rigid and bureaucratic structures: 60 per cent rated themselves as strongly hierarchical (18 per cent of the Japanese did so). Of the Japanese, 73 per cent regarded job specifications as variable and *ad hoc* (27 per cent of the British). Communication flows were also determined by hierarchy in the British organizations, unlike the looser, informal, task-orientated patterns of the Japanese.

The management style of the Japanese subsidiaries seems to have two effects on their (largely British) managers. First, the informal teamwork and group responsibility gives them all a greater sense of commitment than appears among British competitors. Second, their strategies gain in clarity and acceptance as a result of a sequential decision-making process. Marketing plans in a typical Japanese subsidiary are first developed by the British managers, whose 'collective decision' is then conveyed to the Japanese managing director. Once they have accepted the plan, the Japanese act to defend it in the continual dialogue with head office.

Except for their managing directors, the executives of the Japanese subsidiaries were all British, and often recruited in mid-career from UK companies, to which many of them eventually expect to return. The age, education, experience and background of these managers were very similar, on the whole, to those of their counterparts in the UK companies. The training and promotional practices of the two groups of companies were also indistinguishable. Formal planning, control and information systems did not differ greatly – except that the Japanese tended to overlay formal systems with informal daily communication.

The Japanese subsidiaries did not possess strongly-held shared values, or entertain principles of 'sincerity', 'harmony' or 'team spirit', such as are commonly ascribed to their parent companies. (While the subsidiary executives recognized that their parents probably held such values, no attempt was made to imbue UK staff with them.) And finally, not more than a third of these subsidiaries regarded the benefit of life-long employment as applying in any way to their local managers and personnel.

Conclusion

The English think incompetence is the same thing as sincerity.
Quentin Crisp, *New York Times*, 1977

Crisp's claim is cruel but just when comparing British and Japanese competitive success. The study by Doyle *et al.* (1986) found the differences in performance between the Japanese and British companies in the UK market could not normally be attributed to national, cultural, or other innate advantages. They were the result of professional skill. The most successful UK companies were close to the Japanese in their strategies and organization. All averages are misleading, and it is important to emphasize that there were some excellent British companies in the sample, with imaginative management and good prospects. But, overall, their results strongly support the initial hypothesis about Japanese marketing strengths. The British companies, by contrast, were too often finance or production orientated; they were focused on the short term; and their strategies generally failed to reflect the dynamics of markets. Perhaps, most importantly, many of them failed to recognize the dynamics of competition, to realize that in order to win today, companies need to be highly professional, committed and aggressive. It is striking how often British companies were trying to operate a fortress defence although their inevitable failure in holding these fixed positions often resulted in this becoming contracting or hedgehog defences. Very often this was occurring while the companies were highly profitable already, yet they continued to sacrifice market positions in order to gain even higher short-term profits. More worrying than the market share losses were the apparent failures to invest in new product development and fund the early entry into emerging markets. This is particularly true of the traditional British manufacturers of electrical and electronic goods. Most have become licencers of American or Japanese technology who are happy to take large profits by making middle or low quality products for the British market. Financially they are doing well in the short term, competitively they are suicidal.

To describe the domain in which firms compete it

is necessary to add two more dimensions to Porter's original four. One of the constraints is the institutions with which a company associates. In Britain this means the business community (which is short-term and financially orientated) and a comparatively inflexible work force, with equally short-term views. These make it difficult for a British company to take the risks associated with the aggressive pursual of new market and technological opportunities, or the rapid integration of new manufacturing technology and flexible subcontracting into their operations. British firms are competing with other operators without these limitations and so are, maybe, forced into adopting their short-term and defensive strategies.

The second extra constraint to the competitive domian is a firm's technological and managerial expertise. In pursuit of their short-term financial objectives many British firms are finding it cheaper to license technology rather than develop their own. This allows them to follow leading companies cheaply and to exploit some of the local market opportunities. However, even in the British market these firms are easy prey for the world market leaders from whom they have often licenced the technology. There are now cases of British companies whose new product programmes and manufacturing output is almost completely regulated by the Japanese market leader from whom they purchase technology and major components. In effect these firms have been neutered by the Japanese. They are unable to build up overseas sales because they have no licence for these areas. If the Japanese decide to aggressively attack the UK market the British companies have no means of defence other than asking for government protection. It is difficult for them to hold their market in the UK because the Japanese control them there, it is equally impossible for them to counter-attack in overseas markets because they have limited themselves to being a British supplier. One wonders how long a company like Austin Rover would last if its relationship with Honda faltered.

Lack of marketing expertise was evident from the comparison of British and Japanese companies. This can severely reduce the competitive domain within which British firms can manoeuvre. At one level this may mean the firms are unable to analyse market situations and are unaware of the competitive alternatives open to them. At another level it can mean that a company lacks the expertise to implement programmes that have been identified. This low quality of marketing training may be one reason why so many British companies are financially dominated. Despite their limitations, the financial people are the only ones in an organization who are well-trained and have the necessary knowledge to be able to argue their cases. In the land of the blind even the one-eyed accountant is king.

One reason for this British lack of marketing expertise must be their relatively low expenditure on training. America produces about five times the number of MBAs per head of population as Britain. Despite their disadvantage in initial training, firms in Britain spend, on average, a mere 0.15 per cent of turnover in training their employees. This compares with other estimates: 1 per cent of turnover in the United States and 2 per cent of turnover in Japan and West Germany. In explaining Japan's competitive success relative to America, Kotler said it had not occurred because of the Japanese managers' superior knowledge; the Japanese managers read the same books as the American managers. The difference was, the Japanese had put it into action. Britain's failed competitiveness is explained differently, managers have not even read the books.

References

Ayal, I. and Zif, J., 'Competitive Market Choice Strategies in Multinational Marketing', *Columbia Journal of World Business*, Fall, 1978.

Clausewitz, C. von, *On War*, Pelican Classics, 1968.

Cooper, A. C., and Schendel, D., 'Strategic Responses to Technological Threats', *Business Horizons*, February 1976.

Doyle, P., Saunders, J. and Wong, V., 'A Comparative Study of Japanese Marketing Strategies in the British Market', *Journal of International Business Studies*, 17 (1), Spring 1986.

Kotler, P., Fahey, L., and Jatusrinitak, S., *The New Competition*, Prentice-Hall, 1985.

Kotler, P. and Singh, R., 'Marketing Warfare in the 1980's, *Journal of Business Strategy*, Fall 1980.

Levitt, Theodore, 'Marketing Myopia', *Harvard Business Review*, 38,4, July-August, 1960.

Liddell-Hart, B. H., *Strategy*, Praeger, 1967.

Porter, M.E., *Competitive Strategy: Techniques for Analysing Industries and Competitors*, Free Press, 1980.

Porter, M.E., *Competitive Advantage: Creating and Sustaining Superior Performance*, Free Press, 1985.

Sun Tzu, *The Art of War*, Hodder and Stoughton, 1981.

3
Marketing strategy
ROBIN WENSLEY

Introduction

Strategy is one of the most over used words in the business vocabulary. Corporate planners deal with financial strategies, production strategies, R & D strategies, and marketing strategies. Within the domain of marketing, there are product strategies, sales strategies, promotion strategies, advertising strategies, and even copy strategies. It seems as if *all* business decisions are now strategic. This obsession with strategy has lead Pascale (1982) to conclude that 'Our strategy fetish is a cultural peculiarity. We get off on strategy like the French get off on good food and romance'.

Does this excessive use of the term 'strategy' mean that marketing strategy is just another expression for the traditional subject of marketing management? Are strategic marketing decisions really different from other marketing management decisions? What is marketing strategy? In this chapter, we address these questions by providing a definition of marketing strategy, a marketing strategy statement, and strategic marketing decisions. The definitions are then illustrated by reviewing the decision that led to Honda's success in the US motorcycle market.

We then consider both the role and forms of analysis in marketing strategy and some future issues.

What is strategy?

As suggested, the term 'strategy' has often been used indiscriminately in a business context and this usage has resulted in a profusion of definitions:

> A strategy describes the *direction* the organisation will pursue within its chosen environment, and guides the allocation of resources. A strategy also provides the logic that *integrates* the parochial perspectives of functional departments and operating units and points them in the same direction.
> George S. Day, *Strategic Market Planning: The Pursuit of Competitive Advantage*, West, 1984, p.1.

> Strategic planning is the managerial process of developing and maintaining a viable fit between the organisation's objectives and resources and its environmental opportunities. The job of strategic planning is to design the company in such a way that it consists of enough healthy businesses to keep the company going even when some of its businesses are hurting.
> Philip Kotler, *Marketing Management Analysis, Planning and Control*, 5 ed., Prentice Hall, 1984, p. 44.

> Define *strategic marketing* as a process of: strategically analysing environmental, competitive, and business factors affecting business units and forecasting future trends in business areas of interest to the enterprise.
> Participating in setting objectives and formulating corporate and business unit strategy.

Selecting target market strategies for the product-markets in each business unit, establishing marketing objectives, and developing, implementing, and managing program positioning strategies for meeting target market need.

David W. Cravens, *Strategic Marketing*, Irwin, 1982, p. 18.

Strategic marketing management is the analytical process of seeking a differential advantage through: (1) the analysis and choice of the firm's product-market relationships with a view toward developing the best yield configuration in terms of financial performance: and (2) the formulation of management strategies that create and support viable product–market relationships consistent with the enterprise capabilities and objectives.

Roger A. Kerrin and Robert A. Peterson, *Perspective on Strategic Marketing Management*, 2nd ed., Allyn and Bacon, 1983, p. 5.

Strategy is: a scheme or principal idea through which an objective would be achieved.

David J. Luck and O. C. Ferrell, *Marketing Strategy and Plans*, 2nd ed., Prentice Hall, 1985, p. 2.

The strategy concept can be encapsulated into two core elements: the product-market investment decision which encompasses the product-market scope of the business strategy, its investment intensity, and the resource allocation in a multiple-business context.

The development of a sustainable competitive advantage to compete in those markets. This core concept encompasses underlying distinctive competences or assets, appropriate objectives, functional area politics, and the creation of synergy.

David A. Aaker, *Strategic Market Management*, Wiley, 1984, p. 6.

Abell and Hammond (1983), in the first textbook on marketing strategy, decided not to define the term because it was too difficult. Other marketers only define marketing strategy implicitly, in their definition of strategic marketing management.

Part of the confusion concerning the term 'strategy' arises out of its present usage in English language. The word 'strategy' is derived from a Greek term which is roughly translated as the 'art of the general (or commander-in-chief)' (Evered, 1983). Thus, strategy originally referred to the skills and decision-making process of the executive, while 'strategem', translated as 'an operation or act of generalship', referred to a specific decision made by the executive. Over time, the term 'stratagem' has fallen into disuse (in present usage it indicates an artifice or trick) and, now, strategy has a dual connotation – it is both the art itself and the output of practising the art. To further complicate matters, some writers suggest that strategy is reserved for a formal logic, explicitly stated that links together the activities of business; while, others indicate that a strategy can emerge from a set of decisions and need not be explicitly stated (Mintzberg and Waters, 1985). The Kotler, Cravens, and Kerrin and Peterson definitions emphasize the process of strategy, while Day and Aaker emphasize the output of strategy.

In this chapter we will return to the notion of *marketing strategy* as an approach, a process and set of skills, for examining business situations and a *marketing strategy statement* (MSS) as the output of applying this approach. The MSS may be explicitly stated or implicitly derived from observing a set of actions; however, the marketing strategy statement must consider two issues:

- The specific market toward which activities are to be targeted.
- The types of competitive advantage that are to be developed and exploited.

Strategy and business mission

The Luck and Ferrell definition of strategy is similar to the definition of a business mission statement. However, a business mission is a statement that is much less specific than a marketing strategy statement. A mission statement contains an appropriate degree of generality so that it can perform an integrating function of various stakeholders over a long period of time (Ouchi, 1983).

Some examples of mission statements are:

- 'Apple (computers) is not in the game or toy business but in the computer business. What Apple does best is to take a high-cost ideal and turn it into a low-cost, high quality solution' (Apple Mission).
- Levitt's (1960) suggestion that railroads should have defined their mission as being in the transportation business.

● The following principles of Marks and Spencer, the noted UK retailer:

1 To offer our customers a selective range of *high quality well-designed and attractive merchandise* at reasonable prices.
2 To *encourage our suppliers* to use the most modern and efficient techniques of production and quality control dictated by the latest discoveries in science and technology.
3 With the *cooperation* of our suppliers, to ensure the highest standards of quality control.
4 To plan the expansion of our stores for the better display of a widening range of goods (and) for the *convenience of our customers.*
5 To *simplify operating procedures* so that our business is carried on in the most efficient manner.
6 *To foster good human relations with customers, suppliers and staff.*

Marks and Spencer internal document

On the other hand, some 'mission' statements are so narrow that they fail to meet the test of generality but too wide to provide a specific approach for dealing with a target market. For example, consider the mission statement developed by ITT Barton (Pearce, 1982):

The mission (of ITT Barton) is to serve the industry and government with quality instruments used for primary measurement, analysis and local control of fluid flow, level, pressure, temperature, and fluid properties. This instrumentation includes flow meters, electronic readouts, indicators, recorders, switches, liquid level systems, analytical instruments such as titrators, integrators, controllers, transmitters, and various instruments for the measurement of fluid properties (density, viscosity, gravity) used for process variable sensing, data collection, control and transmission. The mission includes fundamental 'loop-closing' control and display devices when economically justified, but excludes broadline central controlroom instrumentation, systems design and turnkey responsibility. Markets served include instrumentation, for oil and gas production, gas transportation, chemical and petrochemical processing, cryogenics, power generation, aerospace, Government and marine, as well as other instrument and equipment manufacturers.

This statement is clearly too narrow and detailed to serve as a mission statement but does not qualify as a marketing strategy statement because it focuses solely on defining target product-markets and does not state the nature of competitive advantages sought. In general, good mission statements are short on numbers and long on rhetoric while remaining succinct. On the other hand some numbers can be useful, such as Toyota's 'Global 10' mission (to have 10 per cent of the world auto market by 1990) (*Business Week*, 1985).

Strategic marketing decisions

Decisions and events can also be labelled strategic, yet again a considerable degree of confusion exists. Many definitions of strategic decisions rely implicitly or explicitly on the notion that such decisions are 'important' at least from a historical perspective (Barwise *et al.*, 1985). However, validity problems arise with any historical reconstruction, thus we need to have some method for recognizing strategic decisions or events before they occur. At this stage we prefer to identify two characteristics of strategic decisions:

● Involvement of a significant resource commitment and thus they are considered to be important because of the level of resources.
● Consideration of competitive activity and a focus on establishing a sustainable competitive advantage.

Marketing plan

While identifying strategic from non-strategic decisions is useful, we do not believe that it is meaningful to distinguish between strategic and non-strategic plans. A plan is, no more and no less, than 'the way it is intended to carry out some proceeding'. The extent to which a plan is strategic or not is therefore the extent to which the proceeding is to be regarded as strategic. We believes that a strategic market plan differs from most market plans, only in the extent to which the former is prefaced by the marketing strategy statement and the analysis used to derive the statement. Of course, some other commentators have identified the key characteristics of a marketing strategy statement but called it a strategic plan:

The Kernel of a strategic plan is the rule that it breaks, the orthodoxy that firm is choosing to challenge. Without a clear definition of the myth that drives the competitors and the truth that is the future touchstone of the firm's own future operating principle, the plan cannot be called STRATEGIC. It's just another of those boring documents that we've all seen (and probably written) full of pious platitudes signifying nothing. As Philip Larkin said of the modern novel recently: 'A beginning, a muddle and an end'.

The other defining property of a strategic plan is that the analytical section is devoted to dispelling the myth by which the competitors live; it cannot, by definition, lead to the truth by which the firm itself is choosing to live. This has to be a jump of the imagination. A plan that doesn't make such a jump is a fraud. In other words a strategy cannot be fully rationalised. It has to be an act of faith. This is the central message of the modern philosophy of science. No general statement, not even the simplest iterative generalisation, can be derived from raw data without some imaginative effort on the part of the mind. Einstein suggested that, 'a theory can be proved by experiment; but no path leads from experiment to the birth of a theory'.

Jules Goddard, *London Business School Journal*, Winter 1985.

The marketing strategy statement

The marketing strategy statement identifies the product-market towards which a business plans to commit resources and the bases upon which the business attempts to develop a sustainable competitive advantage in that product market.

In the remaining portion of this section, we will discuss the three critical concepts embodied in this definition of the marketing strategy statement: the product-market; sustainable competitive advantage; and the commitment of resources.

Product-market space – the competitive arena

A product-market is a group of potential customers with similar needs and sellers who employ similar methods (technologies and marketing programmes) in providing products (or services) to satisfy those needs. A product-market space is a set of product-markets in a specific industry or business domain.

Thus, the product-market space is the commercial arena in which sellers compete against each other for customers. Figure 3.1 illustrates a product-market space for companies in the entertainment business. A variety of entertainment products and services are listed on the left-hand column

	Markets				
Products	Children under 13	Teenagers 13–20	Young adults 21–45	Middle age 46–65	Elderly over 65
Motion pictures					
Network TV programming					
Cable TV programming					
Phonograph records					
Video games					
Operations theme park					
Cable TV operator					
Operating ski resort					
Staging rock concert					

Figure 3.1 *Product-market space for entertainment businesses*

of Figure 3.1. These offerings range from manufacturing tangible products such as motion pictures and video games to providing entertainment 'services' such as designing and/or operating theme parks and ski resorts. A set of market segments based on customer age are described on the top row of Figure 3.1. Each square in the matrix describes a product-market in which a set of firms compete against each other to provide entertainment to a group of consumers.

For example, American International and New World produce low-budget, motion pictures (*Halloween*, *Friday the 13th*) primarily directed towards a teenage market segment; General Cinema and Plitt operate motion picture theatres across the US: MTM Productions (*Hill Street Blues*) and Lorimar (*Dallas*) compete against each other developing programmes for television networks; and Walt Disney and Six Flags operate theme parks directed towards satisfying the entertainment needs of families with children.

The entertainment product-market space shown in Figure 3.1 is only one of many possible representations of the entertainment business. The space could be expanded both in terms of offerings and market segments. Operating a professional soccer franchise or manufacturing toys could be included in the set of offerings. In addition, some offerings could be subdivided. For example, motion pictures could be broken down further by content (G, PG, PG-13, R, X ratings) or method of production (animated, filmed on location, filmed in a studio). Rather than segmenting the market by age, other segmentation variables could be used such as family life cycle stage (young single, young married with no children, full nest, empty nest, elderly, single) or usage situation (entertainment consumed at home versus away from home). However, for this illustration, we will limit our attention to the nine product-market alternatives shown in Figure 3.1.

Consider the strategic marketing decisions facing Walt Disney Productions – a firm that competes in the entertainment business. Should Walt Disney Productions engage competition in each of the fifty product-market alternatives shown in Figure 3.1 or focus on a limited number of alternatives? If Disney focuses on a few alternatives, which product-markets should it pursue? Should it aggressively attack all alternatives selected or pursue a holding action in some alternatives? Notice that all of these questions can be translated into resource allocation decisions. The marketing strategy statement will indicate which product-markets will receive no resources, which will receive limited resources to maintain a holding position, and which will receive substantial resources.

When confronted with these opportunities in the 1950s, Walt Disney Productions adopted a marketing strategy which emphasized theme parks, television programmes and motion pictures directed towards US families with children between 6 and 12 years old (*Business Week*, 1978). Having made the strategic decision to focus on these alternatives, Disney developed a marketing programme to implement its strategy in each product-market alternative. The development of these implementation programmes required a number of additional decisions concerning specific features of the products and services offered, pricing, advertising, promotion and distribution channels. The marketing strategy statement – the selection of product-market alternatives and the allocation of resources – provided the framework for the implementation programmes.

Sustainable competitive advantage

The objective of strategic marketing thinking is to achieve a *sustainable competitive advantage*. Just identifying an exciting product-market opportunity is not enough. The firm must realize that competitors will also recognize these attractive opportunities.

Most marketers are aware of the significant profit potential in products such as premium quality, conveniently prepared, frozen foods; computers for small businesses; robotic and factory automation; and genetically engineered products. However, only firms that have or are able to develop sustainable competitive advantages in these areas will realize these potential profits.

Many firms have been early, but finally unsuccessful entrants, in exciting markets. Some examples of these firms that failed to develop a long-term sustainable advantage are Bowmar in hand-held calculators; Osborne in portable, personal computers; Sinclair in home computers; Texas Instruments in digital watches; Reynolds in ball-point pens; Royal Crown in diet and caffeine-free cola drinks; and Advent in large screen television.

Bruce Henderson (1981), the founder of the Boston Consulting Group, emphasized the importance of understanding competition and achieving competitive advantage:

> A market can be viewed in many different ways and a product can be used in many different ways. Each time the product-market pairing is varied, the relative competitive strength is varied too. Many businessmen do not recognise that a key element in strategy is choosing the competitor whom you wish to challenge, as well as choosing the market segment and product characteristics with which you will compete.

Basis for building a sustainable competitive advantage

Methods for building a sustainable competitive advantage can be divided into three groups:

- *Advantages residing in the organization.*
  Economies of scope
  Intraorganizational synergies
  Flexibility
  Speed of response
- *Advantages residing in a functional area production.*
  Process technology
  Production efficiency
  Scale economies
  Experience
  Product quality
  Research and development.
    Product technology
    Patents
  Marketing.
    Skills in developing new products
    Communication (advertising, sales force) efficiency
    Pricing policy
    Knowledge of customer
    Services provided – credit, technical assistance
    Location
- *Advantages based on relationships with external entities.*
  Customer loyalty
  Channel control
  Preferential political/legislative treatment
  Access to financial resource

While this categorization is somewhat arbitrary, it does illustrate the focus of this chapter. Corporate strategy is concerned with the entire list of potential advantages; however, the primary focus of corporate strategy is on advantages residing in integration of functional areas within the firm. For example, operating a portfolio of business units and exploiting synergies across business units is an important issue in corporate strategy.

Marketing strategy concentrates on competitive advantages based on activities undertaken by the marketing function. In addition, we focus on the advantages derived from relationships typically governed by the marketing function relationships between the firm, its customers, and the distribution channels serving those customers. These sources of advantages arise from activities performed by a number of functional areas within the firm; however, the marketing function is typically responsible for directing the firm's resources toward satisfying customer needs. The marketing function develops long-term relationships with customers, just as the purchasing function creates competitive advantages through supplier relations.

Cost and technology-based advantages often interact with market-based advantages. Low production costs can be translated into low prices. Unique technology can be used to provide customer benefits that cannot be offered by competitors. While within marketing strategy we must examine competitive advantages developed in functional areas other than marketing, our emphasis should be on how these cost and technology advantages map into customer-based, marketing advantages.

Sustainability

The list of competitive advantages is not exhaustive. In fact, any business activity can be developed into a sustainable competitive advantage. The degree to which any business activity can be used as competitive advantage is a function of the ease with which competitors can overcome the advantage. Some advantages seem to be easier to overcome than others. For example, it is difficult for one well-known firm to develop a competitive advantage over others based on access to low cost, financial resources, because capital markets are quite efficient. Thus all large firms have relatively equal opportunies to raise needed financial resources. For these firms, the cost of financial resources levied by capital markets is based on an accurate appraisal of the strategic investment opportunities facing the firms. Thus, a competitive advantage possessed by a firm results in the cost of financial resources rather than the cost of financial resources resulting in a competitive advantage. However, businesses engaging in small, little known product-market opportunities may realize a competitive advantage from being able to secure financial resources from a large, well-heeled parent corporation. The parent corporation, based on its intimate knowledge of the opportunity, will adequately fund the business; while small, independent competitors will be unable to attract commensurate funding from a less-informed imperfect, capital market.

In a marketing context, it is difficult to secure a competitive advantage through pricing. Changes in prices are immediately recognized by competition. Competitors can easily respond to these changes, competing away any short-term advantage that might have been created.

On the other hand, geographic location frequently results in a sustainable competition advantage. There are a limited number of high density traffic sites for retail outlets selling convenience foods. Only one outlet can occupy a specific location. Thus in the USA, once McDonalds has built fast-food restaurants in the best locations, Burger King and Wendy's are at long-term disadvantage when they are located in the second and third best sites. In the UK, however, McDonalds have been successful despite the fact that in principle Wimpy had an earlier opportunity to secure the first quality sites.

Commitment of resources

A marketing strategy involves the *commitment* of resources to a product-market. Typically, a firm must invest in idiosyncratic assets if it wants to build a sustainable competitive advantage in a product-market. In other words, the strategic investments made in a product-market are to a certain extent unique to that product-market – they cannot be easily transferred to other product-markets once the firm has made the investment; it is committed, it cannot easily back out. Owing to their idiosyncratic nature, strategic investments are risky for the firm

and even more risky for competitors who might consider responding.

Marketing strategy and military strategy

Frequently, analogies are drawn between business strategy and military strategies (see Kotler and Singh, 1985; Trout and Ries, 1985; Wensley, 1989). Since as we have already indicated the word 'strategy' is derived from the Greek word defined as 'the art of the general', it may be useful to compare our definition of marketing strategy to the definition of military strategy.

Allocation of resources

Our definition of marketing strategy emphasizes the role of resource allocations. Similarly, a military strategy is primarily concerned with the control and deployment of resources. It provides a framework for military actions during a confrontation. The framework focuses on where and when the point of attack will be made and how personnel and equipment will be deployed across the battlefield. A marketing strategy statement indicates the direction a business plans to take in terms of the products and markets that will be emphasized (the points of attack).

Locus of activity

Rather than deploying troops and equipment across a terrain, a marketing strategy statement is concerned with the problem of allocating product development, sales force, advertising, and promotional activities across a product-market space. Classic military strategy is implemented in physical terrain, which does not change over time. The valleys remain valleys and the high ground remains high ground. However, the product-market 'battlefield' is constantly changing. In addition to external forces of change, such as technology and customer values, businesses are continually changing the product-market space as they attempt to erode away advantages established by competitors. Consider the changes that have occurred in the previously discussed entertainment product-market space over the last ten years, such as the growth of videorecording and the decline of home movies, the penetration of cable TV and cable networks, the video game fad, and the popularity of adult games like Trivial Pursuit. Thus, classic military strategy involves consideration of a more stable environment than the product-market space of marketing strategy.

Objective

In our definition of the marketing strategy statement, we emphasize the objective of building sustainable competitive advantage. Military strategy considers similar objectives, but different authorities have defined it in different ways while von Clausewitz suggested that the objective of war is total domination of the enemy, Liddell-Hart (1967) suggests that a more appropriate objective is a 'better state of peace': this state is realized by achieving a position (an advantage) which is so secure that an enemy would not consider an attack.

In a marketing context, a better state of peace may be achieved by obtaining an increased share in such a manner that competitors would find it unattractive to attempt to regain their lost market share. In other words, the share had been gained through exploiting a competitive advantage that could be sustained.

Grand strategy and corporate strategy

Military strategy is not an end unto itself. It must fit within the grand strategy which reflects the political goals of a country. Military strategy is just one approach to achieve a country's goals. Similarly marketing strategy statement must be considered within a wider framework – often referred to as corporate strategy. However, the military analogy is instructive here since it suggests that we cannot, as is often claimed, see corporate strategy as just the next level which incorporates the various functional and resource strategies (R & D, production, marketing, and human and physical resources). The military analogue suggests that corporate strategy should be primarily concerned with delimiting the domains in which a marketing (competition, external market evaluation) approach should dominate as opposed to domains in which a more internal method of evaluation (and in some cases external cooperation) is to be encouraged. Such an approach might help us to understand more the nature of individual firm behaviour which treats neither approach as totally dominant (*Business Week*, 1985):

> Perhaps the most revealing point that comes out of these essays is how alien the concept of free markets

is to the Japanese. Munemichi Inoue of the Marubeni Trading Corporation, describes how most large companies co-operate with each other in some fields such as resource development and turnkey projects, while they compete fiercely in others. Free competition is not even at issue. The key question is: What Works?

Summary

Thus, a marketing strategy statement indicates a target product-market opportunity and the bases that will be used to defend a position in the product-market. But many strategy or policy statements do not meet these criteria. Many policy statements are simply a set of financial goals. While these objectives may be useful in evaluating strategic opportunities, they provide no direction in terms of what product-markets or competitive approach should be emphasized.

The following policy statement is a good example of such a financially orientated policy statement with little direction.

1 Achieve and maintain 10–15 per cent growth in EPS.
2 To do this while:
   - Increasing dividends
   - Maintaining control
   - Maintaining a strong financial position
   (a) ROI greater than 12–1/2%
   (b) Limiting non-productive investment
   (c) Using debt, but D/E <40%
3 Improve quality of earning by improving:
   - Participation in recognized growth markets
   - Volume in high margin proprietary products
   - Emphasis on marketing position
   - No product/customer more than 15% sales
4 Maintain reputation for:
   - New product introduction from within
   - Market leader in its field of operation
   - Low vulnerability to techno-economic and government factors
   - High level of management expertise
   - Logical grouping of businesses
5 Acquisitions as necessary but:
   - In related areas
   - Less than 30% overseas

On the other hand, Bucy, the chief executive officer of Texas Instruments (TI) decided in 1971 at a strategy meeting that 'we should either get into the consumer market or forget about it' (*Business Week*, 1978).

Prior to 1971, efforts were directed primarily towards supplying semiconductor products to industrial and aerospace customers. TI recognized that technological advances would result in a large, rapidly growing market for consumer electronic products – products for which TI manufactured the critical components. Thus TI decided to put most of its development money for the next few years into the consumer business rather than into computer memories and microprocessors, as its competitors did. They penalized semiconductors – that was the price they paid for allocating their resources toward consumer electronics. In attacking the consumer electronics market with hand-held calculators, home computers, and digital watches, TI focused on building competitive advantages based on low cost gained through large-scale production. This statement by Bucy clearly indicates where emphasis should and should not be placed. In addition, it provides the method by which competitive advantage will be pursued.

Marketing strategy as an explicit set of strategic decisions

Typically, a number of decisions will be involved in translating a marketing strategy statement into practice. This multiplicity of decisions can arise because multiple, and often interrelated, competitive advantages rather than one single advantage are usually required to defend a position in a product-market. Even when multiple advantages are not used, the establishment of one basis of advantage almost always involves a sequence of individual, but related decisions through time.

The success of Honda marketing motorcycles in the US is an interesting example of how a set of strategic decisions result in a marketing strategy.

You meet the nicest people on a Honda

In the business community, the success of Honda motorcycles is frequently used as an example of a successful, explicitly articulated marketing strategy based on using sophisticated analytical techniques. In 1951, Honda was unknown in the US and a minor factor in a highly fragmented, Japanese motorcycle industry. The 575,000 US motorcycles market was dominated by an American manufacturer, Harley-Davidson, and three British manufacturers, BSA, Triumph, and Norton. The image of the motorcyclist was based on Marlon Brando's role in the film *The Wild One* – an unsavoury group of troublemakers who rode large bikes terrorizing the countryside.

Ten years later the US motorcycle market had expanded by 140 per cent. Honda had a 63 per cent market share while Harley-Davidson and the three British manufacturers had less than a 15 per cent market share combined. Honda was directing its marketing effort toward selling lightweight, 50 cc bikes to the young families product-market using an advertising theme 'You meet the nicest people on a Honda'.

In 1975, a report prepared by the Boston Consulting Group (BCG) for the British government identified the reason for the emergence of Honda and the decline of British manufacturers in the US motorcycle market. Case studies based on this report are still used extensively in business policy and marketing strategy courses (Purkagastha, 1981). The BCG report and case studies suggests that Honda developed a low cost competitive advantage in 50 cc motorcycles due to large-scale production of lightweight motorcycles in Japan. When entering the US market, Honda exploited this cost advantage by focusing on a leisure use ('nicest people') segment. It expanded the size of this segment through aggressive pricing and advertising. After realizing significant sales for small 50 cc motorcycles to a leisure segment, it introduced larger motorcycles targeted towards more traditional market segments. Thus, the BCG report attributes Honda's success to a well-articulated strategy directed toward a specific product-market (lightweight motorcycle for a leisure use segment) building on a specific competitive advantage (cost economics).

However, Richard Pascale (1984) interviewed six executives involved with Honda's entry in the US market and found that Honda's success was due to a dynamic, organizational learning process rather than the streamlined, analytical strategic decision-making model suggested in the case studies. The following discussion describes the set of strategic decisions that resulted in Honda's US market strategy.

Technological advantage

In 1949, Sochiro Honda teamed with Tukeo Fujisawa to start producing motorcycles. Fujisawa provided financial resources as well as marketing skills, while Honda was an inventive genius who viewed the company as an outlet for his createive skills. Their initial product had a noisy, two-stroke engine which was not competitive. But, in 1951, Honda designed a four-stroke engine with twice as much horsepower as competitive engines of the same size and weight. Due to the design advantage of this engine, the firm became one of the four or five leading motorcycle manufacturers in Japan.

While Fujisawa was interested in marketing motorcycles with the new engine, Honda saw the engine as an opportunity of achieving a central life ambition – racing motorcycles and winning the motorcycle 'Olympics', the Isle of Man TT race. Fujisawa pressed Honda into adopting the technological advances learned through racing to commercial motorcycles. Eventually, a lightweight but high horsepower 50 cc motorcycle was introduced in 1958 catapulting Honda into first place among Japanese manufacturers.

Marketing entry

After unsuccessful ventures into South-East Asia, Honda was attracted to the US market. Based on a visit to the US, Kihachiro Kawashima, the soon-to-be President of American Honda, was doubtful that motorcycles could ever do well in America given the widespread availability and use of automobiles. But he felt that Honda might be able to secure 10 per cent of 60,000 unit market for imported (largely British) motorcycles. The Japanese Ministry of Finance was even more sceptical, delaying Honda's currency exchange application for six months, and eventually only permitting a $250,000 investment.

Finally, in July 1959, Honda opened a small warehouse in Los Angeles with a $100,000 start-up inventory composed of equal numbers for each of four models: 50 cc; 125 cc; 250 cc; and 305 cc. In terms of dollars, the inventory was weighted towards larger motorcycles. 'Mr Honda was especially confident of the 250 cc and 305 cc machines. The shape of the handlebars on these larger machines looked like the eyebrows of a Buddha, which he felt was a strong selling point'. Forty dealers were established and the larger motorcycles began to sell.

Disaster struck in April 1960. Because motorcycles in the US are driven much further and faster than in Japan, oil leaks and clutch problems developed. While the American Honda group worked feverishly on solving these problems, events took a surprising turn.

Channel relationships

A Sears buyer called on American Honda after seeing people from the company doing errands around Los Angeles using the 50 cc motorcycles. Even though Honda was reluctant to use intermediaries and was not optimistic about the potential for small units, it was desperate and agreed to sell the 50 cc motorcycle through Sears.

As the 50 cc motorcycle began to sell, other dealers approached Honda. Surprisingly, these dealers were in sporting goods rather than motorcycles. While the dealers informed Honda that the 50 cc customers were normal everyday Americans not motorcycle gang members, Honda was reluctant to advertise this segment fearing that it would alienate the traditional, macho market towards which it was directing its attention.

Customer loyalty

In the spring of 1963, an undergraduate UCLA student suggested the theme 'You meet the nicest people on a Honda' in a routine assignment for an advertising class. He passed his paper along to a friend at Grey Advertising who used the idea to solicit the Honda account. While the American Honda management team was divided in terms of this new approach, the commitment of the Honda advertising director swayed the group towards accepting the advertising programme. By 1964, one out of every two motorcycles sold in the US was a Honda.

Honda's success in the US was the result of a technological breakthrough in engine design and some fortuitous events, one of which, the failures of the 250 cc and 305 cc motorcycles, had surprisingly positive consequences. While the role of good fortune should not be underestimated in the success of any marketing programme, the Honda example, at least as it is described above, is also clearly atypical of strategic decision making by many Japanese firms. Japanese firms tend to undertake substantial analyses before embarking on a programme of international market entry (Kotler and Faney, 1982).

Similarly, Honda has maintained its initial success in the US over the years by consistent actions to sustain a competitive advantage based on distribution and brand image in addition to low cost realized through high volume production. The distribution and image advantages arose from the initial decisions to distribute through Sears and to advertise Honda motorcycles for the average American.

Specific distribution and advertising decisions in the Honda example had substantial, long-term strategic implications. They resulted in establishing bases for sustainable competitive advantages and subsequent financial performance. The willingness to make these decisions also involved significant commitments to the 50 cc – leisure segment of the American Honda team and to the US motorcycle market by Honda in Japan.

When the American Honda group decided to distribute motorcycles through Sears, it committed itself to a new strategic direction that would have been difficult to reverse. The Sears decision probably alienated the motorcycle dealers through which Honda originally distributed its larger motorcycles. Had the market served by Sears not developed, Honda might have had difficulty re-establishing satisfactory distribution through suspicious motorcycle dealers. In addition, the advertising positioning towards a leisure segment, potentially alienated the traditional macho motorcycle segment. Thus, once Honda began to pursue the 50 cc – leisure segment product-market, they were committed to that marketing strategy.

In addition, corporate Honda demonstrated a strong commitment to the US motorcycle market. Even when confronted by the prospects of a limited market and early problems, it continued to support the American Honda group.

The role of an explicit statement of strategy

Returning to the Walt Disney Productions illustration, the chief executive officer, after reading this introduction, might respond: 'What is all this marketing strategy stuff? Our objective is to make as much profit as we can. We want to get as much of the consumer entertainment dollar as possible, and we will offer any form of entertainment to anybody who will pay a price that makes money for us'. This perspective would be similar to generals indicating that their strategy is to gain as much territory as possible and ordering the troops to simply charge ahead in any direction they can. Such global, non-directive approaches are not successful in a marketing context or a military context. They often do not result in a marketplace position or a battlefield position that can be defended against competitive attack. By spreading resources across a wide range of alternatives, it is typically impossible to develop a sustainable competitive advantage for any single opportunity.

On the other hand, we must be careful of too much oversimplification. In practice, coordination is rarely costless and often comes hand-in-hand with direction. To return to our analogue of the generals: there was considerable debate between the US and UK commanders over the plans for D-Day as to whether one major frontal assault would actually be better than a whole series of smaller scale invasions which would only be further reinforced and supported if they individually achieved a degree of initial success. In this way 'charging ahead' becomes 'testing the various markets'!

In general, at least at the business unit level the strategic marketing direction that a business plans to pursue needs to be made explicit in terms of specific product-market directions, because success in achieving a sustainable competitive advantage does depend upon people working together so that their efforts are mutually reinforcing. Without an explicit marketing strategy statement, the marketing efforts of a business can work at cross purposes. Advertising campaigns can be directed towards a product-market, but the sales force may fail to call on retailers and wholesalers supporting that product-market. Products may be developed for markets that are not compatible with the business channels of distribution. Thus, the strategic marketing statement provides a vehicle for communicating the business future direction and coordinating efforts throughout the organization.

In addition, an explicit marketing strategy statement allows a business to respond more effectively to changing market conditions. When conditions change, the current marketing strategy and the reasons for the current strategy can be re-examined.

The implications of the changing conditions can be identified and the business can then determine what, if any, changes need to be made in its marketing strategy statement.

There is a danger however that such examples of the need for explicit strategy statements are taken too much at face value: they certainly do imply a rather naive view of most organizations and perhaps overestimate the likely impact of such statements. In practice, the explicit statement provides the underlying logic that guides commercial action in the relevant domain: it provides an effective basis for the discussion of such individual actions within a wider context. Such discussions take place not only between functional executives but also between various levels in the managerial hierarchy.

Focus of strategy development

Level of decision making

Strategic decisions in the sense we have used the term (significant resource commitments, consideration of competitive activity and sustainable advantage) can be made to some extent at all levels in the firm from the chief executive officer (CEO) to the individual sales person. In addition, they can be made in each functional area and in each of the business units. While strategic decisions can be made throughout the corporation, from a normative perspective where should these important decisions be made? Should they be the purview solely of people at the top levels of the corporation or should this responsibility be given to people at lower levels? When attempting to answer these normative questions, one is faced with a classical trade-off between developing a globally optimal strategy based on limited information versus a set of locally optimal strategies based on more complete information (Boxer and Wensley, 1985).

The chief executive officer and corporate planners are in a position to consider all the synergies between business activities directed toward product-markets in which the firm participates. From this global perspective, these people are in a position to develop an 'optimal' strategy that exploits these synergies. However, the information available to corporate planners is limited by the cognitive capacity of the planners and the homogenized nature of the in-

formation flowing up from lower levels in the organization.

On the other hand, people at lower levels in the organization have more detailed information, but they are largely unaware of the relationship between their activities and other activities within the firm. While these people are able to make more informed decisions, their decision will only be 'optimal' for their limited domain.

Historical trend

Over the last twenty years, the rate of change in political, economic, and technological events has increased dramatically. This rapidly changing environment spawned books like *Future Shock* and a growing interest in strategic considerations. Business people needed to develop strategies for coping with the growing uncertainties they face – new technologies with communication, bio-engineering and electronics, and production methods; changing government policies; and increased domestic and foreign competition.

In addition to enormous changes in the business environment, the increased complexity of the business organization fostered a need for explicit strategy statements. Between 1949 and 1970, the majority of the *Fortune* 500 companies shifted from single product, functional organizations to multidivisional, multiple industry and even multinational corporations (Rumelt, 1974). Prior to this change, strategic direction could be provided by a key idea in the head of the entrepreneur. Modern businesses now require explicit strategic statements to coordinate the activities of complex organizations facing rapidly evolving environments.

During this period, strategic direction was determined at the highest level of the corporation. Professional planners became dominant figures in their companies and the influence of operating managers on the strategic direction of their businesses declined rapidly.

However, the role of the corporate planner is now changing. Responsibility for strategic decision-making is now shifting from a corporate staff function to the line business unit managers (Armstrong *et al.*, 1984). Many firms feel that strategic insights from a top-level perspective are limited because they lacked intimate knowledge of the dynamics in the product-market space and the bases for competitive advantage in the space. For example, corporate planners at General Electric (GE) recognized some major environmental trends that would impact on GE's home appliance business. They foresaw the internationalization of markets and the potential entry of Japanese manufacturers, the rising oil prices and the emphasis on energy efficiency, and the shrinking sizes of both houses and families. However, the corporate planners arrived at some incorrect implications for product-market strategies based on these observations. They predicted an overall decline in the refrigerator business and a need to develop smaller, better insulated refrigerators. Because the planners were not in contact with the marketplace or technology, they did not realize that while homes were getting 'smaller, the sizes of the kitchens were not shrinking. In addition, families with working women, a growing segment, wanted larger refrigerators so that they could shop less frequently. Finally, technology suggested that the greatest gains in efficiency could be realized by improving compressors, not insulation.

Relationship between corporate and market strategy

The 'appropriate' level for strategic decision making is a function of the number of product-markets in which the firm operates and the degree to which activities between product-markets are interrelated. At one extreme, strategic decision making may be restricted to the highest levels, when a firm operates in a few, highly-interrelated product-markets. In this situation, there is a substantial overlap between corporate strategy and marketing strategy. In fact, the only difference is that marketing strategy (as we define it) focuses on a limited set of competitive advantages – advantages based on the performance of the marketing function and relationships under the control of the marketing function (customers and channels) – while corporate strategy must consider a wider set of business activities and relationships. Even, in this relatively simple situation, it may be appropriate to develop separate strategies for each functional area and each type of relationship, if there is little synergy between the separate activities.

More complex firms that operate in many product-markets face the dilemma of how much emphasis to place on the integration capability of top-level managers versus the insights of low-level managers.

Dynamic nature of marketing strategy

Coping with a changing environment

A marketing strategy must be dynamic if it is to effectively cope with an inherently dynamic environment. New technologies develop, customer needs change, and competitors react to decisions made by the firm. Regional markets become global markets. Technological and regulatory change bring new competitors into competition against more traditional suppliers.

The Disney, Texas Instrument and Honda examples mentioned previously illustrate the evolutionary nature of marketing strategy. The phenomenal success of Walt Disney Productions was, in part, due to the fact that the 6 to 13 year old segment of the population, Disney's target market, grew from 14.7 per cent of the US population in 1950 to 18.2 per cent of the population in 1960. But this segment is beginning to decline. In 1980, it accounted for only 15 per cent of the US population, and by 1990 it is expected to fall to 12 per cent. Realizing this change in the environment, Walt Disney Productions facing a declining product-market, altered its product-market focus towards the growing segment of 21 to 24 year old adults. To implement this new approach, Disney has made changes in its marketing mix. PG rated movies, such as *Splash*, are replacing traditional G rated movies, thrill rides like *Space Mountain* are being added to the theme parks, and entertainment offerings are being directed towards new markets – Japanese theme parks and US adult centres (Epcot Centre) are pursued (Ross, 1982).

Texas Instruments' strategy of focusing on consumer electronic product-market was largely unsuccessful. By shifting its emphasis from the semiconductor market, TI allowed Intel to gain a strong position in electronic memory markets. However, TI was unable to exploit a cost advantage in digital watches and home computers because consumer needs shifted from low price to design (watches) and support services (home computers).

Clearly, Honda's marketing strategy evolved through a set of decisions, some of which appear fortuitous. These individual decisions evolved into a coherent strategy from a post-hoc analysis, but certainly may not have been as clearly directed when they were made, although they were all taken within the context of a broad and sustained commitment to US market entry.

Static nature of planning process

The dynamic, evolutionary nature of marketing strategy is often disregarded. The emphasis placed on a formal planning process reinforces a relatively static view of marketing strategy. The process advocated begins with a detailed audit of the environment which includes identifying a checklist of variables including the economic, political, technological, competitive, and customer environments. Then, the strengths and weaknesses of the firm are examined. This audit yields a set of strategic opportunities, although the methods for deriving the opportunities from the information collected are often not clearly stated. Then, the opportunities are analysed in more depth using a variety of analytical techniques which includes portfolio matrices, experience curves, and product life cycles. This more detailed analysis produces what is often called 'a marketing strategy' – a target product-market – and a level of resources required to achieve a strategic objective. The objective, typically market share, is established and an implementation programme is developed to achieve the objectives. The final step in the process is to evaluate the results of the implementation programmes. If the implementation programme is achieving the objective, changes are unnecessary. However, a re-analysis is indicated if the objective is not being realized. This re-analysis could involve simply reformulating the implementation programme or beginning the entire planning process again beginning with a new strategic audit (Andrews, 1980).

While the final evaluation and control step introduces a dynamic element, this approach suggests that a marketing strategy is developed by a thorough analysis at one point in time. The dynamic nature of a marketing strategy evolving from a series of strategic decisions is thus not emphasized in most models of strategic development even though reports of strategy development in actual organizations suggests that most strategies are developed incrementally (see Mintzberg et al. 1985; Quinn, 1980).

There is a significant role for the process of strategy review which has been summarized above triggered either by external or internal events or by some form of regular review cycle. The latter mechanism can be important because it is often difficult to recognize clearly the events which actually undermine the viability of the current approach. On the other hand, it is important also to recognize that the dynamic and evolutionary nature of the competitive market requires that each major resource decision also involves the application of specific competitive marketplace forms of analysis, on the basis of the best available information at the time of the decision. The degree to which in any particular situation one chooses then either the strategy evolves from a series of individual decisions taken on their own merits at the appropriate time or the decisions themselves are prescribed by the previously developed strategy statement remains an issue.

Analysis in marketing strategy

Most writings in the area of marketing strategy have focused on the various forms of analysis that are available or are in the process of being developed. Indeed, it has been recognized as rather an irony that many of the techniques of strategic analysis popularized by Boston Consulting Group and later by the writings of Michael Porter, although very directly related to the issue of market evaluation, were actually initially developed outside the domain of marketing in both an academic and a practitioner sense (see Day and Wensley, 1983).

There was also, particularly in the early days, a near universal avoidance of issues of actual influence and the politics of decision making. Despite the fact that such concerns were clearly on the overall agenda of strategic analysis (see Wensley, 1979) and even more so public policy analysts many of the proposed approaches appeared to presume that the analysts could divorce themselves from any issues of internal politics while dominating any discussions about future direction for the enterprise.

This fact, however, also did mean that the techniques themselves tended to be developed within a broadly economic framework: a clear and extensive focus on the nature of competitive reaction but at the same time a tendency to espouse relatively simple and naive models of actual market behaviour. The challenge for those who nowadays find themselves involved in marketing strategy analysis is to recognize the expectations placed upon them while attempting to develop more realistic market models and a better appreciation of the role of analysis in the overall decision-making process. The degree of this challenge should not be underestimated: in a very real sense both pressures result in a focus on situation – or context – specific knowledge and action. Hence by definition the procedures and practices are less easily presented in a generalized and universal form.

Good analysis and bad analysis

If we conduct any form of analysis within a wider political context (even if it is with a small 'p' rather than a larger one) we should also be concerned with the legitimacy of the analysis. At a simple level the legitimacy of such analysis will depend on both its own basis and the use to which it is put. Good analysis in these terms is analysis which is conducted with an appreciation of these concerns while bad analysis avoids such issues.

It has previously been suggested that the basis of many of the available techniques for marketing strategy analysis is dubious in terms of either or both of their theoretical underpinnings and their empirical validity (Wensley, 1981), particularly in the case of the various 'box' approaches to product market selection. However this fault does not lie exclusively in marketing strategy writers. Michael Porter (1980, pp. 42–3) whose writings must on any account be regarded as highly influential in this field spent a considerable amount of time emphasizing his notion of 'generic' strategies. One of the key assumptions that underpinned such a classification was the general view that being 'stuck in the middle' was not a long-term viable strategy:

> The firm stuck in the middle must make a fundamental strategy decision . . . Once stuck in the middle, it usually takes time and sustained effort to extricate the firm from this unenviable position . . . In some industries, the problem of being caught in the middle may mean that the smaller (focused or differentiated) firms and the largest (cost leadership) firms are the most profitable. This implies a U-shaped relationship between profitability and market share.

Given the obvious importance of this relationship to his overall approach we would expect that some strong evidence would be produced that this U-shaped relationship actually existed. However, all Porter (1980, p. 43) offers us as evidence is:

> The relationship appears to hold in the US fractional horsepower electric motor business. There GE and Emerson have large market shares . . . Both are believed to earn high returns in motors, Baldor and Gould (Century) have adopted focused strategies . . . The profitability of both is also believed to be good. Franklin is in an intermediate position . . . its performance in motors is believed to follow accordingly. Such a U-shaped relationship probably also roughly holds in the automobile industry when viewed on a global basis, with firms like GM (low cost) and Mercedes (differentiated) the profit leaders. Chrysler, British Leyland and Fiat . . . are stuck in the middle.

Now while it remains true that the area of strategic decision making is often strongly influenced by the use of analogies, we must surely be very cautious of an approach which masquerades as a general one yet is based on a pair of very imperfectly presented examples.

Good analysis on the other hand raises questions rather than answers them, encourages those involved to recognize the regularities in the phenomena that they are considering and also provides the opportunity for a critical evaluation of the particular form of analysis itself. Finally, however, good analysis is that which encourages effective decision making by those who use it: it is useful in a constructive way. Herein often lies a very real problem: the simplicities of the Boston Box may now be widely recognized but the language of 'cash cows' and 'dogs' still often dominates strategic discussions. Abell and Hammond inadvertently explained the appeal of such approaches because of the way in which they simplify the enormous complexity in a modern multidivisional and diversified business. But such simplification can itself be 'false': however appealing the simple choices that are presented are false choices. More importantly the caveat 'use with care' which is often the response to such concerns is itself misleading. One is still proposing that the strategy options are presented within an unsubstantiated framework and at the same time failing to specify in any reasonable terms the conditions under which the approach might not apply.

Facts, lies and doubts

As Disraeli recognized a rather long time ago the most dangerous lies are those that masquerade as fact, yet at the same time any notion of analysis is built on regularities and rules, in other words, facts. In the particular area of understanding the long-term process of competitive and market evolution which is the essential prerequisite for effective analysis in market strategy we have few facts, a number of lies and many doubts.

A fact: risk matters

Marketing strategy deals essentially with the notion of sustainable competitive advantage. As such it deals with actions against the future 'state of nature' both in terms of the marketplace itself and also ones competitors. This future is inherently risky and uncertain. We must always trade-off the potential returns from any action against the risks attached to it. Even more importantly we cannot accept any statement of facts about previous events and outcomes unless they incorporate as a central notion the issue of risk. For instance, Biggadike (1979) conducted a study in which he claimed that those who aimed for a significant scale of market entry stood a better chance of long-term financial success than those who aimed for a market foothold. His data showed something different and rather less significant: those who get a larger share of the market, though intention or luck we cannot tell, tend to have better financial results than those who do not! Of course, we could look more closely at his data and recognize that certain state transitions show different distribution patterns than others and be able to argue that the incremental market entry strategy is infeasible under certain conditions but this requires a much more elaborate analytical framework than the ones often used by strategy analysts.

Another fact: variance matters

It is a general truism that any explanatory model only explains events with a degree of error. In marketing strategy this general problem is often a very severe one. Some writers avoid the problem by ignoring it: they presume a relationship holds with certainty much as Michael Porter's U-curve that we referred to previously. Others, including many who have worked with the PIMS data base, skate over the problem by confounding the issue of statistical significance with the issue of the proportion of the variance actually explained. It seems somewhat arrogant to suggest it but it would appear that much of the strategic marketing research on the PIMS data base has been reported in a way that ignores some basic issues in statistical analysis. In particular, with a very large data base the problem is not finding a relationship which is statistically significant (all relationship is almost without exception significant) but one which explains a significant proportion of the variance in the dependent variable. It has indeed taken us a long time to recognize that the relationship between market share and profitability only explains at best 10 per cent of the variance in profitability which leaves 90 per cent to be explained by other means (Wensley, 1981).

Finally: expectations matter

The third key fact is that expectations, of both ones competitors and ones customers matter in our understanding of their behaviour and in particular their responses to our actions. The 'rational expectations' approach in economics has been rightly criticised because it can be used to formulate a Catch-22 situation in which all actions are ineffective because the results are instantaneously anticipated by the other players. In marketing, there is no need to indulge in such arcane debate because it is clear that product and service markets remain very imperfect in the strict sense. (More detailed comparisons between product and financial markets and the implications of both the similarities and differences are to be found in Barwise et al. (1987)). On the other hand, one of the common failings in much marketing analysis has been to ignore or underestimate the impact of competitive response (Weitz, 1985) as well as the extent to which in many markets we need to consider the behaviour of active 'customers' rather than passive 'consumers'. In many traditional marketing texts the distinction between customer and consumer has been merely used in situations in which the financial agent (the adult) is not the actual consumer (child). What we are proposing is a much more significant difference between a view of the market as composed of consumers and a view of the market place as individuals and organizations making explicit choices among a portfolio of offerings and often configuring them in new ways for their particular requirements. Such a view has of course always been much more accepted in industrial marketing practice than in the more archetypal consumer markets.

A lie: the universal money machine

It should by now be clear that the one most pernicious lie is that characterized by the 'universal money machine', a simple form of analysis that claims to make money across time and different markets. Such claims are often to be found in the marketing strategy articles from 'invest in growth markets' to 'put more resources into advertising and branding'. This is not to say that such advice might well be very sound in a particular context and at a particular time but merely that there is no reason at all to believe that it is universally true. Indeed any attempt to show that it is has almost certainly failed to incorporate the effect of one or more of the key 'facts' that we discussed above: the triple influences of risk, variance and expectations. This recognition that there is no universal money machine can sometimes be misinterpreted as a much stronger assertion that there is no role for analysis. However, particularly in product and service markets the very nature of the markets in that participants are technically price setters rather than price takers means that there is often a critical role for careful analysis to avoid substantial overpricing and bidding for assets. The problem lies in the fact that this alone is not enough and that just as any competitive activity that incorporates a degree of uncertainty and luck, success cannot be guaranteed. Indeed, life may be even more disturbing than this. McKelvey (1982) points out that not only do the top downhill skiers have to rely on a degree of luck to win alongside their undoubted skill but that also they often technically ski 'over the edge' so that their balance is unstable. In much the same way in market competition irrational behaviour by technically skilled firms may be the only way they can succeed.

A doubt: the significance of market share

The continuing debate about the significance of market share in marketing strategy represents both the problems and the opportunities that arise when we try and shift the focus away from the very general notions incorporated in our list of 'facts' above towards the form of prescription and advice for marketing practitioners more represented by the abortive hunt for the universal money machine. Ever since the original *Harvard Business Review* article by Buzzell, Gale and Sultan in 1975 there has been a strong suggestion that the concept of market share, if not an actual money machine, was a key element in more effective business performance. Indeed the article itself was suggestively titled: 'market share: a key to profitability'. Many years later we are arguably more wise, in that much more research and theoretical development has taken place but also, ironically, more rather than less confused.

Indeed, the current state of our knowledge is perhaps best summarized by the title of an article on the subject in the *Journal of Marketing*: 'Is Market Share All That It's Cracked Up To Be?' (Jacobson and Aaker, 1985). The more diagnostic perspective is, however, underrepresented and can be seen more clearly in the notion of 'strategic management accounting' as developed by Simmonds (1981). What is perhaps more clear is that in various ways if market share is a key at all it is one in the sense that it opens up a way of thinking about and discussing issues of competitive market position in practice and as a result of such discussions and debates the participants may be much better informed to take key marketing strategic decisions.

Keep it simple and sensible

Astute readers will have noticed that to a considerable extent the 'facts' discussed above are of a different order from the 'lies'. The facts are merely statements of issues which must form part of our analytical assessment of any particular marketing strategy, the lies in their various ways represent attempts to collapse such an assessment into one particular dimension and even to prescribe the outcome of the assessment itself. In reality we cannot avoid the fact that issues of analysis in marketing strategy are multidimensional and fraught with uncertainty. The key question, therefore becomes how to fit our analysis into this context of the overall marketing strategy process.

Multiple simplicity versus complexity

If the process of marketing strategy development involves multiple dimensions then this should be reflected in the forms of analysis that we use. Such a consideration should lead us to use multiple analytical frames rather than a single one, however complex and integrative we may claim it is. Moreover, if the individual analytical frames that we apply are relatively simple and hence transparent to those in the decision-making process there is a much better chance that the twin issues, of both the implications of the analysis and its relevance will actually be discussed and evaluated.

Analysis and process

The issue of relating analysis to process also raises a further issue: much of the actual debate between those involved in the actual decision is inevitably conducted within the terms of their collective and individual 'decision structures' (Barwise *et al.*, 1987). To avoid therefore the problem of conducting an analysis which however elegant has limited if any impact on the decision process we must be as concerned with understanding the nature of these individual decision structures at least as much as with the analysis itself.

We have also suggested that a focus on analysis from the point of view of its impact on the decision process implies a much greater concern for both the diagnostic and dialectical nature of analysis. We should look to analysis as a way of raising further questions rather than merely providing naive and simplistic answers. We should also look to analysis as a means to challenge preconceptions and presumptions.

Looking to the future

The future holds great promise for both the practice and the theory of marketing strategy and in the final section we will consider some of the principle areas where change and development might take place. The challenge lies in the fact that such changes will only take place effectively if marketing practitioners and academics themselves change and take the opportunities that are offered. If we do not we may witness a repeat of the events in the late 1960s and 1970s in which major changes in approach to the management of the firm particularly with respect to

its product markets took place essentially outside the marketing domain.

The future for marketing strategy

Being strategic

Advocates of the case teaching method in marketing have long recognized that the method is designed to emphasize that marketing is in the end about doing, or, in other words, about action (see Simmonds, 1982). Hence, despite the concern repeated in this article for 'strategic thinking' (see Morrison and Lee, 1979), this, of itself, is not enough: we need in the end 'strategic action' as well. Just as in our case study teaching, the nature of strategic action, or 'being strategic' involves responding to the balance between analysis and action because we have to recognize that many of the market uncertainties can only be resolved, even partially, by action itself. Indeed there is a strong argument that if being strategic means acting in a way which recognizes the very uncertainty of the competitive commercial world in which we operate, then it should also itself be 'uncomfortable' in that such uncertainties are heightened rather than disguised.

The potential impact of IT

Information technology or IT has become one of the mega-buzzwords of the late 1980s. The general notion, if the DTI is to be believed is the interaction between computing, communication and control technologies. It is already very apparent that individual authors have adopted the term IT to their own idiosyncratic purpose and this article is no exception. There is little doubt that the dramatic expansion in both marketing data availability and processing capability can have a very significant effect on the actualization of various marketing strategy approaches, particularly in the key areas of customer focus and a better understanding of complex market structures involving independent intermediaries at various levels.

Achieving customer focus

The basic unit of marketing exchange can be defined as:

The process of resource transformation to produce a product or service offering to a particular customer in a specific use situation.

We can therefore consider the following three types of specialization or focus as generic strategy types, alongside the common one of a pure volume and cost approach based on a standard product:

- Product/resource specialization.
- Context/use situation specialization.
- Customer/end user specialization

Until recently, the problem with such a schema has been that we had little available in terms of stable, reliable and long-term data upon which to assess let alone implement such a focus. The advent of IT means that such opportunities will now arise.

However, although we can view this sequence of forms of focus as a process of deconstruction we can also reconstruct the options and choices from any level and a different structure will emerge, in terms of both relationships and boundaries. In practice much of this redefinition takes place through independent intermediaries often merely broadly desribed as the distribution channel.

Researching market structure

We will need, therefore, to develop a much better way of describing the behaviour of such distribution channels, or in fact, more generally, the complex market structure in which most firms now find themselves operating. Such approaches may help us both to understand the ways in which particular market structures aid or hinder innovations and developments within the market as a whole as well as providing a basis upon which we can readdress in a more systemic and analytical way one of the other most popular buzzwords in the current strategy vocabulary: the notion of the niche (Boxer and Wensley, 1983).

The organizational challenge

The issue of the form of market focus cannot be divorced from the issue of how the firm itself is organized. It is inevitable that a clearer definition of the options in terms of market focus will also emphasize the concerns which have been previously expressed under the general notion of the 'market-centred' organization (see Hannan, 1978). On top of

this, a broader recognition of the need to exploit and organize around local market knowledge will raise new challenges for organizational design itself as well as related issues of remuneration and ownership (see Boxer and Wensley, 1986).

Conclusion

As we have suggested earlier the most significant issue for marketers themselves will be the extent to which they respond to the new opportunities in both the theory and practice of marketing strategy. It is clear that the development of new market based strategic approaches and the data analysis to support them will not result in the simple and convenient and generalizable distinctions that have so appealed to previous strategic analysts, as well as many of their clients. Instead we will be forced to face more directly the degree of fuzziness and overlap in any way of segmenting a marketplace – or to be more accurate any way of clustering individual customers (see Doyle and Saunders, 1985). We will always find ourselves dealing with tendencies rather than absolutes and forms of analysis that make it much more difficult to avoid this uncomfortable fact. Many of our colleagues, both within and without the broad area of marketing may prefer not to face such issues and be tempted back to the simplicities of previous approaches despite their lack of empirical support. If we fail the challenge we can expect the major developments in strategy despite the fact that they will relate to a deeper understanding of market behaviour to be unencumbered by the label *marketing strategy*.

References

Abell, Derek F. and Hammond, John S., *Strategic Market Planning*, Prentice-Hall, 1983.

Andrews, Kenneth R., *The Concept of Corporate Strategy*, rev. ed. Irwin, 1980.

Armstrong, L., with L. Helm, J.B. Treece, W.J. Hampton, M. Edid, R. Brandt and W.J. Holstein, 'The New Breed of Strategic Planners', *Business Week*, September, 1984, pp. 52–7.

Barwise, P., Marsh, P., Thomas, K. and Wensley, R., 'Research on Strategic Investment Decisions', in H. Thomas and J. McGee (eds), *Strategic Management Research: A European Perspective*, Wiley, 1985.

Barwise, P., Marsh, P., Thomas, K and Wensley, R., 'Strategic Investment Decisions', *Research in Marketing*, vol. 7, 1987.

Biggadike, R., 'The Risky Business of Diversification', *Harvard Business Review*, May-June 1979, pp. 103–11.

Boxer P., and Wensley, R., 'Niches and Competition: The Ecology of Market Organization', *London Business School Research Papers in Marketing*, 8318, 1983.

Boxer, P., and Wensley, R., 'The Need for Middle-out Development of Marketing Strategy', *Journal of Management Studies*, March 1986.

'Texas Instruments Shows US Business How To Survive In The 1980's', *Business Week*, 10 September 1978, pp. 66–92.

'Can Disney Still Grow on Its Founder's Dream?' *Business Week*, 31 July 1978, pp. 58–63.

'Toyota's Fast Lane', *Business Week*, 4 November 1985, pp. 42–6.

Book review in *Business Week Management Challenge*: *Japanese Views*, L. C. Thurow, MIT Press, 21 October, 1985, p. 17.

Day, G. S., and Wensley, R., 'Marketing Theory with a Strategic Orientation', *Journal of Marketing*, 47, Fall 1983, pp. 79–89.

Doyle, P., and Saunders, J., 'Market Segmentation or Positioning in Specialised Industrial Markets', *Journal of Marketing*, 49, Spring 1985, pp. 24–32.

Evered, Roger, 'So What is Strategy?', *Long Range Planning*, 16, Fall 1983, pp. 57–62.

Hannan, M., 'Re-organise Your Company Around Its Markets', *Harvard Business Review*, May-June 1978, pp. 131–42.

Henderson, Bruce D., *Henderson on Corporate Strategy*, Abt Books, 1981, p. 8.

Strategy Alternatives for the British Motorcycle Industry, Her Majesty's Stationery Office, 30 July 1975.

Jacobson R., and Aaker, D.A., 'Is Market Share All That It's Cracked Up To Be?' *Journal of Marketing*, 49 (Fall 1985), pp. 11–22.

Kotler, Philip, and Singh, Ravi, 'Marketing Warfare in the 1980's, *Journal of Business Strategy*, vol. 1, 1981, pp. 30–41.

Kotler, Philip and Fahey, Liam, 'The World's Champion Marketers: The Japanese', *Journal of Business Strategy*, vol. 3, Summer 1982, pp. 3–13.

Levitt, Theodore, 'Marketing Myopia', *Harvard Business Review*, 38, 4, July-August 1960, pp. 26–34.

Liddell-Hart, B. H., *Strategy*, 2nd ed., Praeger, 1967.

Mtron Magnet, 'Troubled House at Disney', *Fortune*, December 10, 1984, pp. 57–64.

McKelvey, Bill, *Organizational Systematics: Taxonomy, Evolution, Classification*, University of California Press, 1982.

Mintzberg, Henry and Mattush, Alexandra, 'Strategic Formulation in Adhocracy', *Administrative Science Quarterly*, 30 (June 1985), pp. 160–97.

Mintzberg Henry, and Waters, James A. 'Of Strategies, Deliberate and Emergent', *Strategic Management Journal*, 6, Fall 1985, pp. 257–72.

Morrison, J. R., and Lee, J. G., 'The Anatomy of Strategic Thinking', *The McKinsey Quarterly*, Autumn 1979, pp. 2–9.

Ouchi, William, *Theory*, Addison-Wesley, 1983.

Pascale, R. T., 'Perspectives on Strategy: The Real Story Behind Honda's Success', *California Management Review*, 16, Spring 1984, pp. 47–73.

Pascale, R. T., 'Our Curious Addition to Corporate Grand Strategy', *Fortune*, 25 January 1982, pp. 115–16.

Pearce II, John A., 'The Company Mission As A Strategic Tool', *Sloan Management Review*, Spring 1982, p. 17.

Purkagastha, D., 'Note on Motorcycle Industry – 1975', 9–578–210 *Harvard Business School*, 1 December 1981.

Quinn, James B., *Strategies for Change: Logical Incrementalism*, Irwin, 1980.

Ross, Irwin, 'Disney Gambles on Tomorrow', *Fortune*, 4 October, 1982, p. 68.

Rumelt, Richard P., *Strategy, Structure and Economic Performance*, Harvard University, 1974.

Simmonds, K., 'Strategic Management Accounting', *Management Accounting*, April 1981, pp. 26–29.

Simmonds, K., 'Strategy and Marketing: A Case Approach', Philip Allan, 1982.

Trout, Jack and Ries, Al, *Marketing Warfare*, McGraw-Hill, 1985.

Weitz, B., 'Introduction to Special Edition on Competition', *Journal of Marketing Research*, 1985.

Wensley, J. R. C., 'The Effective Strategic Analyst', *Journal of Management Studies*, October 1979.

Wensley, R., 'Strategic Marketing: Betas, Boxes or Basics', *Journal of Marketing*, Summer 1981, pp. 173–82.

Wensley, R., 'The Market Share Myth', *London Business School Journal*, Winter 1981, pp. 3–5.

Wensley, R., 'Marketing Action on the Military Front', *Journal of Marketing*, 53(3), July 1989, pp. 128–30.

4
Organization for marketing
PETER SPILLARD

Introduction

There is a distinct danger in learning about marketing that the technology of the discipline is seen to be deterministic. That is to say that merely by getting the techniques right and then building them into strategic or tactical plans the successful outcome envisaged inevitably just happens. If it fails to do so, then such failure is laid at the door of technique or chance. The result is that effort is devoted to eradicating technical errors rather than asking more fundamental questions.

One of these fundamental questions has to do with the organizational context in which problems and opportunities are seen, information interpreted, plans drawn up and programmes executed. This chapter aims to address this question and in doing so throw light on the very important role an organization plays in drawing up and moderating the outcome of marketing plans.

So as to lay the foundation of what the discussion that follows is all about, it seems sensible to begin with a definition.

In a formal sense an organization is a more or less permanent grouping of people established to undertake specific tasks in order to achieve a given set of objectives. Such objectives may or may not be explicitly stated and may or may not be completely agreed. It is also the case that on occasions, especially after the passage of time, the objectives originally established become lost, ignored or modified.

That definition is based on the metaphor that an organization is an instrument for action; a machine. There is another definition based on the metaphor of the organization as a playground. Under this more subjective definition it is seen as an arena where games are played, tricks hatched, territory fought over, empires built, satisfaction and power sought, battles won or lost, ritual and tradition carried forward, development and survival techniques honed, and relationships and alliances formed, broken and reformed. Language, lore and codes of conduct are established and reinforced by practice and sanctions. Informally a pecking order and a social system emerge from day-to-day activity and intercourse.

These things, irrespective of the instrumental aspects of an organization, are what gives the structure and activities their human character. The organization is thus seen as an end in itself where people derive satisfaction and a purpose in life; in other words, where they get their kicks. It becomes a source of stimulation and excitement for its members who may strut, plot, posture and deceive if it suits them and if they are permitted. On the other hand, they may be so motivated that they subjugate or direct all this to the common good, or indeed they may just lie low and satisfice. Whether they do one or the other depends in the end on the effectiveness, quality and values of the playground's leaders whose task is to substitute a shared meaning based upon organizational rationalities rather than one based on the idiosyncrasies of individual members.

This second, more difficult, definition to grasp, based on the playground metaphor, is mentioned simply because if some people in an organization base their behaviour accordingly then those who act as if it is mainly an instrument designed to make and execute decisions will be puzzled when outcomes do not always reflect intentions. Such intentions frequently become the focus for new behaviour in the organizational playground rather than the cause of rational executive action. Or, of course, the intentions can be ignored altogether and the old games just go on being played! Plans can thus be aided or harmed.

Whichever metaphor is adopted, the instrumental or the playground, the specific components of an organization are:

- People – their number, degree of commitment, background, skills, knowledge, character and drives.
- A mission and set of objectives. These may be stated or unstated, but together they define the tasks to be achieved.
- The logics and boundaries of the various specialisms.
- The hierarchy through which power is exercised.
- A control system to audit and influence executive outcomes.
- Information flows to enable decisions to be made.
- Procedures and systems for undertaking defined tasks.
- A portfolio of rewards and punishment to secure compliance and initiatives.
- A set of values to give the the structure a spirit, a culture and an ethos.
- A boundary which defines the limits of the organization.
- Linking mechanisms through which to relate to other organizations.

All these components need to be assessed and matched together in a harmonious 'whole'. A bureaucratic organization, for instance, will possess characteristics along all these dimensions that will distinguish it from a loose organic one. It will tend to be staffed by bureaucratically minded people who are risk averse, led from the centre with formal power exercised vertically downwards, operate within tightly bounded specialisms well defined 'by the book', and subject to formal control systems and prescribed information flows. Procedures will be laid down and any deviation from them punished. The values will be professional, conformist and institutionalized.

There is a continual but often, in these changing times, frustratingly fruitless pursuit of the ultimate harmonization between all these components. The ideal is never reached; it is nevertheless constantly sought.

Furthermore, and for marketing especially, there has to be a recognition that every organization possesses a history written in terms of the complete set of components. Every one of them has been set up and reinforced over time. The striving for harmony itself has had to take place over time. And if one set is appropriate to one time and not to another or to one marketing strategy and not to a different one, then the result is a fundamental and often catastrophic mismatch between organization and the tasks confronting it.

That is why a failure on the part of the marketing technologists to recognize the significance of their enterprises' organizational make-up can often lead to error. It cannot just be taken for granted.

Since it involves a process of grouping, an organization can be studied at whatever degree of aggregation constitutes a group. It is thus possible to review organizational concerns which cover at the lowest level of aggregation matters such as the best way to structure a local sales force or a product launch team right up to the highest, such as the ideal way to structure an entire company better to cope with changing market demands of the 1990s. Indeed one could go even further than that and talk about an organization for marketing an industry or even an entire nation. It is all a matter of boundaries.

For practising marketing managers, of course, all this means that they have to consider the subject at every level. The higher up the hierarchy they are the greater involvement they have with organizational matters simply because the bulk of the structure is at their level or below. Yet at the same time because of its essentially interlocking nature they seldom have complete discretion to design or change their own operation's structure without affecting that of their colleagues. This is especially so in marketing because of the essential way in which it has to relate laterally to other functions both internally and externally. It is even more so because, unlike the more self-contained functions like accounting, production or sales, the designers of marketing structures are faced with such a bewildering choice. That is why the study of organization for marketing is complex.

The reason why it is not merely complex but also important is because the manner in which a group of whatever size is organized affects the results of the activity of that group. An ineffective system produces ineffective action; or sometimes no action at all. Only recently, for instance, has British Airways begun to recover from the imposition of the old BOAC culture and structures upon the very different characteristics needed for successful marketing of the airline's short-haul routes. It has taken almost a generation to put right.

In the case of the UK motorcycle industry it never was put right. The lowly status accorded to marketing and the pre-eminent position given to the engineering and traditional accounting functions in the hierarchy of each firm ensured that the Japanese threat was hardly recognized until it was too late, let alone effectively countered. The recent GEC 'Nimrod' AEW project debacle may well have been due significantly to the way in which the group is traditionally split into distinct SBU profit centres. It is interesting to note how Boeing, the makers of the winning AWACS system, has for a long time incorporated properly matrixed 'project' structures into its organizational design.

Organizational matters, then, can affect both the outcome of mergers and acquisitions as well as the success of individual firms within an industry. That is why, having already established that the subject is complex, it is also important.

The rest of this chapter is designed to highlight a few of the more fundamental issues that need to be addressed when designing or redesigning a system for more effective marketing. It begins with a look at one of the more controversial of these issues: the extent to which an enterprise's structure should be determined only after a strategy has emerged. Clearly if the determination of strategy itself requires or is affected by organization, then to that degree strategy follows structure; but if it is argued that organization is an instrument for carrying out a strategy then, if differing strategies require differing structures, the reverse is true.

Following that debate the tasks of marketing are studied to see how they may determine structural outcomes. These are noted both from the point of view of the nature of marketing itself as well as from that of the firm which selects particular tasks either by its strategy or by its culture and style of operating. The effect of the market environment is then assessed as a factor determining the choice of structure. The various ways in which marketing activities may broadly be grouped into structural units are noted and the choices of their location in the hierarchy analysed. Finally, suggestions are put forward for easing the introduction of specialist marketing units and radically new marketing strategies.

By the end of the chapter it is hoped that the links between strategy and structure are better understood and a greater understanding of some of the more important principles which determine marketing organization will have been generated.

Academic references have been kept to the very minimum.

The strategy/structure issue

One of the properties of an organization is the set of objectives which it is established to attain. A major component of an enterprise's objectives has to do with the establishment of strategic approaches for selecting markets and designing propositions to put to them. Traditionally the view is that having chosen its strategic route an organization is then established to undertake the task of actually executing the strategy. This is what might be termed the 'instrumental' view. Various respected academics, led in 1962 by Alfred Chandler in the US, have shown that in the cases they reviewed, structures did indeed after a time follow strategies. The cases of Du Pont, General Motors and other large US enterprises were cited in evidence. Indeed, the argument has a certain logic to it; after all if an organization is set up to do something it seems obvious that what is to be done must, to some extent, determine how the tasks that follow should be organized.

A logical extension of this argument would be to say that every time a firm changes its marketing strategy it must also think of changing its marketing structure. If, given the essential task of marketing to keep in tune with the ever increasing dynamics of the marketplace, a firm's strategy is constantly having to shift, then so is its structure.

But constantly to change the organization causes confusion and a possible breakdown of the essential predictability and stability that it needs to possess. To do the job well every aspect, including all those properties mentioned in the introduction to this chapter, would need to be reconsidered and made to operate once again in a new harmony. Changing any one property demands changes in all the others. Such disturbance may be more than can be tolerated if the structure is to retain its integrity and effectiveness over any length of time.

We are therefore led to the conclusion that if continual reshaping is to be avoided, the pattern that is initially established must be capable of handling more than one strategy and must also be capable of flexibility over time. We are faced, then, with a dilemma. On the one hand, an organization to be efficient has to be specifically tailored to the tasks confronting it. On the other hand, if it does this well and if the tasks then change, it will soon become inappropriate. Designing the ideal solution, therefore, is always a matter of trade-off and compromise between one ideal and another.

What follows is that in times of extreme environmental or market change an enterprise might be so reluctant to adapt itself that it deliberately or intuitively ignores certain strategic marketing alternatives that may be open to it. That may be the reason why firms in the UK motorcycle industry failed so dramatically. It was not so much that they were incompetent at what they had chosen to do; rather that they were following the wrong strategy in the changed circumstances of Japanese competition and a new market environment. In a sense it could even be argued that they had chosen a market segment (the traditional and declining UK 'kick-start, throbbing engine, xenophobic, golden-age' brigade) and were serving it very well by emphasizing old-fashioned engineering virtues. The trouble was that a whole new and much larger segment was opening up which the UK firms despised, were not set up to manage or cater for and were pretty confident would soon come around to recognize the folly of its ways and once again buy British. It never did!

The UK motorcycle industry is by no means the only example of a set of firms which chose their strategy on the basis of their structure. One finds similar examples all over the place.

Amstrad, under Alan Sugar, possesses a structure centred around the character of the founder – a self-made businessman from humble beginnings in the East End of London. As a result, Amstrad's strategy is itself opportunistic, entrepreneurial, 'mould-breaking' and expansionist. It is not based on scientific or technological breakthroughs and heavy research. It is international in scope, centred on value for money, a bit 'down-market' and with an emphasis on developing existing technology and getting costs down by shrewd buying and distribution. IBM's strategy by contrast is now quite different and in turn derived from its own set of characteristics – large, defensive, institutional, monopolistic, cautious and political. In the case of both firms their strategy is determined largely by what they organizationally already are. IBM had to establish a completely new division in Florida, for instance, to develop and launch its PC range simply because the demands on the respective structures, the new and the traditional, were so different.

The recent spate of privatization in the UK, coupled with the exhortations of government to the remaining state enterprises to become efficient and to attain results in cash-target terms, provides still further examples of the interaction between strategy and structure. With new strategies imposed by government all such organizations have gone through sometimes quite traumatic structural changes.

The Post Office, for example, has traditionally been regarded as a public service. Run on monopoly lines as an administrative authority, rather than as a business, and protected by legislation from direct competition, it was structured until 1985 like most service administrations on a regional basis. Marketing was a head office staff function rather than a sharp-end business function serving operational line units. Given its regional hierarchy and its 'welfare' or service nature it attracted people who were comfortable in such a structure, used systems and procedures that were civil service in nature and adopted reward/punishment codes, control mechanisms and values compatible with its standing and nature as a monolithic, reliable, stable, state-run, monopolistic enterprise.

To expect this particular corporation with its harmonious interlocking structure suddenly to behave like a dynamic entrepreneur by taking risks, being opportunistic and innovating in the marketplace can only be described as unreasonable. Its whole organizational logic prevented this from happening. Change would have had to have come about by diktat; it would never have been generated spontaneously. A comfortable strategy with the necessary fine-tuning was the most that could be expected under the old regime.

With the advent of competition in parcels traffic, with the hiving off of the telecommunications operation to British Telecom and with the imposition of profit expectations by central government, all this had to change. But the marketing strategies necessary to cope with this now much more opportunistic and dynamic set of tasks could not even begin to be thought out, let alone implemented, without a degree of organizational change.

New blood, much more used to the hurly-burly of the marketplace, was recruited under Ron Dearing at the top. Rather than regional structures more appropriate to the old 'welfare' strategy being allowed to continue, a whole set of business unit structures was introduced in 1985. Special managers in charge of parcels traffic, letter traffic, counter services, girobank and ancillary services were introduced each with their own objectives and marketing staff dedicated to the particular business function. The old regional set-up was disbanded altogether in the hunt for more sharp-end competitiveness and the development of a business rather than an administrative focus. At the same time 'service' aspects of the business – transport, technological back-up, estates management, personnel, management accounting and so on – all had to be reorientated to the new approach and

much trauma and conflict, not least with the relevant trade unions, both caused and faced.

The same kind of strategy/structure debate has been going on for years in British Rail. That enterprise has at frequent intervals, and to the dismay very often of the people who actually have to run the network, been structured on the basis of region (Midland, Southern, etc.), routes (London–Edinburgh with feeder services, etc.) type of goods carried (passengers, parcels and the different types of freight) type of service offered (hotel, ship, catering, trains) and now type of customer (commuter, intercity, rural traveller, industrial buyer). Logically, the service can be structured on any of these bases. To do so on all of them at once is, of course, impossible; so an element of choice between them is inevitable. The difficulty with industries like BR is that the criteria for making the choice are so pluralistic and the advantages of one scheme over another so difficult to measure and prove that the final decision is often based upon whim, rather than on any obviously rational and more permanent foundation. The role, tasks and responsibilities of marketing thus change with each successive new chief executive wishing to make his mark en route to a knighthood.

Which, then, causes which? Does structure cause strategy or does strategy determine structure? And in any case does the answer matter?

The answer does matter, if only because managers often conditioned to the instrumental 'rational, scientific' view that organizations are there to do their bidding need to be aware that this is not always the case. Sometimes, through a process of resistance, subordinates can very effectively warp strategy. On other occasions they can very effectively initiate strategy 'bottom-up' to reflect their own capabilities and vested interests. Lessons learned in the playground are powerful indeed. On yet other occasions the organization may not be capable of movement to a different set of strategies simply because of the commitment in plant, raw material, customers and so on that it is already geared towards for some time in the future. Spillard (1985) elaborates this theme and examines the case for strategy sometimes following structure.

Perhaps though it matters less which causes which in general terms, because it is so difficult, and may even be futile, to discover the universally dominant factor. One cannot say with certainty that structure always follows strategy or vice versa. What one can look for, however, is a set of contingencies which would help managers in marketing decide in what circumstances one follows the other. In either situation though, it can be said at the outset and with no doubt whatsoever that the two are inextricably linked. Both need to be in complete harmony if perfection is to be achieved. The only trouble is that if they are in such harmony to begin with then if strategic change is necessary which demands a different logic altogether, the more integrated is present structure with present strategy the more difficult it will be to achieve a new integration around the new set of marketing tasks made necessary by the new strategy.

The task, role and function of marketing

The marketing task

From the discussion in the previous section, it is clear that different enterprises, or the same one at different times, face differing marketing tasks. These may be due to decisions taken within the enterprise (in the case of Amstrad, for instance) or to external influences (as in the case of the Post Office). Such tasks may thirdly be due to the fundamental functions for which marketing is responsible in general. In whatever way they are caused the effects are similar; if an organization is designed to create concerted action, then the tasks facing marketing have a direct link with the emerging organizational form.

To take the 'fundamental' tasks first. Laid firmly at the door of the function of marketing are the responsibilities for ensuring:

- That the enterprise is aware of the nature of and changes in the marketplace. These have to do with competitive, regulatory, economic, sociological, technological, behavioural, political and structural forces all of which if not properly assessed may adversely affect future corporate prosperity.
- That the firm consciously takes these factors into account in formulating a sustainably competitive strategy. It can do this by ignoring them,

controlling or influencing them if it can, adapting to them or as a last resort by market withdrawal.
- That activities under its direct control (the so-called core activities) are undertaken effectively and efficiently. Such core activities are selling, advertising, sales promotion, market research, and the design of tactical marketing propositions to put to its chosen market. By such means is a sustainable competitive advantage achieved in tactical terms.
- That activities over which it wishes to exert an influence in the construction of such propositions, are properly designed and integrated. These concern overall business strategy, new product development and new market ventures of any kind.

These tasks imply that marketing occupies a boundary role. It operates at the interface between the corporate system and a very important part of its environment: the marketplace. To perform this role effectively it needs to be well informed about both of the systems which it links – the corporate and the market.

Quite apart from the vital boundary role performed in managing the relationship between its own organization and the marketplace, marketing also fulfills the role of coordinating the enterprise's internal functions around a market logic. Links with accounting, production, finance, personnel, purchasing, R&D, sales and distribution all have to be forged and maintained. The different logics possessed by all these functions and therefore the people managing them need reconciliation, amendment and constant review. Thus marketing also performs an internal boundary role.

During times of undergoing rapid adaptation and change when an enterprise alters its strategic marketing plans, it is often the case that marketing has to influence actions within the organization by 'invading' the spheres of influence traditionally held by other functions. Decisions about production scheduling, quality control, design, buying, customer service, credit policies and pricing all need to be influenced by input from the marketing manager. Yet all of these are traditionally viewed as the rightful domain or territory of others. On occasions marketing therefore has to play an incursive role. These ideas are depicted in Figure 4.1.

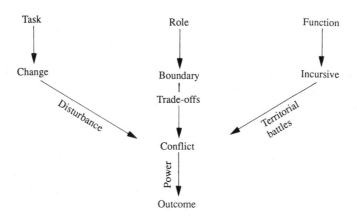

Figure 4.1 *A model of marketing conflict*

Marketing's *task* is to manage change; this brings about disturbance to the status quo. Its *role* is one of boundary management; this brings about the need to negotiate trade-offs and compromises. Third, marketing's *function* is incursive; this brings about battles over territory and domain.

All these essential characteristics of marketing result in different forms of conflict. This is resolved by the use of power or compromise, both inside and outside the organization.

Marketing managers must possess sufficient power over colleagues to induce them to change just as much as they possess it, say, over outside distributors. The internal political system is often crucial in determining marketing effectiveness. It also affects the actual outcome of marketing decisions and the vested interests which are served.

Power can be exercised by:

- Coercion.
- Withholding rewards.
- Upholding sanctions.
- Emphasizing knowledge and expertise relevant to the achievement of generally agreed group objectives.
- Control over scarce resources.
- Maximizing the extent to which others are dependent on marketing – while minimizing the reverse.
- Expanding territorial influence over decision making by establishing the 'legitimacy' and acceptability of marketing.

- Personal influence and game playing.
- Force of argument.

Because of marketing's boundary role and corresponding lack of 'line' authority it is difficult, except over its own core activities, to exercise power through the first three of these methods. Any structure for marketing must, therefore, contain mechanisms of influence and control that are not dependent on coercion, punishment or reward. On the contrary they must be able to influence the functions with which they link through a system of power that is less direct. This is not to say that the exercise of these less direct forms of power generates less conflict and difficulty; if anything more intractable problems may be created simply because they are less easily resolved through overt line power. This is a topic to which we will return towards the end of the chapter.

Essential to the success of marketing then, is the capability it has for exercising power not through force, but through negotiation. Indeed when performing its boundary role both within the corporate system as well as between that system and the marketplace the activity of negotiation and the skill with which the activity is performed are crucial to success. It is up to marketing to see that the structure is designed so as to facilitate such negotiation.

All this implies that marketing organization is 'soft' in nature whenever it has to interact with an external or internal environment. Boundaries are loose, constantly shifting and frequently ill-defined and open to debate. It follows from this that the responsibility and area of influence of marketing tend to be both diffuse and lacking in structual integrity, at least in the sense of possessing a well bounded and undisputed sphere of influence.

Because marketing so often acts at the boundaries of other groups' activities and achieves what success it does through pursuing its objectives effectively by a process of negotiation, most of what it claims to influence is subject to dispute by other groups. These groups are put on the defensive by the very act of marketing trying to influence the outcome of decisions which they traditionally have regarded as their own.

Such boundary disputes are common in marketing and only to be expected in an organization struggling to match itself as well as it can to changing market conditions. They derive from the fundamental nature of the task of marketing wherever it is found.

The innovative versus the maintenance role

Within marketing itself, as well as in its relations with other parts of the enterprise, some roles demand the performance of a maintenance function for which efficiency is the main index of success. These roles usually have a short planning horizon and are typified by units responsible for maintaining sales records and customer contact, dealing with complaints and after sales service, order processing, the collation of routine market information, sales administration and product management. Activities typically the responsibility of the brand manager, the sales person, the administrative clerk or the sales statistician would fall into this 'maintenance' category.

Other activities by contrast are more to do with innovation, creativity and a longer time horizon. They mean performing roles that have to handle larger groups within different departments, at different levels in the hierarchy or even outside the firm altogether. New market ventures, strategic marketing decision making and the initiation of radically new courses of action would all involve the performance of roles demanding strength in innovation.

Each of these roles, the maintenance and the innovative, constitutes a different set of tasks: yet most of the effect of marketing action is dictated by the way in which these two essential, yet contrasting, roles are performed and integrated. Indeed, not merely are they contrasting, they are also conflicting. A maintenance role implies:

- Short time horizons.
- Attention to detail and administration.
- Standardization and routinization of tasks.
- An emphasis on efficiency and productivity.
- The establishment of and discipline over procedures.
- Clear unambiguous objectives capable of easy monitoring.
- An orientation towards tradition and precedence.
- Tight definitions of territory and legitimate activities.
- Elimination of disorder, uncertainty and the questioning of objectives.
- Service to a clientele, either inside or outside the enterprise.
- An emphasis all the time on feedback and control.
- Above all, the protection of the status quo, subject only to changes that increase efficiency.

An innovatory role implies dealing successfully with fresh problems and unplanned requirements that are not easily coped with by an organization used only to maintaining a system in a traditional way. An organisation for successful innovation needs:

- Open lateral channels of communication rather than constrained and vertical.
- To encourage the unusual rather than the routinely conforming solution.
- Plenty of ideas people rather than day-to-day operators.
- A loose structure centred upon the expertise of the moment, rather than upon a preordained hierarchy.
- To be governed by task rather than precedent.
- To tolerate mistakes rather than punish them.
- To reward by results rather than by status or length of service.
- To be decentralized, diversified and fluid rather than centralized, standardized and static.

- To run 'loosely' rather than 'tightly'.
- Less reliance on precedence and hierarchical status as sources of power.
- A culture and set of values excited by innovation and change.
- Young people, with courage, drive and flair who are awkward to manage except through shared values and with committed enthusiasm.
- A cosmopolitan outlook centred on the future.

From the above lists it will easily be seen how innovation demands a structure which is much less defined than that demanded of a maintenance organization with its demand for order. At the same time though it needs to be mission-led, self-driven and subject to general control, otherwise it will degenerate into chaos. The drive for a 'maintenance' system comes from its bureaucratic character; that for an innovatory one derives from shared values and the new task in hand.

If marketing is involved with administration and service, as it was in the Post Office before the recent reorganization into business units, then it needs to be organized as a routine. In that way feedback is generated which will allow better administration and an improvement in service. The ideal structure for such an operation would, therefore, be the opposite to that appropriate to an innovative stance; mechanistic rather than organic.

Under the new regime at the Post Office, marketing is now decentralized, often run by people with new skills brought in specially from outside rather than by existing staff being retrained, subject to less rigid control from above and made particular to the needs of each business operation. Techniques have been borrowed from marketing in other product areas and, indeed, from other countries. The climate toward competition is gradually changing; albeit slowed down a little by the large mass of staff who are in post at middle and lower operating levels and who are used to performing under the rules and conditions of the old maintenance regime.

Welfare versus business objectives

There is a developing literature in marketing which broadens the subject's boundaries to include its operation in 'not-for-profit' organizations. It pro-poses the view that whether the major corporate mission is to make a profit or not, marketing may be just as relevant. If the function's primary role is to ensure a successful match between what is offered and what is demanded, then so long as that corporate body has to compete with others for a clientele's patronage, marketing has a contribution to make. So much is beyond doubt.

Rather more difficult to accept, though, is that even among so-called 'for profit' enterprises there is always a mixture of objectives between out-and-out profit maximization and what might be called a welfare or service orientation.

Earlier in this chapter it has already been seen how the Post Office has altered its balance away from a stance towards public service or administration and more towards profit making. Performing arts companies, too, are having to become more businesslike in their behaviour in order to survive, much to the chagrin of the more purist of their members. So are many of the nation's charities and service institutions.

Because a businesslike ethos with its emphasis upon profit making is so different in kind from a welfare or service-led type it demands different skills, different sets of values, different systems and specializations and even a different type of control system (more 'other-directed', for instance, than 'inner-directed'). In fact, it argues for a radically different set of organizational properties altogether. Marketing, although generally responsible for identical boundary managing tasks, has to work through different political structures and to employ different performance criteria.

One further, but important, point needs to be made. A welfare orientation is not merely tenable in relation to the outside world, the marketplace. It is also possible to see welfare objectives at work internally. If an enterprise depends heavily upon a profession or a particularly powerful work group, be it medical, engineering, accounting, educational, trade union, or any other, the interests of the marketplace and, therefore, the pursuit of business objectives are in danger of becoming subordinated to those of the group. In such a case it can be seen that the welfare interests are internal in character – more to do with looking after the concerns of the firm's own staff and their particular perspectives and interests. This gives rise to all sorts of organizational, not to say marketing, problems, within the enterprise. Most of them have to do with warping the customer orientation that marketing insists upon. Instead, a set of self-serving objectives is created in the midst of which concern with the customer frequently gets lost. The point of saying all this is that when an enterprise for whatever reasons suddenly chooses, or is forced by political diktat, to change its orientation from 'welfare' (be it external or internal in character) to 'business', enormous stress is put upon every aspect of the organization. Conflict becomes acute and there is a strong risk of disintegration. Current difficulties facing the Cooperative Movement, Covent Garden Opera House, the Water Authorities, British Rail and, recently, the Coal Board, British Steel and British Leyland all illustrate the point well. The resulting conflict is about values or ends and may very well involve the root purpose of the enterprise. If marketing is seen to be the cause of such conflict then its difficulties in managing the change in task become acute.

The style of marketing

There has recently been a sudden upsurge of interest in management cultures. This is mainly because of a realization that not only do certain tasks demand different approaches and philosophies but also because the values held to be important by people in an organization determine what it is they wish to do and how they wish to see it carried out – or at least what it is they will tolerate before becoming obstructive. A few management consulting firms have even found that an understanding of management culture is a 'product' that can be sold to their clients. 'Change your culture,' they say, 'and all your problems of dealing with the marketplace will be reduced.' In this sense, at least, they recognize the importance of the contribution that correct organization can make to marketing success.

The notion of culture has already been referred to in an earlier section when the differing needs of maintenance versus innovatory tasks and business versus welfare objectives in different marketing units were identified. But it goes much further than this.

As a function, marketing itself demands that certain values are held by those practising it. Chief among these is the belief that the purpose of production is not merely to serve the interests of those who are producing but, more importantly, of those who are consuming. Values, therefore, which involve identification with buyers, customers, distributors, influential forces in the marketplace, all of them trending into the future, are extremely important to encourage if success in the marketplace is to be ensured.

This set of values, together with those that permit and encourage innovation and new ideas as well as an aggressive competitive will to succeed, constitute the spirit of marketing. If this spirit is absent the firm will not survive long in a tempestuous, volatile and hostile marketplace. Yet it is this very style of management, so necessary for organization, that so often brings difficulty when working at the boundary with functions in an enterprise which may demand different styles – those more to do with running an efficient ship, for example. A good organization has to manage these conflicts successfully and have systems within it which manage to make the best use of both sorts of cultures each with its particular role to play.

What, then, are the dimensions of managerial style and which ones are appropriate for marketing in helping it perform its various tasks?

Each of the following dimensions can be regarded as a continuum along which it is possible, given valid measuring instruments, to place a unit's style and culture.

Risk-seeking – risk-taking – risk-tolerant – risk-averse – risk-avoiding

It is easy to over-generalize here by stating that an organization in total can be positioned along this continuum. Very often an enterprise is used taking risks in one field of activity, say, in technology, but is averse to taking them, say, as far as marketing is concerned. Clive Sinclair's various operations illustrate this point quite well. Clearly if a marketing strategy or set of tasks demands the taking of risks, then management style in key areas which affect success also demands people, attitudes and systems which are at least risk-taking. Maintenance tasks on the contrary demand a style more at the risk-averse end. Style must fit task within every marketing unit.

Analytically rational – seat of the pants judgemental

Some management teams seldom take action without research, forecasting, analysis and deep consideration of alternatives using a rational, scientific approach; while others take decisions more or less instantly and base them upon flair, hunch, judgement and feeling. Most would probably fall between these two extremes, behaving in one way when faced with one particular set of uncertainties or problems and another when confronting a different set. A judgemental style implies tolerance of error; a rational style would try to eliminate error. This has implications for the selection of people, for the system of control and sanctions as well as for the information flows, values and skills that are so necessary to blend together.

Fully democratic – cabalistic – autocratic

The number of people involved in decision making as a proportion of the total membership is another indication of style. So is the frequency with which one style is adopted in comparison with the other; and over which matters the particular style is employed. Democratic styles demand open communication, joint decision making structures and collective responsibility to be built in to the resulting marketing structure. Autocratic styles require perfect knowledge, submissive executives and a sound staff function.

Coercive – reward-based – group esteeming – self-actualising

This is a dimension of style which is concerned with the reward/punishment system. At one end objectives are achieved through fear of the punishment that will be meted out by superior powers in authority. The style then leads through motivation to achieve by the giving of rewards or inducements (money, promotion or status, for instance) through the kind of satisfaction with a job well done stemming from belonging to an appreciative group to, at the other end, the motivation that is essentially 'inner driven'. Whether innovation is more readily induced through external or internal drives is a debatable issue far beyond the scope of

this chapter. Each organization, though, will have its own beliefs about this and if innovation is a task to be performed it will design structures, systems and sanctions based on these beliefs. Such beliefs may have their foundation in the personal views of the chief executive or senior manager of the marketing operation.

Traditional – conformist – radical

This is a dimension that is especially all-embracing. It may apply to any element of the marketing mix (the product styling, the channels of distribution, the discount structures or to the advertising 'treatments', for instance, to the market research and planning techniques used in individual units) or, in more general terms, to the overall outlook of an organization in the way it behaves towards its total environment.

Parochial – cosmopolitan

It is hard to avoid being pejorative here (or indeed in some of the other dimensions of style) but no such intention is meant! This dimension is concerned with the reference points an organization uses or the benchmarks against which it compares itself and is a function both of a set of attitudes and perceptions as well as more operational collection of attributes to do with the scope of the business and the geographical areas in which it deals.

Expansionist – passive – content

This is an aspect of managerial style which relates to the strategic mission itself. A strategy, whether formulated explicitly or held implicitly, can be identified as being proactively expansionist and concerned with change and growth, reactively passive and less ambitious or content with things as they are. Again it is clear how, if this is the firm's strategy, style must follow. Sometimes (shades of the strategy-structure debate mentioned earlier) it may be that an organization staffed by expansion-minded people will generate an expansionist strategy. Which is egg and which chicken is another debatable point. The argument is circular and it is very important indeed for anyone contemplating a radically new strategy with existing managers to break into the circle effectively. The point at issue is where to start; with the people that make up the structure, or with the strategy. British Rail at one point in its history began at the people end by recruiting a whole batch of ex-Shell managers who were then given the task of deciding strategy; Marley probably decided upon a strategy of going into car leasing and then found the people.

Aggressive – incursive – defensive

Military metaphors, these! They have to do with the competitive stance adopted and may, like the dimensions just mentioned, be linked with several other factors such as the nature of the people staffing the organization, the environmental opportunities and threats, size and the strategic mission.

Businesslike – hybrid – welfare

This dimension has been touched earlier on in this chapter. It is mentioned again here because of the close link between this aspect of style and the marketing task carrying the same label. A welfare task tends to attract welfare-minded people, structures and systems interested in service, professionalism, altruism and accountability to a public that is outside the enterprise itself. A businesslike task, on the other hand, attracts profit-minded people accountable to profit-seeking stakeholders.

Rugged – neutral – 'polite'

More an aspect of acculturalization brought about by cloning than anything else, this dimension reflects the preferred behaviour of the ruling group. The contrast between the 'let it all hang out', 'tell it like it is' rough and tumble, crude, vigorous, masculine, often simple and uncivilized style of some organizations and the effortlessly urbane, stylish, witty, clubby atmosphere of others is marked. The stereotypical view of, say, Australian managerial style held by the larger public school staffed, UK enterprises (and, let it be said, the other way round too!) provides perfect and frequent illustrations of the operation of this particular dimension of style. So, too, do the contrasting images of the more heroic self-made north-country managerial cultures and those of the prosperous, more institutionalized south. Each system holds to different yet very particular codes

of ethics, behaviour and what is regarded as acceptable and unacceptable conduct and rules of social intercourse. These contrasting styles affect, for instance, the degree of trust given to subordinates and, therefore, the control systems that are appropriate.

Future – present – past

Occasionally when involved with the marketing management of a firm one is struck by the time-orientation of the people involved. Managers in one firm may constantly refer to the old times, the 'golden-age' and a constant need to get back to the way things were (or at the least, a hope that they will return some day). If this attitude prevails within structures for marketing then opportunities which involve striving towards some future view of the world will not be sought. And if they are they probably will not be achieved, simply because no one is mentally committed to them. In contrast, other organizations set themselves very much in the future and wish even to make it happen; being quite happy to overturn the attitudes, practices and needs of past times. Again the UK versus the Japanese view of the motorcycle market illustrated this well.

'Heavy' control – selective control – finger tip control

The manner in which top marketing managers keep tabs on their subordinates and operations is frequently a matter of personal style not solely dictated by circumstances. Psychologists have much to say about the roots of such style, but its effects upon levels of fear on the one hand and being able to influence performance on the other are quite marked. Reporting systems, staff selection, morale, and the willingness to work beyond the call of duty and to take initiatives are all affected.

Professional – mixed – amateur

Marketing, because it is not an activity which can be regarded as scientific in that it possesses a body of immutable laws, is vulnerable to being practised in a very amateurish way. There is a feeling that anyone with a bit of common sense can do it, especially if he/she has some background in sales!

There is also the danger that this activity is ignored altogether as something important in running a business. 'A good product will sell itself. All we need are some good engineers, a couple of accountants and a managing director with flair.' This attitude and these structures ignore the fact that although marketing is not a science it never-the-less possesses a body of practice based on specialized, professionally executed and soundly based knowledge. Some organizations in their structural design and style recognize this and others possessing a sense that the well-intentioned amateur will suffice do not. The latter will fail to establish a disciplined, well-integrated consistent structure for marketing. They will maybe give accounting or production the status of lead function in their organization merely out of ignorance or prejudice.

Metaphoric – idiosyncratic

Finally, but not forming a continuum, there are two important aspects of style that cannot be ignored. One can be called 'metaphoric' and the other 'idiosyncratic'.

There are organizations, because the units within them need to be bonded together yet differentiated from others, that adopt their own organizing metaphors. Phrases such as 'we run a tight ship', 'marketing is like warfare' or 'at Procter and Gamble we don't have problems, we have concerns' succinctly epitomize the way an organization sees itself. From the organizing metaphor – a ship, a plane, a battle or even, as on occasion one hears, a biological organism surviving and developing in a hostile environment (a sort of marketing Darwinism) – stems the everyday language and the acceptable practices used by the organization. A view of the world emerges which by analogy derives from the metaphor. Firms using a military one will talk about 'securing our resources', 'consolidating our position', 'beating the enemy', 'a war of attrition' and so on. Military style practices will be rewarded and military-type management praised.

Idiosyncratic styles are just what the name implies – peculiar to an individual person. If that person happens to be powerful then his/her style may pervade a whole organization. Even divisional or departmental heads will display such idio-syncrasies. Howard Hughes and other movie and oil moguls, David Alliance at Coats-Viyella, Alan Sugar at Amstrad or Clive Sinclair and many other less publicly known, but to marketing managers (because they organizationally sit on top of them), similarly important people provide ample illustration of the significance of idiosyncrasy. Some managements, like Marks and Spencer, idiosyncratically hardly recognize marketing as a separate activity at all! Procter and Gamble has its own version of it and many firms think it is just to do with selling and price-cutting. All these are idiosyncrasies that reflect themselves in a myriad of ways throughout the components of an organization identified in this chapter's introduction.

The point of identifying these fourteen components of organizational style is not to say that in all cases effective marketing requires one certain profile of styles above all other possible profiles. Some are prerequisites for marketing success and others, so to speak, are optional. Quite clearly the actual mix of styles needed depends on the marketing tasks which the enterprise either requires or confronts. A task implying penetration of new markets with new products by a small firm interested in growing would clearly demand quite a different set from the task facing a well-established large monopolist sitting on top of a captive, stable home market. Rather, the point is to emphasize the need for styles to be consistent and compatible, not only with each other, but with the rest of the organization's total properties mentioned in the introduction. Style is too important to be ignored as a major component but it has to be in harmony with the others and with the strategic tasks that marketing sets for itself. This is not to say that styles have to be identical across the entire system; merely that they need to fit the chosen marketing stance, or at least not offend it. The totality of an organization's style and purpose constitutes an ideology; and organizations with a strong, consistent and relevant ideology invariably succeed better than those without.

Market factors and their effect on organizational design

So far the discussion has centred upon the way in which a firm's own objectives and characteristics condition the types of structures for marketing that should emerge. The fundamental boundary managing nature of the task of marketing has also been noted.

A third factor affecting structural design now needs to be studied; the effect of the market environment itself. This can either be selected by an enterprise in the way that British Airways, for instance, chooses to operate in the package tour business, or it can impact upon it in the way, for example, that an airline faces competition from other airlines and transport systems.

A market can be classed for present purposes in various ways:

By degree of hostility.
By degree of diversity.
By complexity.
By restrictiveness.
By dynamism and rate of change.

The best way of looking at links between markets and organizational structure is to do so by making certain propositions that have stemmed both from observation and research. These now follow. They owe much to the work of Khandwalla (1977).

1   *'The more hostile, complex and fast changing the external environment, the more strategically important to management are uncertainty absorption and avoidance mechanisms (like market research, forecasting, advertising and vertical integration), the more risk-taking and organic is the top management style and the greater is interdepartmental conflict.'*

At this stage it is important to emphasize that there is a difference, more than merely subtle, between complexity and uncertainty. The grid in Figure 4.2 may help to illustrate this with some examples.

Charles Letts, one of the major UK diary publishers, faces a stable, predictable market. Diary sales are linked fairly closely to population size; diaries are bought seasonally once a year, are simple in concept and vary surprisingly little in design. Brand awareness is strong and conservatism in style is high. Furthermore, until recently, the environment was strongly influenced by a Trade Association dominated by the three major publishers: Letts, Collins and T. J. and J. Smith. Until

	Complexity	
	Low	*High*
Low	Diary publishing	Hospital equipment
	e.g. Charles Letts	e.g. Charles Thackray
Uncertainty		
High	Popular record production	Communication
	e.g. Polygram	e.g. Cable and Wireless

Figure 4.2   *The complexity/uncertainty matrix*

fairly recently, too, the distribution channels were not dominated by powerful retail groups. Control over the marketplace, then, was relatively high. The technology of diary production is simple and varies little over time; products are standardized and trade channels fairly well organized and stable. In short, 'a diary is a diary, is a diary . . .'. Marketing was passively defensive and it is the publishing technologies and mentality which predominate. All this argued for a mechanistic, centralized structure.

By contrast, Cable and Wireless faces a world ruled by diplomacy, nationalism, politics, war, economics, high technology, intense competition and rapid innovation. The costs of R & D, production and pre- and after-sales service are enormous. Products are non-standard and usually tailor-made to the needs of large, powerful buyers who in turn are heavily influenced by unpredictable 'non-task variables' (diplomatic pressure, international funding, political loyalties and reciprocal trading), none of which has any direct bearing upon the economic cost/functional benefit relationships associated directly with telecommunication equipment. Cable and Wireless's environment then is highly complex as well as uncertain because it faces a turbulent, hostile, diverse, technically complex and circumscribed market. Some form of divisionalization is therefore necessary in order to cope with complex market differentiation.

Charles Thackray, an important UK supplier of medical and surgical equipment, faces an environment which is technologically highly complex.

The need for the development of advanced drugs and medical hardware which can be guaranteed a life cycle long enough to cover the high cost of their development means heavy investment in risky ventures and a great range of technologies and processes to master. The stringent controls over the sale of drugs and equipment make the environment even more complex; so does the incidence of disease and the state of social priorities and resource availability world-wide. The regulatory climate and the way medical practice is organized and funded throughout the world market merely add to the difficulties. At the same time, though, the uncertainty facing Thackray is, by comparison with Cable and Wireless, fairly low. Diseases and surgical practices are well documented, the state of the art is well known and population size and morbidity rates are predictable. State health services help to guarantee a secure market and so too do product licensing procedures. Channels are well organized and (in the UK at any rate), resale prices are maintained. Advertising is controlled and most products, once produced, are standardized. The medical profession, being conservative and in constant touch, helps prevent too many risks being faced solely due to uncertainty. The proportion of staple drugs and equipment, too, is very high. The major uncertainty stems from predicting the surgeons of the future and the demands they will make for new equipment. A product-group structure would therefore seem sensible. This falls short of full divisionalization but does enable the company to manage complex product and service differentiation.

Polygram, a leading producer of popular records and music, faces the problem of a highly volatile market with short product life cycles, a high fashion element, and ever changing idols. Cynics would say, though, that the industry is capable of considerable manipulation of its market. The industry justifies this by saying that it happens precisely because of the high uncertainty of spotting winners among the hundreds of new solo artists and groups that emerge each year. A personality based structure is called for simply because the key skill, based upon the flair for judging future stars, is so fundamentally rooted in individual ability.

It may be easy to say, as the state of current thought would have it, that dynamic environments call for organic structures and mechanistic ones for stable structures. It is infinitely more difficult to indicate what an ideal organization should be and do, if it faces one of the intermediate environments

(a low uncertainty/highly complex or high uncertainty/simple environment). Broadly speaking, the first of these intermediate types requires the ability to scan and make sense of present inter-relationships between environmental components and the second, the ability to predict; a longitudinal rather than latitudinal capability in other words.

2 *'As the hostility of the market increases, there is initially an increase in the coercive authoritarian style of top management and then a decrease in it, and there is an initial decrease in the investment in staff-based, sophisticated information generating and processing activities, and then an increase in them.'*

3 *'As market hostility increases, the outputs and operations of the organization become more standardized, and the practice of 'human relations' for securing the cooperation of personnel decreases'.*

4 *'The more diverse the market, the greater is the internal differentiation in the structure of the organization, and the more the organization seeks integration through employing a sophisticated control and information system, standard operating procedures and a participatory style of management at top levels'.*

5 *'The more differentiated the task environment of the various subsystems of the marketing organization, the more internally differentiated is the structure, and the more it must resort to complex modes for keeping its operations coordinated or integrated'.*

6 *'The more technologically complex the external environment, the more its top management adopts an optimization and planning oriented style, the more sophisticated and complex is the organization's control and information system, and the more automated and computerized are its operations'.*

7 *'The more restrictive the market environment, the more planning and optimization oriented is the style of top management'.*

8 *'As the market becomes more restrictive, there is at first an increase and then a decrease in the coercive orientation of top management'.*

9 *'Simple, stable markets demand centralized bureaucracy of the classic kind; complex but stable ones tend towards decentralized bureaucracy; simple but dynamic markets argue for centralized organic structures and complex dynamic ones for decentralized organic.'*

There is an almost entropic reversion to a bureaucracy inherent in all large organizations. The ideal environment seems usually to be of the simple stable type because this gives full opportunity to maximize standardization, simplification and specialization of processes, thus bringing in train low costs, an ordered system and a quiet life. Hence, even if the environment is in fact getting more turbulent, there is often a refusal to admit it and, having therefore to face the inevitability of destabilizing the structure. There is further an almost pathological unwillingness to admit increased dependence on the environment, since that is seen to imply weakness, impotence and a lack of faith. A macho attitude to the market leads dangerously to the denial of its uncertainty and complexity, and ultimately to a refusal even to acknowledge the true role of the marketing function in assessing and managing it. The organization then ceases to learn; and without learning it cannot adapt successfully.

10 *'Large regulated monopolies with long planning horizons and heavy increments of investment, such as British Telecom, possess marketing units dedicated especially to analysis, long range planning and at the same time, other units whose task is to regulate short-term demand and to optimize plant utilization.'*

11 *'Oligopolistic industries depend heavily upon non-price competition and, therefore, emphasize product modification, advertising, distribution and selling. Marketing is frequently the lead function simply because the current market place and the battle for market share are the prime preoccupations of the organization.'*

Since one of the major functions of marketing is to ensure that the supplier is in tune with its market environment, and because one aspect of that environment for firms dealing with other enterprises is the customer's own organization, it follows that the seller's organization must to some degree reflect that of the buyer. This is especially the case if the buyer has a high degree of power over the seller, such that they can insist upon the seller conforming.

The phrases 'organizational mating' and 'relationship marketing' have been coined to indicate the process by which this matching is achieved and also provide a rationale for its existence.

Enterprises which succeed by establishing and maintaining long-term stable relationships with a small number of customers (industrial firms with large buyers or consumer firms with large retailers for instance), often do so by establishing formal structures which mirror those existing in their customers. Top management meet top management, marketing directors liaise with procurement directors, accountants meet accountants, sales engineers meet production engineers, representatives meet purchasing agents and so on. Not only that, but procedures and systems may also become integrated; so may informal mechanisms such as social events and management style. Which organization adapts to which is often determined by relative power, but more often by a process of gradual cementing.

In cases where there is only one major customer, the process of mirroring that customer's organization is relatively uncomplicated and few compromises need to be made. Where there is, however, a high degree of heterogeneity among customers' organizations and systems, the problem of reaching the correct structure to cope with that variety becomes more complex. If the number of customers is few, one response might be to set up separate subunits at the interface with each, but to achieve homogeneity by proper use of internal coordinating structures not impinging directly upon the more important customers.

In consumer marketing the role of the key account manager and in industrial marketing the sales engineer, are two roles reflecting the notion of organizational mating. Both are boundary roles interacting with key functional components of both customer and supplier with the task of securing and maintaining a pair-bond.

It is not merely with organizations who buy from the firm that compatibility needs to be ensured. So also does the fit with those with whom the firm is associated as a partner in say, a joint venture or as a client or customer of an advertising agency or market research bureau. It is not always that one can count on the luxury, deriving from one's power, of having other systems adapting their structure and processes to suit one's own. The choice of advertising agency, joint venture partner or even an acquisition is frequently made partly upon grounds of mutual organizational compatibility.

Structural groupings involving marketing

Since an organization for marketing requires its members to group into specialisms, it is clearly necessary to look at the possible ways in which such groupings can be structured. It will be left until the next section for a study to be made of the specific location of marketing groups.

Thompson (1967) states that organizations set boundaries around their activities which he calls domains. These include all the activities over which they have total control using whatever discipline is appropriate, whether mechanistic, organic or whatever. They select these core activities because their successful performance conditions the success of the enterprise; they also reflect the distinctive competence of the organization which sets it apart from competitors and at the same time maximizes its advantage over them. Such crucial activities it carries on 'in-house', leaving the less crucial to be undertaken by others with which it establishes links. These may be suppliers, distributors or facilitating firms such as financial, transportation or other service organizations. In doing this the firm also stakes out customer domains, or markets and product offerings to serve them which are distinct from those offered by competitors.

In choosing to contract-out some of its activities, the firm become dependent on others and, therefore, without line authority over them, has to exert some degree of control or influence by the use of power or agreement. This ensures its survival in a hostile environment and guarantees it the markets and resources it needs. Such control can be exercised by contracting, coopting or coalescing.

One further consideration determining the choice of activities to be undertaken within the firm is recognized by Thompson, too. He implies that firms will tend to contract-out those activities which are not only unable to be undertaken internally on a sufficient scale to be economic, but also which can only be bought-in in quantum amounts. One could also add the reason that some activities are undertaken in-house for reasons of commercial secrecy. That is why in marketing many firms subcontract their advertising, distribution and market research needs but retain in-house their selling, product design and market planning

capabilities. Unless it is big enough to keep an advertising and distribution outlet facility fully occupied (or unless it is so crucial to success that even if it is only partially used it is still worth keeping to itself) a firm will usually rely upon other organizations to provide that kind of service.

Thompson also attempts an explanation of why activities within a firm are grouped in the particular way they are – be it by functional area, region, market, business unit or product. He does this by isolating three types of interdependence between activities (see Figure 4.3).

First, there is the type of interdependence that exists solely because if one unit of the firm performs inadequately it does not directly affect any other part; it merely leads to a less than adequate performance by the firm as a whole. This is because each unit is discrete and, therefore, separated from all others. A failure of the southern sales force, for instance, does not affect the performance of the northern simply because they do not depend on one another. They are only mutually affected if head office, because of the south's failure, has to cut back on the resources available to the north. Such a relationship Thompson labels 'pooled interdependence'.

Then there is the type of interdependence which takes a serial form. The sales force depends on the factory for reliable delivery of products to sell to customers. Such interdependence is not only pooled; it is also sequential.

Lastly, there is the type which is not only pooled and sequential but where in addition the output of each unit becomes the input for the other. The sales force depends on the firm's advertising to help it sell but also provides a merchandising capability on which the agency depends for the effectiveness of its sales promotional campaign. Such interdependence Thompson calls 'reciprocal'.

As one moves from pooled through sequential to reciprocal interdependence, the tasks of coordination and control get more complicated. On this basis, Thompson proposes an explanation of activity grouping. Firms, he says, group first by those activities which are reciprocally interdependent. This is because if they were broken up and reorganized in any other way the costs of coordination and control would far out-weigh any benefits of scale that might result. At the second level, firms

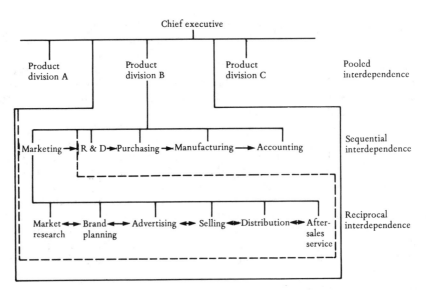

Figure 4.3 *A pattern of marketing interdependence*

group those activities which are sequential and at the third or highest level those which are merely pooled.

By grouping activities in this way a hierarchy of groups is created which in a marketing context may resemble Figure 4.3. Other patterns are, of course, possible depending on the precise interrelationships within each firm and their frequency.

Such a structure minimizes the costs of control and coordination while at the same time encourages economies of scale, specialization and effectiveness.

This particular contingency, resource dependence, is extremely important in determining the basis of divisionalization that a firm should adopt; for instance whether it should be ordered firstly by region, product, function or market. It also determines at what level the various marketing tasks should be undertaken and what the role and responsibilities of marketing should be. It is precisely because the three types of interdependence are not hierarchically ordered in the same way in different firms that one finds the variety of divisional forms that one does.

The particular units identified in Figure 4.3 are, of course, specialist. That is to say they demand organizational properties that are similar within them but different from the others. Hence they are structured separately yet linked in ways Thompson

explains. Traditionally, of course, they each possess their own hierarchy – the sales force, for instance, just like a division, could be organized by region, product, clientele or function; and precisely the same concerns about costs of coordination and control under the various methods determine which pattern finally emerges.

Recently companies such as Procter and Gamble and APV (a major UK multinational grouping of food and drink processing equipment manufacturers) have been faced with the choice of whether to organize by product, by region, by technology or by market. They discovered that it was impossible to choose any one dimension as paramount; in Thompson's terms, they all involved reciprocal interdependence.

The solution adopted by APV in 1988 (and P&G have chosen roughly the same solution) was to split the global market into domains based on the manufacturing subsidiaries. The chief executive of each subsidiary has four major responsibilities:

● That of a technical R & D centre of excellence with the duty of new product development in a given product arena across the globe. Each product arena is based upon the needs of a particular type of customer; for example breweries or bakeries.

- That of a sales region whose duty it is to sell and distribute the entire group's range of products within his region.
- That of a coordinator keeping watch on and developing total group marketing activities in a particular area of the globe.
- That of an advisor to other regions on matters to do with their centre of excellence arena.

The plurality of performance criteria that this organizational pattern involves does cause problems, particularly on the bottom line performance of any particular region, but close control by the group headquarters plus the benefits for global marketing that undoubtedly follow keep these to a minimum.

Alternative locations for the marketing function

Defining marketing as the function which is responsible for constructing the programme of propositions to put to the enterprise's chosen market, its precise location is subject to a variety of choices. Each of these locations has its own rationale and the choice ultimately made depends upon a variety of contingencies.

At board level

The first of these locations is at the level of the main board. Where strategic marketing is the subject at issue or when negotiations with customers are about the securing of very large orders in proportion to the size of the organization – or in other words when any aspect of marketing is so important as to determine the future health and direction of the enterprise – then this aspect of the marketing function is executed at board level. The choice of an advertising agency, a major distributor or the decision to undertake large, risky new ventures would all be matters for board decision, subject of course to professional advice from lower down. Major personnel and budget allocation decisions would also be made here, the precise nature depending on the firm's size and degree of centralization.

The points at which decisions of a lower order would be permitted to be taken further down the hierarchy would depend on certain contingencies however. Among these are:

- The quality of middle and senior marketing managers.
- The variety and distinctiveness of markets dealt with.
- The routineness of marketing decisions.
- The style adopted by top management.
- The dynamics of the market environment.
- The frequency with which decisions need to be made.
- The perceived importance and risk attached to decisions.
- The novelty of the decisions to the organization.
- The degree and quality of information upon which to base decisions.

Within a staff unit reporting to the board

Sometimes the more contemplative, speculative and cerebral aspects of the marketing function are undertaken by a specially established staff group without line responsibility. As a think tank, as a provider of long range information or merely as a unit which maps out alternative courses of action and their likely outcomes this type of group performs a very useful function. Frequently, a unit such as this forms part of a larger strategic planning unit reporting directly to the chief executive.

On other occasions a staff group may play a service role for operating divisions. In this role it would be responsible for:

- A corporate market research capability.
- Corporate public relations.
- Major publicity events, such as exhibitions or sponsorship deals.
- Advising operating divisions about advertising, product design, the application of marketing models, training and so on.

Whether a unit such as this is in fact established also depends upon various contingency factors, among which are:

- The extent to which divisions should and do already possess such capabilities themselves.

- Whether the enterprise is facing long-run turbulence and market uncertainties.
- Whether the enterprise is planning orientated.
- The degree of standardization of marketing problems and solutions across divisions.
- Size.
- Complexity.
- Differentiation necessary between the line and staff 'cultures'.

Within each operating division or strategic business unit itself

Where an organization possesses operating divisions, whether based upon regions, products or clientele and irrespective of whether each has its own production facility, line marketing may be located within them. Unless each division is strategically autonomous – in which case strategic marketing matters will also form part of their brief – their marketing responsibilities are basically tactical in nature. Design and execution of marketing programmes within agreed annual or rolling budgets and within strategic parameters laid down at board level will be their main activity. Their focus will be upon the dimension along which they are divisionalized – a singe geographical area but marketing a variety of products to a variety of customers; a single product group marketing one product but to a total geographical market and a whole variety of customers; or a single customer group marketing a variety of products over a total geographical market.

Such divisionalization arises when a large organization is engaged with numerous markets which themselves are so heterogeneous that coordinating their different needs and programmes becomes costly, difficult and time-consuming. Flexibility, profitability and competitive advantage are all lost as a result. The choice of dimension along which to divisionalize can be made according to Thompson's rule concerning resource dependency that has been referred to earlier. Each division must be ideologically and structurally homogeneous within itself yet clearly differentiated from its neighbours. This difference, made necessary by the characteristics of each division's chosen market clearly means that each needs to have its own specialized marketing operation.

Matrixed with other structures and functions

On occasions an organization's total tasks may get highly complicated yet at the same time be incapable of being simplified by being split up into separate parts such as divisions or business units. This is usually because the market and other subenvironments are not capable of being differentiated either. All must be coped with by a single organizational mechanism. Typically matrices occur in large organizations undertaking one or two massive projects for industrial customers or where the product or service being sold is itself highly complex, demands a variety of resources to put together, requires complicated sets of different skills and knowledge to deploy and is sold to undifferentiable or constantly changing classes of customer not easily grouped together. An example of a full matrix structure is shown in Figure 4.4.

Each sector on the matrix is equally critical to success, demands close cooperation and sharing of information with all other sectors, is complex and has to handle a lot of uncertainty. Furthermore, each dimension has a heavy responsibility for acting as a listening post in its own particular sphere of operations. In this way the enterprise is guaranteed a high degree of knowledge about a very complex environment. The system is designed to handle and even generate conflict so as to resolve differences between the factional interests that would otherwise dominate. The end-result in an effective matrix organization is the successful integration of all inputs necessary to generate profitable business. In an ineffective one it is endless, pointless and acrimoniously destructive meetings resulting in confusion, plummeting morale and the playing of politics. All this means that plans are not fulfilled and there is a reversion to another type of structure; usually of an antithetical, highly centralized, authoritarian kind.

In a matrix, marketing is everywhere! It appears at board level, as a resource input, in project management and in the executive units at the peripheries. It also provides a programming, negotiating, servicing and control capability at the centre. The result is that all those functions, wherever they are, that could contribute to sustainable competitive advantage do so effectively.

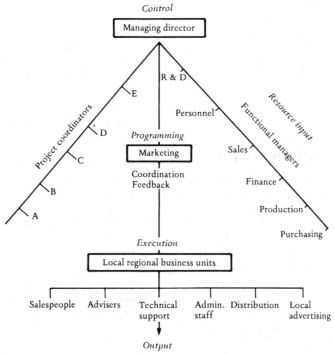

Control

Managing director

R & D

Project coordinators   E   *Resource input*   *Functional managers*

Personnel

D

Programming

C   Marketing   Sales

B   Coordination
Feedback   Finance

A   Production

Purchasing

Execution

Local regional business units

Salespeople   Advisers   Technical   Admin.   Distribution   Local
support   staff   advertising

Output

Figure 4.4 *A full matrix structure*

Fully integrated location

From all that has been said so far, and especially in the last section on the matrix form of organization, it can be seen how the activity of marketing is located in many places. This is because the function contributes to the health of an organization at every level. It also has many aspects, each with its own specialism and body of knowledge, which affect the outcome of all those decisions that directly or indirectly affect custom. Marketing is everywhere from the top at board level right down to the activities of individual sales people, service engineers or counter clerks. It is also present laterally across the organization affecting and being affected by R & D, production, purchasing, personnel and accounting and all other functions whose activities contribute to long-run market success. It also needs to influence many outside organizations upon whose performance in the marketplace depends – advertising agencies, distri-

butors, agents, suppliers, facilitators and so on. Linking structures need to be devised to connect all these thereby constructing a network which together makes up what might be called the 'extended' organization. Product management, market management, brand management and key account management are typical of such linking or coordinating devices. Organized around a product group, market, brand or customer 'logic' these roles are played out very much at the boundaries between internal functions, external agencies and the marketplace. In such a way is integration achieved.

More systemically, though, marketing may not be located everywhere so much as permeate everywhere. The distinction is more than subtle. Particularly in service industries, where so much depends upon interpersonal effectiveness at the point of sale or in marshalling a product specifically tailored to need, a marketing philosophy needs to be held at all levels, especially at the point of contact with the customer. When that state of affairs is reached the ultimate in integration has been achieved. At that point there may be no need, except in strategic, sales and staff functions, for there to be a marketing unit at all. It will have worked itself out of a job.

Conflicts caused by the introduction of a new organization for marketing

A chapter called 'Organization for marketing' would hardly be complete without considering the organizational difficulties of and recommendations for the introduction of new marketing strategies and structures into an enterprise. That, then, is the purpose of this final section.

It is important to realize that well before a specialist section dealing with the function of marketing is introduced into a firm some kind of marketing activity must have existed already. Products were even then designed, made, priced, promoted and distributed. There were probably activities called pre- and after-sales service and there would have been, if not market research, then at least a degree of market planning going on. This total set of activities which a professionally run marketing department would see as its prime concern would of course have been undertaken by a variety of other functions in the enterprise. They would probably have been uncoordinated and primitive though. Sales, advertising and rudimentary market research would have been the province of the sales department; pricing a matter for accounting and production people; distribution, production scheduling, after-sales service and quality control probably looked after by a mixture of sales and production units.

The first difficulty facing the introduction of a concentrated and specialist marketing unit can now be seen. Its roots go back to the ideas of Robert Ardrey and other naturalists when they discuss territoriality. Marketing has to invade the territory previously occupied by other specialisms and take some of their influence and status away. That is inevitable. Yet the skill with which it is done can determine the future success of the unit. There will be disputes about roles, about resource allocation, about status, about priorities and about objectives and the criteria by which success is judged. All this makes for conflict. Not that conflict is always bad; if essential changes are to be brought about then conflict is inevitable and may even be necessary to generate. Provided it is managed sensibly and destructive disintegrative conflict avoided, then all will be well. Territorial conflict, then, is the first difficulty to be faced when introducing marketing; activities traditionally and legitimately the province of other functions are suddenly 'captured' by marketing's incursive behaviour; and such behaviour will be resisted.

In this respect it is important to see marketing as an innovation within the organization. Its introduction will certainly be seen as such by other departments and managers. Some will welcome the innovation (among whom will presumably be those with the power to have brought it in!), but many will not. Still more will fail even to understand the nature of the innovation.

Because marketing when first introduced is an innovation that can be either adopted or rejected, it is useful to look at innovation theory to see if that body of knowledge can help ease its acceptability. The crude checklist that follows has its roots in such theory:

1 Understand first of all what the present organization was set up to do. Analyse its logic and the business principles that lie behind it. What is the status quo and how is it politically reinforced? How does the present structure reflect the present strategy? Not until this homework has been done will it be clear what changes are necessary to fit a new strategy or the establishment of a market orientation. At least then it will be possible to gauge the size of the task ahead.

2 Highlight the problems already existing in the organization that marketing and no one else can help solve. Make these problems future based, new and appear from directions that existing functions could have difficulty in recognizing and handling. They must also be significant along dimensions that existing functions and managers already recognize as important. Without overdoing it, create a feeling that unless change is initiated a crisis

will develop soon. The provision of stark information that shocks is better than any amount of system improvement in information management, for instance.

3 Emphasize that the skills and knowledge that marketing brings are additional rather than substitutional. That way others will not feel so threatened.

4 Help others achieve objectives set in their own terms rather than those of marketing. Sales people will wish to see sales increase and customers more satisfied; service people will wish to see fewer trivial and avoidable breakdowns; production people a more predictable workflow, research and development people fewer commercial failures and so on. Look for common concerns rather than differences.

5 Make marketing successes visible to the whole organization. Internal public relations is often more important than external. Emphasize the importance of the contribution of all departments to such success so that no one feels alienated or ignored.

6 Pick areas of the firm's operation where results can be achieved quickly, selectively and without asking for too many changes at once. Succeed by degrees so that others will more readily accept the demands made by marketing in changing existing practices when they come to be made in their areas.

7 Encourage an expansionist culture so that when the inevitable territorial battles do come there is room for all 'combatants' whose collaboration is essential to develop within the organization.

8 Make sure that people leading the marketing functions are champions of their cause but at the same time sensitive to the politics of change. Ensure of course that having been chosen they are given full backing by those with the ultimate power.

9 Try to ensure that marketing works with the organization by being compatible, at first, with existing cultures, systems, people behaviour, strategies, styles and objectives. Later, as change is made effective, the organization will itself begin to moderate all these things; but throughout the changes compatibility is still to be aimed for, even though marketing may be leading the evolution.

10 Ensure that any changes asked for are simple to understand and to put into practice. Talk in the language of those whom it is wished to influence. Understand their point of view, even if it is not entirely agreed with. Achieve a 'belongingness' rather than indifferent, arrogant isolation.

11 Bring conflict out into the open (although this may depend upon the style of management that happens to be current. It may work more in the USA and Australia than in the UK and Japan, if one accepts the notion of national managerial cultures!).

12 Convert the influential managers and people first, but existing fiefdoms represent powerful vested interests.

13 Understand that old habits die hard and especially so when the organization has been successful over a long time. Appeal to the younger, more cosmopolitan, better educated and hungry members of the organization. They will be the ones more open to innovatory change.

14 Force people to face marketing realities. Bring out the results of research into present activities that may be disturbing and worrying.

15 Make the future seem less fearful and more predictable and controllable. Have a vision which people can understand, welcome and work towards.

16 Gradually begin to change the norms of the organization to fit the new reality of customer orientation and the need for change in the hunt for sustainable competitive advantage. The reporting systems, control data, decision-making processes and even whole bits of the structure may need altering. This needs the careful exercise of power.

17 Aim for organic structures conducive to change and innovation. Loosen up the system. Establish task groups and begin to 'matrix-in' marketing with the other structures. Do not ignore the fact that the existing set-up still needs to operate well so that today's concerns are not sacrificed for tomorrow's.

18 Minimize the extent to which conflict is resolved by the use of organizational force (recourse to higher authority, threats, or fear, for instance). The way enemies will not be

created among important people whose collaboration is needed later. There is also the danger of creating powerful alliances against the innovation.

19 Reduce the frequency of conflict if it is to do with 'ends' rather than 'means'. Get agreement early to all important issues to do with strategic objectives.

20 Increase such frequency if it is to do with 'means', so that changes in operating practices do take place.

21 Get agreement to strategies and objectives which are superordinate to individual departmental ones. Do not allow vested interests to dictate overriding goals of the organization. Divide and rule if necessary, but do it subtly!

22 Prevent unholy alliances from forming against you by anticipating where they might exist and then neutralise them. Watch particularly for those fighting rearguard actions and beware too of snipers emerging from foxholes behind the advance!

23 Increase the extent to which people transfer across functions and are members of groups whose interests overlap. Develop open communication. Look for good future managers as change agents and setters of the new style and purpose.

24 Create a net balance of dependency upon marketing such that people need its contribution more than it needs them.

25 Have courage and keep going over the long term. Introducing any innovation effectively is not easy and much resistance needs overcoming. There will be set-backs inevitably and at times all the world will seem to conspire against you! At such times it is important to know who your friends are (and not only in your own organization!) Look for outside help in times like these.

Conclusion

Once marketing has been accepted and resistance to its introduction reduced, then of course, its job organizationally speaking, is not finished by any means. There remains the task of continually managing change in the marketplace and dealing with the inevitable effects upon the organization. Here conflict is endemic; chronic rather than acute. It has to do with minor disturbance more than cataclysmic change and can be handled lower down the hierarchy by product managers, market managers, venture groups and various liaison devices between the functions. Difficulties are over means rather than ends.

There may come a time though, when the market changes so much and so quickly or a political or other environmental shift happens so suddenly that the whole marketing task of the organization needs reappraisal. The consequences are especially significant if the new task is diametrically opposed to the previous one. On pages 56 and 57 the notion of continua of marketing tasks was introduced. Each of these can be regarded as a dimension of a matrix which could be called a marketing stance matrix. If a change of stance necessitates or results in a violent movement along one continuum (say from risk avoiding to risk seeking, defensive to aggressive, welfare to business or maintenance to innovation), then the organizational consequences are serious enough. If there are simultaneous moves from one end of a continuum to another along several dimensions at once, then the organizational trauma is dramatic. The whole 'set' of the organization and its component units needs reorientating in every aspect – values, culture, systems, skills, styles, structure and people. An entirely new organism will need to emerge. Ask Cable and Wireless, British Airways, British Telecom, our national orchestras or the Burton Group. Do not ask (because they are not around) BSA. At times like this the case for saying that structure follows strategy is most powerfully put. But that is where we came in!

References

Ardrey, R., *The Territorial Imperative*, Collins, 1967.

Bacharach, S. B. and Lawler, E. J., *Power and Politics in Organizations*, Jossey-Bass, 1980.

Bakker, C. B. and Bakker-Rabdan, M. K., *No Trespassing!: Explorations in Human Territoriality*, 1973.

Burns, T. and Stalker, G. M., *The Management of Innovation*, Tavistock, 1961.

Chandler, A. D., *Strategy and Structure*, MIT Press, 1962.

Channon, D. F., *The Strategy and Structure of British Enterprise*, Macmillan, 1973.

Child, J., *Organization: A Guide to Problems and Practices*, 2nd ed., Harper and Row, 1984.

Davis, S. M. and Lawrence, P. R., *Matrix*, Addison Wesley, 1977.

Doyle, P., 'Management Structures and Marketing Strategies in UK Industry', *European Journal of Marketing*, vol. 13, 1979, pp. 319–31.

Galbraith, J. R., *Designing Complex Organizations*, Addison-Wesley, 1973.

Galbraith, J. R. and Nathanson, D. A., *Strategy Implementation: the Role of Structure and Process*, West, 1978.

Gupta, A. K., Raj, S. P. and Wilemon, D., 'A Model for Studying R & D – Marketing Interface in the Product Innovation Process', *Journal of Marketing*, vol. 50, 1986, pp. 7–17.

Hall, R. H., *Organizations: Structure and Process*, 3rd ed., Prentice-Hall, 1983.

Hall, W. K., 'SBUs: hot new topic in the management of diversification', *Business Horizons*, February 1978, pp. 17–25.

Handy, C. B., *Understanding Organizations*, Penguin, 1976.

Kaldor, A. G., 'Imbricative Marketing', *Journal of Marketing*, April 1971, pp. 19–25.

Khandwalla, P. M., *The Design of Organizations*, Harcourt Brace, 1977.

Lawrence, P. R. and Lorsch, J. W., *Organization and Environment*, Graduate School of Business Administration, Harvard University, 1967.

Mintzberg, H., *Designing Effective Organizations*, Prentice-Hall, 1983.

Miles, R. E. and Snow, C. C., *Organizational Strategy Structure and Purpose*, McGraw-Hill, 1978.

Morgan, G., *Images of Organization*, Sage, 1986.

Payne, A. F., 'Developing a Marketing-Oriented Organization', *Business Horizon*, May/June 1988 pp. 46–53.

Peters, T. J., 'Strategy Follows Structure'. Developing Distinctive Skills' *California Management Review*, vol. 26, no. 3, 1984, pp. 111–25.

Pfeffer, J., *Power in Organizations*, Pitman, 1981.

Rogers, E. M. and Shoemaker, F. F., *Communication of Innovations*, 2nd ed., Free Press, 1971.

Rogers, K., *Managers: Personality and Performance*, Tavistock, 1963.

Ruebert, R. W., Walker, O. C. and Roering, K. J., 'The Organization of Marketing Activities. A Contingency Theory of Structure and Performance', *Journal of Marketing*, vol. 49, 1985, pp. 13–25.

Ruebert, R. W. and Walker, O. C., 'Marketing's Interaction with Other Functional Units', *Journal of Marketing*, vol. 51, 1987, pp. 1–19.

Rumelt, R. P., *Strategy, Structure and Economic Performance*, Graduate School of Business Administration, Harvard University, 1974.

Souder, W. E., 'Disharmony between R & D and Marketing', *Industrial Marketing Management*, vol. 10, 1981, pp. 67–73.

Spillard, P., *Organization and Marketing*, Croom Helm, 1985.

Thompson, J. D., *Organizations in Action*, McGraw-Hill, 1967.

Weinrauch, J. D. and Anderson, R., 'Conflicts between Engineering and Marketing Units', *Industrial Marketing Management*, vol. 11, 1982, pp. 291–301.

Weitz, B. and Anderson E., 'Organizing the Marketing Function', *Review of Marketing*, (B. M. Enis and K. J. Roering eds.), American Marketing Association, 1981.

Wensley, R., *Organization Issues in Marketing Strategy*, London Business School Occasional Paper, 82/3, 1982.

5
Planning the marketing function
MALCOLM McDONALD

Introduction

In this chapter we address principally the issue of strategic marketing planning although, as will be seen, most of the principles involved apply equally well to the total strategic corporate process.

The chapter is in three sections. The first section describes the widespread ignorance about strategic marketing planning and confusion about the difference between strategic marketing planning and sales forecasting and budgeting, which encourages business people to perpetuate an essentially parochial and short-term view of business. It also describes the resulting commonality of operational problems, which centre around declining organizational effectiveness and confusion over what to do about it.

The second section describes the marketing planning process itself and concentrates on the key steps – the marketing audit and the setting of marketing objectives and strategies.

The third section concludes by describing the necessary ingredients for success in the design and implementation of marketing planning systems.

Strategic planning myths

Marketing's contribution to business success in manufacturing, distribution or merchanting activities lies in its commitment to detailed analysis of future opportunities to meet customer needs and a wholly professional approach to selling to well-defined market segments those products or services that deliver the sought-after benefits. While prices and discounts are important, as are advertising and promotion, the link with engineering through the product is paramount.

Such a commitment and activities must not be mistaken for budgets and forecasts. Those of course we need and we have already got. Our accounting colleagues have long since seen to that. Put quite bluntly, the process of marketing planning is concerned with identifying what and to whom sales are going to be made in the longer term to give revenue budgets and sales forecasts any chance of achievement. Furthermore, chances of achievement are a function of how good our intelligence services are; and how well suited are our strategies; and how well we are led.

The simpler environment of the 1960s and early 1970s, characterized by growth and the easy marketability of products and services, has now been replaced by an increasingly complex and abrasive environment, coupled with static or declining markets.

The difficulty faced by many companies stems from the realization that the old methods no longer work. Even worse, it is beginning to dawn on many that in those halcyon years, they were hardly manag-

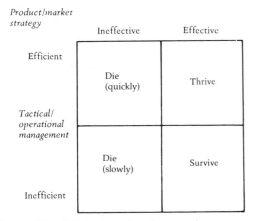

Product/market strategy

	Ineffective	Effective
Efficient	Die (quickly)	Thrive
Inefficient	Die (slowly)	Survive

Tactical/ operational management

Figure 5.1   *Marketing planning matrix*

ing at all – rather they were being dragged along by the momentum of growth, and all they were doing was riding the wave.

Of course it was always necessary, even in those days, to understand the day-to-day operational basics and manage them well, but there was not the same need for a disciplined, systematic approach to the market.

This brings us to the starting point in marketing planning – an understanding of the difference between strategy and tactics and the association with the relevant adjectives, 'effective' and 'efficient'.

Figure 5.1 shows a matrix in which the horizontal axis represents strategy as a continuum from ineffective to effective. The vertical axis represents tactics on a continuum from inefficient to efficient. Those firms with an effective strategy and efficient tactics continue to thrive, while those with an effective strategy but inefficient tactics have merely survived. Many such firms have devoted much of their time and energy to shedding unnecessary and inefficient peripheral activities and are once more moving towards the top right hand box. Many, of course, have gone bankrupt.

Those firms to the left of the matrix are destined to die. It is in circumstances like this where the old style management fails.

By failing to grasp the nettle of strategic orientation, many companies have become, and many more will become, casualties and their place will be taken by companies that are comfortable driving with the new orientation. Already, companies led by chief executives with a proactive orientation that stretches

beyond the end of the current fiscal year have begun to show results visibly better than the old reactive companies with only a short-term vision.

Appreciation is growing among directors and managers of the necessity of having a vision of where their companies should be going, with this direction properly articulated in business plans that identify and develop their distinctive competence. Where this is not happening, plans are developed from a purely financial basis, are mainly extrapolative, and can be likened to a sailor steering by the wake in busy and choppy waters. Not only that, but since most operational managers prefer selling the products they find easiest to sell to the customers that offer the least line of resistance, this approach is tantamount to an extrapolation of the firm's own inefficiencies. Certainly, however, this approach has very little to do with the business of properly understood market-centred opportunities. On the other hand, it is easy to understand why so many companies prefer this mode of management.

Many strategic planning departments of the past, bulging with highly paid management scientists, wafted out the results of their models and brainstorming in a platonic haze that was inevitably distanced from the 'coal face' and the real world of operational managers. The gap between long-term strategic and short-term operational plans grew wider, until finally the bubble burst with the onset of the recession and much of this kind of planning was exposed as the farce that it has always been. Alas, the recession was also accompanied by a return to old, well-tried and tested management methods. Strategic planning was out and the tactical manager returned, at least for a time.

Today, however, the new breed of top executives are taking everyone in their company through an often traumatic period of cultural change from operational to strategic modes. These people have rightly dismissed the arrant nonsenses which arose out of earlier approaches to strategic planning and which understandably got planning a bad name.

The new emerging culture places a much greater emphasis on scanning the external environment, the early identification of forces emanating from it, and developing appropriate strategic responses. The difference this time round is that all levels of management are involved, with the resulting intelligence coming from the market rather than from the heads

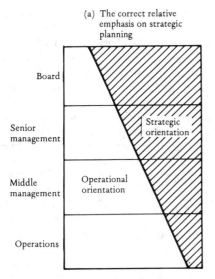

(a) The correct relative emphasis on strategic planning

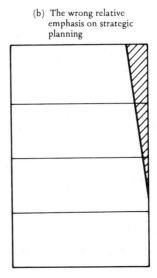

(b) The wrong relative emphasis on strategic planning

Figure 5.2 *Emphasis on strategic planning*

of a remote group of planners with little or no operational involvement.

Figure 5.2(b) shows the old style of company in which very little attention is paid by any level of management to strategy. It will be seen that lower levels of management do not get involved at all, while the directors spend most of their time on operational issues. Figure 5.2(a) shows that all levels of management are involved to some extent in strategy formulation.

There are three distinct yet interdependent stages involved in developing a strategic marketing capability in an organization. These are:

1 Establish a disciplined framework (or logic) for undertaking the marketing planning process.
2 Underpin this framework with a meaningful marketing intelligence function.
3 Undertake the necessary steps inside the organization to convert the words on paper (plans) into actionable propositions on the ground. When this behaviour is being achieved on a consistent basis, then a new culture has been established.

These three stages are not achieved without considerable pain to participating executives because they are being called on to think and act in ways which are radically different from the experiential norms of earlier years.

If they make the transition successfully, they will feel ownership over their strategic and operational plans and will thus ensure that they are implemented with enthusiasm and dedication.

To summarize, two main themes are emerging among the better companies. These are:

1 Acceptance of the need for a strategic orientation among key executives, and this tends to be exhibited in their day-to-day behaviour.
2 A growing understanding of the nuances involved in successfully embedding the desired new orientation into the corporate culture of the organization.

What is strategic marketing planning?

Let us begin by reminding ourselves what is it. It is a logical sequence and a series of activities leading to the setting of marketing objectives and the formulation of plans for achieving them. It is a management process.

Conceptually, the process is very simple. Strategic marketing planning by means of a planning system is, *per se*, little more than a structured way of identifying a range of options for the company, of making them explicit in writing, of formulating marketing objectives which are consistent with the company's overall objectives and of scheduling and costing out the specific activities most likely to bring about the achievement of the objectives. *It is the systemization of this process which is distinctive and which lies at the heart of the theory of strategic marketing planning.*

The precise steps in this process and how they work are the subject of the second section in this chapter.

Naivety about strategic marketing planning

We have just rehearsed with you the notions that virtually any textbook would offer should you care to re-read it. We have long been bemused, however, by the fact that many meticulous strategic planning companies fare badly while the sloppy or inarticulate in marketing terms do well. Is there any real relationship between strategic marketing planning and commercial success? And, if so, how does that relationship work its way through?

There are, of course, many studies which identify a number of benefits to be obtained from marketing planning. But there is little explanation for the commercial success of those companies that do not engage in formalized planning. Nor is there much exploration of the circumstances of those commercially unsuccessful companies that also have formalized marketing planning systems, and where the dysfunctional consequences are recognized, there is a failure to link this back to any kind of theory or rational explanation.

It is very clear that the simplistic theories do not adequately address the many contextual issues in relation to marketing planning, which may well account for the fact that so few companies actually do it.

In fact 90 per cent of companies in a recent study did not, by their own admission, produce anything approximating to an integrated, coordinated and internally consistent plan for their marketing activities. This included a substantial number of companies that had highly formalized procedures for strategic marketing planning.

So what are the benefits? The main ones are:

- Coordination of the activities of many individuals whose actions are interrelated over time.
- Identification of expected developments.
- Preparedness to meet changes when they occur.

- Minimization of non-rational responses to the unexpected.
- Better communication among executives.
- Minimization of conflicts among individuals which would result in a subordination of the goals of the company to those of the individual.

Indeed, many companies have a lot of the trappings of sophisticated strategic marketing planning systems but suffer as many dysfunctional consequences as those companies that have only forecasting and budgeting systems.

It is crystal clear that for any marketing planning system to be effective, certain conditions have to be satisfied, which we shall deal with in detail in the third section of this chapter.

Operational problems resulting from the forecasting and budgeting approach

The following are the most frequently mentioned operating problems resulting from a reliance on traditional sales forecasting and budgeting procedures in the absence of a marketing planning system:

Most frequently mentioned problems

1 Lost opportunities for profit.
2 Meaningless numbers in long-range plans.
3 Unrealistic objectives.
4 Lack of actionable market information.
5 Interfunctional strife.
6 Management frustration.
7 Proliferation of products and markets.
8 Wasted promotional expenditure.
9 Pricing confusion.
10 Growing vulnerability to environmental change.
11 Loss of control over the business.

It is not difficult to see the connection between all of these problems. However, what is perhaps not apparent from the list is that each of these operational problems is in fact a symptom of a much larger problem which emanates from the way in which the objectives of a firm are set.

The meaningfulness, hence the eventual effectiveness, of any objective, is heavily dependent on the quality of the informational inputs about the business environment. However, objectives also need to be closely related to the firm's particular capabilities in the form of its assets, competences and reputation that have evolved over a number of years.

The objective-setting process of a business is central to marketing effectiveness. What the research has demonstrated conclusively is that it is inadequacies in the objective-setting process which lie at the heart of many of the problems of companies.

Some kind of appropriate system has to be used to enable meaningful and realistic marketing objectives to be set. A frequent complaint is the preoccupation with short-term thinking and an almost total lack of what has been referred to as 'strategic thinking'. Also, that plans consist largely of numbers, which are difficult to evaluate in any meaningful way, since they do not highlight and quantify opportunities, emphasize key issues, show the company's position clearly in its markets, nor delineate the means of achieving the sales forecasts. Indeed, very often the actual numbers that are written down bear little relationship to any of these things. Sales targets for the sales force are often inflated in order to motivate them to higher achievement, while the actual budgets themselves are deflated in order to provide a safety net against shortfall.

Both act as demotivators and both lead to the frequent use of expressions such as 'ritual', 'the numbers game', 'meaningless horsetrading', and so on. It is easy to see how the problems listed in the table begin to manifest themselves in this sort of environment.

Closely allied to this is the frequent reference to profit as being the only objective necessary to successful business performance.

This theme is frequently encountered. There is in the minds of many business people the assumption that in order to be commercially successful all that is necessary is for the 'boss' to set profit targets, to decentralize the firm into groups of similar activities, and then to make managers accountable for achieving those profits.

However, even though most British companies have made the making of 'profit' almost the sole objective, many of our industries have gone into decline, and ironically, there has also been a decline in real profitability. There are countless examples of companies pursuing decentralized profit goals that have failed miserably.

Here it is necessary to focus attention on what so many companies appear to be bad at, i.e. determining strategies for matching what the firm is good at with properly researched market-centred opportunities, and then scheduling and costing out what has to be done to achieve these objectives. There is little evidence of a deep understanding of what it is that companies can do better than their competitors or of how their distinctive competence can be matched with the needs of certain customer groups. Instead, overall volume increases and minimum rates of return on investment are frequently applied to all products and markets, irrespective of market share, market growth rate, or the longevity of the product life cycle. Indeed there is a lot of evidence to show that many companies are in trouble today precisely because their decentralized units manage their business only for the current profit and loss account, often at the expense of giving up valuable and hard-earned market share, failing to invest in R & D and running down the current business.

Thus, financial objectives, while being essential measures of the desired performance of a company, are of little practical help, since they say nothing about *how* the results are to be achieved. The same applies to sales forecasts and budgets, which are *not* marketing objectives and strategies. Understanding the real meaning and significance of marketing objectives helps managers to know what information they need to enable them to think through the implications of choosing one or more positions in the market. Finding the right words to describe the logic of marketing objectives and strategies is infinitely more difficult than writing down numbers on a piece of paper and leaving the strategies implicit. This lies at the heart of the problem. For clearly, a numbers-orientated system will not encourage managers to think in a structured way about strategically relevant market segments, nor will it encourage the collection, analysis and synthesis of actionable market data. And in the absence of such activities within operating units, it is unlikely that headquarters will have much other than intuition and 'feel' to use as a basis for decisions about the management of scarce resources.

How can these problems be overcome?

This raises the difficult question of how these very complex problems can be overcome, for this is what baffles those who have been forced by market pressures to consider different ways of coping with their environment.

The difficulty remains of how to get managers throughout an organization to think beyond the horizon of the current year's operations. This applies universally to all types and sizes of company. Even chief executives of small companies find difficulty in breaking out of the fetters of the current profit and loss account.

The problem, particularly in large companies, is that managers who are evaluated and rewarded on the basis of current operations find difficulty in concerning themselves about the corporate future. This is exacerbated by behavioural issues, in the sense that it is safer, and more rewarding personally, for managers to do what they know best, which in most cases is to manage their *current* range of products and customers in order to make the *current* year's budget.

Unfortunately, long-range sales forecasting systems do not provide the answer. This kind of extrapolative approach fails to solve the problems of identifying precisely what has to be done today to ensure success in the future. Exactly the same problem exists in both large diversified companies and in small undiversified companies, except that in the former the problem is magnified and multiplied by the complexities of distance, hierarchical levels of management, and diversity of operations. Nevertheless, the problem is fundamentally the same.

Events that affect economic performance in a business come from so many directions, and in so many forms, that it is impossible for any manager to be precise about how they interact in the form of problems to be overcome, and opportunities to be exploited. The best managers can do is to form a reasoned view about how they have affected the past, and how they will develop in the future, and what action needs to be taken over a period of time to enable the company to prepare itself for the expected changes. The problem is *how* to get managers to formulate their thoughts about these things, for until they have, it is unlikely that any objectives that are set will have much relevance or meaning.

Accordingly, they need some system which will help them to think in a structured way about problem formulation. It is the provision of such a rational framework to help them to make explicit their intui-

tive economic models of the business that is almost totally lacking from the forecasting and budgeting systems of most companies. It is apparent that in the absence of any such synthesized and simplified views of the business, setting meaningful objectives for the future seems like an insurmountable problem, and this in turn encourages the perpetuation of systems involving merely the extrapolation of numbers. There is also substantial evidence that those companies that provide procedures for this process, however informal, have gone some considerable way to overcoming this problem. Although the possible number of analyses of business situations is infinite, procedural approaches help managers throughout an organization at least to consider the essential elements of problem definition in a structured way. This applies even to difficult foreign markets, where data and information is hard to come by, and even to markets which are being managed by agents, who find that these structured approaches, properly managed, help *their* businesses as well as those of their principals.

However, there are two further major advantages enjoyed by these companies. First, the level of management frustration is lower and motivation is higher because the system provides a method of reaching agreement on such difficult matters as an assessment of the company's distinctive competence and the nature of the competitive environment. The internecine disputes and frustration which we all experience so often in our business lives is largely the result of an almost total absence of the means of discussing these issues and of reaching agreement on them. If a manager's boss does not understand what his/her environmental problems are, what his/her strengths and weaknesses are, nor what he/she is trying to achieve, and in the absence of any structured procedures and common terminology that can be used and understood by everybody, communications will be poor and the incidence of frustration will be higher.

Second, some form of standardized approach which is understood by all considerably improves the ability of headquarters management not only to understand the problems of individual operating units, but also to react to them in a constructive and helpful way. This is because they receive information in a way which enables them to form a meaningful overview of total company activities and this provides a rational basis for resource allocation.

To summarize, a structured approach to situation analysis is necessary, irrespective of the size or complexity of the organization. Such a system should:

- Ensure that comprehensive consideration is given to the definition of strengths and weaknesses and to problems and opportunities.
- Ensure that a logical framework is used for the presentation of the key issues arising from this analysis.

Very few companies have planning systems which possess these characteristics. Those that do, manage to cope with their environment more effectively than those that do not. They find it easier to set meaningful objectives, are more confident about the future, enjoy greater control over the business, and react less on a piecemeal basis to ongoing events.

In short, they suffer fewer operational problems and are as a result more effective organizations.

The marketing planning process

In the first section of this chapter, we made it clear that marketing planning is essential when we consider the increasingly hostile and complex environment in which companies operate. Hundreds of external and internal factors interact in a bafflingly complex way to affect our ability to achieve profitable sales. Managers of a company have to have some understanding or view about how all these variables interact, and managers try to be rational about their business decisions, no matter how important intuition, feel and experience are as contributory factors in this process of rationality.

Most managers accept that some kind of formalized procedure for marketing planning helps sharpen this rationality so as to reduce the complexity of business operations and add a dimension of realism to the company's hopes for the future. Because it is so difficult, however, most companies rely only on sales forecasting and budgeting systems. All too frequently, however, the figures bear little relationship to the real opportunities and problems facing a company. It is far more difficult to write down marketing objectives and strategies.

Marketing objectives and their relationship with corporate objectives

It would be useful to begin by discussing the relationship between strategic marketing planning and corporate planning.

There are five steps in the corporate planning process. As can be seen from Table 5.1 the starting point is usually a statement of corporate financial objectives for the long range planning period of the company, which are often expressed in terms of turnover, profit before tax, and return on investment.

More often than not, this long range planning horizon is five years, but the precise period should be determined by the nature of the markets in which the company operates. For example, five years would not be a long enough period for a glass manufacturer, since it takes that period of time to commission a new furnace, whereas in some fashion industries, five years would be too long. A useful guideline in determining the planning horizon is that there should be a market for the company products for long enough at least to amortise any capital investment associated with those products.

The next step is the *management audit*. This is an obvious activity to follow on with, since a thorough situation review, particularly in the area of marketing, should enable the company to determine whether it will be able to meet the long range financial targets with its current range of products in its current markets. Any projected gap can be filled by various methods of product development or market extension (to be discussed later).

Undoubtedly the most important and difficult of all stages in the corporate planning process is the third step, *objective and strategy setting*, since if this is not done properly, everything that follows is of little value.

The important point to make is that this is the time in the planning cycle when a compromise has to be reached between what is wanted by the several functional departments and what is practicable, given all the constraints that any company has. For example, it is no good setting a marketing objective of penetrating a new market, if the company does not have the production capacity to cope with the new business, and if capital is not available for whatever investment is necessary in additional

Table 5.1 *Strategic marketing planning and its place in the corporate planning cycle*

Step 1	*2 Management audit*	*3 Objective and strategy setting*	*4 Plans*	*5 Corporate plans*
	Marketing audit Marketing	Marketing objectives, strategies	Marketing plan	
	Distribution audit Stocks and control; transportation; warehousing	Distribution objectives, strategies	Distribution plan	Issue of corporate plan, to include corporate objectives and strategies; production objectives and strategies, etc., long-range profit and loss accounts; balance sheets
Corporate financial objectives	*Production audit* Value analysis; engineering development; work study; quality control; labour; materials, plant and space utilization; production planning; factories	Production objectives, strategies	Production plan	
	Financial audit Credit; debt, cash flow and budgetary control; resource allocation; capital expenditure; long-term finance	Financial objectives, strategies	Financial plan	
	Personnel audit Management, technical and administrative ability, etc.	Personnel objectives, strategies		

capacity. At this stage, objectives and strategies will be set for five years, or for whatever the planning horizon is.

Step 4 involves producing detailed *plans* for one year, containing the responsibilities, timing and costs of carrying out the first year's objectives, and broad plans for the following years.

These plans can then be incorporated into the *corporate plan*, which will continue long range corporate objectives, strategies, plans, profit and loss accounts, and balance sheets.

At this point it is worth noting that one of the main purposes of a corporate plan is to provide a long-term vision of what the company is or is striving to become, taking account of shareholder expectations, environmental trends, resource market trends, consumption market trends, and the distinct-

ive competence of the company as revealed by the management audit.

Such a corporate plan, containing projected profit and loss accounts and balance sheets, being the result of the process described above, is more likely to provide long-term stability for a company than plans based on a more intuitive process and containing forecasts which tend to be little more than extrapolations of previous trends.

The headquarters of one major multinational company with a sophisticated budgeting system used to receive 'plans' from all over the world and coordinate them in quantitative and cross-functional terms such as numbers of employees, units of sale, items of plant, square feet of production area, and so on, together with the associated financial implications. The trouble was that the whole complicated edifice was built on the initial sales forecasts, which were themselves little more than a time-consuming numbers game. The really key strategic issues relating to products and markets were lost in all the financial activity, which eventually resulted in grave operational and profitability problems.

So what is a corporate objective and what is a marketing objective?

An objective is what you want to achieve. A strategy is how you plan to achieve your objectives.

An objective will ensure that a company knows what its strategies are expected to accomplish and when a particular strategy has accomplished its purpose. In other words, without objectives, strategy decisions and all that follows will take place in a vacuum.

Following the identification of opportunities and the explicit statement of assumptions about conditions affecting the business, the process of setting objectives in theory should be comparatively easy, the actual objectives themselves being a realistic statement of what the company desires to achieve as a result of a market-centred analysis, rather than generalized statements born of top management's desire to 'do better next year'. However, objective setting is more complex than at first it would appear to be.

Most experts agree that the logical approach to the difficult task of setting marketing objectives is to proceed from the broad to the specific. Thus, the starting point would be a statement of the nature of the business, from which would flow the broad company objectives. Next, the broad company objectives would be translated into key result areas, which would be those areas in which success is vital to the firm. Market penetration, and growth rate of sales, are examples of key result areas. The third step would be creation of the subobjectives necessary to accomplish the broad objectives, such as sales volume goals, geographical expansion, product line extension, and so on.

The end result of this process should be objectives which are consistent with the strategic plan, attainable within budget limitations, and compatible with the strengths, limitations, and economies of other functions within the organisation.

At the top level, management is concerned with long-run profitability; at the next level in the management hierarchy, the concern is for objectives which are defined more specifically and in greater detail, such as increasing sales and market share, obtaining new markets, and so on. These objectives are merely a part of the hierarchy of objectives, in that corporate objectives will only be accomplished if these and other objectives are achieved. At the next level, management is concerned with objectives which are defined even more tightly, such as: to create awareness among a specific target market about a new product; to change a particular customer attitude; and so on. Again, the general marketing objectives will only be accomplished if these and other subobjectives are achieved. It is clear that subobjectives *per se*, unless they are an integral part of a broader framework of objectives, are likely to lead to a wasteful misdirection of resources.

For example, a sales increase in itself may be possible, but only at an undue cost, so that such a marketing objective is only appropriate within the framework of corporate objectives. In such a case, it may well be that an increase in sales in a particular market sector will entail additional capital expenditure ahead of the time for which it is planned. If this were the case, it may make more sense to allocate available production capacity to more profitable market sectors in the short term, allowing sales to decline in another sector. Decisions such as this are likely to be more easily made against a backcloth of explicitly stated broad company objectives relating to all the major disciplines.

Likewise, objectives should be set for advertising, for example, which are wholly consistent with wider objectives. Objectives set in this way integrate the advertising effort with the other elements in the marketing mix and this leads to a consistent, logical marketing plan.

A business starts at some time with resources and wants to use those resources to achieve something. What the business wants to achieve is a corporate objective, which describes a desired destination, or result. How it is to be achieved is a strategy. In a sense, this means that the only true objective of a company is, by definition, what is stated in the corporate plan as being the principal purpose of its existence. Most often this is expressed in terms of profit, since profit is the means of satisfying shareholders or owners, and because it is the one universally accepted criterion by which efficiency can be evaluated, which will in turn lead to efficient resource allocation, economic and technological progressiveness and stability.

This means that stated desires, such as to expand market share, to create a new image, to achieve an x per cent increase in sales, and so on, are in fact strategies at the corporate level, since they are the means by which a company will achieve its profit objectives. In practice, however, companies tend to operate by means of functional divisions, each with a separate identity, so that what is a strategy in the corporate plan becomes an objective within each department. For example, marketing strategies within the corporate plan become operating objectives within the marketing department and strategies at the general level within the marketing department themselves become operating objectives at the next level down, so that an intricate web of interrelated objectives and strategies is built up at all levels within the framework of the overall company plan.

The really important point, however, apart from clarifying the differences between objectives and strategies, is that the further down the hierarchical chain one goes, the less likely it is that a stated objective will make a cost-effective contribution to company profits, unless it derives logically and directly from an objective at a higher level.

Corporate objectives and strategies can be simplified in the following way:

Corporate objectives
- Desired level of profitability.

Corporate strategies
- Which products and which markets (marketing).
- What kind of facilities (production and distribution).
- Size and character of the staff/labour force (personnel).
- Funding (finance).
- Other corporate strategies such as social responsibility, corporate image, stock market image, employee image, etc.

It is now clear that at the next level down in the organization, i.e. functional level, what products are to be sold into what markets, become *marketing objectives*, while the means of achieving these objectives using the marketing mix, are *marketing*

strategies. At the next level down there would be, say, *advertising objectives* and *advertising strategies*, with the subsequent *programmes* and *budgets* for achieving the objectives. In this way, a hierarchy of objectives and strategies can be traced back to the initial corporate objective. Figure 5.3 illustrates this point.

How to set marketing objectives

The Ansoff matrix (the brainchild of Igor Ansoff), can now be introduced as a useful tool for thinking about marketing objectives.

A firm's competitive situation can be simplified to two dimensions only – products and markets. To put it even more simply, Ansoff's framework is about what is sold (the 'product'), and who it is sold to (the 'market'). The matrix in Figure 5.4 depicts these concepts.

It is clear that the range of possible marketing objectives is very wide, since there will be degrees of technological newness and degrees of market newness. Nevertheless, Ansoff's matrix provides a logical framework in which marketing objectives can be developed under each of the four main headings. Common sense will confirm that it is only by selling something to someone that the company's financial goals can be achieved, and that advertising, pricing, service levels, and so on, are the means (or strategies) by which it might succeed in doing this. Thus, pricing objectives, sales promotion objectives, advertising objectives, and the like should not be confused with marketing objectives.

Marketing objectives are generally accepted as being selected qualitative and quantitative commitments, usually stated either in standards of performance for a given operating period, or conditions to be achieved by given dates. Performance standards are usually stated in terms of sales volume and various measures of profitability. The conditions to be attained are usually a percentage of market share and various other commitments, such as a percentage of the total number of a given type of retail outlet.

There is also broad agreement that objectives must be specific enough to enable subordinates to derive from them the general character of action required and the yardstick by which performance is to be judged. Objectives are the core of managerial action, providing direction to the plans. By asking

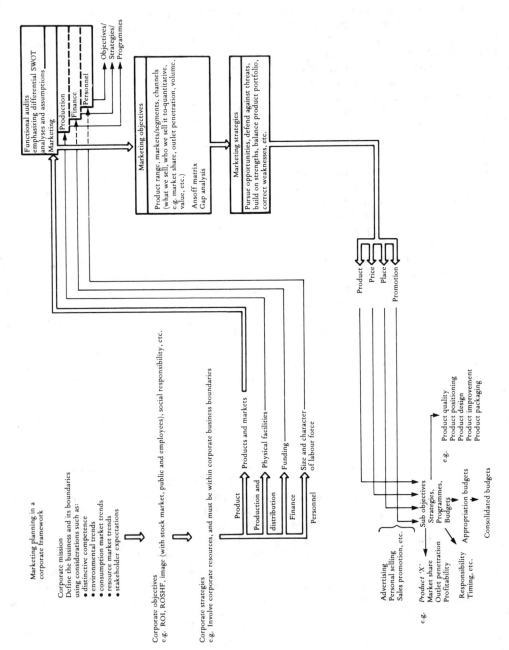

Figure 5.3   *A hierarchy of objectives and strategies*

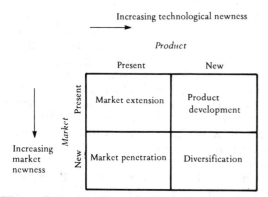

Figure 5.4 *Ansoff matrix (a)*

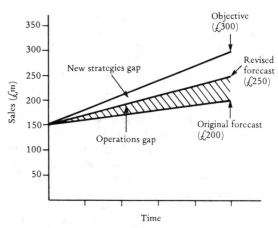

Figure 5.5 *Gap analyses*

where the operation should be at some future date, objectives are determined. Vague objectives, however emotionally appealing, are counter-productive to sensible planning, and are usually the result of the human propensity for wishful thinking which often smacks more of cheerleading than serious marketing leadership. What this really means is that while it is arguable whether directional terms such as 'decrease', 'optimize', 'minimize' should be used as objectives, it seems logical that unless there is some measure, or yardstick, against which to measure a sense of locomotion towards achieving them, then they do not serve any useful purpose.

Ansoff defines an objective as 'a measure of the efficiency of the resource-conversion process. An objective contains three elements: the particular attribute that is chosen as a measure of efficiency; the yardstick or scale by which the attribute is measured; and the particular value on the scale which the firm seeks to attain.'

Marketing objectives then are about each of the four main categories of the Ansoff matrix:

1 *Existing products in existing markets*. These may be many and varied and will certainly need to be set for all existing major products and customer groups (segments).
2 *New products in existing markets*.
3 *Existing products in new markets*.
4 *New products in new markets*.

Simply defined, product/market strategy means the route chosen to achieve company goals through the range of products it offers to its chosen market segments. Thus the product/market strategy represents a commitment to a future direction for the firm. Marketing objectives, then, are concerned solely with products and markets.

Figure 5.5 illustrates what is commonly referred to as 'gap analysis'. Essentially what it says is that if the corporate sales and financial objectives are greater than the current long-range forecasts, there is a gap which has to be filled.

The 'operations gap' can be filled in two ways:

1 Improved productivity, e.g. reduce costs, improve the sales mix, increase prices.
2 Market penetration, e.g. increase usage, increase market share.

The 'new strategies gap' can be filled in four ways:

1 Reduce objectives.
2 Market extension, e.g. find new user groups, enter new segments, geographical expansion.
3 Product development.
4 Diversification, e.g. selling new products to new markets.

If improved productivity is one method by which the expansion gap is to be filled, care must be taken not to take measures such as to reduce marketing costs by 20 per cent overall. Portfolio analysis, which will be discussed later in the book, will indicate that this would be totally inappropriate to some product/market areas, for which increased marketing expenditure may be needed, while for others 20 per cent reduction in marketing costs may not be sufficient.

As for the other options, it is clear that market penetration should always be a company's first option, since it makes far more sense to attempt to increase profits and cash flow from *existing* products and markets initially, because this is usually the least costly and the least risky. This is so because for its present products and markets a company has developed knowledge and skills which it can use competitively (asset-based marketing).

For the same reason, it makes more sense in many cases to move along the horizontal axis for further growth before attempting to find new markets. The reason for this is that it normally takes many years for a company to get to know its customers and markets and to build up a reputation. That reputation and trust embodied in either the company's name or in its brands, is rarely transferable to new markets, where other companies are already entrenched.

The marketing audit should ensure that the method chosen to fill the gap is consistent with the company's capabilities and builds on its strengths. For example, it would normally prove far less profitable for a dry goods grocery manufacturer to introduce frozen foods than to add another dry foods product. Likewise, if a product could be sold to existing channels using the existing sales force, this is far less risky than introducing a new product that requires new channels and new selling skills.

Exactly the same applies to the company's production, distribution, and people. Whatever new products are developed should be as consistent as possible with the company's known strengths and capabilities. Clearly, the use of existing plant capacity is generally preferable to new processes. Also, the amount of additional investment is important. Technical personnel are highly trained and specialist, and whether this competence can be transferred to a new field must be considered. A product requiring new raw materials may also require new handling and storage techniques which may prove expensive.

It can now be appreciated why going into new markets with new products (diversification) is the riskiest strategy of all, because *new* resources and *new* management skills have to be developed. This is why the history of commerce is replete with examples of companies which went bankrupt through moving into areas where they had little or no distinctive competence. This is also why many companies that diversified through acquisition during periods of high economic growth have since divested themselves of businesses that were not basically compatible with their own distinctive competence.

The Ansoff matrix, of course, is not a simple four-box matrix for it will be obvious that there are degrees of technological newness as well as degrees of market newness. Figure 5.6 illustrates the point. It also demonstrates more easily why any movement should generally aim to keep a company as close as

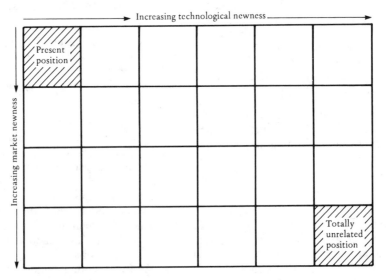

Figure 5.6 *Ansoff matrix (b)*

possible to its present position rather than moving it to a totally unrelated position, except in the most unusual circumstances.

Nevertheless, there are certain phenomena which will inevitably force companies to move along one or more of the Ansoff matrix axes if they are to continue to increase their sales and profits.

The strategic marketing planning process – the steps

Figure 5.7 illustrates the several stages that have to be gone through in order to arrive at a marketing plan. This illustrates the difference between the *process* of marketing planning and the actual plan itself, which is the output of the process.

Experience has shown that a marketing plan should contain:

- A brief market overview.
- A summary of all the principal external factors which affected the company's marketing performance during the previous year, together with a statement of the company's strengths and weaknesses *vis-a-vis* the competition. This is what we call a SWOT (i.e. strengths, weaknesses, opportunities, threats) analysis.
- Some assumptions about the key determinants of marketing success and failure.
- Overall marketing objectives and strategies.

- Programmes containing details of timing, responsibilities and costs, with sales forecasts and budgets.

Each of the stages illustrated in Figure 5.7 will be discussed in more detail later in this chapter.

The dotted lines joining up steps 5, 6 and 7 are meant to indicate the reality of the planning process, in that it is likely that each of these steps will have to be gone through more than once before final programmes can be written.

Although research has shown these marketing planning steps to be universally applicable, the degree to which each of the separate steps in the diagram needs to be formalized depends to a large extent on the size and nature of the company. For example, an *undiversified* company generally uses less formalized procedures, since top management tends to have greater functional knowledge and expertise than subordinates, and because the lack of diversity of operations enables direct control to be exercised over most of the key determinants of success. Thus, situation reviews, the setting of marketing objectives, and so on, are not always made explicit in writing, although these steps have to be gone through.

In contrast, in a *diversified* company, it is usually not possible for top management to have greater functional knowledge and expertise than subordinate

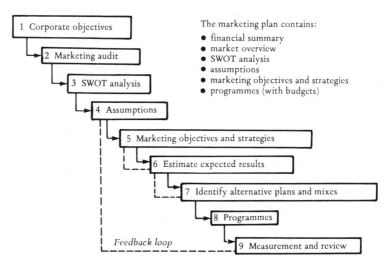

Figure 5.7   *The strategic marketing planning process*

management, hence the whole planning process tends to be more formalized in order to provide a consistent discipline for those who have to make the decisions throughout the organization.

Either way, however, there is now a substantial body of evidence to show that formalized planning procedures generally result in greater profitability and stability in the long term and also help to reduce friction and operational difficulties within organizations.

Where marketing planning has failed, it has generally been because companies have placed too much emphasis on the procedures themselves and the resulting paperwork, rather than on generating information useful to and consumable by management. Also, where companies relegate marketing planning to someone called a 'planner', it invariably fails, for the single reason that planning for line management cannot be delegated to a third party. The real role of the 'planner' should be to help those responsible for implementation to plan. Failure to recognize this simple fact can be disastrous. Finally, planning failures often result from companies trying too much, too quickly, and without training staff in the use of prodedures.

We can now look at the marketing planning process in more detail, starting with a look at the marketing audit.

It is important to remember that at this stage we are describing the *process* only, rather than what should actually appear in a marketing plan. So far we have looked at the need for marketing planning and outlined a series of steps that have to be gone through in order to arrive at a marketing plan. However, any plan will only be as good as the information on which it is based, and the marketing audit is the means by which information for planning is organized.

What is a marketing audit?

There is no reason why marketing cannot be audited in the same way as accounts, in spite of its more innovative, subjective nature. A marketing audit is a systematic appraisal of all the external and internal factors that have affected a company's commercial performance over a defined period.

Given the growing turbulence of the business environment and the shorter product life cycles that

Table 5.2 *Conducting an audit*

External audit	Internal audit
Business and economic environment	*Own company*
Economic	Sales (total, by
Political, fiscal, legal	geographical
Social, cultural	location, by
Technological	industrial type,
Intra-company	by customer, by
The market	product)
Total market, size,	Market shares
growth and	Profit margins,
trends (value/	costs
volume)	Marketing
Market	information
characteristics,	research
developments	Marketing mix
and trends;	variables: product
products, prices,	management,
physical	price,
distribution,	distribution,
channels,	promotion,
customers/	operations and
consumers,	resources
communication,	
industry practices	
Competition	
Major competitors	
Size	
Market shares	
coverage	
Market standing	
and reputation	
Production	
capabilities	
Distribution policies	
Marketing methods	
Extent of	
diversification	
Personnel issues	
International links	
Profitability	
Key strengths and	
weaknesses	

have resulted, no one would deny the need to stop at least once a year at a particular point in the planning cycle to try to form a reasoned view on how all the many external and internal factors have influenced performance.

Sometimes, of course, a company will conduct a marketing audit because it is in financial trouble. At times like these, management often attempts to treat the wrong symptoms, most frequently by reorganizing the company. But such measures are unlikely to be effective if there are more fundamental problems which have not been identified. Of course, if the company survived for long enough, it might eventually solve its problems thorough a process of elimination. Essentially, though, the argument is that problems have first to be properly defined. The audit is a means of helping to define them.

Two kinds of variable

Any company carrying out an audit will be faced with two kinds of variable. There is the kind over which the company has no direct control, for example economic and market factors. Second, there are those over which the company has complete control, the operational variables, which are usually the firm's internal resources. This division suggests that the best way to structure an audit is in two parts, internal and external. Table 5.2 shows areas which should be investigated under both heads. Each should be examined with a view to building up an information base relevant to the company's performance.

Many people mistakenly believe that the marketing audit should be some kind of final attempt to define a company's marketing problem, or, at best, something done by an independent body from time to time to ensure that a company is on the right track. However, many highly successful companies, as well as using normal information and control procedures and marketing research throughout the year, start their planning cycle each year with a formal, audit-type process, of everything that has had an important influence on marketing activities. Certainly, in many leading consumer goods companies, the annual self-audit approach is a tried and tested discipline.

Occasionally, it may be justified for outside consultants to carry out the audit in order to check that the company is getting the most out of its resources. However, it seems an unnecessary expense to have this done every year.

Objections to line managers doing their own audits usually centre around the problem of time and objectivity. In practice, a disciplined approach and thorough training will help. But the discipline must be applied from the highest to the lowest levels of management if the tunnel vision that often results from a lack of critical appraisal is to be avoided.

The next question is: what happens to the results of the audit? Some companies consume valuable resources carrying out audits that produce very little in the way of results. The audit is simply a data base, and the task remains of turning it into intelligence, that is, information essential to decision making.

It is often helpful to adopt a regular format for the major findings. One way of doing this is in the form of a SWOT analysis. This is a summary of the audit under the headings of internal strengths and weaknesses as they relate to external opportunities and threats, as illustrated in Table 5.2.

The SWOT analysis should, if possible, contain no more than four or five pages of commentary, focusing only on key factors. It should highlight internal strengths and weaknesses measured against the competition's, and key external opportunities and threats. A summary of reasons for good or bad performance should be included. It should be interesting to read, contain concise statements, include only relevant and important data and give greater emphasis to creative analysis.

Where relevant, the SWOT analysis should contain life cycles for major products and for market segments, for which the future shape will be predicted using the audit information. Also, major products and markets should be plotted on some kind of matrix to show their desired position over the full-planning method.

Having completed the marketing audit and SWOT analysis, fundamental assumptions on future conditions have to be made. It would be no good receiving plans from two product managers, one of whom believed the market was going to increase by 10 per cent and the other who believed it was going to decline by 10 per cent.

An example of a written assumption might be: 'With respect to the company's industrial climate, it is assumed that industrial overcapacity will increase from 105 per cent to 115 per cent as new industrial plants come into operation, price competition will force price levels down by 10 per cent across the board; a new product will be introduced by our major competitor before the end of the second quarter.' Assumptions should be few in number. If a plan is possible irrespective of the assumptions made, then the assumptions are unnecessary.

The next step is the writing of marketing objectives and strategies. This is the key to the whole process and undoubtedly the most important and difficult of all stages. If this is not done properly, everything that follows is of little value.

It is an obvious activity to follow on with, since a thorough review, particularly of its markets, should enable the company to determine whether it will be able to meet the long range financial targets with its current range of products. Any projected gap has to be filled by new product development or market extension.

The important point to make is that this is the stage in the planning cycle at which a compromise has to be reached between what is wanted by various departments and what is practicable, given all the constraints upon the company. At this stage, objectives and strategies should be set for five years ahead, or for whatever the planning horizon is.

An objective is what you want to achieve, a strategy is how you plan to achieve it. Thus, there can be objectives and strategies at all levels in marketing, or advertising, for pricing, and so on.

Point to remember

The important point to remember about marketing objectives is that they are concerned solely with products and markets. Common sense will confirm that it is only by selling something to someone that the company's financial goals can be achieved; pricing and service levels are the means by which the goals are achieved. Thus, pricing, sales promotion and advertising objectives should not be confused with marketing objectives.

As already stated, the latter are concerned with one or more of the following:

● Existing products in existing markets.
● New products for existing markets.
● Existing products for new markets.
● New products for new markets.

They should be capable of measurement, otherwise, they are not worthwhile. Directional terms, such as 'maximize', 'minimize', 'penetrate' and 'in-crease', are only acceptable if quantitative measurement can be attached to them. Measurement should be in terms of sales volume, value, market share, percentage penetration of outlets and so on.

Marketing strategies, the means by which the objectives will be achieved, are generally concerned with the 'four Ps':

1 *Product*: deletions, modifications, additions, designs, packaging, etc.
2 *Price*: policies to be followed for product groups in market segments.
3 *Place*: distribution channels and customer service levels.
4 *Promotion*: communicating with customers under the relevant headings, i.e. advertising, sales force, sales promotion, public relations, exhibitions, direct mail, etc.

Having completed this major planning task, it is normal at this stage to employ judgement, experience, field tests and so on to test out the feasibility of the objectives and strategies in terms of market share, sales, costs and profits. It is also at this stage that alternative plans and mixes are normally considered.

General marketing strategies should now be reduced to specific objectives, each supported by more detailed strategy and action statements. A company organized according to functions might have an advertising plan, a sales promotion plan and a pricing plan. A product based company might have a product plan, with objectives, strategies and tactics for price, place and promotion, as required. A market or geographically based company might have a market plan, with objectives, strategies and tactics for the four Ps, as required. Likewise, a company with a few major customers might have a customer plan. Any combination of the above might be suitable, depending on circumstances.

There is a clear distinction between strategy, and detailed implementation or tactics. Marketing strategy reflects the company's best opinion as to how it can most profitably apply its skills and resources to the marketplace. It is inevitably broad in scope. The plan which stems from it will spell out action and timings and will contain the detailed contribution expected from each department.

There is a similarity between strategy in business and the development of military strategy. One looks at the enemy, the terrain, the resources under command, and then decides whether to attack the whole front, an area of enemy weakness, to feint in one direction while attacking in another, or to attempt an encirclement of the enemy's position. The policy and mix, the type of tactics to be used, and the criteria for judging success, all come under the heading of strategy. The action steps are tactics.

Similarly, in marketing, the same commitment, mix and type of resources as well as tactical guidelines and criteria that must be met, all come under the heading of strategy.

For example, the decision to use distributors in all but the three largest market areas, in which company sales people will be used, is a strategic decision. The selection of particular distributors is a tactical decision.

The following list of marketing strategies (in summary form), cover the majority of options open under the headings of the four Ps:

1 *Product*:
   ● Expand the line.
   ● Change performance, quality or features.
   ● Consolidate the line.
   ● Standardize design.
   ● Positioning.
   ● Change the mix.
   ● Branding.
2 *Price*:
   ● Change price, terms or conditions.
   ● Skimming policies.
   ● Penetration policies.
3 *Promotion*:
   ● Change advertising or promotion.
   ● Change selling.
4 *Place*:
   ● Change delivery or distribution.
   ● Change service.
   ● Change channels.
   ● Change the degree of forward integration.

Formulating marketing strategies is one of the most critical and difficult parts of the entire marketing process. It sets the limit of success. Communicated to all management levels, it indicates what strengths are to be developed, what weaknesses are to be remedied, and in what manner. Marketing strategies enable operating decisions to bring the company into the right relationship with the emerging pattern of market opportunities which previous analysis has shown to offer the highest prospect of success.

What should appear in a strategic marketing plan

A written strategic marketing plan is the backdrop against which operational decisions are taken. Consequently, too much detail should be avoided. Its major function is to determine where the company is, where it wants to go and how it can get there. It lies at the heart of a company's revenue-generating activities, such as the timing of the cash flow and the size and character of the labour force. What should actually appear in a written strategic marketing plan is shown in Table 5.3.

Table 5.3 *What should appear in a strategic marketing plan*

1 Start with a financial summary which illustrates graphically revenue and profit for the full planning period.

2 Now do a market overview:
   Has the market declined or grown?
   How does it break down into segments?
   What is your share of each?
   Keep it simple. If you do not have the facts, make estimates. Use life cycles, bar charts and pie charts to make it all crystal clear.

3 Now identify the key segments and do a SWOT for each one:
   Outline the major external influences and their impact on each segment.
   List the key factors for success. These should be less than 5.
   Give an assessment of the company's differential strengths and weaknesses compared with those of its competitors. Score yourself and your competitors out of 10 and then multiply each score by a weighing factor for each critical success factor. (eg. CSF 1 = 60, CSF 2 = 25, CSF 3 = 10, CSF 4 = 5).

4 Make a brief statement about the key issues that have to be addressed in the planning period.

5 Summarize the SWOTs using a portfolio matrix in order to illustrate the important relationships between the key points of your business.

6 List your assumptions.

7 Set objectives and strategies.

8 Summarize your resource requirements for the planning period in the form of a budget.

This strategic marketing plan should be distributed only to those who need it, but it can only be an aid to effective management. It cannot be a substitute for it.

It will be obvious from all of this that not only does budget setting become much easier and more realistic, but the resulting budgets are more likely to reflect what the whole company wants to achieve, rather than just one department.

The problem of designing a dynamic system for setting budgets is a major challenge to the marketing and financial directors of all companies. The most satisfactory approach would be for a marketing director to justify all marketing expenditure from a zero base each year against the tasks to be accomplished. If these procedures are followed, a hierarchy of objectives is built up in such a way that every item of budgeted expenditure can be related directly back to the initial financial objectives.

Specific purpose

For example, if sales promotion is a major means of achieving an objective, when a sales promotion item appears in the programme it has a specific purpose which can be related back to a major objective. Thus every item of expenditure is fully accounted for.

Marketing expense can be considered to be all costs that are incurred after the product leaves the factory, apart from those involved in physical distribution.

When it comes to pricing, any form of discounting that reduces the expected gross income – such as promotional or quantity discounts, overriders, sales commission and unpaid invoices – should be given the most careful attention as marketing expenses.

Most obvious marketing expenses will occur, however, under the heading of promotion, in the form of advertising, sales salaries and expenses, sales promotion and direct mail costs.

The important point about the measurable effects of marketing activity is that anticipated levels should result from careful analysis of what is required to take the company towards its goals, while the most careful attention should be paid to gathering all items of expenditure under appropriate headings. The healthiest way of treating these issues is through zero based budgeting.

We have just described the strategic marketing plan and what it should contain. The tactical marketing plan layout and content should be similar, but the detail is much greater, as it is for one year only.

In the last section in this chapter, the planning process is put into the context of different kinds of organizational structures, and the design and implementation of systems are described.

Marketing planning systems design and implementation

In this final section we look at some of the *contextual* issues of strategic marketing planning.

The truth is, of course, that the actual process of marketing planning is simple in outline. Any book will tell us that it consists of: a situation review; assumptions; objectives, strategies; programmes; and measurement and review. What the books do not tell us is that there are a number of contextual issues that have to be considered that make marketing planning one of the most baffling of all management problems.

Here are some of those issues:

- When should it be done, how often, by whom, and how?
- Is it different in a large and a small company?
- Is it different in a diversified and an undiversified company?
- What is the role of the chief executive?
- What is the role of the planning department?
- Should marketing planning be top-down or bottom-up?
- What is the relationship between operational (one year) and strategic (longer term) planning?

Requisite strategic marketing planning

Many companies currently under seige have recognized the need for a more structured approach to planning their marketing and have opted for the kind of standardized, formalized procedures written about so much in textbooks. These rarely bring any benefits and often bring marketing planning itself into disrepute.

It is quite clear that any attempt at the introduction of formalized marketing planning requires a change in its approach to managing its business. It is also clear that unless a company recognizes these implications, and plans to seek ways of coping with them, formalized strategic planning will be ineffective.

Research has shown that the implications are principally as follows:

1 Any closed loop planning system (but especially one that is essentially a forecasting and budgeting system) will lead to dull and ineffective marketing. Therefore, there has to be some mechanism for preventing inertia from setting in through the over-bureaucratization of the system.

2 Planning undertaken at the functional level of marketing, in the absence of a means of integration with other functional areas of the business at general management level, will be largely ineffective.

3 The separation of responsibility for operational and strategic planning will lead to a divergence of the short-term thrust of a business at the operational level from the long-term objectives of the enterprise as a whole. This will encourage preoccupation with short-term results at operational level, which normally makes the firm less effective in the longer term.

4 Unless the chief executive understands and takes the active role in strategic marketing planning, it will never be an effective system.

5 A period of up to three years is necessary (especially in large firms) for the successful introduction of an effective strategic planning system.

Let us be dogmatic about requisite planning levels. First, in a large diversified group, irrespective of such organizational issues, anything other than a systematic approach approximating to a formalized marketing planning system is unlikely to enable the necessary control to be exercised over the corporate identity.

Second, unnecessary planning, or overplanning, could easily result from an inadequate or indiscriminate consideration of the real planning needs at the different levels in the hierarchical chain.

Third, as size and diversity grow, so the degree of formalization of the marketing planning process must also increase. This can be simplified in the form of a matrix.

The degree of formalization must increase with the evolving size and diversity of operations. However, while the degree of formalization will change, the need for an effective marketing planning system does not. The problems that companies suffer, then, are a function of either the degree to which they have a requisite marketing planning system or the degree to which the formalization of

	Company size		
	Large	Medium	Small
High	High formalization	High/medium formalization	Medium formalization
Medium	High/medium formalization	Medium formalization	Low formalization
Low	Medium formalization	Low formalization	High informalization

Market/product diversity

Figure 5.8 *Planning formalization*

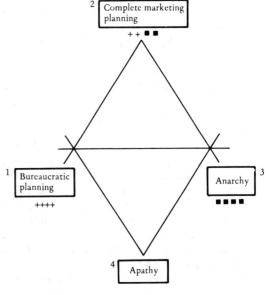

Key
+ Degree of formalization
■ Degree of openness

Figure 5.9 *Four key outcomes*

their system grows with the situational complexities attendant upon the size and diversity of operations.

Figure 5.9 explores four key outcomes that marketing planning can evoke. It can be seen that systems 1, 3 and 4, i.e. where the individual is totally subordinate to a formalized system, or where there is neither system nor creativity, are less successful than system 2, in which the individual is allowed to be entrepreneurial within a total system. System 2, then, will be an effective marketing planning system, but one in which the degree of formalization will be a function of company size and diversity.

Creativity cannot flourish in a closed-loop formalized system. There would be little disagreement that in today's abrasive, turbulent, and highly competitive environment, it is those firms that succeed in extracting entrepreneurial ideas and creative marketing programmes from systems that are necessarily yet acceptably formalized, that will succeed in the long run. Much innovative flair can so easily get stifled by systems.

Certainly there is ample evidence of international companies with highly formalized systems that produce stale and repetitive plans, with little changed from year to year and that fail to point up the really key strategic issues as a result. The scandalous waste this implies is largely due to a lack of personal intervention by key managers during the early stages of the planning cycle.

There is clearly a need, therefore, to find a way of perpetually renewing the planning life cycle each time around. Inertia must never set in. Without some such valve or means of opening up the loop, inertia quickly produces decay.

Such a valve has to be inserted early in the planning cycle during the audit, or situation review stage. In companies with effective strategic marketing planning systems, whether such systems are formalized or informal, the critical intervention of senior managers, from the chief executive down through the hierarchical chain, comes at the audit stage. Essentially what takes place is a personalized presentation of audit findings, together with proposed marketing objectives and strategic and outline budgets for the strategic planning period. These are discussed, amended where necessary, and agreed in various synthesized formats at the hierarchical levels in the organization before any detailed operational planning takes place. It is at such meetings that managers are called upon to justify their views, which tends to force them to be more bold and creative than they would have been had they been allowed merely to send in their proposals. Obviously, however, even here much depends on the degree to which managers take a critical stance, which is much greater when the chief executive him/herself takes an active part in the process. Every hour of time devoted at this stage by the chief executive has a multiplier effect throughout the remainder of the process. And let it be remembered we are not, repeat not, talking about budgets at this juncture in anything other than outline form.

One of the most encouraging findings to emerge from research is that the theory of marketing planning is universally applicable. While the planning task is less complicated in small, undiversified companies, and there is less need for formalized procedures than in large, diversified companies, the fact is that exactly the same framework should be used in all circumstances, and that this approach brings similar benefits to all.

Role of the chief executive in strategic marketing planning

When the role of the chief executive in strategic marketing planning was examined, it was found that few have a clear perception of the:

- Purposes and methods of planning.
- Proper assignments of planning responsibilities throughout the organization.
- Proper structures and staffing of the planning department.
- Talent and skills required in an effective planning department.

The role of the chief executive is generally agreed as being:

- To define the organizational framework.
- To ensure that strategic analysis covers critical factors.
- To maintain the balance between short- and long-term results.
- To display his/her commitment to planning.
- To provide the entrepreneurial dynamic to overcome bureaucracy.
- To build this dynamic into the planning operation (motivation).

In respect of planning, the chief executive's principal role is to open up the planning loop by means of his/her personal intervention. The main purpose of this is to act as a catalyst for the entrepreneurial dynamic within his/her organization, which can so easily decay through bureaucratization. This is not sufficiently recognized in textbooks.

When considering this in the context of the reasons for failures of strategic marketing planning systems, it is clear that, for any system to be effective, the chief executive is required to be conversant with planning techniques and approaches, and to be committed to and take part in the marketing planning process.

Role of the planning department in strategic marketing planning

This raises the important question of the role of the planning department, which is:

- To provide the planning structure and system.
- To secure rapid data transmission in the form of intelligence.
- To act as a catalyst in obtaining inputs from operating divisions.
- To forge planning links across organizational divisions, e.g. R & D and marketing.
- To evaluate plans against the chief executive's formulated strategy.
- To monitor the agreed plans.

The planner is a coordinator who sees that the planning is done – not a formulator of goals and strategies.

Marketing planning cycle

The schedule should call for work on the plan for the next year to begin early enough in the current year to permit adequate time for market research and analysis of key data and market trends. In addition, the plan should provide for the early development of a strategic plan that can be approved or altered in principle.

A key factor in determining the planning cycle is bound to be the degree to which it is practicable to extrapolate from sales and market data, but generally speaking successful planning companies start the planning cycle formally somewhere between nine and six months from the beginning of the next fiscal year.

It is not necessary to be constrained to work within the company's fiscal year; it is quite possible to have a separate marketing planning schedule if that is appropriate, and simply organize the aggregation of results at the time required by the corporate financial controller.

Planning horizons

It is clear that one- and five-year planning periods are by far the most common. Lead time for the initiation of major new product innovations, the length of time necessary to recover capital investment costs, the continuing availability of customers and raw materials, and the size and usefulness of existing plant and buildings, are the most frequently mentioned reasons for having a five-year planning horizon.

Many companies, however, do not give sufficient thought to what represents a sensible planning horizon for their particular circumstances. A five-year time span is clearly too long for some companies, particularly those with highly versatile machinery operating in volatile fashion-conscious markets. The effect of this is to rob strategic plans of reality. A five-year horizon is often chosen largely because of its universality. Second, some small subsidiaries in large conglomerates are often asked to produce strategic plans for seven, ten and sometimes fifteen years ahead, with the result that they tend to become meaningless exercises.

The conclusion to be reached is that there is a natural point of focus into the future, beyond which it is pointless to look. This point of focus is a function of the relative size of a company. Small companies, because of their size and the way they are managed, tend to be comparatively flexible in the way in which they can react to environmental turbulence in the short term. Large companies, on the other hand, need a much longer lead time in which to make changes in direction. Consequently, they tend to need to look further into the future and to use formalized systems for this purpose so that managers throughout the organization have a common means of communication.

How the marketing planning process works

There is one other major aspect to be considered. It

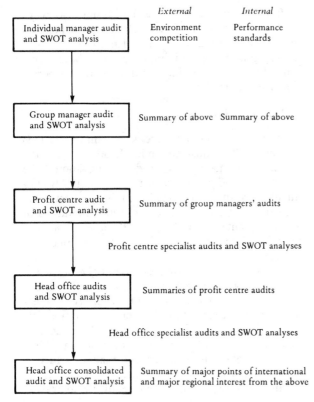

	External	*Internal*
Individual manager audit and SWOT analysis	Environment competition	Performance standards
Group manager audit and SWOT analysis	Summary of above	Summary of above
Profit centre audit and SWOT analysis	Summary of group managers' audits	
	Profit centre specialist audits and SWOT analyses	
Head office audits and SWOT analysis	Summaries of profit centre audits	
	Head office specialist audits and SWOT analyses	
Head office consolidated audit and SWOT analysis	Summary of major points of international and major regional interest from the above	

Figure 5.10 *Hierarchy of audits*

concerns the requisite location of the strategic marketing planning activity in a company. The answer is simple to give. Strategic marketing planning should take place as near to the marketplace as possible in the first instance but such plans should then be reviewed at high levels within an organization to see what issues have been overlooked.

It has been suggested that each manager in the organization should complete an audit and SWOT analysis on his/her own area of responsibility. The only way that this can work in practice is by means of a *hierarchy* of audits. The principle is simply demonstrated in Figure 5.10.

Figure 5.10 illustrates the principle of auditing at different levels within an organization. The marketing audit format will be universally applicable. It is only the *detail* that varies from level to level and from company to company within the same group.

Figure 5.11 illustrates the total corporate strategic and planning process. This time, however, a time element is added, and the relationship between strategic planning letters, long-term corporate plans and short-term operational plans is clarified. It is important to note that there are two 'open loop' points on this last diagram. These are the key times in the planning process when a subordinate's views and findings should be subjected to the closest examination by his/her superior. It is by taking these opportunities that marketing planning can be transformed into the critical and creative process it is

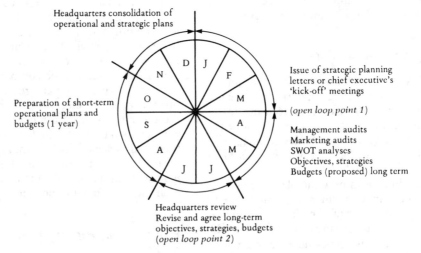

Figure 5.11 *Strategic and operational planning*

supposed to be rather than the dull, repetitive ritual it so often turns out to be.

Since in anything but the smallest of undiversified companies it is not possible for top management to set detailed objectives for operating units, it is suggested that at this stage in the planning process, strategic guidelines should be issued. One way of doing this is in the form of a *strategic planning letter*. Another is by means of a personal briefing by the chief executive at 'kick-off' meetings. As in the case of the audit, these guidelines would proceed from the broad to the specific, and would become more detailed as they progressed through the company towards operating units.

These guidelines would be under the headings of financial, manpower and organization, operations and, of course, marketing.

Under marketing, for example, at the highest level in a large group, top management may ask for particular attention to be paid to issues such as the technical impact of microprocessors on electromechanical component equipment, leadership and innovation strategies, vulnerability to attack from the flood of Japanese and European products, and so on. At operating company level, it is possible to be more explicit about target markets, product development, and the like.

Conclusion

In conclusion, we must stress that there can be no such thing as an off-the-peg marketing planning system and anyone who offers one must be viewed with great suspicion.

In the end, strategic marketing planning success comes from an endless willingness to learn and to adapt the system to our people and our own circumstances. It also comes from a deep understanding about the *nature* of marketing planning, which is something that in the final analysis cannot be taught.

Success comes from *experience*. Experience comes from making mistakes. We can minimise these if we combine *common sense* and *sweet reasonableness* with the structures provided in this chapter and the *models* provided in later chapters. But be sure of *one* thing, above all else. By themselves, the models will not work. However, if you use the models sensibly, strategic marketing planning becomes one of the most powerful tools available to a business today.

PART TWO

The framework
of marketing

6
Environmental analysis

DOUGLAS BROWNLIE

No man is an island, entire of itself

J. Donne

Introduction

The author is about to embark on an evangelistic
mission. Of course, claims of this sort are not unusual in the still emerging and occasionally prescien-
tific discipline of marketing. Indeed, the covers of
this text are widely separated by the writings of some
notable marketing evangelists. However, the term
accurately describes what the author hopes to
achieve in an overview of a topic that, although
having origins as a *methodology* in the field of
strategic management, is founded on a resolute
attitude to business given early expression in the
marketing concept.

Echoes of Donne's simple phrase are to be heard
in Levitt's (1983) writings when he says that the
marketing concept '. . . alerts us to a world of constant change where survival requires studying and
responding to what people want and value, and
quickly adjusting to choices provided by competition, which often comes from outside the industry in
which it finally occurs'. Organizations then, like
people, are creatures of their environment and participants, albeit unwilling, in its processes. They, too,
spend much of their life learning how to cope with
the complexity, hostility, unforeseen traumas,
vagaries and opportunities generated by their environment. Isolation and survival would seem to be
mutually exclusive conditions.

Levitt's message reminds we marketing evangelists of our claim that by heightening the firm's
sensitivity to and willingness to take advantage of
environmental change, a marketing orientation provides a means of survival in a turbulent and competitive market. Rudimentary business acumen may
already have suggested something similar to the
reader: i.e., that a sound business proposition takes
advantage of prior knowledge of the broad currents
of change in the marketplace, principally customers,
competitors, suppliers and regulators. But, as more
experienced readers will agree, the possession of
detailed knowledge and acute analytical skills is a
means to an end, i.e. decision making and action.
Unfortunately, between knowledge and corresponding action lies the confounding influence of
managerial attitudes.

Earlier chapters have suggested that the realization of a marketing orientation is, in practice, often
inhibited, not by failures of the systems, technology
or methodologies of marketing, but by disabling
management attitudes which often express themselves as resistance to change, conservatism, suspicion and prevarication. As many battle-scarred
marketing executives will testify – even those who
may be awash with consumer studies, competitor
evaluations, demand forecasts, political commen-
taries, technology forecasts, stockmarket reports,
economic forecasts, etc, – the mere possession of

information about the changing business environment is a necessary, but not a sufficient condition to ensure *sensitivity*, *alertness*, and *alacrity*.

Management attitudes have a vital role to play in creating an organizational climate that enables the firm, not only to operate what should in effect be an *open window of perception* on the past, present and prospective business scene, but also to act on the insights it provides. Readers will therefore be disappointed if they expect the methodology of environmental analysis and forecasting to be described herein as a panacea for the problems of understanding and coping with the increasingly competitive and turbulent environment of the late 1980s. Methodology alone will not guarantee success.

Writers in the field of strategic management have added little to the basic notion, implicit to the marketing concept, that an *alertness* and *sensitivity* to the external business environment is an essential ingredient of success and longevity. However, they do add a broad view of the elements of environmental change as they manifest themselves at the level of industries. The view encompasses both proximate and remote product, supply, labour and capital markets, as well as the technological economic, social and political forces that can interfere with their operation. Clearly such a view is appropriate to an area that deals with issues having a greater impact on the formulation of strategies and plans at corporate level, than at business unit level.

The broad view has precipitated the evolution of a robust organizing framework for strategic management*. It is capable of integrating methods of information retrieval, processing and dissemination into a global strategic decision-making regime. Moreover, it incorporates the managerial dimensions that have often been overlooked in the vain hope of finding simplex solutions to the complex problems of formulating and implementing strategies and plans in large organizations.

It may become evident that despite the overwhelming need for a factual basis to the diagnosis of strategic problems, the author is proposing an argument against a wholly technocratic view of strategic management. To which could be added the corollary that the reductionist thinking that gave us n-step strategic planning models has little more of any consequence to add to our understanding of how the firm is best able to manage the process of formulating and implementing its responses to environmental change. But, there is no denying that strategic management involves the execution of a number of tasks, some of which can be conveniently grouped together in a step-wise fashion – even if the implied sequence and repressive order grossly oversimplifies the reality.

It will become clear that the tasks of environmental analysis and forecasting have key roles to play in formulating strategy, irrespective of your views on how the process should be organized. Indeed, it could be argued that environmental analysis and forecasting is the starting point of any planning regime whose purpose is to determine how the firm should prepare for and respond to environmental change. Strategic management not only requires knowledge of all aspects of the firm's operations. Above all it requires a knowledge and understanding of changes in the business environment that presently or prospectively will have an impact on the firm.

Environmental analysis and forecasting is responsible not only for *generating* an up-to-date data base of information on the changing business scene. It also has the job of alerting management to what is happening in the marketplace, the industry and beyond by *disseminating* important information and analyses to key strategic decision makers and influencers. However, the conversion of the awareness such dissemination will create into interest, and ultimately to some form of action, is an overtly and

---

* The model is finding application in the context of strategic marketing management where the tasks of environmental analysis and forecasting are subsumed within the external audit. The external audit searches the firm's current and prospective 'marketing environment' for indicators of trends and events likely to have an impact on its competitive marketing edge. It also evaluates the extent and nature of the impact so that marketing threats and opportunities are diagnosed. A marketing threat is any issue, trend or event that, in the absence of pre-emptive or retaliatory action by the firm, will have a detrimental impact on its competitive position. A marketing opportunity is any issue, event or trend that looks likely to have the potential to enhance the attainment of the firm's marketing goals by creating new markets or generating the growth to expand existing ones. The increasingly popular concern for dietary health and physical fitness is causing growth in some product markets and decline in others, thus illustrating that opportunities for one firm may be threats to another.

covertly political process which can emasculate the most penetrating analyses – particularly where vested interests are threatened and top management support absent.

The preceding paragraph asks the reader to take a step outside the realm of the environmental analyst and forecaster and to enter that of the strategic decision maker. The tasks of gathering, analysing and disseminating information and making a decision which uses the information, are often organized as discrete activities. Environmental analysts and forecasters are likely to be members of the corporate or marketing planning staff, or top management aides, i.e. decision influencers, but rarely decision makers. Indeed, the 'boffinesque' role in which they often find themselves cast may do little to enhance the credibility and esteem attributed to them by leading edge strategic decision makers. They will be keen to place their own interpretations on what the expert analysts and forecasters have to say – unless, of course, they have an impeccable track record, in which case the experts may find themselves being elevated to the status of a 'delphic oracle'. But, in the absence of any other intelligence gathering activity, whether systematized or personal, environmental analysts and forecasters will, by means of the perceived importance of the information they generate, be in an enviable position to influence strategic decision makers' perceptions of the firm's competitive position and the options available to it. Students of history will recognize that many a bloody political intrigue was spawned by the jealously guarded, and often misused privilege of proximity to the seat of power which was conferred on privy counsellers and advisors. Thus, in addition to the technical skills demanded of environmental analysts and forecasters, astute political skills could be said to be the hallmark of an effective operator.

It is being argued that the careful collection, analysis and communication of information on the business environment can contribute greatly to the accurate diagnosis of the firm's competitive position and of the feasible strategy alternatives available to it. This chapter introduces a methodology that provides an *enabling mechanism* whereby this contribution can be made. It is also being argued that to realize the full potential of the mechanism requires a supportive managerial environment which is openly endorsed and promoted by top management. But the firm must be prudent in its attempts to surmount the disabling attitudes which can be held by executives who operate the mechanism as well as those who have to make use of its output. Mistrust, prevarication, conservatism, secrecy, etc., can impede the operation of the mechanism thereby undermining the value of its contribution.

The author has gone to some length to argue that the efficacy of any strategic planning system – marketing driven or otherwise – is not a function of methodology alone. Skilled environmental analysis and forecasting is thus of little consequence in a firm whose management is either unwilling or unable to respond to *signals of coming* environmental change.

The text that follows constructs an argument in favour of the view that *formal environmental scanning*** provides a general methodological framework within which the tasks of environmental analysis and forecasting can be conducted.

It is also argued that in so doing the tasks become an integral part of the mechanism by means of which firms formulate strategies and plans at the corporate and business unit level. The text goes on to describe a general approach to environmental scanning which may be used by corporate and marketing strategist alike; what benefits the author believes it brings to practising firms; what management problems are likely to be encountered, and how possibly to surmount them.

Three important premises

As you might expect from an evangelist, the argument in favour of formal environmental scanning is

---

* The term environmental scanning is often used interchangeably with others such as environmental analysis, environmental forecasting, competitive intelligence gathering, external search, environmental surveillance, strategic marketing information retrieval, etc. The author prefers to use the term 'environmental scanning' to encompass the varied information gathering, analysis and dissemination activities that firms pursue in order to keep up to date with changes in the business environment. Clearly the purpose of these activities is not merely to keep track of environmental changes. Without the adjunct of reliable environmental forecasting, there is no basis for strategic planning. Environmental scanning activities range from highly structured and regularly conducted reviews and forecasts of major trends, issues and events in the business environment, to the irregular 'tip' acquired by means of insider access to a network of private and personal contacts, or even by means of espionage.

not proposed on the basis of scientific findings. Given that empirical evidence is mixed and partial*, acceptance of the argument is a matter of some judgement and faith.

The strength of the argument is founded on what the author believes to be a widespread and often unrecognized acceptance of the three basic premises which are discussed below. All three are derived from a currently prevailing paradigm which relates the constructs of strategy, structure, environment and performance in a formulation which verbally states that a *firm's performance is a function of its environment, its strategy and its structure*. Of course, this paradigm is not new, it having been conceived of in an early form by Mason (1939) in the field of industrial economics. Mason postulated that market structure influences the conduct of organizations, and that their conduct, in turn, affects their performance. In its current form the paradigm synthesizes the findings of empirical research in the more recently established areas of business policy, marketing and organizatonal theory, much of which was stimulated by Chandler's (1962) working hypothesis that an organization's structure as well as its strategy determines its performance.

Premise 1

The first premise holds that *the determinants of success are dictated by the business environment:* the interplay of social, politial, technological and economic trends and unforeseen events produces a flux of circumstances and issues to which firms must respond if they are to ensure survival and prosperity.

Students of marketing will readily subscribe to the view that any robust explanation of business success will have as its foundation the tenet of alertness and responsiveness to the opportunities and constraints precipitated by a turbulent business environment. The marketing concept enshrines such a view. Indeed, the business literature in general, and the marketing literature in particular, is replete with cases of firms whose decline (success) can be attributed to their disregard (high regard) for this tenet.

The merit of this view has gained impact with the publication of the results of recent empirical studies

Table 6.1 *Cherished assumptions now thought obsolete*

- Inflation will never exceed 5 per cent p.a.
- Energy will always be cheap and abundant.
- The price of oil will never exceed $2 per barrel.
- Import penetration of home markets will never exceed 15 per cent.
- The primary aim of business is to make money.
- Strict financial control is the secret to good administration.
- Market growth of 10 per cent p.a.
- Workers do not have an important impact on productivity or product quality.
- The consumerist movement does not represent the concerns of a significant portion of the buying public.
- Success comes from having the resources to quickly adopt innovations successfully introduced by others.
- Frequent styling changes are more important to customers than product quality.

of the management philosophies and practices currently finding application in high performing firms. By demonstrating that successful firms display a heightened alertness and responsiveness to

---

* Partiality and inconclusiveness are not untypical of research findings in an area undergoing early empirical study: that early researchers employ different research approaches and problem definitions is in no small way responsible for this. Indeed, definitions of formal environmental scanning commonly vary along the following dimensions: the extent to which it is organized into a set of structured activities, with its own staff, and including the formal use of techniques such as multiple scenarios and delphi studies; the periodicity of the scanning activities, i.e. on a continuous, irregular or regular basis; and the extent to which both corporate and divisional management become involved in the activities. Research approaches have either been small scale in depth case studies, or large scale cross-sectional surveys. Most research is of a US origin.

environmental change, it could be argued that the work of Peters and Waterman (1982), Goldsmith and Clutterbuck (1985), and Hooley *et al.* (1983) not only vindicates the tenet, but accords it the status of a motherhood.

Despite the lessons of Peters and Waterman, the history of many firms reveals that success and excellence remain temporary and elusive phenomena. Indeed, by the time Peters and Waterman had their book published in 1982, some of its 'excellent' firms (including Caterpillar Tractor and Hewlet Packard) were already experiencing difficulties. The easily replicated research model used by the authors is capable of generating partial explanations that have validity only for those firms under study, and at the time in question. Consequently, as time passed and the environmental circumstances of several of the participating firms altered for the worse, unless a timely response was achieved, one could only expect a subsequent fall from the heady performance levels previously used by the writers as indicators of success and excellence. But, the value of Peters and Waterman's work is not merely that it attributes success to the possession of particular management characteristics – the replication of best management practice then being open to aspiring paragons. But, moreover, it represents a stimulus to the popularization of the view that the search for universal prescriptions of success and excellence is a quest for the managerial equivalent of a holy grail. In so doing it lends support to the contingency school of thought and its deterministic view of the relationship between an organization's environment and its performance.

Once achieved, the firm must continue to pursue them as they evolve over time; otherwise, the proud possession, or pursuit of factors that were once associated with success will undermine the firm's competitive position as they become inappropriate to a business environment that has moved on. Consequently, at the heart of the firm's strategic management efforts must be the constant monitoring of the business environment. It then becomes possible to validate or update the assumptions underlying the firm's strategic thinking, thereby keeping it abreast of the factors that determine success and excellence. Questions of efficiency (doing things right) are dealt with by means of the internal appraisal of strengths and weaknesses, whereby unit cost often becomes the aggregate measure of performance. Questions of effectiveness (doing the right things) can only be answered with respect to the expectations the marketplace has of any business sector. Environmental scanning provides a means of keeping in touch with the marketplace and thereby to deal with questions concerning the validity, cogency and consistency of the firm's strategic thinking.

The decline of once great industrial empires can be partly attributed to a failure to re-examine and challenge the basic assumptions that serve the firm, and may have done so for years. Some of the seemingly unassailable pre-1974 assumptions that have come to serve firms badly are listed above in Table 6.1. Compare these assumptions with the key environmental trends of the 1980s which are listed in Table 6.2.

Table 6.2 *Key environmental trends for the 1990s*

- Continuing slowdown in international growth.
- Splintering markets.
- Irreversible inflation.
- Uneven distribution of world resources.
- Increasing exports from newly industrialized countries.
- Technological maturity and the growth of new science-based industries.
- Shortening product development cycles.
- Shorter product development cycles.
- Globalization of markets for products, services and capital.
- Increasing capital intensity.
- Declining fixed to variable cost ratios.
- Emergence of the multilocal company.

Adapted by the author from Ohmae (1982) and Lorenz (1986.)

Premise 2

The preceding positivist view of the environment-firm relationship is to some extent qualified and modified by the second premise. It states that *the firm's response to environmental change represents a fundamental strategic choice.* The relationship is not considered to be unequivocally unidirectional in nature – the firm in all cases being the passive recipient of the dictates of the environment. It could be argued that most firms have some measure of control over their fate, even if environmental change is difficult to predict, and timely responses to it even more difficult to realize. A two-sided view of the dependencies on which the relationship is based would also attribute an active role to the firm. This view may have more appeal to those who would argue that the firm has the potential to exercise control by means of the decisions it takes in response to changing environmental circumstances.

The firm is dependent on its environment for supplies, manpower, financing, equipment, regulation, sales, etc. Consequently, environmental considerations will tend to constrain the firm's choices about what its business mission should be; what business it should be in; on what basis it should compete; and in what product-markets. But as the constraining forces are influenced by the waxing and waning of environmental trends, issues or events, strategic choices will become available to the firm. It will then be able to decide, not only the manner of its response, but also the particular set of external circumstances it wishes to define as its business environment. The principal strategic decision will then be to choose which of the following policy options to adopt: first, to adapt to the new demands being imposed on a particular product-market, whose operation is being influenced by social, economic, political or technological changes; or, second, to actively seek another business environment in which the comparative advantage the firm derives from its current structure and mix of skills and resources is still relevant. The pursuit of the former policy option will invoke a strategy based on innovation or diversification; the latter will call for some form of market development.

Clearly, the boundaries of the firm's external environment should firstly be derived from the scope and purpose of its business mission and then set in terms of specific information to which the firm requires access for strategic planning and decision-making purposes. The relevant business environment in any strategic decision-making situation could then be said to consist of the set of uncontrollable variables that affect the outcome of the decision to be made.

The breadth of the view the firm chooses to take of its business environment has implications for the complexity of the tasks of environmental analysis and forecasting and thus its resource requirements. A broadly defined business mission is associated with a diversified, multiproduct, multimarket firm. It would involve environmental scanning in a very broad area of operation from which a perspective on international political and economic issues, events and trends may be called for by corporate planning. On the other hand, a narrowly defined business mission may focus the efforts of environmental scanning more on domestic issues concerning immediate events and trends in proximate product markets. The firm's environmental scanning activities should cover as many relevant aspects of the business environment as the available resources will permit, particularly those aspects having an impact on the assumptions being used by the firm in its strategic planning and decision making.

Premise 3

Firms subject themselves to the inconvenience, expense, rigour and pain of strategic planning in order to acquire more control over the outcome of any course of action they choose to pursue. Thus, in accordance with Bacon's dictum that 'knowledge itself is power', the third premise holds that *a knowledge of the business environment must precede the acquisition of any degree of control over it.*

The present reader is likely to have witnessed the popularization of terms such as espionage, infiltration, moles, security leaks, early warning, electronic surveillance, counter intelligence, insider dealing, etc. Although evocative of the anxiety and duplicity of our age, the popularization of the vocabulary of the spy lends some credence to the view that the possession of information is itself a factor endowment, and as such it should be treated as a valuable national asset. It is only one small, but logical step to argue that since the gathering of information precedes its possession and dissemination, then this activity also contributes to the generation of wealth.

To the student of military strategy the preceding

Table 6.3   *Sources of information on the business environment*

Location	Types	Sources of information on business environment
Inside the company	Written	Internal reports and memos, planning documents, market research, MIS.
	Verbal	Researchers, sales force, marketing, purchasing, advisors, planners, board.
	Combination	Formal and informal meetings, e.g. working parties, advisory committees.
Outside the company	Written	Annual reports, investment reports, trade association publications, institute yearbooks, textbooks, scientific journals, professional journals, technical magazines, unpublished reports, government reports, unpublished papers, abstracts, newspapers, espionage.
	Verbal	Consultants, librarians, government officials, consumers, suppliers, distributors, competitors, academics, market researchers, industry bodies, journalists, spies, bankers, stockbrokers.
	Combination	Formal and informal meetings, membership of government working parties and advisory boards, industry bodies, trade associations.

view will represent a familiar and even hackneyed line of thought. After all, history offers many examples of battles which could be said to have been fought and won on the basis of 'superior' information. In planning the deployment and employment of his army's resources, the general relies on the intelligence provided by lines of communications which may have a political origin in his own state, but will certainly infiltrate enemy territory and institutions. By means of the intelligence so provided the general hopes to better prepare himself for the ensuing conflict and to enhance the likelihood of his victory – i.e. to gain some control over the outcome of the conflict.

One message that should by now be ringing clearly is that effective management, military or otherwise, cannot occur in an information vacuum. Indeed, it could be argued in the context of marketing that management is about the conversion of information (much of which will relate to the business environment) into revenue.

In the corporate context the tasks of intelligence gathering, surveillance and monitoring are overseen by environmental scanning. It is responsible for managing lines of communications by means of which a flow of information is maintained between important elements of the business environment and the firm's strategic decision makers and influencers. Figure 6.1 depicts the flows of information between the elements of the business environment, environmental scanning, the firm's

management information systems and its strategic decision makers.

Early attempts at strategic planning are likely to

Table 6.4   *The relative importance of sources of environmental information*

1   Verbal sources of information are much more important than written sources. 75 per cent of information cited by executives was in verbal form.

2   The higher the executive in the organization, the more important verbal sources became.

3   Of the written sources used, the most important were newspapers (two-thirds), then trade publications, then internal company reports.

4   The major sources of verbal information are subordinates, then friends in the industry, and very infrequently superiors.

5   Information received from outside an organization is usually unsolicited.

6   Information received from inside the organization is usually solicited by the executive.

7   Information received from outside tends to have a greater impact on the decision maker than inside information.

8   The outside sources used varied according to the job of the manager. Thus, marketing managers talked more to customers.

9   The larger the company, the greater the reliance on inside sources of verbal information.

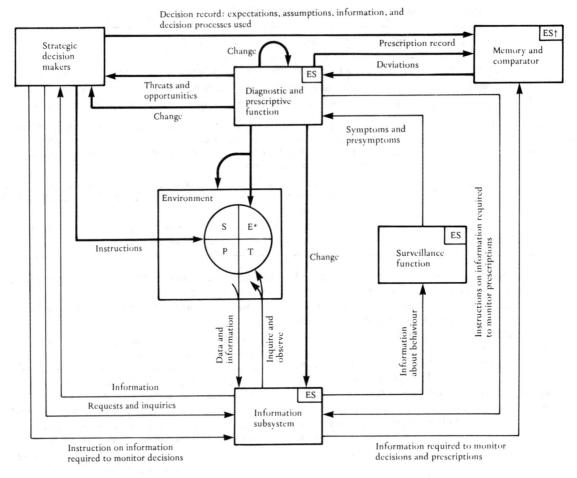

* The organization's window on the social, economic, technological, and political elements of the business environment
† Activities in which environmental scanning is directly involved

Figure 6.1 *Linking environmental scanning and decision making via information flows*
Adapted by the author from Ackoff (1981).

be loosely based in order to be sensitive to a wide spectrum of information. Emphasis will be placed on developing insights into emerging strategic issues. The later drive towards further systematization aims to improve the efficiency of the strategic planning process by making it more routine and predictable. The format of the input and planning documents will be standardized. A formal timetable will govern the timing of data preparation and the meeting of contributing line managers. It can be argued that the drive towards administrative effi-

ciency will suppress the creativity of strategic planning. A balance may have to be achieved between the opposing forces of administration efficiency and strategic planning effectiveness.

As in the military context, the corporate intelligence service will also provide early warning and careful tracking of possible environmental threats in order that a timely response is conceived and executed. Table 6.3 indicates corporate sources of information on the business environment; Table 6.4 comments on their relative importance. Table 6.4

also suggests that to enhance the impact of its work, environmental scanning should not only seek top management support, but also its involvement in order to implicate or consult all key decision makers and influencers at corporate and divisional level.

In recent years the emergence of information technology has encouraged the firm to carefully re-examine the purpose, structure, productivity and accessability of its management information systems, including those governing elements of the business environment. The outcome has often been re-organized data bases which involves further systematization of the tasks of collecting, analysing and disseminating information on the business environment. The demanding task of organizing a data base governing important elements of the firms environment is made more so by the character of pertinent information – which, it is safe to assume, will often possess several of the following characteristics:

● Poor structure.
● Irregular availability.
● Provided by unofficial sources.
● Qualitative in nature.
● Questionable credibility.
● Ambiguous definitions.
● Opinion based.
● Difficult to quantify.
● Insecure methodology.
● Likely to change.

A major impact of information technology has been to change the nature of the information problem facing many firms from being one of under-supply to over-load. The important question in many instances is becoming not the quantity of information, but its quality. Such change will place greater emphasis on management skills in the processing of information from many different sources.

The root *causes* of environmental change may be impossible for any one firm to know and, therefore, to predict and control. But, in the short to medium term the *effects* of such change often manifest themselves as incremental adjustments to the basis of competition. Such adjustments will often coincide with, or even precede, the general recognition of a symptom of some underlying change in the business environment. For instance, the declining annual demand for a consumer durable product could be a symptom of the declining real value of consumers'

disposable incomes. Under these circumstances customers may prefer to delay their replacement purchases by prolonging the useful life of the item they already own. The underlying causes will have origins in the macroeconomic policies being implemented by the government of the day. They will, in turn, be contingent on the domestic and international economic pressures being exerted via the balance of payments and the exchange rates. Of course, all participants in the product market will be equally exposed to the symptom. However, they will not be equal in their ability to respond to the changing circumstances. Firms will have access to differing resource bases, which will include different degrees of managerial imagination and creative flair. Thus, participants will be constrained in different ways in the adjustments they choose to make to their marketing strategies. Over a prolonged period the accumulated effect of such adjustments is to precipitate structural change in an industry via new entrants, withdrawals, product and process innovation, product substitution, etc. But in the shorter term control over effects is not only possible, but desirable.

The unresolved planning dilemma

It has been argued that the ability to exercise control in the firm's current product-markets is derived, at least partly, from a comprehensive and reliable customer, supplier, competitor, regulator and investor knowledge. The successful development and upkeep of the knowledge base is thought to be the principal task of formal environmental scanning – one to which the functions of marketing, purchasing, sales and finance have a major contribution to make. However, in the long term more is expected of it. For instance, as the firm looks away from its existing product markets for future growth opportunities within and outside its current sphere of operation, knowledge will be required of a new and unfamiliar business environment having its own unique set of technological, economic, political and social trends. In so doing greater demands will be made of environmental scanning.

Growth brings with it challenges which will have implications for almost all aspects of the firm's operations, not only environmental scanning. The performance of the overall strategic planning regime may be exposed to scrutiny if a successful outcome is not realized. Much is at stake: the credibility of the strategic planning function; its influence over and support from top management; the goodwill accorded to it by powerful divisional managers; the continuity of its resource base, etc.

A disenchantment with strategic planning has been expressed in some quarters by writers such as Hunsicker (1980). It has its own roots in the persistence of two related trends: the apparent failure of strategic planning in its bid to successfully guide the firm towards new opportunities and away from emerging threats; and the growing sophistication of the strategic planning process itself. The writer takes the view that both these trends have their origin in a firm adherence to the belief that *certainty in strategic decision making can be bought at the price of greater detail*. Faithful followers of this belief may be predisposed to explain the failure of their firm's strategic planning efforts in terms of what they consider to be the inadequately detailed information on which the firm's analyses and forecasts of strategic change are based. This explanation may have appeal for some, given the many imponderables in the business environment which add to the uncertainty of strategic decision making. Nevertheless, remarks such as that which follows do little to convince the author that greater detail is the answer: '. . . if only more attention had been devoted to establishing precise estimates of future inflation, interest rates, GNP growth, etc. . . . .'

If an answer is ever to be found to the problems of coping with a turbulent business climate, the author believes it is unlikely to be found merely in the adoption of increasingly sophisticated strategic planning systems. Lenz and Lyles (1985) in their study of such systems observed that unless their evolution was overseen by top management, they tended to increasingly take a form that stifled creative thought and frustrated top management by placing burdensome demands on its time and by becoming increasingly rigid, bureaucratic, quantitative and formal. That the strategic planning process of many firms has evolved into a very sophisticated analytical mechanism is attributed by Lenz and Lyles to the following factors: the professionalization of the planners job by making strategic planning a science; the unqualified acceptance and misapplication of techniques for strategic analysis; the drive for administrative efficiency; and the excessive emphasis on quantification for strategic decisions. Lenz and Lyles further argue that the conventional approach to strategic problem solving – which dissects the problem into smaller and smaller pieces – can undermine the potency of the firm's strategic thinking by denying it the coherence of the broad view.

Support is growing for what some would consider to be a counter-intuitive argument. It holds that the provision of increasingly detailed information on which to base strategic analyses and forecasts generates more ambiguity than certainty. This view represents a backlash to the school of thought which favours ritualistic rationalism. It is not a rejection of the virtues of ritual and rationality. But, rather a concern that the obsessive pursuit of these virtues occurs at the expense of creativity, innovation, flexibility and entrepreneurship – which are, after all, the hallmarks of adaptability and survival. Supporters share the concern that the basic purpose of strategic planning is not to promote the evolution of a ponderous planning apparatus by means of which the firm may often find itself the unwitting victim of 'paralysis by analysis'. But, it is to provide a systematic rather than 'seat of the pants' approach to the formulation of the strategies and plans by means of which the firm responds to a changing environment. A successful strategic planning system will, of necessity, exhibit a blend of the virtues of ritual and rationalism on the one hand, and, on the other, creativity, innovation and imagination. This calls for a commitment to strategic planning that pervades the firm and offers the first step towards the strategic management approach. Lenz and Lyles suggest that such a blend may be achieved by means of developing a planning culture, as is proposed by the strategic management school of thought; by using strategy review sessions to encourage probing and creative thinking; and by auditing the performance of strategic planning on a regular basis.

Therein reside the horns of the unresolved planning dilemma. Firms need to plan to survive. Planning involves being organized, systematic, comprehensive and rational. But, firms also need to adapt to survive. Adaptability involves flexibility, creativity, innovation, imagination and flair. And never shall the twain meet?

What environmental scanning can accomplish

Whatever is achieved by environmental scanning will largely depend on the purpose the firm has in mind for it. Small firms may require to be kept up to date with regulatory and economic trends likely to have an immediate impact on its day to day business prospects. Larger firms will share the requirements of the small firm, but will also expect information broader in scope and of a futures orientation.

Corporate level environmental scanning is likely to be charged with the responsibility of monitoring, interpreting and forecasting issues, trends and events which go far beyond the customer, market and competitive analyses that most firms perform as a matter of routine. In this context environmental scanning will be expected to provide a broad but penetrating view of possible future changes in the demographic, social, cultural, political, technological and economic elements of the business environment. In so doing it should seek to arm the firm's strategic decision makers and influencers with the information, analyses and forecasts they consider pertinent to the formulation of the strategies and plans which govern how the firm will respond to a changing business environment. It should also provide a basis for questioning the assumptions which underpin the firm's strategic thinking and for generating new assumptions.

Jain (1985) suggests that environmental scanning's principal accomplishment must be to enable the firm to deal with environmental change. In his view the goal can only be achieved by means of making the following contributions to the firm's strategic management.

- Helping the firm to capitalize on early opportunities, rather than lose these to competitors.
- Providing a base of objective qualitative informa- which can be defused if recognized well in advance.
- Sensitizing the firm to the changing needs and wishes of its customers.
- Providing a base of objective qualitative information about the business environment that strategists can utilize.
- Providing intellectual stimulation to strategists in their decision making.
- Improving the image of the firm with its public

by showing that it is sensitive to its environment and responsive to it.
- Providing a continuing, broad-based education for executives, especially strategy developers.

In a recent empirical study of formal environmental scanning in ninety American corporations, Diffenbach (1983) reported that participants found there to be seven types of payoffs from the activity. His findings suggest that although environmental scanning is widely practised and found to be important by many of those who do it (73 per cent) a significant number of respondents did not do it (27 per cent), or did it but did not find it very useful (28 per cent). Table 6.5 lists a selection of the comments Diffenbach received from respondents on the subject of the payoffs of organized environmental scanning.

Defining the business environment

Churchman (1968) defines the environment of a firm as 'those factors which not only are outside the system's control but which determine, in part, how the system performs'. In theory at least the business environment is then thought to include all those factors that exert a direct or indirect influence on the firm in any perceptible way. Given such an unbounded definition one could argue that the rest of the world then constitutes the firm's business environment. Clearly, to take such an indiscriminating view has no operational value. The task of environmental scanning can only be made manageable by taking a very selective and carefully considered view of the environment. It will eliminate much of the rest of the world from the firm's immediate attention.

The boundaries of the firm's environment must be structured in such a way that they enable the scanner to identify important from less important factors and to determine an appropriate time scale for forecasting changes. One would expect there to be factors that deserve to be continuously monitored because of their immediate impact on the industry. These would include users, distributors, suppliers, competitors for customers and suppliers, work force, government regulators, trade unions, product and process developments, etc. (see Baker (1985, Chapter 4) and Jain (1985, Chapter 6) for a full discussion of the elements of the business environ-

Table 6.5 *Payoffs of organized environmental scanning*

Increased general awareness by management of environmental changes

- Improved ability to anticipate long-term problems and make adjustments earlier than otherwise.
- Increased responsiveness of operations programmes to environmental concerns.
- Awareness of top level management to a range of possible futures and how they might affect the company.
- A noticeable tendency for managers to ask themselves if the same approaches used in the past will work in the future.
- Disposition to acting in advance of change.

Better strategic planning and decision making

- Plans and decisions that reflect a greater awareness of political events and economic cycles, and therefore more flexibility and adaptiveness.
- Development of contingency plans.
- More disciplined planning.
- Broadened scope of perspectives, so that one can understand the relevance of external conditions to the business of the company.
- Lengthened planning/decision horizon.
- Gradual and continued incorporation of environmental factors into the corporate decision-making process.
- Improved ability to allocate strategic resources to opportunities created by environmental change.
- Improved ability to anticipate long-term problems and make adjustments earlier.
- Divisions' product plan awareness of social trends, ecology, shifts in population age profile, geographic migration, and the position of women.
- Wide acceptance of the necessity for a common set of environmental assumptions as a basis for formal planning activities.
- Avoidance of crises.

Greater effectiveness in government matters

- Better government relations and understanding of the role of government.
- Greater success in winning government contracts.
- Ability to take proactive (rather than reactive) positions on government regulatory matters earlier.
- Time to adapt products to noise and pollution regulations.
- Anticipation of government restrictions on medical equipment led to extra effort to develop foreign markets.
- Orderly response to federal legislation and reporting requirements.

Better industry and market analyses

- Higher quality of predictions in market and product forecasts.
- Greater confidence in product forecasts.

- Recognition of possible declining markets and resultant rejection of capital investment for manufacturing facilities to supply those markets.
- Early detection of developing shifts in trends from either excess capacity or insufficient capacity in an industry.
- Stimulus for corporation and groups to assess more variables which affect product lines.
- Identification of changes in buyer criteria due to social changes.
- Reorientation of marketing programme to reflect sun belt growth.
- Ability to anticipate future needs for new products, e.g. increasing oil and gas exploration creates need for (drilling) systems usable in a wide range of water depths and operating environments.
- Research efforts toward products filling needs created by government and social pressures (e.g. development of diagnostic tests as hedge against malpractice litigation).

Better results in foreign businesses

- Major investment in foreign countries.
- Positive results of overseas investment and market participation.
- Ability to anticipate changes in international markets and ways of doing business in foreign countries.

Improvements in diversifications and resource allocation

- Ability to concentrate our resources in businesses that will be attractive to the corporation in the long term.
- Shifts in production portfolio – away from those products subject to increasing government and social pressures (e.g. 'polluting' processes, 'dangerous' products) toward those less vulnerable to such pressures.
- Guide to acquisitions process.
- Contributed to policy development with respect to expansion and allocation of capital funds.
- Major diversification which helped company ride out rough time in the aluminium business.

Better energy planning

- Ability to predict economic dislocations resulting from OPEC embargo and to deal flexibly with exchange rates.
- Better energy planning for production facilities.
- Correct anticipation of energy trends in the mid-1960s and consequent development of new energy-efficient glass forming process.
- Identification of potential impact of energy shortage over six years ago (about 1971) and the development of marketing programmes and product lines around ability to help customers reduce energy consumption – action led to strengthened market position.
- Development of additional back-up energy sources.

Note. This table lists a selection of the comments on the payoffs of organized environmental scanning obtained by Diffenbach's (1983) survey of US industry practice.

Table 6.6   *Framework for analysis of the wider business environment*

Cultural	Including the historical background, ideologies, values and norms of the society. Views on authority relationships, leadership patterns, interpersonal relationships, nationalism, science and technology.
Technological	The level of scientific and technological advancement in society. Including the physical base (plant, equipment, facilities) and the knowledge base of technology. Degree to which the scientific and technological community is able to develop new knowledge and apply it.
Educational	The general literacy level of the population. The degree of sophistication and specialization in the educational system. The proportion of the people with a high level of professional and/or specialized training.
Political	The general political climate of society. The degree of concentration of political power. The nature of political organization (degrees of decentralization, diversity of functions, etc). The political party system.
Legal	Constitutional considerations, nature of legal system, jurisdictions of various governmental units. Specific laws concerning formation, taxation, and control of organizations.
Natural resources	The nature, quantity and availability of natural resources, including climatic and other conditions.
Demographic	The nature of human resources available to the society; their number, distribution, age and sex. Concentration or urbanization of population is a characteristic of industrialized societies.
Sociological	Class structure and mobility. Definition of social roles. Nature of social organization and development of social institutions.
Economic	General economic framework, including the type of economic organization – private versus public ownership; the centralization or decentralization of economic planning; the banking system; and fiscal policies. The level of investment in physical resources and consumption.

Adapted from Kast and Rosenweig (1974).

ment). Dill (1958) considers the origin of such factors to be the 'task environment' which he defines as 'the more specific forces which are relevant to decision making and transformation processes of the individual organizations'.

The concept of the task environment opens the environmental scanner's 'window on the world' on to the firm's immediate product and supply markets; and on to current influences on its position within them. But, a wider view would also cast attention towards remote areas where developments could be under way which in the longer term would impinge on the firm's position in its current product and supply markets. For instance, substitute products and processes often originate as spin-offs from technological developments that have been made by firms without the task environment. Clearly it is important to look further afield than the task environment. Kast and Rosenzweig (1974) have suggested a framework by means of which the wider business environment can be divided into areas for study and analysis. Table 6.6 reproduces this

framework. Table 6.7 outlines some of the broad social issues that firms might expect to impinge on their European activities in the late 1980s. Environmental scanning would be expected to follow developments of these issues (and others of a technological, political, cultural and economic nature) and evaluate the impact they are thought likely to have on the firm.

The complexity of environmental scanning, considered by Ansoff (1984) to be determined by two factors: the degree of environmental uncertainty as perceived by the firm and measured by the rate of change in the business environment; and the degree of environmental complexity also as perceived by the firm and measured by the range of activities in which the firm is currently and likely to be prospectively involved, can only be reduced to manageable proportions by first defining boundaries of the business environment which reflect the firm's common thread. However, within the firm itself operates a process of selective perception and attention by means of which irrelevant 'stimuli and noise' can be

Table 6.7 *Key European social issues for the 1980s*

Issues	Characteristics
Low growth and uncertainty	Political instability; higher energy prices; lower economic growth; decline of basic industries; protectionism; high levels of inflation; high levels of unemployment; fluctuating financial markets.
Political uncertainty and insecurity	Political stability in Europe; war and revolution in the third world; international terrorism; urban riots.
Rise of the multinationals	Giant firms; size and diversity; professional management; shareholder power; reform of the board.
Employee participation and trade union power	Works councils; trade unions; bigness and alienation.
Rise of the organized pressure group	Consumer protection; environmental pollution; women's rights; ethnic minorities; protection health
Growth of government	Protectionism; growth of public ownership; economic planning; industrial policy.
Social political pressures on business	Lower profits and slower growth in productivity; economic impact of regulation; pressures on top management for the greater disclosure of information, improvement of the working environment; product safety improvement, reduction of environmental pollution, participative decision making, etc.

Adapted from Taylor and Ferro (1983).

screened out. Given that there are just too many environmental stimuli at any one time for the firm to pay adequate attention to all of them, environmental scanning could be defined as the process in which environmental stimuli are selected and organized into patterns which are meaningful to the firm in the light of its current and future needs and interests. In humans, sensation and perception act as two screening stages – what remains thereafter is at best a partial representation of the reality. Ansoff argues that in the firm the screening process operates by means of three filters (see Figure 6.2) the first of which is controlled by environmental scanning, so that it provides the firm with a view of the business environment which is selective and necessarily partial.

The techniques used by environmental scanning to collect, synthesize and analyse information on the business environment can be viewed as a filter (the surveillance filter in Figure 6.2) through which information must first pass on its way to the firm's decision makers. The organization and control of environmental scanning is thus of considerable importance to the firm since it determines the width and strength of the overall screening effect.

It is not the purpose of this chapter to acquaint the reader with the details of environmental analysis and forecasting techniques. They can readily be found in a voluminous literature on the subject (see Brownlie and Saren, 1983). Table 6.8 lists a number of the more important techniques and relates them to the environmental condition in which their application could be appropriate. Conventional methodologies such as marketing research, demand forecasting, economic indicators and industry studies are also used.

Ansoff argues that the choice of environmental analysis and forecasting technique is too important to be left to the environmental scanning specialist, as it is often done in practice. In his view the user of the output of environmental scanning should have an overriding influence on the choice of technique. Consequently, knowledge of the applicability of the technique is more important to the user than knowledge of the details of the technique's execution. He suggests that the filter which is operated by environmental scanning should be sufficiently open to capture a realistic view of the firm's environment. Distortion and oversimplification are thought to occur where a restrictive filter operates.

The information provided by environmental scanning will pass through two additional filters

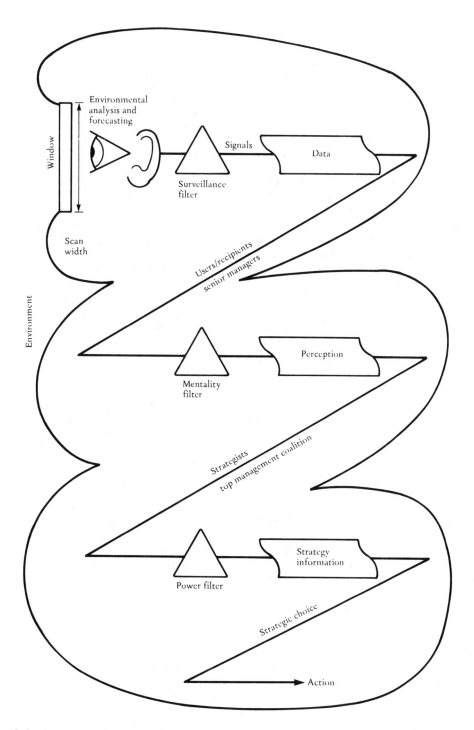

Figure 6.2   *Selection, perception and attention in the firm*

before it becomes part of the information on which strategic decisions are made. The first of these (the mentality filter in Figure 6.2) operates by virtue of the mental success models that are utilized by those managers who receive and act on the incoming environmental scanning information.

The accumulation of successes and failures that managers experience over time is thought to allow them to form convictions about things that work and those that do not. By means of this empirically tested 'world model' experienced managers are then able to cope with the volume and complexity of the information they receive from all sources, including environmental scanning. But, as Ansoff argues, this model of bounded rationality will serve managers badly when they are presented with the novel signals which arise when variables and relationships in the firm's environment are changing. Ansoff remarks that under such circumstances '. . . the manager will filter novel signals which are not relevant to his historical experience, and thus fail to perceive the shape of the new environment; the newly important variables; the new relationships; and the new success factors'. In this way he believes that success will breed failure in a turbulent business environment as managers attempt to cling onto an obsolete model. Thus, the operation of the mentality filter can seriously impede the firm's ability to react to signals of coming environmental change even where environmental scanning has picked them up.

Ansoff argues that in terms of environmental turbulence a strategic and creative mentality must be cultivated in participating managers in order to suppress the effect of the mentality filter. But, even where this is so, novel information will not necessarily be incorporated into strategic decision making. For this to occur, appropriate managers must also possess the power to convince the dominant coalition of top managers to pay heed to the information being imparted by environmental scanning.

It is not unusual for a strategic and creative mentality to be received with hostility by peers and indifference or rejection by superiors. As Ansoff notes, 'to assure a firm-wide acceptance of a new mentality it is essential that top management be the leading practitioners of this mentality'. If top management lack the appropriate mentality, they will persist in preventing vital novel signals from affecting strategic decision making. In this way the third filter (the power filter) operates.

By means of Ansoff's three filters, one can easily appreciate why some firms procrastinate and others seem ignorant of the need for a response to environment change.

State of the environmental scanning art

Ansoff argues that the historical development of management systems follows the evolution of the firm's environment. He characterizes the managerial approach of firms in the stable environment of the early 1900s (i.e. a period when events in the business environment were familiar; the pace of change slower than the firm's ability to respond; and the future visible) as management by post facto control of performance; and in the turbulent environment of the 1980s (i.e. a period when events were discontinuous and novel; the pace of change quicker than the firm's ability to respond; and the future not at all visible and very surpriseful) as management by flexible and rapid response. Management systems would seem to have evolved in response to two trends: the increasing *discontinuity*, *complexity*, and *novelty* of the environmental challenges firms face; and the decreasing *visibility* of the future changes in the business environment. The growing impact of these trends is largely responsible for the widespread following which the strategic planning credo has acquired in the wake of the post 1974 trauma. A consequence of this has been first, to draw attention to environmental scanning as an important element of strategic planning; and, second, for environmental scanning itself to evolve in response to the challenges confronting the firm and its planning system.

Diffenbach (1983) traces the early evolution of environmental scanning to the mid-1960s, at which time the business environment was generally being studied only for the purpose of making economic forecasts. Only in more recent years does he consider there has been an appreciation of the need to look beyond short-term market conditions to the wider technological, economic, political, social, cultural and demographic elements of the business environment. He identifies three distinct evolutionary phases, each of which marks a growth in the scope, systematization, futures orientation and top management recognition of environmental scanning activity. Changes first began to occur during what

Table 6.8 *Environmental analysis and forecasting techniques*

Techniques	Percentage of companies reporting use of techniques (n = 66)	Applicable environmental turbulence level		
		Low	Medium	High
Expert opinion	86	•	•	•
Trend extrapolation	83	•		
Alternate scenarios	68	•	•	•
Single scenarios	55	•		
Simulation models	55	•		
Brainstorming	45		•	•
Causal models	32		•	•
Delphi projections	29			•
Cross-impact analysis	27			•
Input–output analysis	26	•		
Exponential forecasting	21	•		
Signal monitoring	12	•	•	•
Relevance trees	6		•	
Morphological analysis	5		•	•

Adapted from Ansoff (1984) and Diffenbach (1983).

Diffenbach terms the *appreciation* phase. It was precipitated by an upsurge of academic and professional interest in environmental analysis. It spawned a number of publications advocating the broad view of the business environment – in opposition to the then popularly held view that the firm's environment be bounded by short-term market conditions. The awareness and interest so created led to the second phase – that of *analysis*. 'It involves finding reliable sources of environmental data, compiling and examining the data to discern trends, developments and anticipating the future.' Interests in environmental analysis and forecasting techniques (see Table 6.8) grew during this phase. The third and current phase is that of *application*. It is concerned with integrating the output of environmental scanning into the firm's strategic decision making.

A pioneering investigation of environmental scanning was conducted by Aguilar in 1967. In this now classic study the process of environmental scanning was originally conceptualized. In his research Aguilar interviewed 137 managers from forty-one chemical firms in the US and Europe. He found a lack of a systematic approach to environmental scanning which was still being reported in the more recent research of Thomas (1980), Fahey *et al.* (1981) and Stubbart (1982). The research revealed that the participants collected sixteen types of information about their business environment: Aguilar classified them into the five groupings displayed in Table 6.9.

Aguilar's study concluded that for environmental scanning to make an effective contribution to the formulation of strategy it must be conducted in a systematic fashion. He frequently found environmental scanning effort to be fragmented and inhibited by the failure of participating managers to gather and disseminate information that users considered important; and to make use of accessible information that already resided within the firm. His proposals for overcoming the 'fractionalization' of environmental scanning effort called for top management involvement in the definition and execution of scanning activities; greater coordination and integration of these activities with strategic planing; and greater support for these activities, not only from top management, but also from line managers.

Despite the considerable body of strategic planning literature which addresses environmental

Table 6.9   *What information do managers need on the business environment**

Market tidings

Market potential	Supply and demand consideration for market areas of current or potential interest: e.g. capacity, consumption, imports, exports.
Structural change	Mergers, acquisitions and joint ventures involving competitors, new entries into the industry.
Competitors and industry	General information about a competitor, industry policy, concerted actions in the industry, and so forth.
Pricing	Effective and proposed prices for products of current and potential interest.
Sales negotiations	Information relating to a specific current or potential sale or contract for the firm.
Customers	General information about current or near-potential customers, their markets, their problems.

Acquisition leads

Leads for mergers, joint ventures, or acquisitions	Information concerning possibilities for the manager's own company

Technical tidings

New products, processes, and technology	Technical information relatively new and unknown to the company.
Product problems	Problems involving existing products.
Costs	Costs for processing, operations, and so forth for current and potential competitors, suppliers, and customers, and for proposed company activities.
Licensing and patents	Products and processes.

Broad issues

General conditions	Events of a general nature: political, demographic, national, and so forth.
Government actions and policies	Governmental decisions affecting the industry.

Other tidings

Suppliers and raw materials	Purchasing considerations for products of current or potential interest.
Resources available	Persons, land, and other resources possibly available for the company.
Miscellaneous	Items not elsewhere classified.

Source: Aguilar (1967).

* Market tidings (52 per cent) was found by far to be the most popular category of environmental information that participants looked for, followed by technical tidings (17 per cent) and broad issues (12 per cent). He also identified four approaches, i.e. *undirected viewing, conditioned viewing, informal search* and *formal search*, to the collection of environmental information and two principal sources of such information (see Tables 6.3 and 6.4).

Table 6.10   *A typology of environmental scanning systems*

	Irregular	*Periodic*	*Continuous*
Impetus for scanning	Crisis-initiated.	Problem-solving decision/ issue orientated.	Opportunity finding and problem avoidance.
Scope of scanning	Specific events.	Selected events.	Broad range of environmental systems.
Temporal nature	Reactive.	Proactive.	Proactive.
(a) Timeframe for data	Retrospective	Current and retrospective	Current and prospective
(b) Timeframe for decision impact	Current and near term future.	Near term.	Long term.
Types of forecasts	Budget-orientated.	Economic and sales orientated.	Marketing, social, legal, regulatory, culture, etc.
Media for scanning and forecasting	Ad hoc studies.	Periodically updated studies.	Structured data collection and processing systems.
Organization structure	Ad hoc teams.	Various staff agencies.	Scanning unit, focus on enhancing uncertainty handling capability.
	Focus on reduction of perceived certainty.		
Resource allocation to activity	Not specific; (perhaps periodic as 'fads' arise).	Specific and continuous but relatively low.	Specific continuous and relatively substantial.
Methodological sophistication	Simplistic data analyses and budgetary projections.	Statistical forecasting orientated.	Many 'futuristic' forecasting methodologies.
'Cultural' orientation	Not integrated into mainstream of activity.	Partially integrated as a 'stepchild'.	Fully integrated as crucial for long-range growth.

scanning, scepticism still surrounds the extent to which it is finding application in firms. The purpose of Diffenbach's (1983) study was to make some progress towards answering the doubts of the sceptics. The earlier work of Fahey *et al.* (1981) shared this motivation. As a result of their in-depth study of the environmental scanning practices of twelve large American firms, they proposed a typology of models of scanning, as shown in Table 6.10.

The reader will observe that the models represent increasing degrees of systematization, sophistication and resource intensity. *Irregular* systems respond to environmentally generated crises. They are found in firms where the strategic planning culture is not well established. Their emphasis is on finding solutions to short-term problems. Little attention is paid to evaluating future environmental changes.

The *periodic* model is more sophisticated, systematic, proactive and resource intensive. It entails a regular review of the task environment and some

elements of the wider environment. A forward view is taken.

The *continuous* model emphasizes the ongoing monitoring of the business environment, rather than specified issues or events. It draws on the expertise of marketing, sales, purchasing, etc. It operates a clearing house for environmental information and uses regular information systems for analysis and dissemination. A long-term view of environment change is taken.

Fahey *et al.* concluded though that the models they were proposing did not find widespread application in US corporations. They noted the trend towards greater sophistication, but added that the impact environmental scanning had so far demonstrated did not appear to warrant the major deployment of resources it requires. Of course, the empirical studies of Thomas (1980) and Diffenbach (1983) provide evidence that persuades them to take the opposite view.

Table 6.11 *Propositions on environmental analysis and diagnosis*

- A firm whose strategy fits the needs of the firm's environment will be more effective.
- The major causes of growth, decline and other large scale changes in firms are factors in the environment, not internal developments.
- Most top managers gather information about the environment verbally, primarily from subordinates, friends or acquaintances in the industry. Written information, forecasting and management information systems are not significant sources of information for analyses by top managers, but their use may be increasing.
- The more information contacts the strategist seeks, the better environmental analysis. In large organizations, the contacts are primarily internal. In smaller organizations, the contacts are normally external.
- The more sectors and the more factors that are analysed, the more effective is the environmental analysis.
- The more dependent the enterprise is on a sector of its environment (technological, competitor, geographic, supplier, socioeconomic and government) the more it will focus its environmental analysis on that sector.
- The more developed the sector, the more a firm will focus on that sector of the environment.
- The more hostile the sector, the more vital the analysis and diagnosis of that sector of the environment.
- The more volatile and uncertain the sector, the more the diagnosis will focus on that sector.
- The greater the time pressure and cost of search, the less likely it is that in-depth diagnosis will result.
- The greater the complexity of the environment, the more sectors managers must focus on.

Adapted from Glueck and Jauch (1984).

As a result of their work with US industry in the area of strategic management, Glueck and Jauch offer a number of broadly based propositions concerning the corporate use of environmental analysis and diagnosis. These are abstracted in Table 6.11.

The paradox of environmental scanning is that by the time sufficient information has been collected to enable a well informed environmental analysis to be made, it may be too late for the firm to respond before the threat strikes, or the opportunity passes. Ansoff proposes an approach to strategic management (see Figure 6.3) which in his view overcomes the paradox by enabling the firm to develop a timely response to partially predictable events which emerge as surprises and develop very quickly. At its heart is the continuous monitoring of the firm's external and internal environment for signals of the evolution of *strategic issues* which the firm considers able to influence its operations. Ansoff's unit of analysis is then the strategic issue rather than the conventional elements of the business environment. Ansoff's solution to the paradox is a 'graduated response' based on the amplification of and flexible response to weak signals. As he contends, 'instead of waiting for sufficient information to accumulate, the firm should determine what progressive steps in planning and action are feasible as strategic information becomes available in the course of the evolution of a threat or opportunity'. This is a necessarily incomplete discussion of Ansoff's views. Readers are strongly recommended to refer to part 5 of his text for a comprehensive discussion of the subjects of weak signal management and strategic issue analysis.

In the author's view the state of the art in enviromental scanning theory is likely to reside somewhere within Ansoff's holistic views on strategic management. The current practical state of affairs in UK industry is more difficult to determine and one still wonders if there has been any widespread evolution in the application of formal environmental scanning post-Aguilar (1967).

Environmental scanning procedures and problems

The firm's environmental scanning procedures will evolve over time as its commitment to them and experience of them changes. It is unrealistic for the firm that is about to embrace environmental scanning for the first time to expect to operate a foolproof system from the outset. Several technical and managerial constraints will impede the progress of environmental scanning efforts (see Table 6.13). Of course, the firm can shorten the evolutionary period by ensuring top management involvement in the commissioning of the system.

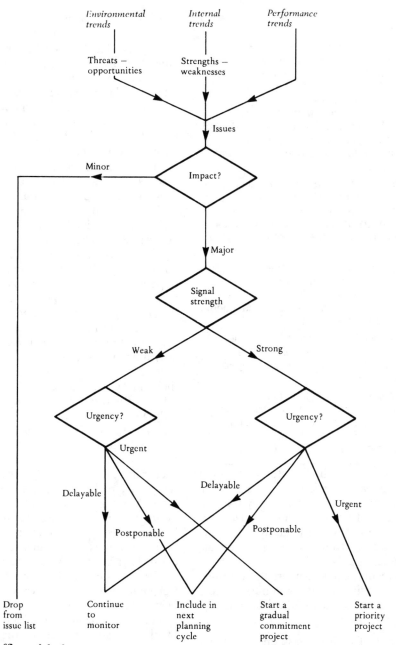

Figure 6.3 *Ansoff's model of strategic issues analysis*

The provision of top management support throughout the evolutionary period helps ensure that a viable system emerges from early efforts which are likely to be directed towards the installa- tion of a system that is likely to be modelled on an ideal scanning procedure such as that shown in Table 6.12. An established strategic planning cul- ture should also help expedite matters by providing

Table 6.12 *A typical sequential model of the ideal scanning procedure*

1 *Monitor* broad trends, issues and events occurring in the firm's task environment. This can be complemented by means of identifying a core list of relevant publications and assigning them to volunteers who report important articles to environmental scanning for further study. Selected areas of the remote environment should be reviewed from time to time. External consultants may be employed.

2 *Identify* trends etc., which may have significance for the firm. A scanning team of senior executives should determine and implement the criteria by means of which *relevance* is established. Weak signals may not be amenable to screening in this way.

3 *Evaluate* the impact of significant trends, etc., on the firm's operations in its current product markets. Those having a significant impact will either be *threats* or *opportunities*. Line managers should participate in the evaluation.

4 *Forecast* the possible future directions of the significant trends, etc., and *examine* the new opportunities and threats they appear likely to generate.

5 *Evaluate* the impact of these threats and opportunities on the firm's long-term strategies. The output of steps 3, 4 and 5 can be summarized by means of the environmental threat and opportunity profile shown in Figure 6.4.

a receptive organizational climate. But, this cannot be guaranteed. Even strategic planners are apt to react to a threatening newcomer in a way that ensures their territorial boundaries and organizational prerogatives are preserved – particularly if the newcomer is to be funded from the existing strategic planning resource base.

Top management involvement in the commissioning of the environmental scanning system should focus on the definition of the following system parameters:

● The boundaries of both the task and the wider business environment.
● The appropriate time horizon for future studies.
● The allocation of responsibility for environmental scanning.
● The degree of formality circumscribing environmental scanning.

To define *the boundaries of the firm's environments* in terms of concrete measures is an almost impossible task for all but the smallest of one-product firms. Nevertheless, environmental scanners need practicable guidelines by means of which they are able to separate relevant from irrelevant environmental information. Such guidelines should be determined in consultation with members of the top management team that is responsible for the formulation of long-term strategies and plans.

But there are no hard and fast rules for making the distinction between relevance and irrelevance. Both Stubbart (1982) and Diffenbach (1983) found firms to be continuously frustrated in their efforts to arrive at a workable definition of their business environment. The nub of the problem is one of achieving a balanced view of the scope of the firm's environment. In order to avoid misdirecting effort to peripheral and irrelevant issues it must not be too wide in scope. Nor should it be a narrow, data dependent, econometric but relevant, if myopic, view. Clearly the problem will be exacerbated in diversified firms which will possess several relevant environments (see Table 6.13). The opportunity cost of the constricted view of the firm's environment may greatly exceed the actual cost of scanning areas of the wider business environment – particularly where weak signals are to be detected.

Given the difficulty firms experience in establishing the preceding parameter, it is not surprising that they tend to focus on familiar environments – preferring to study remote environments on an ad hoc basis, perhaps with the assistance of consultants. A similarly conservative view is often taken of *the appropriate time horizon* for the future studies to be conducted by environmental scanning. Diffenbach's research (1983) found that such studies were considered by divisional management to be more useful the shorter the time horizon they took. Corporate management tended to take a longer view.

The time horizon should, in theory be determined by the investment cycle of the industry and the nature of the product or service it provides. For example: in the oil industry a scanning term of twenty-five years is not unusual; in the fashion industry a period of four years is more appropriate. The time horizon of environmental scanning should then exceed the duration of the firm's strategic

Environment sector	Event/ issue	T*1	O*2	Weighting*3	Importance*4	Impact on company strategies*5			E −	E +
						S_1	S_2	S_3		
Technology	1								*6	*6
	2									
Political										
Economic										
Social										
etc.										
					Σ −	*6				
					Σ +	*6				

*1 Threat

*2 Opportunity

*3 Indicated the degree to which the event is judged to be a threat or opportunity. On an ordinal scale from 1 to 5, where 1 represents a weak T/O; and 5 a strong T/O.

*4 Indicates the degree to which the weighted event has, or will have, an impact on the firm's strategies. On an ordinal scale from 1 to 5, where 1 represents a little impact; 5 a great impact.

*5 The impact each event has on each of the firm's strategies is calculated by multiplying the weighted score by the importance score. A large positive (negative) score represents a strong opportunity (threat).

*6 The row sums indicate the degree to which each event/issue is thought to enhance (+) or inhibit (−) the success of the firm's strategies.

The column sums indicate the degree to which each strategy is itself thought to pose a threat or opportunity to the firm, given its predicted environment.

*7 The value in constructing an ETOP profile is largely to be found in the debate that follows the planners environmental appraisal, when the firm's managers assimilate, debate and develop their own ideas of the organizations threats and opportunities.

Figure 6.4 *Displaying the firm's environmental threat and opportunity profit*

plans. If the firm operates a policy of waiting to see what the industry leaders get up to, then environmental scanning activities may be easily resourced. But, they will provide a narrow, reactive view which is biased towards the short term. A proactive regime will be more demanding of middle and top management abilities, especially in multiproduct-multimarket firms where a variety of time horizons might apply.

The *responsibility for environmental scanning* can be allocated in three different ways. *First,* line managers in functions such as purchasing, sales and marketing can be asked to undertake environmental scanning in addition to their other duties. These managers are likely to be able to provide information on the business environment and should, therefore, contribute in some way to any environmental scanning system. But, the first approach suffers disadvantages such as those that follow: the demotivating resentment the line managers may feel towards this additional imposition on their time; the requirement for specialist analytical, research and forecasting skills which line managers are unlikely to possess; the possibly incompatible mentalities of the roles they are asked to play – creative and farsighted thinker on the one hand; hard-headed operator on the other (see Table 6.13).

The *second* approach is for environmental scanning to be made part of the strategic planner's job. The division of the strategic planning labour in this

Table 6.13 *Deterrents to effective environmental analysis*

Interpretation
The problem is that of interpreting the results of environmental analysis into specific impacts on the company's businesses and into specific responses to be made by the businesses. Included is the problem of the results not being in useful or sufficiently precise form.

- Difficulty of structuring studies in a way that results can be seen to be relevant and meaningful to decision makers today.
- Difficulty of reacting because information from environmental analysis is so intangible with regard to timing and impact.
- Difficulty of assessing the implications of general environmental trends for our specific businesses before they exert themselves.
- Difficulty of translating environmental analysis into relevant business terms, e.g. ROI impact.
- Difficulty of quantifying the impact of major threats and developing alternatives to these threats.
- Difficulty of developing the path from assumption to implication to action, e.g. the tendency to relax or stop after stating the assumption, rather than follow through to an action program.
- Difficulty in seeing the impact of environmental trends on short range operations, i.e. the gradual, accumulative nature of trends can be deceptive.
- Lack of sufficient involvement by top management for them to not only understand the conclusions of environmental analysis but also to internalize them and change behaviour accordingly.
- Difficulty of translating potential opportunities into action plans, e.g. conversion of traditional furniture ideas into new lifestyle furniture concepts.
- The time and analysis required to apply information to our specific situations, e.g. impact of probable energy shortages or price increases on our market for automotive components.
- Difficulty of institutionalizing environmental planning into the formal planning processes of the company so that division strategies reflect the process.
- Difficulty of follow-up planning, e.g. we have pushed ahead on programmes in spite of warning signals that should have alerted us to severe problems.
- Identifying impacts on businesses, particularly when negative.

Inaccuracy/uncertainty
The problem is that either the output of environmental analysis is inaccurate, too uncertain to be taken seriously, or both.

- Uncertainty due to the dynamics of the market place.
- Inaccurate depicting of environmental events.
- So many false predictions.
- Inability to predict the future, e.g. past experience revealed inability of experts to predict the extent of inflationary forces.
- Difficulty of properly characterizing uncertainties in understandable and meaningful terms.
- Difficulty of forecasting the magnitude of the impact of a future trend.
- The moving target syndrome, e.g. especially regarding governmental activity.
- Difficulty of predicting social aims, e.g. no-growth v continuing growth, etc.
- Discontinuities in environmental forecasting for which no company can make satisfactory assessments.

Short-term orientation
The problem is that the preoccupation with short-term matters pre-empts attention to environmental analysis.

- Pressure of short-term events, which tend to soak up some of the resources nominally or usefully committed to environmental planning.
- Dislike for spending money today to help solve a speculative problem tomorrow.
- The reluctance to consider more than the short term because that is where the rewards are.
- Competition between short and long term, i.e. most environmental problems emerge slowly and require solutions which only become effective over similarly long periods of time.
- Organization structures and tasks that force managers to focus on the immediate, short-run elements of their jobs, e.g. budgets are for limited periods of time and encourage concern with this year's results, and maybe next year's.

Lack of acceptance
The problem is that environmental analysis is not accepted within the company.

- Some degree of skepticism as to the possibility of success with environmental analysis – more so at lower levels than at the top.
- Lack of understanding of the usefulness of environmental analysis.
- Difficulty of environmental analysts convincing line managers that the former's output is applicable to the latter's problems.
- The 'we already know our business' attitude on the part of operating management.

Table 6.13 *contd.*

- A suspicion in the practical world of business decisions that scenarios and possible occurrences are impractical and somehow dangerous.
- The 'we have been successful without it' attitude.
- A resistance to change in forecasting methods.
- The presumption by too many executives that each of them can be their own expert in assessing environmental impacts upon the company.
- Lack of commitment and personal involvement of line executives.
- The difficulty of breaking the patterns of thinking in the past.

Diversified businesses
The problem is that diversified businesses mean multiple relevant environments which make environmental analysis too complex.

- Difficulty of applying corporate expertise in environmental analysis at the operating level due to the great diversity of our operations.
- Complexity due to multiple and decentralized organization.

- Need for too large a corporate staff to keep abreast of environments for decentralized, autonomous businesses, and unwillingness of line managers to support a fulltime staff for environmental surveillance at the division level.

Misperceptions
The problem is one of narrow, limited or invalid perceptions of the external environment shared by executives.

- Tendency of managers to think in non-discontinuous terms.
- Unpreparedness of managers, because of education or basic interest, to deal with social, political, and cultural aspects of a rapidly changing environment (many managers are knowledge reductionists rather than holistic).
- Traditional inability to think in world market terms (instead of 'plant countries') when considering trends and factors of a social, political, technological and economic origin.

Source: Diffenbach (1983).

way leads to specialization which may also have some drawbacks. Stubbart (1982) argues that the task of environmental scanning '. . . cannot be easily abdicated to technical specialists at corporate headquarters. Because these specialists do not have to answer for the results of business unit performance, they often do not understand the technical requirements of the unit's business. And, most importantly, these specialists do not have a system for defining, measuring and interpreting a business unit's environment more accurately than the unit's own management can'. It may then be desirable for both planners and line managers to be involved in environmental scanning.

The *third* approach is to establish a separate organizational unit which is responsible for conducting regular and ad hoc scanning at all levels; and for channelling its results to those in the firm for whom they may have some relevance. The US firm General Electric is known to operate such a unit and to fund its activities by charging recipients for the environmental information scanning provides.

The latter approach may represent a theoretical ideal. However, combinations of the first two

approaches are most popular with all but the very large diversified firms who can afford to underwrite the operation of a separate unit. Combinations often operate by means of a temporary scanning team. It is likely to be set up on an ad hoc basis to oversee the study of the impact that a controversial environmental trend, issue or event is thought likely to have on various areas of the firm's operations. The team membership may consist of both line (SBU) and general (corporate) management. Line managers will scan the product market, while top managers scan the wider environment. Line managers may even be temporarily seconded to a staff position for the duration of the study. They will often be closely involved in determining the impact of environmental changes on areas of the firm's operations in which they are experienced. Consultants, either internal or external, may be used where the impact of environmental change is thought likely to threaten the vested interests of line managers in some way.

There is no clear agreement about the best way to assign responsibilities for environmental scanning. Every firm will experience unique circumstances that merit taking a particular approach which an

Table 6.14 *Attributes of a formal approach to environmental scanning*

- Environmental trends, events and issues are regularly and systematically reviewed.
- Explicit criteria have been established that can in turn be used to evaluate the impact of environmental trends.
- Scanning activities are guided by written procedures.
- Responsibility for scanning activities has been clearly assigned.
- Scanning reports, updates, forecasts and analyses are documented in a standardized format.
- Such documentation is generated on a regular basis and disseminated to predetermined personnel according to a timetable.
- The application of formal techniques such as delphi studies and multiple scenarios.

---

off-the-shelf environmental scanning system may be incapable of embracing. However, researchers do agree that firms should involve managers of various levels in environmental scanning activities. It could be argued that only by doing so can environmental scanning hope to become an effective and well integrated contributor to the firm's strategic decision-making regime.

Whatever the means by which responsibility for environmental scanning is assigned, the author argues that the bearers should still have the following tasks to undertake:

- To monitor trends, issues and events in the business environment and study their possible impacts on the firm's operations.
- To develop the forecasts, scenarios and issues analyses that serve as inputs to the firm's strategic decision making.
- To provide a destination to which environmental intelligence can be sent for interpretation, analysis and storage.
- To construct a means of organizing environmental information so that a library or data base on environmental developments can be easily accessed.
- To provide an internal consulting resource on long-term environmental affairs.
- To disseminate information on the business en-

vironment by means of newsletters, reports and lectures.
- To monitor the performance of environmental scanning activities and to improve it by applying new tools and techniques.

It is not only problematic to decide who is to be responsible for environmental scanning. The *degree of formality* that is to circumscribe its activities is also a matter for top management concern. The view that the firm takes will depend on the extent to which top management feels it necessary to be able to exert some control over the day to day activities of environmental scanning. Control may be a problem where responsibility for these activities is devolved to line managers whose own day to day responsibilities are likely to take precedence over what they may consider to be marginal 'blue sky' and 'ivory tower' exercises. This problem is likely to be exacerbated where no formal system for collecting, analysing and disseminating environmental information has been agreed. The lack of commitment and scepticism that line managers will often express about environment scanning can only be dealt with by means of training and involvement (see Table 6.12).

Yet, some firms are content to take an informal approach to environmental scanning, relying on key executives in sales, marketing, purchasing and finance to keep abreast of changes in the business environment through newspapers, trade literature, conferences, exhibitions, and personal contacts. Other firms prefer to organize their scanning efforts into a series of structured and pre-planned activities for which specified staff bear responsibility. The difference is really one of degree. Table 6.14 indicates attributes that a formal (informal) approach to environmental scanning is likely to possess to a great (little) extent.

Diffenbach's research found larger US firms to be more likely to take a formal approach to environmental scanning. This is not surprising given that such firms are also more likely to take a broad view of their business environment, competing as they will do in a number of markets with a number of products. But, the informal approach is not only the prerogative of the small one-product firm. Diversified firms may prefer to take an informal approach to such scanning activities as long-term forecasting, the generation of alternative scenarios, issues analyses and the management of weak signals. These activities demand a degree of creative thinking that can best be stimulated in an informal environment – even if the output of the process is subjected to a more formal treatment.

Conclusion

This chapter provides an overview of environmental analysis; the collection, analysis and communication of information on the business environment. The author sets out a methodology whereby environmental analysis can be put into practice, but cautions that the possession of information about business conditions is a necessary but not sufficient condition to ensure sensitivity, and alacrity. Managerial attitudes have a crucial role to play in creating the right organizational climate which enables environmental analysis to reach its full potential and full value to the organization.

References

Ackoff, R., 'Beyond Prediction and Preparation', *Journal of Management Studies*, vol. 18, no. 1, 1981, pp. 59–69.

Aguilar, F.S., *Scanning the Business Environment*, Macmillan, 1967.

Ansoff, H. I., *Implementing Strategic Management*, Prentice Hall, 1984.

Baker, M. J., *Marketing Strategy and Management*, Macmillan, 1985.

Brownlie, D. T. and Saren, M. A., 'A Review of Technology Forecasting Techniques and their Applications', *Management Bibliographies and Reviews*, vol. 9 no. 4, 1983.

Chandler, A., Jr., *Strategy and Structure: Chapters in the History of The American Industrial Enterprise*, MIT Press, 1962.

Churchman, C. W., *The Systems Approach*, Delacorte Press, 1968.

Diffenbach, J., 'Corporate Environmental Analysis in large US Corporations', *Long Range Planning*, vol. 16, no. 3, 1983, pp. 107–16.

Dill, W.R., 'Environment as an influence on Management Activity', *Administrative Science Quarterly*, vol. 13, March 1958.

Fahey, L., King, W. R. and Narayanan, V. K., 'Environmental Scanning and Forecasting in Strategic Planning – The State of the Art', *Long Range Planning*, vol. 14, no. 1, February 1981, pp. 32–9.

Glueck, W. F. and Jauch, L. R., *Business Policy and Strategic Management*, McGraw Hill, 1984.

Goldsmith W. and Clutterbuck, D., *The Winning Streak*, Weidenfeld and Nicolson, 1985.

Hooley, G. J., West, C. J. and Lynch, J. E., *Marketing in the UK. A survey of current practice and performance*, Institute of Marketing, 1983.

Hunsicker, J. Q., 'The Malaise of Strategic Planning', *The Management Review*, March 1980, p. 8–14.

Jain, S. G., *Marketing Planning and Strategy*, 2nd Ed., South-Western Publishing Company, 1985, p. 250.

Kast, F. E., and Rosenzweig, J. E., *Organisation and Management: A Systems Approach*, 2nd Ed., McGraw Hill, 1974.

Lenz, R. T. and Lyles, M. A., 'Paralysis by Analysis: Is your Planning System becoming too Rational?', *Long Range Planning*, vol. 18, no. 4, 1985, pp. 64–72.

Levitt, T., *The Marketing Imagination*, Free Press, 1983.

Lorenz, C., *The Design Dimension: Product Strategy and the Challenge of Global Marketing*, Blackwell, 1986.

Mason, E., 'Price and production policies of large-scale enterprises', *American Economic Review*, 29, 1939, pp. 61–74.

Ohmae, K. *The Mind of the Strategist: Business Planning for Competitive Advantage*, Penguin, 1983.

Peters, T. and Waterman, R., *In Search of Excellence. Lesson from America's Best Run Companies*, Harper and Row, 1982.

Stubbart C., 'Are Environmental Scanning Units Effective?', *Long Range Planning*, vol. 15, no. 3, June 1982, pp. 139–45.

Taylor, B. and Ferro, L., 'Key Social Issues for European Business', *Long Range Planning*, vol. 16, no. 1, 1983, pp. 42–69.

Thomas, P. S., 'Environmental Scanning – the State of the Art', *Long Range Planning*, vol. 13, no. 1, February 1980, pp. 20–28.

7
Consumer behaviour

GORDON R. FOXALL

Introduction

Marketing management inevitably rests upon some conception or other of how customers behave and of the consequences their reactions to product, price, promotional and distribution strategies are likely to have for the attainment of corporate objectives. In affluent, competitive economies, successful marketing depends above all on matching the marketing mix which results from the integration of these strategies to the willingness of consumers to buy and on doing so more effectively than one's rivals. The consumer-orientated management which results from such matching is a response to the enormous discretion exercised by purchasers in these economies. Moreover, the choices made by consumers have consequences not merely for competing companies within a given, traditionally-defined industry; because of the high levels at which discretionary income is running, companies are increasingly forced to compete across the conventional boundaries of markets and industries. An increase in income or wealth, say, through maturing of an endowment policy, might be put towards a second home or a new car, or spent outright on a new wardrobe, school fees or landscape gardening. Some or all of it might be saved. The provider of each of these services competes not with known rivals in the same trade or profession but with each of the others, whose disparate businesses involve entirely separate responses to the creation and fulfilment of demand. The scale and nature of consumer choice are nowadays such that the survival and growth of firms depends upon marketing managers having a thorough and accurate understanding of their customers' behaviour.

In the marketing context, the term 'consumer behaviour' refers not only to the act of purchase itself but to any prepurchase and postpurchase activities which are of interest to the marketing manager. Prepurchase activity might consist of the growing awareness of a need or want, and a search for and evaluation of information about the products and brands that might satisfy it. Postpurchase activities include the evaluation of the purchased item in use and the reduction of any anxiety which accompanies the purchase of expensive and infrequently-bought items like consumer durables. Each of these has implications for purchase and repurchase and they are amenable in differing degrees to marketer influence. Engel, *et al.* (1986, p. 5) define consumer behaviour as 'those acts of individuals directly involved in obtaining, using, and disposing of economic goods and services, including the decision processes that precede and determine these acts'. Simple observation provides limited insight into the complex nature of consumer choice and researchers have increasingly sought the more sophisticated concepts and methods of investigation provided by the behavioural sciences in order to understand, predict and possibly control consumer behaviour more effectively. Psychology, social psychology and sociology are the disciplines most widely employed in this endeavour which has become a substantial academic industry in its own right.

Whole volumes are devoted to the presentation of the results of this research activity and succinct summaries are also available. This chapter seeks to avoid the duplication of these sources by delineating carefully the scope of the research findings it discusses. The themes covered embrace the broad components of consumer research – individual consumer decision making, patterns of aggregate buying behaviour over time, and personal determinants of choice and style of decision making. But the topics which illustrate them have been chosen deliberately in order to exemplify the current status of consumer research as a subdiscipline of marketing and to show how relevant consumer research can be to the practice of marketing.

Academic consumer research has been successfully applied in marketing in numerous ways, some of which are described in this chapter. But, overall, the effort expended by consumer researchers has not been matched in the quality and quantity of applicable insights and techniques made available to managers. Behavioural scientists in marketing have generally assumed that what they take to be the rational process of consumer decision making can be explained and predicted by means of concepts derived from the mainstream disciplines and have proceeded to investigate consumer choice in terms of cognition, perception, attitudes, personality traits, learning and memory and so on (from psychology) and social class, group dynamics, culture and so on (from social psychology and sociology). But, on the whole, they have been more effective in putting forward conceptual propositions and grand-theoretical comprehensive models than in conducting empirical research appropriate to establishing bases for both the refinement of academic theories and practical marketing planning and operations (Foxall, 1980a; Jacoby, 1978). Even in standard texts, it is not unusual for authors to discuss at length the potential of concepts such as attitudes and personality for consumer research and marketing decision making, only to conclude somewhat wistfully that the necessary links between these concepts and managerially-relevant aspects of consumer choice have yet to be convincingly demonstrated.

Sometimes the conclusion they draw is that concepts like these should be abandoned because of the lack of their demonstrable contribution to understanding or action. But such dire conclusions are avoided in this chapter. First, it argues that the established models of the rational, highly involved consumer should not be abandoned but that consumer researchers should seek to understand better its highly limited scope of application and, similarly, examine the value of alternative, low involvement approaches. In this way, it stresses the situation-specific nature of consumer behaviour which is often neglected. Second, it presents research evidence of useful links between personality and consumption, demonstrating that when the level of analysis and measure of personality are appropriate, and where the research questions are not naive, managerially-useful results can be obtained from the application of behavioural science to marketing. Third, it returns to consumer decision-making, linking it to consumers' personality-based determinants of preferences for quite different styles of problem-solving. This discussion of consumers' cognitive styles is illustrated by recent findings with respect to consumer innovativeness which demonstrates again the value of carefully planned and executed behavioural research for managerial decision making.

Consumer decision making

Several attempts were made during the 1960s to integrate the various partial theories, unrelated research findings and behavioural science concepts which had previously been presented rather haphazardly into general explanatory frameworks which could be used by academics (and sometimes managers) to understand and predict consumer behaviour. Economists, who had previously dominated model-building in this area, generally considered consumer behaviour in terms of a single act, the act of purchase itself, and post-purchase reactions. The three major 'comprehensive' models of consumer decision making (Nicosia, 1966; Engel *et al.*, 1968; Howard and Sheth, 1969) attempt to trace the psychological state of individual purchasers from the point at which they become aware of the possibility of satisfying a material need by purchasing and consuming a product to their final evaluation of the consequences of having done so.

The comprehensive models assume that observed consumer behaviour is preceded by intrapersonal psychological states or events (attitudes, intentions, and so on) in terms of which it may be both described and explained. Moreover, they depict these psychological events as the outputs of the processing of information, taking for granted that consumers seek and use information as part of their rational problem-solving and decision making processes. Thus, in his 'bare bones', summative representation of consumer decison making, Howard (1983) accepts that buyer behaviour is 'largely determined by how the customer thinks and processes information'. The central causal chain of his summative consumer decision model is the familiar information–attitude–intention–purchase sequence assumed by the comprehensive models. All of the models which have been described are founded upon such a rational decision sequence. They credit consumers with considerable capacities for receiving and handling quantities of information and undertaking extensive prepurchase searches and evaluations. They rely heavily upon the idea of cognitive decision making in which information is received and classified by the individual and, via mental processing, transformed into the attitudes and intentions which determine brand choice and related aspects of purchase and consumption. Consumer information processing has sometimes been described as analogous with that of computers; the consumer has been depicted in terms of a 'central control unit' and the cognate elements of information technology. Whatever the details of explanation, however, hypothesized decision makers use evaluation criteria to predict the outcomes of each available option in terms of their objectives; employ decision rules or other methods of comparative evaluation in order to decide upon a course of action; receive and process information, storing it in and retrieving it from memory – all in the course of making a decision or solving a problem before purchasing a brand (Olshavsky and Granbois, 1979; see also McGuire, 1976).

The Nicosia model

In the earliest of the major models, Nicosia considers the manner in which a consumer reacts to news of a new brand. Potential purchasers, previously unaware of the brand's existence, become aware of it by means of a persuasive advertising message. Now aware of a hitherto unnoticed want, they search for and evaluate the alternative means of satisfying it, including the advertised item. The model consists of a flow diagram which also portrays the act of purchase, the consumer's experience gained in using the brand and the feedback which the firm receives through monitoring buyer behaviour.

In the first stage of the decision sequence, the attributes of the firm and of the consumer are understood to determine the advertiser's promotional message and its reception and comprehension by the prospective buyer as it permeates his/her perceptions and predispositions. The consumer is assumed to perceive the physical stimuli presented by the message, and to employ conscious or unconscious cognitive processes in order to interpret and attach meaning to them. This procedure is known as internalization and may result in the formation of an attitude towards the advertised brand. If it does, the sequence continues.

In the second stage, consumers' attitudes towards the product are assumed to determine the nature of their search and evaluation behaviour as they identify and appraise alternative brands. The search process may involve the internal retrieval from memory of information about similar acts of purchase and consumption undertaken previously, the reputation of the manufacturer and retailer, and so on, which creates a psychological context for the message. It may also include the external investigation of these factors through advertising messages, window shopping, other consumers, etc. The process of search may result in consumers being motivated to purchase the item. Assuming that this is the case, the model considers the circumstances under which the motivation to buy actually prompts purchase. Whether or not it does so depends upon situational factors including the availability of the advertised and alternative brands, in-store prompts (such as point-of-sale advertising) and personal selling. Purchase leads on to the storage and/or consumption of the product, the consumer's subsequent judgement of its value and the modification of his/her atittude towards it. The experience of purchase and consumption modifies the customer's psychological state, while the feedback of consequential market intelligence to the firm completes the model by altering the firm's attributes.

The Engel–Kollat–Blackwell model

The model of consumer behaviour originated and developed by Engel *et al.* (1968) has been developed over the five editions of their standard text. Its central explanatory device is the decision sequence comprising problem recognition, search, alternative evaluation, choice, and outcomes. The recognition of a problem may result from internal factors such as changes in motivation or from external information from advertisements or personal selling; in either case, it is consumers' perception of a discrepancy between their actual situation and an ideal which prompts further action. The consumer's first decision is to search for information, internally from memory, externally from such buyer-dominated sources as neighbours and friends who might have bought similar products/brands to that in question and from market-dominated sources like advertisements. The search process identifies several possible sources of resolution of the problem and the consumer next evaluates the alternatives, setting evaluative criteria by which products and brands can be compared in terms of desired outcomes or goals. The products of this decision process are the beliefs, attitudes and intentions which influence choice.

Problem recognition, search and evaluation are aided by an active information processing sequence involving exposure, attention, comprehension, yielding/acceptance, and retention. All of this activity is supported by the functioning of short- and long-term memories. Choice, determined by the outcome of the information process-aided decision sequence may have satisfying or dissonant outcomes for the consumer which influence future purchasing. Engel and Blackwell (1982) also point out that environmental influences may affect the decision sequence acting on the consumer's motivation and intention, and that unpredictable factors (such as the non-availability of the desired brand or insufficient funds) may result in modification of the actual choice made by the customer.

The Howard-Sheth Model

This model comprises four sets of variables: the inputs, stimuli which inaugurate the process of buyer behaviour; perceptual constructs, hypothetical factors which explain the cognitive activity of consumers in terms of information processing; learning constructs, which signify the products of information processing; and outputs, not only purchase itself but its perceptual and learning correlates. The inputs consist of commercial and social stimuli which impinge upon consumers. The model divides them into three classes: significative inputs are such factors as quality, price, distinctiveness, service and availability as they influence the consumer directly through the attributes of the product; symbolic inputs relate to the same factors as they are portrayed in the mass media and by sales people and thus influence consumers indirectly; and social inputs include family, reference group and social class influences which consumers internalize before they can affect the decision process. The effects of these stimuli on the individual's perceptual field include 'stimulus ambiguity' (feelings of dissonance and uncertainty which is reduced by a search for additional information) and 'perceptual bias' (which results from the consumer fitting the available information into his/her existing mental set). In the process of learning, consumers' motives, attitudes, and comprehension of the product determine the degree of confidence they have in the item, their purchase intentions and their actual purchase behaviour. The extent to which buyers are satisfied with their purchase feeds back as modifying information which affects their attitudes, confidence and purchase intentions.

Evaluation

The comprehensive models have been criticised on several counts (see, for example, Foxall, 1980b; Lunn, 1971; Robertson, 1974; Tuck, 1976). One of the most widespread criticisms has been that the models assume too rational a consumer and that observed consumer behaviour does not resemble that which they describe. Atkin (1984, p. 210) describes the way in which models of this type portray the consumer who is persuaded by advertising to choose a particular brand. The consumer is typically depicted as 'devoting attention to the ad, critically perceiving the content (perhaps derogating the source, ignoring certain appeals and challenging some arguments), evaluating the personal relevance of the benefits offered, forming an attitude, and executing a purchase.' The models suggest that consumers are highly involved with the advertising message, able to detect important differences between branded versions of the same product, and that they become committed to one or other brand because its unique attributes are significant to the consumer. When the prospective buyer is confronted with numerous alternative brands, he/she experiences inner conflict which can only be reduced by cognitive activity (Hansen, 1976). Only after having made many purchases do customers reach the stage of being able to make routine responses and when they do so they are assumed to favour a single brand each time they buy (Howard and Sheth, 1969).

Although the models reviewed above have proved useful in educational settings as means of organizing disparate knowledge, each depicts a somewhat arbitrary arrangement of psychological, social, economic and behavioural variables, providing a plausible but untestable view of consumer behaviour. Explanations of this kind could be replicated almost endlessly, each version showing a unique arrangement of explanatory constructs encircling the ubiquitous attitude – intention – behaviour sequence. Each version would be as feasible as any other in the absence of clear-cut rules for making the constructs operational and testable. The comprehensive modeller's keenness to present schemes which generate 'fruitful hunches, ideas and new hypotheses' appears to have led to looseness and vagueness of exposition rather than to the development of empirically testable hypotheses (Tuck, 1976).

What empirical testing of relationships drawn from the models has proved possible has had disappointing results. The Engel–Kollat–Blackwell model was never intended to be tested in this way but a derivative of the Howard–Sheth model was the subject of an extensive research project (Farley et al., 1974). Of the thirty-seven separate tests involved, only twenty-four generated any positive evidence for the model; most of these dealt, however, with parts of the model rather than the whole thing. Moreover, what evidence exists for the model

is 'highly fragmentary, based for the most part on bivariate relations'. None of the relationships tested was confirmed by all the studies which dealt with it and no study shows other than a weak relationship (Holbrook, 1974). Whether the reason for the poor results is that the posited relationships do not hold or that the model is not sufficiently well-specified to enable better testing to take place is an open question. The development of alternative models based on different assumptions about the nature of consumer choice is indicated and has received a major impetus with the wider recognition that consumer behaviour should be depicted as uninvolving or, at least, much less involving than the comprehensive modellers assumed.

Low involvement consumer behaviour

At about the time that the comprehensive models were coming into being, Krugman (1965) suggested that television advertising does not create strong prepurchase attitudes towards purchase but at the most small – possibly undetectable – changes in perception. At this stage, advertising does no more than inaugurate a process of slow and unenduring learning which is not sufficient to allow consumers to discriminate between the advertised brand and its competitors. The learning that results from watching televised commercials is, like the learning of things that are nonsensical or unimportant, uninvolving. It is not until the consumer is in a situation where purchase is possible that this perceptual learning comes to the fore and makes brand differentiation possible. If attitudes are formed at all during this process, it is after purchase and consumption have taken place. Even then, because of the low level of personal concern usually evoked by specific brands within a product class, brand attitudes are likely to be extremely weak.

A television viewer's degree of involvement in what he/she is watching is defined by Krugman in terms of the number of connections he/she makes mentally and unconsciously between what is being watched and his/her personal experience. Robertson (1976) uses the term commitment to denote his mental reaction to a brand (rather than an item of mass communication); an individual's commitment to a brand is a function of his/her perception of the number and salience of the attributes which allow him/her to discriminate between it and other similar brands. There is evidence that under conditions of low media involvement/low brand commitment consumers:

- Make far less use of information than the comprehensive models suggest.
- Show little sign of prepurchase decision making based upon the rational processing of information.
- Use brand trial in order to obtain information about and evaluate brands.
- Exhibit multibrand purchasing within a small repertoire of brands which share attributes (or characteristics) which are common to all members of their product class.

Limited prepurchase information processing and decision making

Consumer research conducted over the last decade or so suggests strongly that consumers have very limited capacities for receiving and using information, that they do not as a rule undertake rational, comparative evaluations of brands on the basis of their attributes or make final judgements among brands on the basis of such outputs of complex information processing as attitudes and intentions. From an empirical investigation of consumers' understanding and use of additional information about the nutritional value of food products, provided on the product labels, Jacoby *et al.* (1977) concluded that 'the vast majority of consumers neither use nor comprehend nutrition information in arriving at food purchase decisions'. An earlier study (Jacoby *et al.*, 1975) reached the conclusion that, whilst the increased availability of information led to consumers' reporting greater satisfaction and less confusion, it also resulted in their making less economically rational decisions. This is not to argue against the provision of information: presumably consumers need to be educated in its uses and benefits (cf. Scammon, 1977). But it does suggest that the idea that consumers are natural information devourers should be qualified.

Consumers' comparatively small use of prepurchase information is not confined to the situations in which they purchase nondurables such as food. Olshavsky and Granbois (1979) and Robertson (1976) cite numerous studies which indicate that consumers drastically limit their search for information about durable products like furniture and cars, and services such as those of general practitioners. Most visit a single store, failing to consult advertising, using restricted price information, considering only one make, and employing perceptions of the manufacturer's reputation, and packaging rather than making evaluations of the product/service attributes to arrive at judgements of quality. The whole decision sequence assumed in comprehensive modelling appears to be absent from many instances of consumer buying. Situational variables, group pressures and the physical arrangement of instore displays influence consumer choice at the point of sale. Many purchases of a make or brand seem not to be preceded by a decision process at all, even on the first occasion (Olshavsky and Granbois, 1979). There is also evidence that the expected outcomes of rational decision making – such as strong brand attitudes – are not present even when products have been purchased on many occasions (Lastovicka and Bonfield, 1982; Foxall, 1983, 1984a).

Brand evaluation through trial

Some early models of consumer response to advertising failed to distinguish trial from repeat purchase: they depict the effects of advertising in terms of a sequence of prepurchase mental states which apparently culminates in the habitual purchase of the promoted brand. Lavidge and Steiner (1961) portray this 'hierarchy of effects' sequence as awareness–knowledge –liking –preference –conviction–purchase, while Colley (1961) speaks of a 'marketing spectrum' which involves unawareness – awareness – comprehension – conviction – action. These models suggested that consumers' evaluations of competing brands could be carried out even before a purchase had been made on the basis of information supplied by the marketer. The comprehensive models are more sophisticated than this, recognizing the importance of repeat buying and the consequences of initial purchase and consumption for subsequent purchase behaviour. But they continue to accent the prepurchase psychological processing of information, especially that supplied by producers, as customers' primary method of evaluating brands. Where there is low commitment to

Table 7.1 *Duplications for Kelloggs brands*

Weeks 1–13		Corn Flakes	Rice Krispies	Special K	Raisin Bran	Froot Loops	Bran Flakes
		\multicolumn{6}{c}{% who also bought Kelloggs}					
Buyers of							
Nabisco Shredded Wheat	%	33	29	18	13	5	5
Kelloggs Corn Flakes	%	(100)	27	13	12	7	5
Kelloggs Rice Krispies	%	29	(100)	18	14	10	5
Kelloggs Special K	%	22	26	(100)	16	6	6
Kelloggs Raisin Bran	%	30	31	24	(100)	6	5
Kelloggs Froot Loops	%	27	33	14	9	(100)	4
Kelloggs Bran Flakes	%	28	27	23	11	5	(100)
Average Kelloggs brand*	%	27	29	18	12	7	5

* Excluding the 100%s.

Source: A.S.C. Ehrenberg and G.J. Goodhardt, *Understanding Buyer Behavior*, Wiley, 1988.

brands, however, it is customers' experience with the brand, their use of it during a period of trial which might involve one or several purchases, which determines whether or not that brand becomes part of the repertoire from which they buy regularly. Ehrenberg and Goodhardt (1980) present a simplified model of consumer behaviour which contains three phases of purchasing and consuming – awareness, trial and repeat buying. Simple as this appears, it has proved a valuable device in both theoretical debate and commercial research (e.g. Ehrenberg, 1974; Tauber, 1981). Repeat buying, which is of enormous significance to the success of consumer goods, is shown as a function of trial purchase and consumption. Trial itself is a function of awareness. The awareness trial and repeat buying approach emphasizes that awareness of a new brand, and any other mental states it engenders, are not alone sufficient to guarantee the adoption (repeat purchase) of the advertised brand. Rather, awareness results at best in curiosity and trial, and it is only when the brand is in use that evaluations and comparisons are possible.

Multibrand purchasing

Most non-durable product classes comprise several brands which are so similar to each other in terms of their basic attributes that consumers do not discriminate among them. Thus it is hardly suprising that consumers do not on the whole show total loyalty to any one brand but select from a small set of tried and tested brands which are close substitutes. There is a great deal of evidence that consumers behave in this manner. The markets for established non-durable products are characterized typically by more or less stable sales, at least in the short to medium term; the buying behaviour of individuals usually involves several brand choices but the aggregate level of market sales and brand shares is stable and predictable. Customers may change brands often – the vast majority frequently do make substitutions – but not in the sense of irrevocably switching brands, never again buying that which is 'rejected' (Ehrenberg, 1972). Buyers of a given product class typically choose several brands over a sequence of purchases. Table 7.1 summarizes this multibrand purchasing for ready-to-eat breakfast cereals over a typical quarter year. Various proportions of those respondents who purchased Nabisco Shredded Wheat during this period also purchased other brands during the same thirteen weeks. Similar duplication of purchasing is also apparent for the other brands. There is no indication here that the majority of consumers are brand loyal in the sense of always purchasing a particular brand. Nor is any brand segmentation suggested. Consumers buy brands from their repertoire, 'some perhaps less often than others, but each fairly consistently over time' (Ehrenberg and Goodhardt, 1988). In the absence of some radical change in the behaviour of a manufacturer – such as the introduction of a more acceptable brand into a complacent market – patterns of repeat buying tend to be predictable in the aggregate even though individual customers appear to be buying haphazardly from week to week or month to month.

The incursions of Rowntree's Yorkie into the moulded chocolate bar market and Tetrosyl's Tetrion into the do-it-yourself filler market are obvious examples of abrupt changes in consumer behaviour but they are the exceptions rather than the rule. Some consumers, of course, are totally loyal in the sense that they buy only one brand and never try its competitors; but they make up only a small proportion of most markets.

Summing up

The major implication of this discussion is that consumer researchers should recognize more readily the variety inherent in consumer decision making and explore the domains of applicability of the comprehensive and other models of choice. This requires not so much a radical conceptual departure as a re-emphasis on the establishment of a plurality of frames of reference based on the situational determinants of choice. In the book that introduced their model, Howard and Sheth (1969) noted that consumer decision making differs according to the strength of attitude towards the available brands in a product class. Extended problem solving occurs when attitude strength is low, when the product class under consideration is poorly defined and when consumers are unable to discriminate among the available brands. Consumers actively seek information in order to reduce their high brand ambiguity and engage in extensive deliberations before purchasing, considering many brands before deciding which to buy. They are heavily dependent upon advertising which is powerful in prompting purchases. At a later stage, having tried some brands within that product class, consumers develop a moderately-strong attitude towards brands and, although there is still some ambiguity about their attributes and capabilities, and still some consequent search for information, choice criteria are shaping

up, brand comprehension is increasing and customers know a few brands well, favouring each about equally. This second stage in consumer decison making is called limited problem solving. The third and final stage, routine response behaviour, occurs when consumers have developed strong attitudes towards brands through experience with several. Brand ambiguity is low and buyers are able to dicriminate among brands, showing strong preference for one (or possibly two) within a clearly-defined evoked set. There is little or no external search for information and what does come their way is subject to selective attention and perception. Customers appear to buy on impulse but this is only because they have well-developed predispositions towards the available brands.

Full recognition of the different modes of consumer decision making requires a willingness to employ, as appropriate, different models for each. The aggregate level of analysis employed by Ehrenberg and Goodhardt involves a more descriptive approach of the operation of whole markets rather than an explanatory approach based on individual decision making which is the foundation of the comprehensive models. The aggregate-descriptive approach has also found numerous practical applications in such areas as market evaluation and new product development (Ehrenberg and Goodhardt, 1988). Moreover, consideration of the painstaking empirical research conducted by these authors leads to the conclusion that low involvement is by far the most prevalent mode of consumer choice and that models based on this insight deserve far greater attention than they have hitherto received.

Personality and preference

It is reasonable to suppose that individuals' personalities – their distinctive patterns of outlook, mannerisms and behavioural responses – should influence their product and brand choices, that there should be consistency between buyers' characteristic ways of responding to the environment and their reactions to specific opportunities to purchase and consume. In those situations where consumers carry out extensive prepurchase decision making, their reception and handling of information and the outputs produced in the process would be influenced by their unique pattern of responses. And, in situations from which such extended problem solving were absent, the process of choice would be directly shaped by personality factors.

The possibility of using measures of personality to guide marketing action, for example in segmenting markets psychographically, tailoring new brands to the susceptibilities of innovative consumers, and repositioning mature brands, has encouraged a large volume of research. Few significant relationships which would be of interest to marketing managers resulted from this research which concentrated upon the search for links between aspects of consumer choice (such as brand selection) and highly specific personality traits (such as assertiveness, anxiety, and sociability). Hardly surprisingly, personality research in the marketing context fell into a state of neglect; the number of empirical studies executed dwindled and some consumer behaviour texts omitted the subject altogether. However, the investigation of personality types, broad bundles of complementary traits which describe an individual's general pattern of behavioural response (e.g. extraversion) has often shown more promise in the quest to describe and predict consumer behaviour.

Personality is generally understood as a concept which accounts for the apparent consistencies and regularities of behaviour over time and across a variety of situations (Pervin, 1984). As such, personality constructs explain those aspects of behaviour which are relatively stable across situations and, as a result, predictive of future behaviour. Personality has also been understood as the 'unique way in which traits, attitudes, aptitudes, etc. are organized in an individual' (Marx and Hillix, 1979) and this draws attention to the ways in which individuals differ from one another through the peculiar configuration of traits and other characteristics each possesses. Marketing interest in the study of personality derives however, from the possibility that, in spite of their uniqueness as individuals, members of groups and aggregates may possess a given trait or type in common with each other; such groupings might then become the basis of separate market segments and justify special marketing action. While individuals might not always be uniform and predictable in their patterns of choice in different situations, it might be possible to make sense of and to forecast the general reactions of broadly-defined groups and classes of purchaser.

Personality research in marketing

For many years, consumer researchers failed to find more than a handful of significant relationships between measures of personality and aspects of consumer choice despite a great many empirical investigations. Particularly disappointing was the fact that personality measures often turned out to be less accurate predictors of consumer behaviour than more traditional segmentation variables such as social class, age and previous patterns of choice. The following selective review of the resulting literature provides the flavour of this short-lived but intensive research programme.

Two classic studies which attempted to link traits of personality with product use concern the ownerships of different brands of motor car. Both investigations were carried out in the US and, among other things, involve car owners' preferences for Fords or Chevrolets. Evans (1959) cites as the stimulus for his research the fact that, while mechanically and in terms of design, these makes of car were almost identical, advertisers had tried to create very different brand images for each, based on what they assumed were the profiles of car buyers. Likely Ford owners were popularly portrayed as independent, impulsive, masculine and self-confident, while probable Chevrolet buyers were presented as conservative, thrifty, prestige-conscious, less masculine, and moderate. A standard personality test (the Edwards personal preference schedule) was administered to respondents who owned one or other of these makes of car in order to measure these personality traits and any others that might be relevant.

On the basis of the personality test scores alone Evans successfully predicted whether an individual owned a Ford or a Chevrolet in 63 per cent of cases, just 13 per cent more than would have resulted from a chance allocation of the respondents to ownership of one or other make. Using only socioeconomic measures, he was able to make correct predictions of 70 per cent of the respondents' ownership patterns. The result of a third and final trial in which he used a combination of both measures, failed to increase the accuracy of his allocation of the respondents beyond that of the first trial based on personality measures alone. Clearly, measures of personality show little promise for the segmentation of the particular submarket investigated here. A part rep-

Table 7.2 *Personality traits and product usage*

Product/behaviour	Associated traits(s)	Correlation coefficient
Headache remedies	Ascendency	-0.46
	Emotional stability	-0.32
Acceptance of new fashions	Ascendency	0.33
	Sociability	0.56
Vitamins	Ascendency	-0.33
	Responsibility	-0.30
	Emotional stability	-0.09
	Sociability	-0.27
Cigarettes	None of the four	
Mouthwash	Responsibility	-0.22
Alcoholic drinks	Responsibility	-0.36
Deodorant	None of the four	
Automobiles	Responsibility	0.28
Chewing gum	Responsibility	0.30
	Emotional stability	0.33

Source: Derived from W.T. Tucker and J.J. Painter, 'Personality and product use', *Journal of Applied Psychology*, 45, 1961.

Table 7.3 *Personality and product choice: some examples*

Product/brand	Traits	Results
(a) Fords/Chevrolets	Achievement, defence, exhibition, autonomy, affiliation, intraception, dominance, abasement, change, heterosexuality, aggression.	Allowed correct prediction of 13 per cent more buyers' choices than random allocation alone would give.
(b) Car types	Activeness, vigour, impulsiveness, dominance, stability, sociability, reflectiveness.	'No personality differences between Ford and Chevrolet owners'. Low activity related to low convertible ownership.
(c) Magazines	Sex, dominance, achievement, assistance.	Less than 13 per cent of purchase behaviour variance explicable in terms of personality for magazines or cigarettes.
Cigarettes	Dominance, aggression, change, autonomy.	
(d) Toilet tissue	Forty-five traits	Personality of no value in prediction of brand loyalty, number of units purchased or colour of tissue.
(e) Private brands	Enthusiasm, sensitivity, submissiveness.	Less than 5 per cent of purchase variance explained by these three traits; other traits of no value.

Source: Derived from F. Evans, 'Psychological and objective factors in the prediction of brand choice', *Journal of Business*, 39, 1959; R. Westfall, 'Psychological factors in predicting brand choice', *Journal of Marketing*, 26, 1962; A. Koponen, 'Personality characteristics of purchasers', *Journal of Advertising Research*, 1, 1960; Advertising Research Foundation, *Are There Consumer Types'?* ARF., 1964; J.G. Myers, 'Determinants of private brand attitude', *Journal of Marketing Research*, 4, 1967.

lication of this research by Westfall (1962) which used an alternative test of personality, the Thurstone temperament schedule, also failed to distinguish satisfactorily between Ford and Chevrolet owners.

Although cars have featured in a number of surveys, a wide range of products and brands has been included in tests of consumers' personality traits and marketplace choices. Tables 7.2 and 7.3 show some of the results which can be summarized as follows: there is a mass of evidence that personality traits are linked with product and brand choice but the statistical associations produced by researchers are, in the main, very weak. Correlation coefficients of the order of $r = 0.3$ or below are extremely common in studies of this kind, indicating that personality traits account only marginally for patterns of consumer choice and that they are unlikely to provide a general basis for managerial action. The vast majority of the many dozens of investigations which have sought to measure the association of personality with product and brand choice have been summed up by Kassarjian and Sheffet (1982) who comment that 'if correlations do exist they are so weak as to be questionable or perhaps meaningless'.

There are several reasons for the poor showing of consumer research in this field which derive principally from the insensitivity of many researchers to the theoretical and methodological implications of personality testing in the context of marketing. Consumer researchers have generally appropriated standard psychometric tests from other areas of behavioural research and practice even though such tests often produce valid and reliable results only within their original spheres of application – frequently the clinical settings within which the psychologists who devised them worked. On the whole, the validity and reliability of the tests employed had not been established either in the context of economic behaviour or across a sufficiently wide range of human behaviours and situations to justify the tests' application in consumer research. Ignoring the theory-ladenness and methodological etiquette inherent in the test instruments they have 'borrowed', several researchers have arbitrarily amended inventories and assumed that their sensitivity, established in one realm of investigation, will transfer automatically to another, quite disparate, research domain. As Kassarjian (1971) pointed out in his first review of the accumulated empirical evidence, it is remarkable that investigations in which personality constructs were 'taken out of context and studied independently of other cognitive or physical variables' managed to account for as much as 5 to 10 per cent of the variance in observed consumer behaviour.

Another factor which accounts for the poor performance of previous research is the level of analysis at which so much of it proceeded. Many researchers have sought strong relationships between traits of personality which can vary so much from individual to individual and which are usually broadly defined, and precise aspects of consumer choice such as brand choices which are frequently highly situation-specific and precise. This optimistic approach was never likely to do justice to the general proposition that personality and purchase/consumption choices are consistently related.

The possibility that trait theorists have been looking in the wrong place for applicable information has led some researchers to substitute personality type variables in their marketing investigations.

Many of the results of this work have been rather more encouraging for consumer research. Cohen (1968), for instance, used the research framework derived by Karen Horney from her psychoanalytical work, which classifies individuals as compliant, aggressive or detached types. Compliant individuals are anxious to be with others, to receive love and recognition, help and guidance. Such needs may make them overgenerous and oversensitive so that they shy away from criticism and allow others to dominate them. They are essentially conformists. Aggressive people tend to be achievement-orientated, desire status and see life as a competitive game. They seek the admiration of others by being outgoing in their behaviour and often display 'leadership qualities'. Finally, detached individuals try to separate themselves from others both emotionally and behaviourally: they do not seek responsibility or obligations and do not try to impress.

In practice, of course, individuals possess traits derived from each of these types but they tend, nevertheless, to score more highly on one dimension and can be categorized accordingly since the three types contain sufficient unique traits to be conceptually distinct from the others. In consumer tests, Cohen was able to match these personality types with product/brand preferences and usage rates. For instance, highly compliant people were more likely than less compliant individuals to use mouthwash, to prefer Dial soap, and to drink wine at least several times each month. Those respondents scoring high on aggression bought more men's deodorants (preferring Old Spice) than low scorers on this dimension. Both compliant and detached people drank tea rather more frequently than aggressives. Specific preferences for TV programmes and magazines were also identified. Aggressive individuals, for example, preferred exciting programmes such as *The Untouchables* and *The Fugitive* and magazines like *Playboy* and *Field and Stream*. Compliant individuals chose programmes such as *Dr Kildare* and *Bonanza* and typically read *Readers' Digest*. The detached respondents had more mixed and ambivalent preferences.

It is important to note that Cohen found no statistically significant relationships for a range of products including cigarettes, dress-shirts, men's hairdressing, toothpaste, beer, diet products and headache remedies. Nevertheless, this study tends to resurrect the concept of personality as a possibly useful variable for consumer research, at least at the level of the type. Another typology of behavioural types is found in Riesman's *The Lonely Crowd*, a research-based work which classifies individuals in terms of their broadly-based social character. Three such classifications are suggested: tradition-direction, the orientation of individuals whose values and behaviour are rooted in the past, inner-direction, shown by those who have a strong personal sense of correct behaviour, and other-direction, exhibited by those whose cues for behaving in particular ways, whose values and attitudes, are largely acquired from others. Kassarjian (1965) conducted an experiment based on the last two of these categories (reasoning that tradition-direction would not be important among the American college students who were the subjects). He constructed pairs of advertisements for a given product or service such that in each pair one advertisement contained a built-in inner-directed appeal, the other an other-directed appeal. Respondents tended to choose the advertisements which corresponded to their social character as the most likely to influence them. Both groups expressed the view that most people were likely to be influenced by other-directed appeals, though neither group showed greater or significantly different media exposure or preferences.

While neither of these pieces of research suggests a breakthrough in consumer research, they do indicate that personality types provide a more appropriate level of analysis than do traits, and that the investigators were using psychometric tests of greater relevance to the economic behaviour involved in consumer choice. Further evidence that when appropriate tests are applied in consumer research and when those tests are applied with theoretical insight and methodological precision, far more useful results for marketing management can be obtained derives from Allsopp's application of Eysenck's measures of personality to beer and cider consumption.

Personality and beer and cider consumption

Allsopp (1986a) employed several personality tests derived from the work of Eysenck (1952, 1960; Eysenck and Eysenck, 1969, 1976) in an investigation of the determinants of on-licence beer and cider consumption among young men in Britain. The research was based on two samples, of 174 apprentice craftsmen who attended college on a block-release or day-release basis, and of 173 full-time students on degree courses in engineering, business, food technology and other subjects. All respondents were males and aged between 18 and 21. Each completed a retrospective diary of their consumption of alcoholic beverages during the week ending the day before the research took place, and answered questions about their general leisure interests and pursuits, in addition to completing tests of the following dimensions of personality.

Extraversion–introversion

Extraverts are sociable, need others to talk to, like excitement, taking risks and are active and impulsive; introverts, by contrast, are quiet and retiring, reserved and cautious (Eysenck and Eysenck, 1975). The expectation was that high scorers on the extraversion (E) scale would consume more alcohol than low scorers: the extraverts would be more likely to seek and find stimulation in on-licence alcohol consumption than introverts.

Emotionality

High-scorers on this neuroticism (N) scale are anxious, moody, easily depressed, over emotional, worriers; in short, emotionally unstable. Low scorers, the emotionally stable, are calm and even-tempered, do not worry as a rule and react emotionally only slowly and temporarily. The relationship which should be expected between emotionality and alcohol consumption is unclear from Eysenck's theory. The anxiety which is typical of the higher scorer might manifest in more drinking because of the relaxation this provides; alternatively, it might inhibit drinking in social situations with their peculiar stresses.

Tough-mindedness

High-scorers on the psychoticism (P) scale are extremely antisocial, insensitive, even psychotic. While the high range of the scale is suitable for clinical applications, it is not directly relevant to consumer research. However, the low to medium range of the scale measures degrees of self-centredness, independence, innovativeness, and

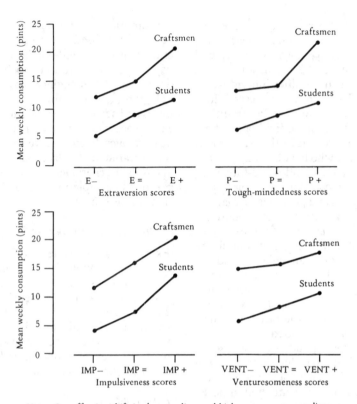

Note: Cut-off points defining low, medium and high scorers on personality scales different for craftsmen and students.

Figure 7.1 *Mean weekly consumption for low, medium and high scorers on four personality scales*
Source: J.F. Allsopp, 'The Distribution of On-licence Beer and Cider Consumption and its Personality Determinants Among Young Men', *European Journal of Marketing*, 20, (3/4), 1986, p. 56.

risk-taking and these are directly relevant (Allsopp, 1986b). The expectation guiding the research was that medium scorers would be greater on-licence consumers of alcohol than low-scorers on account of these characteristics.

Impulsiveness and venturesomeness

Impulsiveness (Imp.) and venturesomeness (Vent.) scales measure personality factors which involve sensation-seeking. They also correlate closely with the E and P dimensions. It was expected that high scorers would consume more alcohol than low scorers.

The results indicate several significant relationships between the personality dimensions investigated and the on-licence consumption of beer

and cider (see Table 7.4). While the levels of correlation are not out of the ordinary for personality research in marketing, the relationships they indicate are strong and enable marketers to make distinctions between groups whose purchase potential differs importantly. The results for emotionality (N) are not significant – perhaps the two theoretically possible effects cancelled each other out. Nor is the correlation of Vent. scores and consumption significant in the craftsmen sample. As the figures show, however, the relationships which are significant indicate strong differences between the higher and lower scorers in the expected directions.

In Figure 7.1, the scores for three subsamples of each of the craftsmen and student samples are shown for the four scales that produced significant results. The three subsamples represent for each sample

Table 7.4 *Correlations between total beer and cider consumption and E, P, N, Imp. and Vent.*

	Craftsmen	Students
E	0.23**	0.29***
P	0.26***	0.33***
N	−0.09	0.04
Imp.	0.28***	0.44***
Vent.	0.06	0.17*

***p<0.001 (two-tailed)
**p<0.01 (two-tailed)
*p<0.025 (two-tailed)

Source: J.F. Allsopp, 'The Distribution of On-Licence Beer and Cider Consumption and its Personality Determinants among Young Men', *European Journal of Marketing*, 20 (3/4), 1986, p. 55.

approximately equal groupings of low, medium, high scorers. In the case of the students, high scorers consume about twice as much as low scorers in the E, P and Vent. scales, and about three times as much on the Imp. scale. Among the craftsmen, high scorers on the E, P and Imp. scales consume about twice as much as the low scorers; in the case of the Vent. scale, where the relationship is non-significant, high-scorers consume about a fifth more than low-scorers.

Figure 7.2 shows the combined effect of the two higher order dimensions, E and P. For both craftsmen and students, the greatest consumption is found among those scoring highest on both scales (E+P+) and the smallest among those with the lowest scores on both scales (E−P−). Among the craftsmen, compared with the lowest scoring group (E−P−), the highest scoring group (E+P+) consume three times as much beer and cider, while the second highest scoring group (E=P+) consumes twice as much as the lowest scoring group. The student sample shows greater differences: the E+P+ group accounts for about three and a half times as much consumption as the E−P− group, while the E=P+ group drinks three times as much as the E−P− group.

Figure 7.3 indicates the levels of consumption reported by the higher scorers on all of the relevant scales. (For this analysis, the samples were each divided into two subsamples of approximately equal size.) In the case of the craftsmen, those scoring high on two or three of the significant scales consumed about twice as much as those scoring high on none or one. In the case of the students, those scoring high on four scales drank about four times as much beer and cider as those scoring high on none.

As Allsopp points out, the results are especially interesting in the design of 'pub atmospheres' since it is reasonable to expect that different personality groups are attracted to quite different physical and social environments. Moreover, the personality types which are clearly related to on-licence alcohol consumption have also been shown to be related to

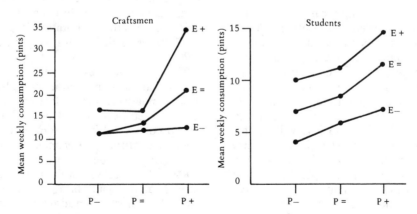

Note: Cut-off points defining low, medium and high scorers on E and P different for craftsmen and students.

Figure 7.2 *Mean weekly consumption for nine personality groups categorized by combinations of extraversion (E) and tough-mindedness (P)*
Source: J.F. Allsopp, *ibid.*, p. 57.

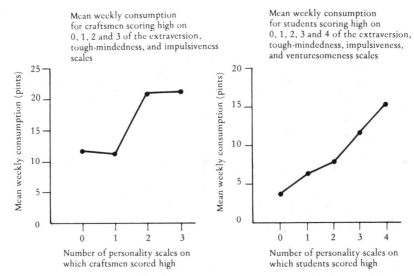

Figure 7.3 *Levels of Consumption reported by higher scoring groups*
Source: J.F. Allsopp, *ibid.*, p. 58.

preferences for specific leisure interests such as sports. This is also relevant to pub marketing and the use of the Eysenck personality questionnaire would also allow pubs to be assessed on whether they were successful in attracting the appropriate customer groups (Allsopp, 1986a).

Cognitive style and consumer innovativeness

The importance of identifying the earliest adopters of innovations has long been apparent to marketing managers. These consumer innovators create the markets for new brands and products by displaying them in use to the majority of the consumers of any brand or product, who are more conservative. These later adopters make up the bulk of most markets, however, and are essential to the commercial success of innovations. While they are less willing than innovators to initiate the diffusion process for new brands and products, they readily adopt items which have been made socially acceptable by others.

Most marketers find it worthwhile to accelerate the diffusion of their innovations and one means of doing this is to minimize the time that elapses between the launch of a new product and its initial acceptance by innovative customers (Baker, 1983). It is necessary, therefore, to tailor the launch

marketing mix of innovations to the requirements and susceptibilities of the primary market composed of these earliest adopters. There are also benefits for the marketer in identifying the potential innovators for his/her new product early in the new product development process in order that such consumers can be adequately represented in concept and product tests. If the potential innovators are not impressed with the innovation, it is unlikely that the social dynamics required for effective diffusion will occur. Care must, therefore, be taken to ensure that their reactions to novel brands/products are heeded at all stages of the innovative sequence (Midgley, 1977).

All of this assumes, of course, that such potential innovators can be identified and by means which make it relatively straightforward and inexpensive for manufacturers to assess their specific reactions to new products. Although some progress has been made in identifying the economic and social characteristics of consumer innovators in general (Foxall, 1984b), the ideal way of doing so for the purposes outlined above would be a psychometric test which isolated potential initial adopters by measuring their unique personality traits or types.

Unfortunately, the comments made above with respect to personality testing in marketing in general apply equally to research which has attempted to

Table 7.5 *Characteristics of adaptors and innovators*

Implications	Adaptors	Innovators
For problem solving	Tend to take the problem as defined and generate novel, creative ideas aimed at 'doing things better'. Immediate high efficiency is the keynote of high adaptors.	Tend to redefine generally agreed problems, breaking previously perceived restraints generating solutions aimed at 'doing things differently'.
For solutions	Adaptors generally generate a few well-chosen and relevant solutions, that they generally find sufficient but which sometimes fail to contain ideas needed to break the existing pattern completely.	Innovators produce numerous ideas many of which may not be either obvious or acceptable to others. Such a pool often contains ideas, if they can be identified, that may crack hitherto intractable problems.
For policies	Prefer well-established, structured situations. Best at incorporating new data or events into existing structures or policies.	Prefer unstructured situations. Use new data as opportunities to set new structures or policies accepting the greater attendance risk.
For organizational 'fit'	Essential to the ongoing functions, but in times of unexpected changes may have some difficulty moving out of their established role.	Essential in times of change or crisis, but may have some trouble applying themselves to ongoing organizational demands.
For potential	The Kirton Inventory is a measure of style but not level or capacity of creative problem solving. Adaptors and innovators are both capable of generating original, creative solutions, but which reflect their different overall approaches to problem solving.	
For collaboration	Adaptors and Innovators do not readily get on, especially if they are extreme scorers. Middle scorers have the disadvantage that they do not easily reach the heights of adaption or innovation as do extreme scorers. This, conversely is a positive advantage in a team where they can more easily act as 'bridgers', forming the consensus group and getting the best (if skilful) out of clashing extreme scorers.	
For perceived behaviour	Seen by Innovators: as sound, conforming, safe, predictable, relevant, inflexible, wedded to the system, intolerant of ambiguity.	Seen by Adaptors: as unsound, impractical, risky, abrasive; often shocking their opposites and creating dissonance.

© Kirton 1985; reproduced with the written permission of M.J. Kirton 1986.

identify consumer innovators psychometrically (Pizzam, 1972; Kassarjian and Sheffet, 1982). Once again, there has been a tendency for researchers to assume naively a simple and direct relationship between personality traits and innovative purchasing, to approach the problem at the wrong level of analysis and to take little care in the selection of appropriate measurement instruments. The expectation that a single trait or even a group of traits would be strongly correlated with innovative adoption but weakly associated with later adoption was surely overoptimistic. However, as the research des-

cribed below indicates, it is possible to identify the psychological make-ups of consumer innovators in managerially useful ways if care is taken in the level of analysis and the test chosen.

Adaptors and innovators

The theory of cognitive style and the measure of adaptive and innovative style of information processing, decision making and problem solving advanced by Kirton (1976, 1977) stand out as relevant to the identification of consumer innovators. Kirton's adaption-innovation theory was developed in the context of economic behaviour in organizations. It proposes that individuals characteristically exhibit one of two distinct styles of problem solving and decision making. Extreme adaptors confine their problem solving endeavours to the frame of reference in which they perceive the problem to have arisen. They tend to produce better ways of accomplishing familiar tasks and their solutions can be unobtrusively implemented within established organizational structures and working practices. Extreme innovators, by contrast, are less likely to seek solutions that can be readily accommodated within the context within which the problem is given. They tend, as a fundamental expression of their problem solving style, to evaluate the frame of reference within which the problem is presented and, as they seek solutions, they redefine and reconstitute both the problem and the context of its origin. Thus they tend to produce different ways of organizing, deciding and behaving which entail radical change, the ramifications of which extend well beyond the initial problem.

The theory assumes that everyone can be placed upon a continuum the polar extremes of which are these extremely adaptive and extremely innovative styles of problem solving. It predicts that adaptors will adopt solutions which improve technical efficiency but involve practices and objects which are similar to those previously employed for the same purpose; solutions by innovations, however, are likely to require some realignment of objectives and plans, and the incorporation of novel activities, techniques and objects (Foxall, 1986c). Table 7.5 summarizes the characteristics of adaptors and innovators and their mutual perceptions.

Since cognitive style is conceptualized as being consistently related to behaviour, it should correlate well with dimensions of personality which have themselves been shown to be stable. The large amount of research which has now been conducted for the Kirton adaption–innovation inventory (KAI) in this regard takes the form of correlations of scores on the KAI and established personality inventories. Such evidence is now available in the form of over sixty correlations, produced by more than twenty independent scholars in some eight countries, involving over twenty different psychological tests (Kirton, 1987a). In summary (Kirton, 1987b):

The innovator tends to be more extravert, less dogmatic, more tolerant of ambiguity, more radical, more flexible, more creatively motivated, more creatively self-perceptive, more assertive, expedient, self-assured, undisciplined, independent and sensation-seeking than the adaptor; with more self-esteem, liable to risk-taking, needing (and liking) less structure, and is more spontaneous. The adaptor is more controlled, less stimulating, more steady, reliable, prudent and probably more often seen as right and dependable, better able to fit into teams, get on with authority, be sensitive to policy and mores; be more realistic, efficient and orderly. Neither type (extreme) is likely to be any more or less neurotic, more or less likely to reach high position (except in conditions unfavourable to type), be more or less intelligent, resourceful, original, creative and generally regarded in worldly terms as successful.

The cognitive styles of adaptors and innovators are measured by the KAI, a psychological test which asks respondents to indicate the degree of ease or difficulty with which they feel they could consistently maintain specified adaptive and innovative behaviours over time (Kirton, 1977). The behaviours which comprise scale items include responding favourably to the stimulation of change and adherence, by preference, to the established rules.

The KAI has been shown to have a high degree of predictive validity in the sphere of economic problem solving (Kirton, 1984, 1987a, 1987b). Moreover, several of the correlates of the KAI listed above are psychological and behavioural factors which have been associated in the diffusion literature with the adoption of new ideas, practices and products. Relative to later adopters, innovators tend to be less dogmatic, more able to cope with abstractions, ambiguity and uncertainty, less fatalistic (and presumably therefore more likely to be flexible, self-controlled and unsubjugated) and higher in achievement motivation and aspiration (Rogers, 1983). Many of the descriptions of innovators in Table 7.5 are thus likely to apply accurately to consumer innovators (Foxall and Haskins, 1986), and the two surveys of innovative purchase which are described below were undertaken on the basis of this expectation.

The first investigation (Foxall and Haskins, 1986) was conducted among a quota sample of 101 female supermarket shoppers in southern England. In addition to completing the KAI questionnaire, each respondent indicated the frequency with which she

Table 7.6 *Product categories for food innovation study*

Group	Criteria	Product classes from which innovative brands were selected
1 'Discontinuous new brands'	KAI mean of buyers of innovative brand is significantly greater than that of non-buyers *and* significantly exceeds that of members of female general population whilst that of non-buyers does not.	Garlic salad dressing. Instant decaffeinated coffee. Low calorie, sugar-free snack biscuit.
2 'Dynamically-continuous new brands'	KAI mean of buyers exceeds that of non-buyers for each brand but not at a significant level; mixed patterns of variation from mean of female general population.	Mixer sherry. Fibre-rich cereal. Reduced fat sausages. Battered haddock steaks. Drinking yoghurt. Savoury wheat crackers.
3 'Continuous new brands'	KAI mean of non-buyers exceeds that of buyers, though the difference is significant only in the case of the cream and vegetable oil spread; KAI mean of non-buyers significantly exceeds that of general female population in each case, while that of buyers does not.	Reduced fat cheddar cheese. Cream and vegetable oil spread. Mixed fruit drink. Cheese sauce granules.

Source: Derived from G.R. Foxall and C.G. Haskins. 'Cognitive Style and Consumer Innovativeness: An Empirical test of Kirton's Adaptation-Innovation Theory in Food Purchasing, *European Journal of Marketing*, 20, (3), 1986, pp. 63–80.

had purchased thirteen new brands of established food products which had been introduced within the preceding four months. In common with most research into personality and consumer choice, only an extremely weak correlation was found between the measure of cognitive style and the number of new brands purchased ($r = 0.09$). However, an independent panel of consumers had rated the thirteen brands in terms of their continuity/discontinuity as compared with established members of the product classes investigated. The definitions of continuity, dynamic continuity and discontinuity employed for this purpose were based on those of Robertson (1967). *Continuous innovations* are least disruptive in their impact on consumption behaviour compared with their current alternatives (for example line extensions and alterations to existing products such as fluoride toothpaste); *dynamically continuous innovations* have some disruptive influence on consumption behaviour but do not change established patterns of behaviour fundamentally (for example an electric toothbrush); and *discontinuous innovations* have considerably disruptive impact on consumption behaviour or are

associated with a basic change in life style or consumption habits (for example new items which are distinct from existing offerings in terms of taste, function or content such as videorecorders or microwave ovens).

When, during the analysis of the results, the thirteen brands were examined in terms of this classification, consumers' KAI responses exhibited the three clear patterns of continuity/discontinuity shown in Table 7.6.

Clearly the discontinuous new brands are purchased by consumer innovators with a tendency towards an innovative cognitive style; continuous new brands by consumer innovators with a tendency towards an adaptive style of decision making and problem solving. A third, intermediate group of new brands (the 'dynamically continuous' innovations) were purchased by consumers whose cognitive styles showed a mixed pattern of adaptiveness and innovativeness.

The success of this two-pronged attempt to uncover links between cognitive style and innovative buying is encouraging. The pattern identified goes beyond the naive assumption that has guided most

Table 7.7 Product categories for healthy eating study

Group	Criteria	Products
1 'Discontinuous new products'	KAI means of buyers of these products is significantly more innovative than that of non-buyers and significantly exceeds that of the female general population.	Wholewheat rice. Wholewheat snack biscuit.
2 'Dynamically-continuous new products'	KAI means of buyers exceeds that of non-buyers for each product but not significantly; for all but two products, KAI means of both buyers and non-buyers significantly exceed that of the female general population.	Wholewheat bread. Low calorie soft drinks. High-fibre cereal. Semi-skimmed milk. Low-fat/low sugar yoghurt. Sunflower margarine. Decaffeinated coffee. Sugar-reduced jam. Tofu. Calorie-reduced salad dressing. Sugar and starch reduced baked beans. Saccharine-free sweetener. 300-calorie meal. Tuna packed in brine.
3 'Continuous new products'	KAI means of non-buyers of each product exceeds that of buyers but none of the differences in means is statistically significant; for five of the eight products, KAI mean of buyers does not differ from that of the female general population.	Calorie-reduced soup. Low-fat sausages. Sunflower cooking oil. Skimmed milk. Low-fat cheese. Wholewheat potato crisps. Low-sodium salt. Low-fat cream.

Source: Derived from G.R. Foxall and C.G. Haskins. 'Cognitive Style and Discontinuous Consumption', *Journal of Food Marketing*, 3(2), 1987, pp. 19–32.

previous research that there would be a simple, direct association of personality factors and purchase by introducing the mediating variable of brand continuity/discontinuity. While the research confirmed the importance of Robertson's qualitative distinction, however, there remained the anomaly that the relationship between cognitive style and the number of innovations purchased was curvilinear. Purchasers of up to three new brands were, on average, adaptive, while purchasers of four or five innovations were innovative. This finding is consistent with the expectation that innovativeness measured by the KAI would be positively related to the degree of consumer innovativeness measured in terms of the number of innovations purchased. However, the mean score of the small number of purchasers of six or more new brands contradicted this in being clearly adaptive.

The second investigation (Foxall and Haskins, 1987) was intended to examine further this result using a larger sample and a larger group of related product innovations. A quota sample of 345 female supermarket consumers supplied information relating to their purchases of so-called 'healthy-foods', products which had been available for some time in specialist health food stores but which had recently been introduced to a wider public through supermarket outlets and heavily promoted as part of a campaign of healthy eating. The products were, therefore, assumed to be novel for the respondents at least in the context of supermarketing and the research was intended to clarify the relationship between cognitive styles and innovative purchases of these products.

Overall there again emerged a weak correlation between innovativeness and purchase ($r = 0.01$) but the twenty-four products examined could once again be categorized according to the degree of continuity/discontinuity suggested by the cognitive styles of respondents. Table 7.7 shows, however, that the relationship is somewhat less clear-cut than in the case of brands. The sample of 'healthy eaters' shows, none the less, a more distinct curvilinear relationship between cognitive style and the number of innovations purchased. The mean KAI score of purchases of up to two new products was distinctly adaptive, while that of purchasers of four to fifteen was distinctly innovative. However, the score of the relatively few purchasers of sixteen or more innovative products was highly adaptive again.

Once the basic assumption that consumer innovators will always be innovators in Kirton's terminology is abandoned, however, the results become far more interesting from the scientific and the practical marketing viewpoint. Innovators would be expected to purchase impulsively, independently, perhaps haphazardly: it is only to be expected that they would choose several innovations experimentally, being attracted mainly towards the more discontinuous items, especially at the brand level where marketers stress the novelty of their offerings in order to distinguish them from the other members of the product class which are likely to be similar if not identical in physical formulation. These innovators are not likely to display the routine purchasing, based on systematic and assiduous searching out of related items. Adaptors, however, can be expected to be suspicious, at least initially, of innovative products or brands. However, it is the adaptor rather than the innovator who is likely to become 'converted' to a way of life which involves purchasing many novel items within a product range – and this is exemplified in the purchase of the largest number of 'healthy-eating' food products by consumers, albeit rather few, whose mean KAI score was quite adaptive. Similarly, in the case of the new brands, the innovator is likely to be a trier, impulsively experimenting but not becoming loyal either to brands or to new brands in general, while those consumers who do become careful searchers for novel foods are more likely to be adaptive.

To summarize, two effects have been found. First, a qualitative difference among innovations, based on their continuity-discontinuity, has been found, confirming Robertson's tripartite classifica-tion and permitting its operational measurement; the purchasers of the more discontinuous innovations tend to be more innovative, while purchasers of the more continuous are adaptive. This qualitative effect is stronger in the case of new brands than products. Second, a quantitative difference in the behaviours of adaptors and innovators is apparent in that the purchase of the largest numbers of innovations is accounted for by consumers who tend towards adaptiveness. This effect is stronger in the case of products.

The results suggest that launch marketing mixes must appeal to both innovators and adaptors who each make further purchasing by later adopters socially acceptable in different ways and to different types of consumer. The importance of the concept of cognitive style is that it links research on consumer decision making with that on personality. Again, it draws attention to the diversity inherent in consumer decision making and explains the underlying ways in which personality influences decison making with respect to new products and brands (Foxall, 1987).

Conclusion

For at least two decades, consumer research has been based on a single model of human choice behaviour which has dominated our ideas of how purchasing and consumption occur. This has led to widespread reliance on the notion of the rational buyer whose behaviour is understood primarily in terms of his/her cognitive processing of information, the outcomes of which are the attitudes and intentions that determine store and brand choice. Perusal of the contents of the main journals in the field (such as the *Journal of Marketing Research* and the *Journal of Consumer Research*) provides evidence that this is where the vast bulk of research effort is concentrated. The perceived failure of this model consistently to deliver accurate predictions of consumer choice at the managerially useful level of the individual brand or store has recently led to interest in non-cognitive theories and frames of reference for the study of consumer choice: for example, psychoanalytical theory (Debraix and Vanden Abeele, 1984), behaviourism (Kassarjian, 1978; Nord and Peter, 1980; Rothschild and Gaidis, 1981; Foxall, 1986a, 1986b); and emotional rather than intellectual depictions of choice (Holbrook and O'Shaughnessy, 1984). This chapter has not pursued these lines of investigation which are anyway at an embryonic stage of development. Rather it has argued that rather than overthrow current understanding of consumer behaviour, it is necessary to evaluate critically the dominant frame of reference in order better to understand its nature and scope, to determine where it applies and, equally important, where alternative approaches should be encouraged. Academic consumer research is undergoing a revolution from within, and in order to maximize the benefits of past research and ensure that useful research is conducted in future, it is necessary to appreciate and appraise both current theory and the results it has spawned.

Therefore, without detracting from the successes of consumer researchers in marketing, this chapter has pointed to some of the biases that have underlain academic research into consumer behaviour. Its main conclusions are as follows. First, although consumer researchers have been successful in constructing models of consumer decision making based on cognitive psychology's insights into human information processing, these have often been untestable and, in any case, applicable to relatively few buying situations (Bagozzi, 1984). Their abstract theoretical nature renders their propositions of limited use to marketing managers. Above all, researchers have failed to specify the range of consumer buying to which the models refer and have generally ignored other forms of less involving choice. Fortunately, other researchers have avoided this highly theoretical approach and have concentrated on the description of buyer behaviour in the aggregate, a strategy which has produced more managerially-relevant results and elucidated aspects of consumer choice which are not apparent from the work of the grand theorists. Secondly, concepts which have obvious relevance to other areas of behavioural science (clinical psychology, for instance) have been enthusiastically and uncritically employed in consumer research. The result of trying to use standard tests of personality in consumer behaviour research has been a host of weak correlations between trait measures and aspects of brand or product choice. Not only have the findings of such research lacked usefulness, they have often led researchers to abandon the attempt to find meaningful relationships.

Most consumer behaviour texts discuss personality, for example, in terms of what might have been but end limply with the sad conclusion that the promised associations with consumer choice have not been discovered. Consumer research that has treated individual concepts as separate entities and failed to integrate them has contributed to this disjointedness. The consumer research discussed in this chapter has demonstrated, however, that this need not be the case if researchers are willing to adopt a more professional approach to the development of their discipline.

References

Allsopp, John F., 'The Distribution of On-Licence Beer and Cider Consumption and its Personality Determinants among Young Men', *European Journal of Marketing*, 20(3/4), 1986a, pp. 44–62.

Allsopp, John F., 'Personality as a Determinant of Beer and Cider Consumption among Young Men', *Personality and Individual Differences*, 7, 1986b, pp. 341–7.

Atkin, C. K., 'Consumer and Social Effects of Advertising', in B. Dervin and M. J. Voigt (eds) *Progress in Communication Sciences*, Ablex, 1984.

Bagozzi, Richard, P., 'A Prospectus for Theory Construction in Marketing', *Journal of Marketing*, 48, 1984, pp.11–29.

Baker, Michael J., *Marketing Development*, Penguin, 1983.

Cohen, Joel B., 'The Role of Personality in Consumer Behaviour', in Harold H. Kassarjian and Thomas S. Robertson (eds), *Perspectives in Consumer Behaviour*, Scott Foresman & Co., 1986, pp. 220–34.

Colley, R. H., *Defining Advertising Goals for Measured Advertising Results*, Association of National Advertisers, 1961.

Debraix, C. and Abeele P. Vanden, 'On the Demise of the Thinking Machine. The non-cognitive revolution in consumer research', paper presented at the EIASM Conference 'New Challenges in Management Research', Leuren, Belgium, 1984.

Ehrenberg, Andrew S. C., *Repeat Buying*. North Holland, 1972.

Ehrenberg, Andrew S. C., 'Repetitive Advertising and the Consumer', *Journal of Advertising Research*, 14, 1974, pp. 25–34.

Ehrenberg, Andrew S. C. and Goodhardt, Gerald J., *How Advertising Works*, JWT/MRCA, 1980.

Ehrenberg, Andrew S.C. and Goodhardt, Gerald J. (with Gordon R. Foxall), *Understanding Buyer Behaviour*, John Wiley, 1988.

Engel, James F. and Blackwell, Roger D., *Consumer Behaviour*, 4th ed., Dryden, 1982.

Engel, James F., Kollat, David T. and Blackwell, Roger D., *Consumer Behaviour*, Holt, Rinehart and Winston, 1968.

Engel, James F., Blackwell, Roger D. and Miniard, Paul W., *Consumer Behaviour*, 5th ed., Dryden, 1986.

Evans, Franklin B., 'Psychological and Objective Factors in the Prediction of Brand Choice: Ford versus Chevrolet', *Journal of Business*, 32, October 1959, pp. 340–69.

Eysenck, Hans J., *The Scientific Study of Personality*, Routledge, 1952.

Eysenck, Hans J. *The Structure of Human Personality*, Methuen, 1960.

Eysenck, Hans J. and Eysenck, Sybil B. G., *Personality Structure and Measurement*, Routledge, 1969.

Eysenck, Hans J. and Eysenck, Sybil B. G., *Manual of the Eysenck Personality Inventory*, London University Press, 1975.

Eysenck, Hans J. and Eysenck, Sybil B. G., *Psychoticism as a Dimension of Personality*, Hodder and Stoughton, 1976.

Farley, John U., Howard, John A. and Ring L. W., (eds), *Consumer Behaviour: Theory and Applications*, Allyn and Bacon, 1974.

Foxall, Gordon R. 'Academic Consumer Research: Problems and Potential', *European Research*, 8, 1980a, pp. 20–3.

Foxall, Gordon R., 'Marketing Models of Buyer Behaviour: A Critical Review', *European Research*, 8, 1980b, pp. 195–206.

Foxall, Gordon R. *Consumer Choice*, Macmillan, 1983.

Foxall, Gordon R., 'Evidence for Attitudinal-Behavioural Consistency: Implications for Consumer Research paradigms', *Journal of Economic Psychology*, 5, 1984a, pp. 71–92.

Foxall, Gordon, R., *Corporate Innovation: Marketing and Strategy*, Croom Helm, 1984b.

Foxall, Gordon R., 'The Role of Radical Behaviourism in the Explanation of Consumer Choice', *Advances in Consumer Research*, XIII, 1986a, pp. 187–91.

Foxall, Gordon, R., 'Theoretical progress in Consumer Psychology: The Contribution of a Behavioural Analysis of Choice', *Journal of Economic Psychology*, 7, 1986b, pp. 293–315.

Foxall, Gordon R., 'Managers in Transition: An Empirical Test of Kirton's Adaption-Innovation Theory and its Implications for the Mid-career MBA', *Technovation*, 4, 1986c, pp. 219–32.

Foxall, Gordon R., 'Consumer Innovativeness: Novelty-seeking, Creativity, and Cognitive Style', in Elizabeth C. Hirschmann (ed.), *Research in Consumer Behaviour*, vol. 3, Greenwich CT: JAI Press, 1987 (in press).

Foxall, Gordon R. and Haskins, Christopher G., 'Cognitive Style and Consumer Innovativeness: An Empirical Test of Kirton's Adaption-Innovation Theory', *European Journal of Marketing*, 20 (3/4), 1986, pp. 63–80.

Foxall, Gordon R. and Haskins, Christopher G. 'Cognitive Style and Discontinuous Consumption: The Case of "Healthy-Eating"', *Journal of Food Marketing*, 3, (2), 1987, pp. 19–32.

Hansen, Flemming, 'Psychological Theories of Consumer Choice', *Journal of Consumer Research*, 3, 1976, pp. 117–42.

Holbrook, Morris B., 'A Synthesis of the Empirical Studies', in Farley *et al. Consumer Behaviour: Theory and Applications*, Allyn and Bacon, 1974, pp. 229–52.

Holbrook, Morris B., and O'Shaughnessy, John, 'The Role of Emotion in Advertising', *Psychology and Marketing*, 1, 1984, pp. 45–64.

Howard, John A., 'Marketing Theory of the Firm', *Journal of Marketing*, 47, 1983, pp. 90–100.

Howard, John A. and Sheth, Jagdish N., *The Theory of Buyer Behaviour*, Wiley, 1969.

Jacoby, Jacob, 'Consumer Research: A State of the Art Review', *Journal of Marketing*, 42, 1978, pp. 87–96.

Jacoby, Jacob, Chestnut, R. W. and Silberman, W. S., 'Consumer Use and Comprehension of Nutrition Information', *Journal of Consumer Research*, 4, 1977, pp. 119–28.

Jacoby, Jacob, Speller, D. E. and Kohn, C. A., 'Brand choice as a function of information load', *Journal of Marketing Research*, 11, (1), 1975, pp. 63–9.

Kassarjian, Harold H., 'Social Character and Differential Preference for Mass Communication', *Journal of Marketing Research*, 2, 1965.

Kassarjian, Harold H., 'Personality and Consumer Behaviour – A Review', *Journal of Marketing Research*, 4, 1971, pp. 409–18.

Kassarjian, Harold H., Presidential Address, *Advances in Consumer Research*, 1978.

Kassarjian, Harold H. and Sheffet, Mary J., 'Personality and Consumer Behaviour: An Update', in Harold H. Kassarjian and Thomas S. Robertson (eds) *Perspectives in Consumer Behaviour*, Scott Foresman & Co., 1982, pp. 160–80.

Kirton, Michael J., 'Adaptors and Innovators: A Description and Measure', *Journal of Applied Psychology*, 61, 1976, pp. 622–9.

Kirton, Michael J., *Manual of the Kirton Adaption-Innovation Inventory*, National Foundation for Educational Research, 1977.

Kirton, Michael J., 'Adaptors and Innovators: Why New Initiatives Get Blocked', *Long Range Planning*, 17, 1984, pp. 137–43.

Kirton, Michael J., 'Adaptors and Innovators: Problem-solvers in Organizations', in K. Gronhaug and G. Kaufman, (eds) *Innovation: A Crossdisciplinary Perspective*, Wiley, 1987a.

Kirton, Michael J. 'Adaptors and Innovators: Cognitive Style and Personality', in S. G. Isaksen, (ed.) *Frontiers of Creativity*, Brearly Ltd, 1987b.

Krugman, H. E., 'The Impact of Television Advertising: Learning Without Involvement', *Public Opinion Quarterly*, 29, (4), 1965, pp. 349–56.

Lavidge, R. J. and Steiner, G. A., 'A Model for Predictive Measurements of Advertising Effectiveness', *Journal of Marketing*, 25, 1961, pp. 59–62.

Lastovicka, J. L. and Bonfield, E. H., 'Do Consumers Have Brand Attitudes?' *Journal of Economic Psychology*, 2, 1982, pp. 57–76.

Lunn, J. A., 'A Review of Consumer Decision Models', ESOMAR, 1971.

McGuire, W. J., 'Some Internal Psychological Factors Influencing Consumer Choice', *Journal of Consumer Research*, 2, 1976, pp. 302–19.

Marx, Melvin H. and Hillix, William A., *Systems and Theories in Psychology*, McGraw-Hill, 1979.

Midgley, David F., *Innovation and New Product Marketing*, Croom Helm, 1977.

Midgley, David F. and Dowling, Graham R., 'Innovativeness: The Concept and its Measurement', *Journal of Consumer Research*, 4, September 1978, pp. 229–42.

Nicosia, F. M., *Consumer Decision Processes*, Prentice-Hall, 1966.

Nord, William R. and Peter, John P., 'A Behaviour Modification Perspective on Marketing', *Journal of Marketing*, 44, 1980, pp. 36–47.

Olshavsky, R. W. and Granbois, D. H., 'Consumer Decision-Making: Fact or Fiction?' *Journal of Consumer Research*, 6, 1979, pp. 93–100.

Pervin, Lawrence A., *Personality*, 4th ed., Wiley, 1984.

Pizzam, A., 'Psychological Characteristics of Innovators', *European Journal of Marketing*, 6, 1972, pp. 203–10.

Robertson, Thomas, S., 'The Process of Innovation and the Diffusion of Innovation', *Journal of Marketing*, 31, January 1967, pp. 14–19.

Robertson, Thomas S., 'A Critical Examination of "Adaption Process" Models of Consumer Behaviour', in J. N. Sheth (ed.) *Models of Buyer Behaviour*, Harper and Row, 1974, pp. 271–95.

Robertson, Thomas S., 'Low Commitment Consumer Behaviour', *Journal of Advertising Research*, 16, 1976, pp. 19–24.

Rogers, Everett, M., *Diffusion of Innovations*, 3rd ed., The Free Press, 1983.

Rothschild, Michael L. and Gaidis William C., 'Behavioural Learning Theory: Its Relevance to Marketing and Promotions', *Journal of Marketing*, 45, 1981, pp. 70–8.

Scammon, Debra L., ' "Information Load" and Consumers', *Journal of Consumer Research*, 4, 1977, pp. 148–55.

Tauber, E.M., 'Utilization of Concept Testing for New Product Forecasting', in Y. Wind, V. Mahajan, and R. N. Cardozo, (eds) *New Product Forecasting*, Lexington, MA: DC Heath, 1981, pp. 199–213.

Tuck, Mary, *How Do We Choose?* Methuen, 1976.

Westfall, Ralph, 'Psychological Factors in Predicting Product Choice,' *Journal of Marketing*, 26 April, 1962, pp. 34–40.

8
Organizational buying behaviour
PETER W. TURNBULL

Introduction

An understanding of the organizational buying process is fundamental to the development of appropriate industrial marketing strategy. The organizational buyer is influenced by a wide variety of factors both from outside and within the organization. Understanding these factors and their interrelationships is critical to the competitive positioning of the business, to the development of appropriate market and product development plans, and to the management of the whole marketing task of the business.

Increasingly, companies are recognizing the significant impact which professional procurement can have on profitability and the British manufacturing industry is increasingly buying-in components and subassemblies, rather than manufacturing in-house. For example, some telecommunications equipment manufacturers now buy in items accounting for up to 80 per cent of total cost. Thus, even a 2 per cent procurement saving can have a marked effect on profitability or give the company a significant price advantage in the marketplace. Additionally, professional purchasing also helps secure long term and improved sources of supply.

This growing importance and recognition of purchasing makes it imperative for industrial marketers to also increase their professionalism. A crucial,

element of such professionalism is, as consumer product marketers have so long recognized, the understanding of buying behaviour. However, in industrial markets this is more difficult than in consumer markets and requires an understanding of various academic disciplines which underlie the polygot area we term organization buying behaviour. To be effective marketers must address a number of key questions:

- Who are the key participants in purchasing?
- What process and procedures are followed in choosing and evaluating competitive offerings?
- What criteria are used in making buying decisions?
- What sources of information and influence are used?
- What organizational rules and policies are important?

These and other questions must be considered and answered if the industrial marketer is to be truly professional.

This chapter attempts to provide a framework of understanding by which these questions can be addressed. The most important theoretical and research contributions of the last two decades are briefly reviewed to give a fairly comprehensive picture of the current state of the art in the study of industrial buyer behaviour.

It will become apparent through the course of this chapter that organizational buying is a complex process. Attempts to oversimplify this process ultimately result in a loss of understanding of the dynamics of the process and its constituent elements. However, it is worthwhile to begin with the analysis of organizations buying structures.

Organizational buying structures

An organization is a group of people pursuing a common aim through coordinated activities. Organizations are characterized by structure, activity and goals. By analysing organizational buying in the light of these three factors it is possible to highlight the essential elements of organizational buying behaviour.

A major characteristic of organizational buying is that it is a group activity. It is comparatively rare that a single individual within an organization will have sole responsibility for making all the decisions involved in the purchasing process and commonly we find a number of people from different areas of the business and of varying status involved. This group is usually described as the *decision-making unit* or *buying centre*.

A major challenge facing industrial marketers and sales people is the identification of these key individuals who constitute the buying centre, the roles of these individuals and the various factors that may influence its constitution.

Composition of the buying centre

Much research has focused upon the size and structure of the buying centre, Alexander *et al.* (1961) found that in 75 per cent of the firms they interviewed, three or more people became involved in the buying process. Anyon (1963) suggested that there was an average of six people involved, while Hill and Hillier (1977) point out that in situations where certain expensive products are being purchased for the first time, as many as forty people may become involved in the purchase decision.

While interesting, generalizations such as these are of little practical help. The industrial marketer will be more concerned to discover who are the

influential people in the different stages of the decision-making process and the areas in which their influence lies.

Shankleman (1970) in a study of the purchase of capital equipment, writes:

> The managing director would agree to the equipment budget for the research department expressed solely in terms of money. The research manager would decide which of the various requests for money should have priority and the section head would decide which of the various items should be bought on the basis of a detailed study of reports made by his team.

Similarly, in an earlier study, Thain (1959) concluded that top management made the fundamental policy decision whether or not to buy but the operational staff decided what to buy.

The structure of the buying centre can also be examined in the light of the different roles of the individuals who constitute it. Webster and Wind (1972) suggest the major roles found in buying centres to be:

- Users.
- Influencers.
- Deciders.
- Gatekeepers.

Klass (1961) also identifies four roles and lists the functional departments that would be involved in each role:

- Contributors: foreman, supervisors, sales managers, promotions personnel.
- Participants: engineers, R & D, chemists, product advisors.
- Responsibles: purchasing department and agents.
- Deciders: directors of purchasing, plant managers, company executives.

However, these categories are rather rigid and make no allowances for differences in buying situations. Klass's categories especially assume a relationship between functional roles and their contribution to the buying process that can by no means be taken for granted.

Hill (1972), rather than analyse the structure of the buying centre through the roles of the participants, suggests an analysis on the basis of functional units:

- Control unit: responsible for policy making which influences buying.
- Information unit: responsible for providing information relating to the purchase.
- Buying unit: those persons with formal responsibilities for negotiating contracts.
- User unit: anybody within the organization who will use the product or service.
- Decision-making unit: those people within the buying centre who between them will arrive at a decision.

Hill believes that in reality only the control, information and decision-making units are important in influencing the buying decision.

It is apparent that there may be many sources of influence on the buying decision, both formal and informal. By piecing together the suggestions of the various research studies into the composition of the buying centre, it is possible to draw up the following list of roles that may be performed:

1 Policy makers.
2 Purchasers.
3 Users.
4 Technologists.
5 Influencers.
6 Gatekeepers.
7 Deciders.

Policy makers

A company may adopt certain general policies in its buying which may affect the purchase behaviour of a single item. For example it may be company policy to only purchase from British suppliers, or suppliers within a range of fifty kilometres, or for certain items to be multiple sourced.

Purchasers

The purchaser is here defined as the person or persons who have formal authority for ordering the product or service. A considerable amount of research has been completed investigating the importance of the purchasing agent in influencing buying decisions. For example, Weigand (1968) has pointed out that the purchasing agent may be no more than a clerical officer and his/her influence on the buying decision may consist of nothing more than filling in the necessary forms to complete the order.

Feldman and Cardozo (1968) and Lister (1967) are among many authors who have pointed out that the purchasing agent's role is dependent upon the management's philosophy towards purchasing. Where this is seen as important the purchasing agent will play an influential part in decision making.

James (1966), Marrian (1965) and Strauss (1962) indicated that the purchasing agents' perception of their own role and status would be major determinants of the influence they exerted. Ambitious purchasing agents will try to enhance their role and will see their prime function as keeping management continually aware of technical developments through the provision of regular information. In addition, ambitious purchasing agents seek to become involved in all phases of the decision-making process. Kettlewood (1973) in a study of the freight transport market where purchasing agents had little authority found that the desire to simplify work was a major determinant in the behaviour of the purchasing agent.

Nevertheless, it is important to identify the individual who will be primarily responsible for the final ordering of the service. Any assessment of the importance of the purchasing agent must consider the organization's attitude towards the purchasing function, together with the level of risk associated with the purchase. In all instances these considerations are liable to be situation specific and suppliers must, therefore, become aware of the differences between their customers.

Users

These are those people who actually operate the product or service. In certain instances their role will coincide with that of the technologist. It is likely that users will be primarily concerned with product performance and ease of use. Weigand (1966) suggests that users with expert knowledge may exert sufficient influence to override certain commercial considerations such as price or delivery times.

It is therefore important that suppliers should establish good relations with all members of a firm who have contact with the service they provide, and ensure that a high level of service is maintained throughout all their operations.

Technologists

These are the people with the specialist knowledge which enables them to differentiate between the performance of the different products or brands. They are primarily concerned with the technical aspects of the various products or services and these considerations will be of prime importance in their assessment of them. Technologists are likely to be people with professional qualifications and in seeking to influence them suppliers should be aware of the specialised nature of their influence on the buying centre.

An important finding of the International Marketing and Purchasing (IMP) Project Group in studies of purchasing in Western Europe was that purchasing staff and technologies in Germany and Sweden were more highly qualified than their counterparts in Britain. Thus British suppliers operating in these export markets faced more technologically demanding customers. German customers were very critical of the technical competence of British companies and this created a barrier to entry for British exporters (Turnbull and Cunningham, 1981).

Influencers

Webster and Wind (1972a) define this category as:

> Those who influence the decision process directly or indirectly by providing information and criteria for evaluating alternative buying actions.

Influencers thus include anybody who has an influence on the buying process both within and outside the organization. As a category this is too wide to be of any functional use since it can embrace such a wide range of people. However, it does point out that there can be substantial inputs from a wide range of different functions into the buying process.

Gatekeepers

The concept of gatekeeper comes from the theory of opinion leadership and communications flow. A gatekeeper is a person who regulates the flow of information and thus plays a major part in determining the attitudes of other members of the buying centre towards a product. It is possible that the role of gatekeeper will be performed by an individual who has another role within the buying centre, for example the purchasing agent.

Deciders

These are the people who have the formal authority for approving the purchase. It is likely that they will occupy senior management positions and therefore, as Shankleman (1970) pointed out, be concerned only at the policy making level.

These categories are useful indicators of the different areas of interest in the buying centre. A production engineer will view a machine purchase in a different way to a finance director. The transport manager will also take a different view to that of the managing director when the purchase of fleet cars is considered. We should note, however, that these roles can overlap and may vary according to the nature of the purchase and the stage of the buying process.

Having discussed basic purchasing structure, it is important to be aware of the factors that will influence that structure. The next section therefore examines the major variables which determine the composition of the buying centre.

Determinants of the buying centre

It has already been pointed out that the role of the purchasing agent is dependent upon the organization's philosophy towards the purchasing function and is therefore situation specific. While it is possible to suggest certain determining characteristics of the composition of the buying centre, it should be emphasized at the outset that the buying centre's composition will depend upon the specific purchase situation. In practical marketing terms such knowledge can only be built up through extensive contact between suppliers and buyers. The importance to suppliers of knowing their customers cannot be overemphasized.

While there are a host of variables which can determine the composition of the buying centre, they can broadly be categorized into market, company and product factors.

Market factors

Wallace (1976) identifies two features relevant to the study of organizational buying. First, those processes which characterize organizations and their members in their purchasing activity and second, those characteristics which differentiate organizational buying markets from consumer markets. It is these characteristics that are referred to here as market factors.

Products and services are often technologically complex and this, combined with bulk purchasing, leads to many industrial purchases being of high value. Also, industrial markets are characterized by derived demand and marketing thus requires careful evaluation of the secondary markets which influence demand for the primary product. Furthermore, many industrial products are highly concentrated and there tend to be greater differences between buyers. Markets can be either geographically concentrated or concentrated through the size of the firms. As a result, communication channels between industrial buyers and sellers tend to be shorter than in consumer markets.

Finally, many industrial markets are characterized by reciprocal trading arrangements between firms which may inhibit buying practice and make it difficult for new suppliers to enter some markets.

Each individual market will have its own characteristics and the companies that purchased from or within that market will organize their buying departments to meet the particular conditions that prevail. The organization of the buying centre to meet these market characteristics will vary depending upon the size of the company and the service being purchased.

Company factors

Sheth (1973) suggests three major company variables that will influence the composition of the buying centre: company size, degree of specialization and company orientation. It can be expected that as company size increases the greater the number of buying influences. Additionally, we can generally expect a higher degree of purchasing expertise in large organizations.

A study sponsored by *The Financial Times* (1974) concluded that most companies operating several establishments 'claimed to operate a centralized purchasing policy for the products covered by the survey'. The research indicated that, although no company admitted not having a clear policy on these matters, companies do in fact vary their practice according to convention or convenience, even within the framework of a centralization or decentralization policy. Sheth (1973) concludes that the greater the degree of centralization, the less likely the com-

pany will tend towards joint decision making.

Organizations with several operating subsidiaries, particularly if these are overseas, will have to have an overall policy regarding centralization. Even where control is highly centralized, subsidiaries may, nevertheless, be given varying degrees of freedom in choosing suppliers of specified product categories. The degree of centralization may therefore be vital to both the composition of the buying centre for these services, and also relevant to the development of a strategy for international marketing.

Finally, Sheth (1973) suggests that the composition of the buying centre will be dependent upon the company orientation. If a company is technology orientated the buying centre is likely to be dominated by engineering people who will, in essence, make the buying decision.

These various research findings highlight the necessity for a supplier's marketing management to know the policies and buying routines of its customers. By studying both existing and potential customers, suppliers can develop marketing strategies targeted to the important buying influences.

Product factors

Weigand (1966) defines a product as 'a variety of promises to perform'. Perfomance will be judged according to the expectations that the individual has of the product and it is important to remember that different people and organizations will have different perceptions of the product. As Alexander *et al.* (1961) have pointed out.

> The broad basic differences between types of goods arises not so much from their variations in their physical characteristics as differences in the ways in which and the purposes for which they are bought.

The product variable embraces a number of characteristics, including product essentiality, technical complexity, value of the purchase, consequence of failure, novelty of the purchase and frequency of the purchase.

Where a product is central to an organization's operations it is likely that the purchase will be decided upon jointly by all the parties concerned. This is also likely to be true in instances of high capital expenditure. In both of these instances the consequence of failure may be severe and so where the possibility or the consequence of failure are perceived to be higher it is likely that purchase decisions will be shared.

Bauer (1960) coined the term 'perceived risk' and Cyert and March (1963) applied the concept of risk avoidance as one of their basic concepts explaining the behaviour of the firm. They suggest that, in order to avoid uncertainty and failure, organizations avoid the necessity of having to anticipate events in the future by emphasizing short-term feedback; and impose standard operating procedures to ease the burden of decision making.

Hill and Hillier (1977) use the term 'risky shift' to explain how members of a group take decisions involving a higher degree of risk than they would do as individuals. The 'risky shift' concept is central to the composition of the buying centre and highlights the point that its composition will vary as a result of the characteristics of the product being purchased and particularly in relation to the perceived risk of the buying situation.

Buying situation

However, product complexity will be situation specific. Product complexity should not be regarded per se but rather related to the purchaser's technical knowledge and expertise. Knowledge and expertise will arise out of previous experience with the product and consequently lead to a reduction in risk perception. It can therefore be logically concluded that a major determinant of the composition of the buying centre will be the organization's previous experience of the product and the supplier.

Prior experience of the product or supplier will be a determining factor in risk perception. Robinson et al. (1967) define three 'buy classes' which are dependent on previous experience: new buy; modified rebuy; and straight rebuy. These buy classes influence both the composition of the buying centre and the buying process itself.

New buy In this situation the organization has no previous experience of the product or supplier. Consequently perceived risk will be high and purchase decisions will be more likely to be made by senior management.

Modified rebuy The company already has prior experience of the product but the particular purchase situation demands some degree of novelty. This may arise due to different specifications in a product or through change of supplier.

Straight rebuy This usually entails the routine reordering of products on the basis of decisions that have been made previously. There will be little risk perception in these instances and the purchase decision will be taken by lower management. In such cases there may not be a discrete decision at all but only in relation to the establishment of the order routine. It is usually very difficult to break the inertia of routine reordering and a 'new' supplier will have to demonstrate strong reasons to the buying organization to justify the extra risk and effort of changing supplier.

Robinson et al. link the buy classes to what they term buy phases or stages in the decision-making process. These stages constitute the last of the variables influencing the composition of the buying centre.

Stage in the buying process

Organizational buying decisions are not discrete but result from a variety of stages which interact, and upon which the final decision depends. As previously noted the composition of the buying centre will vary as a result of the particular activity taking place. Product users may provide the stimulus for a new purchase. In specifying the characteristics of a new product, technologists and finance people may be involved. The purchasing department may collect information about new products which will then be evaluated by the users and technologists and finance people. In deciding which alternatives should be short listed the finance department may become involved again, and the final selection may be made at board level where all the company interests will be represented.

During the last twenty years many writers and researchers have attempted to categorize the stages of the buying process. Fisher (1969) categorizes three stages; Cunningham and White (1974) also suggest three stages which lead to the final patronage decision; Dewey (1960) suggests a five-stage framework; Webster and Wind (1972a) classify four basic stages. The similarity of the stages suggests some universal pattern of organizational buying. However, all models assume a discrete and ordered process which is unrealistic in practice. Empirical findings have always shown that stages can occur simultaneously or out of sequence etc., depending on the particular buying situation.

Thus any attempt to examine the process in separate stages inevitably gives the false impression of a series of sequential steps. Nevertheless such an examination is valuable in so far as it reveals a pattern of activities which call for different responses from suppliers. The successful supplier will recognize and meet the needs of these activities at the appropriate times.

Despite the fundamental criticisms of the various buying stages models there is no doubt that buying is a dynamic and sequential process which the industrial marketer must make every effort to understand. Perhaps the clearest and most useful classification of the organizational buying process is that suggested by Luffman (1974) who proposes five basic steps: stimulus; specification; search; evaluation; and selection. These stages embrace the major activities and will be used to further examine this aspect of organizational buying behaviour.

Stimulus

The stimulus to purchase arises from the organization becoming aware of a problem which results in their needing to make a purchase. Webster (1965) ascribes five reasons why such a need may arise,

1 Dissatisfaction with present products or services.
2 Change of business.
3 Need for cost savings.
4 Curiosity.
5 Organizational policy decision.

The stimulus to purchase and all ensuing purchase activities are directly attributable to the attempt to satisfy the organization's objectives. The stimulus to purchase a given product or service may arise as a result of some other activity or event that has taken place and affected the organization.

Cambell (1966) however questions the traditional view of the organization passively waiting for problems to appear. He suggests that in many organizations there are positive efforts to identify problems and to seek improved performance during the ordinary course of the organization's activities, including reviews of purchasing which serve to stimulate the buying process.

Specification

Having identified that the problem can be solved through purchasing, the organization must then specify the exact nature of the product that will meet their requirement. Specifications can refer either to the product itself and/or to the supplying company and will usually be made on the basis of previous decisions made within the buying centre.

However, recent research has indicated that there is often substantial contact between buyers and sellers and that the supplier may be able to significantly influence the buyer with relation to specifications (Hakansson, 1983). For example, capital equipment and bank services may be specified as a result of extensive negotiations. Nevertheless the purchasing company may have certain minimum 'threshold' criteria which have to be fulfilled before a supplier can even be considered as a potential supplier. Specifications may be a part of overall corporate policy but there are likely also to be certain specifications which relate to the particular purchase situation.

Search

Searching for information is a major way of reducing risk and the search for alternative products or suppliers is liable to be most extensive when risk perception is high. Cyert and March (1973) suggested that search, like decision making itself, was problem directed. They made three basic assumptions about organizational search. First that search is motivated by a problem. Second that search proceeds on the basis of a simple model of casuality, until driven to a more complex one. And third, that the search would be biased by the searcher's perceptions of the environment. The frequency of search is a function of how well present suppliers and products are meeting organizational goals and one reason for frequent search is 'to keep present suppliers honest' by comparing them with alternatives.

The collection of information usually has a cost, either financial or in terms of effort or time expended. Buckner (1967) found that suppliers usually only examine a limited range of suppliers.

Table 8.1   *Percentage of respondents finding each source important by stage in the buying process*

	Awareness	Interest	Evaluation	Trial	Adoption
Salespeople	84	90	64	70	56
Trade journals	90	38	22	16	8
Buyers in other companies	18	22	28	16	8
Engineers in other companies	26	34	44	20	18
Trade associations	42	24	14	4	8
Trade shows	76	38	16	12	4

Adapted from Webster (1965).

Limited search can particularly be ascribed to the cost of information gathering. White (1969) however, indicated that a major reason for limiting search, was work simplification or avoidance. Three comments relating to the depth of search stand out from White's work into the purchasing of machine tools:

1 'We obtained three quotes: two for consideration and one to make up the quota.'
2 'I am required by the finance people to buy the cheapest. I therefore obtain a quotation for the machine I want and two more expensive ones.'
3 'In a company where the works manager makes the final decision: We get four. The buyer always does. I suppose it's his job but I only look at one.'

The search process may therefore be governed in many instances by satisficing rather than maximizing motivations, particularly in purchase situations where risk is not felt to be high.

Organizational search is a continuous process of data gathering which may relate specifically to products or generally to economic trends or markets. Search relating specifically to purchase situations may occur simultaneously with other stages in the decision process as a continuous activity or else as a series of sequential steps. Webster's research (1965) clearly showed how different sources of information are used at each stage in the adoption process (see Table 8.1).

Thus, from Table 8.1, advertising in trade journals would appear to be the most efficient method of gaining awareness for a product but sales people are more efficient at generating interest. The research also demonstrated a decreasing reliance on external sources as people become increasingly aware of the product.

Evaluation

Hill and Hillier (1977) suggested that evaluation may be comprised of two main stages. The first is that of selecting companies to tender and the second is the final selection of product and supplier. This idea concurs with Weigand (1968) who talks about an approved list of suppliers from which the purchasing agent is at liberty to select on the basis of price, delivery and a variety of other negotiable factors.

Evaluation must obviously be made against some predetermined criteria, often relating to both product and supplier. Green *et al.* (1968) scaled a number of product and supplier attributes or char-

Table 8.2   *Importance of different criteria in evaluating products*

Performance characteristic (Ranked in order of preference)	Scaling value
Quality/price ratio	3.61
Delivery reliability	2.94
Technical ability and knowledge	1.95
Information and market services	1.86
General reputation	1.65
Geographic location	1.63
Technical	1.61
Extent of previous contact	1.44
Importance of client (reciprocity)	0.61
Extent of personal benefits supplied to buyer	—

Source: Green *et al.* (1968).

acteristics and obtained the following ranking on a Thurstonian scale (see Table 8.2).

These findings were borne out by Cunningham and White (1974) who suggested that various attributes were essential if a supplier was to be even considered but that other factors would decide which supplier was ultimately selected. The former they termed qualifying factors and the latter determining factors. White found that a favourable reputation for delivery, reliability and service were important prerequisites for increasing the chance of being seriously considered as a potential supplier. The strongest determinant of a buyer's patronage decision is his/her past experience which relates to the buyer's perception of the supplier's reputation.

Particular product or supplier attributes and their relative importance will obviously vary according to the product and the buying situation. Previous research into product and supplier evaluation seems to indicate that evaluation is a two step process where products and suppliers are measured against some kind of preconceived set of criteria.

This necessarily brief discussion of buying stages underlines several of the models of buying behaviour discussed later in this chapter. Before moving on to this topic, however, it is necessary to consider the last characteristic of organizations – the motivations and objectives of the organizations and their members.

Buying goals

The role of the buying process as a problem solving activity was suggested by both Cox (1966) and Cambell (1966). The whole purchasing process is designed to meet certain aims or objectives on both the organizational level and the individual level. These objectives, it is suggested, can relate either directly or indirectly to the buying task.

However, a variety of factors can intervene between the original purchase objectives and the final buying decision. The cost of searching for the product or service that exactly fits the purchase specifications may be prohibitive, or, alternatively, such a product or service may not be available. White (1969) indicated that in some instances a major determinant of buying behaviour is the desire for work simplification.

Therefore in many instances both organizations

and individuals may be pursuing 'satisficing' rather than maximizing courses of action in their behaviour whereby a compromise will be reached between the attainment of the purchasing objectives and the actual purchase.

Models of industrial buying behaviour

The purpose of modelling buyer behaviour is to clarify the relationships between various inputs, such as selling, previous experience or competitor activities, and outputs which are the purchase or rejection of a product or service from a particular source.

Many models have been proposed and an excellent summary of these is made by Webster and Wind (1972b) in their book, *Organisational Buying Behaviour*. The authors define four main categories of model:

1   Task related.
2   Non-task related.
3   Complex.
4   Multi-dimensional.

Task related models

These are based on the view that the desire for rational or optimal outcomes is a fundamental determinant of behaviour. These models focus on concepts such as lowest purchase price; lowest total cost; constrained choice; rational economics; and materials management.

Non-task related models

With non-task related models the perspective shifts from the demands of the task to be accomplished to the personal interests that might be affected by the outcome. Examples of the key concepts used in non-task related models include:

● Individual desire for ego enhancement or personal gain.
● Desire to avoid risk in decision making (Bauer, 1960; Newall, 1977).
● Gratification of buyer and seller through a dydactic relationships (Evans, 1963; Bonoma and Johnston, 1978).

- Lateral relationships between buyer and colleagues (Tosi, 1966).
- Relationships with significant other persons from within the company and their effect on transmission and interpretation of information (Webster, 1969).

Complex models

In the late 1960s several more comprehensive models were postulated, incorporating a large number of variables. For example, the *decision process model* (Wind and Robinson, 1968) depicts decisions as occurring over a considerable period involving segmented stages, i.e. 'problem alternatives' and 'selection'.

The *compact model* (Robinson and Stidsen, 1967) attempts to establish general rules that govern the decision process. Three dimensions of influences are proposed: organization structure; elements of the buying process; and the characteristics of individuals. However, in this model no reference is made to the exchanges and negotiation occurring between parties.

We can criticize these models for adopting only a partial approach and even the more complex models fail to cover many of the important points observed by Webster and Wind. Moreover, many are theoretical rather than realistic. They are of limited practical use to the marketing or purchasing practitioner.

In an attempt to be more realistic, Robinson *et al.* (1967) proposed the *buygrid model*. This is based on empirical observations of buyer behaviour in companies. In Table 8.3 we see that decisions are thought to vary on two dimensions. First the stage of the decision (or 'buyphase') and second the nature of the decision itself (the 'buyclass').

The buygrid model offers certain improvements over earlier models. For example it recognizes that buying is often repetitive. However, Ferguson (1979) comments that the buygrid model had only a limited capacity to predict outcomes when he applied it to examples of decision making. In most situations he observed that the proposed systematic decision process was often 'short-circuited'. To overcome these objectives we must turn to the more comprehensive models which incorporate a wider range of variables.

Table 8.3   *The buygrid model*

Buyphases	Buyclasses		
	New task	Modified rebuy	Straight rebuy
Identification of need	X	X	X
Determination of requirement	X	n/a	n/a
Specific description of requirement	X	n/a	n/a
Search for potential sources	X	n/a	n/a
Examination of sources	X	n/a	n/a
Selection of source	X	X	X
Order routine established	X	X	n/a
Evaluation of performance feedback	X	X	X

n/a – not applicable.
Source: Robinson, *et al.* (1967).

Complex multidisciplinary models

Clearly the models previously described are inadequate both as descriptive representations of reality and as predictive tools. Several models have been developed which attempt to overcome these problems. In an early attempt to integrate various dimensions of consumer buying behaviour Howard and Sheth (1969) developed a behavioural model based on social, psychological, cultural and economic variables.

Subsequently Sheth (1973) proposed a complex model specifically for industrial buyer behaviour, which integrates a large number of variables into one comprehensive model which is briefly described below.

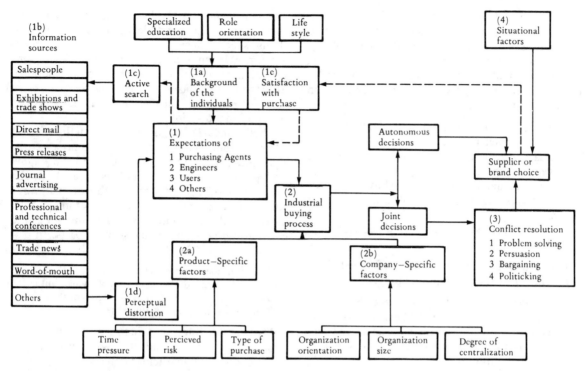

Figure 8.1 *Sheth model of organizational buying behaviour*
Source: J. Sheth, 'A Model of Industrial Buyer Behaviour', *Journal of Marketing*, vol. 37, no. 4, October 1973.

The Sheth model

Sheth's model of industrial buyer behaviour outlined in Figure 8.1 proposes four broad categories of variables:

1 The psychological world of the decision makers.
2 Product and company variables.
3 Structure and methods for problem solving.
4 Situational factors.

Psychological world of the decision makers

The decision makers' perception of the product's ability to satisfy both implicit and explicit criteria such as quality, delivery time, price, reputation, etc., will vary in accordance with their roles, education, life style, past experience and knowledge of the product and suppliers. This background which constitutes a sort of 'black box', leads to individual perceptual distortions which will influence each person's approach to the buying task.

Product and company variables

Product specific factors include perceived risk, type of purchase (new or rebuy situation) and time pressure.

Perceived risk and purchase situation have been discussed previously. Time pressure refers to the possibility that decisions may need to be made within a time limit. Sheth suggests that the shorter this time limit the more likely that the decision will be made autonomously.

Company factors include company orientation, company size and centralization, the influence of which has already been discussed.

Structure and methods for problem solving

The decision makers' psychological world and the various product and company variables will lead to the buying task being solved by a particular method. Sheth suggests that these methods can be summed up as either joint or autonomous decision making.

Joint decision making results in conflict between the decision makers and the third stage of Sheth's model concentrates on the reasons for and resolution of this conflict. Conflict may stem from:

(a) Disagreement on expectations about the suppliers or their products.
(b) Disagreement about the criteria with which to evaluate suppliers or products.
(c) Fundamental differences in the buying goals or objectives among the members of the buying centre.
(d) Disagreement about the style of decision making.

For each of the above bases of conflict the following forms of conflict resolution apply,

(i) *Problem solving* Increased search for information and further deliberation about existing information. This additional information is then presented in such a way that conflict is minimized.
(ii) *Persuasion* An attempt is made to show the dissenting member(s) how their criteria are liable to result in corporate objectives not being fulfilled.
(iii) *Bargaining* The fundamental differences between the parties are conceded and a decision is arrived at on a 'tit for tat' basis. This will either result in a compromise or else allow an individual to make the decision autonomously in return for some favour or promise of reciprocity in future decision making.
(iv) *Politicking and backstabbing* These, according to Strauss and Sheth are common methods of problem solving in industrial buying.

According to Sheth, problem solving and persuasion benefit the eventual decision and therefore the organization, while bargaining and politicking are non-rational and inefficient means of problem solving and the decision, the decision makers and the organization suffer in consequence.

Situational factors

Sheth argues that industrial buying decisions are often determined by 'ad hoc' situational factors and not by any systematic decision-making process. Thus, specific decisions are a result of certain environmental considerations, such as price controls, the economic environment, strikes, promotional efforts or price changes. These factors can often intervene between the decision-making processes and the final decision.

Sheth's model is not intended to be definitive, but offers a framework which draws attention to the dynamics and complexity of organizational buying and presents the relevant factors in a systematic way. The model concentrates on the internal workings of the buying process and does not incorporate external influences and tells us nothing about the relationship between the constituent parts. In discussing the situational factors, Sheth wrote:

> What is needed in these cases is a checklist of empirical observations of the ad hoc events which initiate the neat relationship between the theory or the model and a specific buying situation.

We should note here that a universal buying process does not exist and the model's value lies in its application to particular buying situations or organizations. In this manner it can contribute towards a better understanding of the complexities of organizational buyer behaviour.

The Webster and Wind model

Webster and Wind's (1972a) model outlined in Figure 8.2 stresses the role of the individual as the real decision maker in the organization. Therefore the individual's motivation, personality, perception, learning and experience are all vital to the actual decision process. This model is truly comprehensive however and honours concepts from the fields of individual, organizational and social psychology, economics, management, sociology and politics.

Webster and Wind recognize the existence of a buying centre and argue that organizational buying is a multiperson process subjected to and influenced by the aggregate behaviour of a number of people, and also by the interaction between them. The activities of both individuals and the collective buying centre are influenced by a variety of factors, some of which are related to the buying task (task variables which include rational and economic motivations) and non-task variables (a variety of

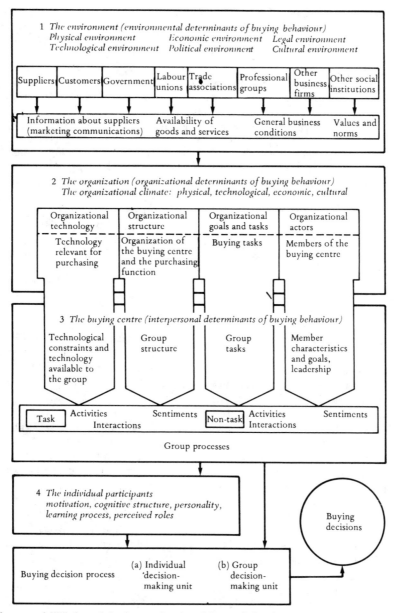

Figure 8.2 *Webster and Wind model of organizational buyer behaviour*
Source: F. Webster and Y. Wind, 'A General Model of Understanding Organizational Buyer Behaviour', *Journal of Marketing*, vol. 36, no. 2, April 1972.

emotional or non-rational reasons for purchasing decisions).

Webster and Wind suggest that the final buying decision is dependent on influences exerted from four spheres:

1 The general environment.
2 The organization.
3 Interpersonal influences.
4 The influence of the individual.

Table 8.4   *A complex model of factors affecting industrial buying decisions*

Level of influence on behaviour	Source of influence	Types of constraints to behaviour that emerge
1 The firm's environment	Physical, legal, economic, technical, political, cultural, suppliers, customers, governments.	Information, products and services, business conditions, values, norms.
2 The organization	Business climate, physical climate, technological climate, economic climate, cultural climate, structure of work, personnel, organizational goals.	Technology relevant for purchasing, organization of the buying centre, buying tasks, members of the buying centre.
3 The buying team	Technological constraints, buying group structure, buying group tasks, member characteristics, member goals.	Task and non-task: ● activities. ● interactions. ● orientations.
4 The individual	Motivation, cognition, personality, learning, roles.	Buying decision process, individual DM unit, group DM unit ↓ buying decision.

Based on Webster and Wind (1972b).

An abridged version of the model is shown in Table 8.4.

At the most general level we have the firm's environment. This comprises the wide and complex system of institutions that make up the social and industrial infrastructure. By dictating needs, norms and laws this level of influence affects the practices of the firm and the individual.

Below the firm's environment we encounter the organization's internal environment. Decision making occurs against a background of the firm's technology, the way work is organized, the firm's objectives and goals and the character of individuals themselves.

The third level of influence proposed is that of the decision-making unit. At this level the roles performed by participants in the decision make a major contribution to the eventual outcome. Thus the roles of 'influencer', 'order placer', 'decider', 'gatekeeper' and 'user', may all be present.

Although we might presume the buying centre to have a common set of expectations and the decision itself may be the outcome of several different collective processes, such as bargaining, consensus negotiation and game strategy. Several writers have commented on tactics used by individuals to promote their own interests. For example, Strauss (1962) suggests that purchasers may avoid or enforce company rules or use political or personal persuasion. Walton and McKenzie (1965) stress the importance of distributive and integrative bargaining plus attitudinal structuring in achieving a 'common front'.

The fourth and lowest level of influence – that of the individual – highlights the fact that all behaviour is ultimately conducted at at personal level. Thus motivation, cognition, personality, experience and learning may all affect the outcome of the decision process.

Webster and Wind's model focuses our attention on a number of significant features that are particularly relevant in international marketing. Thus, at the most general level foreign trading partners may well come from very different environments. The organizational environments of buying and selling firms may also be different or disjointed. As a result understanding may be poor and communication difficult.

At the second level the model accounts for the fact that firms in different cultures may have very different working climates. In addition the way work is organized could be disparate.

At the third level, the model recognizes the possibility of conflicts of interest and the influence of 'significant others'.

Perhaps of great interest at the individual level of influence their model highlights the fact that personal processes and capabilities will affect the outcome of decisions. Thus training and experience, cognition, personality and motivation will all affect sales and buying performance. Clearly, important differences in personal factors such as these are more likely in different foreign markets.

In essence Webster and Wind's model is one of the most comprehensive of its kind and considers a wide range of decision related factors and variables. However, it is still of limited practical help to the marketer. This is because it does not concentrate on the units of analysis that are fundamental to the real life processes that are occurring with prospective and ongoing buyer–seller relationships (i.e., the relationship between individuals and the nature of what is exchanged).

Although it covers a multitude of determinant factors, what is lacking is a focus on the processes that are most important in the long- and short-term aspects of a buying decision. No reference is made to the personal relationships and the atmosphere of the relationship that may evolve between buyer and seller.

Seeking to resolve this issue, the International Marketing and Purchasing (IMP) Group developed a model of industrial marketing and purchasing as an interactive process based on long-term relationships.

The interaction approach

The *interaction approach* (Turnbull and Cunningham, 1981; Hakansson, 1982) focuses on the most basic elements of the decision process. It stresses the necessity that marketers are perceptive and flexible in the definition and satisfaction of customer needs. This is done by placing greater emphasis on the processes and relationships which occur between and within buying and selling organizations. Hakansson (1982) emphasizes the following points to distinguish their approach:

- Buyers and sellers are seen as active participants in the transaction. The buyer is thus not limited to a passive role and can seek to influence the nature of the marketing inputs that are offered.
- Buyer–seller relationships are often long term in nature, tend to be based on mutual trust rather

than a formal commitment and often start months or even years before money and goods are exchanged.
- Complex patterns of interaction evolve between and within the companies and their different departments.
- Because of the complex nature of relationships, marketers and purchasers may be more involved with supporting and maintaining these, than with actually buying and selling.
- The links between buyers and sellers may become institutionalized.

From these observations industrial purchasing decisions may be seen to vary as a function of four main areas of variables.

The interrelationship of these four key areas is illustrated in Figure 8.3.

In the brief description of the four areas which follows, we shall observe how the interaction model stresses the importance of the individual and the level of his/her interpersonal and intercompany skills.

The interactive process

Relationships between buyers and sellers can be broken into a series of episodes. Each episode contributes to the overall relationship which will be developed over a greater period of time. These episodes can be considered in terms of elements of exchange. For example, the exchange of the actual product or service, the exchange of information, the exhange of money or social exchanges. The greater the extent of uncertainty concerning these elements, the more likely that increased interaction will take place to resolve these uncertainties and allow the parties to become familiar with each other and develop mutual trust.

The occurrence of episodes over time can lead to the interaction becoming routinized and to preconceptions regarding the role set of both individuals and organizations. Such routine patterns of behaviour may become characteristic of a single relationship or else of a whole industry.

Mutual adaptations may occur between buyers and sellers which will result in cost reductions or some other advantage. The existence of such adaptations can serve to bring each party closer together. This can therefore act as a major influence on chang-

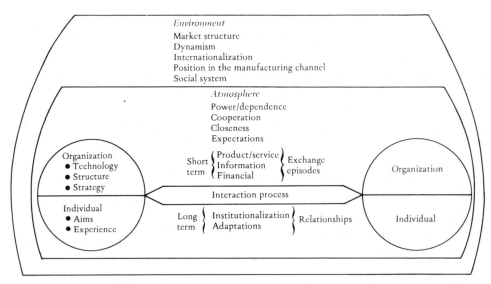

Figure 8.3   *Main elements of the interaction model*
Source: H. Hakansson (ed.), *International Marketing and Purchasing of Industrial Goods*, John Wiley, 1982.

ing marketing or buying policies.

The participants

Interaction occurs between organizations and individuals and is dependent on the nature of the organization and its members. Relevant factors may be the firm's technology, size, experience or structure or the individual's motives, attitudes and perceptions. These factors have already been discussed at some length in previous sections.

The environment

The interaction process takes place in the general prevailing environmental conditions which will determine certain norms of behaviour and values. Particularly relevant factors may be the market structure, social systems or economic conditions.

The atmosphere

The products of a relationship is the atmosphere which result from the various exchanges and adaptations. The atmosphere refers specifically to the degree of closeness between the buyer and seller which will be reflected in the level of conflict or cooperation in their interaction.

The nature of the atmosphere can be planned.

The development of a close relationship with a 'good atmosphere' may result in advantageous conditions for the buyer and seller. However, in order to avoid power dependence, where one party becomes vulnerable to the power of the other, the 'closeness' of the atmosphere may be regulated.

The interaction model focuses on the relationships between individuals both within and between firms. It portrays dynamic and developing relationships, which approximate to the reality of organizational purchasing, in a way that none of the previous models are able to do. In so doing it presents a more complex picture of organizational buying and offers a challenge to the researcher to find a universal pattern of relationships from which to build a comprehensive model.

Since it is unlikely that any single model can include sufficient variables to allow for the complexities of thousands of different relationships, it would seem that future models of buyer behaviour should attempt to incorporate patterns of interaction that are characteristic either of similar purchasing situations or else of particular industries.

In reviewing various models of buyer behaviour an attempt has been made to bring together the various elements of organizational buyer behaviour that were discussed under the headings of organizational structures, activities and goals. No single model adequately explains all the complexities of the organizational buying process and this in itself is a warning against any attempt to construct simplistic models. However, taken together, the three complex models provide a framework for empirical research into the buying process as each of the relevant areas is treated with different emphasis in each model.

Conclusion

The industrial marketer can no longer presume that the company will be a sole or dominant supplier for ever. Existing relationships must be maintained and strengthened to protect against growing competitive pressures. Equally important, to survive in the increasingly international competitive environment of the next decade, suppliers must aggressively seek to establish new relationships both in domestic and foreign markets.

These twin strategies – defending the existing customer base and proactively seeking new accounts – have a common fundamental requirement, the knowledge and understanding of how organizations buy.

Understanding the dynamics of organizational buying behaviour is essential to all major strategic and tactical planning in industrial marketing: the identificaton of profitable segments and motivating those individuals with product and service offerings appropriate to their needs. Thus every action of the industrial marketer is based on the probable response of organizational buyers in relation to price, product, distribution, advertising and promotion.

Industrial marketing is characterized by complex interaction processes both within the marketing and purchasing companies and between these companies. High technological and financial dependencies are common in industrial markets. These dependencies lead to extensive involvement and interchange over long time periods. Thus purchasing is a multiphased and multiobjective process. Due to the complex multidisciplinary, multifaceted nature of the buying process the aim of researchers to develop comprehensive but testable and normative models is still not yet fully achieved.

References

Alexander, M., Cross, T. and Cunningham, S., *Industrial Marketing*, Richard Irwin, 1961.

Anyon, G., *Managing an Integrated Purchasing Process*, Rinehart & Winston, 1963.

Bauer R. A., 'Consumer Behaviour as Risk Taking' in R. S. Hancock (ed.) *Dynamic Marketing for a Changing World*, Proceedings of 43rd Conference, American Marketing Association, 1960.

Bonoma T. V. and Johnston, W., 'The Social Psychology of Industrial Buying and Selling,' *Industrial Marketing Management*, vol. 7, no. 4, 1978.

Buckner, H., *How British Industry Buys*, Hutchinson, 1967.

Campbell, R., 'A Suggested Paradigm of the Adoption Process', *Rural Sociology*, vol. 31, December 1966.

Cox D.F. (ed.) *Risk Taking and Information Handling*, Harvard University Press, 1966.

Cunningham, M., and White, R., 'The Behaviour of Industrial Buyers in their Search for Suppliers of Machine Tools', *Journal of Management Studies*, May 1974.

Cyert, R. and March, J., *A Behavioural Theory of the Firm*, Prentice Hall, 1963.

Dewey, R., *How We Think*, DC Health and Co, 1960.

Evans, F. B., 'Selling as a Dyadic Relationship', *American Behavioural Science*, vol. 6, May 1963.

Ferguson, W., 'An Evaluation of the Buygrid Analytical Framework', *Industrial Marketing Management*, vol. 8, no. 1, 1979.

Feldman, W., and Cardozo, R. N., 'The Industrial Revolution and Models of Buyer Behaviour', *Journal of Purchasing*, 4, November 1968.

Fisher, L., *Industrial Marketing*, 2nd ed., Business Books, 1969.

'How British Industry Buys', *The Financial Times*, November 1974.

Green, P., Robinson, P. and Wind, Y. 'The Determinant of Vendor Selection. The Evaluation Function Approach'. *Journal of Purchasing*, August, 1968.

Hakansson, H. (ed.), *International Marketing and Purchasing of Industrial Goods*, John Wiley, 1982.

Hill, R., 'The Nature of Industrial Buying Decisions', *Industrial Marketing Management*, vol. 2, October 1972.

Hill, R. and Hillier, F., *Organisational Buyer Behaviour*, Macmillan 1977.

Howard, N. and Sheth, J., *Consumer Buyer Behaviour*, John Wiley, 1969.

James, B., 'Emotional Buying in Industrial Markets', *Scientific Business*, Spring 1966.

Klass, B., 'What Factors Influence Industrial Buying Decisons', *Industrial Marketing*, vol. 14, May 1961.

Kettlewood K., 'Source Loyalty in the Freight Transport Market'. Unpublished MSc. dissertation, *UMIST*, 1973.

Lister, P., 'Identifying and Evaluating the Purchasing Influence, *IMRA*, August 1967.

Luffman, G., 'Industrial Buyer Behaviour: Some Aspects of the Search Process', *European Journal of Marketing* vol. 8, no. 2, 1974.

Marrian J., 'Marketing Characteristics of Industrial Goods and Buyers' in A. Wilson (ed.), *The Marketing of Industrial Products*, Hutchinson 1965.

Newall, J., 'Industrial Buyer Behaviour: A model of the Implications of Risk Handling Behaviour for Communication Policies in Industrial Marketing', *European Journal of Marketing*, vol. 1, 1977.

Robinson, P., Faris C. and Wind, Y., *Industrial Buying and Creative Marketing*, Allyn and Bacon, 1967.

Robinson, P. J. and Stidsen, B., *Personal Selling in a Modern Perspective*, Allyn & Bacon, 1967.

Shankleman, E., 'Study of Industrial Buying Decisions', *New Scientist*, September 1970.

Sheth, J. 'A Model of Industrial Buyer Behaviour', *Journal of Marketing*, vol. 37, no. 4, October 1973.

Strauss, G., 'Tactics of Lateral Relationship – The Purchasing Agent', *Administrative Science Quarterly*, vol. 7, September 1962.

Thain, D. H., 'How Industry Buys – With Conclusion and Recommendations on Marketing to Industry,' National Industrial Advertisers Association of Canada, 1959.

Tosi, H.L., 'The Effects of Expectation Level of Role Consensus on the Buyer-Seller Dyad', *Journal of Business*, October 1966.

Turnbull, P. W. and Cunningham, M. T., *International Marketing and Purchasing*, Macmillan 1981.

Wallace, A., 'A study of the Buying Process for New Products by Intermediate Marketing Organisations in the Channels of Distribution for Grocery Products', unpublished Ph.D thesis, UMIST, 1976.

Walton, R.E., and McKensie, R.B. (eds.), *A Behavioural Theory of Labor Negotiations*, McGraw Hill, 1965.

Webster, F.C., 'Modelling the Industrial Buying Process', *Journal of Marketing Research*, vol. 2, November 1965.

Webster, F. and Wind, Y. 'A General Model for Understanding Organisational Buyer Behaviour', *Journal of Marketing*, vol. 36, no. 2, April 1972a.

Webster, F. and Wind, Y. *Organisational Buyer Behaviour*, Prentice Hall, 1972b.

Weigand, R., 'Identifying Industrial Buying Responsibilities', *Journal of Market Research*, vol. 3, February 1966.

Weigand, R., 'Why Studying the Purchasing Agent is not enough', *Journal of Marketing*, vol. 32, no. 1, January 1968.

White, J., 'Some Aspects of the Marketing of Machine Tools in Great Britain,' unpublished Ph.D. thesis UMIST, 1969.

Wind, Y. and Robinson, P., 'Generalized Simulation of the Industrial Buying Process', Marketing Science Institute Working Paper, June 1968.

9
Market research

DAVID F. BIRKS

Introduction

The later chapter on marketing information systems clearly demonstrates the need for marketers to take a strategic perspective of the information function. The findings from ad hoc market research studies are a vital component of a marketing information system. The requirement of ad hoc market research does not mean that the marketer has not planned information needs to support his/her marketing planning. The marketer may envisage the strategic decisions that need to be made but may have difficulty in translating this into a distinct information requirement making it difficult to plan support; ad hoc research can supply the answers. There may also be complete surprises for the marketer, totally unpredictable events, new situations that planned information support cannot help with; again ad hoc research can supply the answers.

Standard market research texts from the USA or the UK focus primarily on the research process, descriptions of techniques and means of analysing quantitative data. Little regard is given to the problems of defining research problems before applying techniques, the rationale for the use of quantitative and qualitative techniques and the relationships between the marketer and the market researcher.

Market research is examined in this chapter from a 'non-technician's' perspective. Many excellent

marketing decisions are made without market research, many marketing opportunities have been squandered even after the strict adherence to market research processes. In both of the above instances the reverse can also be claimed. Thus, the chapter commences by examining the purpose of market research and by showing its limitations.

Without a thorough and accurate evaluation of the marketing problem to be solved and its translation into a research problem, techniques however well practised may be of little use or even may be harmful. An analogy to this is the medical doctor prescribing treatment after a cursory examination of the patient, the medicine may be even more dangerous than the condition it is supposed to cure. In market research, much can be done in problem definition by good negotiations at the onset. However, there is no set technique for this process. The chapter continues by outlining the process of diagnosing problems and the interaction of marketer and researcher.

Marketing problems in many instances are not easily defined, uniform and controllable, neither are the research tasks that ultimately help solve them. Many variables from quite disparate subject areas interact to form marketing phenomena. Explaining, understanding and predicting marketing phenomena can be achieved with the support of quantitative and/or qualitative methods, depending entirely upon the nature of the problem under study. Thus, the rationale, benefits and limitations of quantitative and qualitative methods are presented. There is also discussion on how the two approaches can interlink and support each other.

Marketers are continuously conducting 'research in action' as part of their daily life in making sense of situations and forming intelligent opinions of potential outcomes. This process is outlined as a basis for showing the nature of the task facing market researchers beyond being technicians that brings them closer to markets. This continues with an evaluation of the characteristics required of the ideal researcher. The chapter concludes by evaluating what marketers can do to help market researchers help them. Market research should not be seen as a passive gathering of historical data but as dynamic and creative. The marketer has a key role to play in this process.

In context

All organizations face change in their environment with resultant changes in their markets and in their ability to satisfy their markets. Each organization is faced with new marketing problems and opportunities in their existing and potential markets. Marketing decision makers or marketers cope with these challenges in a variety of ways. Some take decisions intuitively or after consultation with close colleagues, others use internally generated data from a planned marketing information system, while others commission ad hoc market research to give support. There can be no hard and firm rules about how and when a marketer seeks support for marketing decisions, as the term 'marketing decision' covers a vast array of contexts, personalities, time scales and risks. The support needed by marketers varies with the scale and nature of the decisions they are taking. In short, market research is not the panacea for all the ills of the marketer:

> High risk, substantial uncertainty, high levels of investment and a vacuum of information are the conditions which breed a demand for externally generated market information and not all companies confront these situations all the time. (Hooley and West, 1984)

The need for externally generated marketing support has arisen from the distance between decision makers and consumers and the increasing speed of change of markets. In order to illustrate the distance between decision maker and consumer, the following example highlights what gaps can be overcome by market research.

Consider a grocer's shop in days of our parents or grandparents (or ourselves), where it served general provisions in a local community. The grocer could meet his customers on a daily basis. He would get to know their likes and dislikes of certain products (how thick the ham should be cut for Sunday tea), what could be afforded, who sought credit (and who never paid their debts). Beyond these observations and in the course of daily business, the characteristics of customers would be gleaned, what they enjoyed at the cinema, what public houses they frequented, where they went for holiday, how Emily was faring at her new school. With these observations of his customers, built up over many years, the grocer was armed with information that would allow him to manipulate many marketing variables. Who would be the likely takers of a new line of continental mustard? How much would he get away with price rises on certain items. Who would notice the rise. How to move slow shifting stock to certain customers. The grocer could alter his approach to different customer types based on what his experience told him would give him the greatest success. His 'picture' of different consumer types would be an amalgamation of demographic, geographic, psychographic, psychological and behavioural characteristics, though it is not contended they were classified and measured in this manner. What allowed the grocer to build such a strong picture of his customers was his closeness to them. There could be an empathy between the parties, an intellectual and emotional understanding that was intuitively built up and reinforced on a daily basis. In a stable environment such as this, externally generated market information could do very little unless either the grocer or his customers changed.

If the grocer were to build a network of small shops, and an office to manage their activities, which he controlled, a distance would emerge between himself and the consumer. He may afford to live in a very large house away from the shop's community bringing a *geographical distance*. Being the head of the organization, the cues or signals that he picked up daily may be coming to him second or third hand, there being an *organizational distance* from the consumer. Finally, by missing the daily contact with customers and mixing with other business individuals an *intellectual* and *emotional distance* can build up. These distances can occur in any organization and if marketers perceive that the distance between themselves and customers create high risk, substantial uncertainty in decision making or a high level of investment is required, then market research may help them.

The second need for externally generated marketing support highlighted earlier was the increasing speed of changes of markets. Again, with the example of the grocer in days of yore, a slow moving, stable environment allowed forecasting horizons to be kept to short time spans. The speed of change in competition, new products, demographic and cultural changes in customers, legislation and the local economy allowed the grocer to proceed with tactical measures and perhaps resignation through good and lean times. The grocer with vision would have been able to see which major environmental changes affected his customers' expectations *and* his ability to satisfy these expectations.

Again, should the lone grocer go on to build his empire, two things could happen. First, he might be able to exert an amount of influence on the environmental factors that can change his customers. Second, he might be faced with a greater number of environmental factors *and* a subsequent greater number of interrelationships of environmental factors that have the dual effect of changing customer expectations and his ability to meet or exceed those expectations. If that environment were to include more competition (in manners beyond just price), a greater number of new products and processes, dramatic shifts in the demographic make up of consumers, great changes in purchasing power of consumers (to name but a few factors) then maintaining an understanding of salient environment factors and their interrelationships could prove to be difficult.

In understanding a slow moving environment, the marketer may be able to highlight salient factors, their interrelationships and subsequent effects, perhaps even by trial and error. Trial and error or experimentation may be perceived as high risk and full of uncertainty in an environment that is fast moving. High levels of investment in such circumstances may again warrant the use of external marketing support – market research.

In the two key areas that highlight a need of support for marketing decision makers, i.e., distance from consumers and speed of change, the words 'market research may help' warrant further explanation. The marketer may see the examples as being too general and far removed from the specific problems faced in marketing decision making. From this point it would be fruitless to try and list all potential marketing problems that market research could help with. The purpose of the marketing decision maker is outlined to allow a better context in which to examine the purpose of the market research function.

The purpose of market research

In a short definition the purpose of the marketer can be described as: 'designing and delivering market mixes that meet or exceed the expectations of selected target markets'.

In a sentence the role seems straightforward but it hides a most complex task that may be broken down into two sections:

1 The ability to continually foresee both in the short and long term the expectations of existing and potential markets, i.e., to be able to design marketing mixes that make the most out of opportunities or overcome problems caused by new market requirements and/or changes to new markets.
2 The ability to generate and coordinate integrated effort throughout the organization to enable the delivery of planned marketing mixes in a manner deemed to be the optimum for selected target markets, i.e., the ability to exploit and/or make the most of strengths and weaknesses within the organization.

A key word in the above two abilities is the word 'planning' or the ability to forecast.

Realistic marketing planning implies knowledge of the present and future state of the market, in so far as the future can be predicted.   (Arpi, 1970)

In marketing, not all (if any at all) of the decision maker's activities can be modelled with clear causal relationships:

> The marketing manager is rarely in a good position to estimate the sales rate resulting from different combinations of prices, and messages, and media, sales call strategies, and product styling and packaging investments. The problem is that marketing effort works through a maze of highly unpredictable behavioural relationships, rather than through a fairly stable set of technological relationships. (Lilien and Kotler, 1983)

The marketers being required to forecast, perceives the risk and uncertainty of a situation in their own way. Support from market research may or may not be required – nothing is concrete. However, uncertainty cannot be completely eliminated in marketing forecasting:

> No method known to man can entirely eliminate uncertainty. But scientific method, more than any other procedure, can minimize those elements of uncertainty which result from lack of information. By doing so, it reduces the danger of making a wrong choice between alternative courses of action. (Jahoda et al., 1951)

The words 'scientific method' describe the rigours and discipline expected of the practitioners of market research in reducing uncertainty:

> Without scientific orientation, marketing research would have little validity, it would deteriorate into subjective and biased assessments of market behaviour. Hence an objective posture and systematic methods of enquiry are vital constituents of marketing research. (Chisnall, 1986)

Up to this point it has been claimed that the marketer is continually looking to the future, faced with uncertainty as to the outcomes of various situations which could be affected by his/her distance from the consumer and/or the speed of change in markets. The marketer perceives risk or uncertainty in different manners but may use market research to reduce uncertainty. Market research can help provide an objective evaluation of a situation by adopting a systematic procedure to investigate marketing phenomena.

This is the widely held view of the role of marketing research which is encapsulated in the following 'approved' definition of marketing research from the American Marketing Association (1987).

> Marketing research is the function which links the consumer, customer and public to the marketer through information – information used to identify and define marketing opportunities and problems; generate, refine and evaluate marketing actions; monitor marketing performance and improve understanding of marketing as a process.
>
> Marketing research specifies the information required to address these issues; designs the method for collecting information; manages and implements the data collection process; analyses the results; and communicates the findings and their implications.

From this definition the fundamental roles of support for the decision maker may be derived as:

1   Defining the nature and scope of target markets

Characteristics of target markets are a vital foundation for marketing mix design. Where are the consumers located geographically? What behavioural or lifestyle characteristics do they possess? What expectations do they have of the products or services they consume (or would like to consume)? What is their ability to purchase different products or services? In what circumstances do they purchase and consume products or services?

Knowledge of these characteristics helps marketers to 'build a picture' of their markets and to overcome any physical or psychological distance that may exist between marketers and their markets.

2   Understanding factors that can change target markets and the firm's ability to satisfy those target markets

In order to conduct effective marketing planning an understanding of the nature of the firm and consumer's environment is required. This does not mean that marketers need to understand the total marketing system (which would be impossible) but to understand the *salient* subsystems within the total system that have the greatest effect on their own firm's performance and those that have the greatest effect upon the cognitive, behavioural or physical features of target markets.

Knowledge of the salient features of the marketing system for an individual firm can help to identify the growth or demise of a market and the potential of new markets.

3   Testing marketing mix features as 'expected' by target markets

With a 'picture' of target markets and a knowledge of the firm's capabilities, marketers can design what they believe will be an optimum mix, one that will induce the greatest levels of satisfaction throughout a target market. Because of the time taken to plan and deliver a marketing mix, the marketer will make assumptions about the expectations of a target market. Even with the 'scientific' support of market researchers, potential consumers may be unable to conceptualize or even express their expectations of a product or service at the time when the marketing mix is planned. Thus, for example, when a product is being formulated, the market researcher can test various formulations to see which features best suit different types of consumer. As well as testing individual marketing mix components, the interactions of various marketing mix components can be tested.

4   Monitoring the effect of marketing activities

After a marketing mix has been targeted to a group of consumers, the market researcher can help to assess the effects of those efforts. Whether the effects of those efforts have been a success or a failure is immaterial (from the perspective of furthering our understanding of marketing phenomena), what is important is to know *why* certain marketing mix efforts had a certain effect or outcome. This further helps to understand better the expectations of consumers in target markets, and what factors can have an effect on their expectations (including those within the marketer's control and those without).

Market research supports marketers by increasing their knowledge of marketing phenomena related to their problems. The key constructs of

problems can be identified, as can the interrelationship of these constructs and the strengths of such interrelationships. By helping marketers to further their understanding, the foundation of better planning and forecasting can be made.

The limitations of market research

The message is clear enough – if marketers have a gap in their knowledge, if they perceive risk and uncertainty in decision making and cannot find support within their organization, then they can gain support from externally generated market research. However, there are cases where the use of market research support has resulted in failure and it is worth examining the limitations of market research.

Lehmann (1989) points out two areas of misconception of the role of marketing research:

1 Market research does not make decisions. Research's role is not to make decisions. Rather, research takes data about a confusing/uncertain market and rearranges them into a different form which hopefully makes the market more understandable and consequently good decisions easier.
2 Market research does not guarantee success. Research at best can improve the odds of making a correct decision. Anyone who expects to eliminate the possibility of failure by doing research is both unrealistic and likely to be disappointed. The real value of research can be seen over a long period where increasing the percentage of good decisions should be manifested in improved bottom-line performance and in the occasional revelation that arises from research.

There is a reminder here of the long-term benefits of doing research, i.e., that the results of a study may help decision makers with an immediate problem, but by building their knowledge they can also have long-term benefits:

Decisions are not hallowed for all time. Nothing stands still: actions change as a result of new information; information alters as actions change. The process is dynamic and continuous. Thus, ultimately, decision making is about improving the quality of decision – through better information, better understanding, more insight. (Vineall, 1979)

Beyond the misconceptions of the role of market research, other authors show why the simple concept of the market researcher supporting the marketer may be flawed.

Historically, much market research has been undertaken on behalf of new products, and yet their success rate, across a wide range of product categories, has been poor. Why is this? If market research is as useful as market researchers believe it to be, there should have been more successes and fewer failures. (Sampson and Standen, 1983)

They go on to admit that it is unreasonable to blame research for every failure. They postulate two reasons for the rejection of research findings by marketers:

1 Blind optimism/disbelief in research – many patently bad products have been launched because marketing management did not believe their research findings.
2 Political pressures within an organization to launch a 'borderline' case.

Luck *et al.* (1978) give further reasons why marketers reject research findings which go beyond the confines of product testing:

1 Invalidity of research methods. If the decision maker suspects the accuracy or appropriateness of the methods for the problem faced, lack of confidence would lead to rejection.
2 Faulty communication, so that the findings are difficult to comprehend or utilize – or unconvincing.
3 Irrelevance of the findings to the perceived problems, in the view of the decision maker.

If marketers have experienced any of the above rejections to research, they can easily support their case by questioning the time taken to conduct research (and the possible consequences of delays in decision making), the cost required (not only in paying for market research but in managerial effort) without strong methods of evaluating the return on investment, and the support that can be given from a researcher who may know little if anything of the context and environment in which

the decisions are to be made. They could point to examples such as the launch of California Cooler (and the entire 'cooler' wine industry in the USA) 'which was launched with absolutely no marketing research' (*Business Week*, 1984) and contend that high investment decisions of great risk and uncertainty have succeeded without market research while others have failed with the use of market research (the reverse is also true).

There are many indicators in the reasons for rejecting research of problems of communication between the marketer and researcher and further in the assumptions of the parties, responsibilities and expertise.

It is sometimes said that if management commissions market research, and at the end of it the results only tell it what it already knows, then the fault lies with management for posing the wrong questions or problem in the first place. This may be realistic if one takes a narrow view of the manager's and the researcher's separate responsibilities but not if one considers that they have a joint commitment to solve the problem. (Ward, 1971)

If there are problems in the acceptance of research findings with indications that communication and awareness of the roles of each party are a problem, then it is logical to examine this issue at the foundation of the research process, i.e., the initiation of a piece of research, and to examine the roles, competences and responsibilities of the marketer and the market researcher.

The intitiation of effective research

From a theoretical perspective the initiation of market research is a most straightforward procedure. Most market research texts devote just a few pages to the process. In basic terms, if marketers perceive that they require support from a market researcher, they outline the nature of their marketing problem, the background to the evolution of the problem and their decision-making constraints in the form of a research brief (which may be in a written or oral format). Following this, the researcher translates the marketing problem into a research problem and outlines how the problem may be solved, what it will cost and how long it will take. Both parties ensure that the other's perspective is clear. (The above perspective does not account for the vagaries of the most simple of research tasks to the highly complex, which will be tackled later.) For what ostensibly seems to be a straightforward task, much can go wrong:

> Studies of research success and failures point again and again to close collaboration between researcher and client as the single most important factor predicting a good outcome. (Andreasen, 1985)

> The underlying problem of poor research outcomes can often be traced to the quality and quantity of interface between the manager who is using the research and research professionals. (Aaker and Day, 1980, p. 59)

Debomy (1989) taking an extreme and even controversial perspective, argues that market researchers 'have no idea what a company's strategy can be, or even no idea what marketing is'. On the other hand, 'clients, even when they are qualified researchers by training or experience, can never be as competent as their institute counterpart in designing and conducting research, and are even often unable to define a set of research objectives on their own'.

The problem may stem from the format of the research brief. There is an infinity of different cases, and a multiplicity of different circumstances (company structures, relationships with in-house and outside researchers and project types, time-scales and budgets). These must influence the exact format of the research brief (Greenhalgh, 1983). Therefore there can be a great variety of means of the marketer actually communicating the nature of the marketing problem. More fundamentally, however, is the marketer's conception of the marketing problem he/she faces. Without a clear definition of the marketing problem, subsequent stages become of limited value or even of damage to the organization. Of course there are instances where the definition of the marketing problem is so straightforward that it would be insulting to question the validity of a problem statement, though this is not always the case.

> There is a tendency to assume that the manager always has a clear understanding of the management problem and that, therefore, the only difficulty is in communicating the understanding. This

is often not true; the manager is perhaps more likely to approach the researcher with problems that are not clearly defined. In this case the initial task of the researcher is to help develop a commonly understood and agreed definition of the management problem. (Tull and Hawkins, 1987)

The validity of the conclusion of the above statement is based on three premises. The first is the marketer's conception of how clear the marketing problem is – why bother to involve other parties into the diagnosis when it is so obvious? The second lies in the marketer's willingness to allow another party to help in the process of problem diagnosis, i.e., the trust and confidence that exists between the parties. The third lies in the expertise of the market researcher, i.e., what they can bring to the process of problem diagnosis:

> The expertise of the market researcher is often misunderstood by management. He is an expert in the techniques of market research. He may also be a very rounded person, with wide knowledge and considerable wisdom in business matters. But, on the other hand, he may be a very narrow specialist whose judgement is no worse and no better than that of the man who has commissioned him to carry out the work. (Ward, 1971)

A very simple model of these factors illustrates a basic dichotomous scale that shows tendencies of the clarity of the marketing problem (Figure 9.1).

Problem perception

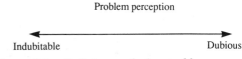

Indubitable   Dubious

Figure 9.1 *Defining marketing problems*

If a marketing problem is to be placed at a point on the dichotomous scale, much depends upon the marketer's ability to observe cues and signals and thus form a diagnosis. If the diagnosis does not match 'reality' then regardless of the sophistication of market research techniques, the solution could be wrong and harmful. If the marketer perceives the problem to be indubitable he/she may simply see the researcher as a 'supplier' of techniques. If the marketer perceives the problem to be tending towards the dubious he/she may use the market researcher (as one of many potential sources) to help in problem diagnosis before a suitable research technique is decided. There is no formula to say when the researcher should be involved in problem definition; again it all rests upon the marketer's perception of risk and uncertainty.

A key word in the process of defining marketing problems and how dubious they are is 'diagnosis'. While diagnosis now has a chiefly medical context, in its essence it is not a medical term at all, but has a vastly broader meaning. From its derivation diagnosis means to distinguish. This involves discrimination (King, 1982). To those involved with the definition of marketing problems on a daily basis the ability to 'distinguish' or 'diagnose' may become innate and simple to complete. For others not used to the process it may be arduous and difficult to conclude. From a medical analogy:

> While it may take 20 minutes of teaching rounds for the doctors and students to arrive at a tentative diagnosis, experienced clinicians typically formulate initial hypotheses within 15 seconds of talking with a new patient.   (Elstein *et al.*, 1978)

What must be considered from such a statement is what process does the diagnostician go through enabling him/her to reduce the formulation of hypotheses from twenty minutes to fifteen seconds? What is involved in problem setting rather than problem solving?

> In real world practice, problems do not present themselves as givens. They must be constructed from the materials of problematic situations which are puzzling, troubling and uncertain . . . although problem setting is a necessary condition for technical problem solving, it is not itself a technical problem.   (Schon, 1988, p. 66)

Schon sees the process of problem setting as one in which, interactively, we *name* the things to which we will attend and *frame* the context in which we will attend to them. In learning to diagnose problems, the 'naming' and the 'framing' are explicit but as we gain experience of this process it becomes part of our everyday actions. Schon describes this process in the workday life of the professional.

> The workday life of the professional depends on tacit knowing in action. Each competent practitioner can recognize phenomena, families of symptoms associated with a particular disease,

pecularities of a certain kind of building site, iregularities of materials or structures. . . .

Or the behaviour of competitive salespeople, the intensity of competition in sales promotion terms, the innovativeness of a new product:

> . . . For which he cannot give a reasonably accurate or complete description. In his day-to-day practice he makes innumerable judgements of quality for which he cannot state adequate criteria, and he displays skills for which he cannot state the rules and procedures. Even when he makes conscious use of research-based theories and techniques, he is dependent on tacit recognitions, judgements and skilful performances. (Schon, 1988, p. 69)

Schon sees practitioners as developing a repertoire of expectations, images and techniques. They learn what to look for and how to respond to what they find. What they look for and find may be signs that are very subtle and difficult to describe. In everyday action the tacit knowing of relevant signs allows the practitioner to 'name' and to 'frame' but not in all cases in an explicit manner. Polanyi (1967) invented the phrase 'tacit knowing', the following exemplifies what he means by the term tacit knowing:

> If we know a person's face, we can recognise it among a thousand, indeed among a million, though we cannot usually tell how we recognize a face we know. Similarly we recognize the moods of a human face without being able to tell 'except quite vaguely' by what signs we know them. (p. 4)
> When we learn to use a tool, or a probe or a stick for feeling our way, our initial awareness of its impact on our hand is tranformed into a sense of its point touching the objects we are exploring. (p. 12)

If there is something that is puzzling, troubling and creating a risk in a marketing decision, as marketers make sense of it they reflect on the understandings (built up of much tacit knowing) which have been implicit in their action. Given a problem, their understandings surface, are criticized, restructured and embodied in further action. The pragmatic nature of the work of the marketer means that the process of 'reflection in action' is central to dealing with situations of uncertainty, instability and uniqueness. If a situation arises, however, where the marketers' 'reflections' are insufficient to allow them to progress they may perceive high risk and seek market research support.

In the initiation of research, consideration must be given to the role of market researchers in their task of understanding the diagnosis of the problem and setting out a suitable research strategy. Krum *et al.* (1988) contend that communication at the initiation of research could be improved and that market researchers prefer a more active consulting role at that stage:

> Before a research project can begin there must be a clear statement of the problem and objectives. Should researchers take a consulting or an engineering approach at this point? A consultant questions and advises while an engineer forges ahead and designs the requested project. (Krum *et al.*, 1988)

The distinction is not so clear cut. Problem diagnosis is not either simple or complex nor are the relationships that allow the intiation of a research project. Figures 9.2, 9.3 and 9.4 set out different stages of interaction between the marketer and the researcher showing what each party brings to the relationship and the problems that may ensue.

Figure 9.2 illustrates the situation where marketers have a clear understanding of what their problem is and what must be done to resolve it. This case matches the description of research work at British Gas (Johnson, 1983) where the organization employs market research staff and little creative design work is needed at the initiation of a project:

> What is mainly needed is an efficient system for the collection and processing of data.

It also matches much of what happens in the USA according to Barnard (1984):

> It is perhaps not accidental that American research agencies are normally referred to as suppliers. Much ad hoc research is designed by the client company which submits a fairly (or very) detailed specification to the research supplier.

Marketers do not have to be explicit in their diagnosis of the problem but to translate that into a specific detailed research brief. Here, researchers are being used for their technical skills, only perhaps competing against other researchers to fulfill the detailed specification. 'Objective' in the market researcher's sense means having no political persuasion within the organization under study, no favoured hypothesis or pet theory to prove (it is not intended to open up debate on the nature of objectivity in social science investigations and the aims of trying to become 'detached' from what is being measured). Keeping researchers away from the problem definition stages also allows marketers to couch the nature of the problem in terms that fulfil their political objectives. The researcher being objective in such a process gives credence to the findings:

> The technical adequacy of market research is not the only issue determining whether or not the research will be perceived as useful. Clearly the political acceptability of certain findings also will influence the use of research. (Deshpande and Zaltman, 1984)

Similarly, the researcher is kept out of the interpretation of the findings. Not knowing the context of the initiation of the research, the market researcher could only comment on findings that have occurred in similar cases in the past to which he has been privy:

> The external research supplier may not be as privy to the insider's views and hence has a more difficult task of extracting an understanding of what market research can accomplish. (Deshpande and Zaltman, 1984)

Though the process outlined in Figure 9.2 may be speedy and allow the marketer much control over the process, problems may occur in the 'translation' of marketing problem into a research problem. Problems may occur in defining the initial marketing problem but the marketer may use any specialists within the organization or without, such as ad agencies, a research buyer, or consultants.

Figure 9.3 illustrates a greater amount of co-operation between the marketer and the market researcher. Here the marketer may find difficulty in translating the marketing problem into a research problem and thus presents a less detailed brief. In order to do this the marketer is having to be explicit about the 'names' and 'frames' of the diagnosis of the problem.

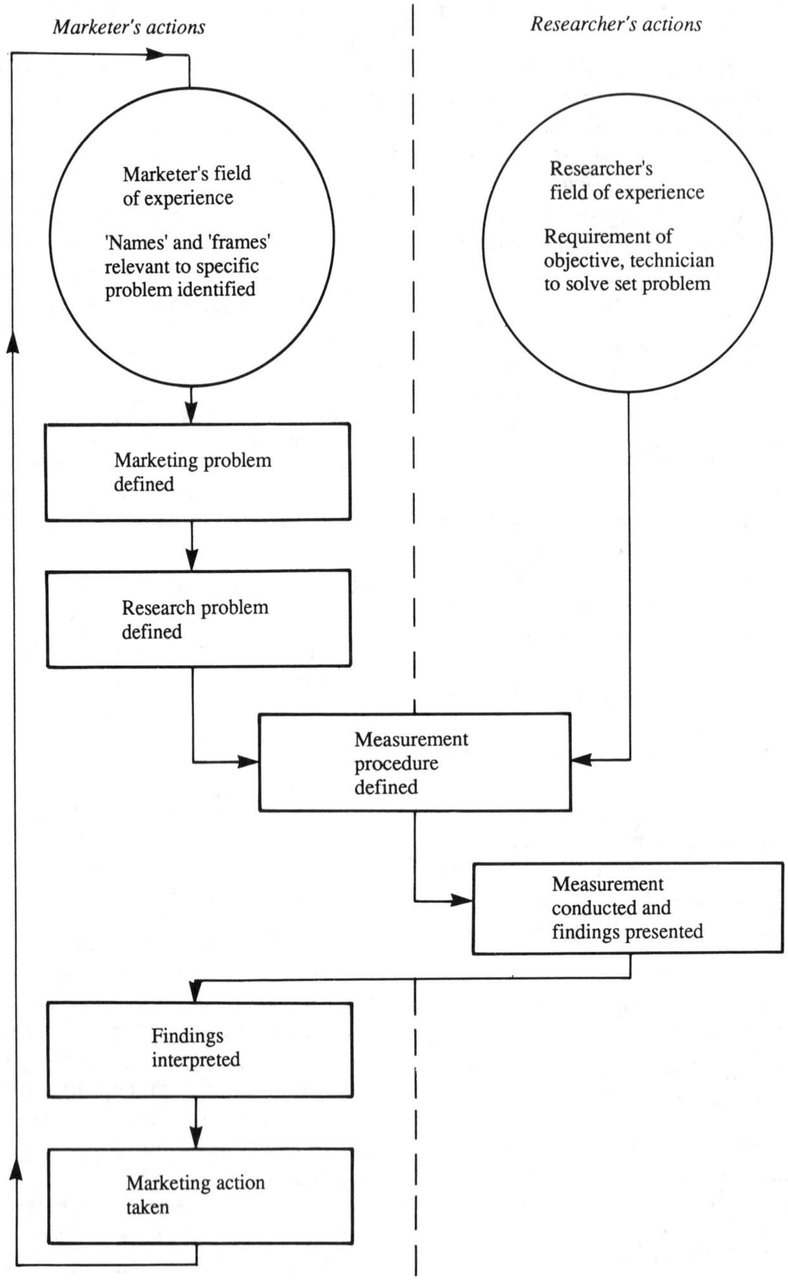

Figure 9.2 *Marketer–researcher interaction: marketer dominated*

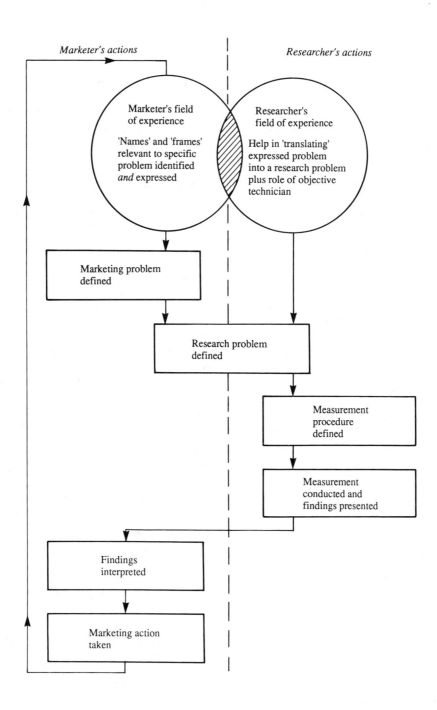

Figure 9.3   *Marketer–researcher interaction: researcher dominated*

Having to be explicit about diagnosis may help the marketer's own understanding of the problem but need not be more successful than coping with uncertainty by 'reflection in action'. The key issue here is that the market researcher has now become privy to the field of experience of the marketer and the marketer has the chance to explore the techniques that the market researcher may have used in similar situations in the past. The extent of overlap in the fields of experience is crucial:

> The researcher frequently does not observe the symptoms (names and frames) first-hand but is presented with them by a client, possibly together with an explanation (i.e., the problem). There is a double danger here in selectivity of both clients' and researchers' perceptions influencing the inference of the problem . . . the psychology of perception indicates that we are likely to bias our perceptions in accordance to our expectations (and thus not see some symptoms at the expense of others).   (Elliot and Christopher, 1973)

The danger of the above is that researchers may perceive the nature of a marketing problem through their means of fulfilling the research problem, i.e., their ability to use research techniques in order to achieve a particular outcome. In other words, the research technique can ultimately define the nature of the marketing problem:

> The research specialist who is not management-orientated will often accept the request for research help without clearly establishing the need for research. This person may fail to ask perceptive questions regarding the decision situation and be uncritical of whether research will facilitate the decision-making process. In addition many specialists are concerned with the technical sophistication of the research design and methodology than the information needs of the management. This focus leads any researcher to look for decision situations where they can apply the latest techniques.   (Kinnear and Taylor, 1983)

Marketers may have contacted the researcher with a known specialism in a technique considering that their knowledge is the most relevant to their marketing problem. If the researcher's practice becomes increasingly tacit, spontaneous and automatic, this brings benefits of specialization. There are dangers in this:

> As a practice becomes more repetitive and routine, becoming increasingly tacit and spontaneous, the practitioner may miss important opportunities to think about what he is doing . . . he can then be selectively inattentive to phenomena that do not fit his 'knowing in action'.   (Schon, 1988)

The key issue is a perceived need to set firm research objectives, the translation from marketing objectives causing the problem. Tentative, exploratory work may help illuminate both the marketing and research problem definitions:

> Despite the importance of research objectives, they are not and should not be the focal point of the dialogue between the manager and the researcher. If objectives become the focal point, the emphasis is subtly shifted towards the researcher's needs, rather than on the manager's point of view. The predictable result is a narrowly defined statement of objectives that misses important features of the strategic issue.   (Aaker and Day, 1980, p. 62)

They contend that both parties suffer in such a situation: the researcher having only a narrow undertanding of the reasons for the research; the manager not knowing fully what they want and may have partially or incorrectly defined their problems or decision alternatives to be evaluated.

Alt (1980) in his scathing attack on the UK market research industry contends that much damage can occur by taking an 'operationalist' perspective of solving marketing problems.

Kinnear and Taylor (1983) also highlight the problems of such an approach in the later stages of the research process:

> This emphasis on technique results in technical jargon and standardised ways of presenting research findings which tend to inhibit the management research communication process, especially in the reporting of research results.

However, this approach could bring the ideal support for the marketer. The specialist researcher could well have experienced a similar marketing problem in the past, thus finding it relatively simple to translate the problem into a research problem and then apply the technique. The interpretation of the research findings do not necessarily have to be completed by the marketer as in Figure 9.3, they could be a combined effort.

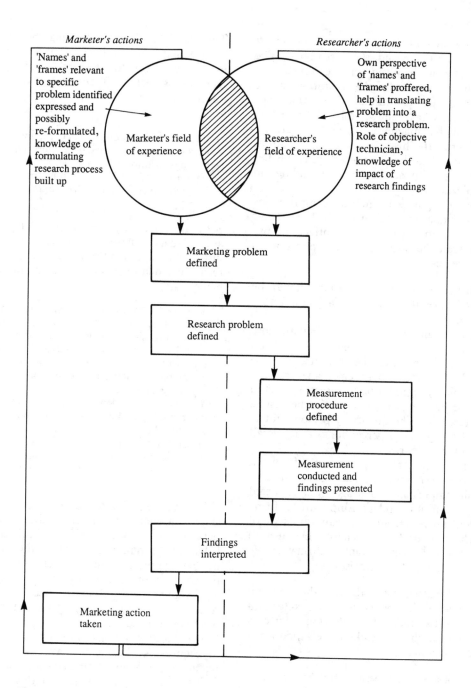

Figure 9.4 *Marketer–researcher interaction: interacted effort*

Figure 9.4 shows a greater combination of effort between the marketer and the researcher. The researcher is now involved in the process of diagnosis, which results in the definition of the marketing problem. The initial brief at this stage may be vague which allows the researcher to present alternative diagnoses based on a greater understanding of the history, context and politics of the decisions to be supported plus his/her knowledge of the impact of research findings in other organizations.

The layout of Figure 9.4 matches the implications of the Deshpande and Zaltman (1982) study of research users into the factors that affect the use of market research information. The implications of their study were:

1   The structure of an organization should be examined carefully to detect any inhibitory effects on research use.
2   Managers should provide researchers with more information about the decisions to be made on the basis of the research they produce.
3   Personal interaction between managers and researchers is very important in creating trust in the researcher and consequently in the results of the research. The quality of personal interaction affects manager perceptions of the overall quality of the report itself.
4   Providing a research agency with feedback about the use/non-use made of research is especially important if that agency is expected to have a continuing relationship with the firm.
5   Researchers who favour an exploratory style of research should be especially sensitive to managers' tendencies to want confirmatory research containing few surprises.

Vineall (1979) concurs with the view that building up a close relationship between the marketer and researcher is of value. The following advice is proffered to research users seeking the support of a qualitative researcher:

> There is considerable benefit to be obtained in choosing qualitative researchers who have experience in analysing marketing and advertising problems and experience in the market in question. Establishing a long-term liaison with researchers will increase their value.

The benefits of the close liaison go beyond the need for a strong problem diagnosis at the onset. In the interpretation of the research findings, the researcher is better placed to observe relevant information and demonstrate their marketing impact.

> If the working relationship between marketing and market research is a good one, interpretation of the findings will be a joint operation so that the significance of the findings is fully (marketing) and properly (market research) exploited. (Crimp, 1985)

In any research project there is an over-abundance of data (quantitative and/or qualitative) and distilling this data into a manageable report can result in much of its original meaning or richness being lost:

> The verbal presentation and written report provided by a researcher, however carefully and conscientiously constructed inevitably can only feed back a limited and researcher structured representation of the data as the basis for the researcher's understandings and conclusions. The relevance and usefulness of this to the client's decision making depends significantly upon the communicative skills and orientation of the researcher. For some clients and researchers, particularly those who have, over time, developed a relationship of mutual trust and confidence, such a situation may not represent an issue. (Jones, 1981)

Beyond the taking of marketing action, feedback allows the marketer and researcher to build their fields of experience. Marketers building a knowledge of formulating research related to their marketing problems, the researchers understanding the constitution of marketing problems. The overlap in their fields of experience grows and the researcher's ability to support the marketer effectively is improved.

There are limitations to the model of interaction in Figure 9.4. Problems may exist in finding a researcher in whom the marketer can build up confidence and trust, or in fact this process may take many years. In many organizations there exist research buyers who mediate between the user and researcher, as well as helping to find the researcher with the correct technical skills for a particular job they may form a barrier between the user and researcher in building up trust and confidence. It could also be argued that the close contact with the marketer, knowing the context of decision making and the history behind the marketing problem could be achieved by using in-house researchers who could then write specific research briefs and develop the relationship as detailed in Figure 9.2. In certain circumstances, though, the external agency may be able to draw on marketing and research experiences from a wider or different perspective that may be of use, they could have distinct technical skills and they may help overcome particular organizational political problems.

Finally, Figure 9.4 might be regarded as describing the role of the marketing consultant rather than the market researcher. Much depends upon our experiences and subsequent perceptions of what a market researcher is. Certainly, within the industry efforts are being made to change the market researcher's image.

> Taking an active role in strategy development was one strong way in which other marketing services integrated themselves into the day-to-day business of their clients. Isn't research admirably placed to do the same? We of all people know the play of ideas; and in assessing the trade-offs we have a feel for what you can change and what you can't. (Berry and Fisher, 1987)

In 1987 the Market Research Society commissioned Touche Ross (as objective outsiders) to investigate the 'Challenge to Change' in the research industry. Comments on the impact of that report:

> They agreed that other professions like accountancy, management consultancy and strategic planning could erode our markets – often buying in *our* services on the cheap . . . we could end up further away from the real decision makers – consigned to trade forever in the twilight world of the big company middle manager. . . . Market research professionals will be in the mainstream of management consultancy – just like the planning function in advertising agencies. Researchers will have access to more data about their clients – they'll provide a rounder, higher value, value added service. (Morris, 1989)

Choosing the right technique

Beyond defining the marketing and research problem correctly is the issue of applying the most appropriate research technique to the set problem. The previous section highlighted the issue of defining the nature of problems by the means of solving them, i.e., operationalism. This stance involves a tendency to move away from the user's needs towards technical issues.

> . . . faced with a problem, there has been an implicit tendency to twist it to fit the best known technique. Thus research design has become technique design. A natural result of this is that researchers increasingly see themselves as purveyors and proponents of particular techniques. (Blyth and Robson, 1981)

In order to help overcome this issue the rationale and potential applications of qualitative and quantitative methods are evaluated. There is no simple 'black and white' method of demarcating which phenomena should be examined using qualitative or quantitative methods (or 'soft' and 'hard' methods). Uncertainty, biases, errors, differences of opinions, motives and values weaken every link in the chain that connects the diagnosis of a marketing problem to the selection of a research technique. The most appropriate manner in which to evaluate qualitative and quantitative methods is to examine the characteristics that information should possess if it is to be of *practical* value to the decision maker (given their inherent time and cost limitations). The framework for this evaluation is from Peterson (1982).

Information must be:

Accurate, i.e. a *valid* representation of the phenomena under investigation, that has come from a *reliable* or consistent measurement, and that is *sensitive* to differences. Combining these three criteria refers to the degree to which information reflects 'reality'.
Current, i.e., the degree to which information reflects events in the relevant time period, past and present.
Sufficient, i.e., the completeness or clarity of a 'picture' that reflects marketing phenomena under study.

Available, i.e., that access to relevant information can be made when a decision is imminent.

Relevant, i.e., that the support given 'makes sense' to the decision maker, that they can use research findings to build upon their foundation of existing knowledge.

The utopia of generating information that contains all of the above characteristics does not exist in market research except in the realms of basic marketing phenomena where the relevancy of the information could be questioned, i.e., is it too basic to be of any use? Realistically, trade-offs must be made among the above characteristics. Within the characteristic of accuracy there are trade-offs which are primarily caused by what the researcher is measuring (Boyd *et al.*, 1989):

1 The subject of investigation is usually the human being.
2 The process of measuring humans may cause them to change.
3 It is difficult to assess the effect of extraneous variables in marketing experiments and thus their applications are limited.

The choice of measurement devices and the interpretation of their measurements, the complexity of the subject under study, the context or environment in which measurements are taken, all combine to make it difficult (if not impossible) to gain completely objective and accurate measurements. Of all the potential trade-offs, Peterson (1982) contends that 'relevancy is the one characteristic that can never be compromised. To do so would make information useless'.

Relevancy embraces, inter alia, measuring the ability to plan and forecast from research findings, to be able to distinguish real differences in consumers, to know that characteristics are representative of groups of individuals and ultimately build up a stronger understanding or awareness of markets and the forces that shape them. There is no one method that can achieve all these.

A starting point for the evaluation of the purposes of qualitative and quantitative methods can be the classification of 'responses to interviewing' as detailed in Figure 9.5 (Cooper and Braithwaite, 1979). At one extreme it shows that there are issues that consumers can express quickly,

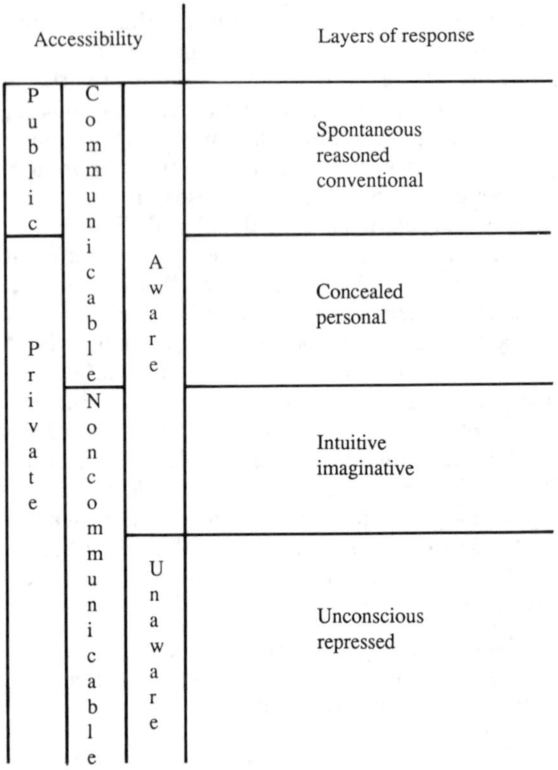

Accessibility			Layers of response
P u b l i c	C o m m u n i c a b l e	A w a r e	Spontaneous reasoned conventional
P r i v a t e			Concealed personal
	N o n c o m m u n i c a b l e		Intuitive imaginative
		U n a w a r e	Unconscious repressed

Figure 9.5 *Responses to interviewing*

that are simple to reflect, of common everyday occurrences. In such circumstances, simple questioning (or self-reporting) in a standardized manner is possible. Further, the same procedure can be conducted in a like manner to a whole array of 'types' of individual such as age groups, social class and intellectual levels. Clearly in such situations quantitative techniques are applicable that allow very detailed *descriptions* of basic characteristics of consumers. At the other extreme are factors that the consumer may not be able to conceptualize, let alone express or be willing to express.

In such circumstances the characteristics of the individual will determine what is the best way to probe and elicit appropriate responses. Nothing is standardized here but the result may be the 'tapping' of the rationale of behaviour in certain individuals. In such situations qualitative techniques are the most appropriate allowing *exploration* to take place as each situation may demand. In between these two extremes could be situations for example that are simple, easy to express but highly embarrassing for the individual (and perhaps even for the interviewer). In these situations it is not so clear which techniques will best reflect the reality of the situation.

It is the situations in between the two extremes where most controversy exists about choosing the most appropriate methods. In recent years much debate has raged about which set of methods best serve the marketer. As has been argued earlier the best method for the marketer is determined by the nature of his marketing problem. The marketing problem does not, however, always give a clear linear route to an appropriate technique.

The rationale of quantitative methods

In the development of explanations of marketing phenomena, quantitative methods can help in building models that highlight key constructs, show their interrelationships and the relative strengths of interrelationship. Different types of scaling are used to build such models. Thus, the first reason to use quantitative methods is to build models that describe marketing phenomena using terms that are universal. Being universal, allows other researchers to build upon findings, set them into other contexts and adjust the findings of other studies. Beyond the description of phenomena, hypotheses can be formulated in models and tested, thus experiments can be conducted. Thus the second reason to use quantitative methods is to test hypothesized situations.

The rules for conducting quantitative research and the means of conducting statistical tests are addressed clearly in all major market research and statistics texts with little difference except in style of presentation. Quantitative data is seen as being 'hard', errors in measurement can be calculated and accounted for and confidence in findings can be calculated. Finally, quantitative methods can ensure a proper representation of the population or distinct subgroups:

> even if 7 out of 10 people interviewed in a qualitative setting express enthusiasm for a particular product or idea, it is entirely possible that in

a broader survey of the market, 7 in 10 might actually reject that same product.   (Goldman and McDonald, 1987)

Quantitative methods support the marketer in answering questions such as the size of markets, their salient features, the distribution of features and especially in assessing the importance of particular features to different consumer types.

> To evaluate responses to advertising, we cannot get away from the question 'How TYPICAL is this response?' Is it MOST of our target group who feel like this, or only an eccentric few? One cannot answer this question from qualitative research alone.   (McDonald, 1988)

If one refers to the start of this chapter and re-examines the four areas in which researchers support marketers, it can be seen that in each area, quantitative methods help in describing and experimenting with marketing phenomena.

The rationale of qualitative methods

In the development of explanations of marketing phenomena, qualitative methods can initially *identify* the key constructs, their relationships and the relative strengths of interrelationship. Thus, qualitative research can help formulate the premises of descriptions which can then be tested on a representative basis. In experimentation, qualitative research can help by identifying relevant independent and extraneous variables.

Qualitative methods may be used for purposes other than to help build models. In the example used at the start of the chapter where the grocer had a strong empathy with his customers, the same sort of understanding can be sought about the underlying dimensions of attitudes, motivations, emotional status, personalities. Here the emphasis is not on establishing what consumers do but why they behave as they do. In many instances the consumer cannot succinctly explain why they behave in a particular manner:

> . . . little credence can be attached to the answers given when informants are asked directly about the reasons for their behaviour – mainly because they themselves do not know and can only rationalize – to get at the '*truth*' it is necessary to take cross-

bearings from a set of indirect approaches in order to arrive at deductions which approximated to that truth. (Henry, 1986)

Building an empathy with consumers means the researcher building up a 'richness' of understanding.

Richness has something to do with 'variety', 'depth', 'realness', and 'colour'. (Fineman and Mangham, 1983)

Developing a richness of understanding of consumers, gaining insights that may be more appropriate in novels, plays, paintings, poems, cartoons, operas, diaries or dreams can be used for two main reasons. The first could be *after* a quantitative study where perhaps a significant difference between consumers has been highlighted or a basic characteristic shown in a target group then the reasons for this may be further elucidated. The second could be as a study in its own right. Marketers could have what they perceive to be a clear description of their target markets and their salient characteristics but they may wish to alter features of their marketing mix but find themselves unable to understand the consumer well enough to know what their reaction would be. A qualitative study in its own right could also be the source of ideas for innovations in all aspects of the marketing mix, the decision maker building on his/her existing knowledge rather than a quantitative study. A summary of the uses of qualitative research is contained in Table 9.1.

The rules for using qualitative methods are not as clear as with quantitative methods. Many of the methods are 'borrowed' from other disciplines in the social sciences and humanities and have been used for purposes entirely different to understanding consumer behaviour. Much of the success of the methods lies in the experience of the researcher, their ability of knowing when to probe, what to probe with, and beyond that to the interpretation of meanings *and* the resultant impact of those meanings for the marketer. All of this is highly subjective but it can allow a passage to the valid issues of consumption for the individual that quantitative techniques may miss, and be highly sensitive to the differences that will sway the individual one way or the other. If these provide

Table 9.1 *A summary of the uses of qualitative research*

1　*To obtain some background information where absolutely nothing is known about the problem area or product field in question.*

2　*In concept identification and exploration.*

3　*To identify relevant or salient behaviour patterns, beliefs, opinions, attitudes, motivations, etc.*

4　*To establish priorities among categories of behaviour and psychological variables like beliefs, opinions and attitudes.*

5　*Defining problem areas more fully and formulating hypotheses for further investigation and/or quantification.*

6　*During a preliminary screening process in order to reduce a large number of possible contenders to a smaller number of probable ones.*

7　*To obtain a large amount of data about beliefs, attitudes etc. as data input for multivariate analysis studies.*

8　*Conducting post-research investigations or post-mortems to amplify or explain certain points emerging from some major study, without having to repeat it on a large scale.*

9　*In piloting questionnaires to test comprehension, word forms, memory factors.*

10　*Where it cannot be discovered in a simple, straightforward way like direct questioning why people behave as they do because the field of enquiry is personal or embarrassing in some way.*

Source: Sampson (1986).

enough information to build upon the marketer's existing knowledge, then the findings are relevant and actionable.

Questions can be raised about the reliability or consistency of qualitative methods as the process can be highly subjective (as opposed to the perceived role of the researcher being highly objective). The issue can be resolved from the perspective of how the results are perceived. If the expectation is that qualitative findings are to be used to develop a rich 'picture' that can be continually enhanced then alternative perspectives are welcomed. If the expectation is that qualitative findings are to be used to form the foundation of quantitative studies then the validation process using reliable techniques clears the issue, but not for Blyth and Robson (1981):

> It is a myth that subjectivity is a source of concern only in qualitative research. Subjectivity is used and must be used in all methods of data collection and interpretation.

And Silverman (1985):

> We cannot put our commonsense knowledge of social structures on one side in the misplaced hope of achieving an objective viewpoint. In an inter-subjective world, both observer and observed use the same resources to identify 'meanings'.

One of the main factors for the usefulness of qualitative research in supporting marketers is the dynamic, exploratory nature of investigation that provides such fresh insights, imitating much of the process of marketing decision making –

> While interviewing, the qualitative researcher is functioning intellectually on a number of levels: listening to the discussion and accepting the data as it is presented; processing this data to set up hypotheses; testing these hypotheses by means of further probing and prompting; and also taking account of the nuances and subtleties of consumer language and expression to explore new relevant avenues of thought not covered in the original research brief. Indeed, the researcher's intellectual approach to the interview needs to be as multi-dimensional as is the data itself, in order to provide *understanding*.   (Blyth and Robson, 1981)

This is compared to the quantitative research process which is the antithesis of the above in that once started a quite rigid approach must be adopted.

Having stated that the approach to one methodology is the antithesis of the other:

> There is no suggestion that qualitative and quantitative research are alternative, or in any way opposed or mutually exclusive, forms of research. Each is to be preferred for different purposes. In practice qualitative and quantitative findings are frequently complementary.   (Vineall, 1979)

> All market research has only one final objective, namely to enhance the quality of marketing strategy and we argue that in pursuance of that objective, all techniques are convergent and have their roots in the same conceptual framework. (Blyth and Robson, 1981)

By applying the criteria of 'relevancy' to the findings of qualitative and quantitative research it is clear that each research type can be relevant first, dependent upon the nature of the marketing problem and, second, dependent upon what the marketer is 'comfortable' in using given the perceived risk or uncertainty.

Having taken the findings of a study (be it quantitative or qualitative), much of the way that the decision maker learns and develops is going to affect future marketing and research problem definitions, perceptions of risk and uncertainty, relationships, i.e., trust and confidence of researchers, and sources of information that can be relied upon.

If market researchers understand how marketers build their knowledge and develop their understanding of markets they have a greater chance of providing effective support. This takes the chapter beyond outlining the areas in which the decision makers can be supported, to look at what abilities the market research should possess in order to offer strong support to a decision maker who is already 'researcher in practice'.

The marketer's reflection in action

When marketers draw on their experience to help with a new situation, they become 'researchers in practice'; they reflect in action. They are not bound by the categories of theories and techniques. For every new situation that is faced, each to some degree different from that faced in the past, they construct a new hypothesis of the unique case. The hypothesis may not be explicit in any way and many of its premises may be loosely defined, but it serves to guide reasoned action and the search for further information. Their search for further information is not limited to a deliberation about means which depend upon a prior agreement about ends. They do not keep means and ends separate, but define them interactively as they frame a problematic situation.

> He does not separate thinking from doing, ratiocinating his way to a decision which he must later convert to action. Because his experimenting is a kind of action, implementation is built into his inquiry. This reflection in action can proceed even in situations of uncertainty or uniqueness because it is not bounded by the dichotomies of 'technical rationality'.   (Schon, 1988)

The 'technical rationality' in the above statement placed in the marketing context refers to the scientific process of building knowledge. Briefly, the process involves: the observation of patterns; the categorization of events; the formation of generalizations of those events creating (testable) hypotheses; the testing of those hypotheses to form general conclusions. Thus from the specific observations made, by inductive reasoning, general conclusions can be made. Beyond these general conclusions, specific situations can be predicted by the use of deductive reasoning. This means building knowledge is bound by technical rules at each stage to ensure the validity of the process and the 'truth' of the output of each stage.

Marketers faced with unique situations, predicting the future, use inductive and deductive reasoning mostly without the strictures of technical rationality, it becomes implicit or part of their reflection in action. Hypotheses are built based upon their past experience and are part of the 'naming' and 'framing' approach to understanding the nature of their markets and environment. In new situations alternative hypotheses may compete with each other with various potential outcomes. This process of reasoning involves: the derivation of consequences of the hypotheses and the comparison of these hypotheses with known facts (or, first, the investigation of 'reality' to discover the relevant facts); the reformulation of the hypotheses in order to generate more nearly exact consequences (if this is necessary); the rejection of the hypotheses if the consequences are too grossly incompatible with the facts; attempts to refine, by simplification and by relating to other areas of knowledge, the basic tenets of the hypothesis and so on. Aspects of this process have been called 'hypothetico-deductive'

reasoning, but the process as a whole is a good deal more complicated (Scriven, 1976).

In short, in order to deal with specific new situations that involve the future, marketers use their own observations or generates observations from other sources, categorizes these observations in different manners to form explanations or the facts upon which they can base deductions. They will accept or reject certain hypotheses based on their confidence in the 'facts' or initial observations and how well the combined facts have been categorized. They will accept or reject certain deductions based on how confident they are in the premises and structural relationship of the premises. It is not a process of following a series of observations through to a conclusion but a constant 'to and fro' of ideas, of interactively searching for cues, testing and taking action and as such is a highly creative process:

> You are forced to accept an argument (premises and structure) only if you cannot think of any other. If you cannot think of another explanation that is comparably plausible, then, until it is ruled out, there is no case. The process of trying to think of alternative explanations of a set of facts – the premises of an argument – is an entirely creative process. It is exactly the process which the great original scientist goes through in coming up with a novel theory. There are no precise rules to guide one in such a search and it requires imagination nurtured by a rich and varied experience to generate the novel hypothesis here. (Scriven, 1976)

In the generation of competing hypotheses and potential outcomes, marketers may make mistakes. First, they may be hasty in their inductive reasoning, leaping to a conclusion on the basis of insufficient evidence. It may be that the number of past observed instances of a certain condition (e.g. the success of a price rise) is far too few or the conclusion far too sweeping. Second, they may be forgetful in induction, overlooking some obvious or well-known facts. Third, they may be 'lazy' in their induction, failing to draw any conclusion at all from the evidence at hand or in failing to draw conclusions as strong as the evidence justifies. All the above inductive mistakes will form weak premises from which to build deductive reasoning. The fourth mistake can occur beyond the above in deduction by forming a poor structure of the truths or generalizations of induction, i.e., making the wrong relationships of meanings.

Hypothetico-deductive reasoning helps marketers to cope with the future. It helps them to cope with dynamic markets and environments. The strength of marketers' plans lie in their crafting of deductive reasoning. They make inferences that allow them to create solutions to novel problems:

> The process of creation can be viewed as one of running things up provisionally, taking a look at them in the light of standards deriving from experience and knowledge, and modifying, rejecting or accepting parts of the whole before moving on to develop other ideas. (Fineman and Mangham, 1983)

The researcher has a role to play in this creative activity, to help avoid the basic mistakes of hypothetico-deductive reasoning, while not imposing a rigid structure of technical rationality that could inhibit the marketer.

Desired skills of an effective researcher

It is generally accepted that the market researcher gets 'close' to the consumer, developing explanations and ultimately understanding why consumers behave as they do. It is naturally expected that the researcher has the technical skills to develop this 'closeness' be they of a quantitative and/or qualitative nature. In order for this closeness to be of any effect it has been argued earlier that the researcher should be part of a growing exchange of experiences with 'client' marketers building up a knowledge of marketing problem definition and the contribution of research findings to the solution of problems, i.e., to be part of the strategic decision-making process. Thus, as well as drawing skills enabling them to get close to the consumer, effective researchers require skills that will allow them to get close to the marketer.

Taking the hypothetico-deductive reasoning explanation as a basic from of the marketer 'in action', the distinct skills of the market researcher may be evaluated. The researcher is not expected to replicate the hypothetico-deductive reasoning process of the marketer but be able to recognize the process existing and be able to help avoid mistakes in inductive reasoning, hypothesis formation and deductive reasoning (when they have the possibility of doing so).

In inductive reasoning it has been stated that the marketer may be 'hasty', 'sweeping', or 'lazy'. In order to help here, the researcher requires skills of *observation* and *synthesis*. The ability to observe involves being able to identify and describe symptoms as distinguished from the problems themselves, symptoms that the marketer has not recognized or experienced before. This involves knowing where to search for such symptoms in an organization (always assuming that one is allowed to search). As well as symptoms emerging from documents in an organization, the experiences of a wide array of individuals can be of help. The elicitation of relevant points that help form descriptions of symptoms may be necessary. In ensuring that the inductive reasoning process proceeds with sufficient evidence, researchers may be faced with a vast array of data from a variety of sources. They must decide what credence may be attributed to these sources. They will be required to help synthesize data, to sort out inconsistencies and make connections between data from a variety of sources:

> The alert market researcher needs to be as inventive as his colleagues in creative departments, since ingenious research is unlikely to flow from the mechanical application of principles to the solution of problems. This creativity should be particularly apparent at the early stages of a project, during problem location and analysis. (Elliot and Christopher, 1973)

The researcher has a role to play in hypotheses that are to be tested. Here the knowledge of appropriate tests (skills, timing, costs) will help to form hypotheses that go beyond mere conjecture. With the results of tests comes the ability to formulate deductive reasoning. The justification of deductive reasoning is made by:

1   The relationship of meanings between the various terms in the statements (the researcher providing support of a *confirmatory* nature).
2   The logical structure of the premises of the argument (the researcher providing support of an *exploratory* nature).

The end result of the development of skills that bring the researcher closer to the marketer is that research no longer becomes passive and historical but a part of the pragmatic process of establishing well-founded expectations of the future, a vital role in strategic decision making.

It is conceded that many of these abilities required of the researcher are of a normative nature. The reality may be more like the situation described by Bailey and Scott-Jones (1988) in their research of research buyers:

> Some research is conducted because somebody is 'getting stuck' (deferring decisions or covering themselves). Such research is often qualitative and tends to be carried out to help research users who do not really know what questions to ask. Our research buyer respondents felt that such research sometimes crossed the boundary from 'political' and became worthwhile.

Beyond this description of the state of affairs in some organizations they went on to list what the research buyer is looking for in the ideal researcher. Note that the research user may have a different perspective and that no priorities or trade-offs were made, though two characteristics were seen as being of paramount importance, the first being personal compatibility, the second being 'objectivity', not only being objective but demonstrating that they are objective. Of the research buyers they interviewed the following characteristics of the ideal researcher were agreed:

- Express things succinctly.
- Express clear conclusions.
- Provide a dialogue with the buyer during the whole of the project.
- Have experience of research.
- Have experience of the project field.
- Make proposals that spark the imagination.
- Provide own ideas.
- Provide a professionally produced oral presentation of findings.
- Show a businesslike approach.
- Appear credible.
- Be discreet.
- Not cost too much.

The list appears to catalogue sources of major disasters that research buyers have been faced with in the past. The overwhelming 'ability requirement' from this list is one of communications to get close

to the *market* and get close to the *marketer*. Martin Simmonds (1982) listed three criticisms of British market research agencies from a survey of marketing management personnel in leading companies:

1 Lack of understanding of market; marketing function; clients business.
2 Poor image; do not project themselves; researchers first; salespeople last; too back room; too academic.
3 No presentation skills; lack of clarity; ambiguous; long-winded; hesitate to make recommendations.

Again much of these criticisms are directed at the communicative skills of the market researcher.

> The ultimate clientele of most market research companies and of professional market research buyers too, tend to be people who have very different mental processes and expectations from market researchers themselves. The gap is considerable and it requires the inner directed market researcher once again to jump outside his own skin and view his data and the world through very different eyes. (Bartrum, 1984)

The marketer, however, cannot afford to wait for an abundance of researchers who can combine technician's discipline with a 'showman's flair'. In large organizations, the research buyer can help (or hinder) to bridge any gaps between the marketer and the researcher and thus lessen the need for the researcher to be a showman, but what of the role of the marketer in the initiation, processing and application of effective market research?

Conclusion

Marketers can take comfort that they may not have to bother with market research at all. If there is no geographical distance between themselves and consumers, no organizational distance, intellectual or emotional distance then there is little use in using ad hoc market research. Add to these conditions a stable environment and no desire to change marketing objectives then the whole notion of market research can be scrapped. These conditions hardly reflect the situation of the vast majority of marketers. Market research can support marketing decisions and reduce risk and uncertainty but if things go wrong it may not necessarily be the fault of the application of techniques. The key question marketers must ask themselves before contemplating market research support is 'have I diagnosed the marketing problem correctly?' If marketers are unsure of the answer to that question then a further question is 'who can help me to better define the marketing problem *and* translate it into a research problem?' For the latter question the answer may lie in the researcher who has experience of ad hoc projects from problem definition through to the interpretation and application of research findings. The onus is on marketers as to whether they perceive the market researcher as just a supplier of techniques or as a means of widening their own experience.

If marketers have been exposed to a limited range of techniques, first they would be wise to question whether they or their research supplier suffers from operationalism and has developed a tendency to define problems through the means of solving them and second, they would be wise to expose themselves to alternative techniques. Being exposed to a wide range of quantitative and qualitative techniques and evaluating the rationale for the use of them as presented by researchers serves a vital purpose. It widens the field of experience of the marketeer helping in marketing and research problem diagnosis. It also serves as a lesson that market research is a joint commitment to solve a problem.

Researchers should not have to become marketers nor marketers become researchers in order to initiate and conduct effective market research. Any barriers that come between them ultimately mean a lengthening of the distance between the marketer and his/her markets. In the same way that the researcher should get close to the marketer, understanding the nature and context of the difficulties, the marketer must be doing the same. Simple linear processes of market research cannot achieve this.

References

Aaker, D. A. and Day, G. S., 'Increasing the effectiveness of marketing research', *Journal of Marketing Research*, vol. 23, no. 2, Winter 1980.

Alt, M., 'Fact and fiction in survey research: some philosophical considerations', *Quantitative Sociology Newsletter*, no. 25, Summer 1980, pp. 6–20.

American Marketing Association, 'New marketing research definition approved', *Marketing News*, 21, January 2nd, 1987.

Andreasen, A. R., ''Backward' market research', *Harvard Business Review*, vol. 63, May–June 1985, p. 176.

Arpi, B., *Planning and Control Through Marketing Research*, Hutchinson, 1970, p. 15.

Bailey, L. F. and Scott-Jones, G., 'What is the research buyer buying?', *Management Decision*, vol. 26, no. 1, 1988, p. 17.

Barker, E. M., *Everyday Reasoning*, Prentice-Hall, 1981, p. 193.

Barnard, P., 'Research in the USA', *Journal of the Market Research Society*, vol. 24, no. 4, October 1984, p. 277.

Bartram, P., 'The communication of results: the neglected art in market research', *Market Research Society Conference 1984*, p. 105.

Berry, T. and Fisher, S., 'Researcher: Get back in your box', *Market Research Society Conference 1987*, p. 380.

Blyth, B. and Robson, S., 'Resolving the hard/soft dilemma', *Market Research Society Conference 1981*.

Boyd Jr., H. W., Westfall, R. and Stasch, S. F., *Marketing Research, Text and Cases*, 7th ed., Irwin, 1989, p. 49.

Business Week, 'The concoction that's raising spirits in the wine industry', October 8th, 1984, no. 182.

Chisnall, P. M., *Marketing Research*, 3rd ed., McGraw-Hill, 1986, p. 6.

Cooper, P. and Branthwaite, A., 'Qualitative technology – new perspectives on measurement and meaning through qualitative research', *Market Research Society Conference 1977*.

Crimp, M., *The Marketing Research Process*, 2nd ed., Prentice-Hall, 1985, p. 32.

Debomy, D., 'How buyers and suppliers can best help each other', *Market Research Society Conference 1989*, 2nd pre-conference workshop.

Deshpande, R. and Zaltman, G., 'Factors affecting the use of market research information: a path analysis', *Journal of Marketing Research*, vol. 19, February 1982, pp. 25–26.

Deshpande, R. and Zaltman, G., 'A comparison of factors affecting researcher and manager perceptions of market research use', *Journal of Marketing Research*, vol. 21, February 1984, p. 38.

Elliot, K. and Christopher, M., *Research Methods in Marketing*, Holt, Rinehart and Winston, 1973, p. 9.

Elstien, A. S., Shulman, L. S. and Sprafka, A., 'Medical problem solving: an analysis of clinical reasoning', *Harvard University Press*, 1978.

Fineman, S. and Mangham, I., 'Data, meanings and creativity: a preface', *Journal of Management Studies*, vol. 20, no. 3, 1983, p. 297.

Goldman, A. E. and McDonald, S. S., *The Group Depth interview – principles and practice*, Prentice-Hall, 1987, p. 8.

Greenhalgh, C., 'How should we initiate effective research?' *Market Research Society Conference 1983*.

Henry, H., 'Motivation Research', *Marketing Intelligence and Planning*, vol. 4, no. 5, 1986, p. ii.

Hooley, G. J. and West, C. J., 'The untapped markets for marketing research', *Journal of the Market Research Society*, vol. 26, no. 4, October 1984, p. 336.

Jahoda, M., Deutsch, M. and Cook, S. W., *Research Methods in Social Relations*, Part 1. Dryden Press, 1951, p. 28.

Jones, S., 'Listening to complexity – analysing qualitative market research data', *Journal of the Market Research Society*, vol. 23, no. 1, January 1981, p. 35.

Johnson, F. J., 'The price and relevancy of accuracy of market research survey data', *Market Research Society Conference 1983*, pp. 1–31.

King, L. S., *Medical thinking: a historical perspective*, Princeton University Press, 1982, p. 91.

Kinnear, T. C. and Taylor, J. R., *Marketing research: an applied approach*, McGraw-Hill, 2nd ed., 1983, p. 28.

Krum, J. R., Rau, P. A. and Keiser, S. K., 'The marketing research process: role perceptions of researchers and users', *Journal of Advertising Research*, vol. 27, no. 6, December 87/January 88, p. 15.

Lehmann, D. R., *Market Research and Analysis*, 3rd ed., Irwin, 1989, p. 14.

Lilien, G. L. and Kotler, P., *Marketing Decision Making: a model building approach*, Harper & Son, 1983, p. 8.

Luck, D. J., Wales, H. C., Taylor, D. A. and Rubin, R. S., *Marketing Research*, 5th ed., Prentice-Hall, 1978.

McDonald, C., 'Understanding needs measurement', European Research, February 1988, p. 6.

Morris, A., *Market Research Society Newsletter*, April 1989, p. 4.

Polanyi, M., *The Tacit Dimension*, Doubleday & Co., 1967, p. 4.

Sampson, P. and Standen, P., 'Predicting sales volume and market shares' in *New product development research contributions to strategy formulation, idea generation and screening product, product testing and final marketing*, ESOMAR, November 1983.

Schon, D. A., 'From technical rationality to reflection in action' in Dowie, J. (ed.), *Professional Judgement: a reader in clinical decision making*, Cambridge University Press, pp. 60–77.

Scriven, M., *Reasoning*, McGraw-Hill, 1976, p. 197.

Silverman, D., *Qualitative Methodology and Sociology*, Gower, 1985, p. ix.

Simmons, K. M., 'The image of the British Market Research Industry in the business world', *Market Research Society Conference 1982*, pp. 1–23.

Tull, D. S. and Hawkins, D. I., *Marketing Research: measurement and method*, 4th ed., Macmillan, 1987, p. 29.

Vineall, M. G., 'Qualitative research: a summary of the concepts involved', *Journal of the Market Research Society*, vol. 21, no. 2, April 1979.

Ward, A. W., 'Information needs in management' in Aucamp, J. (ed.), *The Effective Use of Market Research*, Staples, 1971, p. 23.

10
Quantitative methods in marketing
ARTHUR MEIDAN

Introduction

Marketing was one of the last of the major functional areas of management activity to be entered by quantitative methods and techniques in a systematic way, and only in the last three decades or so was any significant progress achieved. This relative lag of quantitative methods progress in marketing was attributed to a number of factors as listed below:

1 *The complexity of marketing phenomena* This is due to the fact that when stimuli are applied to the environment, the responses tend to be non-linear, to exhibit threshold effects (a minimum level of stimulus needs to be applied before response occurs), to have carry over effects (for example, response to this period of advertising, will occur in future) and to decay with time in the absence of further stimulations.

2 *Interaction effects of marketing variables* This means the impact of any single controllable marketing variable is difficult to determine due to interaction of the variable with the environment and also with other marketing variables. Indeed, most of the variables in marketing are interdependent and interrelated.

3 *Measurement problems in marketing* It is often difficult to measure directly the response of consumers to certain stimuli and therefore indirect techniques are often used – an example is

the use of recall measures to ascertain effectiveness of advertisements.

4 *Instability of marketing relationships* The relationship between market responses and marketing decision variables tends to be unstable due to changes in taste, attitudes, expectations, and many others. These factors make continuous market measurements and revision of decisions crucial to marketing.

5 *Relative incompatability of marketing and quantitative methods personnel.*

In view of the above factors it is therefore not really surprising to find that applications of the quantitative methods in marketing had been slow. Perhaps it could also be due to the fact that marketing dealt more with behavioural rather than technological phenomena. But current development of quantitative techniques has progressed so that a variety of models is now available. These models are utilized by the marketing manager to solve a variety of problems, and virtually for all the quantitative methods, software packages are now available.

There are several ways in which quantitative methods can be used in marketing. One of these ways is through the classification of marketing into decision areas which confront the marketing manager and which include product development, pricing, physical distribution, sales force, advertising and consumer behaviour. However, it is thought to be more appropriate first to classify the techniques which are used in marketing and to fit in the situations where these models are used most frequently. In this way, most of the models and techniques can be analysed. Their validity can be judged from their usage, how accurately they represent the problem environment, their predictive power and the consistency and realism of their assumptions.

In selecting an appropriate method of analysis two major factors should be taken into consideration. First, whether the variables analysed are dependent or interdependent and, second, whether the input data is of a metric or non-metric form. Metric data are measured by interval or ratio scales, while non-metric data are only ordinal scaled. The dependent variables are those which can be explained by other variables, while interdependent variables are those which cannot be explained solely by each other.

Marketing variables are usually interdependent. For example, a firm's objectives are usually interdependent with marketing mix variables; profits usually depend on sales; market share depends on sales; firms' growth depends on profits and sales and vice versa, etc. Also firms' marketing-mix variables such as price, promotion, distribution and product are interdependent.

Since marketing research is very often a multivariate analysis involving either dependent or interdependent variables the major groups of techniques that can be used are as follows (see Figure 10.1):

1 *Multivariate methods*, called so because the various techniques attempt to investigate the relationships and patterns of marketing decisions that emerge as a result of the interaction and interdependence among many variables at the same time.

2 *Regression, correlation and forecasting techniques*. Regression and correlations are methods that can be employed in inferring the relationships among a set of variables in marketing. *Forecasting methods* are mainly applied in forecasting sales and market demand. Sales forecasting methods are a function of an aggregation of non-controllable environmental variables and marketing effort factors, which have to be taken into consideration.

3 *Simulation methods* are a group of techniques which are appropriate to use when the variables affecting the marketing situation (such as competition), require complex modelling and are not amenable to analytical solutions. The importance of the simulation technique in marketing is that it offers a form of laboratory experimentation by permitting the researcher to change selected individual variables in turn and holding all the others constant.

4 *Statistical design theory or stochastic methods* represent consumer response stochastically and allow a multitude of factors that affect consumer behaviour to be included. This means that market responses can be regarded as outcomes of some probabilistic process.

Essentially, there are two main uses of these methods: to test structural hypotheses and to make conditional predictions. They serve as a basis of market measurement and also identify and estimate the parameters of market responses so that structural hypotheses can be tested statistically, for example testing brand loyalty. Regarding conditional predictions, stochastic methods are used for predicting market share or even the time needed for a new product to achieve its ultimate market share.

5 *Deterministic operational research methods* are OR techniques looking for solutions, in cases where there are many interdependent variables and the researcher is trying to optimize the situation. A classical example of such a situation in marketing is when a company producing various products (or parts) is selling them through two different channels which vary with respect to selling costs, typical order sizes, credit policies, profit margins, etc. Usually in such cases the company's major objective is to maximize total profits by establishing optimal sales target volumes and marketing mixes for the two channels (or customer segments) subject to the existing limiting constraints. The various existing constraints can be formulated mathematically assuming linearity of the various functions and then the problems can be solved either graphically, or alternatively algebraically by employing the simplex method.

OR methods assume that chance plays no part and solutions are determined by sets of exact relationships. Under this heading there are linear and non-linear optimization models.

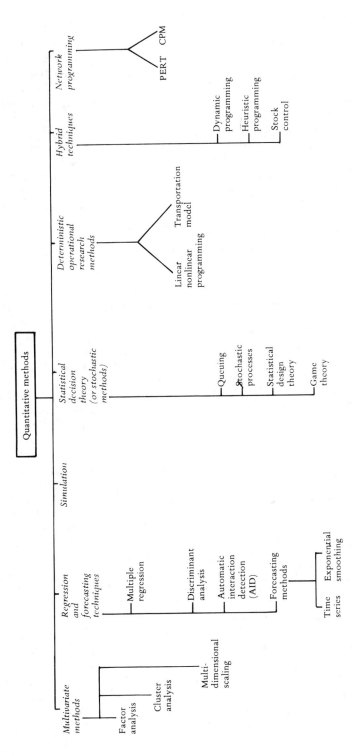

Figure 10.1 *The main quantitative methods in marketing – a taxonomy*

6 *Hybrid models* are methods that combine deterministic and probabilistic (stochastic) properties, e.g. dynamic programming, heuristic programming and stock control. These models are particularly useful in handling distribution problems, as explained below.

7 *Network programming models* are usually used for planning, scheduling and controlling complex projects. There are two fundamental analytical techniques known as critical path method (CPM) and performance evaluation and review technique (PERT). The differences between the two are, first, PERT acknowledges uncertainty in the times to complete the activities while CPM does not. Second, PERT restricts its attention to the time variable, while CPM includes time-cost trade-offs. These two together are also called critical path analysis (CPA) techniques.

The seven groupings of methods above do in no way exhaust the quantitative methods in marketing. There are probably over sixty techniques, models and methods – mainly from the realms of statistics and management science – that could be employed for data analysis and decisions in marketing management. The selection of techniques presented in this chapter is based either on their particular current relevance for handling many marketing problems or/and because of their potential in marketing research and analysis.

Multivariate methods

The multivariate methods in marketing are probably the predominant techniques of the last decade or so, not only because of the wide variety of flexible techniques available in this category, but mainly because they answer the most pressing need of marketing research, which is to obtain the ability to analyse complex, often interrelated and interdependent data.

There are three main multivariate sets of methods: factor analysis; cluster analysis; and multidimensional scaling.

Factor analysis

Factor analysis (FA) is primarily a tool to reduce a large number of variables to a few interpretable constructs. Factor analysis is used for exploration and detection of patterns in the data, with the view of obtaining data reduction, or summarization, which could be more amenable for reaching decisions and taking marketing management actions. The standard factor analytic methods enable the researcher to obtain graphical presentations of the data into three or more dimensions. The software for FA is readily available and is standard in any SPSS package. The input data is collected from respondents and the main limitations are how many factors to extract and the labeling of the emerging factors. Factor analysis could be used for analysing consumer behaviour (Meidan, 1976), market segmentation, product/service attributes, company images, etc.

Cluster analysis

Cluster analysis is a generic label applied to a set of techniques in order to identify 'similar' entities from the characteristics possessed by these entities. The clusters should have high homogeneity within clusters and high heterogenity between clusters and geometrically the points within a cluster should be close together, while different clusters should be far apart.

Cluster analyses are in a sense similar to factor analyses and to multidimensional scaling in that all three are used for reduced space analysis. Cluster analysis is primarily used for segmentation and for decisions on marketing strategies towards different segments and markets (Meidan, 1983), or in situations which involve grouping products, brands, consumers, cities, distributors, etc. The main limitations of this technique are that there are not yet defensible procedures for testing the statistical significance of the emerging clusters and often various clustering methods yield differing results. There are several types of clustering procedures. In Figure 10.2 a hierarchical clustering of variables associated with a marketing strategy for hotels is presented (Meidan, 1983).

Multidimensional scaling

Multidimensional scaling (MS) is a measurement technique concerned mainly with the representation of relationships, differences, dissimilarities (or similarities), substitutability, interaction, etc. among behavioural data such as perceptions, preferences and attitudes.

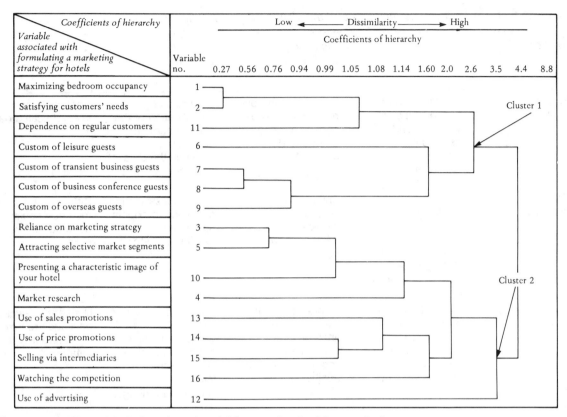

Figure 10.2 *Hierarchical clustering of variables associated with a marketing strategy*
Source: A. Meidan, 'Marketing Strategies for Hotels – A cluster analysis approach', *Journal of Travel Research*, vol. 21, no. 4, Spring 1983, p. 17–22.

The input data on various objects (variables) which are to be analysed, are collected from the subjects (respondents) by a number of direct or indirect questions. The questions can be either of Likert type or alternative asking each of the respondents to rank the variables to be investigated, for example products, brands, characteristics, etc. When the number of variables investigated are n, the number of all possible relationships among these variables (along k dimensions) are $n(n - 1)/2$.

In order to visualize and quantify the overall attitudinal data of these respondents with regard to the n variables investigated along (k) dimensions, the data should be input on to one of the available software packages.

The solution (output) of the MS computer program is of a metric nature, consisting in a geometric configuration, usually in two or three dimensions.

The distances between the variables (objects) and/or respondents (subjects) investigated, which are presented as points in the configuration, represent the (dis)similarity, substitutability, relationship, etc. Multidimensional scaling is used particularly in its non-metric version, the non-metric multidimensional scaling (NMS). The advantage of NMS in relation to say factor or cluster analyses is the ability to see the entire structure as variables together and to obtain metric output, from attitudinal (non-metric) input data. In addition, NMS enables easy comprehension of the results since the decision maker could visualize and assess for him/herself the relationships among the variables.

Multidimensional scaling and non-metric multidimensional scaling in particular have been successfully applied in investigating various marketing problems, for example market research, sales and

Table 10.1 *Main multivariate methods and their marketing applications*

Method	Based on	Marketing applications references	Main advantages	Main limitations
Factor analysis	Identification of relationships among variables and establishing the 'weight' (factor loadings) for these variables.	Determine corporate marketing images, consumer behaviour (Meidan, 1976) and attitudes.	Data reduction, identification of the main constructs (factors) that underlay the data characteristics.	Applicable only to interval scaled data.
Cluster analysis	Developing similarity or dissimilarity measures (coefficients), or distance measures, to establish clusters association.	Primarily for segmentation studies and strategy (Meidan, 1983).	Enable classification of brands, products, customers, distributors, etc.	Different clustering methods could generate different clusters.
Multidimensional scaling	Calculation of the proximity (or alternatively of dominance) among attributes/variables and respondents.	Market research, market share analysis (Doyle, 1972) market segmentation, brand positioning, etc.	Present the entire structure of variables, making easier to visualise and interpret relationship/ similarities among data.	Different software packages required for different types of data input.

market share, market segmentation, determination of marketing mix, consumer buyer behaviour, brand positioning, brand preference, export marketing, etc. A good user's guide to multidimensional scaling is presented by Doyle (1972). Discussion on when to use NMS techniques in marketing research is offered by Meidan (1975).

The three main multivariate methods are compared in Table 10.1.

Regression and forecasting techniques

Regression analysis

Regression analysis attempts to investigate the *nature* (and strength) of relationships, if one exists, between two or more variables in marketing phenomena. It could be used, for example, to establish the nature and form of association between sales

and, say, the number of customers, the nature of competitive activity, the amount of resources spent on advertising, etc. The association between Y (sales) – which is the dependent variable – and the independent variables affecting sales are usually expressed in a mathematical function of the type:

$$Y = f(x_1, x_2, x_3, \ldots x_n)$$

The purpose of regression is to make predictions about scores on the dependent variable based upon knowledge of independent variable scores (Draper and Smith, 1966). The prediction of value of Y requires fitting a regression line and determining r^2, the coefficient of determination, which is the amount of variation explained in a correlation context.

Regression provides measures of association, not causation; yet regression (and correlation analysis) could assist marketing managers in better understanding the implicit relationships among various independent and dependent variables, for example, age, income, education and amount of credit card usage, or various forms of sales people's incentives and their sales calls/or the number of new orders obtained, etc.

Discriminant analysis

Like regression analysis, discriminant analysis (DA) uses a linear equation to predict the dependent variable, say, sales. However while in regression analysis the parameters (coefficients) are used to minimize the sum of squares, in discriminant analysis, the parameters are selected in such a way as to maximize the ratio:

$$\frac{\text{variance between group means}}{\text{variance within groups}}$$

Discriminant analysis is used in marketing for predicting brand loyalty, predicting buying or attempting to predict consumer behaviour in general; this classification method could be used when the data (the independent variables) are interval scales. A good discussion on the uses of discriminant analysis is presented by Morrison (1968). Among the marketing investigations using DA, we have prediction of consumer innovators (Robertson and Kennedy, 1969), the potential of a sales territory, like/dislike of a service, etc. The problem in discriminant analysis is not just to find the discriminant function, but also to make sure whether the function is statistically significant, and what is the relative importance of the predictor variables. The DA (and in particular multiple discriminant analysis, i.e. when we are handling more than two variable groups), requires a computer program.

Automatic interaction detection

The regression analysis mentioned above attempts to identify association between the dependent and independent variables, one at a time. In addition, the assumption is that the data is measured on interval scales.

In many other marketing research situations we need a method able to handle nominal *or* ordinal data and to identify *all* the significant relationships bet-

ween the dependent and the independent variables.

Automatic interaction detection (AID) is a computer-based method for iteratively selecting the independent variables in order to be able to predict the dependent variables. It splits the sample of observations in two groups on a sequential routine, trying to keep the subgroups that emerge as homogenic as possible, relative to the dependent variable. The homogenity is measured by minimizing the sum-of-square deviations of each subgroup member from its subgroup mean.

AID is used in marketing for market segments analysis, analysing the effect of advertising levels on retail sales, predict consumption/sales and brand loyalty (Newman and Werbel, 1973), etc.

The method is not as powerful as regression analysis and since the minimum subgroup size should be no less than thirty, the original sample of objects required must be fairly large (1000 or more). A good discussion on the pitfalls of AID analysis could be found in Doyle and Fenwick (1975).

Forecasting methods

Forecasting methods are mainly applied in forecasting sales and market demand. Chambers *et al.* (1979) classify them in three categories: qualitative techniques; time series analysis, and causal models. In each category there is a series of models; some are suitable for forecasting initial sales and others for forecasting repeat purchases. Consequently one should make clear the differentiation between diffusion and adoption models, although unfortunately the available space here is too short for a detailed presentation.

Probably the most well-known forecasting techniques are the time series methods. These rely on historical data and by definition are of limited application to the forecasting of new product sales. The exceptions are where the sales history of a similar product can give guidance and where the product is only new to the company and not the market. Time series methods include:

1 *Trend extrapolations* which include the naive (sales will continue at the same level or will change by a constant amount each year), through to sketching extrapolation of time series curves by hand or fitting mathematical curves to the data by regression analysis.

Table 10.2 *Regression, automatic interaction detection and discriminant analyses – a comparison*

Method	Based on:	Applications in marketing references	Main advantages/ objectives	Major limitations
Regression analysis	Developing a function expressing the association (or relationship) between dependent and independent variables.	For segmentation, consumer behaviour analysis, sales forecasting.	Enables predictions about a dependent variable, say, sales figures. Provides measures of association between independent variables and certain important marketing dependent variables.	Requires fitting a regression line and determining the parameters. This could be quite complex and lead to certain errors.
Automatic interaction detection	A computer-based sequential routine attempting to classify objects into groups as homogenic as possible, by minimizing the within group sum of squares (Doyle and Fenwick, 1972).	For market segments analysis, assess the effects of advertising on retail sales, predict brand loyalty (Newman and Werbel, 1973), sales prediction, etc.	Suitable for identifying the different variables affecting market segments; determining the importance of each independent variable and the form in which it affects the dependent variable.	Less powerful than regression. Minimum group size should be no less than thirty and the original sample size should be quite large.
Discriminant analysis	Maximize the ratio of variance between group means, not within groups variance.	Predicting brand loyalty, consumer innovators (Morrison, 1968), like /dislike of a service (or product) etc.	Enables predictions of dependent variables.	Identifying the statistical significance of the discriminant function; multiple discriminant analysis *requires* a computer program.

2 *Exponential smoothing* basically involves moving averages, and weighting more recent data. The method is based on the following model:

$$\bar{Q}t + 1 = a\ Qt + (1 - a)\bar{Q}t$$

where $\bar{Q}t + 1$ is Sales in next period, a is the Smoothing constant, Qt is Sales in present period, and $(1 - a)\bar{Q}t$ is the Smoothest sales.

Where $\bar{Q}t$ is found by averaging the sales for the last few previous periods' sales – in other words it is a moving average, *a* is derived by trial and error testing of different smoothing constants between 0 and 1 in order to find the one that gives the best fit of past sales.

In order to select a forecasting technique for new products, the first principle is to match the methodology with the situation. The degree of newness of the product, for example, is crucial as are product and market characteristics, the forecaster's ability, the cost, the urgency and, the purpose for which the forecast is needed. Also critical is the range over which the forecast is operative, the comprehensibility and therefore acceptability of the method to managers. Needless to say, there is no single forecasting method suitable for all products (consumer to heavy industrial) with differing degrees of newness, which is accurate in the short term and in the long, capable of giving early warning of turning points, simple, cheap, fast and acceptable to managers.

The second principle is that at least two methods should be used and one of these should always be the subjective judgement of the forecaster, who must override the formal technique decision when information coming from outside the model clearly shows that the technique's forecast may be at fault.

There are powerful arguments for combining forecasts by different techniques. Methods are selective in the information they use so that a combination of methods would incorporate more information and improve accuracy. Doyle and Fenwick (1976) advocate this and produce evidence of improved accuracy.

Simulation methods

The cost, the time involved and other problems associated with field experimentation, often precludes it as a source of information for particular situations. In such instances it is often desirable to construct a model of an operational situation and obtain relevant information through the manipulation of this model. This manipulation, called simulation, describes the act of creating a complex

model to resemble a real process or system and experimenting with this model in the hope of learning something about the real system.

Simulations represent a general technique which is useful for studying marketing systems and it is one of the most flexible methods in terms of application. Simulation models have been formulated to serve two management functions:

1 Planning.
2 Monitoring and controlling operations.

For planning purposes, such a model may be used to examine consequences of alternative courses of action and market events. As for monitoring and controlling operations, simulation models may be used to generate results which can be compared with actual results.

The term simulation can be interpreted in a broad sense to reflect the variety of meanings ascribed to it by persons inside and outside marketing. Within its broad interpretation, at least two different usages of the term stimulation can be distinguished:

1 Simulation as behavioural modelling (an attempt to recreate the real-time behavioural characteristics of a system).
2 Simulation as a way of introducing and handling uncertainty.

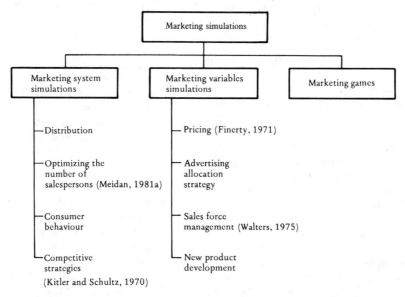

Figure 10.3 *A taxonomy of marketing simulation applications*

Table 10.3 *Simulation uses in marketing (the method, advantages, limitations and when recommended to use)*

Method	Based on:	Marketing applications	Advantages	Limitations
Simulation	Conducting experiments using a model to simulate working conditions of the real system.	(a) Marketing planning (Walters, 1975). (b) Monitoring and controlling (Kotler and Schults, 1970) marketing operations. (c) Distribution, consumer behaviour, retailing, staffing (Finerty, 1971), advertising. (d) Marketing training (Kotler and Schultz, 1970).	(a) A very flexible and simple method easily understood by managers. (b) Saves time and resources. (c) Simulation has found wide applications in the field of marketing.	(a) Tedious arithmetical calculations. (b) Rather costly in computer time.

Marketing simulations can be conveniently divided into three classes (Doyle and Fenwick, 1976). The first deals with computer models of the behaviour of marketing system components, the second deals with computer models on the effect of different marketing instruments on demand, and the third deals with marketing games (a taxonomy of this classification is shown in Figure 10.3). The value and objectives of using simulations, are as follows:

1 To determine the optimizing values of controlled variables.
2 To study transitional processes.
3 To estimate values of model parameters or the model's functional form.
4 To treat courses of action that cannot be explicitly formulated within the model.
5 For initial problem structuring of a complicated problem. This structuring may be effected by breaking down the system (or process being modelled) into a set of subsystems, where appropriate content specialists can be brought in to assist the model's formulation.
6 For training system operators and decision makers, for example simulations in the form of 'business games' have sometimes been quite useful as training devices for demonstrating the interaction of many variables on the game's output and giving the 'player' some feeling of the impact of others' decisions on the results of his/her planned activity.
7 The demonstration of problem solutions. Simulations have often been used to demonstrate the impact of some recommended course of action on the system under study, even though the action selected was based on the solution of an analytical model. The versatility of simulation for use in real world marketing problems is usually more direct than a (seemingly more abstract) set of equations.
8 Running sensitivity tests of proposed solutions. Simulation models provide a rather straightforward means to test the effects of departures of initial assumptions on the effectiveness associated with the best course of action.

Marketing system simulations (Figure 10.3) attempt to reproduce the behaviour of distributors, customers and competitors. Specifically, distribution simulations seek to describe the behaviour of institutions that affect the flow of product from producers to final buyers. Consumer behaviour simulations seek to describe the formation of attitudes and buying behaviour of actual and/or potential customers. Competitive strategy simulations seek to describe the marketing actions and reactions of competitors in an ongoing marketing process.

A firm wanting to adopt a simulation model would have to take into account the market characteristics of the environment it operates in and model on this basis. The design work is carried out by a specialist and does not involve the marketing executives directly, except in the furnishing of information about the market characteristics. As a result, the end product is a model typically characterized in symbolic terms and is completely foreign to the executives' experience, and the utilization of the model will solely depend on the ability of the modeller to persuade the executive of its usefulness. The ultimate criterion of the success of a simulation model is the utilization of the model. An unused model, no matter how elegant, is a failure.

Some of the main characteristics, advantages, limitations and applications of simulation in marketing are presented in Table 10.3.

Statistical decision theory or stochastic methods

In this category there are four methods, all of which are useful in solving marketing problems.

Queuing

This method is of particular relevance to some marketing situations and is used to predict how different systems will operate. More precisely, it explicitly gives expressions relating the design of the system to the length and frequency of queues, average waiting time, the probability of no delay at all, etc. By design of the system is meant that the rate of arrival of 'customers', the number and speed of 'servers' or sales clerks, and the arrangement relating customers to servers is modelled and appropriate planning of the queuing system in operation is possible.

This method is of importance to large retailing institutions such as supermarkets, gasoline stations, airline ticket offices, seaports, airports and other areas where services are available through queuing. A notable problem in retailing institutions is that of making sales force decisions, the reason being the high cost incurred in hiring sales clerks whose services are almost irreplaceable. Since these sales clerks work in situations which can be systematically regulated and accurately observed, techniques can be used to provide management with information so that the optimal size of the sales force can be ascertained. A queuing model to determine the optimum number of sales clerks to be assigned to a floor in a department store so as to maximize profitability, could be determined. The attention should be focused on five main variables:

1 The number of potential customers arriving and requesting service per unit time.
2 The amount of time required by a sales clerk to wait on a customer.
3 The number of items purchased per customer per transaction.
4 The incremental value to the retail establishment of each item sold, i.e. profits.
5 The amount of time the customer is willing to wait for service.

Probability distributions of these variables could be obtained from data gathered empirically, and the situations are then simulated using random numbers. The results obtained from the field studies suggest that simulated results compare quite closely with actual data.

Most research articles state that the use of queuing theory is mainly concentrated on solving problems in retailing institutions where the model helped management to decide on the size of their sales force. Perhaps it was the successful application of this technique in this area of marketing that has contributed to its vast improvements and wide applications. There are, however, limitations to this technique, one of which is that queuing systems must be operated over a sufficiently long period to achieve a steady state solution and it is often difficult to predict the length of time required to achieve this. Another problem is the reluctance of managers to have confidence in this technique, but this can be overcome by making sure the method is thoroughly understood.

Stochastic processes

A stochastic process is a random experiment which occurs over time, the outcome of which is determined by chance. From these random experiments some attributes of interest are observed and numerical values can be given to these attributes according to the probability law. The stochastic process method is commonly used in building brand choice models of consumers. In all, there are three basic types of stochastic process methods; they are the zero-order, Markovian, and learning models, and each has got its own set of assumptions.

The zero-order model assumes that past brand choice has no effect on future brand choice. There are studies on the existence of brand or store loyalties using the zero-order model approach and defined brand loyalty as a proportion of total purchases within a product class that a household devotes to its favourite or most frequently purchased brand. Results suggest the existence of brand loyalty within, but not across, product classes. Consumers were more loyal to chainstores than towards speciality or independent stores and no correlation existed between stores and brand loyalty. The most important implication of these studies was that families concentrated on their brand and store choices more than expected by the chance model (randomly distributed).

The Markov model assumes that only the most recent purchases affect the brand choice decisions. Using the Markovian model one can measure the expected number of periods before an individual would try a particular brand. Further studies propose the segregation of consumers into 'hardcore' and 'switchers' so as to improve the predictive power of the model. They define 'hardcore' customers as those who devote three-quarters or more of their total purchases in a product class to a single brand and who should be treated as a homogeneous population.

Markov models should be used for dynamic market predictions such as equilibrium market shares, average time to trial which is a measure of the attractive power of the brand, and for evaluating the success of new product introduction. Regarding the prediction of market shares using the Markov model, the equilibrium shares will also give some indication of the direction in which the market is heading. This will serve as useful diagnostic information for firms. However, there is no obvious drawback to this: in real market situations, the equilibrium market shares are rarely reached because of competitive activity.

In retailing institutions, the arrangement of equipment, people and goods in the interest of optimizing the use of floor space is of vital importance. Usually retail managers make layout decisions by rule of thumb and common sense. While this method is obviously suitable for small firms, it is a highly complicated task for large department stores. One other area where the Markovian analysis has been used in marketing is in making personal selling decisions where it is used in the modelling of sales effort allocation to customers. Normally, the allocation of sales effort would be between new and old customers and, to decide on the optimum allocation, a Markov model could be used to yield information for controlling sales effort as well as for the determination of the number of times to call upon a prospective customer before dropping the prospective firm altogether.

The third of the stochastic process methods is the learning model which postulates that brand choice is dependent upon a complete history of past brand purchases as the effect of purchasing a brand is cumulative. Therefore, when applied in the brand switching complex, this will mean that purchase of a brand will ultimately increase the probability of purchasing the same brand again. This model could be used in monitoring consumer behaviour. By learning model is meant that the probability of purchase in time $(t + 1)$, is a linear function of the probability of purchase in time. The probability of purchasing a brand increases with past number of purchases of the same brand as indicated by empirical findings.

Statistical decision theory

Decision theory is often used to evaluate the alternative outcomes of different decisions and to find the best possible decision. Associated with the statistical decision theory is the decision tree diagram which portrays the various alternative decisions and their consequences. The game theory, discussed below, is commonly regarded as an analytical approach to decision making involving two or more conflicting individuals, each trying to minimize the maximum loss (minimax criterion).

One other assertion about game theory is that, an important area in marketing where decision theory is employed is the making of advertising decisions where it offers a method of formulating the budget decision. In statistical decision theory probabilities

Table 10.4 *Statistical decision theory or stochastic methods applications in marketing (approaches, advantages, limitations and when recommended to use)*

Method	Based on:	Applications in marketing and references	Advantages	Limitations
Queuing	Probability distribution analysis of data (empirically gathered on how the major factors/variables will affect the situation-problem under analysis). It is an analysis of queuing systems attempting to determine service levels /performance.	(a) Optimize: sales force (Paul, 1972), number of checkouts (Schuchman, 1963), number of attendants etc. (b) Minimize inventory carrying costs; suitable and widely used by chain stores, supermarkets, department stores, gasoline stations, airline ticket offices, ports, airports, etc.	(a) Predicts how different marketing systems will operate. (b) Gives explicit expression relating the design of a system to the length and frequency of queues, waiting time etc.	(a) Must be operated a sufficient length of time to achieve a steady state solution. (b) Manager's reluctance to have confidence in this method.
Stochastic process	A random experiment which occurs over time and whose outcome is determined by chance. This is an analysis of systems with variable/ uncertain components.	(a) For building choice, models checking on customers' loyalty (Cunningham, 1961). (b) Predict buying decisions and future purchasing probabilities.	Might predict flow of customers and future purchase probabilities.	Suitable for short-run predictions only.
Statistical decision theory	This is an analysis of decision making processes where outcomes are uncertain. Probability of each outcome – based upon past data or subjective estimates – is given adequate weight and is taken into consideration for decision making.	For decision making on: budgeting, advertising, pricing test-marketing, new product development, merchandising, optimum mix, etc.	Simplifies the level of analysis and suggests a number of possible outcomes.	Subjective estimation of the probability for each decision might effect the results' validity.
Game theory	Constant sum game solution, use of a maximum criterion to determine, for example, budget/resources allocation. Theoretical analysis of competition/ collusion between organizations.	For decision making by retailing firms, mainly on: pricing (Higgins, 1973), product stock determination and advertising, budget allocations, also for better decision on negotiation processes.	(a) Aids management in decision making. (b) Suggests a useful analytical approach to competitive problems, such as: pricing, advertising outlay and product decisions.	Does not have much predictive power over other quantitative techniques.

of each outcome are either based upon past data or subjective estimates. In addition to this, the value (profit accrued from advertising) of each outcome must also be estimated subjectively. These values are multiplied by their respective probabilities and summed over all outcomes to yield the expected pay off to a certain level of advertising. This process can be repeated for each budget level and the one generating the maximum profit or pay off is chosen. Pricing decisions in advertising is another area where decision theory can be applied. The main disadvantage of this method is the subjective estimation of the probability for each decision.

Decision trees can also be used to decide whether or not to test-market a new product before launching it. Cadbury Schweppes Ltd used this technique to help in deciding the feasibility of test-marketing a new chocolate product. By carrying out a test-market programme of the new chocolate, the earnings obtained exceeded those of embarking on a national launch without prior test-marketing. Riter (1969) used this method for making merchandising decisions, such as finding the optimum mix of sizes and widths of fashion shoes to be ordered especially when the possible alternative choices were very many and carrying high costs.

Game theory

Game theory, when compared with decision theory, has found limited applications in marketing. Nevertheless, it has been applied to retailing institutions in making product decisions. Retailers' decisions to open orders are accompanied by negotiations with suppliers. On the basis of interviews with department store buyers and merchandisers it was concluded that merchants could benefit by applying game theory to this negotiation process. Game theory helps management to decide on its advertising budgets without any prior knowledge of competitors' budgeting decisions.

In pricing advertisements, Higgins (1973) used the game theory to provide solutions. The total reward for all the firms included in the pricing decision study was considered fixed, the decision resting on which product price to lower to generate more sales so as to minimize the maximum loss.

To date, game theory does not have much predictive power over other techniques. It nevertheless suggests a useful analytical approach to such competitive problems as pricing, advertising outlays, and product decisions in marketing. A summary of the four major stochastic methods, their possible applications in marketing (with some references), advantages and limitations, is presented in Table 10.4.

Deterministic operational research methods

Deterministic techniques are those in which chance plays no part and solutions are determined by sets of exact relationships. Under this heading there are both the linear and non-linear optimization models.

Linear programming

Linear programming (LP) is a mathematical technique for solving specific problems in which an objective function must be maximized or minimized, considering a set of definite restrictions and limited resources. The word programming stands for computing or calculating some unknowns of a set of equations and/or inequalities, under specific conditions, mathematically expressed.

Linear programming was originally developed during the Second World War as an aid to decision making in military problems. The method was applied to various theoretical economic problems during the early 1950s and later in the analysis of many business problems, notably production planning and distribution. In the 1960s and 1970s LP was largely applied in marketing management, mainly because of its advantages, i.e. it permits the comparison of a large number of alternative combinations in terms of a single criterion, usually cost efficiency. Linear programming lends itself to the solution of problems in which the elements being compared differ in their characteristics and capabilities, and in their inherent restrictions or limitations. Essentially it involves the allocation of some resource–time, money or materials – among alternative uses under certain limiting conditions or constraints.

It does not provide an ideal solution but only the best possible, given the constraints.

Because it is a mathematical technique, linear programming depends on numbers and thus one of the problem that arises is translating qualitative judgements into mathematical terms. Another essential feature is the use of constraints which may represent realistic limits to certain choices, that may help to balance the previous problem in the mind of a marketing manager who desires practicality. These constraints may be self-imposed (that is a policy judgement) in addition to naturally occurring constraints such as a year consisting of fifty-two weeks. However, it should be remembered that given enough constraints the range of possible decisions could be narrowed down such that the linear programme would come up with a schedule the manager had preselected.

Before the LP technique can be employed in the solution of a marketing problem, five basic requirements must be considered (Meidan, 1981):

1 *Definition of the objective.* A well-defined objective is the target of the solution and the answer to the problem must satisfy the requirements. Objectives such as reduced costs, increased profits, matching of sales force effort to customer potential or improved media selection, can be handled.

2 *Quantitative measurement of problem elements.* A quantitative measurement is needed for each of the elements described in the problem which is an essential condition for applying mathematical models such as hours, pounds (£) etc.

3 *Alternative choice.* It must be possible to make a selection for reaching a solution which satisfies the objective function.

4 *Linearity.* The term linearity describes the problem and its restrictions. Equations and inequalities must describe the problem in a linear form.

5 *Mathematical formulation.* Information must be compiled in such manner that it is possible to translate the relationships among variables into a mathematical formulation capable of describing the problem and all the relations among variables.

A number of techniques is available for solving a formulated linear programme. A graphical solution is possible when there are three variables only. After this the 'simplex algorithm' is used. Possible alternatives are checked through in a logical sequence in an iterative process. In most marketing problems this demands the use of a computer owing to the sheer amount of information that has to be processed.

An example showing the use of LP in determining the best allocation and mix of marketing effort, is presented in detail by Meidan (1981b).

One is faced with four kinds of difficulties in using linear programming models:

1 The first difficulty is in describing the problem mathematically. In an industrial situation, one must know exactly how much one can use of the production resources such as: manpower, raw materials, time etc. Again there may be some elements influencing the events under consideration that one cannot objectively measure.

2 The second problem lies in the interpretation and proper use of the objectively obtained optimum solution. One may need to analyse additional business considerations, over and above the ones used in describing and formulating the problem. Between the preparation of data and the use of the results, there is the laborious computation.

3 Even if the problem had been correctly stated and formulated, technical limitations may exist such as the amount of data a computer can handle or that no solution exists, for example, the number of constraints and/or variables may be too large.

4 A further limitation lies in the reliability of the proposed solution. This could arise when a linear assumption is taken for a real non-linear behaviour of the component. Finally, it is difficult and sometimes impossible to combine two or more objective functions into one optimum solution.

Substantial care must be taken in matching the problem to the particular LP model. The technique should not be emphasized at the expense of the problem and models are no substitute for looking outside it.

This is perhaps best demonstrated by the Sun Oil Company of America, who faced a product mix problem owing to a change in market conditions. The company tried to model the problem of how many grades were needed to sell at its petrol stations, as its previous policy of one grade would rapidly become ineffective. Various solutions were presented but then the president suggested that the problem could be approached in a different fashion. Perhaps the company could continue to market its existing single grade, but provide the facility for a wide range of grades by blending it in the pump with a concentrated octane additive. The implementation of this idea was carried out using a variety of mathematical models to evaluate the strategy and then to set objectives for the marketing plan and its measurement of success.

Linear programming techniques, despite the advent of more sophisticated approaches to similar problems, remain an effective fairly simple way of dabbling in the pool to see if it is acceptable; it also includes a range of modified techniques that may suitably bridge the gap between a tentative start and full computer simulations of marketing plans at a reasonable cost.

LP methods could be – and are – employed in solving the following marketing problems:

Physical distribution

Designing an optimal physical distribution system is dependent on choosing those levels of services that minimise the total cost of physical distribution, whose objective function might read: $C = T + F + I + L$ where C = total distribution cost, T = total freight cost, F = total fixed warehouse cost, I = total inventory cost and L = total cost of lost sales.

Given the objective function, one seeks to find the number of warehouses, inventory levels and modes of transportation that will minimize it, subject to at least three constraints:

1 Customer demand must be satisfied.
2 Factory capacity limits must not be exceeded.
3 Warehouse capacity cannot be exceeded.

The linear programming model has been used in solving distribution problems particularly in the transportation of finished goods to warehouses. The aims were to minimize transport costs subject to certain constraints, such as warehouse costs (Kotler, 1972). Other uses of LP models in marketing include site location, physical distributions and blending products.

Warehouse location

Chentnick (1975) discusses the various methods of locating warehousing systems which are of interest as their usefulness is indicated, thus suggesting the advantage of linear programming in comparison to other methods.

There are six decision areas within the total logistic approach:

1 Facility location (or warehouse/depot location).
2 Inventory allocation.
3 Transportation.
4 Communications.
5 Utilization.
6 Customer service levels.

Broadly speaking, the function of a warehouse can be broken down into five regions:

1 Storage.
2 Assembling of customer orders.
3 Service of customers.
4 Economies of scale by bulk buying and delivery.
5 Processing and final packaging.

These areas reflect the nature of the distribution function as the link between production and marketing, attempting to effect a compromise between the varying demands of its two masters. The importance of warehouse location is reflected in the objective function of total distribution which is usually attempting to optimise the costs associated to each of the decision areas. There are two definable sets which characterise the two methods of solution to the warehouse location problem (Meidan, 1978):

1 The infinite set assumes that the warehouse can be positioned anywhere on the map: obvious slight adjustments can be made later to allow for rivers, mountains, etc. A main assumption is that transport costs are directly proportional to distance (as the crow flies) and this is questionable in many situations.
2 The feasible set assumes a finite number of possible locations and both costs of buildings and haulage can be calculated with a high degree of precision. The obvious problem with this method is one of cost and time employed in collating the necessary data, but the expected benefits of an accurate anaysis can easily offset this initial outlay.

These two approaches include various models but these again can be identified by two distinct groups: first static models, which attempt to answer all or some of the problems contained within a one period optimization model, namely those of:

- Where the warehouses should be sited.
- The number of sites required.
- The physical size.
- Customer allocation to each warehouse.
- A breakdown of the cost areas associated with the plan.

Second, dynamic models, which incorporate linear programming. The objective of linear programming is to set up the relationships among plants, products, warehouses and customers in the form of equations with the aim, usually, to minimize cost, and incorporating constraints.

Delivery planning

Another aspect of the distribution problem is that of delivery planning. Let us suppose there are two factories, X and Y, producing the same product and two customers, A and B, who require the product. Factory X has four tonnes available and factory Y, three tonnes. For simplicity we assume that the customer demand for the product is equal to the supply and that A requires two tonnes and B requires five tonnes. How should the product be distributed in order that transport costs are minimum assuming that only whole tonnes can be despatched? LP could assist in optimizing the delivery planning system.

Media selection

One area in marketing where the linear programming models have been extensively used is in advertising decisions, especially in media mix decisions in a market segment. Higgins (1973), for example, proposed the use of this model for deciding on the optimum paging schedule for colour supplements of newspapers. The range of 'paginations' extended from twenty-four pages to a maximum of eighty pages. He formulated a linear programme, the objective of which was to maximize profitability within constraints such as the number of issues per year and seasonality.

A number of thorny problems confront companies concerning the allocation of advertising resources. Companies would like better analysis of whether they are spending too little or too much on advertising: whether they are timing their advertising expenditures optimally through the year; whether their agency is choosing the best media, and so forth.

We consider here the media selection decision using the linear programming approach. The media selection problem is to allocate a scarce resource among a large number of alternative uses, so that the best possible contribution is made to a central objective, i.e. obtaining the maximum possible impact on the pertinent market target within the given budget. The alternative uses of the appropriation are the many 'advertising units' which must be considered before a specific media schedule is adopted.

When stated in this way, the media mix problem clearly fits the basic structure of the linear programming model. The main constraints are the size of the advertising budget, the minimum and maximum usages of specific media vehicles and media categories, and the desirable minimum exposure rates to different target buyers. The criterion used to measure effectiveness is the weighted number of exposures which is to be maximized.

Marketing mix decisions and budget allocations

The marketing mix refers to the amounts and kinds of marketing variables the firm is using at a particular time and includes price, advertising costs and distribution expenditures, each of which could be subdivided into futher variables. A typical example is given by Jolson (1973). A company is introducing a product which sells for $10 per unit, and every unit sold contributes $2 to the firm's net profits. The marketing manager believes that there are two basic strategies in selling the product: personal selling (via sales people) and advertising. His/her problem is to decide on the correct mix to maximize profits.

There are many other similar examples in the literature. However, they clearly oversimplify the problem by ignoring non-linearities, marketing mix interactions and the reliability of the data. The problem of non-linearity can be overcome by using more advanced techniques such as quadratic (non-linear) programming. Marketing mix interactions are more difficult to overcome since a basic assumption to the techniques of linear and non-linear programming is that the variables are independent.

Product mix and the multiproduct marketing strategy problem

The problem of product mix, i.e. variety and quantity of products produced, is commonly encountered by almost all multiproduct firms during

Table 10.5 *Some major deterministic operational research techniques applicable in marketing (the method, advantages, limitations and when recommended to use)*

Method	Based on:	Applications in marketing references	Main advantages	Major limitations
Linear programming	Objective and constraint linear functions.	(a) Advertising (Higgins, 1973), space optimal media mix allocations. (b) Distribution problems, site location (Kotler, 1972). (c) Budget allocation, new product decision (Wilson, 1975). (d) Blending product mixes. (e) Marketing mix decisions (Jolson, 1973).	(a) Maximize profitability of allocations, subject to constraints. (b) Minimize costs. (c) Aids management in decision making	(a) Difficult to obtain and formulate the various functions. (b) Constraints must be altered as soon as external and/or internal factors change.
Transportation model	Transportation/ allocation matrix ascertaining the minimum costs, routes, quantities supplied etc.	To allocate resources, supply etc. by reducing transportation costs. Suitable particularly for department stores, truck rental firms, transport companies (Budnick *et al.* 1977).	Very suitable for managerial decision making.	Inaccurate in the longer run as a result of changes in costs.
Non-linear programming	Non-linear objective functions and non-linear constraint relationships.	To find the maximum return to a new product search, subject to budget constraint.	(a) When the relationships are non-linear. (b) When the objective function is non-linear while the constraints are linear.	Difficult to establish non-linear relationships.

the planning period. Here the objective is to maximize current profits subject to the various constraints such as its capacity, demand levels and quality. Such problems necessitate the use of linear programming.

An example is the application of so-called blending problems where a number of components are mixed together to yield one or more products; such problems are encountered, for example, in the petroleum industry (blending of motor gasoline), or the steel industry (determination of the charge for a blast furnace). There are usually many different ways in which raw materials can be blended which satisfy the various constraints.

Other marketing management applications for LP

Wilson (1975) cites a number of potential applications of LP including new product decisions, resolving conflict in market segmentation, the choice of a new market from a set of possible alternatives, and gives an example of its use in allocating a sales force to new products.

The allocation of a number of sales people to a product and the size of their territories may be tackled using ordinary integer linear programming. This approach demands a lot of information about the existing market, its future trends, assessment of untapped potential and all the associated costs. Goal programming, on the other hand, may be used when a minimum knowledge of the situation and realistic objectives are available. Here the subjective constraints placed on the model give direction to an objective and hence an area of solutions, i.e. constraints become goals.

The transportation model

The transportation model is a specialized class of linear programming model. Like the linear programming models, its aim is to optimize the use of resources with the exception that it requires separate computational techniques not normally used in other models. However, the model is best defined as the shipment of some homogenous commodity from sources of supplies to a set of destinations, so that the cost of transportation is minimized.

The transportation model seems to have limited application and the area of marketing where it has been used is in making distribution decisions. This limited usage is the result of the way in which the model is formulated. Budnick *et al.* (1977) successfully applied this technique to aid in solving the problem of distributing trucks, at minimum cost, within three metropolitan areas so as to meet demand in different parts of the city where, in some areas, trucks were surplus to demand while other areas were short of supply.

As with other techniques, this model suffers inaccuracy as soon as the costs of transportation change. Very often some of these transportation charges are variable, depending on whether there are breakdowns or unforeseen stoppage of the trucks. If these changes occur this model will give very crude, if not nonsensical answers. The major deterministic operational research techniques and their marketing applications, limitations and advantages, are summarized in Table 10.5.

The hybrid models

Under this category there are three different types of methods used in solving marketing problems: dynamic programming; heuristic programming; and stock control models.

Dynamic programming

As stated by Budnick *et al.* (1977) dynamic programming is a recursive approach to optimization problems which works on a step-by-step basis utilizing information from the preceding steps. The model has been used to aid decision making in areas such as distribution (i.e. the minimization of transportation costs), the distribution of salespeople to various territories (in such a way that maximum profits will be obtained) and determining the best combination of advertising media and frequency under a budgetary constraint.

Indeed the dynamic programming model can serve as a very useful tool for solving problems in marketing. Despite this, there have been some computational difficulties associated with its usage. But with the growing need for sophisticated techniques for solving marketing problems, the dynamic programming model has found its way into some major marketing institutions where computational skills are not uncommon among marketing personnel.

Heuristic programming

Heuristics is commonly defined as the use of rule-of-thumb for solving problems. Therefore heuristic programming techniques are based on orderly search procedure guided by these rule-of-thumbs and are mainly applied to problems when mathematical programming techniques are either too expensive or complicated. However, they do not guarantee optimal solutions. In the past, heuristic programming has been applied rather extensively in certain areas of marketing.

Media selection is a problem of major concern in marketing. This is especially true if one considers the amount of money companies invest in advertising suggested the optimal number of advertisements derive solutions to the problems of media scheduling suggested the optimal number of advertizements to be placed in each medium and the size of each insertion. The number of insertions was determined by graphical methods which attempted to find the point where the marginal returns to the last insertion equals the marginal cost of the advertisements for each medium. Other heuristic models also made use of this 'marginal approach' and included allocating budgets for advertising from time to time so that exposure targets are met for each period.

Table 10.6 *Dynamic, heuristic and network programming applications in marketing (the methods, advantages, limitations and when recommended in use)*

Model	Based on:	Applications in marketing references	Advantages	Limitations
Dynamic programming	Recursive optimization procedure; optimizing on a step-by-step basis.	Solving media selection problems; distribution (minimization of transportation costs; distribution of salespeople to various sales territories.	(a) Maximize the objective over the planning period. (b) Introduces new factors, e.g. 'forgetting time', 'accumulation of intersections'. (c) Wide potential application in industry.	The programming procedure is rather complex; computational difficulties.
Heuristic programming	Orderly search procedure guided by the use of rule-of-thumb. Based on 'marginal approach' or trial and error.	Media selection and scheduling; warehouse location; sales force allocation; decision on the number of items in a product line; suitable for making product promotion decisions.	(a) Good, flexible, simple and inexpensive method. (b) Combines the analysis into the style of decision making and the reasoning used by managers.	Does not guarantee optimal solution.
Network programming (PERT and CPM)	Presents the wide range of critical activities that must be carried out and coordinated. PERT acknowledges uncertainty in the times required to complete activities while CPM does not. PERT deals only with the time factor. CPM refers to the time–costs trade-offs, as well.	Planning, scheduling and controlling complex marketing projects (Bird *et al.*, 1973), e.g. building new stores, new product development (Robertson, 1970) product commercialization, advertising–sales relationships (Johansson and Redinger, 1979), distribution planning (LaLord and Headen, 1973).	(a) Sequences and times of activities are considered, responsibilities allocated and coordinated in large/complex marketing projects. (b) Project time can be forecast and completion time may be shortened.	(a) Difficulties in estimating costs and times accurately particularly for new projects. (b) Of use only when functions and activities can, in fact, be separated.

Selection of warehouse locations is another extremely important decision area in marketing; much effort has been expended in this area and heuristic technique is one of several techniques currently in use for site selection. In sales force allocation, after a firm has established its budget for sales effort, the next decision includes allocating sales effort to customers, sales territories and time. One could use a heuristic procedure for aiding the making of these decisions. The approach determines the minimum time of travel to visit each account and return home. The effect of deviation from the route to examine sales effectiveness was considered and the assumption made was that the effectiveness of visits to a customer depends on the time of visit. With this change in schedule, the opportunity cost of deviating from the minimum time route was compared to the expected increase in sales. The programme therefore considered the time, cost of sales and the expected sales volume in the proposed schedule.

Even though heuristic models are applied to analyse a variety of problems, the approaches are very similar. On the whole heuristic programming has been widely applied in marketing in the past two decades. Perhaps this is attributable to the several advantages of this technique such as its flexibility and that it seeks to give 'good' solutions even though not optimal. Very often, due to realistic problem definitions, good solutions generated by heuristic programmes are better than the best solutions of optimising routines. A summary of the main characteristics, advantages, limitations and applications of dynamic and heuristic models in marketing is presented in Table 10.6.

Stock control models

The distribution side of marketing has been successfully modelled using quantitative methods for a number of years. The objective of the distribution system is to get the right goods to the right places at the right time for the least cost, and involves decisions on such problems as the number, location and size of warehouses, transportation policies and inventories.

In this section, the inventory decision will be discussed but it must be realized that inventory represents only one part of the local distribution network, a complete analysis of which is outside the scope of this text. The inventory decision has two parts to it: when to order (order point), and how much to order (order quantity). These are not independent and can be deduced from a stock control model. The ordering of goods involves costs, such as transportation and handling, which increase the number of orders placed.

On the other hand, the storage of goods also involves costs such as storage space charges, capital costs, insurance costs and depreciation costs. The first decreases and the second increases with the order quantity. The simplest model assumes that demand is constant, shortages are not allowed (no stock-outs), immediate replacements of stocks and a

regular order cycle. If C_s = cost of holding of one unit of stock/unit time, C_o = cost of placing an order, d = demand rate (units/unit time), Q = order quantity in units, t = order cycle time (order point).

Mathematical analysis shows that the total costs (ordering plus stockholdings) are minimized when the following order quantity is used:

$$q^\star = dt^\star = \sqrt{\frac{C_o d}{C_s}}$$

$q^\star$ = is often referred to as the economic order quantity (EOQ). The simplest model can be improved by relaxing some of the assumptions.

Network programming models

Network programming models are the methods usually used for planning and controlling complex marketing management projects. There are two basic methods: critical path method (CPM); and PERT (performance evaluation and review technique).

The critical path analysis method

Critical path analysis, in its various forms, is one of the techniques developed in recent years to cope with the increased need for planning, scheduling and controlling in all functions of management. For a number of reasons this technique is particularly applicable for use in marketing management. First marketing management, by definition, involves the coordination of many other functions and activities: advertising, distribution; selling; market research; product research and development.

Second, much of the work in marketing can be of a project nature, for example new product launch, organization of a sales promotion, setting up of a new distribution system. Finally, in competitive marketing situations, time can be all-important. When a plan is formulated, a statement of the objectives of a project, operation or company is made, along with the policies and strategies needed to each those objectives.

A project is composed of a series of activities directed to the accomplishment of a desired objective. The main difference between projects and production processes is that projects are normally non-repetitive. The decision maker is usually confronted with a unique situation, for which there is neither prior experience nor information for control. The problem that the decision maker faces is that he/she is responsible to complete a project in the minimum possible time, or by a certain deadline. In other words, he/she is responsible to coordinate the activities which compose a project in such a way that all of them will finish in time. One possible solution would be to start each activity as soon as the preceding one is finished; this assumption is incorrect, since it assumes that all the activities of a project are in a sequential relationship, which means that we are not allowed to work with two or more activities simultaneously. CPA is based exactly on the opposite assumption, i.e. that some of the activities of a project are in concurrent relationship, and take place simultaneously. CPA deals therefore with planning, scheduling and controlling. Scheduling is the coordinating, ordering, timing of the activities, decisions and operations required by the objectives, policies and strategies. The advantages to be gained from CPA in marketing are similar to those gained in other functions, except that the centrality of the marketing function, particularly in some consumer goods firms, increases its desirability. The advantages are:

1 It enables more efficient use of resources.
2 The very performance of the exercise requires thought about what is being done and why and how, i.e. a review and consideration of objectives, strategies, policies, priorities, methods and alternatives.
3 The plan can be a method of communicating the objectives, strategies and policies to those involved, which can be an important factor in motivation.
4 Possible problems, along with their effects, can be anticipated to an extent. When such problems do occur, their causes are more easily identified and hence the right remedy more readily chosen.
5 It can enable 'management by exception' to take place, i.e. management need only take action when things are not according to plan. This is important because management time is valuable.
6 It provides a way of measuring performance by

comparing what actually happened with what ought to have happened according to the plan.

The fact that marketing involves the scheduling and coordination of so many tasks means that CPA is an invaluable technique. It ensures that no jobs are omitted and may reveal interdependencies between activities which would not have been seen otherwise. It also enables one to reduce activity and project time at minimum cost.

Its application is however limited to jobs where it is possible to *separate* activities, and it has to be realized that since some activity times are estimates, a degree of subjectivity is introduced. It is not hard to see how a manager of a department might give a pessimistic estimate for an activity in order to ensure that he/she is not going to be pushed hard when it actually comes to performing that activity. Also, some people are genuinely uncertain how long an activity will take. The solution in both cases is to get as many informed opinions as possible and to use PERT to obtain the probability of completing a given task in a given time. For more detailed description on PERT and CPA see Meidan (1978).

In any management function where CPA is used, there are two main considerations which are related. The first is to what extent the activities are broken down and hence how complex the network is and, second, whether the initial cost of implementation of CPA is worthwhile. These considerations are particularly important when the activities are so numerous that computers are required. Nevertheless, if one, for example, is planning to launch a product in a very large market the expense will almost certainly be worthwhile. In addition, even fairly expensive projects could be improved with manual CPA. The actual formulation of the objectives, strategies and policies in a given project will usually be relatively simple. For example, when launching a new product the objective will presumably be to capture x per cent of a given market profitability, and strategy will be that of the marketing mix. The more complex the operation, the more difficult the scheduling of the activities involved, in order to minimize time and cost. The activities in a product launch might include section of brand name, package design, market research, test marketing and installation of new production equipment.

Applications of PERT and CPA in marketing

There are a large number of possible applications of PERT and CPM methods; for new product launch (Robertson, 1970); distribution; planning (Lalorde and Henden, 1973); sales negotiations and purchasing (Bird *et al*. 1973); launching a marketing company/project/department; sales promotions; conference organization advertising campaigns; new stores opening; realign sales territories, etc.

Budnick *et al*. (1977) proposed using network planning for product development, while others suggest the use of CPM to coordinate and plan the hundreds of activities which must be carried out prior to commercialization of a new product. Recently Johansson and Redinger (1979), using path analysis, formulated an advertising-sales relationship of a hairspray product. They suggested that the variables affecting the advertising–sales relationship include advertising, awareness, liking, acceptance, preference and purchase. These variables were linked up by equations, each equation with its possible error terms and 'path coefficients'. Using these equations, the path diagram was constructed. By manipulating the equations, the 'path coefficients' were expressed in terms of chosen coefficients and using empirical data gathered from field studies, path coefficients were ascertained. The variables of the equations were also expressed in terms of other variables to determine their causal link. From the path diagram and formula derived, they were able to determine the advertising sales relationship.

Network analysis is suited to a wide range of applications in management, and in particular marketing where it has increased knowledge of the time-cost relationship, especially in situations where there is uncertainty. It is applied in the introduction of a new product, and also to distribution, purchasing and sales negotiations, etc. Network analysis is easily understood and implemented. Its application does not require specialists but does require the contribution of all the managers, who must not refuse to give the information needed. In return, the technique will enable managers to know when their responsibilities are going to begin and what is expected from them for the completion of a project.

Conclusion

The marketing research literature does not specify which quantitative method is most 'popular'. One can only conclude that the multivariate methods, as well as the stochastic and hybrid techniques and models are widely used. The flexibility of both simulation and heuristic programming models mean that they can be applied to almost any situation where other models fail to give satisfactory results. Although at times no optimum solutions are obtained, they nevertheless give very 'good' results especially when mathematical programming is too expensive and complicated to use. But, all too often, these models are erroneously used when other more accurate techniques are available. Queuing theory, network planning and transportation models are more restricted in their applications in marketing as they are formulated to solve problems in specific areas. Regarding deterministic techniques, these are suitable for finding optimum solutions to problems particularly when set relationships exist between the variables although, in marketing, relationships not influenced by changes in the external environment seldom occur. In summary, the usage of different types of models depends largely on the problem under investigation as well as on the type of data available and their level of interrelationships.

This chapter has attempted to present the application of the main quantitative methods in marketing. A taxonomic structure was adopted and all the techniques were broadly classified under seven headings: multivariate methods; regression and forecasting techniques; simulation methods; statistical decision methods; deterministic operational research methods; hybrid models; and network programming models. Advantages and limitations in the usage of each of these methods were discussed. However the use of different types of methods depends largely on the marketing management situation of the problem under consideration.

References

Bird, M. M., Clayton, E. R. and Moore, L. J., 'Sales Negotiation Cost Planning for Corporate Level Sales', *Journal of Marketing*, vol. 37, no. 2, April 1973, pp. 7–11.

Budnick, I., Mojena, R. and Vollman, M., *Principles of OR for Management*, Richard D. Irwin, 1977, p. 135.

Chambers, J. D., Mullick, S. K. and Smith, D. D., 'How to Choose the Right Forecasting Technique', *Harvard Business Review*, July–August 1979, pp. 45–74.

Chentnick, C. G., 'Fixed Facility Location Technique', *International Journal of Physical Distribution*, vol. 4, no. 5, 1975, pp. 263–75.

Cunningham, R. M., 'Customer Loyalty to Store and Brand', *Harvard Business Review*, vol. 39, 1961, pp. 127–37.

Draper, N. R., and Smith, H., *Applied Regression Analysis*, Wiley, 1966.

Doyle, P., 'Nonmetric Multidimensional Scaling: A User's Guide', *European Journal of Marketing*, vol. 7, no. 2, 1972, pp. 82–8.

Doyle, P. and Fenwick, I., 'The Pitfalls of AID Analysis', *Journal of Marketing Research*, vol. 12, November 1975, pp. 408–13.

Doyle, P. and Fenwick, I., 'Sales Forecasting Using a Combination of Approaches', *Long Range Planning*, June 1976, pp. 61–4.

Finerty, J. J., 'Product Pricing and Investment Analysis', *Management Accounting*, December 1971, pp. 21–37.

Higgins, J. C., 'Some Applications of Operational Research in Advertising', *European Journal of Marketing*, vol. 7, no. 3, 1973–4, pp. 166–75.

Johansson, J. K. and Redinger, R., 'Evaluating Advertising by Path Analysis', *Journal of Advertising Research*, 1979, pp. 29–35.

Jolson, M. A., *Quantitative Techniques in Marketing*, Macmillan 1973.

Kotler, P. and Schultz, R. L., 'Marketing Simulations: Review and Prospects', *Journal of Marketing*, July 1970, pp. 237–95.

Kotler, P., *Marketing Management, Analysis Planning and Control*, Prentice-Hall, 1972, p. 364.

LaLonde, B. and Headen, R., 'Strategic Planning for Distribution', *Long Range Planning*, December 1973, pp. 23–9.

Meidan, A., 'When to Use Nonmetric Multidimensional Techniques in Marketing Research', *European Research*, March 1975, pp. 58–65.

Meidan, A., 'Pub Selection Criteria' in M. J. Baker (ed.), *Buyer Behaviour*, Proceedings Marketing Education Group Conference, Glasgow, 1976, pp. 41–59.

Meidan, A., 'The Use of Quantitative Techniques in Warehouse Location', *International Journal of Physical Distribution and Materials Management*, vol. 8, no. 6, 1978, pp. 347–58.

Meidan, A., 'Optimising the Number of Salesmen' in M. K. Baker (ed.), *New Directions in Marketing and Research*, University of Strathclyde, Glasgow, 1981a, pp. 173–97.

Meidan, A., *Marketing Applications of Operational Research Techniques*, MCB University Press, 1981b, p. 86.

Meidan, A., 'Marketing Strategies for Hotels – A Cluster Analysis Approach', *Journal of Travel Research*, vol. 21, no. 4, Spring 1983, pp. 17–22.

Morrison, D. G., 'On the Interpretation of Discriminant Analysis', *Journal of Marketing Research*, vol. 5, February 1968, pp. 64–9.

Newman, J. W. and Werbel, R. A., 'Multivariate Analysis of Brand Loyalty for Major Household Appliances', *Journal of Marketing Research*, vol. 10, November 1973, pp. 404–9.

Paul, R. J., 'Retail Store as a Waiting Line Model', *Journal of Retailing*, vol. 48, 1972, pp. 3–15.

Riter, C. B., 'The Merchandising Decision Under Uncertainty', *Journal of Marketing*, vol. 31, 1969, pp. 44–7.

Robertson, A., 'Looking Out for Pitfalls in Product Innovation', *Business Administration*, June 1970, pp. 39–46.

Robertson, T. S. and Kennedy, J. N., 'Prediction of Consumer Innovators: Application of Multiple Discriminant Analysis', *Journal of Marketing Research*, vol. 6, May 1969, pp. 156–63.

Schuchman, A., 'Queue Tips for Managers', in *Scientific Decision Making in Business*, readings in OR for non-mathematicians, Holt, Rinehart & Winston, 1963, pp. 300–12.

Walters, D., Applying the Monte Carlo Simulation', *Retail and Distribution Management*, February 1975, pp. 50–4.

Wilson, J. M., 'The Handling of Goals in Marketing Problems', *Management Decision*, vol. 3, no. 3, 1975, pp. 16–23.

to aid the selling process by developing customer targets and call norms, allocating time between customers, pre-call planning and qualifying leads. As selling has increased in sophistication it has become increasingly more marketing orientated, taking a longer term view of profits and considering the long-term satisfaction of customers, rather than immediate sales targets. There is thus no need, particularly with business-to-business selling, to attempt to move the potential customer through all the stages of the purchase decision in one 'hard sell' presentation. If the aim is to build long-term sales relationships, then IT can be used at each stage to support the sales activities. (Figure 11.1)

Computer-generated mailshots, or advertising aimed at obtaining literature requests, will help generate leads avoiding the need for cold calling. A personalized follow up letter, information sheet or brochure will help stimulate interest and a tele-marketer call can help prepare the ground for the actual contact. At the actual presentation portable videos and other audio visual equipment are being increasingly used, such as compact daylight viewers/

projectors for slide based presentations. These are now often the size of a briefcase, have remote control and high definition screens at a low cost.

The combination of lower prices and high power of micros encouraged Ciba-Geigy Pharmaceuticals to supply BBC B Micros to its sales force, to be used in conjunction with printed promotional support material and video. The software program was mainly educational and provided a focus for the discussion and later sales presentation. Philips Lighting and British Gas similarly bought Hewlett Packard portable computers for their sales engineers to take on building sites. The machines were programmed to allow the salesperson to produce a quotation on site, without the need for a 24-hour delay while design and support staff were consulted. The software was designed to prompt the sales-person to ask for all relevant information and provide the quotation while interest was still high. Many other organizations have cut the time between the salesperson stimulating desire and being able to initiate action by allowing sales details of the visit to be entered directly on to a portable. The informa-

Marketer	Method	Prospect
Capture attention	Exhibition. Direct mail/advertising to generate leads to be stored on computer	Problem/need recognition
Arouse interest	Computer generated literature sent out, follow up letter, telemarketer call to gather more information	Information search
Create desire	Interest qualified by telemarketer or salesperson contact, specific sales information designed for prospect given by portable video/terminal	Evaluation
Initiate action	Salesperson contact, follow up letter, ease of ordering and payment essential, as with EFT and credit rating checked by computer	Selection
Demonstrate service	Customer service call, relationship building, future needs noted and entered on data base	Decision implementation
Continued support	Customer service call, automatic follow up letter or telephone call, to generate further qualified leads	Post-purchase process

Source: Modified from L. Loeffler *Marketing News*, March 14th, 1988, pp. 8–9.

Figure 11.1 *A framework for IT-aided selling*

tion can then be transmitted back to the company in the evening via a modem and home telephone. The central computer automatically accepts the data, allowing overnight updating of records and transaction checks. After a sale is made the computer also contributes to the cultivation of long-term customer relationships and hence repeat and cross selling opportunities. A computerized record system therefore allows the company to maintain customer loyalty and satisfaction and contribute to future sales activities.

The use of the computer in sales should not be seen simply as a method of increasing efficiency with the sole aim of reducing costs. Instead they should be used as a long-term investment in competitive advantage, allowing the sales force to be more effective in the sales situation while also allowing a much closer customer relationship. The FPS case study is an example of this.

Financial and Planning Services (Management) Ltd

Financial Planning Services (FPS) is one of the largest independent personal financial advisory services in the United Kingdom, with over 100 offices. The company offers a personal financial management service, offering advice to clients on a wide variety of personal finance decisions, such as tax, life and other assurance, portfolio management, pension schemes, mortgages, etc.

FPS deals with over 270 life companies, but one, General Portfolio, has created a direct computer link which is to the benefit of client, FPS and General Portfolio (GP).

The usual method of servicing clients is a first visit to gather details on the customer's requirements, personal details and financial position, etc. and then returning to the office to organize any quotations required. These are obtained by phoning various life offices, who themselves enter the customer data into their computers which produces a quote. A hard copy of this is then posted to FPS who arrange a second visit with the prospective client.

However, there is a separate procedure for obtaining quotations from GP, involving an IBM micro with disk-drive monitor, printer and accompanying software, funded by GP. This system allows instant quotes to be given on the complete range of GP's products. This system gives both GP and FPS an efficiency advantage over competitors. While the entire financial services market is dependent on computers for storage and retrieval of data this has not resulted in particular firms gaining a competitive advantage. As most companies have applied similar systems for identical functions increased efficiency has resulted but no gains relative to each other.

Where GP has gained an advantage is that by placing its computer system in an 'independent' sales environment GP has a head start over competing life companies. This time advantage has proven to be crucial in the sales environment, giving a much faster customer response and greater convenience to FPS.

GP has gained a large increase of sales from FPS. FPS has managed to improve their conversion of enquiries to sales because of their improved speed of response, and has also reduced running costs. A mutual significant benefit has resulted from the link, which is likely to be formalized to comply with the Financial Services Act, 1988.
Source: Alisdair Findlay.

The use of direct marketing techniques, such as direct mail and telephone marketing, as sales tools in their own right, or as sales support, has increased drastically in recent years. It has been suggested that talking about direct marketing without discussing data bases is like talking about ham without mentioning eggs, and indeed it is the combination of these two elements which give direct marketing the usefulness and sophistication it now has.

The techniques of direct marketing existed long before they were linked to IT and electronic data bases, and were generally seen as the 'poor quality' end of marketing activities. This perception is rapidly changing as major advertising agencies incorporate direct marketing into promotional campaigns and the range of companies reporting success with direct marketing continues to grow.

The features of direct marketing are that:

- Advertising or selling are combined.
- The results are measurable, and therefore effectiveness can be tested.
- It is flexible, in both timing and objectives, and therefore controllable.

- It is complementary to other elements of the promotional mix.
- It is selective, assuming a suitable list or customer data base is available.

The lack of selectivity has contributed to the common criticism of 'junk mail' which the direct marketing industry is trying to live down. Not only are shotgun approaches to the market extremely inefficient they also tend to annoy the uninterested recipient. Such approaches are contrary to the view that the modern marketing approach is to build long-term customer relationships. The growth of relational data bases has encouraged firms to adapt their information systems to include a customer data base that includes much more than simply a list of names and addresses. This customer data base can then be used to drive customer orientated programmes in a personalized, articulated and cost-effective manner (Rapp and Collins, 1987).

Data base marketing is thus a sophisticated form of target marketing which has the ability to target individual customers with a unique communication or sales approach, if required and justified by marketing considerations.

While in theory it would be possible to run a data base manually the amounts of data involved makes this unrealistic in practice. The aim of data base marketing is not simply to sell, as with direct response mail shots or teleselling, but to build up a long-term relationship with existing and potential customers. This means that a company must know its customers not only in terms of a general customer profile or segment, but also by keeping a record of all past transactions and communications between the firm and that customer, and of the individual's responses (if any).

While many large organizations have large customer data bases, such as in the retailing and banking sectors, these have usually been built for financial and accounting reasons and are frequently incapable of providing the information in the form required by marketers. Data base marketing has capitalized on the reduction in cost of hardware, linked to increased memory and improved software, and a change in attitude of users who put pressure on system designers for wider access and better integration of separate data bases.

The collation of information which exists in different sections of the company in different formats, and then merging it to create a customer based file directly accessible by the marketing department is one of the major problems in data base marketing. Possible input to the data bank will be sales data bases, but these are often organized by product rather than customer and may need to be redesigned. Bought in mailing lists, sales enquiries, exhibition visitors, service calls, after-sales contacts and enquiries, as well as details on competitors' customers are all relevant. To this will be added descriptive details of customer/prospect characteristics and then details of all personal sales calls, direct mail shots, exhibition invitations, telephone sales calls etc., along with details of any responses and purchases.

A DBM sytem of this type is clearly expensive to build and maintain and would need to be extremely effective to pay its way. The concept of customer lifetime value is frequently used to justify the investment, rather than a simple immediate comparison of cost against sales created. Customer lifetime value measures the net present value of all future contributions to overhead and profit from the customer. It is estimated not only from initial revenue from sales but after-market revenue from the sale such as maintenance contracts, insurance, after-sales service, upgrades, supplies etc. as well as cross and repeat selling.

The decision as to how much of that lifetime value to invest in acquiring a new customer will depend on the break-even point and required return on investment.

This has previously restricted the growth of data base marketing to products with high unit costs, although some fast-moving consumer goods companies have shown how DBM can be successfully used. The type of companies particularly suited to using DBM (Shaw and Stone, 1988) show one or more of the following characteristics:

- Their market can be divided into identifiable segments.
- Periodic reselling is required to keep customers.
- Cross selling possibilities exist.
- Competitors have created barriers to entry by controlling distribution or have high advertising thresholds.

- Suitable distribution channels or mass-advertising media are not available.
- Customers are identifiable and have a high annual spend.
- The company have a customer orientation and the marketing skills to exploit and control the medium.
- Sufficient investment in time and resources is available.

What is required for DBM to be successful is the development of a coordinated customer communication campaign, where direct marketing is simply one strand of an integrated campaign. The focus should thus be not on the technology or techniques but on the customer. The question is how, by using direct marketing linked to a data base, the company can make finer adjustments to its marketing strategy to increase both its effectiveness and efficiency. In an era when markets are supposedly fragmenting under the pressure of increasing sophistication and competition then a well-constructed customer data base is an essential aid to cost-effective target marketing. The ability of a firm to collect the necessary customer data and use it in its marketing, rather than selling, activities will depend upon its degree of marketing orientation and the sophistication of its existing information systems.

Information provision and IT

The provision of customer related information should be one duty of marketing information system, yet research suggests that the majority of firms have not reached a sufficient level of sophistication in their general market and information acquisition and usage to allow them to benefit from data base marketing (Fletcher, 1981; Oasis, 1989). Information systems tend to follow a hierarchy (Spraque and Watson, 1979) with low-level electronic data processing (EDP) systems being the first stage. An EDP system would have a basic data processing function with no common data base. It could classify, sort, add, and delete information and thus act as an electronic filing cabinet. Next comes an integrated data processing system where users can access information from different sources. If this includes a marketing data base, rather than simply financial and sales figures, and has the ability to analyse data and run simple models, then it enters the marketing information system (MIS) of the hierarchy. At the peak are decision support systems (DSS) or strategic information systems (SIS) which, as the name implies, are capable of aiding the decision maker in making strategic decisions, and as such require sophisticated software, decision models and information flows.

The ideal marketing information system thus differs from lower level systems in that the data base being collected is transformed into information relevant to decisions the marketer has to make. These decisions themselves tend to be of different types, ranging from the simple structured decisions involved in controlling the marketing function (such as checking sales trends, salespeople quotas etc.), to the much more unstructured, qualitative decisions relating to strategic planning.

At the strategic planning level executives are making decisions as to which markets to attack, the nature of competition and competitive advantage, as well as allocating resources to allow the firm to position itself effectively. The information to aid strategic planning decisions therefore tends to be qualitative, general, future orientated, and externally focused. Information for control purposes will tend to be quantitative, detailed, past and present orientated, and internally focused. An information system for marketing purposes should therefore be capable of handling all types of data requirements.

Technology which can facilitate data acquisition, processing and communication is therefore a key management concern. The cost of these activities has, in the past, been a justifiable excuse for many firms who did not want to invest in an information system. Today, however, due to developments in IT and deregulation of telecommunications, these constraints have been reduced, if not removed. The developments of local and wide area networks means it is no longer meaningful to talk about information processing and communications as independent activities. The roles of computing and communications are so entwined that their business value depends on the total system (Hammer and Manqurian, 1987).

The provision of huge external data bases which are easily accessible, and without geographic constraints, has created opportunities for even the smallest firm. The reluctance of industry to adopt this technology, and make use of value added data services (VADS) provoked the Government, in association with British industry, to launch VANGUARD in 1986. This was a consortium of sponsors: Department of Trade and Industry (DTI); the Telecommunications Managers Association, and the IT Users Standards Association whose main purpose was to promote the uptake of VADS in UK businesses (HMSO, 1988). VADS embrace a wide range of time and cost saving facilities for transferring information electronically rather than on paper. It is typically categorized into electronic data interchange (EDI), electronic mail (E-mail), and on-line information services.

It is increasingly the case that it is what a company knows and how it manages this knowledge base, rather than its physical assets, which will determine its market value. The use of VADS is therefore more than just an aid to manipulating the marketing mix, but a strategic marketing resource. There are now over 4,000 commercially accessible on-line data bases worldwide, with 350 of them based in the UK. These can be accessed through host-organizations such as Lockheed Dialog (500 data bases), Datastart (100 data bases), IRS-Dialtech (30 data bases), SDC-Orbit (30 data bases), Pergamon-Infoline (30 data bases) and Datastream (7 data bases). The user, by means of a dial-up telecommunication link to a remote computer, and interactively searches the data base using key words or questions. The output can be displayed on the terminal, or printed out as necessary.

The information providers (IPs), are made up of organizations such as publishers, trade associations, governments, and commercial organizations such as Reuters, Dow Jones, Financial Times, Dun & Bradstreet etc. They gain the benefit of being able to continually update their material in a way which is not possible with printed copy. Marketing managers can therefore check for the most recent research or information to help their decision making, without the delay this would normally entail. Specialized data bases exist which list published research and data on over 130 countries with forecasts, market trends and industry comment.

The disadvantage of VADS to the firm is that there is an initial outlay on equipment (£1,000–£2,500) and data base charges of £40–£90 for a connection fee and then additional charges for data obtained which can make the search an expensive process. At a rate of £2 per minute, as with McCarthy's on-line data base charge, an inexperienced user can incur high costs. This may encourage firms to put on-line access under the control of an information specialist, but the trend is towards 'end-user' computing and distributed systems which allow the organizations members gain experience and ensures the system meets the needs of the users rather than computing technicians.

At present the main users of VADS are advertising agencies and retail organizations who wish to monitor specific markets through access to such things as Mintel, MEAL and BRAD through MAGIC (Marketing and Advertising General Information Centre) and MAID (Media Analysis and Information Database). They also have the marketing sophistication required to make use of the information once it is acquired.

It is not possible for an organization lacking in marketing skills to gain them through the purchase of technology. If a firm does not know how to use a business information library to conduct an environmental analysis, then providing the information on-line will not bring any advantages. If a firm does not have a customer orientation then its customer data base will be little more than a mailing list.

While there are many examples of successful use of IT to gain competitive advantage, there are just as many examples of firms who have failed to gain the benefits expected from investing in IT.

The barriers to the successful use of information systems and IT have been noted by Kemerer and Sosa (1988). Often IT opportunities are not exploited due to a non-supportive corporate environment, particularly when the benefits are qualitative or diffused through the organization as with decision support systems. The high initial investment in hardware, software and training is beyond the reach of many companies, especially when the technology is at the leading edge and unproven.

The difficulties created by the failure of technology to fulfil the salesperson's or vendor's promises can lead to major losses if the functioning of the organization is hindered, but most firms cannot afford to run duplicate systems until the bugs are removed. Kemerer and Sosa give the example of Federal Express Corporation of America, which was forced to stop its zapmail electronic document transmission service after a plague of telecommunication equipment difficulties:

> The telephone lines performed extremely poorly, and transmissions were slow and noisy, making repeat transmissions necessary. This of course caused Federal Express to incur large, unexpected costs. The company nevertheless decided to continue the project and upgrade it. They set up satellite transmission facilities at customer sites and installed rewritten software and more mainframe switching stations around the country. The company also had to request the use of a communications satellite. The FCC approved a satellite launch, but the Challenger Space Shuttle disaster caused the cost of satellites to skyrocket and their launching to be delayed. All of these problems contributed to Zapmail's failure, which in the end meant a $200 million loss for Federal Express. (Kemerer and Sosa, 1988, p. 22)

Even after the IT idea has been successfully developed and implemented other problems arise. It may be copied by competitors, as with ATMs, such that the competitive advantage is lost. The gains in this case may not last long enough to justify the investment, but if competitors use the idea themselves the firm will still have to make the investment simply to catch up.

The system may often be much more expensive to maintain than initially predicted as maintenance, training and enhancement costs are met. Indeed the very success of the system may cause problems as latent demand is unleashed which makes the system oversubscribed almost immediately.

The design of an information system for marketing managers therefore requires an analysis of the uses to which it is to be put, and the benefits a firm hopes to acquire. To make full use of the marketing opportunities which come from the application of IT then the focus should not simply be on the cost benefits available from greater efficiency, but on ways in which IT can be used to give a long-term, sustainable competitive advantage. This requires the marketing manager to consider the strategic role of IT.

IT and marketing strategy

IT is having an influence on the way in which marketing managers conduct their job through the availability of computers and software. These allow the manipulation of data and the better analysis of market conditions and demand. The provision of networks to transmit information regardless of the geographical distances involved, and at a fraction of the cost or time previously involved, has also created new opportunities both for suppliers and users of information.

Many firms, particularly in the US, have realized that the investment in IT should be seen not simply as a corporate overhead to be absorbed as part of the cost of doing business but as a competitive weapon in its own right. This requires senior managers to view IT not as a part of the infrastructure servicing the rest of the organization to be left to computer specialists, but as a strategic resource.

A framework for studying the potential impact of IT on a firm's business has been provided by Parsons (1983). He suggests that senior management must understand how IT may impact upon the competitive environment and strategy of the business if they are to allocate sufficient resources to IT. The three areas he focuses on are industry level, firm level and strategy level (Table 11.1).

Table 11.1   *The three level impact of IT*

Industry level	
IT changes on industry::	Products and services
	Markets
	Production economics
Firm level	
IT affects key competitive forces:	Buyers
	Suppliers
	Substitution
	New entrants
	Rivalry
Strategy level	
IT affects a firm's strategy:	Low cost leadership
	Product differentiation
	Concentration on market or product niche

Source: Parsons, 1983.

Industry level impact of IT

At the industry level IT changes the nature of the industry itself, shortening industry life cycles, changing the nature of the product and services, opening up new markets by erasing geographical limitations and, with new products and services such as home banking, meeting innovative needs. By changing the economics of production, as with the newspaper industry, or the nature and efficiency of distribution, many traditional and fundamental assumptions within the industry must change. This macro-environmental review is a major part of strategic planning and in some industries such as banking, is likely to highlight substantial opportunities or threats created by IT. In some firms this has forced them to re-evaluate their mission statement, or definition of their business.

What business are we in?

One of the essential elements of the strategic process is the answer to the question 'What business are we in?' This definition should then be used to guide the activities of the firm while making strategic choices. One of the consequences of IT is that it encourages, and in some cases forces, a redefinition of the firm's business. As IT allows institutions to offer new services, their traditional view of their business becomes increasingly restrictive. American Express reportedly views itself not as being in the financial services business, but the information business.

American Airlines is an example of a business that has gained a major competitive advantage by selling not airline seats, but information. In 1975 United Airlines offered to link travel agents directly into its Apollo booking system. American Airlines followed with SABRE which had the added attraction of listing over 400 competitors' flights as well. As virtually all America's travel agents book through computerized reservation systems and travel agents provide the majority of the airline business, any system which attracted them would potentially benefit the operating airline. In SABRE's case the attraction for travel agents was that there was now no need to shop around for information as American Airline provided it

through its alphabetical listing of airlines. The fact that American Airlines, listed as AA, came first in the list and was thus most likely to be accessed for details of seat availability was a fortunate coincidence. As competitors offered their own systems the American Government was forced to step in and regulate the area, banning some of the more obvious bias. In a bid to attract the travel agents the airlines improved their systems by including more information, this time on hotel reservations and car rental. The cost of these systems became a major barrier to entry as no airline could exist without access to one. Some decided it was cheaper to use SABRE than build their own, and with a charge for each booking American Airlines recognized that what had started as an aid to efficiency could become a profit centre and marketing tool in its own right. The reservation system allows airlines to recognize frequent fliers, identify traffic trends, and in minutes identify underbooked flights, allowing immediate marketing responses. The effectiveness of marketing tactics used to attract identified target segments can also be easily monitored, all at a fraction of the time and cost possible without the system. The UK airlines have their own system, Travicom, which links with the reservation systems of forty-nine different airlines, including BA's booking system Babs, with 97 per cent of travel agents using it. In 1987 American Airlines objected to the merger of BA and British Caledonian (the owners of Travicom) alleging that B-Cal would stop issuing its tickets through SABRE, that Travicom was biased towards BA, and did not list US rivals, making it difficult for AA to operate in the UK. BA also bought an 11 per cent stake in Apollo, the United Airlines system, and the biggest competitor to SABRE, which brought accusations of unfair competition.

The trend seems to be for consortia to form to develop even more advanced reservation systems, and this has increased the pressure for an international code of conduct. What is clear is that to define a business in terms of the product or basic service being sold is an error, as it restricts corporate vision.

It has been suggested (Abell, 1980) that to specify what business a firm is in, a firm must look at three important areas. First, what customer groups are being satisfied. Second, what customer needs are being satisfied. Third, what technology is being employed to satisfy the customer.

The definition of customer groups tends to be 'What is at present' rather than a 'What might be' question. Unless the customers have unique characteristics, in terms of geography, size or other features which add to switching costs, then poaching by other firms is extremely likely. Similarly with customer needs, competitive advantage can be gained by identifying an unmet need, or by satisfying it to a greater degree than competitors, as did American Airlines; however these gains are often transient. In the past it has frequently been the third criteria, the differing technological base and experience of suppliers, which has followed firms to identify their competitors and thus position themselves. The ubiquitous nature of IT has meant that previously unrelated industries are being brought together by a common technology, making even this criterion redundant. The boundary lines between the technology of information handling and transmission, telephone, newspapers, printing, photocopying, broadcasting, computers, are decaying as IT develops. Facsimile machines now photocopy and transmit, telephones can be used to communicate between computers, electronic newspapers and video magazines are available, and cable networks link television sets and computers. The demarcations between the technology are therefore blurring. Information is frequently a common denominator of many industrial practices and exchanges, such that telecommunications and computers link them all. A definition of a business must therefore be based not on what the supplier thinks is being sold, but what the customer thinks is being bought.

Electronic markets

The potential benefits of IT include enhanced communication, increased efficiency in decision making and better information flows. This allows the extension of markets across geographical and industrial boundaries, and improved relationships between elements of the supply chain.

This can be seen in the creation of electronic markets where computer to computer buying and selling takes place. For computer to computer trading to take place a common communications standard needs to exist, either as an industry standard or by the vendor providing the suitable software and equipment. The creation of an electronic market reduces inefficiencies and improves buyers' access to sellers, while disseminating full, accurate and immediate information. Electronic trading is not new but the most recent development is the network of computer terminals allowing large numbers of people access to remote centralized markets. Perhaps one of the most well-known electronic markets is the buying and selling of stocks and shares. The 1987 stock market crash focused attention on the dangers of 'program trading' where individual traders program their systems to automatically buy or sell shares when prices reach predetermined levels. It was suggested that this automatic selling contributed to the crash when computers themselves created a drop in prices, by their prior decisions, resulting in further automatic sell-offs. During this period of extreme volume and volatility, nine of the twelve computer systems of the New York Stock Exchange broke down at some point, adding to the panic and confusion.

IT makes it so much easier to exchange information that it encourages the growth of geographically dispersed markets, as did its predecessors, the telegraph and telephone. For each exchange to take place a cost is incurred and the more exchanges that take place the greater the potential for cost savings. The customer benefit comes from making more advantageous matches between buyers and sellers. IT can help both buyer and seller to link their needs more closely. By the constant exchange of information, stocks can be reduced and delivery improved, giving benefits to both parties and improving the general efficiency of the market.

Firm level impact of IT

The second level of Parsons' three-level impact of IT focuses on the firm itself. Porter (1985) describes five basic competitive forces which determine a firm's profitability and the nature of competition. These are:

1 The threat of new entrants.
2 The threat of substitute products or services.
3 The bargaining power of suppliers.

4   The bargaining power of buyers.
5   Rivalry among existing firms.

Munro and Huff (1985) have shown how IT has the power to change these competitive forces as in Figure 11.2.

Many of the potential changes brought about by IT require the cooperation of suppliers, buyers, or the intermediaries supporting the firm's interaction with buyers, and these change the complex relationship between the participants. This can affect relative bargaining power in negotiations over price, product, and other decisions during the exchange process.

Buyer/supplier power during exchange

The ability to identify and switch between suppliers can do much to reduce a manufacturer's costs. A few suppliers, of labour, energy, components or whatever can force concessions from a buyer if no choice is available. Conversely, strong buyer groups can force concessions from suppliers if they are the dominant or only users of the producer's products.

There has been considerable interest shown in the changing power balance between suppliers, manufacturers and retailers. Power reflects the degree to which one firm can influence the actions and decisions of another, and has been classified into reward, coercive, expert, reference and legitimate power. Its application by relationship between manufacturers, retailers and buyers has been shown by Guiltiman and Paul (1982):

Alternative power bases available to manufacturers, distributors and buyers

Power base	To a manufacturer	To a buyer or distributor
Reward	Ability to offer product with low prices, quantity discounts, or extra benefits	Ability to offer large buying volume
Coercive	Ability to withdraw product (with the loss of sales) when no comparable alternative is available to buyer	Ability to reject offer (with little or no loss of sales) when no equivalent distribution or buyers are available to sellers
Expert	Ability to offer superior or needed technical assistance	Ability to provide unique distribution support
Referent	Ability to offer prestige brand name	Ability to offer image of quality retail outlet or serve as prestige example of satisfied buyer
Legitimate	Contractual provision that requires distributor to carry full line	Contractual provision that requires seller to provide warranty repair and exclusive distribution

Source: Guiltiman and Paul, 1982, p. 282

Force	IT potential
Buyers	Reduce buyer power by increasing switching costs to buyers, e.g. link technology systems with home banking, computer-to-computer ordering, locking in buyers
Suppliers	Supply chain management by retailers, and JIT manufacturing systems demand much more from suppliers and transfer costs. Suppliers of information, as with EPOS systems controlled by retailers, gain power.
Substitutes	IT creates substitutes for many products and services, as with electronic mail and hard copy letters and communications. IT can be used to shorten NPD processes to duplicate or replace products, and by adding benefits can create unique packages.
New Entrants	Existing entry barriers are often negated, new ones created, by the requirements for investment in computer and telecommunication networks.
Rivals	IT changes rivalry as in IT based consortia (e.g. Unichem) using shared data bases and ordering facilities. New rivals are created.

Source: Modified from M. Munro and S. Huff, 1985.

Figure 11.2 *Competitive forces and potential impact of IT*

From the seller's point of view the three most important kinds of power are reward, referent and expertise. The use of coercion to force the other party to accept the exchange, as when the buyer take the majority of a supplier's production and threatens to change supplier, is unlikely to achieve commitment or satisfaction. IT has allowed greater rewards, or benefits, to be bundled into an offering, thereby increasing reward power. It allows access to data bases and expert knowledge through information systems thus increasing expert power. Similarly, by allowing retailers to conduct direct product profitability analysis of individual items, by the analysis of EPOS scanning data, they now have more information than manufacturers allowing them to use coercive power in refusing shelf space, leveraging one supplier's goods against another, and insisting on just-in-time delivery and flow-through distribution.

The installation of up-to-date scanning equipment has also helped stores improve their image of efficiency and reliability, in the same way that robotics and on-line ordering can improve the image and status of manufacturing firms. Legitimate power only plays a part when the participants of an exchange agree to a long-term relationship to justify the cost of investment.

The parties that take part in an exchange are each attempting to maximize their own utility. If a long-term orientation to the firm's activities is taken, and if future exchanges are valued, then the well being of both parties is an essential aspect of the exchange. This mutual dependence is an essential aspect of such IT linkages as just-in-time (JIT) manufacturing and supply chain management. JIT requires the supplier to produce and deliver to the original equipment manufacturer (OEM) the necessary units in the correct quantities at the correct time, within agreed performance specifications every time (Hayes, 1981). Supply chain management looks at the total supply chain, usually from the retailer's viewpoint, and integrates it using modern electronic data processing and telecommunication tools to support systems integration, functional integration and optimization of inventory and capacity utilization (Houlihan, 1982).

It has been suggested that JIT exchange relationships have the greatest degree of dependency and risk with a tangled web of relations and the need for high communication of both a formal and informal nature (Frazier, *et al.*, 1988). While JIT has received considerable attention in the purchasing, materials and logistics literature, marketing academics do not seem to have recognized the importance of JIT to them.

The introduction of JIT requires reliability from suppliers in delivering quantity and quality and this changes the mix of suppliers who can meet the standards, or want to. Similarly the use of single sourcing makes a manufacturer vulnerable if commitment is required, considering the added costs and skills necessary for the supplier to integrate with the manufacturer systems.

The benefits from this cooperation and commitment can be substantial with examples being given (Stevens, 1988) of one firm achieving a reduction of inventory from 2.8 months to 1.3 months and a labour reduction of 30 per cent. Space was reduced by 5 per cent, work in progress from twenty-two days to one day and production increased by 200 per cent. Stevens gives examples of other UK firms making similar savings.

If links are made with interorganizational information systems then other major improvements in efficiency can be made. General Motors tied its CAD/CAM and order entry systems to its suppliers' production systems. The suppliers' computers communicate directly with General Motors robot-based assembly line in an integrated flexible manufacturing system (Cash and Konsynski, 1985). Another example is of a large retailer who has linked its materials-ordering system with the primary supplier's order-entry system. The supplier with the lowest cost automatically gets the order, and the retailer's computer continually monitors the supplier's finished goods inventory, factory scheduling and commitments to ensure sufficient inventory will be available to meet unexpected demand from the retailer (MacFarlan, 1984).

Houston and Gassenheime (1987) remind us that good marketing management emphasizes the building of long-term relationships, which results in a well-established set of expectations about the nature and outcomes of exchange. This requires a balancing of the various, often conflicting, functional objectives participating firms will have. Relationships are likely to evolve as each party to the exchange develops a dependence, and discrete transactions are transformed into more durable associations supported by shared goals, planning and commitment to the relationship (Dwyer *et al.*, 1987).

JIT and supply chain management could not exist without improved information flow between the participants and IT has provided the technology and software to make this possible. In 1988 agreement was reached on EDIFACT (electronic data interchange for administration, commerce and transport). This created an internationally agreed common language necessary for communication. Previously a domestic common language had been agreed called TRADACOM (Trading Data Communications). This standard had been promoted by the Article Numbering Association (ANA) to improve data exchange between companies allowing direct computer to computer communications between otherwise incompatible systems. It is estimated that 80 per cent of all electronic data interchange (EDI) transactions passing between British companies in 1988 were based on TRADACOM.

Competition

The remaining three competitive forces identified by Porter relate to competition and are the threat of new entrants, the threat of substitute products or services, and rivalry among existing firms.

New entrants are a constant threat to existing firms as they reduce market shares and, by increasing competition, often reduce profitability as they attempt to gain a foothold. In growing industries demand may increase sufficiently to accommodate the new entrants but in a mature industry reduced market shares and sales can well result in the departure of one or more of the less efficient founder firms. Entry barriers, such as the high cost of manufacturing plant, the investment required to build distribution networks, the building of reputation or low cost structures based on experience, all deter new entrants. IT is changing the cost of entry, particularly manufacturing costs.

Mass production with undifferentiated products is no longer necessary to gain economies of scale. Increasing use of computer-controlled manufacturing processes means that greater production variability can be achieved with little or no sacrifice of scale economies. A standard 'core' product can be created with the customization of end products, even if they are configured from identical components. IT has made diversity as cheap as uniformity.

Similarly a new entrant can invest in new technology, learning from the experiences of existing producers, and leapfrog them in terms of cost reduction and productivity. By the time the other firms have caught up, the new entrant may be firmly established in the market and may dominate certain key segments.

As shown in Figure 11.1, IT also creates substitutes for many products and services. Electronic data bases allow quick searching by key words and are replacing library research and consultancy firms, electronic newspapers (such as the experiment by the *Birmingham Mail and Post*). Electronic journals and magazines already exist although they have met with limited market success. IT has mainly been used as a component of a larger product, such as with speedometers in cars and control mechanisms in washing machines, their incorporation bringing cost reductions and improved performance. In some products, such as quartz watches, the cost and performance improvements have been much more drastic making previous products and most of the Swiss watch industry redundant. IT often enables a simplicity of design or construction which allows the cost savings to support aggressive pricing strategies. Alternatively added functions or benefits can be incorporated into the product increasing its value over competitors in the eye of the consumer.

While rivalry is an essential aspect of competition most managers have, consciously or unconsciously, learnt acceptable and unacceptable rules of competition to ensure profitability levels are kept adequate for all.

These cosy arrangements may lead to the formation of cartels and cooperative agreements to keep out new entrants. The danger of new entrants is that they may disrupt the agreements, or disturb the passive state of mind of existing firms. This negative, reactive approach ensures potentially disruptive marketing strategies are not attempted.

IT, by changing the market environment and creating new opportunities and threats, tends to disrupt relationships between market participants. IT allows greater coordination and control of activities regardless of location. The restructuring of operations is frequently possible to allow better matching of competitive strategy and market needs. As discussed earlier suppliers, manufacturers, intermediaries and customers may find that it is worthwhile entering into mutually beneficial agreements. Some competitors may similarly find that they can use each other's facilities, as with American Airlines reservation system and the sharing of ATMs by banks, in a way which improves efficiency while maintaining competition. The balance between cooperation and competition can be a difficult one for firms to achieve and encourage vertical or horizontal integration and takeovers.

Strategy level impact of IT

The third level suggested by Parsons relates to the effect of IT on a firm's strategy and how it attempts to satisfy the market. Marketing emphasizes that the product bought by the consumer is not simply the tangible physical object but the totality of benefits and values which are perceived as flowing from ownership and use of the product. Thus the value of a product is derived from all aspects of the firm's operations which synthesize into the aspects visible to the consumer, summarized in the marketing mix.

Value has been defined as that amount buyers are willing to pay for a product or service, and a business is profitable when the value it creates exceeds the cost involved in performing all the firm's operations necessary to bring the product into being. Porter (1985) has popularized the idea of the value chain to illustrate how a firm creates value. He classifies the activities of a firm into the primary activities involved in the physical creation of the product (such as manufacturing, delivery, sales) and the support activities that service the primary activities and allow them to take place (such as general management, accounting, personnel). All of these independent activities are linked in various ways and contribute to the end product as purchased by the consumer. The efficiency with which they are performed determines the cost and value created. The firm's activities are also part of a wider set of activities which together form the marketing or value system. Suppliers, intermediaries and end users have their own value chains which link together to form a channel transporting and transforming raw materials to final product and end user.

The firm, to gain competitive advantage, must look for ways of improving its own activities, or the linkages between activities, or the linkages between elements of the wider value system. Porter gives examples of how IT is permeating the value chain at every point and transforming both the way in which value activities are performed and the nature of linkages among them.

Management is being improved through information systems and various computer models which improve decision making. Computer-aided design, computerized accounting and costing procedures, electronic mail, on-line search procedures and electronic data interchange all improve the information processing components of the support activities. The primary activities have similarly been affected by such things as automated warehousing, automatic identification techniques, computer-aided manufacturing, automatic order processing, data base and telemarketing, portable computers for salespeople, computerized fault identification for after-sales services etc.

The introduction of IT is frequently cost led rather than market led, resulting in long-term strategic advantage often being lost. Wiseman and MacMillan (1984) have suggested that a 'strategic target' should be chosen on which to focus the advantage gained by IT. Focusing on the value system they suggest suppliers, customers, or competitors. Suppliers include those who provide raw material, capital, labour and services. Customers include users, retailers, wholesalers and distributers. Competitors include existing rivals, potential new entrants, substitute products or any firm competing for scarce resources. They recognize that the linkages in the value system mean that changes in one area will impact upon another, allowing multiple targets.

Once a target has been chosen the strategic 'thrust' or approach must be chosen. Two major generic approaches frequently cited are differentiation and cost. IT can reduce costs in any part of the value chain by reducing waste, improving productivity, identifying marginal customers etc., and this is frequently the spur to IT adoption. In following a differentiation strategy IT is used to add unique features or benefits, or to contribute to existing aspects of the mix in a way which will set it apart from competitors. Parsons (1983) argues that firms pursuing a differentiation strategy are most successful when they establish uniqueness in several categories and gives examples of cost and differentiation strategies as in Table 11.2.

The enhanced value given to a product or service which differentiates it from competition can help 'lock-in' customers, particularly if the 'switching-cost' is high. Once a relationship has been built up, and time, money and effort has been invested in the relationship, then the 'emotional' as well as the financial cost of change can be high. The reduction in cost in any part of the value chain may also be used 'offensively' if it allows flexibility on price structures. An example is an airline seat reservation system where day to day price changes are possible as demand changes.

The choice of a low-cost strategy against a differentiation strategy should be based on how well the application matches the strategic needs of the company and competitive conditions.

Wiseman (1988) points out that while a strategic thrust may initially be very successful, it often has the effect of destabilizing the entire industry. The creation of competitive advantage by the use of IT signals a new era of mega-competition, in which competitors counter-attack by adopting the technology themselves and offer similar or better benefits. Wiseman puts forward the axiom that successful strategic use of IT spurs strategic responses.

It therefore becomes important to capitalize on being first despite the risks of so doing.

In deciding on whether to launch a pre-emptive strike the response lag of competitors must be considered to determine the duration, vulnerability and value of competitive advantage derived from the thrust.

Other strategies include the firm concentrating on a market niche, distinguishing itself by unusual cost or product features. Porter calls this a focused strategy, while marketers will recognize it as a concentrated, rather than differentiated segmentation strategy. As with the differentiated strategy the firm must ensure its competitive advantage is sufficiently entrenched, or the entry barriers and switching costs are sufficiently high, to ensure other larger firms will not be attracted into the

Table 11.2   *IT applications that support generic strategies of firms*

| | Generic strategies | |
	Low cost	Product differentiation
Product design development control	Product engineering systems Project control systems	R & D data bases and professional work project stations Electronic mail CAD Custom engineering systems Integrated systems for manufacturing
Operations	Process engineering systems Process control systems Labour control systems Inventory management systems Procurement systems Quality monitoring systems	CAM Systems for suppliers Quality assurance systems Quality monitoring systems
Marketing	Streamlined distribution systems Centralized control systems Econometric modeling systems	Sophisticated marketing systems Market data bases Graphic display systems Telemarketing systems Competition analysis systems Modelling systems Service-orientated Distribution systems
Sales	Sales control systems Advertising monitoring systems Systems to consolidate sales function Strict incentive/monitoring systems	Differential pricing systems Office/field communications Customer/sales support systems Customer order entry Dealer support systems Customer order entry systems
Administration	Cost control systems Quantitative planning and budgeting systems Office automation for staff reduction	Office automation to integrate functions Environment scanning and non-quantitative planning systems Teleconferencing systems

Source: G. Parsons, 'IT: A new competitive weapon', *Sloan Management Review*, 1983, p. 12.

segment. Substitution will always be a threat to a firm following this strategy, particularly if competitors are allowed to close the competitive gap by their own investment in IT and marketing strategies.

Innovative offerings, which better satisfy the customer, and increased cooperation between suppliers and customers can improve efficiency and hence customer service. A focus strategy therefore uses both low cost and differentiation to satisfy a particular niche in a novel way.

Conclusion

Firms are constantly seeking the competitive equivalent of the Holy Grail. They search for the one technique, philosophy or concept which gives them a unique insight into their industry or the nature of their operations, or allows them by adopting the technique, to gain such an advantage that they may, unlike their less fortunate, or less astute competitors, find the clear path to corporate salvation and long term security. In search of such a technique many false gods are enthusiastically embraced, only for the adherents to realize that the benefits are not as great as claimed, or that negative aspects exist which reduce the overall worth of the idea.

Often these early converts are moving away from the technique even as they are being promoted as disciples of the new order.

Many managers quite rightly suspected that the hype surrounding IT disguised yet another 'flavour of the month' fad, which would be absorbed into existing practices without major effect. While the successes of IT were widely promulgated, the failures received less publicity, and many firms made unwise investments which did not create the competitive advantage expected.

It is therefore interesting to note that the growth of IT, and its incorporation into business practices, has continued despite the problems met. This has resulted from a two-fold pressure. First, the successful use of IT has created such competitive advantage that other firms have been forced to follow if they wished to remain in the industry. The new IT based practice thus becomes the industry standard.

Second, IT is not based on any one technology or technique but an integrated collection of technological advances which allow multiple applications in many different areas of business practice. These tend to be self supporting, creating a synergistic benefit as the firm moves along the experience curve. Disappointment in one area is often compensated by unexpected benefits elsewhere. This is often the case when a cost driven improvement in efficiency gives improved customer service on which the firm can then capitalize.

IT is not a panacea for an inefficient or uncompetitive firm. It will not allow a reactive, production orientated firm to gain major competitive advantage at a stroke. It will not even give long-term competitive advantage if used as part of an integrated marketing strategy.

What it does offer, for firms of all sizes, in whatever industry, selling products or services, is an opportunity to integrate all its business operations in a way which creates maximum added-value for the customer, while keeping in constant touch with the marketplace to identify new opportunities and threats as they arise. It therefore allows firms with a customer orientation to stay level, if not ahead of its competitors, by ensuring that to the best of its ability it is focused on giving maximum customer satisfaction.

It is often said that marketing is too important to be left to the marketing department. Equally, IT is much too important to be left to information technologists. IT and marketing are both integrating approaches which are most successful when accepted throughout an organization, and used for both operational and strategic purposes. Marketing managers should therefore consider as a matter of urgency how IT can be used within their own organization.

References

Abell, D., *Defining the Business: The starting point of strategic planning*, Prentice Hall, 1980.

American Marketing Association, *Marketing News*, vol. 23, no. 9, 1989.

Cash, J., and Konsynski, B., 'I.S. Redraws Competitive Boundaries', *Harvard Business Review*, March/April, 1985, pp. 134–42.

Dwyer, F., Schurr, P., and Oh, S., 'Developing Buyer Seller Relationships', *Journal of Marketing*, vol. 51, April 1987, pp. 11–27.

Frazier, G., Spekman, B., and O'Neal, C., 'JIT Relationships in Industrial Markets', *Journal of Marketing*, vol. 52, no. 4, 1988, pp. 52–68.

Fletcher, K., 'Information Systems in British Industry', *Management Decision*, vol. 21, no. 2, 1981, pp. 25–36.

Guiltiman, J., and Paul, G., *Marketing Management: strategies and programs*, McGraw-Hill, 1982.

Hammer, M., and Manqurian, G., 'The changing value of communications technology', *Sloan Management Review*, vol. 28, no. 2, 1987, pp. 65–71.

Hayes, R., 'Why Japanese Factories Work', *Harvard Business Review*, vol. 59, July/August 1981, pp. 57–66.

HMSO, *Vanguard: Opportunities for Education and Training to Accelerate the Update of Value-Added and Data Services in the UK*, HMSO, 1988.

Houston, F., and Gassenheimer, J., 'Marketing and Exchange', *Journal of Marketing*, vol. 51, October 1987, pp. 3–18.

Houlihan, J., 'Supply Chain Management: the modern approach of logistics', *Focus: The Journal of the Institute of Physical Distribution Management*, vol. 1, no. 3, 1982, pp. 12–16.

Kemerer, C., and Sosa, G., 'Barriers to successful Strategic Information Systems', *Planning Review*, vol. 16, September/October 1988, pp. 20–3; 46.

Loeffler, L., *Marketing News*, March 14, 1988, pp. 8–9.

Munroe, M., and Huff, S., 'Information Technology and Corporate Strategy', *Business Quarterly*, vol. 50, Summer 1985, pp. 18–24.

McFarlan, F. W., 'Information technology changes the way you compete', *Harvard Business Review*, May/June 1986, pp. 98–103.

Oasis, A Report on the Management of Marketing Information, Oasis and Institute of Marketing, 1989.

Parsons, G., 'Information Technology: A new competitive weapon', *Sloan Management Review*, vol. 25, Fall 1983, pp. 3–14.

Porter, M., *Competitive Advantage*, Free Press, 1985.

Porter, M., and Millar, V., 'How information technology gives you competitive advantage', *Harvard Business Review*, July/August 1985, pp. 149–60.

Rapp, S., and Collins, T., *Maxi Marketing*, McGraw-Hill, 1987.

Shaw, R., and Stone, M., *Database Marketing*, Gower, 1988.

Spraque, R., and Watson, H., 'Bit by bit to decision support systems', *California Management Review*, vol. 22, no. 1, 1979, pp. 61–8.

Stevens, G., 'Can JIT work in the UK?' *Logistics Today*, vol. 7, no. 1, 1988, pp. 6–9.

Wiseman, C., and MacMillan, I., 'Information systems as competitive weapons', *Journal of Business Strategy*, vol. 5, pt. 2, 1984, pp. 42–9.

Wiseman, C., 'Attack and counter attack: the new game of information technology', *Planning Review*, vol. 16, September/October 1988, pp. 6–14.

This chapter is adapted from Keith Fletcher, *Marketing Management and IT*, Prentice Hall, 1990.

12
Computers in marketing

STEPHEN T. PARKINSON

Introduction

Many organizations install their first computers to manage large volumes of mundane and repetitive clerical tasks. It is usually easy to justify the application of computer technology to such tasks, given savings in labour costs, increases in accuracy and more rapid data processing times. However the computer can be used in a broader range of applications within the organization. In many companies this potential is gradually being realized with the use of the computer to assist in professional and managerial tasks as well as low level clerical functions.

This chapter reviews the role of the computer in the analysis, planning and control of the marketing effort. It also discusses its administrative and decision support potential. A final section of the chapter discusses auditing the requirement for computer applications in marketing.

Given the wide range of applications of the computer which already exist, it is only possible to provide an overview of the main developments which have taken place in the last few years. A decision has also been taken not to discuss individual aspects of computer technology. Those readers who feel the need for such a briefing are advised to consult one of the standard textbooks on this subject.

The potential of new information technology

Effective information management has a major influence on a company's ability to assess and respond to its competitive position. An effective computer-based approach to information management can create substantial advantages in planning and controlling the marketing effort as the following examples illustrate.

A mail order company knows what each of its customers has bought from its catalogues since that customer made his/her first purchase. It knows the sizes of garments purchased, the styles, and the mix of products bought by the customer. It can link this data to other commercially available data bases which detail patterns of consumption of a wide range of associated products and services. This has provided the company with a very powerful tool for segmenting its markets and targeting its marketing effort.

A major multiple using electronic point of sale (EPOS) equipment for scanning bar code information at the checkout as customers' purchases are registered, knows each day what quantities of each size of each brand have been bought, at which outlets. It can match this information to the timing of local and national promotions to obtain a picture of the effectiveness of these promotions. The same company is developing a consumer panel to improve its market information still further.

Members of this panel will pay for the goods at the checkout using a 'smart' credit card which contains economic and demographic information about the consumer. This data can be matched to individual purchases to create a rich source of continuous data about its marketplace.

An engineering company has a computerized information system which monitors its relationships with its customers on a continuing basis. This system records every contact with the customer from telephone calls which are logged by the switchboard, to information from sales calls, receipt of inquiries, despatch of quotations, and the sale of spares. The same system also records the progress which is being made in manufacturing the customer's order and provides an up-to-date picture of performance against the quoted delivery schedule.

In these examples the computer has become an integral part of the company's marketing information system. It has enhanced the organization's ability to manage its environment. There are many other instances where the application of the computer has lead to similar results.

The development of computer applications

Many of the first commercial applications of the computer were developed to meet the financial reporting needs of a company. These applications included order processing, invoice management, and the preparation of accountancy information. Such applications were designed to help the company to manage large flows of data effectively rather than to provide information in a form which management could use for analysis and planning purposes.

Computerization in many companies was handled by one central department which controlled the flow of information through the organization. This led to the growth in importance of the information department whose role it was to anticipate the needs of user departments and provide appropriate information in a form in which it could be used by operating managers. This has not always led to the most successful or useful information system.

Collins (1983) described such a system which was operated by South Eastern Gas in the late 1960s in these terms:

> Traditionally, systems have been developed along functional lines, that is to say, a system serving customer service was developed within the functional boundary of customer service. Where cross-functional links were required, these were obtained by 'stitching across' from two systems not necessarily originally designed to interface. The primary function of the systems was on the transactions carried out by clerks with fairly limited management information systems derived from the transactions . . . Data was not viewed as a corporate resource but as belonging to the function that owned the system. Hence it was possible for two systems with customer records to have separate files with cumbersome cross linking and updating, if indeed such updating existed at all.

This situation is typical of many computer-based data management systems. Today it is still difficult in many companies to obtain useful managerial information from a centralized data processing system. Information is not seen as a strategic resource, and not managed effectively. In many companies managers with marketing responsibilities are not aware of the potential of the computer to provide information in a form which they need to perform their tasks effectively. At the same time members of the information department are unaware of the format in which data is needed or are unable to supply it in a form in which it can be used.

Even when change is required it may be difficult to implement. In large organizations with a lot of transactions to control, it is frequently difficult to persuade a data processing department to interrupt the flow of data processing to produce new analyses, for example analyses of sales to specific market segments, or the costs of selling to each market segment. This can inhibit the development of new applications.

This situation is beginning to change with the gradual introduction of the microcomputer into many functional areas. The essential difference between the microcomputer and the mainframe or minicomputer is the independence which it offers to the user. A manager who uses a microcomputer to analyse data can operate independently of the mainframe or minicomputer. Data analysis can be controlled by the functional specialist (the information user), rather than the information specialist (the information provider). This encourages experimentation with new applications.

In many organizations microcomputers do not have the capacity to handle the large volumes of transactions which are generated. In the future they may have such capacity, or be linked to mini- or mainframe computers in such a way that they appear to have such capacity. However at the moment in such organizations the main role of the microcomputer may be to pilot new applications locally on small samples of data. Once a manager is able to develop and test an application of a computer to a specific business problem then he/she can see the potential of the computer more clearly. If such applications are successful then they may be developed for the company's mainframe computer.

The introduction of the microcomputer has now allowed many smaller companies to introduce an element of computerization to their own business systems. The potential for the development of the computer in a much wider range of organizational settings has increased dramatically as a direct consequence.

In the finance and accounting area applications of the computer are obvious and immediate. Since the majority of accountancy information is numerical, such data can be analysed easily and effectively. The standard 'spreadsheet' programme is a powerful tool which can simplify and speed up many conventional accountancy tasks. The computer has been rapidly adopted for producing accounts, financial modelling, cost management, and financial control.

In marketing the application of the computer appears to have been slower. Higgins and Opdebeeck (1984) conducted a survey of senior executives responsible for marketing in a sample of 500 organizations chosen randomly from a list of *The Times* Top 1000 companies, banking institutions and building societies. Thirty-eight of the 104 companies which replied said that microcomputers were used in the marketing department to provide information for decision making.

Usage was more likely in the largest companies in the sample (none of the fourteen companies with a turnover of less than £45 million used microcomputers in their marketing department).

The main applications of the microcomputer were to marketing control (annual plan and profitability).

There were fewer applications to modelling (defined as 'a representation of a real life system, using logical and mathematical relationships which can be converted into a form suitable for use on a computer').

In the three years since the Higgins and Opdebeeck study this position has changed with more widespread availability of applications programs developed for specific aspects of marketing management. Many of these applications incorporate decision models. Today there is no need for the marketing manager to develop such models. They can be bought as a standard tool for use on the microcomputer. A review of such 'tools' follows in subsequent sections.

Information management and marketing roles

Marketing is an outward looking function. One of the key roles of the marketing manager is to provide information on changes in the external environment which have implications for the company. Marketing is also future orientated.

It is concerned with decisions about the short-, medium- and long-term direction of the organization. Marketing managers must be able to manage information effectively if they are to succeed in these roles. Table 12.1 identifies some of the major tasks of the marketing manager and the information which is required to undertake these tasks. The computer is being applied in each of these areas as the following pages illustrate.

Table 12.1 *Information and marketing tasks*

Task	Information requirements
Analysing the market	Sales/profit: ● in total ● by product, area, client ● market rates of growth ● cash flows by each segment Client attitudes: ● brand awareness ● brand loyalty Number of customers: ● by product ● by area ● by purchasing patterns

Table 12.1 *contd.*

	Units sold per unit input: ● advertising to sales ratios ● personal selling effort to sales ● shelf space to sales

Defining
marketing
objectives
	Sales/profit performance
	Market share
	Cash flows
	Competitive strengths/weaknesses
	Technical, legal, political, social
	   influences on the market
	Resources and skills in the
	   organization
	Buyer loyalty
	Channel loyalty
	Customer needs and buying power
	Financial position
	Manufacturing competencies,
	   capacity and flexibility
	Research and development
	   strengths

Developing appropriate marketing strategies	Data on current strategies: ● cost ● effectiveness Identification of strategic options ● cost ● potential effectiveness Targets Budgets
Controlling performance	Units sold per unit input: ● advertising to sales ratios ● personal selling effort to sales ratios ● shelf space to sales ratios

Source: L.K. Parkinson and S.T. Parkinson, *Using the Micro-computer in Marketing*', McGraw Hill, 1987.

Managing market information

Customer contacts

Companies interact with their customers and potential customers at a variety of different levels. This interaction ranges from initial response to a direct mail shot, to meeting a company representative, placing an order, paying, and requiring aftersales support of one form or another.

Each of the elements of this interaction can be captured and monitored ('tracked'). One major computer manufacturer has established a system which records each contact with its customers from initial inquiry to installation and aftersales service. This tracking system monitors the frequency and purpose of incoming telephone calls, representative sales reports, response to direct mail and exhibition inquiries, sales invoice and delivery information, and the frequency and purpose of aftersales support. This type of information is analysed in a variety of different ways to monitor the effectiveness of different aspects of the company's marketing programme.

The development of small portable computers which can be carried by a representative has enabled many companies to introduce more effective order processing and handling systems. The representative can enter information on contacts, inquiries and orders directly into his/her own machine. This information can be transmitted to a local sales office or to headquarters for processing. Some small portable microcomputers which are currently available have a telephone link already built into them and do not require a fixed link to transmit and receive information.

One biscuit manufacturer in the UK has issued each of its 100 representatives with such machines. The advantages which it claims are faster order processing and more rapid turnround of enquiries by head office. It is also claimed that this system has lead to considerable improvements in the speed and quality of collection of market research information.

On-line data bases

An on-line data base is a data base which is available to any user with suitable communications equipment to connect to the 'host' computer. Many such data bases are made available to users through a broker service. The user pays a charge directly for the use of this service. Foster and Smith (1986) have classified the data bases which are currently available into eight different types (Table 12.2).

An explosion has taken place in recent years in the business usage of such data bases. The main influences have been greater availability of numeric and/or textual information in electronic form, powerful timesharing computers, and interactive software which allows user-friendly dialogue with the system, and terminals which can transmit and receive in-

Table 12.2 *On-line data bases*

Types of data base	Examples
Company • directory • accounts	Dun and Bradstreet, Key British Enterprises, ICC, Jordans. Datastream, Infocheck.
Business and company news	Informat Business Database, Nexis, Textline, World Reporter.
Prices • securities • foreign exchange • commodities	FT Share Information City-service. Reuter Monitor.
Products and markets	PTS Forecasts: PTS Time series.
Economics and finance	Bank of England Databank, OECD Business Survey. OECD Main Economic Indicators.
Trade	Comex–Eurostat, Tradstat, OECD statistics of Foreign Trade.
Media and consumer data	MEAL, Target Group Index, MAID, Neilsen Retail Index, National Readership Survey.
Business management	ABI/Inform, Business Periodicals Index, HBR/Online, Management and Marketing Abstracts.

Source: Allan Foster and Gerry Smith, *Online Business Source Book*, Headland Press, 1986.

formation effectively and quickly. Better indexing and abstracting systems have made such systems effective and cost economic for many applications.

Several major marketing data bases are currently available to an on-line subscriber through an information broker. These include MEAL (Media Expenditure and Analysis), Target Group Index, BARB, GB Site, and the Nielsen Retail Index. Recently several on-line data base services have been introduced to help the user manage separate files more effectively.

MAGIC offers full text information to the user from Mintel Market Intelligence Reports, MEAL and BRAD, and a variety of other trade publications. MAID is another full text service which allows the user to search for information under a variety of different key headings from several major well known sources. The advantage of using MAID is that it can search all sources simultaneously using key words rather than accessing each source separately. MAID covers the following sources: Economist Intelligence Unit; Euromonitor; Market Assessment Publications; and MEAL. It also provides a 'newsline' data base of indexed material from a variety of different trade journals. MAID was launched in November 1985. Its early users include

several large UK advertising agencies, and multiple retailers.

On-line data bases have several advantages which make them attractive to prospective users. Any organization with a terminal and the necessary communications link can make use of the service. The advantages to the user include faster and more flexible interactive patterns of search, the ability to manipulate data statistically using files drawn from the host and up-to-date information. The cost disadvantages which once characterized such systems appear to be diminishing rapidly as technologies improve.

Managing sales data

The sales data base is one of the most useful sources of information for marketing planning. If the input of information into such a data base is designed effectively, then a wide range of different analyses can be produced. Figure 12.1 illustrates a typical sales entry screen from a package designed by Plusmark of Maidenhead.

Details of each order are entered into the data base. The package can be used to control order scheduling and delivery, inventory management

```
-------------------------------------------------------------------
Plusmark Building Supplies   Order Processing    Sales Order Entry
                             ----------------
Order No.           [000001]
Customer Account    [ABC    ]
Customer Reference  [ABC0001          ]   Available Credit    50000.00
Order Date          [24/12/86]             Account Balance     18500.00
Oue Date            [15/01/87]             Account Currency    Sterling
                                           Currency Rate   [   1.0000]
Deliver to:         [ABC1]                 Invoice to:      [ABC2]
Company Name                               Company Name
Address                                    Address
Post Code                                  Post Code




Additional Disc. % [   5.00]
Payment Terms        [1]         30 Days    30/01/87
Sett.Disc. %       [   2.50]
Sett.Terms           [1]
Delivery Method      [V]         Van
Van Route          [  A1]
Carriage Terms     [  C]         Chargeable
Sales Area:Man     [WEST:JN   ]
-------------------------------------------------------------------



-------------------------------------------------------------------
Plusmark Building Supplies   Order Processing    Sales Order Entry
                             ----------------
Order No.     000001      Customer A/C ABC    Associated British Co.
Order Date    24/12/86    Currency     STER   Available Credit 50000.00

 :Stock Code     :Unit :W/H:Quantity:  Price  : Discount :VAT:   Net
-------------------------------------------------------------------
1:WIDGET         :Gross: 1:      20:    1.20:     25.00: 1 :  18.00
 :               :     :  :       :        :         :   :
 :               :     :  :       :        :         :   :
 :               :     :  :       :        :         :   :
 :               :     :  :       :        :         :   :
 :               :     :  :       :        :         :   :
-------------------------------------------------------------------
 Screw-threaded copper widget            :Total Gross     24.00
                                         :Discount         6.00
                                         :Add. Discount    0.90
                                         :Total Net       17.10
     Due date    :15/01/87:              :VAT              2.56
     Sales Area  :WEST:                  :To Pay          19.66
     Sales Man   :JN  :                  :Margin %        26.00
-------------------------------------------------------------------
```

Figure 12.1 *Sales entry screen*
Source: Plusmark, Maidenhead. Reproduced with permission.

and financial control. It can also be used to provide a wide range of different types of analysis for marketing decision making including:

1 Sales over time of specific products/product groups for control purposes – analysed by type of customer, area, postcode (for Acorn classification).
2 Forecasts of sales – based on previous sales histories.

3 Profitability of specific products/product groups – analysed by type of customers, area, salesperson.

This data base system is typical of many which are now available for micro-, mini- or mainframe applications.

There has also been a rapid growth in the number of external agencies which provide information which can be related to the company's own customer

```
                   CUSTOMER PROFILE REPORT
                   ------------------------
           GROUP                                    CUSTOMERS   $    BASES   INDEX

           A MODERN FAMILY HOUSING FOR MANUAL WORKERS   606   13.8   10.8   127.6
           B MODERN FAMILY HOUSING, HIGHER INCOMES      580   13.2    7.8   167.0
           C OLDER HOUSING OF INTERMEDIATE STATUS       425    9.7    9.6   101.3
ACORN      D VERY POOR QUALITY OLDER TERRACED HOUSING   444   10.1    9.4   120.2
group      E RURAL AREAS                                135    3.1    5.8    52.9
           F URBAN LOCAL AUTHORITY HOUSING              739   16.5   20.9    50.9
           G HOUSING WITH MOST OVERCROWDING             106    2.4    3.2    75.3
           H LOW INCOME WITH IMMIGRANTS                 244    5.5    4.0   138.7
           I STUDENT AND HIGH STATUS NON-FAMILY AREA    120    2.7    3.5    77.9
           J TRADITIONAL HIGH STATUS SUBURBIA           736   16.7   19.0    88.1
           K AREAS OF ELDERLY PEOPLE (OFTEN RESORTS)    191    4.3    5.3    81.9
           U UNCLASSIFIED                                70    1.6    1.8    88.4

           AREA TOTAL                                  4399  100.0  100.0


              NEIGHBOURHOOD TYPES
ACORN
group      GROUP
           A  1 LA & NEW TOWN HOUSING, HIGH WAGE AREAS   94    1.9    1.7   112.3
           A  2 MIXED HOUSING, YOUNG FAMILIES            92    1.9    1.6   116.5
           A  3 RECENT COUNCIL HOUSING                  341    7.8    5.3   146.3
ACORN      A  4 MODERN LOW COST PRIVATE HOUSING          99    2.3    2.2   102.3
type       B  5 MODERN PRIVATE HOUSING, MEDIUM STATUS   335    7.6    6.3   120.9
           B  6 MODERN PRIVATE HOUSING, YOUNG FAMILIES  120    2.9    1.0   293.2
           B  7 MILITARY BASES                          116    2.6    0.5   527.4
           C  8 MIXED HOUSING, OLDER AREAS               59    1.5    1.9    95.9
           C  9 OLDER TERRACES WITH LOW UNEMPLOYMENT    195    1.5    1.3   104.7
No. of     C 10 MIXED DEVEL. MT, OFTEN IN COUNTRY TOWNS 162    3.7    3.5   105.2
customers  D 11 INNER AREAS, LOW QUAL TERRACED HOUSING  155    3.6    3.2   112.2
in ACORN   D 12 LOW QUALITY HOUSING, DECLINING AREAS    280    6.0    5.2   125.0
type       E 13 VILLAGES WITH SOME NON-FARM EMPLOYMENT   61    1.4    2.4    57.9
           E 14 RURAL AREAS WITH LARGE FARMS             41    0.9    1.9    51.9
           E 15 RURAL AREAS WITH OWN-ACCOUNT FARMERS     33    0.3    1.6    46.9
           F 16 PERIPHERAL LOW INCOME LA ESTATES        177    4.0    6.7    60.1
           F 17 SMALL LA FAMILY HOUSES (SCOTLAND + NE)   17    1.9    1.5   116.7
           F 18 URBAN LA ESTATES, LOW UNEMPLOYMENT      115    1.7    3.3    91.3
% in       F 19 TERRACED/LA HOUSES (OFTEN MINING AREAS)  96    2.0    2.1    93.1
ACORN      F 20 LA ESTATES WITH OLDER COUPLES           147    3.3    4.0    93.5
type (A)   F 21 LOW INCOME LA ESTATES (OFTEN HIGH RISE)  72    1.6    1.9    96.1
           F 22 LA ESTATES WITH AGED (OFTEN HIGH RISE)   62    1.4    1.3   109.4
           G 23 LA ESTATES WITH MOST STRESS (GLASGOW)    69    1.6    2.3    69.2
           G 24 TENEMENTS AND NON-PERMANENT DWELLINGS    37    0.9    0.9    93.5
           H 25 VICTORIAN LOW STATUS (INNER LONDON)      77    1.9    1.2   145.9
           H 26 MULTI-LET HOUSING WITH IMMIGRANTS        64    1.5    1.3   111.9
           H 27 TERRACED HOUSING WITH IMMIGRANTS        103    2.3    1.5   156.1
           I 28 STUDENT AREAS/AFFLUENT INNER LONDON      44    1.0    1.5    66.7
% in       I 29 HIGH INCOME AREAS WITH FEW CHILDREN      76    1.7    2.0    86.4
ACORN      J 30 MODERN PRIVATE HOUSING, HIGH INCOME     226    5.1    5.0   102.8
type in    J 31 MEDIUM STATUS INTER WAR PRIV. HOUSING   218    5.0    4.8   103.2
GB(B)      J 32 ESTABLISHED SUBURBS OF HIGH STATUS      138    3.1    3.5    89.6
           J 33 ESTABLISHED RURAL COMMUTER VILLAGES      44    1.0    1.5    66.7
           J 34 VERY HIGH STATUS AREAS                  110    2.5    4.1    61.0
           K 35 AREAS OF ELDERLY PEOPLE, PRIV. HOUSING  149    3.4    3.9    86.8
           K 36 AREAS OF ELDERLY PEOPLE, FLATS & HOMES   42    1.0    1.4    68.2
           U 37 UNCLASSIFIED                             70    1.6    1.8    55.4
Ratio of
A to B     AREA TOTAL                                  4399  100.0  100.0
(Base 100)
                                       BASE    GREAT BRITAIN
```

Figure 12.2 *Acorn analysis of customer data base*
Source: CACI. Reproduced with permission.

data base. For example, the British Market Research Bureau conduct a regular survey of a large sample of consumers to determine what people buy (the Target Group Index). This survey covers a wide range of different consumer products and services. It measures patterns of media exposure of the sample and collects information on attitudes and life style. This information can be matched by computer to the company's own customer data base, to determine what products and services to offer existing customers and how best to reach them.

In consumer markets a company's existing customers can be analysed by Acorn classification. The Acorn classification scheme from CACI is based on an analysis of the population by residential qualification. Each customer can be classified into a specific residential category depending on his/her postcode. The profile of the existing customer base can be matched to the profile of the population as a whole, to measure levels of market penetration and performance. This data can be monitored continuously over time to determine the effectiveness of its marketing activities in each segment.

Figure 12.2 is an analysis which was produced for a company selling off the page and through direct mail. The high indices in group B (modern family housing, high incomes) and group H (low income areas with immigrants) let the advertising department weight their media expenditure in favour of magazines and journals with good penetration in these areas. The company also did an Acorn selected mailing from the voters roll to neighbourhood types B6 and B7.

Using customer data in this way is an effective approach to segmenting the market according to existing patterns of purchase and targeting specific marketing programmes at individual groups with consistent or common sets of characteristics. It is especially useful in helping to 'cross sell' related products into market segments with similar needs. Computer-based approaches are being used increasingly widely by banks and insurance companies to sell a wide range of related services to clearly identified market segments with known purchase histories of similar services.

EPOS systems

In the retail market the development of electronic point of sale (EPOS) systems will have a major impact on the availability and quality of information on the markets for many consumer products in the next few years. EPOS systems installed at individual check-outs read the bar code information on the product and produce a record of all purchases made by the customer. The advantages to the customer include faster checkout operation and less chance of errors being made. An itemized bill with full details of all purchases helps customers to monitor what they have bought.

EPOS systems can provide significant improvements in stock management and control. Items no longer need to be priced individually – a central computer can be updated as price changes are made. Inventory control is improved with up-to-date information on the quantities and sizes of each item sold each day. As information on inventory levels has improved so retailers have been able to move nearer to 'just-in-time' purchasing systems, requiring their own suppliers to become increasingly flexible in the timing and quantity of deliveries, as well as the variety of products.

In addition to enhancing the management of inventory, such systems also have considerable potential as a source of marketing information. Using an EPOS system the retailer can monitor for each customer, date and time of purchase, items bought, prices paid, promotional deals and means of purchase. As a result the retailer is in a better position to monitor the effectiveness of specific promotions, or new product introductions, and can take more informed decisions about the allocation of shelf space to specific brands.

When the information collected by the EPOS system is combined with information on margins from different products then decisions can be made about the relative attractiveness of different items and the amount of shelf space to allocate to each item. Adjustments can be made on a store by store basis where necessary.

Retailers using an EPOS system have access to a great deal of information on trends in the sales of specific products in different locations at different times of the year. External research agencies which have traditionally supplied this type of data by surveying samples of outlets on a regular basis, will find that their data is less up-to-date than that supplied by an EPOS system. One agency has recognized the challenge and has developed its own system, Nielsen ScanTrak, to provide such data.

A report by Ogilvy and Mather (1986, p. 55) describes the advantages of an EPOS system as follows.

> When compared with traditional retail audit data, the most useful and innovative factor about scanning data is not its greater accuracy but that it is collected in real time. The exact date and time of purchase can be identified, in addition to the type of store in which the purchase was made and the geographical location of that store . . . Using scanners retail audits will for the first time actually be auditing sales and not estimating them from recent stock and delivery positions . . . Analysis could distinguish variations in sales levels between competing brands, or in a particular brands' sales from one store type to another, or from one geographical area to another.

As such systems become more widely available the nature of marketing planning will change, for retailers and their suppliers. The data collected by an EPOS system can be stored and analysed by an instore computer, providing the local store manager with a considerable amount of information which can be used in decisions about store lay-out or the evaluation of the effectiveness of local promotions.

It can also be analysed at regional or national level, and used by manufacturers to plan sales promotions and monitor their effectiveness. Ogilvy and Mather (1986, p. 68) believe that this will lead to more precise measures of advertising effectiveness. They comment:

> A by-product of using scanner data as a research tool will be the eventual possibility of live, real time test markets (Adlabs). These can be used for evaluating the sales effectiveness of alternative advertising weights, media strategies or creative approaches. Such data will enable advertising (and indeed all marketing activity) to be made more accountable. In turn this will encourage the more efficient use of marketing budgets by allocating higher proportions to the most cost effective techniques.

Market research applications

Computer applications are developing rapidly in market research throughout the research process from sample design and questionnaire development through to survey analysis and presentation.

At the questionnaire design stage some survey analysis programs now combine word processing capabilities with questionnaire coding facilities. It is possible to design and pilot a questionnaire quickly and effectively using the computer directly. At the same time the data entry structure is defined. The resultant questionnaire can be displayed on a terminal attached to a mini- or mainframe computer, or an independent microcomputer. It can also be displayed on an independent hand-held terminal, which can be used to capture data in a face to face interview. Data from such hand-held terminals can be downloaded into the computer for analysis, or transmitted by telecommunications link to a central computer.

Filters can be automatically programmed, taking the interviewer logically through the appropriate sequence for each respondent. Where randomized presentation of questionnaire items is required (for example in ranking questions), the program can be written in a way that this occurs automatically for each respondent.

Where the company has a computerized data base of potential respondents to work from (customer records or commercially purchased listing), the computer can be programmed to generate a sample to the researcher's specifications. In some telephone interviewing situations each member of the sample is drawn from a computerized data base and dialled automatically. The interviewer then completes the survey. When the original member of the sample refuses to cooperate or cannot be contacted, the computer selects another respondent from the data base to meet the sample specification.

The development of computerized survey analysis has led to considerable improvements in the quality of market research analysis and the speed with which reports can be produced. Early applications were restricted to mainframe computers owned in the main by the larger commercial market research bureaux. Today there are several survey analysis packages which can be used on a microcomputer (for example SNAP). The development of microcomputer-based survey analysis packages enables many small users to analyse market research data quickly and professionally. Some (such as SNAP) allow the user to transfer the data to more sophisticated packages for further analysis. The presentation of the results of the survey can also be improved by transferring data to graphics display packages such as Freelance, which give the user considerable discretion in the way data is presented.

Developing competitive data bases

Competitive information comes in many different forms, including press reports, financial accounts, sales representative reports, details of patents lodged, etc. The amount of information which is available about the competition is often considerable, yet many companies fail to gather such information effectively or use it in marketing planning. It is often the weakest section of many marketing plans.

One of the main problems of developing and maintaining a competitive data base is to relate information from a wide variety of different sources. For example financial reports may be obtained using an on-line service such as Infocheck, sales representatives may file reports as a result of visits to specific customers, press reports may be collected by a clipping service. Each of these elements is likely to be stored in separate files. A relational data base, which brings information together from different sources, allows the user to search for data on specific topics. This can provide a useful way of combining the information from different sources to develop competitive profiles.

Defining marketing objectives and developing the marketing plan

The process of marketing planning can be complex, particularly since a wide range of different inputs is usually required from different sources. Most companies plan across a range of different products and markets which are frequently characterized by high rates of change. An increasing amount of attention has been given to the development of computer-based models which can help this process.

The ideal system would assist the marketing manager in bringing the appropriate information together and organizing it effectively. It would provide guidance on the alternative strategies which are available in specific situations, and would forecast results in terms of sales and profitability. Such a system should also be able to explain its logic and allow 'how' and 'why' questions.

In a survey of marketing practice in the UK, Hooley et al. (1983) found low usage of modelling techniques in a sample of 1800 marketing executives. Only 40 per cent of respondents had tried or were using market modelling techniques on a regular basis; Higgins and Opdebeeck (1984) found only limited use of models implemented on a microcomputer for market simulation, discounted cash flow, sensitivity analysis and econometric modelling.

Since these surveys the picture appears to be changing. An increasing number of microcomputer-based packages are becoming available to assist in marketing planning decisions. Such packages incorporate many of the models referred to by Higgins and Opdebeeck and Hooley et al., but they do not require that the marketing manager actually develops the model. A knowledge of operations research techniques is less important than an appreciation of the package's relevance and limitations in a particular business situation. This represents a major step forward in the potential for applications of modelling to marketing decision taking.

Several microcomputer packages now exist which can be used to help in collating the information. The software can then be used to assist in developing the marketing plan. One of the main advantages of using the microcomputer in this way is that it can assemble a picture of the company's position quickly and consistently.

Standard menus prompt the user to enter the data in a uniform manner, and analytical tools built into the software allow the user to process the data in a variety of different ways. STRATPAC is one package which can be used in this way. The user inputs data on the financial performance of the company as a whole, and for each strategic business unit. A strategic appraisal form must be completed which requires information on cash flow as a percentage of sales, market dominance, projected real industry growth and an index of product quality.

Once this data has been input STRATPAC provides a variety of different options. Where appropriate the program allows the user to develop forecasts of future sales revenue by applying alternative curves to historical data and finding the best 'fit'. STRATPAC also produces a summary financial statement which can be used to develop a wide range of different ratios to analyse the company's financial position.

There is also a facility for conducting sensitivity analyses of the financial models which STRATPAC creates. Using the sensitivity analysis function the marketing manager can explore the impact of change in key variables (such as forecast levels of sales) on the company's position, and identify the key factors upon which performance may depend.

A further set of options in the package allows the user to apply several strategic planning models to the data, for example the Boston Box Model, Shell's Directional Policy Matrix, and Investment Strategy Portfolios.

These analyses require a great deal of data, and are time consuming to complete. If a package such as STRATPAC is used, a great deal of the actual data assembly is done for the user, leaving more time free for analysis. Moreover it is relatively easy to change one or more key variables and see the effect of such changes, without extensive manual recalculations. This facility encourages the user to try out a wide range of different assumptions about market conditions and competitive strengths and weaknesses.

Campaign is another package which provides similar support. This package was developed by PE Consultants as a tool to assist in analysing the client company's business and developing its marketing plan. A series of questions are posed about the company's customers, competitors and organization. At various points in the analysis the package questions the assumptions which have been made about the company's position. Using Campaign, the consultant is able to identify specific options and rate each option according to its attractiveness. The package can also be used in selecting the most attractive marketing plan according to a set of predetermined criteria, and budget that plan.

There are currently few such 'expert' systems to assist in the marketing planning process. It seems likely that such systems will be developed to assist marketing managers, although it is difficult to predict how quickly such development will take place. Davis (1986) has reviewed the current state of the art of such systems. His paper gives a good introduction to their potential in marketing.

Implementation and control

There are a considerable number of reported computer applications in specific areas such as sales management, direct mail, product development, and distribution. It is beyond the scope of this chapter to provide a comprehensive review of these applications. Comment will be limited to some of the most recent developments.

Several software packages have been developed to assist in the management and control of the field sales force. Applications of the personal computer have already been developed to assist in creating and maintaining a customer data base, diary organization, word processing and communication with head office.

Further applications include determining the size of the sales force, territory allocation and journey planning, assessing the efficiency of sales calls and profiling different accounts. The microcomputer can also be used to monitor sales performance against objectives. An example of this type of application is given below.

Many advertising agencies use the computer for media selection and budgeting. The complexities of these decisions and the large amounts of data required (rates for all media, at different space sizes and positions etc.) make the application of computers particularly suitable. One application (MEDIAC) is described by Lilien and Kotler (1983). Applications have also been developed for modelling response to different patterns of advertising exposure. The development of EPOS systems has provided a major new source of data for developing and testing such models (see Ogilvy and Mather, 1986).

The quality of direct response advertising has also improved considerably as a result of the introduction of the computer. A company's existing data base can be extended by buying other related data bases from commercial brokers. The quality of the mail-out can be dramatically improved by personalizing the letter to the individual, using a mail-merge facility. Moreover, information about the customer can be used to identify which customers to send specific offers.

The reply coupon in the mail-out can also be bar coded with information about the characteristics of each recipient from the company's own customer data base. This bar code can be read by a scanning device to determine the characteristics of respondents to specific offers. Analysis of the patterns of response can then be used to monitor the attractiveness of different offers to specific market segments.

There is also a considerable number of reported applications of the computer in the area of physical distribution management. Computers have traditionally been used to process large quantities of orders, invoices and delivery information. They have also been used to maintain information on levels of inventory. Increasingly data from these sources is being used in planning optimum inventory levels and order handling policies. These decisions require information on changes in customer requirements and competitive activity. Such information can often be collected from other data bases (such as the customer data base maintained by sales or marketing).

In some situations companies have developed direct computer links with their suppliers. When stock reaches a specific minimum level, an order is generated automatically for the item. This type of system places considerable pressure on the supplier to provide a flexible response to customer requirements. The diffusion of EPOS systems among major retailers will create further pressure on suppliers to establish such linkages, and to develop the capability of responding quickly and flexibly to changing user requirements.

Ogilvy and Mather (1986, p. 45) present the following scenario for the 1990s:

- More than half of the largest retail branches will be scanning, with the multiples converting their other stores as fast as they can go (as cost creating nuisances).
- Already the 'big six' will have studied in depth their turnover and profit patterns line-by-line, and totally re-appraised their stocking policies.
- All except very large or fast growing sectors will be cut back to 2–3 leading brands, a high quality own-label plus a cheap generic. All low share 'me too's' to be delisted unless they have demonstrably high brand loyalty, or very much larger margins than other brands.
- Shelf allocations and shelf filling totally systematized – no manufacturers' staff allowed in the stockroom or to touch the shelves.
- No sales promotions allowed which require changing the shelf layout or special display material or which cannot be operated by scanner. Other promotions to be negotiated at head office and at long notice.
- All outers and traded units have to be bar coded.

- All regular branch deliveries have to be ordered by computer through head office in line with sales off-the-shelf, and routine plus occasional topping-up orders to manufacturers made electronically through Tradanet.
- Key account negotiations based on the retailer's precise information on trends in store turnover and profitability.

Applications of the computer have been developed for a wide range of other areas such as forecasting, pricing and product development. For a detailed review of such applications and practical examples developed for use on a microcomputer see Parkinson and Parkinson (1987).

Control

The potential for controlling the quality of the marketing operation has been considerably enhanced by the development of the computer. Sales analysis (measuring the variation between budgeted and actual performance) is a common control measure which can be produced easily from a computerized sales data base.

Figure 12.3 illustrates a typical control system. In this example the performance of individual salespeople can be monitored against budget for the current period and the year to date. Such data bases can also be used to analyse the causes of variations between target sales and actual sales. For a description of this process see Hughes and Singler (1984). A decline in sales may not always be the fault of the salespeople. The loss of one important customer, or the decline of one market in a particular territory may be the underlying reason for the decline in sales. Systematic analysis of the sales data base on several dimensions can often indicate where the problems lie.

A computerized marketing control system can also be set up to monitor the costs of specific marketing activities. These costs would normally be established in the marketing plan and form the basis of the marketing budget. Two dimensions of these costs are important – the relationship between budgeted expenses and actual expenses (control factors), and the relationship between marketing expenses and sales achieved (productivity factors).

Each of the control factors can be analysed in terms of specific elements of the budget in the

PLUSMARK BUILDING SUPPLIES	SALES LEDGER	SALES ANALYSIS				DATE 01/02/85			PAGE NO
COMPANY NO 0 PERIOD NO 02 RUN NO 000036									
SALESMAN COMPARISON TO TARGET WITHIN AREA									
SALESMAN CODE NAME	----THIS PERIOD----				----YEAR TO DATE----				
	SALES	TARGET	VARIANCE	%	SALES	TARGET	VARIANCE	%	
AREA - RSOU READING (South)									
GREE NOT TARGETED IN AREA	9.36				9.36				
HERT TED HERTLER-SMITH	2995.12	2500.00	495.12	119.80	2995.12	5000.00	2004.88-	59.90	
HYDE PHILIP HYDE	2326.43	3000.00	673.57-	77.55	2326.43	6000.00	3673.57-	38.77	
AREA TOTAL	5330.91	5500.00	169.09-	96.93	5330.91	11000.00	5669.09-	48.46	
RUN TOTAL	6736.07	11500.00	4763.93-	58.57	6736.07	23000.00	16263.93-	29.29	

*** PRINTING COMPLETE ***

Figure 12.3 *Sales ledger analysis*
Source: Plusmark, Maidenhead. Reproduced with permission.

operating plan (i.e. for individual product/market areas). The computer can be programmed to produce this data automatically, generating management reports as and when required. Trends in specific costs can be monitored and where there are significant deviations from the budget, attention can be given to causes of such deviations.

Productivity ratios can be analysed in a similar way to monitor relative changes in different types of marketing expenditure against changes in sales performance. Comparative data from studies of competitive behaviour can be used to make judgements on appropriate levels of expenditure.

A policy for information management

One of the most striking features of the adoption of any new technology into an organization is the relatively slow rate of acceptance which is often present even for an innovation which offers significant advantages to that organization. Management opinions and attitudes can often play a major role in retarding or accelerating the diffusion of such an innovation into the organization. The development of computer applications in marketing is a situation where this problem has arisen. On the one hand, the majority of today's marketing managers are probably aware that the computer could be applied in marketing but they are not necessarily aware of what its technical capabilities are or, indeed, what it would cost to install and operate such a system. On the other hand, suppliers of equipment are often unaware of the marketing tasks which have to be accomplished.

There still appears to be widespread ignorance among managers of data processing systems of the types of marketing information which are required, and how marketing operates as a substantial business function. In the absence of clear information about what the user actually requires, it is difficult for companies which develop and supply software to specify systems which are attractive to marketing managers.

If the diffusion of the use of computers within marketing in an organization is to be rapid and effective then a policy for information management is required. Organizations which develop information systems in an ad hoc manner often find that they are restricted by decisions which have been taken in another part of the organization. The decision to standardize on one technology can impose severe restraints on the use of other technologies (for example if we have got IBM we stick with IBM).

The organization must decide on how information is to be collected and managed. An important issue is who has the responsibility for updating the information contained in different data bases. The input of information and the subsequent management of that information must be done in such a way that users are convinced that no opportunity has arisen for the quality of the data to become damaged by unauthorized or inept input. Users need to be consulted at the design stage for their perceived requirements. Ginzberg (1981) identifies the failure to consult system users at the design stage as the major reason for the lack of success in developing and implementing an effective computer-based information system.

Collins (1983) also stresses the importance of relating the design of any information system to the business needs of the organization. He discusses how IBM applied a business systems planning approach to define the information system which was needed by his organization (South Eastern Gas). His article contains a useful checklist of questions to be used in auditing the information management requirements of an organization (see Table 12.3).

As organizations begin to look carefully at the data which they have available for marketing decisions and to evaluate the types of decisions which they take, the professionalism of marketing itself will change. In that sense adoption of the computer may lead companies to approach the marketing process in a systematic and planned way. However it is also important to recognize that the analysis of data using the micro- or mainframe computer is only one part of the marketing process. It can help to create a broader set of commonly applied techniques in analysis and planning. Decisions on which markets to attack, how to respond to competition or what types of new product to develop must also be related to the individuals' own knowledge or feeling for the market in which they are operating. In short, the computer is a planning tool not a substitute for planning.

Conclusion

Information is a strategic resource. Organizations

Table 12.3 *Computerized information system: audit checklist*

1. What are your specific responsibilities? Are they different from those indicated on the organization chart?
2. What are the basic objectives of your function?
3. What are the three greatest problems you have had in meeting these objectives? (Not only current problems but problems of the recent past also.)
4. What has prevented you solving them?
5. What is needed to solve them?
6. What value would better information have in these areas (in person hours saved, pounds saved, better opportunities etc.?)
7. In what other areas could the greatest improvements be realized, given better information support?
8. What would be the value of these improvements?
9. What costs may be incurred by inaccurate or untimely information?
10. What is the most useful information you receive? (The best aspects of current systems must be retained.)
11. What would you most like to receive?
12. How would you rate your current information support with respect to:
    (a) Types of information?
    (b) Timeliness?
    (c) Accuracy?
    (d) Cost?
    (e) Consistency?
    (f) Ease of use or clarity of presentation?
13. How are you measured by your superior?
14. How do you measure your subordinates?
15. What other kinds of measurement are you expected to make?
16. What kinds of decisions are you expected to make? What computer aids might help you in your decision making?
17. What major changes are expected in your area in the next year? Over the next two, four or six years?
18. What do you expect and what would you like the results from this study to be?
19. Any additional views or comments?

which manage information effectively have a major competitive advantage. The development of relatively cheap, powerful computers with a wide range of applications software will radically change the way in which companies manage information in the future. Marketing has lagged behind other business functions in the use of the computer. This position is changing rapidly as managers become more familiar with the potential of the new technology, and specific applications are developed.

This chapter reviews some of the main developments in the use of the computer in marketing and draws out the implications of these developments for the marketing manager. It also discusses the main stages in auditing the requirement for computer applications and developing a strategy to introduce the computer effectively.

References

Collins, A. C., 'A Management Strategy for Information Processing', *Long Range Planning*, vol. 16, no. 6, December 1983, pp. 21–8.

Davis, E. J., 'The Use of Expert Systems in Marketing' in *Technology Developments for Problem Solving* ESOMAR, September, 1986.

Foster, A. and Smith, G., *On line Business Source Book*, Headland Press, 1986.

Ginzberg, M.J., 'Early Diagnosis of MIS Implementation Failure', *Management Science*, vol. 27, no. 4, April 1981.

Higgins, J. C. and Opdebeeck, E. J., 'The Microcomputer as a Tool in Marketing Decision Aids', *Journal of the Market Research Society*, vol. 26, no. 3, July, 1984.

Hooley, G., West C. J.and Lynch, J. E., *Marketing in the U.K: A Survey of Current Practice and Performance*, Institute of Marketing, 1983.

Hughes, G.D., 'Computerized Sales Management', *Harvard Business Review*, vol. 61, no. 2, March–April, 1983.

Hughes, G. D. and Singler, C., *Strategic Sales Management*, Addison Wesley, 1984.

Lilien, G. L., and Kotler, P., *Marketing Decision Making*, Harper and Row, 1983.

Ogilvy and Mather Advertising, *The Effects of New Information Technology on the Retailing of Packaged Goods*, Ogilvy and Mather, 1986.

Parkinson, L. K. and Parkinson, S. T., *Using the Microcomputer in Marketing*, McGraw Hill, 1987.

13
Developing marketing information systems

NIGEL PIERCY

Introduction

To the reader progressing through the book it will have become apparent that the process of developing marketing plans and strategies (considered in Part One) is largely built upon the foundation provided by various forms of marketing information and intelligence. Similarly, Part Two has already illustrated the diversity of sources of marketing information which confronts the marketing manager and planner. For example, scenarios from environmental analysis and predictions from models or buyer behaviour, and information from models based on management science and computer modelling techniques abound in a modern marketing analysis.

The critical issue addressed in this chapter is how to build a framework which provides marketing managers with a vehicle for coping with the deluge of marketing information they are likely to face, i.e. a framework for *managing* the marketing information function. In fact, experience suggests the practical problem is not simply restricted to coping with a flood of information. There can be a problem of managerial response to the information problem which can be simply to ignore the potential chaos created by excessive disorganized information and to approach the management of marketing with little or no solid information.

Whether the problem faced is one of information saturation or information *starvation*, the common factor is the basic need to manage marketing information more effectively.

The structure of this chapter involves expanding on this last point regarding information management in marketing – to identify this as an issue of some complexity, which is concerned with the development of information as a 'marketing asset' or resource, but one which may provide a key source of competitive and strategic advantage.

With the strategic nature of the marketing information function established as our point of departure, we examine a process of information systems design for marketing, together with the problems inherent in successfully applying this process. Further insights are obtainable by briefly examining the impact of new information technology on the marketing information function, and the organizational dimensions of information processing in marketing. The chapter then concludes with an agenda for marketing management to use in formulating a marketing information strategy.

This structure is intended to provide answers to what have been found by this author to be the commonest questions raised by managers in this area:

- Why should I manage information?
- So, is the 'marketing information system' the answer to all my problems?

- What is a 'marketing information system' anyway?
- If we want one, how do we go about getting one?
- Has the marketing information system got something to do with new technology?
- Has the marketing information system got something to do with organization?
- What is an information strategy, and why do we need one?

Why manage information?

Perhaps the first response of marketing managers to the proposal that they should devote effort and resources to the development of a marketing information system (MIS), is to question whether this is truly their role in the business, as opposed to that of computer or data processing managers. Indeed, they may be tempted to observe that their function is complex enough with the responsibility for managing staff, distributors and customers, and the marketing mix, without the additional burden of some kind of esoteric information management role.

These questions are quite reasonable and deserve to be confronted at this early stage in the chapter.

The *first* of these issues is whether marketing information management should be a marketing or computer/data processing responsibility. While it may be desirable to call on technical expertise from many sources in developing a MIS (e.g. in the purchase of equipment, or the writing of specialized software) there is growing evidence that there is advantage in having the 'ownership' of the information system located as close to users (i.e. marketing decision makers) as possible.

Indeed, one recent article has entered the plea to managers to 'save your information system from the experts' (Rubin, 1986), and this present author has detailed earlier the case for a 'marketing information analyst' (Piercy, 1981), to be a focus for coordinating management information needs in marketing with the technology of information systems. We return in the penultimate section of this chapter to the organizational issue, but for the moment suggest that for the marketing manager to abrogate responsibility for the information system is highly undesirable.

The *second* question of why information management is as central to marketing as the marketing mix involves a number of key issues: the processing of information may be seen as essential to the marketing department's present-day role; the speed of environmental and technological change is accelerating the urgency of the information problem; information may be seen as a 'marketing asset' involving investment for a long-term return on that investment; and information provides a key source of competitive advantage in developing strategies. These key issues are expanded briefly below.

Marketing as an information function

One recent textbook (Christopher *et al.*, 1980) has proposed that:

> Good information is a facilitator of successful marketing and indeed, seen in this light marketing management becomes first and foremost an information processing activity.

The reasoning underpinning the argument that processing information should be seen as the fifth P in the marketing mix (Piercy, 1983a), is based on a view of marketing as a 'boundary-spanning' activity, i.e. acting as the interface between the core of the organization and the marketing environment (Jemison, 1984). Indeed, it has been argued that it is largely through carrying out this boundary-spanning role, i.e. absorbing environmental uncertainty and interpreting the environment for the rest of the organization, that marketing gains influence in strategic decision making (Piercy, 1986; Lysonski, 1985). This involves, in essence, creating from the pool of information, that the environment represents, a picture of the world which enables others in the organization to forecast and plan. At its simplest, if the marketing department (or, it should be noted, some other subunit) does not convert the uncertainty of the marketing environment into a sales forecast, there is no basis for planning production, manpower or the financing of operations.

In this sense, the management of information is at the very centre of the status of marketing management and the implementation of the marketing concept in a company.

A marketing management problem

However, if we accept that information management is a core responsibility of marketing management, then it is necessary also to agree that it is a responsibility which is difficult to fulfil.

It has already been noted above that the sources of marketing information are diverse, ranging from environmental intelligence to computer models. It must also be said that these sources of information are highly variable in the quality and quantity of what they produce. There is also some suspicion that the impact of computerization, and the more recent new information technology revolution, has been to increase the volume of information which confronts the manager, rather than to control or filter that flow.

The scenario which emerges is often one of considerable complexity and one where handling marketing information is a substantial burden on management. While it is far from providing a universal panacea, the concept of a marketing information system provides a framework which attempts: to identify the different types of marketing information which may be useful in a particular situation; to provide a vehicle for integrating the different sources of information pertaining to a given marketing problem; to coordinate the collection, storage and dissemination of marketing information; and above all else, to match the information sources to management information needs.

Information as a marketing asset

It follows from the points above that information should be regarded as a 'marketing asset', i.e. an intangible, but value-producing resource (Piercy, 1986b). The issue of how to place values on marketing assets and how their value might be shown on a balance sheet or other financial statement remains controversial, but there are a number of implications in viewing information as a marketing asset: it involves investment to create and maintain its value; it should be maintained and protected like any other asset of the business, even though it is intangible; and its value should enter any cost/benefit analysis of information. Indeed, these attributes of the marketing information resource may be linked not merely to supporting management decision making in a positive way, but to the creation of competitive strength.

Information for marketplace advantage

Although there are dangers inherent in over-simplifying the way in which managers use information, which will be commented upon shortly, even the most sophisticated view of the MIS as a decision-support system ignores many of the strategic and competitive implications of developing information systems. The following examples illustrate this point.

First, it is apparent that the information system may provide an aspect of *customer service* and consequent advantage over competitors. Examples of this are well-known. American Airlines and Commercial Union have both opened up their respective markets by placing computer terminals linked to their company information systems at the customer level for on-line inquiries.

Second, the development of an information system has provided various companies with the opportunity to *differentiate* on the basis of how they do business. For example, Metpath, a clinical testing laboratory gives physicians on-line access to medical test results through remote terminals, and achieves competitive differentiation in what had become a commodity market, high brand loyalty; and it erects a technological and investment barrier for new competitors (Wiseman and Macmillan, 1984). One view is that companies should systematically investigate the strategic competitive advantages that they may be able to achieve through the information systems (Ackoff et al., 1985).

Third, developing information systems may create the possibility of *new information-based products*, to be added to the product-line. For example, it has been noted that the marketing information collected by major retailers through laser scanning at the checkout creates a data base, which provides both competitive advantage in negotiating with suppliers and a saleable commodity (Piercy, 1983b). Similarly, Reuters, the news agency, has used its general information system to develop a specialized financial information product for the financial sector (Earl, 1983).

Fourth, information systems development can alter *market structure and competitor relationships*. For instance, Figure 13.1 shows what has been called the 'macromarketing' information system, where consumers, retailers and manufacturers are all potential participants in a distributed information system linked electronically (Piercy and Evans, 1983). This is comparable with the 'manufacturer-distributor

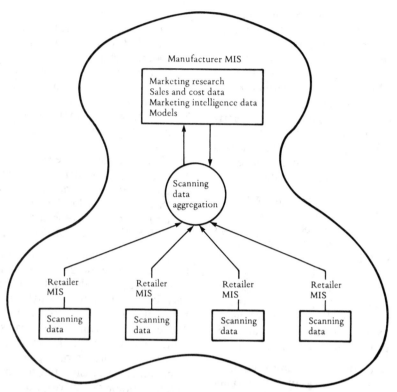

Figure 13.1 *Macromarketing information systems*
Source: N. Piercy and M. Evans, *Managing Marketing Information*, Croom Helm, 1983.

information partnership' which has been described in the industrial market sector (Reddy and Marvin, 1986), and the redrawing of competitive boundaries through 'inter-organizational information systems' (Cash and Konsynski, 1985). While these proposals remain essentially potentials at present, they amount to a potential for a realignment of competitive and distributor relationships of a type with fundamental implications for marketing strategy development.

With the case established that the marketing information function must be viewed strategically, as a critical marketing management task, the chapter can proceed.

A marketing panacea – the answer to all my problems

Before continuing to consider the actual structure of the marketing information system and the development process, there are certain necessary reservations

to be expressed. These points are important to avoid 'over-selling' the MIS to the practitioner and to maintain some practical reality in what follows.

First, it must be noted that information management requires resources – financial, physical and human. Without adequate resourcing and the commitment of managerial effort, no development process is likely to succeed – token efforts will produce token results. In short, there is a cost involved, which may be substantial, although it should clearly be balanced against the value of what may be achieved – and it is hoped that what follows will provide a basis for realistically assessing that value.

Second, for reasons which will be expanded upon shortly there is no clear and obvious relationship between the development of the marketing information function and commercial success – a point which has been reiterated by many (for example Jeuck, 1953; Davidson, 1975; May, 1981). To look for immediate 'bottom-line' impact is to take a simplistic view of how marketing information is used, and to assume that an activity like market research makes decisions rather than simply supporting the decision making process.

This leads to a third point: that the impact of information on decision making is complex and frequently covert. In fact, our understanding of managerial decision making remains limited, although it is apparent that (in the model frequently presumed by the management scientist) marketing information is sought for reasons other than making simple choices between known options using explicit criteria. It has been suggested, for instance, that:

● Managers seek information to justify what has already been decided (Cyert et al., 1956)
● Marketing information may be used to make salespeople 'properly optimistic' (Hardin, 1969)
● Managers may seek information as a way of delaying decisions (Samuels, 1973)
● Marketing information may serve an 'organizational' function, for example providing common ground or a shared frame of reference, acting as a collective memory, or functioning as a stabilizing factor, or even providing reassurance.

One writer suggests 'there are many uses of research which are often discussed as purely irrational or political without further thought. They can, however, be seen to stem from the needs of organizations as such and the really rational approach would align them as legitimate functions which need not be ignored or swept under the carpet' (Channon, 1968).

Not unrelated to this complexity and covertness in the organizational role of marketing information is a fourth point: that information systems development has on occasion led to 'management suspicion and disappointment' (Holtgrefe, 1986). Indeed, one symptom of the information system that embodies unrealistic management expectations is that it is not used by managers themselves. It is hoped that the approach developed here will avoid, or at least minimize, this danger.

In fact, a fifth point should be made: if handled badly, developing a marketing information system may actually damage the existing decision-making processes. Recently, an attempt has been made to identify the adverse 'hidden side-effects' (Haskins and Nani, 1986) of information systems on management decision making. This suggests that:

1 The information system is a constrained set of data, with the result that managers may build a false picture of the world using only that constrained data, so decisions are made with unnecessarily limited information, which is probably the same information set used in earlier decisions.
2 The information in the system may represent the designer's view of the world rather than the manager's.
3 While the data in the system may be frequently changed, the structure or frame of reference of the system may remain static, ignoring the fact that as the world changes so should the configuration of data represented by the information system (Haskins and Nanni, 1986).

However, the conclusion to which we are led by the points above should not be too gloomy! The goal is not to persuade the reader of the impossibility of ever designing an effective MIS, but to highlight the fact that doing the job properly requires resources and extremely painstaking analysis. It is actually quite easy to achieve the appearance of a MIS by changing the names of reports and job titles and designating responsibilities for the MIS (for example, to a junior executive), but this is no more than cosmetic and should be recognized as such. Developing a marketing information system that is genuinely effective requires far more.

If we have now answered the questions of why managing information is a marketing function, and also why it is not information technology's instant answer to all marketing problems, then we can proceed to a discussion of what the MIS *is*, and how it may be *developed*.

The marketing information system – what is it anyway?

Views of what the MIS should actually be are varied, although the structure shown in Figure 13.2 remains largely unchallenged as a view of the components of the system.

To deal with the first of these points, definitions of the MIS are relatively uninteresting and are not quoted here, although is is possible to ennumerate the characteristics which have been associated with the MIS:

- It stores and integrates information on marketing issues from many sources.
- It provides for the dissemination of such information to users.
- It supports marketing management decision making in both planning and control.
- It is likely to be computerized.
- It is not simply a new name for market research!

This said, it is necessary also to recognize that there are many different types of MIS. Graf (1979) distinguishes between:

1 *Data storage and retrieval systems*, which make it simpler to use information by making it readily available. Such a system might involve keying information requests into a visual display unit or other computer terminal to access a magnetic disk file of information, or something much simpler like a card index of research reports, files or sales statistics or a bibliography of publications.
2 *Monitoring systems*, which check progress and may alert management to variations, such as sales or market share falling below target.
3 *Analytical information systems*, which are designed to answer such questions as why something happened, what is likely to happen next, and 'what if' queries, such as what will happen if we reduce prices or if we increase advertising.

At a rather more sophisticated level, we can distinguish between the elements which are associated with:

1 *Current awareness subsystems*, based on sophisticated computer stores of data,
2 *In-depth and crisis information subsystems* involving the use of marketing research techniques.
3 *Incidental information subsystems*, which are similar to what is discussed here as marketing intelligence (Uhl, 1974).

Pursuing the concept of the type of information provided by the MIS, a technically more sophisticated approach (Buzzell *et al.*, 1969) distinguishes between control information, planning information and information for basic research. Control information involves continuous monitoring of marketing activities, for instance reporting exceptions against sales plans and marketing objectives,

and identifying trends, problems and opportunities. Different needs are met by planning information, exemplified by the storing of a base of data about products, markets and so on, or computer simulations, for sales and market forecasting. Basic research information is used to develop cause and effect models of responses to marketing actions.

Returning to the structure of the MIS, the model in Figure 13.2 has been used to study MIS in companies like 3M, Parke-Davies and Beechams (Perdikis, 1984) with some success, suggesting that the model has some general applicability. This model identifies four components of a MIS, in terms of the source and type of information concerned. *Marketing productivity analysis* is concerned with using the information already available in the financial and administrative systems, such as cost and sales data. This is the first case where it may be possible to evaluate the relationship between inputs to the marketing effort (sales time, management effort, promotional budgets, etc.) and the outputs generated (orders received, sales revenue, etc.). While the comparison of inputs and outputs on this basis is necessarily crude it can frequently be highly productive if used properly. The techniques available include: expense and effort to sales ratios (Wilson, 1981); creative sales analysis, e.g. business gains as opposed to business losses to diagnose marginal sales trends (Piercy, 1978); and the development of marketing cost accounting reports which link costs

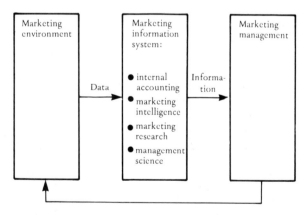

Figure 13.2 *Structure of the marketing information system*
Source: N. Piercy and M. Evans, *ibid.*

and returns to given marketing entities (Barrett, 1986).

Indeed, one recent analyst (Simmonds, 1986) has developed a framework for using accounting tools to measure competitive position. This framework takes basic accounting indicators such as sales, cash flow and so on, and derives a series of indicators of competitive position in the way shown in Table 13.1, which can be interpreted to evaluate the impact of marketing strategies on relative market position in financial terms.

These data sources and the analyses they are capable of producing are available to even the most rudimentary MIS. Here, probably more than anywhere else, the crucial factors are:

● Not to overload managers with vast amounts of information just because it is available.

Table 13.1   *The accounting assessment of competitive position*

	Ourselves	Competitors 1 2 3 . . .	Total market
Basic accounting indications			
Sales volume			
Profit			
Cashflow			
Working capital			
Shareholders' funds			
Sales volume			
Derived competitive position indications			
Price per unit/cost per unit			
Volume increase			
Market share			
Profit percentage			
Working capital/ sales ratio			
Shareholders' funds/ sales ratio			
Relative market share			
Relative cost per unit			

Adapted from K. Simmonds, 'The accounting assessment of competitive postion', in N. Piercy (ed.), *Marketing Asset Accounting*, MCB, 1986.

● To design reports to highlight 'critical success factors' (see below).
● To design information flows to match managers' information needs – both in volume and 'understandability'.

Marketing intelligence involves a variety of types of data, broadly concerned with 'environmental scanning' (Aguilar, 1967). The question of environmental appraisal was studied in Chapter 6 by Brownlie, so relatively little comment is required here. It has long been known that managers come to know the world through a relatively disorganized type of environmental scanning.

More recently, attempts have been made by some companies to formalize the intelligence function, in the way demonstrated in Table 13.2, which describes some of the work done at Levi-Strauss. Others have noted the advantages in formalizing the marketing intelligence function (Piercy, 1978; Vasconcellos, 1985) and provide actionable frameworks for management attention. One such model is shown in Table 13.3.

In spite of such advances, however, there remains the problem that much intelligence is comprised of 'soft' or qualitative data, which are difficult to integrate into the information system, and which are difficult to evaluate in terms of their validity or reliability. However, this is an information source easy to underestimate, and it should be incorporated in our model.

Marketing research represents the . process of generating information around given problems or areas of interest, using either *secondary* or published data sources or the undertaking of *primary* research to generate new data at the marketplace level. This is clearly not the place to attempt a detailed technical study of marketing research techniques (since appropriate sources are given in the references section at the end of the chapter), although there is much to recommend the discipline of a process-based approach to marketing research of the type shown in Table 13.4. The value of this model is that it provides a vehicle for planning research exercises, but also for evaluating and controlling research actually done.

It has frequently been suggested that marketing research often turns out to be a wasteful use of resources: because researchers do not understand

Table 13.2   *Environmental scanning in Levi-Strauss*

Environmental factors	Scanning	Interpretation
Social, for example population changes, leisure time and recreation, fashion trends, preferences for natural fabrics.	For example changing age distribution in US market – monitoring trends in birthrate and population discovers that teenager market segment in the US is shrinking.	Shrinking market potential in largest market segment.
Economic, for example economic growth and inflation, imports to the US, clothing spending, retail changes.	For example imports of jeans to the US – monitoring growth in Far East production and quota agreements suggests import growth in US.	Imports will probably gain a higher share of US market for Levi-Strauss products.
Governmental, for example import barriers, retail price maintenance, metrication, flame-proofing standards in clothes.	For example monitoring US government consumer protection bodies finds reduced budgets and less attention to flammability research, suggesting less chance of new standards for general clothing.	Slowed rate of this environmental force.

Source: N. Piercy and M. Evans, *Managing Marketing Information*, Croom Helm, 1983.

management problems (Leech, 1980); because research is done out of context (Biel, 1967); because of a lack of integration between marketing researchers and managers (Schlackman, 1979); and where there is a lack of communication between researchers and managers leading to 'panic' research too late to help and providing irrelevant information (England, 1980).

In such cases it would seem that the responsibility for problems lies not with the techniques used but the management of the organizational interface between information users (planners, managers) and providers (marketing researchers). Thus our present interest lies not in the techniques of doing research but in terms of Table 13.4 the problem definition and communication stages of managing the research process. In information management terms the critical tests for evaluating marketing research projects lie first, in the ability to specify precise objectives which lead to a list of pieces of information needed for a particular purpose; and, second, in the degree to which useful results are successfully communicated to the sponsors or users of research. In developing the MIS it is necessary to accept that primary marketing research may be the only way to produce needed information (although arguably it is the last resort rather than the first), but that we face problems in:

1   Managing the process of research and the interface with managers,
2   Validating the process,
3   Integrating the findings into the corporate data base or 'memory'.

Management science in marketing is concerned essentially with the application of simulation and model-building techniques for marketing planning and control. The techniques in this area have been considered in two earlier chapters, and our focus here, as with marketing research, is not in techniques of applying these methods but in the problems of managing the information they generate.

In this way it is possible to claim some consensus in what the MIS *is*, in terms of what it should do and what components it should contain. What we have not considered is what mechanisms are available to *integrate* these various components.

In even quite simple cases it is possible to obtain conflicting views about what is happening in the real world, depending on when we stop looking for information and what particular source we tend to favour. For example, in Table 13.5 our view of what is happening in the market is likely to vary according to which level in the channel we investigate and which information source we pay attention to and believe. There are no easy answers to the integration

Table 13.3 *A sequential model of environmental scanning*

Stages	Activities
1 Identify potentially relevant environmental changes.	Selecting environmental forces of likely relevance from technological, social, economic, governmental and natural dimensions.
2 Monitor – determine the nature, direction, rate of change and magnitude of forces.	Collecting and storing intelligence from the environment.
3 Forecast probability of impact, timing and likely consequences.	Extrapolating trends and developing scenarios, for example through Delphi forecasting.
4 Develop and implement strategic responses.	Focus on counterforces.

Source: D.W. Craven, G.E. Hills and R.B. Woodruff, *Marketing Decision Marketing: Concepts and Strategy*, Irwin, 1980.

problem, although it has been effectively analysed as one of the critical issues facing us in designing marketing information systems (Westwood *et al.*, 1975). The problem is largely one of designing an holistic model, such as that provided by Kotler's (1971) marketing information and analysis centre,

Table 13.4 *A processual approach to marketing research*

Stage 1   Defining and clarifying the marketing problem
- Setting the objectives for research.
- Producing a data list, i.e. the specific pieces of data required.

Stage 2   Determining the sources of information
- Can the research objectives be met from secondary published sources – can they be trusted?
- Do the objectives require primary research – if so who or what are the relevant sources?

Stage 3   Designing a data collection strategy
- What measurement method is to be used – observation, personal interviewing, postal questionnaire.
- What type of questionnaire is needed?
- What sampling is appropriate?

Stage 4   Data collection
- Implementing the data collection strategy – interviewing, etc.

Stage 5   Data processing
- Editing, coding and tabulating the data, testing the results.

Stage 6   Communicating results
- Designing reports and presentations which match the research objectives specified in stage 1.

Source: N. Piercy and M. Evans, *Managing Marketing Information*, Croom Helm, 1983.

which functions as 'the marketing nerve centre for the company'. This suggests that to approach the integration problem requires:

1   That the MIS be recognized as a valid entity rather than seen simply as short-term marketing research,
2   Organizational adjustments to incorporate the marketing information system into the administration superstructure of the firm,
3   The use of new technology to reduce the problem to something manageable.

These issues are tackled at the conclusion of the chapter in the context of developing an information strategy in marketing. First, we turn our attention to the need for a developmental process for the MIS.

A marketing information system development process – if we want one, how do we do it?

With a model of the MIS in mind that identifies the components of the system, it is possible to pursue a logical model for developing a MIS and then to show how that logic has to be adapted to the realities of the organization.

Table 13.6 shows a simple model for systems development in marketing, which follows the logic of reviewing the present information system, assessing information needs, and remedying shortfalls. Such a model provides a reasonable basis on which to proceed but its application is unlikely to be free from complications.

Table 13.5   *Evaluating a price-cut*

We reduce the price of a brand in period 1 – what is the result in period 2?

		Information source	Information type	Result	Conclusion
In-company		Accounts office	Sales revenue	No change	Price cut has no effect
		Order processing	Orders received	Increased	Price cut increased orders
		Salespeople	Intelligence	Extra retailer sales	Price cut increased orders
Channel of distribution		Wholesaler warehouses	Stock levels	Depleted	Retailers have increased purchases
		Multiple retailers	Retail audit	Stocks increased	Orders increased but not sales
		Independent retailers	Stocks	Depleted	Consumers purchased more, no additional orders from retailers yet
Buyers		Consumers	Consumer panel	Mixed	We do not know what is happening – we need more detailed analysis

Actual situation – multiple retailers are buying-in at the reduced price, after a period's delay, but are not passing the price-cut on to the consumers, while small independent retailers buying through wholesalers are doing extra business by passing the price-cut on to their customers.

Measurement of current information flows and uses

The problems of measuring current information flows and data uses are primarily but not wholly logistical. In anything but the smallest company, actually finding out what information is generated and what happens to it is a lengthy process of interviewing/questionnaire surveys and flow-charting to describe the complexity of information practices which have evolved over a period of time, with all the idiosyncrasies and historical oddities that this implies.

However, even this apparently innocuous part of the process has been associated with real practical difficulties – market research reports which have been deliberately suppressed; misleading and incomplete responses about data stores; defensiveness and protectiveness about current information practices; and so on (Piercy, 1979).

Developing the MIS must been seen in many cases as an innovation in a company, with all that this implies about the potential for resistance to

Table 13.6   *Simple model of systems development*

Stage 1   Measure present information flows and uses.

Stage 2   Identify marketing management information needs.

Stage 3   Design new information flows to close the gap between 1 and 2.

Stage 4   Reconcile these with the overall information system.

Stage 5   Implement.

Stage 6   Revision.

change. Over and above this, even at this preliminary stage it is important to recognize that information is not a commodity – it is a source of power, of political influence and of organizational status. Actions which may be, or may be perceived to be, threatening are likely to be resisted and manipulated.

In fact, the whole MIS development process has a political dimension, to which we will give attention as an aspect of implementation, but it is necessary to be aware throughout of the need to identify the entrenched interests inside and outside the marketing department (for example sales managers whose 'private files' are their power base; product managers whose major goal is to suppress any information undermining the position of the brands which they champion; the finance department using its 'confidential' cost accounts to maintain a political 'veto' over marketing activities; and so on), and to make allowances for these barriers.

Identifying marketing management information needs

The very core of the MIS development process is the identification of the management information needs which the system is to address, and it is in this area where the most intractable problems emerge. A number of points which emerge as critical issues in this context are discussed below.

Context

A first point of context is to note that any idea of a standard set of marketing management information needs is highly misleading (despite the views put forward in the promotional literature of suppliers of decision support system software). For instance, recent research (Piercy, 1986c; 1986d) has distinguished various forms of marketing department, differentiated by size and responsibilities in the ways demonstrated in Table 13.7 and Figure 13.3.

The finding that marketing departments vary in

Table 13.7 *Marketing department responsibilities*

		%
1	Advertising and marketing research	51
2	Advertising marketing research, trade marketing and sales	21
3	Advertising, marketing research, trade marketing, sales, customer service and exporting	13
4	Advertising, marketing research, trade marketing, sales, customer service, exporting and distribution	15
		100
		(*n* = 130)

Source: N. Piercy, 'The model of organization', *Marketing*, 15 May, 1986d, pp. 21–30.

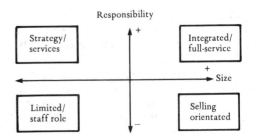

Figure 13.3 *Marketing department types*
Source: N. Piercy, 'The model of organization', *Marketing*, 15 May 1986, pp. 21–3.

these ways suggests emphatically that defining marketing management information needs requires situational study, not standardized models.

A second point of context relates to the continued existence of 'myths' surrounding the use of information in organizations and the danger of creating 'misinformation systems' (Tricker, 1971; Ackoff, 1967). In essence, there are significant dangers in assuming that 'more' and 'faster' are necessarily advantages in designing information availability and flows.

Practical limitations

In addition to recognizing such issues of context it is important to note that there are a number of limitations inherent in what we are actually trying to measure. It has to be said that managers often appear not to know themselves what their information needs are. It is this which provides the fundamental limitation to the process of asking managers to identify their needs for marketing data.

It has been noted that when asked, managers tend to respond that they do not know, they need what they currently receive, or they need everything they can be given. In the end information needs should reflect the task activity of the manager, and in this sense they can be specified only when the decision making process has been modelled. From this, however, there arises a second practical limitation in the sense that some information needs may not be 'knowable' or at least not easily predictable. The model in Figure 13.4 suggests that marketing decisions can be broadly categorized into strategy, planning and operations, each associated with very different types of decision, and by implication associated with information needs which are varied in their

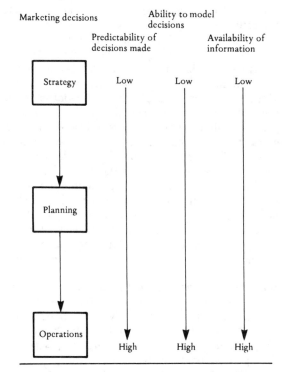

Figure 13.4 *Marketing decisions and information needs*

predictability and the actual availability of the required information.

In practical terms, it is relatively straightforward to model operating decisions in marketing – stock re-order levels, routine price discounts, and the like – and to define information needs in this way. It may even be relatively simple to model the marketing planning process to isolate information needs – market research, competitive changes, results against plan, etc. What remains largely intractable is predicting the information needs of strategic decision makers in marketing on the grounds that (Rockart, 1978a):

> Top executives' activities are dynamic, everchanging, and therefore one cannot predetermine exactly what information will be needed to deal with changing events at any point in time. These executives, are and must be dependent on future-oriented rapidly assembled, most-often subjective, informal information.

Similarly, it has been observed by Mintzberg (1985) that:

It is necessary to look at the content of managers' information, and at what they do with it. The evidence here is that a great deal of managers' inputs are soft and speculative . . . Furthermore, very analytical inputs – reports, documents and hard data in general – seem to be of relatively little importance to many managers.

In short, at the operational and short-term planning level it is possible to predict many information needs and to meet these. As we move from planning to strategy, the ability to predict and programme decisions is far less. At this level the best that can normally be offered is an accessible data base to answer the 'give me everything we know about . . .' request, and some method for highlighting or flagging significant factors for management attention – as with 'critical success factors' approach discussed below.

A third practical limitation, not unrelated to the last point above, is the problem that managers at all levels differ substantially in their problem-solving style, and hence their information needs.

At one level we can observe the apparently unsystematic way in which managers search for, and choose to pay attention to, information, and such phenomena as the 'private' or 'secret' personal filing systems that individuals build.

It may be noted that idiosyncrasy in information use may be inconvenient to the systems designer, but may also be central to a manager's personal effectiveness.

Figure 13.5 *Managers' problem-solving styles*

On a broader front, it has been argued (Mason and Mitroff, 1973) that we should view managerial problem-solving in terms of the process whereby information is organized and evaluated by individuals. The process of information gathering involves making judgements after information has been gathered. This approach implies that the resulting perceived information is heavily dependent on the individual's mental set, memory capacity and other mental processes. This leads to the model in Figure 13.5, which suggests a number of problem-solving styles:

1 Sensation thinkers are applied thinkers who keep systems running and want the organization to be run on facts. They follow the rules and manage many details and facts.
2 Intuitive thinkers are interested in principles and hypothesized relationships, and are more interested in designing things than running them, and need support from others in details and facts. They are orientated towards new problems and also to political coalitions.
3 Intuitive feelers prefer unstructured situations, loosely coupled organizations and few rules or rigid systems.
4 Sensation feelers are pragmatists who deal with problems in a methodological fashion and prefer well-defined rules and decisions based on facts rather than hunches. They dislike abstractions and radical change.

Returning to the axes in the model in Figure 13.4 by way of summary, in terms of information evaluation a distinction is made between a dominant 'feeling' style and a dominant thinking style of problem-solving (Mason and Mitroff, 1973):

A thinking individual is the type who relied primarily on cognitive processes. His evaluations tend to run along the lines of abstract true/false judgements and are based on formal systems of logic. A preference for feeling, on the other hand, implies the type of individual who relies primarily on affective processes. His evaluations tend to run along personalistic lines of good/bad, unpleasant, and the like/dislike.

In terms of information gathering, managers with a dominant sensation style tend to prefer standardized ways of working and routines; they are 'detail people' gathering much data. Those with a dominant intuitive style are impatient with routine details and dislike taking the time for precision in information and perceive the environment as a totality rather than a series of facts (Mason and Mitroff, 1973).

Figure 13.5 suggests that different task roles are typically associated with different problem-solving styles, and thus with information behaviour, but it seems likely that in reality there will be variations in information behaviour within role sets as well as across them. This research would, however, seem to suggest very systematically the nature of the limitation placed on the MIS design by individual problem-solving styles, but by implication also suggests that the solution lies in emphasizing individualized rather than centrally standardized information provision through the MIS.

Thus far, our concern in approaching the task of identifying marketing management information needs has been heavily grounded in the context of making the measurements and the practical limitations which exist. We turn now to the methods available to help solving the problems identified.

Table 13.8 *Measuring marketing information flows*

1 Contact established with key interviewees, who can identify key decision and personnel.
2 Unstructured interviews with decision making participants to identify roles played.
3 Interview data converted to flow charts.
4 Flow charts from interviews are amalgamated.
5 Validity of flow charts tested with original interviewees and others in the company, and modified.

Source: J. Hulbert, J.U. Farley and J.A. Howard, 'Information processing and decision making in marketing organizations', *Journal of Marketing Research*, Vol. 9, no. 2, 1972, pp. 75–7.

Models of analysis

In terms of measurement techniques, a tested process is shown in Table 13.8, involving the use of interviews, questionnaires and flow charts to build a picture of the existing MIS. However, moving from what *is* to what *should be*, requires rather more than this. Two approaches worth noting are Munro's (1978) data analysis/decision analysis and Rockart's (1978) 'critical success factors' models.

Munro's approach offers two complementary methods of analysing managers' information needs. Data analysis involves the study of information flows compared to perceived information needs,

Table 13.9 *Data analysis and decision analysis*

	Data analysis	Decision analysis
Methodology	1 Examine all reports, files, and other sources of information used by the manager. 2 Determine with the manager the use made of each source of information examined. 3 Identify redundant information sources/flows to be eliminated. 4 Identify, with the manager unsatisfied information needs.	1 Identify with the manager major decision responsibilities. 2 Identify the policies and organizational objectives relevant to the decision responsibilities. 3 Examine the steps and processes involved in making each major decision. 4 Develop a flow chart of each decision. 5 Use the flow chart to determine information required at each step in the decision. 6 Identify redundant information and unsatisfied information needs.
Advantages	Incorporates managers' views of information requirements. Effective with structured decisions. Flexibility. Speed.	Links information needs to decisions and objectives. Effective with unstructured decisions. Information can be matched to personal decision-making style. May improve the decision process as well as information flows.
Disadvantages	Managers are relied upon to identify and describe accurately their information needs. Information needs are not linked to decisions and objectives. No established procedures or standards.	Information requirements may change if the manager is replaced. Specifying decision processes is difficult. More time-consuming.

Source: N. Piercy and M. Evans, *Managing Marketing Information*, Croom Helm, 1983.

while decision analysis involves modelling the major decisions made and identifying information needs from these models. The stages in each approach are summarized in Table 13.9. Munro's suggestion is that:

> Where the decision is 'programmed' . . . it is advisable to use data analysis. On the other hand, for decision situations which are poorly understood, data analysis offers no help as the data for such situations is not available . . . the experience of attempting to construct a decision model for poorly understood decision situations frequently results in a greatly improved understanding of both the decision process and information required.

A further attack on the problem of senior managers' strategic information needs is provided by the 'critical success factors' approach (Rockart, 1978), which focuses on 'the limited number of areas in which results, if they are satisfactory, will ensure successful competitive performance for the organization. They are the few key areas where "things must go right" for the business to flourish' (Rockart). An example of the use of this approach is given in Table 13.10.

While they do not provide complete answers, such approaches give a starting point in identifying and classifying different types of information need in marketing.

Designing the information system

To the extent that it proves possible to identify management information needs in the context described above, then much of what remains is re-

Table 13.10 *Analysing critical success factors*

An example: microwave associates

Critical success factors	Measurements
Image in the stock market	Price/earnings ratio.
Technical reputation with customers.	Orders/quotations ratio. Field interviews by salespeople. Changes in the percentage of each major customer's business being obtained
Market success	Market share changes by customer. Market growth rates.
Risk in major bids and contracts.	Experience with similar products. Experience with the customer. Prior customer relationships.
Profit margin on projects.	The profit margin on the bid compared to other projects.
Morale.	Staff turnover, absenteeism, etc. Informal feedback.
Performance against budget on key jobs.	Time against plan. Cost against budget. Profile across major jobs.

Source: N. Piercy and M. Evans, *Managing Marketing Information*, Croom Helm, 1983.

latively straightforward 'gap-filling' using the model of marketing information types in the MIS discussed earlier.

What has become apparent, however, is the need for a design strategy for the MIS (Howard *et al.*, 1975). One approach distinguishes three such MIS design strategies, appropriate in different circumstances.

1   Supplemental strategy: to automate and facilitate information flow and storage, orientated towards data input and output. In situations of high uncertainty and excessive problem solving this approach may be the most useful.
2   Modification strategy: of making information more widely available, orientated towards changing the communications structure. This may be appropriate under conditions of moderate uncertainty and relatively unstructured objectives.
3   Replacement strategy: of replacing information processing and decision rules with new rules and computer systems, which is orientated towards decision processes. This may be appropriate where the environment is stable, and objectives are well-structured because decision processes are likely to be highly routinized.

The underlying point is that the strategy of MIS should be seen as contingent on surrounding conditions and the particular company's situation. This contingency view relates to: the sophistication of what is to be attempted; the scope of developments which are planned; and the expenditure of resources on the MIS project.

Implementation and review

Until this point the concern has been with analysis and planning, but clearly attention needs to be devoted to putting plans into effect in terms of MIS innovations and modifications. Two of the key issues are organization and new technology, and these are discussed below in separate sections of the chapter. At this point, two issues are worth attention: the responsibility for MIS development, and the need for a strategy of change.

MIS responsibility

There are evident attractions in allocating responsibilities for MIS development to individuals or groups, and this author has argued the case for a marketing information analyst, whose role involves studying marketing management information needs, and the ways in which these needs can be met, using the type of methodology discussed in this chapter.

However, when the problems of implementation are concerned, there are two other points to be borne in mind. First, it has been noted by Buzzell *et al.* (1969) that:

Management must decide how to organize MIS development activities. This is a much more complex problem than might be assumed. Sophisticated MIS

Table 13.11 *Scenario writing for information systems development*

Objectives	What are we trying to do?
	What resources are needed?
	Who controls these resources, directly or indirectly?
Problems	What elements are critical?
	Are any of these elements 'owned' by monopoly interests?
	Will their 'owners' cooperate – what is the effect of the MIS on the distribution of 'ownership'?
	Can uncooperative 'owners' be avoided or bought-off?
	Will they respond with delays or token support?
	Will they provide massive resistance?
Games	How are people likely to (a) divert resources, (b) deflect goals, (c) dissipate energies.
	How can this be countered?
Delay	How much delay should be expected?
	What negotiations are necessary?
	What resources are available for negotiation?
	Would project management structures help?
Fixing the game	What management help is needed?
	What resources do they have to help?
	What incentives are there for them to play the 'fixer' role?
	Can a coalition be built to fix the game?

Source: N. Piercy and M. Evans, *Managing Marketing Information*, Croom Helm, 1983.

requires the co-ordinated efforts of a great many departments and individuals.

The implication is that successful implementation may require the involvement of a team, in the form of a committee, working party, project team, and so on. It should also be noted that others have made a substantial case for active user participation in the whole information systems development process – suggesting this to be the key to success in the right company.

Second, as well as the number of people involved, there is some suggestion that the organizational level of the key players may be critical. If we believe that MIS development is important then this should be reflected in senior management involvement. Indeed, Keen (1980) goes as far as to see a senior 'fixer' as the key to coping with the organizational problems inherent in information systems change.

Strategic MIS development

Throughout this consideration of MIS development stress has been placed on the need to take a strategic view. By this it is meant that the whole information function should be tied to the strategic future of the firm. The alternative is a series of ad hoc responses to short-term problems and missing most of the potential gains from information management discussed earlier.

In particular, where MIS change is involved, it has been suggested that we should write a scenario, in the way suggested in Table 13.11, to provide a broad view of the goals and obstacles faced, before becoming involved in purely tactical development actions.

With these points made, and a model for MIS development uncovered, attention now turns to two final issues: the organizational dimension of information systems, and the impact of new information technology.

The organizational dimension

This author has recently produced a full treatment of the issue of marketing organization (Piercy 1985), which was based on the premise that organizational structure and information processing are intimately related problem areas. In this present book, Spillard (Chapter 4) has analysed the major organizational issues, but there are a number of points which should be emphasized here.

Organization for MIS

If the information function is to be regarded as an essential part of the management process in marketing, then it requires formal recognition in the structure. We discussed earlier the question of allocating responsibilities for MIS development, but attention also should be paid to:

● The location of responsibility in the organization, e.g. company-wide versus in the marketing department,

- The need to provide an organizational framework to cope with the integration problem discussed earlier,
- The need to match the structure of the marketing information function with the strategic development of the firm,
- The problems of integrating information specialists with decision makers, which may partly be solved through structural devices.

Organizational barriers to MIS development

At another level, the organization must be recognized as a source of barriers to developing information systems – an issue touched on briefly earlier. At that point we commented on the resistance to change by those who feel threatened, but it is possible to go further to argue that since information provides power, to redistribute information is to redistribute power. To ignore the barriers created by the political infrastructure of the organization is quite simply to ignore the realities of organizational life.

Information and organizational strategy

It is quite normal, though frequently unexpected, for managers to find as they investigate and seek to redesign information systems, that this process throws up major questions about the actual organization of the department and the company. For instance, in one recent case – Agrescco (Shrivastava and Etgar, 1985), it was found that implementing a marketing decision support system created significant structural impact as a byproduct. The information system was associated with changes in work procedures, formal reporting relationships, types of reporting, the decentralization of decision making, and some reallocation of personnel. Individually these changes were small but collectively amounted to a significant structural adjustment directly associated with introducing the information system.

This link is explainable because if we take the information system as the structure we place on our environment, and the organizational structure as the representation in the company of the segmentation of the environment, then it is reasonable that changes in one should lead to changes in the other.

Perhaps the important point to be made is that the development of organizational structure is a strategic issue (Piercy, 1985) and that our thoughts should be directed towards the need for both information and organization strategies in marketing.

New information technology

We close our consideration of developing marketing information systems by attempting to highlight the impact of new information technology on the marketing information function. Indeed, it is virtually impossible in the 1980s to seriously consider the MIS without considering new information technology.

Costs and opportunities

The most obvious new information technology implication is that the costs of the equipment and software needed to power an information system have been radically reduced. The effect is that many information functions which were previously merely theoretical possibilities are now practical realities (Shrivastava and Etgar, 1984).

For example, the Hospital Products Division of Abbots Laboratories has recently implemented a marketing decision support system. With a large product mix and extensive sales records, previously information had existed in the data store but was for all practical purposes inaccessible. Even with simple sales/profit analysis, information that previously took two days manual clerical effort to produce is now available almost instantly on request (Brown, 1985). The company enthuses:

> The systems bundles are sizeable, but the bang for the buck when we're there is stupendous. It can do things we've only dreamed about.

It is clear that new information technology provides initially a major change in the costs of collecting, processing, storing and communicating marketing information which cannot be ignored (Martell, 1986).

The new information technology catalyst

Because of this change in cost, and because of the focus of contemporary management attention on new information technology questions, it is likely that new information technology will prove a powerful catalyst allowing MIS developments to be resourced and implemented.

We saw earlier how new information technology provides a potential for a distributed information system linking the channel of distribution and providing information-based sources of competitive advantage.

It is interesting to speculate that while at present we can only see the impact of the earliest phases of new information technology implementation on marketing – and that impact is already substantial – later phases of new information technology change will have more radical implications for the MIS and for marketing itself (Piercy, 1984; Martell, 1986).

For instance, 'phase one' change may be to give the market researcher a microcomputer and his/her secretary a word processor. 'Phase two' change may involve networking these machines (and others) and possibly removing the secretary from the system, so the researcher produces his/her own reports. But later phases may involve automating data collection and allowing managers to communicate directly with a data base, or in some scenarios automating the decision-making stage as well.

Broad new information technology implications

It is arguments such as this which underline the need for marketing management to comprehend and respond to the underlying pervasive impact of new information technology.

For instance, consider the following propositions as illustrative of the new information technology impacts we have in mind:

- The 'macromarketing information system' and the 'information partnership' contribute potential forms of information-based integration between firms that undermine our assumptions about independence and competition.
- The existence of the company organization as we know it is threatened by the opportunity to locate information and knowledge workers remotely (at home, in the marketplace, etc.) and to work and communicate electronically.
- The familiar hierarchial shape of the company organization is ultimately based on the limited ability of individuals to process information, but the new information technology-based information system challenges this principle. The im-

plication is that the organization becomes far flatter – possibly losing the whole middle management element.
- The reason for having departments is that they specialize – the marketing department is the specialized boundary-spanning function with the marketplace – but the ability to share information through automated data flows and data bases challenges the need to have the same departments.
- New information technology gives management the choice to decentralize more with distributed information processing, but equally the opportunity to centralize control far more effectively than ever before.

It is not possible here to formulate a scenario for the full implications of new information technology. The two points to convey are that it provides a mechanism facilitating and encouraging MIS change, but that such changes may be fundamental and strategic – not simply changing the way we do things, but changing the things we do.

Conclusion

Perhaps the strongest recurrent theme throughout this chapter has been the need for marketing management in the 1980s to take a strategic perspective on the information function.

We have attempted to construct a foundation for this by examining the need to manage information in marketing to create a 'marketing asset' leading to competitive advantage. Accepting that there are substantial practical limitations to bear in mind, and barriers to overcome, we examined a model of the MIS and a process for developing the MIS in-company, involving the realistic measurement of information needs and the design of gap-filling information flows. An attempt was then made to place this process into the context of organizational and technological change.

What this provides is an agenda for marketing management in the development of a coherent, long-term strategy for a critical dimension of marketing. It is suggested that it is only through such a strategic approach that we can appropriately respond to the pressure to manage marketing information and thus to manage marketing itself.

References

Ackoff, R. L., 'Management misinformation systems', *Management Science*, vol. 14, no. 4 1967, pp. 147–56.

Aguilar, F. J. *Scanning the Business Environment*, Macmillan, 1967.

Barrett, T. F., 'Issues in the design of marketing accounting systems' in N. Piercy (ed.), *Management Information Systems: The Technology Challenge*, Croom Helm, 1986.

Biel, A. L., 'Management goals and marketing research: the dilemma of organization', Proceedings: ESOMAR/WAPOR Congress, 1967.

Brown, D. C., 'The anatomy of a decision support system', *Business Marketing*, June 1985, pp. 80–6.

Buzzell, R. D., Cox, D. F. and Brown, R. V., *Marketing Research and Information Systems: Text and Cases*, McGraw-Hill, 1969.

Cash, J. I. and Konsynski, B. R., 'IS redraws competitive boundries', *Harvard Business Review*, March-April 1985, pp. 142–3.

Channon, C., 'The role of advertising research in management decision-making', Proceedings: Market Research Society Conference, 1968.

Christopher, M., McDonald, M. and Wills, G., *Introducing Marketing*, Pan, 1980.

Craven, D. W., Hills, G. E. and Woodruff, R. B., *Marketing Decision Making: Concepts and Strategy*, Irwin, 1980.

Cyert, R. M., Simon, H. A. and Trow, D. B., 'Observation of a business decision', *Journal of Business*, vol. 29, 1956, pp. 237–48.

Davidson, J. H., *Offensive Marketing*, Penguin, 1975.

Earl, M., 'Emerging trends in managing new information technologies', in N. Piercy (ed.), *The Management Implications of New Information Technology*, Croom Helm, 1983.

England, L. R., 'Is research a waste of time?' *Marketing*, 16 April 1980, pp. 56–7.

Graf, F., 'Information systems for marketing', *Marketing Trends*, vol. 2, 1979, pp. 1–3.

Hardin, D. K., 'Marketing research – is it used or abused?', *Journal of Marketing Research*, vol. 6, 1969, pp. 239.

Haskins, M. E. and Nanni, A. J., *MIS Influences on Managers: Hidden Side Effects*, University of Virginia, 1986.

Holtgrefe, G., *DSS for Strategic Planning Purposes: A Future Source of Management Suspicion and Disappointment?*, Vrije University, 1986.

Howard, J. A., Hulbert, J. and Farley, J. U., 'Organizational analysis and information systems design: A decision-process perspective', *Journal of Business Research*, vol. 3, no. 2, 1975, pp. 133–48.

Hulbert, J., Farley, J. U. and Howard, J. A., 'Information processing and decision making in marketing organizations', *Journal of Marketing Research*, vol. 9, no. 2, 1972, pp. 75–7.

Jemison, D. B., 'The influence of boundary spanning roles in strategic decision making', *Journal of Management Studies*, vol. 21, no. 2, 1984, pp. 131–52.

Jeuck, J. E., 'Marketing research: milestone or millstone?', *Journal of Marketing*, vol. 17, 1953, pp. 381–7.

Keen, P. G. W., *Information Systems and Organizational Change*, Massachusetts Institute of Technology, Boston, 1980.

Kotler, P., *Marketing Decision Making: A Model Building Approach*, Holt Rinehart and Winston, 1971.

Leech, M., 'Research's future imperative', *Marketing*, 16 July 1980, pp. 33–4.

Lyonski, S., 'A boundary theory investigation of the product manager's role', *Journal of Marketing*, vol. 49, Winter 1985, pp. 26–40.

Martell, D., 'Marketing information and new technology' in N. Piercy (ed.), *Management Information Systems: The Technology Challenge*, Croom Helm, 1986.

Mason, R. and Mitroff, I., 'A program of research on management information systems', *Management Science*, vol. 19, 1973, pp. 475–8.

May, J. P., 'Marketing research: illuminating neglected areas', *Journal of the Market Research Society*, vol. 23, no. 3, 1981, pp. 127–36.

Mintzberg, H., 'Planning on the left side and managing on the right', *Harvard Business Review*, vol. 54, no. 4, 1985.

Munro, M. C., 'Determining the manager's information needs', *Journal of Systems Management*, vol. 29, no. 6, 1978, pp. 34–9.

Perdikis, P., *Marketing Information Systems for Strategic Planning*, MSc Dissertation, University of Wales Institute of Science & Technology, 1984.

Piercy, N., *Low-cost Marketing Analysis*, MCB, 1978.

Piercy, N., 'Behavioural constraints on marketing information systems', *European Journal of Marketing*, vol. 13, no. 8, 1979, pp. 261–70.

Piercy, N., 'Marketing information – bridging the quicksand between technology and decision-making, *Quarterly Review of Marketing*, vol. 7, no. 1, 1981, pp. 1–15.

Piercy, N., 'Information processing – the newest mix element', in M. Christopher, M. McDonald and A. Rushton (eds), *Back to Basics: the 4Ps Revisited*, Marketing Education Group Conference Proceedings, 1983a.

Piercy, N., 'Retailer information power: the channel marketing information system', *Marketing Intelligence and Planning*, vol. 1, no. 1, 1983b, pp. 40–55.

Piercy, N., 'Marketing and new technology' in N. Piercy (ed.), *The Management Implications of New Information Technology*, Croom Helm, 1984.

Piercy, N., *Marketing Organisation: An Analysis of Information Processing, Power and Politics*, Allen and Unwin, 1985.

Piercy, N., *Marketing Budgeting – A Political and Organizational Model*, Croom Helm, 1986a.

Piercy, N. (ed.), *Marketing Asset Accounting*, MCB University Press, 1986b.

Piercy, N., 'The role and function of the chief marketing executive and the marketing department', *Journal of Marketing Management*, vol. 1, no. 3, 1986c, pp. 265–90.

Piercy, N., 'The model of organization', *Marketing*, 15 May 1986d, pp. 21–3.

Piercy, N. and Evans, M., *Managing Marketing Information*, Croom Helm, 1983.

Rackoff, N., Wiseman, C. and Ullrich, W. A., 'Information systems for competitive advantage: implementation of a planning process', *Management Information Systems Quarterly*, December 1985, pp. 285–94.

Reddy, N. M., and Marvin M. P., 'Developing a manufacturer-distributor information partnership', *Industrial Marketing Management*, vol. 15, 1986, pp. 157–63.

Rockart, J. F., *A New Approach to Defining the Chief Executive's Information Needs*, Centre for Information Systems Research, Massachusetts Institute of Technology, 1978.

Rubin, R. S., 'Save your information system from the experts', *Harvard Business Review*, July-August 1986, pp. 22–4.

Samuels, J. A., 'Research to help plan the future of a seaside resort', Proceedings: 12th Marketing Theory Seminar, Lancaster, 1973.

Schlackman, W., 'The participation concept as a key factor in integrating professional services within the modern corporation', ADMAP, vol. 15, no. 6, 1979, pp. 292–7.

Shrivastava, P. and Etgar, M., 'A decision support system for strategic marketing decisions', *Systems, Objectives, Solutions*, vol. 4, 1984, pp. 131–9.

Simmonds, K., 'The accounting assessment of competitive position' in N. Piercy (ed.), *Marketing Asset Accounting*, MCB, 1986.

Tricker, R. I., 'Ten myths of management information', *Management Accounting*, vol. 49, no. 8, 1971, pp. 231–3.

Uhl, K. P., 'Marketing information systems', in Ferber, R. (ed.), *Handbook of Marketing Research*, McGraw-Hill, 1974.

Vasconcellos, P., 'Environmental analysis for strategic planning', *Management Planning*, January-February, 1985, pp. 23–30.

Westwood, R. A., Palmer, J. B., Zeithin D. M., Levine, D. M., Thio, K. and Charley, R., 'Integrated information systems', *Journal of the Marketing Research Society*, vol. 17, no. 3, 1975, pp. 127–82.

Wilson, R. M. S., *Financial Dimensions of Marketing*, Macmillan, 1981.

Wiseman, C. and Macmillan, I. C., 'Creating competitive weapons from information systems', *Journal of Business Strategy*, Autumn 1984, pp. 42–9.

PART THREE

Managing the marketing function

14
Managing the marketing mix

PETER DOYLE

Introduction

This chapter evaluates the concept of the marketing mix and its main constituent elements and addresses the problems inherent in uniting these into unique and distinctive combinations. Subsequent chapters will then examine the key considerations associated with each of the main mix elements: product development and management; pricing; selling; advertising and promotion; and distribution and service.

In most firms marketing mix decisions are led by the marketing department, but inevitably other functional areas play a key role. Engineering and R & D management are significantly involved in product policy; finance, production and other departments influence pricing and distribution decisions. Hence management of the marketing mix is unlikely to be effective without a marketing orientation forming a common culture throughout the business. In many firms, able marketing decision makers are frustrated by a production-orientated approach and lack of understanding of the marketing concept among other functional areas. These issues are discussed by Baker in Chapter 1.

Marketing mix decisions usually centre around a particular product or service, or closely related group of products and services. However, as Wensley shows in Chapter 3 the decisions are normally circumscribed by strategic considerations. Some products may have been singled out by top management as 'stars' and as such will be more abundantly financed to achieve longer term goals. Other products at the end of their life cycle, might be 'milked' – advertising and support cut-back, and prices pushed up to generate cash flow. The types of portfolio planning techniques discussed in Part One are now a common influence in marketing mix decisions.

In the following pages the essential background to marketing mix management is discussed: target marketing; the differential advantage and the key analyses for developing the marketing mix.

There are two key decisions which are central to marketing management: the selection of target markets which determine where the firm will compete and the design of the marketing mix (product, price, promotion and distribution method) which will determine its success in these markets.

Selection of target markets

A market is defined as the set of actual and potential buyers of a product. In today's rapidly changing environment products and markets have a limited life expectancy. A firm which does not update and change its products and markets is unlikely to be successful for long. A major job of management is to determine which markets offer the business opportunities for profit and growth in the future. Market research is the tool used to generate the information for reaching such decisions. Three areas for research are particularly important. First, the firm will want to estimate the size and growth potential of alternative markets since in general it will prefer to operate in growth rather than mature or declining markets. Second, it will wish to judge the strength of competition in candidate markets. How tough is the competition? Will it be possible to carve out a niche without strong reaction from existing competitors? Third, choice of target market will be influenced by the fit of the market requirements with the firm's own strengths and weaknesses. A heavy engineering company, for example, is unlikely to be effective in switching to fast-moving consumer goods where it lacks technological or marketing expertise. In general, a company will seek product and market opportunities in areas where it has some expertise which can form the basis for a competitive edge.

After a broad market is identified comes the key task of *market segmentation*. *Undifferentiated marketing* (Figure 14.1), a single marketing mix offered to the entire market, is rarely successful because markets are not homogenous but made up of different types of buyers with diverse wants regarding product benefits, price, channels of distribution and service. A market segment is a group of buyers with similar purchasing characteristics. For example, the car market might be divided into an economy segment (buyers looking for a cheap form of car transportation), a status segment, a sporting-orientated segment, etc. In developing a marketing plan, the marketers usually have to design appropriate offers for each segment if they are to compete. *Differential marketing* is the policy of attacking the market by tailoring separate product and marketing programmes for each segment. *Concentrated marketing* is often the best strategy for the smaller firm. This entails selecting to compete in one segment and developing the most effective marketing mix for this submarket. Ford, for example, now pursue a policy of differentiated marketing whereas Volkswagen has traditionally concentrated on the smaller car market.

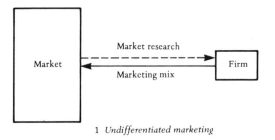

1 *Undifferentiated marketing*

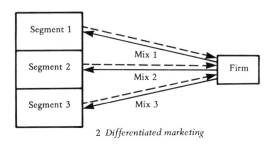

2 *Differentiated marketing*

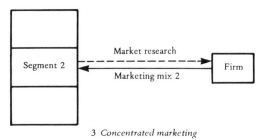

3 *Concentrated marketing*

Figure 14.1 *Marketing segmentation and alternative marketing strategies*

Developing the marketing mix

The marketing mix is the set of choices which defines the firm's offer to its target market. McCarthy (1981) has popularized the four Ps definition of the marketing mix – product, place, promotion and price (Table 14.1). Buyers in the target segment have a set of wants and by research and successful adaption marketers will develop an offer to match them (Figure 14.2). 'Product' includes a number of decision elements as do the other Ps shown in Table 14.1. As emphasized earlier, the marketing mix for one segment may need to be quite different from

Table 14.1 *Components of the marketing mix*

Product	Price	Promotion	Place
Quality	List price	Advertising	Distributors
Features	Discounts	Personal selling	Retailers
Name	Allowances	Sales promotion	Locations
Packaging	Credit	Public relations	Inventory
Services			Transport
Guarantees			

that of another. In tailoring its mix a firm will seek to offer one which target customers will see as superior to that offered by competition. This goal of offering a marketing mix superior to competition is termed the *differential advantage*.

Three key marketing principles

In analysing marketing problems and developing marketing plans three concepts play a central role: marketing segmentation, the differential advantage and positioning strategy.

Market segmentation

Pigou (1932) and Chamberlin (1938) developed the basic theory of market segmentation, showing that where different segments exist with separate demand functions, the monopolist would maximize profits by charging different prices to the two segments. There are many practical examples of this type of price discrimination, for example a public utility charging different rates for business and domestic consumers. The concept of segmentation in marketing, however, is much more general. The marketer recognizes that consumers differ not only in the price they will pay, but in a wide range of benefits they expect from the 'product' and its method of delivery. The firm can discriminate not only in price but potentially in any of the four Ps. For example, the market for electronic calculators is made up of a number of segments including a segment of 'scientific users', an 'office' segment and a 'general public' segment. Each segment is likely to have a different price elasticity but in addition each desires different 'products': the scientific segment requiring more sophisticated features and offices wanting greater robustness for example. The chan-

nels utilized will also vary: scientists will be best sold to via personal selling or specialist journals, offices via specific distributors and the general public through the major retail chains. Similarly, the advertising and promotional strategies will differ in media and message between each segment.

Segmentation is central to marketing because different customer groups imply different marketing mix strategies. The technique of segmenting a market also reveals profit opportunities and 'strategic windows' (Abell, 1978) for new competitors to challenge established market leaders. As a market develops new segments open up and older ones decline. Within most markets is a mix of fierce and relatively weak competitive segments, slow and high growth segments (for example the segment of people wanting large, luxury cars has declined relative to the economy segment). The marketing strategist will be seeking to identify those dynamic segments offering the best growth and profit possibilities.

Differential advantage

Target market segmentation is, however, insufficient for strategic planning since, in general, other companies will also be competing for any segment chosen. To be successful marketers must also develop a differential advantage which will distinguish their offer from competitors in the segment. Only by creating such a differential advantage can the firm ordinarily obtain high profits. In a market where no firm has a differential advantage consumers choose on the basis of price, and price or 'perfect' competition ensures that profits are pushed towards zero. The task of the modern business is to seek what may be termed a 'quasi-monopoly' – to make itself unique to consumers so that they will not switch to

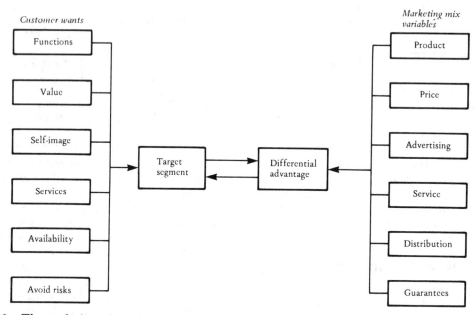

Figure 14.2 *The marketing mix and differential advantage: matching customer wants*

competitors for minor price advantages. High profit firms such as IBM, Marks and Spencer, Avon Cosmetics, Kodak, Yamaha and Procter & Gamble are generally those which have succeeded in creating such consumer preferences. These differential advantages may be obtained potentially via any element of the marketing mix – creating a superior product to competition, more attractive designs, better service, more effective distribution, better advertising or selling, and so on. The keys are understanding that an 'advantage' is based upon research into what customers really value and that a 'differential' is derived from an evaluation of competitive strategies and offers.

Positioning strategy

Positioning is the amalgam of these two earlier principles. Positioning strategy refers to the choice of target market segment which describes the customers the business will seek to serve, and the choice of differential advantage which defines how it will compete with rivals in the segment. Thus Porsche is positioned in the prestige segment of the car market with a differential advantage based on technical performance. The Mothercare store is positioned to serve mothers with young children with a differential advantage based on breadth of merchandise assortment for that target segment. The appropriateness and effectiveness of the positioning strategy is the major determinant of a business' growth and profit performance.

Key analyses for developing marketing strategy

In formulating its choice of target market segment, marketing mix and differential advantage the firm will focus its research in six major areas:

Market analysis

As described earlier, before committing itself further the company should assess the growth and profit opportunities likely to be open to it in the candidate market.

Customer analysis

The firm will need to research how the market is segmented, which of these segments are the most attractive and what are the benefits desired by customers within each of these segments. Knowledge of such factors will be central to designing its product and offer. In addition, to develop its promotional and distribution strategy it will need to determine who are the key people affecting product choice in the buying group (the household or buying organization) and what type of buying process occurs before a decision is reached (for example how information is sought, how alternatives are compared).

Competitive analysis

Developing a differential advantage means making target buyers an offer superior to competition. Clearly, therefore, this strategy requires identifying who the competitors are now and whether new ones may emerge in the future. The marketer needs to judge what their strategic objectives are, how their offer is perceived by buyers and how it may change in the future. Finally, it is crucial to estimate how competitors are likely to react to any strategic initiative on your part. If you introduce a new product or cut prices in an effort to gain market share, is this initiative likely to be nullified by speedy retaliation from competition? (For a thorough discussion of competitive analysis see Porter, 1980.)

Trade analysis

Most companies do not sell all their goods directly to the final consumer but use trade intermediaries – wholesalers, distributors, agents and retailers to do this for them. Such an arrangement offers the company economies in marketing and distribution and the opportunity to sell to wider markets. On the other hand, these intermediaries are normally independent and their commerical goals will not be identical to those of the individual manufacturers they buy from. Thus the company will need to consider how to motivate the trade to give its product preferential treatment in their presentations to the public.

Star *et al.* (1977) suggest the manufacturer's trade analysis should be focused around the following questions:

1. What role does the product play in the trade's merchandise mix (for example traffic generation or margin generation)?
2. How does the trade merchandise the product (for example self-service versus personal selling)?
3. How satisfied is the trade with the marketing and trade strategies of competitors?
4. What differential advantage might be obtained through actions such as generous trade terms, extensive advertising, improved delivery, etc?

Environmental analysis

Strategy formulation needs also to consider the changing environment of the business. Success will be affected by broad changes in the economic, demographic, sociopolitical and technological environment. The major US car companies, for example, which concentrated on large, heavy petrol-consuming vehicles, were severely hit by the Middle East crisis and the rapid rise in oil prices after 1973. In the more immediate marketing environment, management must study the problems and opportunities being created by new consumer tastes, changing patterns of distribution (for example from independent shops to multiple grocery-type shops) and emerging products. Such forces curtail the product life cycle of existing products and necessitate continual strategic innovation and repositioning if the firm is to maintain its viability.

Economic and stakeholder analysis

In assessing a strategy the firm will want to assess the financial implications and its impact on stakeholder groups of importance to the firm. For a business the strategy will need to generate an adequate level of profit to satisfy shareholders and provide for the firm's continuing investment requirements. Since investment generally anticipates profit return, the cash requirements will also have to be considered – can the business finance the marketing strategy? Other stakeholder or interest groups that may constrain the policy include consumerist organizations, the local community, government regulatory bodies, unions and suppliers. The well designed strategy will have considered the impacts on all relevant parties.

Marketing mix decisions

Market research and business appraisal to complete

these six analyses, together with judgements about how the company is to position itself against potential target market segments and to develop a differential advantage are implemented by management decisions on the marketing mix. Important normative rules for optimizing the marketing mix have been developed by economists. These rules stem from the classical model of the firm in which output and price are the only decision variables and where sales are optimized at the point at which marginal revenue equals marginal cost. Dorfman and Steiner (1954) extended this to include other 'marketing mix' variables, namely advertising and product quality. The Dorfman–Steiner theorem showed that short-run profits are maximized where the company balances lower prices, increased advertising expenditure and higher quality products in such a way as to equate:

$$\xi q \frac{P}{C} = \xi = \mu$$

where the first expression is the elasticity of demand with respect to quality improvement multiplied by price over average unit cost, the second is the price elasticity of demand and the third is the marginal revenue product of advertizing.

The Dorfman–Steiner theorem provides an important insight for designing the marketing mix and several studies have tried to estimate and apply their rule (for example, Lambin, 1969; Corstjens and Doyle, 1981). In practice, however, its use is limited for a number of important reasons. In particular, it is extremely difficult to estimate these marginal effects, especially in oligopolistic markets where competitive reaction is a major dilemma and where many variables (advertising, intensity of distribution and price) interact with one another. Also, the firm is generally not seeking to maximize profits solely, but may have a range of strategic goals (growth, risk avoidance, supporting complementary products in the firm's range, etc.). Some of these issues become clearer when the elements of the marketing mix are considered.

Product policy

Economic theory has little to say about product policy because the theory of consumer behaviour treats the products themselves rather than the benefits or characteristics they possess as the direct objects of utility. Under such an assumption little can be said about the key questions of how one product competes with another or how one can develop a superior product. Recently economists have tried to fill this gap by developing a new theory of consumer behaviour which defines a product as a bundle of characteristics which are the ultimate goal of the buyer. As Lancaster (1966) has shown this opens the possibility of a much more fruitful set of insights into consumer behaviour.

Paradoxically this notion that consumers are interested in the benefits provided by a marketer's offer rather than the product itself has always been central to marketing theory. The 'new economics' mirrors an approach which has been long applied in marketing to the study of brand preferences (for a discussion see Ratchford, 1975). To a marketing manager a product is the constellation of benefits generated by the physical product, its design, features, packaging, style and service support which together provide satisfaction to the consumer. It is often said that much of IBM's success was based on its recognition that its cost and complexity will make computers unattractive to industry executives. At the same time, IBM knew that these executives increasingly needed more effective systems for efficiently and rapidly handling and manipulating information. IBM's offer was not a computer but a 'management information system' made up not only of the hardware but software, attractive input/output and related peripherals, technical support, training, installation, operational back-up and easy financial arrangements. The founder of Revlon Cosmetics, one of the most successful consumer goods companies, put the distinction between products and benefits more colourfully when he said 'in the factory we make cosmetics, in the store we sell hope!'

For marketing it is crucial to see how the product's benefits are perceived by consumers rather than how they are defined by production experts. *Product positioning* is a market research technique which seeks to elicit from buyers a description or 'map' of how alternative brands are perceived. Figure 12.3 shows a positioning study by Johnson (1971) of the US beer market. The dimensions (characteristics) buyers appear to use when judging

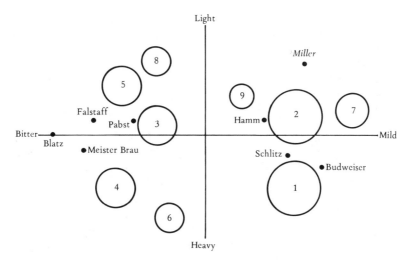

Figure 14.3 *A product positioning study of the US beer market*

beers are lightness and mildness. The circles show the preference of buyers. Since, of course, different segments have differing tastes these are spread, the radius of the circle indicates the estimated size of each consumer segment. Positioning studies have obvious uses in product planning: they show the strengths and weaknesses of the manufacturers' brands along the dimensions which are important to consumers, they show how closely competitive brands are seen and they indicate where different segment preferences are. Such insights have obvious implications for repositioning the product by quality changes, design, packaging or advertising modifications and also for new product development.

Product positioning models suggest seven alternative strategies marketers can pursue by modifying their product or persuasive communications (Boyd et al., 1972):

1 Developing a new brand.
2 Modifying the existing brand.
3 Altering beliefs about the company's brand.
4 Altering beliefs about the competitors' brands.
5 Altering the importance attached to the individual characteristics.
6 Calling attention to neglected characteristics.
7 Shifting consumer preferences.

Pricing policy

The economic theory of price shows that profits are maximized when prices are set to equate marginal revenue and marginal cost. An obvious practical problem is that other variables usually affect demand both independently and interactively with price, for example some studies have shown that advertising increases price elasticity (Frank, et al., 1972). In principle, modern econometrics provides methods of estimation in such circumstances and there have been a number of successful empirical applications published (see Palda, 1969).

In general, however, few firms explicitly follow the economic model in developing pricing policy. Most find estimating the parameters of the demand function too difficult, time-consuming and expensive. In addition, with such a rapidly changing marketing environment, few would expect such parameters to be stable. In practice, management price on the basis of more intuitive judgements about the nature of cost, demand and competition. Pricing is also significantly affected by the firm's objectives. Where the firm has, for example, a long run strategic goal of winning a dominant market share then its price is likely to be significantly lower than for a firm aiming to maximize current profits.

In setting prices the manufacturer has to consider not only its own profitability and the reaction of buyers, but other parties too. The company's distributors must be given an adequate profit margin to ensure that they have sufficient incentive to push the product. The decision maker will also have to consider the likely reaction of competitors to a switch in pricing policy. Not only existing competitors are affected by pricing policy but the level of profit margin is likely to influence the entry rate of new competitors. From time to time, government agencies also affect pricing policy for anti-inflation or anti-monopoly reasons.

Studies show that in practice almost all companies price on the basis of cost-plus. Price is determined by adding some fixed percentage to total unit cost. Unfortunately such findings do not really tell us much without a theory of how the mark-up percentage is determined. The major determinant of the potential mark-up is the product's differential advantage, the greater the perceived value it has over competitive products the more the consumer will pay. The most sophisticated marketing companies like Hewlett-Packard and 3M Corporation calculate this perceived value to the consumer in considerable detail before making a pricing decision (Shapiro and Jackson, 1978). The McKinsey management consulting firm advocates calculating this value by comparing the product's total costs and benefits with those of a 'reference product' for example the market leader.

For example, consider a company seeking to price a new industrial product X in a market where the brand leader is product Y. Users of Y pay £3,000 for the product, another £2,000 to set up the product (for example transportation, engineering, installation) and over the life of the product spend another £5,000 in maintenance and operating costs, making a total life cycle cost of £10,000. Suppose the new product X has features which lower start-up and post-purchase costs to £4,000, yielding a £3,000 life cycle saving. Then the economic value to the buyer of product X is £6,000. That is, the consumer should be willing to pay up to £6,000 for the new product. At £6,000 there would be no incentive to switch from the brand leader. Hence, the supplier might decide to price it at £4,000 to produce a £2,000 'customer savings incentive'.

The most common types of pricing policies firms pursue in practice are the following:

Market penetration pricing

Here the firm prices low, sacrificing short-term profits, to aim at a dominant market share. Circumstances favouring this policy are:

1 Where the market is highly price elastic,
2 Where total unit costs will decline substantially with production experience,
3 Where a low price will discourage new competitors entering the market.

Market skimming pricing

This entails setting high initial prices which yield high profit margins over a relatively small volume and generally for a short period of time. It is a viable option where:

1 A segment of significant size exists which will buy at the high initial price,
2 The firm has limited production capacity or resources with which to expand,
3 The high initial price will not attract an immediate competitive takeover of the market,
4 The high price creates an image of a superior product.

Cost orientated pricing

Most firms, as noted, set prices largely on the basis of product costs. *Mark-up pricing* and cost-plus pricing set price by adding some fixed percentage to the unit cost. *Target pricing* is another cost-orientated pricing approach that sets prices to achieve a certain target return on investment.

Perceived value pricing

Unlike the cost orientated policies, this approach, as described earlier, bases price on demand considerations – on how the buyers perceive the value of the product relative to competition. To be effective this approach requires market research to obtain an accurate picture of the market's perceptions.

Price discrimination

This is another common form of demand pricing whereby the firm seeks to charge different types of customer with different prices for the same or similar product.

Where segments exist with different price elasticities this type of discrimination allows the firm to achieve higher profits. To be successful, customers in the higher price segment must not be allowed to buy from the lower price segment. In addition, the practice should not lead to serious customer resentment.

Companies change their prices and strategies over time. The most common stimuli to price increases are rising costs of increased demand for the firm's product. Price cutting can be initiated from excess capacity in the industry, the loss of market share or because the company decides to strengthen its position in the market.

Promotional policy

After a company has designed a product and offer to match the wants of its target market segment, it needs to communicate this offer to buyers and persuade them to try it.

There are four main tools which may be used to achieve these goals: advertising; personal selling; sales promotion and public relations. In general, before purchasing a product buyers have to be brought through various stages of the communications process. First, they have to be made *aware* of the product's existence. Second, they have to *comprehend* the benefits the product offers. Third, they need to become *convinced* that it will meet their wants. Finally, they have to be brought to the point of making a positive *purchase* decision (Aaker and Myers, 1982).

The different communications tools are frequently used to achieve specific communications goals. Advertising is particularly good at making the market aware of a new product, but it is usually far less effective than personal selling at closing the sale. Personal selling is usually a very costly means of creating awareness and comprehension, but more efficient at stimulating conviction and purchase. There are also differences between consumer and industrial goods. Sales promotion and publicity tend to be used for both types of marketing but because of the larger number of buyers which characterize consumer marketing, mass media advertising is more important there, whereas personal selling is usually the major selling medium in industrial marketing.

Here we shall note the key decision areas in advertising. In planning advertising, marketers, usually in conjunction with their advertising agency, will need to make five decisions. First, they will need a clear definition of the target market segment to which the advertising is to be directed. They will

then need to determine the most effective media (newspapers, journals, TV, radio, posters, etc.) for getting their message to these people. Increasingly, agencies use a computer program to seek an optimum combination of media which will deliver the desired number of exposures to the target audience (Broadbent, 1977). Linear programming, heuristic programming and simulation models have all been used as aids to help planners determine the media mix which maximizes effective exposure subject to budget and other company constraints. The third area for decision is on the form and content of the message or copy to be expressed in the advertising. In general, the advertising agency will try to create a message which will express the differential advantage of the product in a manner which makes it believable, desirable and exclusive. The other two decision areas concern determining how much should be spent on advertising and how the investment should be subsequently evaluated and controlled.

Econometric studies have been widely used to estimate the payoff of advertising and determine the optimum advertising budget. For example, in a study for a major alcoholic drink product, Corstjens and Doyle (1981) used time series data to estimate the demand function of the brand as:

$$q_t = 4.27 - 0.004B_t + 0.245A_t - 1.20P_t + 0.672q_{t-1}$$

where q_t = sales of the brands at time t in units, B_t = industry sales of the product class, A_t = brand advertizing expenditure (in logs) and P_t = price (in logs) of the brand at time t.

This equation explained 85 per cent of the variation in sales of the brand. From this it was possible to calculate the short- and long-term advertising elasticities for the brand as 0.14 and 0.43 respectively. Then using the Dorfman-Steiner theorem (which shows that at the optimal level of advertising, the marginal revenue product of advertising equals the price elasticity of demand), it was shown that the optimal long-term advertising ratio was 13 per cent of sales for this brand.

Distribution policy

Distribution management is concerned with decisions on moving goods from the producer to the target consumers. Decisions about distribution channels are very important because they intimately affect all other marketing mix choices and because once made they are not easily changed. In principle, a manufacturer can choose between selling the goods directly to the consumer and using a variety of distributors and retailers.

The marketing distribution channel undertakes a number of tasks besides the physical transportation and storing of goods. Intermediaries may also undertake market research for the manufacturer, promotion, pricing and negotiation with the customer, and financing the sale and purchase of the goods. Manufacturers use intermediaries to perform some or all of these functions as this often leads to superior efficiency in marketing the goods to the customers. Intermediaries, through their experience, specialization and contacts can often offer the manufacturer more than it can achieve by going direct.

In developing a distribution strategy the manufacturer will make choices about the types of intermediary to use (agencies, distributors, retailers etc.), the number to use, the specific tasks they are to undertake (storage, advertising, pricing, transport, etc.) under which the intermediary will undertake these tasks. Central to the problem of channel management is the recognition that distributors are independent businesses with goals that are at least partially conflicting with those of the manufacturer. Whether the manufacturer can design the channel to meet its own goals depends upon the power it has and the ability to motivate the intermediaries to cooperate. Knowledge of these marketing issues has been enriched by a considerable number of research studies by behavioural scientists (for example Stern and El-Ansary, 1977). One of the remarkable changes in the last two decades has been the growth in power of the major retail chains at the expense of grocery manufacturers. Increasing concentration in grocery retailing has meant that manufacturers depend on the major chains to give them effective distribution and the retailers have not been slow to utilize this power in demanding higher margins and better terms from their suppliers in exchange for cooperation.

In choosing distribution channels the manufacturer will seek intermediaries which meet four criteria. First, intermediaries should be orientated to serving its target market. A manufacturer of fashionwear for upper income women will need to get its product into retail outlets effectively serving such a clientele. Second, the firm will want distributors which help it to exploit its differential advantage. If the product's competitive edge is in sophisticated technology features offering cost savings to buyers, then the manufacturer will need dealers capable of explaining these benefits to prospects. Third, working with a particular channel must be economically rational for the manufacturer. Direct selling with a company sales force is a powerful channel but it is too expensive for companies without a significant market share. Finally, the manufacturer will be influenced by the control and motivation of prospective intermediaries. A distributor selling a wide range of successful competitive products might give insufficient attention to a newcomer's product.

Distribution channels once established are not easy to change. Yet as the manufacturer's circumstances or the market evolves it often becomes necessary to adapt or even radically revise existing distribution channels. When starting out a manufacturer may choose distributors to market its product because this will reduce overhead costs. But if the company grows it is likely to become increasingly financially attractive to switch from distributors to direct selling because the higher overheads can now be spread over a larger volume. In addition, channels, like products, are subject to life cycles and highly successful forms of distribution give way to new forms more effectively geared to today's markets. Variety stores and small supermarkets have lost ground to superstores, catalogue showrooms and discount stores (see Davidson *et al.*, 1976). Such forces mean that the firm must be continually monitoring the performance and prospects of its distribution arrangements and be prepared to adapt them when conditions change.

Conclusion

In today's rapidly changing and highly competitive international environment a business can be successful only if its offer matches the wants of buyers at least as effectively as its best competitors. Marketing management is the task of planning this match. It is based upon the analysis of customers, competitors and distributors, the selection of target market segments and the design of marketing mixes which will provide the firm with a differential advantage. An organization's success in creating a differential advantage determines its international competitiveness and profit performance.

The changing environment – changing wants, new competitors and technologies, different stakeholder pressures on the firm mean that a differential advantage is never secure. Change requires the firm to continually reposition itself by shifting from declining to emerging market segments and renewing its differential advantage by such measures as improving its product features, adapting new technologies or higher levels of service. Businesses which fail to develop such repositioning strategies gradually lose contact with buyers and give way to firms which are more successfully marketing orientated.

References

Aaker, D. A. and Morgan, J. G., *Advertising Management*, *Prentice-Hall, 1982*.

Abell, D.F., 'Strategic Windows', *Journal of Marketing*, vol. 42, no. 2, April, 1978, pp. 21–6.

Boyd, H. W., Ray, M.L. and Strong, E.C., 'An Attitudinal Framework for Advertising Strategy', *Journal of Marketing*, vol. 36, no. 2, April 1972, pp. 27–33.

Broadbent, S., *Spending Advertising Money*, Business Books, 1977.

Chamberlin, E. H., *The Theory of Monopolistic Competition*, Harvard University Press, 1938.

Corstjens, M. and Doyle, P., 'Evaluating the Profitability of Advertising for Heavily Advertised Brands', *European Journal of Operational Research*, vol. 8, no. 3, November 1981, pp. 249–55.

Davidson, W. R., Bates A. D. and Bass, S. J. 'The Retail Life Cycle', *Harvard Business Review*, vol. 54, no. 6, November 1976, pp. 94–105.

Dorfman, R. and Steiner, P.O., 'Optimal Advertising and Optimal Quality', *American Economic Review*, vol. 59, June, 1954 pp. 817–31.

Frank, R.E., Massy W. F. and Wind, Y., *Market Segmentation*, Prentice-Hall, 1972.

Johnson, R. M., 'Market Segmentation: A Strategic Management Tool', *Journal of Marketing Research*, vol. 8, no. 1, February 1971, pp. 15–23.

Lambin, J. J., 'Measuring the Profitability of Advertising: An Empirical Study', *Journal of Industrial Economics*, vol. 17, no. 2, April 1969, pp. 86–103.

Lancaster, K. J., 'A New Approach to Consumer Theory', *Journal of Political Economy*, vol. 74, no.2, April 1966, pp. 132–57.

McCarthy, E.J., *Basic Marketing*, Irwin, 1981.

Palda, K. S., *Economic Analysis for Marketing Decisions*, Prentice-Hall, 1969.

Pigou, A. C., *The Economics of Welfare*, Macmillan, 1932.

Porter, M.E., *Competitive strategy*, Macmillan, 1980.

Ratchford, B.T., 'The New Economic Theory of Consumer Behaviour: An Interpretive Essay', *Journal of Consumer Research*, vol. 2, September 1975, pp. 65–75.

Shapiro, B.P. and Jackson, B.B., 'Industrial Pricing to Meet Consumer Needs, *Harvard Business Review*, vol. 56, no. 6, November 1978, pp. 119–27.

Star, S.H., Davis, N.J. *et al.*, *Problems in Marketing*, 5th ed., McGraw-Hill, 1977.

Stern, L. W. and El-Ansary, A. I. *Marketing Channels*, Prentice-Hall, 1977.

15
Product development and management
MICHAEL J. THOMAS

Introduction

Product development and management is a major responsibility, perhaps preoccupation for most marketing managers, as the product or service offerings of a company (or an organization) determine the nature of the business and the marketplace's perception of the business. In this sense it is the core of the marketing management function. As such it is tempting to cover an enormous variety of topics, all of which might reasonably be included under the umbrella of product development and management. It is not my intention to do this and readers seeking further information and enlightenment should consult the key readings at the end of this book.

This chapter will concentrate on a limited number of topics, all of which I judge to be of paramount importance. These topics are product development, strategic management of the product mix, the product life cycle, portfolio management, productivity analysis and the future of product/brand management.

Product development

It should not be a matter for disagreement. In the environment of global competition and accelerating technological development and innovation that is the reality of the contemporary trading environment, every company must be thinking about product development. Every marketing company has to be alert to quickly developing opportunities – it must focus on markets or product categories which it can suitably exploit, consistent with company objectives, resources, capabilities and strengths. Overriding consideration must be given to securing a competitive advantage. But before going any further I want to lay two markers down. First, a quotation from the Annual Report of the Boston Consulting Group, 1982. It is about the nature of competitive advantage.

In the real world of business competition, each survivor is uniquely superior to all others in some significant way, no matter how subtle the difference. That competitor dominates his unique niche or his life cycle is short.

The nearly infinite possible combinations of customer characteristics, costs, logistics, methodology, etc., make it possible for vast numbers of competitors to co-exist. And each competitor may simultaneously be defending its niche against multiple unique antagonists.

Market share and industry structure are ambiguous terms when such a complex spectrum of individual differences is woven into a web of relationships in which no given competitor has exactly the same competitors as any other.

Strategy development starts with the task of identifying the comparative differentials for each competitor that constitutes a constraint. The next step is to determine the tradeoffs and match-ups that make competitive equilibrium possible. The strategy itself must aim at enlarging either the scope or the depth of the competitive advantage.

Ability to adapt to changing competition determines each competitor's life cycle. The web of customers, suppliers and competitors and the external environment of resources and conditions are constantly shifting. When any competitor adapts to each shift, then the equilibrium between competitors is changed too. Each must adapt. Your competitor is your environment. As a consequence, the whole competitive network is constantly evolving.

Every competitor that survives must be superior to all others with respect to some unique combination of external conditions. Every company dominates its own unique competitive segment. That domination may be by a thin margin, but if a competitor fails to be superior on its own turf, it will inevitably be crowded out.

Second, a cautionary note to demonstrate if nothing else proper humility and understanding by a marketing man that the market pull model to which most of us subscribe is not without its problems. The quotation is from an American source (*The McKinsey Quarterly*, Autumn, 1972). In the UK it would be possible to argue that the technology push model has been a frequent source of commercial failure. Thus I want the discussion that follows to be read in the context of there being no 'one best way'.

Strict adherence to the marketing concept has damaged American business. It has led to a dearth of true innovation and it has shifted the strategic focus of the firm away from the product to other elements of the marketing mix, elements that can be manipulated very successfully in the short run but which leave the business vulnerable in the longer term.

A market-driven new-product strategy provides little encouragement for technological discoveries, inventions, or significant breakthroughs; the 'technology push' model has given way to the 'market pull' model.

The market pull model generally yields good results, especially for industries such as packaged goods. And it seems to work in the short run. But whether such a model is desirable for a company or an entire industry in the long run, and whether it suits high-technology and more complex product classes, is certainly debatable.

A market-oriented R & D strategy necessarily leads to low-risk product modifications, extensions and style changes. Product proliferation, a disease of the 1970s, has been one result. Market-derived new product ideas will usually result in the ordinary.

Though the metaphor of war and the thoughts of Clausewitz can be overdone, it is useful to delineate the search for competitive advantage in the following terms:

- Choose where to fight, do not let the enemy pick the battlefield.
- Employ superior forces in number and quality.
- Concentrate your forces on the decisive point.
- Employ surprise to increase your advantage.
- Maintain the strength of your troops to keep fighting longer.
- Once victory is achieved, do not let the enemy recover.

These strictures need a context. Choosing where to fight is about excellence in marketing intelligence, marketing research and technological originality. Knowing your competitors better than they know themselves, understanding their strengths – the sources of their competitive advantage – and weaknesses will help to pinpoint where to fight. Your forces, the combined forces of new product development teams and the teams that take new products to launch need to be better than those of your competitors – in number and quality. Product search and development should not be spread over too wide a field. Though there will always be room for speculative endeavours, in general the goal should be clearly defined, the precise nature of the competitive advantage that is being sought defined. Surprise can involve execution and timing. Execution done without the world knowing precisely what is going on, and timing of launch and commercialization done with extreme care. Continuous support of the troops is vital. Victory does not usually come in the short term, rarely is the quick preemptive strike a characteristic of market success. Sustaining your initial advantage and building upon it is something the Japanese understand much better than many of their competitors, while sacrifice of short-term profit for medium-term market leadership is much to their liking. And once victory is achieved, then it must be sustained by continuous marketing support – when the brand becomes more important than the product.

The marketing/R & D interface is critically important to new product development, and one or two comments about it are in order. The long and well-documented history of new product failures in this country is replete with examples of products coming to market without any clear analysis of the nature of the need or want they are supposed to meet. Technology push has a bad track record in the UK. Sinclair's electric tricycle is a recent example of the beast. New product development requires constant communication between marketing, general management and the R & D team. Marketing research is the tool for analysing the marketplace and the possibilities for innovation and new product development; research and development is where the technical expertise for translating these possibilities into products lies; general management gives direction, thrust and resources for this to be done. R & D should not however be reactive to intelligence from the marketplace. R & D can and should be proactive in producing ideas, but these ideas must be subject to marketplace evaluation before they proceed along the development path. In the best of all possible worlds R & D and marketing departments are in continuous interaction. Some R & D ideas will not pass muster on commercial grounds, some marketing ideas will not be translatable into real products, but the right creative climate needs to be nurtured, and that will only come from mutual respect between R & D and marketing managers.

New product development is perhaps better understood by more companies than ever before. But the best companies are still in a minority. Neither is new product development the exclusive preserve of in-house development, there are a number of very creative product development agencies and their value as sources of new ideas should not be overlooked.

What can we say by way of generality about new product development? The textbooks are replete with checklists, which will not be repeated here. The following points are worth making:

1 New products are a way of getting new and keeping old customers.
2 New products are an effective way of obtaining a competitive advantage.
3 New products are a source of both growth and hope in the perceptions of both employees and other stakeholders. An innovative company is more exciting than a conservative company.
4 Good marketing research and ongoing marketing intelligence are a prime source of new pro-

duct ideas, because research and intelligence should be generated from the battlefield, from consumers in the marketplace. And good marketing research is not just head counting, it is about diagnosis, it helps you understand what makes consumers tick, what motivates customers, how they think about their problems for which your products may provide a solution.

5 Good marketing research should give you information about what your competitors are doing, and what your customers think about them.

6 Technical and marketing development should move along together, one should never lead the other for very long. The marketplace is dynamic, a good opportunity defined yesterday needs to be retested tomorrow.

7 Never lose sight of the target market, your defined competitive advantage, the customer benefit you intend to provide and promote. Positioning is critical.

8 The ultimate test is repeat purchase rates, not one-time trials.

9 Test marketing is an attractive insurance policy but reaction times are accelerating, so test market exposure means that your competitors will know exactly what you are up to. Surprise is lost.

10 Implementation is crucial. A good idea can be ruined by poor implementation. The opportunity created by implementation cannot be recreated. You have only one chance to get it right. Attention to detail in market launch will make it harder for competitors to jump in – leave them no opportunity that you could have exploited.

11 Do not start on the first rung of the learning curve every time you embark on a new product development. Everyone learns from experience and from mistakes. Every development and launch needs to be fully recorded and evaluated. Mistakes will occur, the sin is not to learn from them.

12 Minimize risk if it can be done sensibly. Amstrad is currently demonstrating remarkable fleetness of foot in getting quickly into markets and out again if necessary. Alan Sugar subcontracts a great deal of his new product manufacture. Global procurement is a fact of life in

today's world, as is risk reduction by joint development. Do not ignore either possibility.

We have until now concentrated our thoughts on new product development, but product development is not always about new products. The care and nurture of old products is in fact a development strategy and one requiring great skills if competitors are constantly biting at your heels. The Mars bar stands as a monument to the success of old product development. Rowntree Mackintosh and Cadbury continuously try to weaken Mars bar's hold as market brand leader, but with little success. Mars Fun Size and Mars Big Bar are successful developments of a theme that have strengthened the product's hold on the market, a hold that is the result of continuing care and attention to marketing detail. The story is repeated with other Mars confectionery lines.

Product development also encompasses foreign market development. Though the term global product is glibly used, a good marketing manager knows that while the core product may be exportable and marketable internationally, the product must be marketed in terms appropriate to each overseas market. Again Mars serves as a good example. Another Mars product, Snickers, a successful bar in North America, has been sold for over a decade in the UK as Marathon. Earlier this year Mars renamed Marathon – it is now called by its global brand name – *Snickers*.

New product development is either a process internal to the company, or a subcontracted activity. But new products can be acquired, so development by acquisition must be considered as a strategy. It can be a relatively inexpensive and fast way of diversifying the company's total product offering, or of obtaining an entry into a new market. But as Beechams and Boots have both demonstrated it can also be a costly business, particularly if you are acquiring established brand names. The cost may be worth it in the long run providing it is part of coherent business development strategy.

One final point is to be made in this discussion of product development. We have earlier referred to market research's role in analysing the marketplace, and customers needs and wants. Customers are not always ultimate consumers. In our love affair with the marketing concept we too glibly suppose that ultimate consumers are the relevant reference point and source of information to whom access must be

had directly. But in the UK market of the 1990s, very significant changes in the balance of power as between manufacturers, retailers and ultimate consumers are taking place. Retailers have been acquiring more and more power, at the expense of the manufacturer certainly, but also at the expense of the consumer. Such power over the consumer is in one sense benign because the consummate skill of the Sainsburys and the Marks and Spencers is to give their customers what they think they want. But such powerful retailers have great power to mould and fashion taste. I do not suggest for one moment that they abuse this power, and at the end of the day consumers do have a choice, alternative stores at which to purchase their food and clothing. Nevertheless, the increasing power of private label over national brand, and the internationalization of retailing (and of franchising of retail outlets) must mean that product development must take note of the participants, both consumers and the distributors who make access to consumers possible.

Strategic management of the product mix

Product development takes place within the context of strategic management of the product mix. Marketing directors of any company have responsibility for management of the total product/service offering, that offering being composed of an array of new, growing, mature and perhaps declining products or services. Marketing directors must maintain some kind of optimality within their portfolio of products and services, that optimality being defined at corporate level in terms of corporate mission, and in such specific terms as growth targets, return on investment, return on assets managed, specific market share gain, working capital targets and cash flow prescriptions. Their agents for achieving optimality will be their product group managers and their brand managers. I do not intend to say much about strategic planning in general, since I cannot do better than recommend Chapter 3 in Michael Baker's *Marketing Strategy and Management* (Macmillan, 1985). What I do want to do is to explore in a little more depth than does that chapter, two tools of strategic marketing management, namely the product life cycle concept, and portfolio analysis.

The product life cycle and product policy management

The product life cycle concept has for long been a cornerstone of product policy management. Yet it is still poorly understood. What follows is an attempt to clarify its current status.

The product life cycle derives from a biological metaphor, namely that all 'living things' go through a cycle of birth, growth, maturity and inevitable decline and death. Product forms, product classes and brands are likened to 'living things' in this context.

A product is born as a result of research and development activities bearing fruit in the form of a product launch. During the introductory stage, sales are relatively slow as demand is developed among the innovators in the marketplace. During the growth stage, the increasing rate of diffusion leads to a more rapidly expanding demand. When the market ceases to expand, the maturity stage is reached, the rate of sales growth levels off, competition becomes stable, and repeat purchasers constitute the major component of sales. Finally as new, more innovative products reach the market, decline sets in, and eventually the product is withdrawn from the market.

'Forget the product life cycle' was the command made in a now famous article (Dhalla and Yuspeh, 1976). Their command was based upon conceptual and operational arguments.

The conceptual arguments were that:

- Products are not living things, hence the biological metaphor is entirely misleading.
- The life cycle of a product is the dependent variable, being a function of the way in which the product is managed over time. It is certainly not an independent variable.
- The product life cycle cannot be valid for product class, product form and for brands – indeed an important function of a brand name is to create a franchise that has value over time, permitting changes to take place in the product formulation.
- Trying to fit product life cycle curves into empirical sales data is a sterile exercise in taxonomy.

The main operative arguments include:

- The four phases or states in the life cycle are not clearly definable.

- It is impossible to determine at any moment in time exactly where a product is in its life cycle hence:
- The concept cannot be used as a planning tool.
- There is evidence that companies who have tried to use the product life cycle as a planning tool have made costly errors and passed up promising opportunities.

In the face of these powerful arguments, what can be said about the product life cycle? Clearly it is not a universally valid model, but rather an ideal type from which fundamental insights into the behaviour of most product forms over time can be deduced, but which in application needs very careful handling. It may be more valid in one product category than in another. For many product categories there is empirical evidence that sales over time show the classic form. Thus we can argue that as a means to an end – that end being more sensitive management of the product over time, no sensible product manager should ignore the intellectual inheritance represented by the product life cycle literature. Using the product life cycle concept is a means to creating an optimal life cycle, rather than being controlled by it. Sales history is a fundamental tool of the product manager, but sales history is not the only variable controlling the future of the product. As Michael Porter (1980) has demonstrated, the context in which the product life cycle is applied is also significant. Porter focuses on the nature of the industry in which the product is located, suggesting that the evolution of the industry from emergent to declining is as least as important as the stage in the life-cycle of the particular product that is the subject of analysis.

In summary, the product life cycle, as amended by Porter, is a versatile framework for organizing contingent hypotheses about appropriate strategic alternatives, and as a means for anticipating the consequences of the dynamics of the served market. It can help in the formulation of market share strategies since it provides a means for viewing trends in primary demand as well as basic competitive patterns. But it cannot provide a means for managing by formula.

Portfolio analysis and product policy management

Portfolio analysis has in the last ten years loomed

Table 15.1   *Porter's evolutionary stages v traditional PLC approach*

Stage description		Strategic action	
Porter's categories and descriptions	*Traditional PLC descriptions*	*Porter's suggestions*	*Traditional PLC advocates*
Emerging industry Uncertainty among buyers over product performance, potential applications, advantages of rival brands, likelihood of obsolescence Uncertainty among sellers over market wants, technological developments	*Introduction (pioneering stage)* Customer awareness of product low Limited distribution Sales slow Few competitors	*Emerging industry* Strategy to take into account five forces of: • threat of entry • rivalry among competitors • pressure of substitutes • bargaining power of buyers • bargaining power of suppliers	*Introduction* Stimulate primary demand (among early adopters?) Selective distribution Advertising to create awareness of product's potential
Transition to maturity Falling profits for industry Slowing growth Customer knowledgeable about the product Less product innovation Competition in non-product aspects of the offering	*Growth/maturity* Competition intense Slowing growth Consumer knowledge and preferences mature Widest ever distribution	*Transition to maturity* New segments or cater more closely to wants of some segments More efficient organization Closer dealer relations	*Growth/maturity* Market penetration or hold/defend via market segmentation Service emphasized Selective demand advertising
Decline Competition from substitutes Changing wants Demographic factors affecting markets	*Decline* Competition from substitutes Customer changing to new products Distribution shrinking	*Decline* Seek pockets of enduring demand or Divest	*Decline* Seek new product uses Changes to revitalize product Simplification of product lines

Source: John O'Shaughnessy, *Competitive Marketing*, Allen & Unwin, 1984.

very large in the literature of strategic management. In this section I want to engage in a reduction exercise in an attempt to understand the contribution that portfolio analysis can make to product policy as it affects product lines and product mix management. A practical approach is discussed at length in Linneman and Thomas (1982). All I wish to do here is to argue that portfolio analysis can be used by marketing directors to evaluate their brand managers' plans. Both the growth-share matrix and the market-attractiveness business position matrix types lend themselves to analysis of lower level units (strategic business units (SBUs) can be defined as individual products). Much of the data needed by

marketing directors to develop their operational strategy using portfolio analysis should be prepared as part of the brand manager's plans as outlined by Bureau (1981). The information required by marketing directors from the brand managers will depend *in part* on an interrelated mix of:

1   Perceived critical success factors.
2   Corporate yardsticks.
3   Divisional mission and role(s).
4   Processing facilities.
5   Data availability.
6   Portfolio model chosen.

It is essential that marketing directors develop a

proforma step by step procedure for all brand managers to follow so that information is sufficient and compatible to develop their portfolio analysis. A proforma type information need approach alongside knowledge of the 'game rules' for the final analysis will help reduce the occurrence and severity of conflicts. Brand managers might reasonably argue that the final univariate or composite dimensions chosen were inappropriate for their particular product(s) and/or market segment(s). On the other hand, definitional problems may mean product-market boundaries could be drawn to paint a picture which supported their budget proposals.

The product-market segment level portfolio analysis would have to 'fit' with both corporate requirements planning timetable and objectives. Critical success factors which vary between divisions must be even more likely to vary at the product-market segment level. To assess the efficacy of plans marketing directors will not just wish to develop a static portfolio picture but will need brand managers to provide information on past, present and future portfolio locations for their products. These in turn will have to be put against a time scale *beyond* the brand managers' *annual* plan in order to examine the longer range portfolio implications of the product-market segment promotional proposals. It is, also, very likely that they will have to develop for 'corporate', three different scenarios: best case, most probable and worst case, which will have to be translated into information requirements at the product level.

Marketing directors' objective in using portfolio analysis to assess the efficacy of brand managers' plans would be to facilitate decisions on the allocation of finite resources between the managers and to ensure that the combined plans will meet the divisions' mission and objectives. Portfolio analysis would thus aid the assessment of the efficacy of those plans by relating individual operational marketing plans to key composite or univariate dimensions, bringing together all the brand managers' plans to see if each location, direction, projected results etc. will meet divisional needs, and aid visualization such that 'missions' can be applied to each plan which in turn can be compared with proposed budgets and promotional plans to measure likely effectiveness and appropriateness.

At the first level, directors can check the basic soundness of each plan against its position on the portfolio display; bearing in mind that the portfolio display facilitates visualization rather than serving as an analytical and prescriptive tool in itself. At the second level, they can assess the mix and balance of those plans and if they are appropriate for their needs. In effect, the efficacy that is being assessed is not so much whether it is likely to achieve the *brand manager's* desired and forecast results, but more the efficacy of the overall mix of brand manager plans. At the next level, they can then assign missions and strategies to each plan appropriate to the overall division's needs. Product lines, brands, segments etc. and associated plans would then have been assigned clear roles to play in their long- as well as short-term divisional strategy. They could then compare those assigned roles to see how they match with the marketing mixes, expenditures and other functional commitments proposed in the individual brand manager's plans. Haspeslagh (1982) maintains that resource allocation is what portfolio analysis is about, hence marketing directors will be able to relate plans to missions to test efficacy of the former – do the custodial, harvesting, phased withdrawal, penetration, divestment, acquisition and new product/opportunity development decisions relate to the brand managers' plans or do some of the latter have to be revised in the light of the portfolio analysis. Again the efficacy of the plans and justification for marketing expenditures are being assessed in relation to required portfolio roles.

The actual portfolio displays do not provide strategic answers for resource allocation problems between brand managers. But they aid visualization, communication and decision making at the level of both marketing directors and their team of brand managers.

Product policy and productivity analysis

Every marketing manager should have available to him/her information about every product in his/her product line/mix. The dimensions of this information are suggested by the listing in Table 15.2.

Table 15.2 provides a basis for marketing productivity meaurement.

This use of productivity measurement in relation to the marketing function is relatively new. The

Table 15.2 *Product audit information*

Product	Market

Characteristics of product
 ● description
 ● principal users
 ● role played by product in company objectives and strategy, e.g. complete existing line.
	Segment
	 ● description
	 ● size
	 ● location
	 ● growth potential
	    numbers buying
	    amount bought per occasion
	    frequency of purchase.

Production of product
 ● raw materials and their availability
 ● warehousing needed
 ● inventories required
 ● whether product requires specialist plant, specific skills, aptitudes and attitudes
 ● technical know-how.
	Customers
	 ● reasons for buying.
	 ● use of product
	    how? when? with? what?
	 ● relative importance of quality, price, convenience, shape, weight, size, style, packaging
	 ● how reached?
	    media
	    channels
	 ● coverage
	 ● goodwill

History of product ● time series of sales ● seasonal pattern of sales ● costs and profitability.	

Future
 ● vulnerability to obsolescence
 ● anticipated future sales trends
 ● anticipated future costs and profitability.
	Competition
	 ● names of rivals
	 ● comparison on the following:
	    share of the market
	    pricing policies
	    prices to different groups
	    warranties

Product performance compared with objective set for it	credit policy
	    advertising
	    expenditure by region and media

Effect of withdrawing product
 ● on strategy
 ● on profit
 ● on suppliers
 ● on customers
 ● on employees.
	distribution
	    channels
	    sales organization
	    accounts where strong
	    service
	    services offered
	    training of staff
	    quality of service
	    flexibility in speed of response to competitive action.

Source: John O'Shaughnessy, *Competitive Marketing*, Allen & Unwin, 1984.

central role of marketing can be expressed as the management of consumer demand and the translation of this demand into sales and profits. Marketing productivity analysis is an important tool in evaluating the performance of the marketing department in carrying out this role. It measures the efficiency with which marketing inputs are used to generate target levels of marketing outputs.

Two aspects of marketing productivity can be identified. The first is directly related to the management of the marketing mix. The analysis of cause and effect relationships between marketing inputs and outputs forms the basis for the development of an optimal marketing mix, in terms of type and level of investment and allocation to the various marketing segments. To quote Sevin (1965):

> The ratio of sales or net profits (effect produced) to marketing costs (energy expended) for a specific segment of the business.

Marketing productivity is a measure of the profit responsiveness by segment to different levels of marketing investment.

Alternatively, the concept of marketing productivity focuses on the idea of efficiency. It focuses on the need for greater control over the productivity of marketing budgets. Measurement of marketing productivity is related to the establishment of 'standards of performance' to the process of planning for reduction in the amount of financial and/or physical resources used in the attainment of these standards. The task is one of analysing and improving the efficiency of the marketing function without jeopardizing present or future sales volume – and profit targets.

Market response function

The productivity of a company's marketing performance is related to the success with which an organization can link its product mix to the various segments it serves.

Every marketing executive has to make judgements as to which elements of the marketing mix he/she will have to use to achieve the marketing objectives. Marketing productivity analysis assists marketing/product managers in determining the impact of varying levels, types and allocation of marketing resources on sales and net profits. By careful analysis of the costs of marketing inputs and their allocation to the various segments, marketing managers can begin to assess the profit-generating capacity of each segment. This then becomes the manager's yardstick to measure the productivity of the company's marketing operations, the cornerstone for the control of all marketing operations.

Control function

With increasing pressure on company profits, the need for greater control over marketing expenditure and efforts becomes more critical. Marketing productivity analysis can play an important role as a control instrument as it relates the inputs of the marketing operation to the results achieved and to standards of performance. The focus is, therefore, on the efficiency with which these inputs are utilized. A framework for productivity improvements can be set up. This framework would include:

- Profitability control.
- Volume control.
- Expense control.

The subject of control is developed at greater length in Chapter 21 by Jack Bureau.

Profitability control

All companies should attempt to calculate the profitability of each of its products and/or product class, of its customers by account size and, of each of its sales territories (and export markets). Simple profitability measurement is less desirable than a return on investment standard.

The use of this 'return on investment' ratio is based on the availability of a group of ratios, which are developed to evaluate and diagnose profitability by segment and for the company as a whole. Widespread use is made of these ratios, because of their importance in formulating effective strategies, as well as in assessing performance.

Volume control

The second area of control is related to the achievement of volume goals. Whereas with profitability control the inputs and outputs were expressed in monetary terms, the focus is shifted to non-pecuniary measures of performance. Measures, such as a 'minimum order volume for a customer to be profitable', 'minimum order volume to support a retail/outlet/distribution channel', 'sales volume achieved in new markets' are relevant.

By establishing standards of performance on levels of volume per product, per customer, per salesperson, etc., a basis is developed for evaluating the productivity with which these standards are achieved.

Expense control

A third area where productivity analysis can be

employed as a control technique relates to the measurement of expenditure efficiency of the various components of the marketing budget. Marketing budgets are prepared on the basis of financial inputs which are associated with the realization of volume targets.

Input to output ratios are to be applied to monitor the level of marketing expenditure in relation to sales goals to ascertain whether the company is overspending or not. The key ratio is seen to be 'marketing investment to operating profit' which is fully specified in Figure 15.1.

$$\frac{\text{sales}}{\text{total marketing investment}} \times \frac{\text{operating profits}}{\text{sales}}$$

These secondary ratios can be further broken down:

$$= \frac{\text{operating profit}}{\text{marketing investment}}$$

This ratio is fully defined in Figure 15.1.

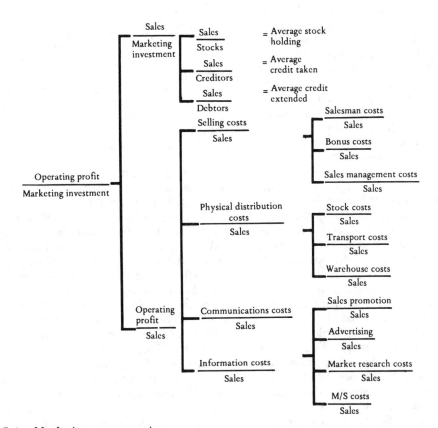

Figure 15.1 *Marketing expense ratios*
Source: R.M.S. Wilson, *Management Controls and Marketing Planning*, Heinemann, 1979.

The analysis of the productivity of marketing expenses only has value when compared to standards of performance. The use of standards and tolerance limits makes it possible for the marketing managers to pinpoint those areas which require their closer attention.

The second and third areas of control over marketing are combined into 'performance accounting'. Its purpose is to match the performance of centres of responsibility against company plans, standards and budgets.

These centres are seen as the basic collection units for both cost and revenue data and, therefore, serve as a basis for marketing productivity analysis.

A full discussion of the techniques for implementing performance analysis can be found in my research report 'Marketing Productivity Analysis' published as vol. 4, no. 2, 1986 of *Marketing Intelligence and Planning*, the journal edited by myself. This is available as a report from MCB University Press, 62 Toller Lane, Bradford, BD8 9BY. The report describes in detail how to measure the contribution of each product and product line to the profitability of the company. This is a technique that uses the concept of functional marketing expenses, which are allocated to each product/product line. Product and loss statements for each product/product line can be calculated, and unprofitable products/product lines identified. On the basis of this information, marketing managers can shift marketing inputs to the more profitable entities. Under the contribution margin approach, only those costs are considered that are directly related to the marketing of a single product and which would disappear should the company drop that product, or segment of the business. This is only acceptable for internal accounting purposes. For general financial reporting, a full costing system is required.

There are some operational difficulties in implementing a contribution approach. First, future costs are more relevant to decision making than historical costs. In most companies, current costs are used, as these are the best estimate of the future costs. Second, in evaluating the use of scarce resources, the criteria should be opportunity cost rather than actual costs. Third, a method has to be developed for assigning promotional activities to each segment relative to the impact in the period

under analysis. Despite those problems, a contribution approach holds great advantages over the traditional full costing approach in facilitating the evaluation of possible alternatives. As it stands now, it is not yet possible to provide management with information on the productivity of the marketing inputs. To improve marketing decisions, it becomes necessary to relate demand-generating marketing efforts directly to the gross margin produced by the marketing effort. This can be achieved by restructuring of the familiar contribution income statement as documented in Table 15.3 below.

Table 15.3 *Contribution margin approach*

Revenue
  Less: Variable manufacturing costs
          Other variable costs directly
            traceable to the segment
          _____

Contribution margin
  Less: Fixed costs directly traceable
            to the segment
          _____

Segment net income
_____

The development of this marketing productivity-based management accounting system is based on the work of Feder (1965).

The objective of the reconstructed contribution income statement is to link the marketing investment to the level of profits generated. This enables the calculation of marketing productivity ratios, as responsiveness of sales and profits can be directly related to marketing activities.

For this purpose the layout of the income statement is revised into the form shown in Table 15.4.

The rationale behind this version of presenting management accounting data is that it provides marketing/product managers with two focal points for control, namely gross and net marketing earnings. The gross marketing earnings (GME) are the internal criteria for marketing control, as the figure these represent is the measure of responsiveness of profits to direct marketing inputs.

Second, after deducting the marketing overheads from this GME figure, we arrive at the contribution

Table 15.4 *Revised income statement layout*

Sales
  Less: Standard variable manufacturing
              costs
  _____

Standard profit contribution
  Less: Direct marketing costs
              Advertising
              Sales promotion
              Selling
              Distribution
  _____

Gross marketing earnings
  Less: Marketing overheads
  _____

Net marketing earnings
  Less: Company overheads (including
              variances)
  _____

Net profits before tax

made by the marketing department, in terms of the net marketing earnings (NME) to the company's overheads and profits. This NME figure is the external focal point of the marketing control system. It is used by corporate management to evaluate the marketing function.

Third, using standard costs (when variable costs are predictable and vary with the given base) implies the possibility of variances, and these variances are taken out of the marketing productivity calculations by bringing them under the heading of company overheads.

This approach is directed primarily at the analysis of product/product-line profitability. As such, it can be used by marketing directors to evaluate the productivity of the marketing operations under their control.

The future of product/brand management

The preceding discussion was focused on ways in which marketing managers can focus on and hence control both the balance of their product portfolio and the performance of each product and product line. Heretofore, many companies have used the product or brand management system as a means

for bringing into existence a system for close control over each product in the product line. Every brand manager was held responsible for planning, coordination of the marketing mix and hence for decision making in respect of his/her own brand. Product/brand managers focus on:

1   Establishing the product's marketing objectives.
2   Planning the marketing, product and packaging activities to achieve product objectives.
3   Determining an expense budget for each of the marketing activities.
4   Scheduling the marketing activities, especially for type, frequency and timing of promotion.
5   Establishing ongoing measurement and control review procedures.
6   Communicating the plan to ensure understanding by those who will implement it, especially the sales force.
7   Creating and maintaining enthusiasm for the plan.
8   Monitoring progress and effectiveness of performance according to pre-established standards.
9   Specifying corrective action when plan and performance are at variance.
10 End-of-year report to management.
11 Post-mortem plan re-evaluation for learning purposes.

Thus the strength of the system may be summarized thus:

1   It is a means for providing each product with a product champion.
2   Product/brand managers devote their full attention to improving the performance of their brand, thus providing vigorous product-by-product leadership.
3   It has a proven track record as a training ground for the marketing managers of tomorrow.
4   Most successful marketing companies have used the system.

In recent years, however, a rather long catalogue of problems associated with the product/brand management system has developed. The catalogue would include the following points:

1 Product/brand managers are jacks of all trades, masters of none.
2 It is an expensive management system, only the most successful products can sustain the burden of management costs.
3 It is a myopic management system, in that brand managers are young and intensely ambitious, hoping that brilliant short-term performance will be sufficient to provide promotion – few brand managers expect to stay with any one brand for more than three years.
4 The problem of responsibility (for the profit of the brand) without authority creates many problems, particularly at the interfaces with other functions, most particularly with the sales force, and the advertising agency.
5 It is a system that encourages number crunching, leaving too little time for strategic thinking.
6 It is not conducive to effective product development since it tends to be product orientated rather than market orientated.
7 Where companies sell to many markets, through dissimilar distribution channels, and where customer motivation differs considerably from one segment of the market to another, then a market manager system is superior to a product management system.
8 And finally, and perhaps most critically, significant changes in the balance of power are taking place in many consumer markets which may threaten the future of the product/brand management system as it has functioned heretofore. This development is due to the rise of the power of the retail chains. National account management is necessary when a manufacturer is selling to one of the major retail chains, and as such chains dominate food retailing, and increasingly clothing, electrical goods, and indeed most of our high streets and out of town shopping centre developments, then the future of the product/brand management system must evolve, perhaps retrogressively. From those days when product managers were almost the managing directors of their own 'brand based' company, perhaps the future offers not much more than gopher status, running about doing their national account managers' bidding. In this sense the sales management function is gaining power at the expense of the product management function. Above all, the needs of both ultimate consumers and increasingly the retailers who are becoming the arbiters of consumer preferences, need to be better managed.

Product policy needs to be refocused, on markets, market segments, and segment productivity and profitability. The competition of the future will be for space on retailer's shelves and retailers, the best of them anyway, have a sharp eye for productivity.

Conclusion

Product development and management is a pervasive topic and one which forms the core of the marketing management function. Thus aspects of product policy are to be found in every chapter of this book. The purpose of this chapter was not to give a necessarily shallow overview of product development and management but instead to select some areas to discuss in more detail. Six topics are discussed; the development of old and new products, managements of the marketing mix, the relevance of the product life cycle, the uses of portfolio management and productivity analysis and the future of product/brand management.

References

Bureau, J.R., *Brand Management*, London, Macmillan, 1981.
Dhalla, N.K. and Yuspeh, S. 'Forget the product life cycle', *Harvard Business Review*, January-February, 1976, pp. 102–12.
Feder, R. A., 'How to measure marketing performance', *Harvard Business Review*, May-June 1965, pp. 132–42.
Haspeslagh, P., 'Portfolio planning: uses and limits', *Harvard Business Review*, vol. 60, 1, 1982.
Jones, J. P., *What's in a name*, Gower, 1986.
Linneman, R. D. and Thomas, M. J. 'A Commonsense approach to portfolio planning', *Journal of Long Range Planning*, vol. 15, no. 2, 1982, pp. 77–92.
Lorenz, C., *The Design Dimension*, Blackwell, 1986.
Porter, M., *Competitive Strategy*, Free Press, 1980.
Sevin, C.H., *Marketing Productivity Analysis*, McGraw-Hill, 1965.
Sowery, T., *The Generation of Ideas for New Products*, Kogan Page, 1989.
Thomas, M. J.. *The Marketing Handbook*, 3rd edn., Gower, 1989, particularly Chapters 16, 17, 20, 21.

16
Pricing

JOHN WINKLER

Introduction

How does the publisher price this book?

First of all, the publisher has a feel about the 'market price'. Most books of a certain kind fit into a slot. Who determines where the slot is? No one person does, there is a sort of consensus in the trade.

But someone added up the costs of production, found that this book would be expensive to produce and that meant the publisher had to move it up to a higher slot than usual.

But then someone else said, 'This is a special book for the Institute of Marketing. It will sell to practitioners. They will buy it for their companies so the price can be quite high'.

'Ah, but it will also sell to members and they will not pay so much if they buy it personally. And should we not sell it at a lower price to members than to bookshops?'

'Don't forget the students. These people have to buy it for themselves. The teachers of marketing will not recommend it if it is expensive. Why do we not produce a limp cover version and sell it at a cheaper price?' 'Will that not take sales away from other copies?' 'Well, launch it later, then.'

I was not present at any of these conversations. But you can have odds of £100 to £1 on them taking place.

Every practitioner of marketing has been there before. The most critical factor in business, in its effect upon profits in the short term, is price. And the study of price, which should be as scientific as you can get, turns out to be a mass of hurried judgements, and guesswork.

And every country where a free market exists is the same. The US is no different to the UK: no more sophisticated in its techniques. The same is true in the Far East. And in Switzerland, Sweden and South Africa. The same price seminar programme can be run in every single country without change.

Put simply, pricing decisions are often arbitrary, usually hurried, sometimes a mess and seldom tested. But when executives use their experience to set prices, there is a series of different and often conflicting factors to take into account.

This chapter describes these directions, these thrusts of argument. There is the cost argument, what the market will bear argument, and what the competition will do argument.

On top of this, the prices must be sold. Setting prices to sell shampoo out of Tesco shops is one thing. Setting up the complex deal to sell the whole product range to Tesco is a totally different matter.

So the pricing decision cannot be divorced from the way in which the prices will be negotiated. This also is covered in this chapter.

How to set prices – pricing systems

Standard costing is the usual system upon which prices are based in most companies. No one is against companies preparing their costs, business cannot be run properly without such systems. But as a sole means of settling prices, the system is full of flaws. Let the standard cost price be the *lowest* unit price you are willing to accept. That is a good starting point; but then add margins to it. If the standard cost throws out prices which are too high, then the market will find you out, and you will have to reduce them or pull out of the market. So it will seldom price things too high for the long run. But it often does price things too low – and the market never tells you this. Even strong sales figures will not reveal the price is too low – they could be strong for a host of reasons, and low price does not necessarily mean big volume orders – unless the price is very much lower than the average.

Marginal pricing works only if you can guarantee that the whole costs of your entire business can be covered by your normal sales at full selling prices. Then you can use a marginal price if you want. The problem occurs when it is very difficult to establish a standard cost system, because the fixed costs in the business are a very high proportion of the total costs and they are very difficult to allocate between different products or services. Then you may have to cost out variables, add on a margin for luck to cover your overheads and that is your selling price. Dangerous, as you can see, but sometimes unavoidable, particularly when accountants are employed under a strict master who will not allow them to make sensible guesses as to overhead allocations. 'that's for the crystal ball merchants in the marketing department,' says the chief management accountant. 'Only record exactly what you can measure.' It is a bit Jesuitical, and not very helpful.

Paying for the actual costs of production plus an agreed allowance for profit, on very large orders – defence contracts for example, or local authority work – this may be one way to cover the costs and stay in business. It appeals to the customer's sense of morality, but he/she will want to see the justification for the figures just the same. The system can disguise a great deal of skulduggery in the presentation of the data, and can hide a lot of waste.

Product analysis pricing shows what customers would have to pay if they arranged to have the product made for themselves. It sets a target of costs and a target for price. It uses past pricing and bidding data, and is an excellent system for a jobbing business such as a printer to use. Most companies have an element of jobbing work somewhere in their production process, and this pricing system can be very useful.

Standard cost pricing

This is a lovely logical system which most companies use and which does not work at all well, but they seldom find this out. There is something to be said for it but not a lot.

Adding together the variable cost, the fixed cost and the profit per unit provides a selling price.

Table 16.1 *Standard cost pricing*

Step 1 Set up a system of 'standard' costs based on an assumed 'normal' rate of output over a number of years. All fixed and variable costs should be added, and the total divided by the number of units to be produced. This gives you the average cost per unit. The following costs should be included:

(a) Cost to design (including building and testing preproduct prototype, if appropriate).
(b) Production (labour and materials).
(c) Depreciation on research and development and plant investments.
(d) Overhead.
(e) Rent.
(f) Insurance.
(g) Handling and packaging.
(h) Storage.
(i) Cost of building and carrying stocks.
(j) Advertising expenses (assuming you use a percentage of sales for determining advertising budget).
(k) Delivery.
(l) Installation, services.
(m) Warranty service costs.
(n) Patent royalty.

Step 2 To total cost add a set percentage of cost (based on experience) to cover selling, merchandising and administration costs, plus a 'normal' profit to arrive at preliminary price.

Step 3 Compare preliminary price with the going market price for a similar product, and adjust slightly if needed.

Nothing could be simpler, except that it is an inferior method of setting prices.

The first problem is that it assumes that costs are the thing which cause people to buy. But the market is not the least bit interested in cost. It is interested in getting what it wants at a competitive price.

Using the standard cost system, full cost accounting, full cost pricing, call it what you will, if your fixed costs are treated on a percentage basis, then if you manage to get your fixed costs down then your selling prices go down. You reap no advantage. Actually, you will lose by it, because the profit is usually calculated on a percentage basis also. As your selling price goes down, so will your actual profit per unit (but not your magic percentage).

A further problem is that using the standard cost system, if you produce products at too high a cost, compared to competition, then you will have to reduce your price anyway – because your product will not sell. But if you produce products below the cost of your competition, then the market will not tell you that you are too cheap. Have you ever heard buyers tell you that they will voluntarily give you more money on account of your efficiency? And you will not *necessarily* sell more, just because you are cheaper.

Another problem is, if you call your factory labour a 'variable' cost, this assumes that if you sell 10 per cent more than planned, then you will employ 10 per cent more labour. But you will not. You will keep your existing labour and give them overtime rates. If your sales go down by 10 per cent less than forecast, then the assumption is that your labour bill will go down by 10 per cent. But it will not. Try sacking 10 per cent of your staff one week, and putting them back on the next.

But there are more problems. The entire system is based upon forecast sales. But how do you know how many sales you are going to get? And will your sales be affected by your price – yes, they will.

Standard cost pricing is inflexible. It is anachronistic. It is based upon a historical view of past costs leading to tomorrow's prices. It is altogether a weak system to use, but on the other hand, it may be a less weak costing system than any of the others which follow. To provide a base line figure, standard costing may be acceptable. To measure profitability, standard costing may be acceptable. But to rely on it, *and on nothing else* to set selling prices is completely unacceptable. Yet many companies do just this.

Cost-plus-profit systems of pricing

Now this is a much healthier system because at least you may be guaranteed to stay in business.

In many types of business, cost-plus-profit formulae are the only sensible way to contract for business. Big deals can often be handled this way. IBM in London has a deal with a major hotel group so that all its visiting executives stay in a certain hotel at special 'cost-plus' rates. The contract is valuable to the hotel group, but IBM insists on examining the quarterly profit and loss accounts from the hotel. It makes it very difficult to manipulate invoices. When selling, the companies using cost-plus-profit formulae, like to identify every possible item of cost, and this leads to tortuous accounting and calculation, particularly with the semivariable costs such as repairs and renewals or delivery costs, which rise and fall with significant changes in the level of production, but are not directly associated with every small change in the level. When buying under this system, companies

Table 16.2 *Drawbacks of cost-plus pricing*

- Difficult, in advance, to determine such costs as construction, material price changes, and similar costs.
- Difficult to allocate joint costs to specific products.
- Not based on realistic profit goal or market share objective.
- Ignores elasticity of demand.
- Generally disregards competition.
- Buyers are more concerned about the cost and value of product to them than about production and selling costs to supplier.
- Does not distinguish between out-of-pocket and 'sunk' costs.*
- Difficult to determine 'fair' return.
- Ignores capital requirements and return on investment.
- Many costs vary with volume, and volume depends on price charged.

* Those which are spent, regardless of production level.

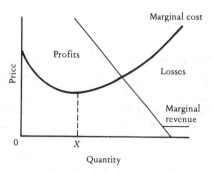

Figure 16.1 *Marginal pricing*

like to be able to identify and verify costs for themselves; they like as little as possible to be costed in as direct and more absorbed on the profit. But they must take care that they are not being charged with someone else's costs, and that they are not subsidizing a wasteful production system.

Marginal pricing

If cost-plus-profit will generally keep you in business, then this can easily put you out of it. Marginal pricing provides the intellectual rationale for accepting the lowest possible price, and is exceptionally dangerous when uncontrolled. Every weak salesperson, when faced by a big buyer who is squeezing him/her hard on the price, will come back to his/her management with something like the following argument.

'This buyer is not going to pay our full price for this big order because he can get it cheaper elsewhere. Do we want to do the business or not? If we give him a price reduction, then we are making some money on the deal, over and above our variable costs. Would you rather have this money, or would you rather not have it?' Faced with this logic, a manager under pressure will usually agree that it is better to do the low price deal than not.

The problem concerns a misconception about costs. The costs of making the product include the materials and other variable costs, but they also include the costs of running the business as a whole, salaries, rents, administration and the like. It is all of these costs which must be recovered in the long run by all the deals which are done.

Marginal pricing throws all of these fixed costs into a pot and calls it 'Contribution to overhead and profit'.

The basic theory of marginal pricing is that price is set at a point where marginal cost equals marginal revenue.

Marginal cost is the increase in total cost as a result of producing and selling one more unit of a product. In Figure 16.1 you can see that from zero production up to a volume of X, marginal cost decreases; then begins to increase. X represents the point where economies of scale have been exceeded. After this point, marginal costs tend to increase.

Marginal *revenue* is the additional amount received as a result of selling one more unit of a product. Note on the figure that marginal revenue decreases as quantity increases. This is because of the supply and demand theory that people will buy greater quantities of a product at lower prices.

When you should never use marginal pricing

If you are going to consider a marginal price, well below your full costs, then these are the principal factors to take into account. *Never* do it if it will set a precedent for the long run with your big customers. *Never* do it if the news of the low price deal will spread in the market and other customers will want the same. *Never* do it if it commits you to extra capital cost in the short run, or in the long run. *Never* do it if it uses up scarce resources you need elsewhere. *Never* do it if you have to sacrifice some full profit business to fit it in. *Never* do it if it costs you cash flow as well, by giving credit. *Never* do it if it will undermine the position of you or your salespeople in the market. *Never* delegate discretion on marginal prices down the line.

If you must do a marginal cost deal

Dump the product or service well away from your usual market, and away from your usual customers. Clear your excess stocks. Turn it into a cash up front deal. Keep a particular competitor under pressure in his/her own patch – but be careful because he/she might do the same to you. Do it on a once-off basis; repeat business should be done at normal prices. Make sure that one person controls all the marginal price decisions.

The proper role of costs in pricing

No one is suggesting that we abandon costing procedures in a business – that would be a ludicrous proposition. What is being promoted hard is the idea that costs alone should not determine selling prices.

But the company still needs its costing system to show which products make money and which do not make money. Costs are needed to evaluate the profitability of the assortment. The sales offices must be encouraged to push the products which show high profits or which the factories need to fill up their production lines. The sales offices must know which are the least profitable products for the company, so that these can be held back. That is the proper role of costs in the pricing mechanism; to show how much money is being made, what is profitable and what is not profitable.

The danger in costing systems is the use of percentages to indicate 'profitability'. Just because one product produces a 'profit' of 45 per cent does not mean that it is more profitable than another which produces 35 per cent. This is a very difficult idea for some people to understand, particularly if they have been working under this assumption all their lives.

Product analysis pricing: a technique for bidding

Many companies produce non-standard products, which are custom built, or suited to a particular local market. Local market conditions might be changeable, and competition erratic. So the company's pricing decision will have to be taken down the line at the local level.

The decision is always difficult because buyers are usually experts. They specify tightly their requirments and submit them to companies for tender.

They will select the quotation which is around the lowest, from among those companies meeting the specifications. So the buyer's position is very powerful.

In this case, your pricing decision must be market orientated. This requires a target price to be set initially, based upon your need for the work, the volume of the order, and the likely level of competitive bids. The actual price to be quoted should be a little higher than this, to allow for manoeuvre.

A pricing data sheet is prepared showing the allowance for materials, for bought-in components and for any special features required. These are all costed at the market value, i.e. the sum which customers would pay for these things if buying themselves.

This sum is compared with the deals which have been done by your company in the recent past over similar product groups. The figures are compared, discussed with sales and the target price is selected.

Finally, the decision to bid. At the selected target price, are you better off taking the job or refusing it? To answer this you must consider the alternatives. Do you have an alternative use for that production capacity; or will it lie idle? Will taking the job tie you up in some way so that you will be unable to take on other more profitable work?

How much will this contract provide for future business with this customer, what prestige will the contract bring, and so on? The system has the advantage of flexibility. It handles non-standard production well. It looks principally at the market, particularly in the form of past evidence of similar work, to see what jobs have been won or lost at what prices. It takes account of how much you need the work, and how much volume is involved in the deal. It sets limits for costs. It is quick and it avoids the abominations of percentages.

Market-related pricing systems

There is more profit to be made from selling many

Table 16.3 *Market-related pricing systems*

Pricing system	Purpose
'Moral' pricing	Based upon a notion of justice and fairness.
Pricing costs	Easing through psychological price barriers.
Promotional pricing	Used as the basis for forcing the sales of the product.
Skimming the market	Slicing off the top segment of demand with high prices.
Prestige pricing	The psychology of using extremely high price to add a special appeal.
Penetration price	To force high market share through low prices.

at a sensible price than in selling one at a high price.

Morality is an idea that often enters peoples' minds when prices are discussed – it is one of a series of market-related pricing systems which are sometimes used. When an organization favours a particular pricing system, it seldom does so to the exclusion of all other systems. With market-related systems, the costs are calculated also and usually form the company's floor price.

Moral pricing

'Moral pricing' is used principally by monopolist organizations such as local and national government and institutions where costs are particularly difficult to identify, and where the subject may be socially or politically sensitive.

For example, the faculty of the University of Sussex met the representatives of trade unions in order to discuss how a proposed children's creche facility was to be priced. Five different price levels were agreed upon – one level for single parent families (the lowest), one level for married students, another level for members of the faculty, and so on. The prices were all based upon an idea of affordability and justice. They had hardly anything to do with cost.

Around the world there are many organizations who cannot price up to what the market will bear because of their philosophy. Charity organizations will often price their everyday functions and products low. But when they run a special event to attract the wealthy, then they price the tickets to their 'all star' functions very high indeed because they are appealing to rich people 'who can afford it'.

The problems associated with a 'moral price' system are caused by the fact that many such prices are so low as to make an organization unprofitable, so it pushes other prices up higher to compensate. Or the services and facilities may suffer because there are insufficient funds to pay for their maintenance and renewal. The decisions are based upon individual judgement, notoriously suspect when committees are involved. It also involves the exercise of power or patronage by a monopolist supplier – always an unhealthy base for morality.

Pricing points

Many industries use pricing points, particularly in distributive trades. If you want to sell a 300 ml pack of quality shampoo to chemists' shops, then you will price it to allow buyers a percentage margin if they sell it in their shops at 49p per pack. If you want to get extra displays and more sales effort from their managers, then you will have to offer buyers a promotional discount whereby they can sell it at 39p. They will not sell it at 45p nor at 40p. They want to get below the next pricing point.

It happens with contracts at large prices also. A contract which should be costed at just over £10,000,000 for a short section of new road, may be submitted at £9,950,000 just to get it under the psychological price barrier. And it works, it works really well. Look out for pricing points in your own price lists. If you are in the habit of rounding off your quotations to even sums, then do not do it. Chip the price just below the round figure so that the first digit they read is lower than the one you were planning.

Pricing points are often difficult to handle. Notice that if you want to promote your shampoo down to a selling price of 39p in the shop, you may have to cut your selling price to buyers by 20 per cent – that is a big, big price cut. So what you might do is to introduce a different pack size of perhaps 200 ml in order that shopkeepers can sell at their 39p pricing point and you still make your money. Then, of course, you will get fragmentation of the market by size, and the retailers will complain. You then have to force them to take your full size range. Life can be difficult with this system, particularly in small unit sizes and prices. Your only consolation is that life can be difficult with any other pricing system also.

Promotional pricing

Promotional pricing systems can be used by companies to fill up slack demand. For example, it is much cheaper in Britain to use the telephone for making calls at the weekend; or even during the afternoon, than it is to use the telephone at the peak hours of weekday mornings. You can get cheaper holidays in major hotels out of the main summer season.

Promotional pricing can be used by retailers and manufacturers to force the market either to sell more, to hold their market position or to make more profit for someone.

Promotional pricing techniques are also used to clear special problems of excess stocks, and low selling lines. Each year, winter and summer, the clothing trade and the department stores hold their sales. The schemes started originally as a means whereby retailers sold their out-of-season lines, their ends of ranges, their awkward sizes. But the whole scheme became so profitable that nowadays the shops and stores negotiate to buy in 'specials' and actively buy for their sales twice a year from suppliers, who often make special sale lines as well as clearing their own stocks. The discounts offered in the sale are often 30 per cent or more on the usual prices, but large sales volume is moved in a short period of time. For many groups of shops, if it snows in January, and rains in July, then they lose money on the whole year's trading. This will kill their sales upon which they rely for their profit.

The advice on using promotional pricing is, in general, do not use it unless you are forced to use it. Find some other way to clear your problem – dump the excess stocks in markets outside your mainstream markets if you can. If you succeed with your discount pricing, then you will encourage your competitors to follow suit, so in the end everyone sells the same as before but at lower profit. And you will encourage buyers to shop around for better 'deals'; you will make your salespeople's job more difficult because they will find themselves unable to sell unless they can offer a special price. You will encourage your customers to switch from paying the full price to paying the discount price.

Skimming and prestige pricing

These two techniques are similar. Both operate at the top end of the market. One is designed to sell high quality at low financial risk; the other seeks to do the same but by using the price itself to promote the idea of status and prestige.

There is always a small group of people who are willing to pay high prices for what they want. They may have a very strong need for a particular product.

New products, entering new markets which have not seen the like before, generally use a skimming price technique. This allows them a profit at a low manufacturing level. It is their hedge against things going wrong. The risk is minimized. Practically all radical new products start by a price skimming technique. It is the competitors which bring the prices down as they copy their way into the market.

There is a demand at the top end of every market. And the price skimmers go for it. They do not sell huge volume, but they do not need substantial manufacturing plant nor great overheads. They make money, and they sleep at nights. Their market sectors tend to be more stable in bad times than the major market sectors. They sell to people with money. Generally, they have less hassle about price than those who sell to people without money.

This is a very comfortable way of business for a small specialist company without large resources. For such a company which can produce brilliantly at the top quality end which some people want, the skimming price or the prestige price system is recommended. But notice one proviso; the quality produced must be relevant to what some people want. It is not a question of producing what the technicians call 'quality'. It is not quality for its own sake. It is quality which is relevant to the performance which the buyer wants. And the quality for such producers must extend to everything they do; it must extend to their switchboard; the efficiency with which they handle correspondence; the truth of their sales story and so on. This is the way to a successful and profitable life – not *the* most profitable life, because in terms of absolute cash profits, you need more sales volume. But it is a good life.

Penetration price

Penetration pricing technique is where the market is undercut significantly and in such a way as to make it impossible for competitors to respond. As a result, there is a major increase in sales volume. It is an attractive idea in logic; but it is the route to disaster for most companies if they are forced into it.

A penetration price technique is dangerous, but it can be successful provided that managers know exactly what they are doing. A company with massive resources can use it with comfort. But a good rule of thumb is this; if your proposed very low price in the market does not succeed in gaining you extra business, will the move seriously damage the rest of your business as a whole? If the answer is that you cannot afford to fail, then do not do it.

So, if you are thinking of a penetration price technique, then you must be brave. You must perceive that the market can be distorted for all time out of its present shape. You must perceive that a large number of new users will come to you and you will open up a substantial new market, previously untapped. The existing competition must be unable to compete with you on your price. You must have some technology available to you which is beyond the capacity of your competitors. And you must cut deep. Very deep. Do not even think in terms of 15 or 25 per cent. You must think of 40 per cent off the existing prices or even more. Maybe as much as 75 per cent off. (Less in food, more in durables.)

That is the penetration price technique. Have you the nerve for it?

Surveying the market

I wish there was a way in which this section could be more helpful to you – but most of the answers from market research are inadequate. The reason why companies do not use prices based upon what the market will bear is that there is no truly adequate way of measuring what the market will bear. You cannot ask 3000 housewives in a survey what they think they will pay for a new type of toothbrush. They do not know the answers themselves until they are actually buying it.

In some industries there is enough competitive information published with great frequency so that the volume sales of a product at any given price can be predicted with accuracy. In commodity trading, for example, all that is necessary is to study the market reports.

In consumer markets, specialized market information can sometimes be drawn from panel studies such as those provided by AGB Ltd. If individual purchases of toothbrushes are measured by a panel over a period of time, it may be technically possible to identify how the market will respond to price promotions. A market test in one area may be used for predicting market reactions across the country.

In industrial markets the research techniques available are extremely limited. They are also costly and time-consuming. The element of management judgement in setting market-related prices is extremely high in industrial marketing.

The best rule is to remember that the key factor at the end of the day will be judgement based upon experience of the market. Use every piece of evidence which can be gathered and which is reliable to assist in this judgement. Every time there is a price change then record the results. Measure the market and its various segments, compare the competitors' prices serving those segments.

In America, in the UK and on the Continent, many research companies have attempted to assist with specialized market trial techniques or other direct research methods into pricing questions. The applications are very limited and the results are often rather abstract and uncertain. But do investigate the technical possibilities of using market research – there may exist a valid technique in your particular market. But do not let your researchers become too excited about data based upon small samples. Forty respondents are not going to tell you how to price your industrial product with any degree of reliability – and it may cost you £3,000 to interview these if the product is in any way technical.

In consumer markets try to avoid asking people about their future intentions, or their opinions about price. Better to conduct some kind of trial on an orderly basis and then observe their behaviour. After this you can ask for their opinions.

Competitor-related pricing systems

The price leader

Most markets are divided into segments of varying kinds. Some segments offer high quality, high levels of service, and take high prices. Others offer as little as they can and price it low. There are others in between. There are distinct kinds of buyers involved for each segment. In each market sector, you will find a 'price leader'. This is the company in the market which is used by its competitors as a yardstick for comparison. Commonly, it is the market leader, the biggest selling product in that segment of the market but this is not always necessarily so. It is the one who tends to make the first move on prices, up or down, and its competitors tend to follow.

If you use competitive pricing as your principal technique, then pick the price leader in your segment. Against it, if you offer a discernible product difference, a distinct improvement which the market definitely wants (not what you think it should want) and you can sell this difference hard, then take a premium price a shade over your chosen competitor. Do not pick all the competitors – just pick the key company and go for it, on its weakness in product or service performance.

If you offer nothing over your competition but what you offer is comparable to what it offers, then chip under it on price by between 10 and 15 per cent. It must be that size of discount against it if you do not offer any advantage. If you yourself are the price leader, then maintain your psychological domination over your competitors using a little reward and punishment. Be nice to them when they do something you like or behave the way you want them to behave. Turn nasty when they do not behave properly. If you are going to turn nasty, then turn very nasty indeed, so they will not do it again. Otherwise they will begin to enjoy setting you up.

Market share pricing

This is very similar to the penetration price technique with very deep discounting. Remember that competitors will not sit back and let their sales go without a fight, and some of them will fight dirty. You are going to start a price war -- the buyers will see to that. 'Sorry, can't do business today,' they smile, 'just had a good offer in from a rival. You can have the business, but you'll have to beat their price.' And that is the way the price war starts.

Do not do it in a high technology market – the market is more price sensitive towards the bottom end with 'me-too' products. A twin segment strategy can be quite useful for a market share pricing technique. This is where your profits are secured by your operations in the high price, high value sector of the market, but you dump out your B grade product or your second brand to keep the competition down.

Discount pricing

This is different from promotional pricing in that the discounts are used as a way of life. The technique is to set an artificially high price, and then to discount off it. Discount prices can be formally published as a series of offers for a given time or for a given quantity.

Discounts might not be published, however. In which case, if buyers do not ask, then they do not get. So professional buyers handle their interviews with care. They pull in two or three companies for quotations and find out what they can get from each of them. Then they pull in their chosen company and squeeze it to give all the concessions the others have offered to them. So the bargaining hassle begins.

Everyone knows that car dealers will reduce the price of a secondhand car. But the buyer has to negotiate it. Dealers will give away as little as they can. But they will still discount if asked. Luckily for the salesperson, not every car buyer has the courage to ask.

Advice on discount pricing: do not publish discounts if you can avoid it. You will do better if you negotiate them individually. Second, if you are discounting, then vary the terms a lot. Put a time limit on every deal and then renegotiate it. Whatever you do, do not let your discounts become rooted in the structure of your price list, otherwise you will give away money for nothing. If you must do this, because everyone else does it, then set the prices higher than usual and show even bigger discounts. But generally keep the situation as flexible for yourself as possible.

Negotiated prices

Here we have the full range of manoeuvre at work. Each party starts in a situation of some uncertainty about the other, which gradually becomes clarified. Each party is conscious of its alternatives – buyers seek to maintain competition for their business for as long as possible and will use this leverage in discussion. Sellers use the uniqueness of their proposition and its relevance to the buyer's situation in order to back their demands for price. Buyers raise price as soon as they can in the discussion – sometimes demand it in writing before discussion. Sellers seek to announce their price as late as possible in the discussion, once the buyer's excitement has been aroused. Buyers will seek to get as many extras as possible included in the overall price. Sellers will seek to unbundle the package and price each of their

Table 16.4 *The do's and dont's of discounting*

Do's	Dont's
Keep your aim in mind.	Offer discounts because everyone else does.
Make surcharges if they will not pay.	Offer settlement discounts if there is another way of getting yourself paid.
Be creative with your discounting.	
Use discounts to clear stocks.	Copy everyone else.
Put time limits on the deal.	Discount when there is no need.
Discount for extra business.	Publish discounts for all time.
Make sure discounts are passed on.	Let them stick in the trader's pocket.
Discount only to survive in mature market.	Give them away automatically.
Use different discounts for different groups.	Discount with a new product.
Keep flexibility, keep reviewing.	Use on discount for all purposes.
	Let the chief give the money away.

items separately. Buyers will seek to leave their requirements open on some matters until after the agreement has been signed so they add them in at no cost later. Sellers will seek to have some part of the agreement left open-ended, so that they can add bits and pieces to their prices later.

Tendering

One of the most difficult problems facing managers will be the price at which to submit a tender. When several companies offer very similar products or services, then a large customer, typically a local authority or government department, may ask several firms to bid for the contract.

Companies usually seek to find out all they can about the expectations of the customer before submitting their bids, but it is in the nature of things that customers are very reluctant to give out information about competitors' bids or other factors involved. Once the specification has been drawn up and offered to the market, then it is too late for a

supplier to do much about it. On the other hand, it has been known often enough in the past for news of a forthcoming tender to be leaked to suppliers well in advance. Suppliers' technical experts then have a vested interest in getting behind the purchasing department to the people who will be concerned with drawing up the specification. If these people can be influenced by technical arguments to draw up the specification in such a way that very few companies – perhaps only one company – can meet it, then the bid can go in at full price in the clear knowledge that it is the only one which can be accepted. The opportunity to do this may be limited, but it may be worth trying where possible.

Equally, there may be other small advantages which can be promoted. For example, it is not always the lowest tender which is accepted. If two tenders are close to each other and one of them comes from within the local authority area, then the local firm will usually get the contract. If one company can offer a reciprocal trading arrangement with the large customer, then this will give it an edge.

If, in handling the contract, suppliers can show that they will use local labour which will help the employment situation in a local authority area, then this will give them an edge on price. Look at the features of your proposition which lie outside the specification itself and promote these.

Pricing in action

Price negotiation

Your business will be concerned with its main customers. Call them national accounts or key accounts or what you will, the fact is that relatively few of them will account for an enormous proportion of your income. If you make profits at the rate of, say, 5 per cent on your turnover; if you can negotiate an extra 1 per cent on the price from all the accounts which are responsible for half of your total business, then you will have increased your total profit by 10 per cent. If you could negotiate a 10 per cent increase from these key accounts, then you will have doubled your total profit.

Consequently, you must pay attention to how you deal with these key accounts – they are all likely to be shrewd and tough buyers who know how to use their power. You must match them in skill.

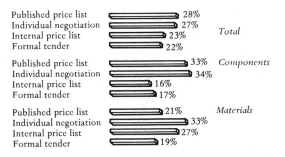

Published price list	28%	
Individual negotiation	27%	
Internal price list	23%	*Total*
Formal tender	22%	
Published price list	33%	*Components*
Individual negotiation	34%	
Internal price list	16%	
Formal tender	17%	
Published price list	21%	*Materials*
Individual negotiation	33%	
Internal price list	27%	
Formal tender	19%	

Considerable price discretion is used within industry as indicated by the figures for the 'internal' price lists and the prices negotiated individually.

Figure 16.2 *Pricing systems used for different types of product*

In setting up the deal, remember that a few things are important all the way through. The first of these could be called *style*. If you are going to deal with major customers over the years ahead, then realize that they will learn how to handle you, just as you will learn how to handle them. If you are too sharp, too tough, too cunning, or simply inefficient, then they will know the next time. So you may get away with something the first time, but they will remember and will seek revenge upon you. The style of approach used on the first deal should set up the relationship for the future.

Suppose that you meet these big prospects for the first time. They might be very aggressive. They might insult you or your company. They might use competition ruthlessly against you, or they might press hard against your weakness. If you give in to this pressure, they will always use the same style upon you. So it might even pay you to withdraw nicely from the deals, with great courtesy, leaving yourself a way back for later.

If you have the courage to do this, it may pay handsome dividends for the future. If you do business later, they will modify their behaviour to you, because they know now that you cannot be browbeaten. Of course, you may lose the deals altogether and never get back in! That is the risk you take. But remember, there is also a risk in staying there and putting up with this pressure, because they will screw down your deals for ever and a day.

Search for *collaboration*, not conflict, is the second point to remember. From time to time, you will get into conflict with your key accounts, a complaint, a

clash of will, but if your relationship with them is friendly and cooperative, then it can withstand this kind of pressure. At the start, you cannot afford conflict, however, particularly if you are in a very strong position. If you use your power brutally, then they will either withdraw, or get their own back on the next deal. But to achieve collaboration you will have to sense what they want from you. You will also have to know what you want from them. This means that you must explore their situation, find out their background, and assess their needs *before* you make your own presentation.

So the general rules are to watch your style and your integrity. If you say something, mean it, and deliver all you promise. Look out for the things they want from you, and be concerned with the things you want from them. Try and get into a position where, later, you can begin to exchange the two. Ask for all you think you might possibly get. Be brave.

Now let us set up the deal in four stages. Define the objectives, what you want. Position the deal in their minds. Get to the first offer. Keep them hooked on your big ideas.

Make a list of all the things you want from them; all the volume of business, in all your product groups, from all of their sites, over a period of time.

So get your objectives sorted out and hold on to them – your top one, your expected one, and the bottom line. And if you settle for the bottom line call this 'failure' – after all, it is next to not getting the business at all. Do not persuade yourself it is success just because you have landed a piece of business at any price.

Now there is a problem, because if you go in too high too soon and stick to these early big demands, then if they are thinking of something much less, they will be offended or frightened and will walk away. If you have been too strong, then you will lose them. If you do not know how they are going to react to what you want, then do not make an explicit demand, rather suggest it instead. Get the idea floated in their minds. Talk about the deals done elsewhere. Give them reassurance that this is a perfectly normal deal for them. And give them a little time to get used to your idea if they are not expecting it. One good technique is to ask them not to make up their minds now, but to think about it all first and to sleep upon it. Some quite big ideas need to be mulled over, tell them this, it is quite true. You

Table 16.5 *Eight guidelines to follow*

1 Keep your price until the end.
2 Make them open, if you can.
3 Make them do the work.
4 Sandwich your price between benefits.
5 The price should be non-negotiable.
6 Show them the penalties of not buying.
7 Do not squeeze too hard against weakness.
8 Let them win something.

can use the technique even in the same meeting. Get the big idea out into the open, float it around, and say that you would like to discuss this with them, not now but a bit later. This will allow time for the idea to take shape in their minds without closing them off against you. If you hit them with a big idea, and ask for an immediate decision, they will say no and you will have the devil of a job to unseat them.

Finally, keep them hooked on to your big ideas. Give them reassurance that although the idea may appear big to them, it is quite normal. Keep in contact with them – if they walk away and mean it, then you will have to go after them. In this case, ask them for their counter proposal, make them bring their own ideas out into the open. Find a way to be persistent, nicely, firmly.

Progress payments

Your price will have a different value to you depending upon when you get paid. If they give you £1,000 in a year's time, it will be worth much less than if they give it to you now. For example, if they give it to you now, then you could bank it and earn perhaps 10 per cent or more on it, so that it will be worth £1,100 in a year. And inflation will damage the value of money you receive in the future.

So your price must be fixed up with your terms. If you have a long manufacturing lead time, or if you are going to incur heavy costs at the beginning of the contract, but it will not be completed for a long time, then it could pay you to devise a system of progress payments. It is common with many construction projects to ask for one-third payment at the start, one-third during and one-third on completion. The system could be applied in many other money intensive projects. Another way of solving the financial problem is to ask the customers to pay for the costs of the materials themselves and to pay you just for

working on them. If cash flow is your problem, then think creatively about how you set your terms on large orders.

Price presentation

Ease them through the price pain barrier. Talk discounts. Talk terms. Talk savings. Talk about anything but price.

The first thing to realize about price presentation is that it is very painful for buyers to have to think about it. They get very excited, we hope, at what you are going to give them – your product, your service, the benefits you offer them. They get gloomy at the thought of what they have to give in exchange, the price. So you must ease them through the pain barrier, give them an aspirin.

Table 16.6 *Handling price resistance*

When they say	You say
They have not got the money.	What is their budget?
	What is their cash?
	Look at your terms.
	They will actually *save* money.
	Your cost is a small part of their total cost.
	What are they spending now?
Your competitors are cheaper.	Some are more expensive.
	But look at the cost savings to them.
	Show the reason for the difference.
	Compare product differences.
	Miniaturize price differences.
It is not worth it. You are charging too much.	How much is too much?
	Everyone pays the same.
	Look at the returns to them from your offer.
	The unit price is very small.
	What else would they spend their money on?
	But look at the discount they will receive.

Table 16.7 *Checklist of mechanical possibilities* (Whether prices are negotiated, estimated, or contracted for, they might include specific provision for the following)

Relation to list prices
- Net price quotations to distributor.
- Less discount to distributor.

Provision for resale prices
- Suggested prices.
- Recommended resale prices.
- Advertised resale prices.

Pricing extras, replacement parts and repairs
- Separate charges.
- Inclusive with original purchase or with main product.

Discount structure
- Cash (for quick payment of invoices).
- Quantity (for large purchases).
- Trade (for being at certain level in distribution process).
- Promotional (e.g. co-op advertising).

Delivery/transportation
- Prepaid or COD.
- Base point (i.e. prices are calculated from a specified point, regardless of where shipment originated).
- Cost of insurance and freight (CIF).
- FOB factory (free on board) – buyer's pay cost of transportation to their location, plus the same base price paid by all other buyers.
- FOB destination – seller's pay cost of transportation to buyer's location.
- Freight equalization – distant buyer is quoted a delivered price consisting of FOB factory price, plus delivery charges from location closest to customer.
- Delivery included.

Other items affecting quoting
- Guarantee and warranty service.
- Installation charges.
- Service/maintenance charges.
- Allowances (e.g. promotional, co-op advertising).

On price; be prepared. There is no substitute for knowing the market, and knowing the competition. Calculate the benefits you convey upon the other party. Calculate in particular the things you offer (including your own personal advice and skill) which your competitors do not offer, and then force these into their minds. When they argue over your price, these are the things you use to hold them. Calculate all the other little ways you can

ease them through the price pain barrier; through payment terms, through discounts, through extra services just for them. Be honest; but you can put your prices in the best light by showing them that competition is more costly in the long run, that they are spending this kind of money on other things, that your extra quality justifies the extra cost, that they are not being overcharged.

Be creative and imaginative with your price presentation. Do not be afraid of high price, be proud of it. Use your high price to make your quality argument for you. Do not be defensive about price – they will rarely buy the cheapest in the market so someone has to win with a higher price. It could be you. If they want you they will pay.

Price bargaining tactics

Here is how to get what you want out of a complex deal. Remember you are not fighting a battle, you are working towards a solution which is good for you and them. That is the first rule. The second is to know what you want, and be able to have a good guess at what they want. Next, you must decide whether you are going to bundle up all that you want in a package, or break it up into separate bits. Then you go for the exchange.

Table 16.8 *Bargaining: points to look for*

Collaborative bargaining	: Not conflict bargaining
Set your objectives	: Do not play it as it comes
Sort out the bits you want	: Do not do all the giving
If they break up their demands	: You bunch them
If they bunch their demands	: You break them
If you . . . then we . . .	: Do not give it away

Pricing management

Handling fierce price competition

Most price wars are started by buyers. Sensing that the market is soft, and that the suppliers need the business badly, they search widely. Suppliers weaken on their price to get the business. This makes buyers even more determined. The news gets around and the war has started.

At first, buyers enjoy the price war, they enjoy

their power. But later they come to hate it – it is time-consuming, difficult, demanding. They are never sure they have got the best deal. They long for a return to stability.

At first, the salespeople hate the price war. They suffer badly. Later, when they get more power from their managements to deal on their own accord, they come to enjoy it. They enjoy the thrill, the hunt for new business at any price. They have an edge on their own management. 'Do you want to do the business, or don't you,' they say to their chief. 'Well, you've got to give me the authority to deal at their price then.'

Here are eight rules for waging a price war through discounts, based upon the principles enunciated by von Clausewitz last century for the waging of a real war.

Table 16.9 *The principles of waging war*

1   Select and maintain the aim.
2   Use surprise.
3   Maintain morale.
4   Take offensive action.
5   Secure your defences.
6   Maintain flexibility.
7   Use a concentration of force.
8   Use an economy of effort.

How to minimize the damage caused by a price war

Make sure the demand is stronger than the supply

During a recession you must move. It is fatal to stand still. You are going to move in the end anyway because the market will shift you if you do not move voluntarily.

You can move either up-market or down-market. You can add either extra value or strip the product to its core and sell it cheap.

Whatever you do, whether you move up or you move down, remember the golden rule that you should try and aim to ensure that the demand in the market will, in the long run, exceed your resources. That way it puts you in a position of power and control. Your order books will be full and you will get the prices you want with minimum discount.

If your cash flow is good, your profit record is excellent so that you can borrow money in the market should the need arise and, provided that the underlying trend in your market is towards growth, then it can pay you to expand your facilities, knock the price down radically and hammer the competition to the edge of the market. But to do it, you need a discount of at least 25 per cent on the normal selling price in the marketplace, and you may need much more than that. It requires a strong nerve and great courage, but the profits can be considerable.

The alternative is to cut the business back, concentrating on the things you do extremely well and getting rid of all the marginal activities, positioning yourself in a specialized position in the market.

Work your margins and your price

In desperation, to minimize the losses caused by a severe price fight, then carry out the following actions.

1   Strip away every item of spare cost on the central product which is under attack. You must get this bare product price down to compete with and to hold competitive volume. But strip all the associated services and back up from it.
2   Charge extra for everything connected with the product. Charge for delivery. Charge for installation. Charge for service, consulting, commissioning. Make extra charges for special favours, strip the credit facility away. Offer the economy package which is the bare bones of the product with everything else charged as an extra; or the deluxe package with the service all-in plus a few extras. This way your customers will have a choice, and your salespeople have something with which to compete.
3   Walk around your stockroom, your depots. Examine the product range in detail. Raise the small products in price. Raise the slow-moving products in price. Raise the add-on products in price. Raise everything you can but keep the central price fight product down in price – let the rest of the range pay for it.
4   Look at your invoices. List out all the things you could possibly charge into them. Could you charge for telephone calls, administration, handling, telexes, storing? Have this list of items printed on your invoices and then pick up the

costs separately and charge them out. You might easily find an extra 5 per cent or more from this move alone.

Notice that we are talking about the problem of your company's survival. We do not normally need to be so aggressive as this, but in a price fight the pressure is severe, and the margins are so thin that they must be worked hard.

It is not a technique which is designed to build respect and authority. It is damaging to a company's reputation, but in an extreme situation companies at the margin of survival will adopt the practice of 'buy it and cook it'. The procedure is to price as low as is necessary to land the business, then having landed it, work up all the extras afterwards. Add on extra services, sell more volume to the account, tie them up. Builders know the technique well. Ask a roofing specialist for a quotation for a new garage roof and the average small jobber will give you a low price. As soon as he has got off the old roof, he will show you how the joists have sunk, how the wood has rotted and how the rain cannot run away effectively because the central joist is not man enough for the job. 'Whoever built your garage did a hurried job on it. Took short cuts. What do you want us to do?' What will you do? You will pay up, that is what you will do.

And very large building contractors will use the same technique when they have to when bidding for contracts against low price competition.

How to stop a price war

Unless you have 60 per cent share of the market or more, you are unlikely to be able to stop it. And even then, you might not be able to do so. Your only alternative, if you have a lower market share, is to persuade two or three companies whose share adds up to 70 per cent or more of the market, that it is in everyone's interest to stop it. This may run foul of the Monopolies Commission, but if the alternative is going broke, then some companies will do it.

One American marketing professor, D. S. Leighton, (1967) has noted that group behavioural responses are necessary to resolve unstable market situations. To resolve price wars requires a significant and respected leader of the market to indicate the way, added to a mature set of relationships in which each competitor acknowledges and respects the qualities of the others in specialist sectors of the market. Prices are stabilized as a result of competitors having a shared interest in the future of the market as a whole. There must also be a willingness among everyone to penalize deviant behaviour on the part of one member.

Price wars exhaust themselves in the end. Mergers push dying companies together. Capacity is reduced. Companies begin to behave sensibly, others pull out of the industry. And when the price war is over, everyone heaves a sigh of relief.

Making price changes to force your market share and profits

Increasing the price; leader or follower?

The ability to raise a price is to a large extent determined by the ability to control the supply into a given market. You become the 'price' leader by being strong in the marketplace. The price leader is usually, but not always, the market leader. The price leader is the major producer whom the others respect for its knowledge and experience, for the way it manipulates the market, or else they fear it and its retaliatory powers should they step out of line on price.

For the individual company in the specialist market looking for a price leadership position, the following questions must be asked:

- How much control can be exercised over the market; how far can competitors be influenced to move in line?
- How would such control or influence be exercised; what sanctions exist against someone who steps out of line?
- How far is it possible for customers to reject the price increase; have they another source of supply to move to quickly? Is there a substitute product?
- How long will it take to get into a price leadership position; can it be done in three months – a giant supplier with 60 per cent share of the market might achieve the goal simply by warning everyone of its moves and publicising them widely? Or, in the case of a fragmented market where upwards of a dozen suppliers must be cajoled along to conform, the influential approach might take five years or more to build

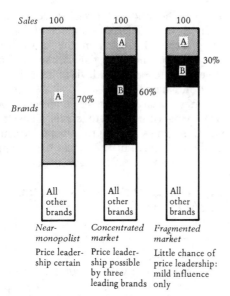

Figure 16.3   *Price leadership*

the necessary respect for the leader.

Price leadership depends upon having accurate information and speedy communications. The moment that someone of significance makes a move on price or discount, then the price leader must know instantly. It must feedback this knowledge to its competitors in the trade rapidly before they hear of it from other sources. This will increase its power – the competition may then become slightly dependent upon it for such information.

In markets which are characterized by aggressive hostile competitors, as many markets are, then there is little hope of collaboration unless the three top competitors can put together above 60 per cent share of the specified market.

In all other cases than the establishment of price leadership, then individual suppliers must make shift with their own resources as best they can.

Putting up your prices

Just because your costs are rising, it does not mean that you can necessarily pass them on in the form of price increases. What the market will bear has got very little to do with costs; it has a great deal to do with the nature and strength of demand.

The first question to ask is whether your customers must absorb your price increase out of their own profits, or whether they themselves pass them on. They will resist, and resist strongly, any price increase which comes out of their own pocket. Their greatest resistance will be against the price increases of products which form a high proportion of their manufacturing costs.

A six-point guide to making price increases

Put the prices up when everyone else does

Hide yourself in the forest. Suppliers often make a great mistake by holding back on a price increase for a few weeks while the rest of the industry goes up, thereby hoping to gain an advantage in extra business. But, the rest of the competition successfully persuades the trade that all the prices are going up, so the trade is reluctant to switch suppliers in the short term; second, when the prices do go up, suppliers make the price increase all by themselves in a cold spotlight of attention. Many of their customers will think they have put prices up twice, and competitors will not disabuse them of this notion. Third, the rest of the trade will not trust the suppliers again. They will be cold shouldered from the councils of war.

Do not hold back: if the others are putting up their prices, then you should go with them. The only exception to this is where you plan a penetration price technique, so that when the others go *up* you put your prices *down*, advertise them widely and aggressively, and make up your losses with increased volume. But this is the strategy of the brave, or the foolish. If you are going to do this, then you must do it so fiercely that you can be certain of driving some of the competition out of the business altogether, because they cannot afford to compete with you. If you have the resources of Fort Knox, then try it. Or if you have unlimited government funds to call upon, then try it – the taxpayer will pay if it goes wrong.

Not too much at any one time

People have a mental yardstick they use when checking prices. Move outside this measure and you will be subjected to cries of immorality, profiteering and all-round greediness unless you can prove yourself innocent.

The common measure of acceptable price increases is the general rate of inflation. Buyers will mentally tolerate price increases which are below or at the general level of price increases in the country; at this level, the need to demonstrate the case remains and buyers will always complain about the price increase proposed. But the increase will generally go through, provided that others are moving by about the same amount.

Difficulty is experienced when a particular company or an industry as a whole needs to push up its prices significantly higher than the general rate of inflation. An increase in the price of an important commodity; a weakening of the currency; or a rapid surge in fuel costs may have a sharper impact upon some industries than upon others. If the price of silver increases, it hardly makes the lead story in the business pages (the price of gold is a much sexier story for journalists). But if you are a professional photographer, you will read the news about silver prices with gloom – sooner or later it will affect your costs dramatically.

So if the industry must move with significantly higher prices than inflation, then it must make a very sound case for it. It must also use warnings and signals in order to get the market used to the idea of forthcoming increases.

Not too often

Keeping your head low down when price increases are about is a good idea, and relatively small, but frequent increases, is one way of doing this. Over a period of time, regular buyers will notice if price increase notifications from the same supplier seem to come flooding through the door at short regular intervals. How often is too often? Well, raising the prices once a week every week is too often.

Generally, a quarterly phasing seems to be as frequent as is acceptable for a company moving slightly higher than the competition. It is always a trade off between frequency and size of increase. Many industries have a tradition of once a year increases across the board. While this provides good cover for a supplier, the routine is too inflexible and does not leave enough room for individual movements against the stream. There is always a lag between the time when a company's cost increase are incurred and the company's ability to put up the prices. This drag must be paid for out of profits. The problem is badly compounded when a company finds it must wait for a price increase until the annual move of the industry.

Get the customers used to small but fairly frequent moves in price. Remember also that prices need not always move upwards; see next point.

Move something down, when you move something up

Companies panic when they move prices. Their need for the extra money is at the top of their minds, and they become insensitive to their customer's position. That is silly, very silly.

Find some economy for them if you possibly can. Point out that there are cheaper products in your range which they could buy. Point out that they can buy smaller sizes if they want to keep their cash payments level. Point out that you have just *lowered* the price of one or two small products in your range. Wherever you can effect economies in production, then you should show that you will pass on these savings to them. It all helps to create less friction, and prevent seizing up. What is seizing up? When the customer throws out your price increase, and throws out your product also, and buys from a competitor in your place, that is seizing up. Prevent it.

Look after your key accounts

Remember that 80 per cent of your profits are in the hands of relatively few customers. These customers you must pay attention to. Give them advance notice, give them a chance to stock up at the old price. Find a way to give them a little more time than the others. The rule is that price increases from you are non-negotiable. Buyers will always assume that you will negotiate them. Your position is that you will never negotiate on the price *increase* but you will negotiate on other factors. Your position should be that the prices to your key accounts must go up with all the others at the same time. However, you are prepared to give them a special promotional deal, or rebate, or allowance, or incentive – you can call it what you like – but basically, what you give them is the extra money back for a period of, say, four weeks.

It is very important indeed that you make price increases non-negotiable to customers. The big ones will always give you a very hard time. They will bureaucratize their power. 'Sorry, pal, we have this memo from head office to say we are not allowed by our company policy to accept any price increases from suppliers for the next three months.' That is very nasty, but it is also a game of bluff.

That is why you must have a counter ready. Give them a moratorium on the price increases for a month or even two, but only if they order their usual amount from you. And ensure that their invoices carry the new prices from day one, but also show the rebate you have called 'special allowance' or some other such elegant phrase. Then it is easier to keep them on the new prices later but to drop the special allowance. The expiry date of the special allowance should be shown on the invoice. Otherwise they will insist it be kept in for ever as a discount. Better to make it a credit note if you can, and not show it on the invoice at all. If they will not play at all on the price increases, then you will have a lot of trouble. If you are in a strong market position then run a bluff; be happy in the knowledge that most relationships with key accounts last for a long time in practice although the ride can be bumpy. If you are weak, then work harder at it, take care to mix up the deal, give yourself something to negotiate with which they would like to have, but which can be withdrawn if they do not play.

Provide sound – and true – explanations

Some companies show their ineptitude when it comes to telling their customers about price increases. Either they are arrogant, or they creep. It is nervousness which does the damage. They are frightened of losing their customers. So they do not put forward their best arguments. Here is the way to do it.

First, add up all the cost increases and show them as percentages against, say, a year ago. Do not fake the figures, the customers will be suspicious enough anyway and they will spot a lie a mile off. Itemize one or two details (show them a photocopy of your petrol price per litre, or whatever was your big cost problem a year ago, compared with the petrol price today).

Demonstrate that the price increase you are imposing is much less than the total of all the cost increases.

Look realistically at your figures; look at the improvements you have made to your business. If it were not for these improvements, then the customers would be paying a lot more. And that is the literal truth. So why not tell them?

When the price increase means survival this is what to do

In a recession, companies must make price increases in order to survive. The first thing to do is to cut away all the waste, improve the productivity, take the overheads right down to the bare minimum, and run the business as tight as a drum. Now plan your price increases. (Whatever you do, in a recession, do not do it the other way by trying to claw back all your losses from the market through price increases at first, and then taking your cost savings for the difference. This is a sure way to lose your entire business. It is the way of the weak company.)

Table 16.10 *Ten ways to increase 'prices' without 'increasing' prices*

---

1 Revise the discount structure.
2 Change the minimum order size.
3 Charge for delivery and special services.
4 Invoice for repairs on purchased equipment.
5 Charge for engineering, installation, supervision.
6 Make customers pay for overtime required to get out rush orders.
7 Collect interest on overdue accounts.
8 Produce less of the lower margin models in the product line.
9 Write escalator clauses into contract.
10 Change the physical characteristics of the product.

Putting your prices down

This is an art in its own right. If you want to make money out of putting your prices down, then you must do two things. You must put your prices down when everyone else is staying up – stand clear of the forest to be noticed – and you must advertise the price reduction like glory. It is no good just hoping that the market will come crashing to your door just because of your price reduction. Nothing much will happen unless you blast it out to all and sundry. Drop your prices in a big lump – do it once – do it suddenly, without warning and put the maximum pressure on the competition. Have *their* key accounts lined up for your salespeople and a secret sales plan for each of them to attack your competitors at their most vulnerable points with your new prices immediately. Go for new volume business. Pick off your new target customers one by one.

Do not expect them to come to you, they will not. Left to themselves, they will go back to their existing suppliers and squeeze them for lower prices with the news of your low prices. You will have to make a strong personal selling effort to win them over to you. Give your sales force all the backing you can afford. It is an expensive business putting down your prices.

Organizing for pricing decisions

Try to give your people down the line as little discretion to vary price as possible. They will have to have some – but make sure that they always make the customers struggle for the discount. The best way to do this is to make sure that they have to struggle for permission to give it themselves. They will not like being strapped down like this, but it is the only safe way.

In small organizations with few people, chief executives can control prices easily. As the business grows, they employ other people. The business becomes less sensitive, less flexible. The business is bigger, more complicated. The product range is wider. The business serves a wider range of markets. Costings are too complicated to be carried in the head. The business ends up with an organization structure. There are committees. Departments get in the way of each other. Salespeople cannot get a hearing in the higher reaches of power.

So the further the business organization removes itself from the market, then the less sensitive it is to the marketplace. And that has a direct impact upon pricing decisions.

Make sure you have a good analysis about the market, about the competition and about your costs and profits. Make sure that this analysis comes

together in the same place at the same time; and ensure that doubtful data from the marketplace is verified independently. Sales information is a fair source provided you do not believe everything the buyers tell you; check the information using several different people.

Strategic pricing decisions relating to market share goals or margin goals should be reserved for top management decisions using recommendations from below.

Be sensible about transfer pricing and make sure that savings are shared between the buying and selling divisions within the same group, otherwise resentment breaks out because one division feels that the other has all the advantage. If you must load the price to a division because you want to take offshore profits, then give them a token allowance in their annual performance assessments.

Make sure that any discount given to customers is given to them by the salesperson handling the account, and not by the salesperson's manager. The manager him/herself should be much more difficult on price than the salesperson when both are in front of customers. This way, customers want to deal with the salesperson in future, not with the manager.

So make everyone work hard for the things they feel they must give away, and publish to the field force the total amounts given to the customers by the field salespeople.

The pricing decision

The general decision on margins as a whole should be set by general management. A basic requirement of the business should be to improve efficiency and to reduce the unit cost over a period of time, so as to maintain the gross margin. Another should be to trade your prices effectively in the market.

Within the general framework of pricing policy, the marketing management team can now set prices for products and markets based upon market data; policy guidelines on costs and margins, and management accounting information. Some multiproduct companies have a management account function built into their marketing department structure, and this is an ideal system because it brings together the costing skill with the market analysis without destroying the element of 'feel' or intuition which is such a vital part of the pricing process.

Conclusion

Various aspects of pricing are discussed in this chapter; price setting, presentation, negotiation, bargaining and management. To put the message of

For establishing pricing policy

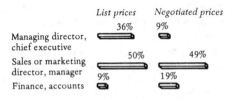

For calculating actual selling price

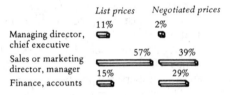

Figure 16.4 *Who has the primary responsibility?*

this chapter into practice have a pricing policy agreed by top management, known down the line and acted upon. Base it ultimately upon some notion of a suitable profit return upon investment. This will translate into an average gross profit return across the board needed for a given volume of sales. This 'average' now needs to be modified because you will need to earn higher margins on some product ranges to compensate for the lower margins on other product ranges. Add this requirement to the need for new product development; match it to market potential; add in the market and competitive pricing data, and you will have a pudding to delight the cookers of your books and the marketers of your products when they come together to set prices and discounts.

References

Brown, W. and Jacques, E., *Product Analysis Pricing*, Heinemann, 1965.

Industrial Market Research Ltd, *How British Industry Buys*, 1975.

Leighton, D.S., *New Developments in Pricing Strategy*, Bradford Management Centre, January, 1967.

17
Selling

JOHN LIDSTONE

Introduction

A sales force is *one* of the most effective marketing tools that can be used by a company to create and keep customers. But since the cost of keeping a salesperson on the road is high, marketing management must first ask the question, 'what cost-effective role does the sales force play in achieving the company's marketing objectives?' Behind this question is the unspoken one, 'if we did not have a sales force, would we have ever invented one?'

For most companies the answer has been to recognize three stark facts of economic life:

1 A sales force is an expensive marketing tool that must be directed selectively towards very specific objectives, markets and customers.
2 Salespeople must produce profitable, not just voluminous, results to justify the financial investment.
3 In the fight for markets and for sales revenues, the role of the sales force is of crucial importance.

Throughout the world thousands of men and women are employed in selling products, services or ideas. In the highly competitive environment in which the majority of firms have to sell their products today, salespeople are often the spearhead of a company's total marketing efforts.

They carry the main responsibility for getting through to the customer and securing the order.

Vast financial resources are committed by commercial enterprises on the assumption that they will succeed in doing so.

As the managing director of a major manufacturer, summing up the challenge facing his company at the end of a national sales conference said: 'After our clever marketing men and women have put their plans to bed, after production has made what our marketing researchers have told us people have told us people want and will buy, we are not in business until you (the salespeople) have sold these products again and again to our existing customers and to new ones. That is the importance of the sales force'.

Why do we need salespeople?

The art of persuading people to buy products, services or ideas is as old as the history of mankind. What is constantly changing is the marketplace in which salespeople and the companies employing them operate. Selling is like art. It mirrors the age in which it is practised. Historically, salespeople were employed to sell the products or services that companies decided to supply. This production-minded approach was only successful while the entrepreneurs who created them did not have too many competitors or, while products were in short supply, their salespeople could almost push goods on to customers or were persuasive enough to influence them to buy what the manufacturers had made.

Today this is no longer true. The development of the *marketing concept* has produced the greatest and most marked change in the attitudes of manufacturers and those who sell their wares to their greatest assets – their customers and potential customers. Most of the products and services we need have become plentiful, supply often outstripping the demand for them. Competition has not only become acute and ruthless between companies but has intensified between countries such as those in the European Economic Community, Japan, others in the Third World and America.

The secret of survival – let alone of success – in business has turned from the manufacture of products as such to the prediction of what people need and will want to buy.

Thus the development of the marketing concept – the creation of customers and keeping them satisfied – has led to the need to find out what people want and then make it rather than the traditional approach of making things and then trying to sell them. This approach, by no means new, recognizes that customers create a business and satisfied ones are the cornerstones of its continued existence.

But the development of this customer-facing attitude and policy, however rigorously and imaginatively pursued, does not alone answer the problem of how to survive. What one company decides to do can also be done by others. The knowledge, skills and information among competing manufacturers large and small today are similar. What one company spends millions of pounds or dollars on over several years and invents today, others can imitate tomorrow. And patent laws, as the British pharmaceutical industry, record and film industries and makers of pocket calculators and other electronics goods have discovered to their cost, are no insurance against the pirating of their products. So another fact of commercial life has had to be recognized. That imitation is quicker and cheaper than invention and less risky. Similarly, the costs companies incur producing and distributing their products and services tend to be identical as are their ultimate selling prices to the buyer.

The marketing environment

The environment in which manufacturers, commercial, industrial and services companies operate and compete with each other is characterized by three factors.

Similarity of products and services

The products and services offered by competing companies tend to be similar if not frequently identical in appearance and advantages. Indeed in many of the fast-moving consumer products such as foods and paper tissues, brand leaders stare across at themselves from opposite shelves in supermarket and self-service shops, except their twins are called 'own label' and are virtually the same product. There is little to choose between similar makes of mass-produced motorcars. In the electrical gadgets field the only difference between transistor radios, pocket calculators and tape recorders in similar price brackets is the manufacturer's name. Take the back off and all share a common origin – Japan or another far eastern source of cheaply produced printed circuitry. The catalogue of identical products is endless. Services such as banking and packaged holidays reflect the same pattern of similarity.

Similarity in prices and discounts

The prices charged by companies for similar products and services also tend to be alike. New and/or superior products and services are charged at a premium. This happy state of affairs lasts until a competitor enters the same market and starts to encroach on sales. Then prices are reduced. Thus with some very notable exceptions, in the vast majority of products and services we buy (detergents, petrol, food, clothes, banking and insurance) those offered by competing companies tend to be alike in product and service benefits and in prices we pay or discounts we are allowed if we are the distributor. And this is true whether we are marketing in London or Lisbon, in Scunthorpe or Singapore, since multinational companies develop transnational specifications for their products and parity of standards.

Presentation to the customer

The main difference between competing manufacturers, servicing companies, supermarket chains and multiple stores is in the way they communicate with their customers. It is the one area of the company's three things offered (products, prices, presentation) where the greatest control and direct influence can be brought to bear; in the *presentation* of products, services and ideas to the customers or consumers by means of public relations, advertising, packaging, direct mail, telephone selling, exhibitions and the sales force. But however good all the other methods of communication are, in the majority of companies the bulk of the presentational effort is carried out by the sales force (see Figure 17.1).

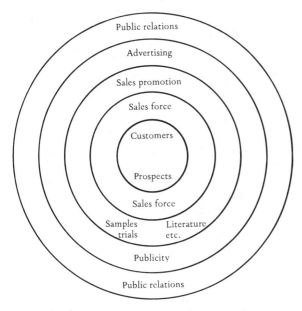

Figure 17.1 *Circles of influence*

The importance of the sales force becomes self-evident when you consider that in some markets the only difference between competing companies is the relative quality of their sales forces. In markets such as office equipment and life assurance, buyers' decisions are more often than not determined by who calls on them, what they say and how they say it. In many markets, the sales force is the only significant advantage a company has over its competitors.

The changing nature of selling

There are other changes taking place that affect the role and the importance of the sales force. Six major changes can be seen.

The development of the market concept

During the 1960s, companies developed marketing departments which almost to the exclusion of other people, had the responsibility of 'looking at our business through the consumer's eyes and providing products and services to satisfy their needs at a profit'. Now we are passing through a stage in which such a concept not only involves the whole firm but all *functions* worry and give priority to the needs of the customer. But moving on again, prodded by an articulate and increasingly sceptical public, towards broadening the marketing concept, everyone in a business enterprise and not least the sales force is going to worry more about the *well being* of customers, rather than just whether our products satisfy their needs – which marketing research has hitherto neatly identified.

The growth of multinational companies

The EEC has changed the approach of many capital goods' producers, chemical manufacturers and retail stores towards their markets. A market or sales territory covering three or four countries rather than counties or cantons has become a common feature for many companies.

Companies are tending to become larger but less numerous

Takeovers and mergers bear ample and almost daily testimony to this development. Before 1939 there were over forty car manufacturers in the UK. Today there are only four major ones. At the beginning of this century every town of any size boasted its own brewery; today there are only ninety-nine in existence and this number is decreasing yearly. Such a development means that no company and, in particular, no salesperson can let down such organizations in its product quality or in its service and hope to retain the business. For the salesperson whose job is to develop and maintain business with such giant organizations, the implications are stark. The attitude of 'I was just passing by so I thought I would pop in to see if there was any business' is thankfully rarely heard by customers when salespeople call on them. But no less dangerous now is the attitude of salespeople to a call that failed in its objective either through lack of planning, seeing the wrong buyer or discussing the wrong product to meet a particular customer requirement: 'Oh well you can't win them all. I will get the order the next time round.' There will *not* be a next time for salespeople who have not done their homework before they call on customers. This is true of more and more marketing situations.

Buyers are becoming increasingly powerful

Following from the previous factor, the buyers of your products and services in the companies, manufacturers and retail shops/chains to whom your salesperson has to sell are, because of their purchasing power and the size of their orders, becoming much more powerful. Matching this increased power and influence they are also becoming much more sophisticated in their knowledge of the products of their suppliers; in financial knowledge and the effect on profitability of their buying; in negotiating the purchase of supplies, and furthermore in their own marketing and selling. A Swiss chemical company, an electronics group and one of the world's largest car manufacturers have taken the education of their purchasing officers to the point where they are given selling courses alongside their company's own sales force so they have a better appreciation of the selling techniques used by salespeople who call on them.

Competition

Competition between these giant organizations is increasing as each seeks to defend or expand market shares and control the key factors that influence prices and buyers' decisions. For example, manufacturers of motorcars, tyres and car accessories own or virtually control their distributor outlets. Every company, particularly multinationals competing with home based companies, is going to exploit every opportunity to expand at the expense of others.

The role of the salesperson

These factors of economic life and changes in the marketing environment do not lessen the importance of the sales force. On the contrary they mean that the sales force will have a more decisive influence on the success of marketing plans as their work becomes more specific. Companies have recognized

that customers create a business, but only by keeping them satisfied can a company prosper. If they do not, others will. This means that every sales force must be recruited and selected, trained, motivated and developed to perform as skilfully as it can its prime and vital task – the reason for its existence – to identify the needs of customers and satisfy them.

Customers are becoming more sophisticated in their tastes, more knowledgeable about the products and services they buy or reject, and more critical and conscious of those who supply them. The salespeople who sell them must be more professional.

The marketing environment in which companies operate implies that salespeople will be needed as *never* before to perform a vital but changing function. Where once the salesperson was a jack of all trades selling everything to everyone, he/she must now specialize, performing fewer tasks but more effectively and efficiently. Some companies are appointing salespeople to deal with just one major customer or to look after a particular sector of a market. The sales force and each member of it will be the spearhead and apex of a triangle through which more costly and tailored resources will flow.

New products, new technology and new techniques, mean that the salespeople must be creative in their selling rather than just react to customers and their needs. People's needs do not change, but the means of satisfying them do. However large companies become, they will ultimately succeed or fail, like the corner shop by their abilities to identify, anticipate and satisfy customers' requirements profitably. Likewise salespeople must be trained, motivated and controlled in such a way that they become more skilled in identifying and satisfying customers' needs faithfully, efficiently and constantly.

Techniques of selling

Before examining the selling techniques salespeople use, the selling process first needs to be understood. Indeed, what is selling?

What is selling?

It is widely believed – and among many sales managers too – that selling has a mystique of its own and cannot be analysed. The dramatic rise of some of the washing machine empires during the 1960s and the more recent growth of financial and unit trust opera-

Table 17.1   *The nine categories of sales position*

Type of position	Sells	Job characteristics
1 Inside order takers	Usually serve behind a shop counter. Customers have made up their minds to buy, e.g. groceries, hardware. They serve them; they may suggest alternatives.	Little opportunity for creative selling but may trade-up choice; main job requirements are to be reliable, of good appearance and courteous.
2 Van salespeople	Mainly deliver food and non-food products, e.g. fuel-oil, coal, laundry, soft drinks, milk, bread, etc.	Reliability. A pleasant manner and good service are more important than aggressive selling. Few do any creative selling.
3 Manufacturer's salespeople calling on retail trade	Sell food and non-food products to shops, supermarkets, cash and carry, e.g. detergents, hardware, food, books, etc.	Mostly repeat selling; a pleasant manner, good service and reliable to follow a regular journey cycle; little scope for creative selling.
4 Goodwill builder 'missionary salespeople'	Educate potential users of the product or users to widen or increase their use of it, e.g. pharmaceutical products to doctors, brewery representatives, and specifier's products (architects, engineers).	Usually cannot take orders but build a climate of awareness in which the benefits of a specific product or service will be favourably considered when the need arises.
5 Technical salespeople	Sell electronic equipment, industrial products or highly engineered component parts to original equipment manufacturers.	Major emphasis is their technical know-how. Often too preoccupied with technical details: tend to forget their job is to sell. Far better to employ someone who can sell than an engineer who might or might not!
6 Creative speciality salespeople of tangibles	Sell consumer durables that are often desirable but not essential, e.g. washing machines, cars and educational books.	Have to make the prospective customer dissatisfied with existing product or situation before they can begin to sell their product. This requires a highly structured selling presentation and they are salespeople who face many refusals; a sales job often truly described as 'hard' selling.
7 Creative speciality salespeople of intangibles	Sell intangibles which are often desirable but not essential to life, e.g. advertising space, life assurance, stocks and shares, incentive schemes and banking services.	Usually more difficult than the previous category because the product is less readily dramatized; its benefits come later or are difficult to comprehend. A very hard selling job requiring persistence and a highly structured approach.
8 Political or indirect salespeople	Sell products or services to large users: fuel-oil contracts, flour to bakeries, cement to local authorities, chemical aggregates such as sand, gravel, etc.	Usually little or no differences between competing products or services offered. Salespeople only have themselves to be better at looking after the needs of the buyer; he is a wheeler-dealer, sometimes a skilled negotiator, and sometimes a politician.

Table 17.1   *contd.*

Type of position	Sells	Job characteristics
9 Multiple salespeople	Sell products or services to groups of people such as committees, boards of directors, project teams of engineers, e.g. computers, technological products for defence equipment, research or consulting services, pension schemes and merchant banking.	The most difficult and skilled selling job; the salespeople usually make presentations to several people with different, rather than similar needs. Usually more people say 'no' to their propositions than say 'yes'. They must have presence, charm and a highly-developed empathy.

Notes:
Categories 1 to 5 are usually highly structured in every aspect of the sales job, e.g. who to see or is seen, what to do and how to do it, the procedure for completing sales administration.
Categories 6 and 7 much less structured yet need to be to combat the high amount of refusals which reduce the cutting edge of selling skill.
Categories 8 and 9 are very little structured. Also very few people are qualified to do this selling successfully. That is why they earn a lot of money as a rule.

tions have been attributed to the wizardry of born salespeople aided by occult powers. This mystery even remains when some of the most successful practitioners write books about selling, largely because they do not understand it and so cannot explain what they do and how they do it.

Although selling is different from all other business activities it is possible to define and set out certain features which are common to all sales situations. It is then possible to say what basic requirements a person needs to become a salesperson. Many sales managers believe that if a person can sell, say, grocery products they will be equally successful selling industrial products or intangibles such as insurance. While all sales managers can quote success stories to prove their point, there are, nevertheless, dangers in taking this assumption (or wishful thinking) too far. Selling is not a unitary vocation in which people start at a certain basic level sales job and automatically graduate through stages to different and more complex types of sales activity. Paradoxically, many of the most difficult sales jobs are the easiest to obtain, for example, selling speciality products such as household hardware, life assurance, or encyclopedias. They have also been the graveyard of thousands of sales careers.

Nine distinct types of sales position can be classified as shown in Table 17.1. Most sales jobs are combinations of one or more of these categories, particularly those such as technical adviser or bank manager. A closer look at these categories, however,

reveals an important distinction which must be taken into account when considering the training a particular type of salesperson requires.

The differences relate to the extent to which each sales job is structured, for example how precisely every aspect of the sales job is defined, spelt out, journey cycled and supervised. As a generalization, sales positions in the first five categories are highly structured; the next two far less so, while the last two categories have very little job structure.

A visit to a customer can be a mixture of many different situations: some simple ones of physical delivery, others involving high level complicated negotiation. The person who can adapt to and gain business in such variable situations can be regarded as a professional salesperson of the highest order.

Why do people buy things?

It is easier to understand the true nature of selling and define the basic requirements for a professional salesperson if one first analyses the reasons why people buy, because in the nine categories of sales position there are basic needs common to all customers. The answer to the question 'what makes people buy?' is the cornerstone of selling technique because it enables salespeople to plan how they can make themselves, their company and their products or services interesting to each of their customers.

If we look at early 'primitive' society we find people took actions to satisfy their basic needs. The

Table 17.2 *Order of importance*

Customers		Salespeople	
1	Themselves Satisfaction of their needs, e.g. mortgage to buy a house, new machine to increase production	1	Themselves Their company Their products Their ideas
2	*Their needs* and the benefits which satisfy them	2	*Their product* and making their customers buy it
3	The *salesperson* Salesperson's company Salesperson's products Salesperson's ideas	3	*Benefits* to their customers
4	*Buying* from the salesperson	4	*Customers' needs* Benefits which satisfy their customers' needs

ultimate goal was simply to survive. To achieve this other needs, such as those for food, shelter, clothing and sex had to be satisfied. Nowadays these basic needs manifest themselves in many different ways. Nevertheless, whether at work (acting as a buyer for the firm) or at home (buying for the family) people judge products, services, ideas and other people in the light of their own needs. We can state quite simply that: *people buy things and take actions to satisfy their needs.*

In most selling situations there are two people: a customer who has needs and a salesperson who has products or services. Customers never buy the products or services a salesperson offers but what the products or services do to satisfy their needs. These end results or benefits are the links in the chain that leads to a sale. When a salesperson has no benefits to offer in the products he/she presents or in the language in which he/she describes them, then there is no sale. People will buy from a salesperson and take the actions desired by the salesperson if they know that by doing so they will receive benefits which will satisfy their needs.

What are the basic requirements of a salesperson?

The desire to satisfy particular needs is a characteristic common to anyone in a buying situation, whether he/she is the purchasing director of a major engineering group of companies or a pensioner. There are also certain characteristics which should be common to all salespeople. Like the nine categories of

sales position, there will, of course, be big differences in their degree and emphasis, but the basic characteristics are the same. Two factors make these characteristics necessary. The first is that sales situations are for both salespeople and customers unnatural social relationships. The second is that the things which are important to customers are not always seen as important from the salespeople's viewpoints, particularly if they have had little or no sales training. The result can, understandably, end up in the conflict of priorities shown in Table 17.2.

Customers are most unlikely to see things from salespeople's points of view. *Everyone is to him/herself the most important person in the world.* Therefore to be successful salespeople have to be able to see things from customers' points of view and demonstrate through their words and actions that they have done so. Their chances of success are greater if they can understand the needs of the people they talk to and make them realize that they can help them fulfil these needs. The ability to do this depends on a combination of innate personality characteristics and acquired knowledge which can be summarized under four headings: the right job attitude; product or service knowledge; sales technique, and work organization.

The right job attitude

Salespeople need to have a job attitude which combines the twin attributes of enthusiasm and empathy. Enthusiasm means wanting to establish themselves, prove themselves, be accepted by others

Table 17.3   *Product analysis (agricultural tractor example)*

Customer needs	Benefits that will satisfy customer needs	Product features from which the benefits are derived
1 Rational		
Performance – must be able to work fast with a variety of implements	Plenty of power, particularly at low speeds	A 65 BHP diesel engine with high torque at low rpm. Wide range of matched implements available
Versatility – must cope with a variety of soil and cultivating conditions	Can travel at a wide variety of speeds	A 10-speed synchromesh gearbox – four wheel drive available for very difficult conditions
Simplicity – must be easy to drive	Simple and speedy implement changeover. Easy to drive	Quick-attach linkage with snap-on hydraulic couplings. Ergonomically placed levers and pedals
Low cost – must be economical to run	Low fuel consumption	Efficient engine design with improved braking and fuel injector system. Good power/weight ratio
Reliability – must be able to operate continuously and be serviced quickly	Well-proven design with all basic snags removed. Local dealer with 24 hour parts service	More than 10,000 units already in operation. Wide dealer network with factory-trained mechanics backed by computerized parts operation
2 Emotional		
Security – fear of making wrong decision	Most popular tractor on the market – 10,000 farmers cannot be wrong	Largest company in the industry with good reputation for reliability and value for money
Prestige – desire to gain status in the eyes of others	Chosen by those engaged in best agricultural practice	Favoured by agricultural colleges and large farmers

Notes:
1   The product analysis should be completed from left to right. Only when the needs have been identified can the appropriate benefits and the relevant features be selected.
2   If salespeople work from right to left not only will they lose their buyer's interest as they talk about items which may not be of interest, but also they will have no basis for selecting which benefits to stress.
3   This example is not intended as a complete analysis. That can only be done with a specific buyer in mind as each person has an individual need pattern. Performance will be most important to one farmer, low cost to another.
4   It will be noted that some of the product features are so technical as to be almost meaningless to the layperson. This is one of the greatest dangers for industrial salespeople. Unless they translate their trade jargon they will fail to achieve understanding and thus cannot be persuasive.

and exercise control over the decisions made by others. Empathy involves the capacity for reacting to the experiences and emotions of others without necessarily taking their side; of wanting to help. To some extent these attributes cancel each other out, but successful salespeople combine the two in such a way that they meet the needs of customers and achieve their own sales objectives.

Product or service knowledge

Product knowledge is too often taken for granted by companies and by salespeople. Sadly, experience of hearing countless hundreds of salespeople talking unintelligible gibberish does not support this complacency. Salespeople are usually given inadequate knowledge and it is slanted towards the company and not to the customer. Every salesperson must be taught about products from the customer's point of view. This is a very difficult concept to grasp. Buyers buy to satisfy their needs. These needs are satisfied by the benefits of the product or service; these benefits are derived from technical features of

Table 17.4 *The buying sequence*

How people buy	How to sell	
	Sales objective	Sales technique
1 I am important	To explore and identify customer's needs	Opening the sales interview
2 Consider my needs		
3 How will your ideas help me?	To select and present the benefits which satisfy the customer's needs	The sales presentation
4 What are the facts?		
5 What are the snags?	To prevent by anticipating snags likely to arise or handle objections raised so that the customer is satisfied with the answers	Handling sales objections
6 What shall I do?	To obtain a buying decision from the customer or a commitment to the proposition presented to him/her	Closing the sale
7 I approve		

the product or service. Salespeople should analyse everything they sell in this order before they meet a customer. In this way their thinking and their orientation will be towards the customer. No exercise repeated at regular intervals with each salesperson will yield the sales manager more sales than analysing product in terms of

Customer's needs → Customer benefits → Product features

Table 17.3 illustrates how this is carried out.

Sales technique

Selling skill is too often viewed as a natural ability or talent rather than a technique that can be acquired. A successful salesperson is one who has mastered the art of persuasive communication. Sales technique involves understanding people's logical and emotional reactions to a sales presentation.

Salespeople are frequently subject to refusals. There are always more people who say 'no' to salespeople than 'yes'. This tends to demoralize salespeople because they may feel this refusal of their product as a social rejection of themselves. Selling technique consists of doing and saying those things which will reduce the risk of refusal and make it easier for salespeople to reach their sales objective.

Sales interviews should be prepared, not played by ear. Such preparation gives the salespeople more control over the sales interview.

The sales interview is usually considered to pass through the stages of identifying customer needs, creating interest and desire for the benefits that are offered, overcoming or preventing objectives, and closing the interview by getting a buying decision.

How sales technique is applied to the buying sequence through which every sale passes is illustrated in Table 17.4.

Work organization

Salespeople must develop good work habits and be organized to make the other basic requirements of good salesmanship as effective and productive as possible. This involves classifying customers and prospects, planning customer meetings in advance, analysing sales interviews afterwards to improve future meetings, journey planning to avoid wasting unnecessary time travelling, and reporting activities accurately and when required.

A definition of selling

It is important for sales managers and their salespeople that both know what selling is and agree a common definition to concentrate their minds and inspire their efforts to put it to work.

The types of selling done in all nine categories is usually *personal*. Even when faced by a group of

Table 17.5 *Action planning checklist*

	Evaluation	*Action and timing*
1 What is the company's definition of selling? If there is none, write one.		
2 What category(ies) of sales positions (see Table 15.1) are employed in the sales force?		
3 How are these different categories of sales position structured to ensure that the salespeople are: (a) Trained regularly? (b) Motivated? (c) Controlled?		
4 What actions have been taken to analyse products on a 'customer needs: customer benefits' features basis, (see Table 15.3) to ensure that salespeople communicate with customers from a needs viewpoint? If no actions are taken, make the necessary decisions by writing them down now.		

people, salespeople are selling to *individuals* each with their own particular needs, preferences and prejudices. Customers want to be assured that salespeople understand their needs and their point of view. Salespeople can only achieve this if their communication with the customer is *two-way*. In the eyes of many customers there is little difference between the products and services offered by competing companies. They have to be *persuaded* that there are differences which will help them.

Drawing all these factors together enables a definition of selling to be made as follows:

Selling is personal individual persuasive two-way communication aimed at achieving planned sales objectives.

Interviewing techniques

The structure of the sales interview

For simplicity the sales interview can be broken down into its component parts:

1 Preparation
2 Opening
3 Presentation
4 Objections handling
5 Closing

This is the structure around which salespeople should build the flesh of their interviews so that the

problems of tension, nervousness, lack of appeal to customer needs and woolly talk are reduced. An example of a structured format for planning a sales interview is illustrated in Figure 17.2.

The benefits of having a structure

Many salespeople and some managers discount the need for planning the sales interview. They will argue that because one cannot foresee what the customer will do or say, planning and preparation are pointless. This is making perfection the enemy of the good, because to some salespeople such preparation implies a muzzle on the mouth. But can salespeople play sales interviews off-the-cuff when the company's turnover depends on the way they communicate with customers, who are short of time, and when competitors are also after the business?

Preparation

The cornerstone of preparation is the proper use of customer records. Too few salespeople regard such records as an aid to their selling, more as a chore that head office insists they maintain. The benefits to the salesperson of an effective record system will be the information it provides about the needs, habits, idiosyncracies of customers and prospects, the numbers and types of decision makers in a business who can influence the sale, the products they use and do

	Objectives	Methods
1	Specific objective(s) of call is?	
2	Plan to see .... who has the need and authority to make a buying decision	
3	My opening will be designed to	
4	My presentation will aim to	
5	I anticipate that the following objections will arise : (a) .... (b) .... (c) .... (d)	
6	I want to obtain the following decision(s) from the buyer: (a) .... (b)	
7	To support my sales presentation I need the following equipment, visual aids and correspondence:	

Figure 17.2 *How sales interviews should be structured*

not use, and why, and a host of other data. Customer records will help salespeople to identify the *correct* objectives for a sales interview and enable them to plan how best to achieve them. The benefits of preparation can be summarized as follows:

1 It gives salespeople confidence because they know what they plan to do and how they are going to do it.
2 It makes them think ahead. They know in advance the broad lines of their plan, so that when carrying it out they can concentrate on listening to the customer and not become preoccupied with what to say next.
3 It enables them to talk in a positive way and from the customer's point of view.
4 It gets more business in the limited time there is available for selling.

What should salespeople prepare?

Salespeople should think about the following factors when preparing each sales interview.

1 *Call objective(s)*. Is it clear that salespeople have a definite purpose for the call which will promote the sale of the company's products or services? If not why are they calling? General statements such as 'to sell our range of equipment' is not good enough or precisely defined. It fails to identify customers and their individual requirements. The more specifically an objective is stated the greater the likelihood of success, for example: 'To reduce this customer's loss of production time by getting him to install our XJ1 Mechanical Handler.'

2 *Opening words*. After the usual introductory courtesies, how are they going to get down to the purpose of his call so that the customer is made to think and talk about his needs or problems?

3 *Presentation*. What benefits will he offer? Will they meet this particular customer's needs? What evidence will he use to prove the benefits he offers, for example third party reference success stories? What visual aids can he use to illustrate his story? Has he brought them with him?

4 *Objections handling*. What objections is the cus-

tomer likely to raise? How will he answer them?

5 *Closing*. How is he going to close the interview and get a buying decision or commitment? Does it match his call objective?

If salespeople do all these things consistently then they are doing a good job for their company. If not, they are falling short of their potential and both salespeople and their companies are the losers.

How successful sales interviews should be conducted

While the preparation provides a call strategy, how is that plan to be implemented to achieve a successful sales interview?

Opening

First impressions can be crucial. The unnaturalness of the sales situation sets up tension for salespeople and customers. Planning will help to put salespeople at ease. Their opening should put customers at ease also, and do much more. At the start of sales interviews the salespeople want to achieve four objectives:

1 Create a good impression
2 Gain the customer's individual attention.
3 Explore the customer's needs.
4 Get the customer talking about them.

Let us examine each of these objectives in turn:

Creating a good impression

Do they say and do those things which create a warm, friendly atmosphere which makes the business part of the interview run as smoothly as possible? Do they command respect? Are they polite without being servile?

Gaining the customer's attention

Do they make customers listen because they want to and not because they have to?

Exploring customer's needs

This is one of the most vital stages of the interview. Before any real communication can proceed, customers must be given the time, opportunity and reasons to express themselves. This can best be done by asking carefully directed but open-ended questions which get them talking rather than making monosyllabic 'yes' or 'no' replies.

The questions chosen and the words used will dictate the area of need salespeople want to concentrate on or explore. If the questions begin with: How? What? Where? When? Who? Why? Which? then they will invite and encourage comment from customers. Such questions should allow comment and not require justification or defence.

An example of the open-ended questioning technique

A bank manager is anxious to obtain the account of the owner of a firm who he knows is planning to step up production dramatically and is going to need money to do it. The bank manager has been granted an interview with the managing director, whose account is held by another bank. The introductions have been made and the interview begins:

Managing director: 'Do you know this is an unusual experience for me. I usually have to come and see my bank manager and not for the most agreeable of reasons. You must want something.'

Bank manager: 'No Mr Head, the purpose of my visit is to find out whether I can help you. Let me explain. This report in last week's *Echo* about your proposed expansion plans (here manager opens newspaper and shows to Mr Head) was it correct?'

Managing Director: 'Yes except they did not say how much overseas business we hope to win.'

Bank manager: 'That is most interesting. My congratulations. Tell me how much increased production do you plan?'

Managing director: 'At least 25 per cent by next December.'

Bank manager: 'How much will this cost?'

Managing director: 'Our first estimate is about £282,000'.

Bank manager: 'How do you plan to raise that kind of finance?'

Managing director: 'I was wondering whether you might have some proposals we could consider?'

As soon as the answers indicate an area of *need* which salespeople can meet and satisfy, they are in a position to sell benefits to the customer. The greatest single failing of salespeople is their inability to understand the concept of needs, and their reluctance to identify them. Yet knowledge of and identification of each customer's needs are the prerequisite of all successful selling.

Presentation

If salespeople are successful in establishing customers' needs or identifying their problems, they are halfway to success. Customers will be interested but they want to know whether the salespeople's propositions will produce benefits which satisfy their needs to solve their problems. During the presentation, the meaty stage of the interview, salespeople often fall into the trap of talking about product features.

Some examples of what salespeople say about their products or services which they fondly (and also foolishly) think will appeal to the customer now follow. All are true.

Example one

A valve salesperson is selling plug-type valves containing a chemical, the benefit of which is that it keeps the valve permanently lubricated and therefore trouble-free. He is talking to a sewerage works superintendent.

Salesperson: 'And above all, the best thing about these valves is that they are low Mu.'

The result of the call was no sale.

Example two

A sausage salesperson is selling a brand of sausages in a small shop which has just been bought by a married couple new to the retailing business. The sausages are pork and in packets of eight. The benefit, if there is one, is obscure:

Salesperson: As you are wanting to start with a good balanced stock of popular sausages you will want some pork eights, won't you?'

The result of the call was no sale.

Example three

A salesperson is selling corporate credit cards to the general sales manager of a company employing ten export sales executives. He has worked out that if the general sales manager gives his salespeople credit cards the benefit to them will be the convenience of not having to carry considerable sums of money with them on each tour. But this is not a benefit as such to their manager.

Salesperson: 'The great benefit to them, of course, and to you too, is that they need never carry large amounts of cash in future on their overseas visits. That must make it worthwhile mustn't it?'
General sales manager: 'It may be worthwhile to them but as it appears to offer me no tangible improvement on savings I think we will carry on as we are.'

Do salespeople think and talk about benefits?

Remember, benefits are the desirable results from the customer's point of view and, in business terms, from the points of view of all the other people the customer is concerned with – customers, staff, and their families. Benefits do not include any of the following:

1 The technical features of a product or proposition: 'This boiler has a thermal capacity of 85 000 BTUs'. 'This unit trust policy includes life cover.'
2 The way a product is packed.
3 The price of the product or service.
4 The methods of operation.

Benefits are the desirable results produced by these various features for any person who uses the product. Their effectiveness and their appeal depend on the extent to which they satisfy a customer's needs or problems. People buy products, services, and ideas, for what they *do*, not for what they are.

Do salespeople use third-party references?

In other words, do they make skilful use of the satisfaction experienced by other customers who have bought the product or service? In particular, do they focus upon the benefits they are getting? To prevent the choice of any third-party references backfiring on them, do they mention people or firms who: Are respected by the customer? Are faced with the same conditions?

Do they use stories to illustrate their argument?

Do they explain what other companies or customers have actually said about their experiences, either with or without their company's products?

Do salespeople ask progress test questions?

A productive sales interview involves two-way communication. It is important that salespeople get feedback from customers to confirm if they have heard, understood and agreed so that any doubts can be cleared up and questions answered. Do salespeople during the presentation check these things by asking questions such as: 'Am I right in thinking this is what you want?' 'How does this strike you?' 'What would your family think about that?'

Do they use visual aids?

Models, catalogues and leaflets add variety to their presentation and pictures to their words. Do they: Keep visual aids hidden until needed? Stop talking when the customer is looking at them? Remove them after use to minimize distraction?

As a brief summary, check the presentation against these points. Do salespeople: Talk about benefits related to the customer's needs? Use third-party references? Use stories to illustrate their argument? Ask progress test questions? Use visual aids?

Objections handling

Sooner or later in the majority of sales interviews, objections will be raised. Obviously salespeople must know the answers. But knowing them and putting them across to the customer's satisfaction are two different things.

Winning an argument may satisfy the ego but is not very productive. First, are salespeople aware of the existence of the raised emotions which accompany an objection and do they take steps to remove or reduce unfavourable emotions either by listening to the objection without interruption or by 'sparring'? By the latter is meant pausing after hearing the objection out, answering customers by saying the objection is understandable and deserves serious consideration, and playing back customers' questions to clarify full understanding and to check if it is the only objection preventing the customers deciding to buy. The 'sparring' technique is illustrated in Figure 17.3. Having 'sparred' with customers, do salespeople use the right methods to overcome the particular objections raised?

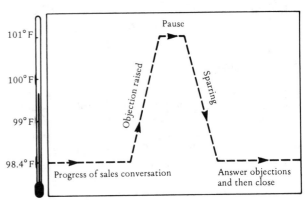

Figure 17.3 *Sparring the objections*

Closing

Closing the sale by asking for a buying decision is one of the weakest areas of sales techniques. It needs to be the strongest. There are two main problems.

The first problem is in salespeople's minds – their fear of social rejection. In a free society where customers can usually buy from at least two suppliers salespeople cannot escape rejection from time to time. Yet unless they close the sale successfully, their chances of achieving their preset objectives are nil. Putting it bluntly: 'If you cannot close you cannot sell.'

The second problem is that salespeople believe the close is divorced from the actual progress of the sale and that the presentation will be sufficiently beguiling for customers to buy without being asked. This rarely happens. The close only converts acceptance of the idea, plan or product into action. The close is also important for customers. They need this help to reassure them in the decision they want to make or have made.

What is a close?

A close is the achievement of the preset objective of salespeople's calls. In most industries it is the signing of the order. Some salespeople work in industries, particularly the goodwill builders – category four – where the nature of the trade makes it difficult to physically obtain the order at the end of the sales interview. Pharmaceutical representatives promoting ethical drugs to doctors, brewery representatives, manufacturers of building products promoting their products to architects, surveyors and town planners, etc., are examples of this.

Whatever the sales situation there are major indications that customers have 'bought' and can be asked to commit themselves in words. These indications include:

1 When they actually say they will buy the product or write it into the specification.
2 When they ask searching 'buying' questions about the in-use characteristics of a product: the type of service most relevant to their type of business; in the case of a doctor speaking to a pharmaceutical representative, questions about the dosage, side effects of a drug, etc.
3 When customers name the product in the context of using it to solve a problem or getting it to solve someone else's need that they are concerned with.
4 When they ask if they can have a demonstration or a trial.

When to close

The close should be attempted by salespeople immediately acceptance of the idea is shown. This acceptance may be customers' outright statements that they want to order. More often their acceptance will manifest itself in the form of *buying signals* or buying questions such as questions about the success rates other people have achieved with the product, its side effects, in-use characteristics, or the method of payment; also discussions about the order size or guarantee period, etc. The tone of voice, hesitancy, posture, the calling in of another person to give an opinion or to have a look or admire, are also signals.

If salespeople have checked each step of their presentation to ensure understanding and agreement they are better able to judge the psychological moment of acceptance and to close.

How to close

At the close it is imperative that salespeople should concentrate on customers and the satisfaction of their needs or problem, and not on the product. There are many techniques for closing. Salespeople must know how to employ them and which ones will be most effective in any given sales situation. The important point is that salespeople must close clearly, confidently and persuasively. Their choice is very much dependent upon the type of persuasion needed with particular customers. Here are the most widely used and most effective ones:

The direct request: 'May I go ahead and place an order for two machines?'

Immediate gain from immediate decision: 'By opening a deposit account immediately you can get the maximum benefit from present interest rates now.'

Alternatives: 'Which of these two models do you prefer, the green one or the white one?'

Assumption: 'You have obviously already decided what to do. The only problem we have to deal with now is the quantity you are going to need to commence production next month, isn't it?'

Third party reference: 'Bloggs and Partners, similar to yourselves, have invested in this system and have been able to reduce staff costs. Would it not benefit you to do the same?

Summary close: 'There are four benefits you can enjoy . . .' (then list them one by one keeping the most important to the end).

Closing on a question or objection:
Doctor: 'What preparation do you offer?'
Salesperson: 'How will you want to use it?' (Not '20 × 25 and 200 × 25 mg, or in suspension of 4 oz'.)

After the close

The close is made when the objective of the sales interview has been achieved. If salespeople fail to do this, do they keep the initiative by mentioning or arranging another meeting?

If they succeed, do they give customers a feeling that they have achieved something worthwhile and not been bested?

Do they provide this reassurance by repeating the main benefits customers will obtain from the decision they have made?

Conclusion

It is a sobering thought that the survival of some of the largest corporations ultimately depends upon the persuasive tongues of a handful of men and women scattered throughout the country!

Dealing with a variety of individuals, subjected to

unnatural social encounters, separated for long periods from their superiors, these salespeople can easily develop bad selling habits which can spoil their performance. Few salespeople actually sell, that is expose themselves to the danger of getting business, for more than 20 per cent of their working day. The tools of selling are the salesperson's words and actions. They are in direct competition with salespeople from other companies. They use words to gain business. Their words can also lose business.

Let us now examine the prime responsibility sales managers carry for training and developing their sales personnel to maintain their selling skills at the level needed to succeed.

Managing a sales force

Sales managers are responsible for getting planned sales objectives achieved *through* the efforts of their salespeople and not *for* them. This means that sales managers must build and maintain a sales team which will be *stable*, *productive*, and *satisfied*.

Difficulties facing sales managers

Getting planned sales results presents sales managers with certain difficulties which they must recognize and deal with if they are to be successful in obtaining them.

Initially they should recognize the fact that the salespeople they manage are normally *geographically spread*. They usually work from home and spend the greater part of their working lives in unsupervised situations. This causes problems of communication, motivation and control.

What should also be recognized is that *selling is a social skill* and salespeople are employed to use it to persuade customers to part with their own or their firm's money in exchange for products, services, or ideas. This is a socially unnatural situation and one which frequently brings customers and salespeople into conflict, particularly those who sell consumer-durable products such as cars, double glazing, or encyclopedias, or intangibles such as advertising, insurance, etc. The things that are important to customers are their needs, their problems and their requirements. Naturally, these are not as important from salespeople's points of view. They will tend to talk about their company, their products, and even the orders they need. As a result, salespeople are frequently rejected at the start of a sales interview or refused an order at the end of it. *This erodes their selling technique.* If salespeople are to be productive, sales training must be given as an essential and continuous process to repair morale and eroded technique.

Every sales manager looks for that elusive gold mine 'the born salesperson' but few find them. There may be one or two star performers, but most sales forces are largely made up of average salespeople. Yet to combat resistance from customers and competition from other companies their selling must be *above average* to gain business. Sales training must be directed at creating the performance difference needed (see Table 17.6).

Sales managers must recognize that those who choose selling as an occupation are usually the least equipped to cope with the strains that go with it. Selling attracts many people who have failed in their first choice of career either through lack of

Table 17.6 *Four difficulties facing sales managers*

Difficulties	Implications
1 Sales force – geographically spread	● Communicating ● Motivating ● Controlling
2 Selling – a developed social skill	● Keeping high standard of skill
3 Customers – often refuse salesperson's proposition	● Loss of morale ● Erosion of selling technique
4 Sales force unsupervised for over 90 per cent of the time	● Providing frequent leadership to repair morale ● Training to develop selling skill

Table 17.7 *The sales manager's job*

Prime job objective: to achieve planned sales objectives through the efforts of the sales force

Key tasks	Knowledge	Skills
1 Train and develop new salespeople		
2 Train and develop experienced salespeople on a regular basis		
3 Appraise and evaluate sales performances of the sales force on an individual basis		
4 Motivate the sales force to achieve planned sales objectives		

opportunity or of application to pass the necessary examinations. Such people often need constant, strong leadership, yet the very nature of the job makes it difficult to supply. People who choose selling are usually very sociable individuals who enjoy and need constant companionship. Yet selling is socially one of the most lonely jobs a person can choose.

The training functions of sales managers

What then must sales managers do to get the sales results they need through their sales force, bearing in mind that they will be judged by the sales they multiply through them and not by the amount they sell for them? In order to build and maintain a stable, productive, and satisfied sales force and to overcome the difficulties that stand between them and their goals, sales managers must carry out four specific functions (see also Table 17.7):

1 Train and develop new salespeople.
2 Train and develop experienced salespeople on a regular basis.
3 Appraise and evaluate the sales performance of their team so that necessary action can be taken to ensure achievement of planned sales objectives.
4 Motivate the salespeople to achieve their sales objectives.

In carrying out these four functions they will be providing the two ingredients essential to sales success: leadership and support for people faced with a lonely life and isolated from day-to-day contact with

the company; and training to develop their skill and combat the constant wearing-down process caused by customer contact. Bear in mind that *if managers cannot train, they cannot manage.*

The main cause of failure among sales managers

Managers can only be successful if they recognize that their role is that of a teacher not of a salesperson. They must develop others to sell and not seek frequent opportunities to show off their own prowess as a salesperson. This is the fundamental difference between being a salesperson and managing salespeople. It is also one of the root causes of failure among sales managers.

They are usually promoted because they have shown they are good salespeople. Yet as sales managers that is the one thing they must resist doing. If then they had not been trained to train others, what do they do?

Frequently they see their job as getting out with their salesforce and involving themselves in their sales calls. The better they are as salespeople, the more they will be tempted to take over the sales interview in the mistaken belief that somehow this will teach them how to sell. Rarely will it improve the selling skills of the salesperson they accompany.

Sales managers must be able to sell

To be successful they do not need to be brilliant salespeople. Nevertheless, they should be competent ones. They must understand the principles of selling and how to apply them so that they can impart this knowledge to their salespeople. During the course of training new salespeople, they must be able to show by example the standard of salesmanship they want their salespeople to reach and exceed; only if their own standard is above average can they expect above-average performance from those who emulate them. And while they should not try and outshine their star salespeople their own selling must command respect from the whole sales force to enable them to follow their leadership. Salespeople have scant respect for sales managers who 'can easier teach twenty what were good to be done, than be one of the twenty to follow mine own teaching' (*The Merchant of Venice*, Act 1, Scene 2).

Conclusion

The two major influences on all salespeople are their customers and their sales manager. While their customers are the source of their sales and success, sales managers are the lynchpin in that relationship. They multiply and improve the presentation of the company and its products through the salesforce. Through their skilful training they counteract the erosion of selling technique which customers have on their salespeople. Through their training they lead and manage their salespeople towards the company's objectives and in doing so satisfy the needs of each salesperson. *But if they cannot train they cannot do any of these things.*

The material from this chapter is based on extracts from John Lidstone, *Training Salesmen on the Job*, 2nd ed., Gower, 1986.

18
Branding
PETER DOYLE

Introduction

The role and valuation of brands has recently become a controversial issue. Not only is the importance of successful brands emphasized by marketing managers, but some financial executives have developed a new enthusiasm for brands, having seen that their inclusion in the balance sheet enhances shareholder funds, reduces company gearing, and so facilitates further growth by acquisition. This paper explores five key questions about brands:

1 What is a successful brand?
2 What is the value of a brand?
3 How are successful brands built?
4 What are the comparative advantages of buying brands versus building and developing them internally?
5 What are the logic and economics behind brand extension strategies?

The successful brand

Before defining a brand, it is first necessary to define a *product*. The concept of a product is not straightforward. First, products and brands are mistakenly often associated only with fast-moving consumer goods. But today, the most rapidly growing and profitable products are in services: financial; retail; and management services. Also, besides products and services, people, places and ideas can be thought of as 'products'. Politicians, movie-stars and privatization schemes are now marketed in much the same way as Coca-Cola or Crest toothpaste.

Second, products mean different things to people *inside* the business, than they do people *outside*. Inside, to the firm's managers and accountants, a product is something produced in the factory or the office. It is about materials, components, labour costs, quality and output specifications. But outside, to the consumer, a product is something different – it is a means of meeting his/her needs or solving their problems. These needs and problems are as likely to be emotional and psychological as functional and economic. It is a product's ability to meet these needs and aspirations which creates its value. The value of a product is not what the producer puts in, but what the consumer gets out. As the chief executive of Black and Decker put it, 'Our job is not to make ¼ inch drills, but to make ¼ inch holes'. Or the chairman of Revlon Cosmetics, 'In the factory we make cosmetics, but in the store we sell hope'. Similarly, IBM has always maintained it 'doesn't sell products. It sells solutions to customers' problems' (Rodgers, 1986).

A product then is *anything which meets the needs of customers*. When several companies are offering rival products, they will want to identify and distinguish their particular offering. This is called 'branding', so there is a Black and Decker brand, a Revlon brand and an IBM brand. But the focus here is not on brands *per se*, but on successful brands. Just because people are aware of a specific brand does not mean that is is successful. People recognized brands like the Sinclair C5, the Ford Edsel, the Co-op, or Wimpy restaurants, but they did not develop preferences for them. The recent Landor survey (1989) found, for example, that British Telecom was in the UK's top ten brands for awareness, but in terms of esteem it was rated number 300. BT has been referred to as a strong *negative* brand. It was known for all the wrong reasons.

A positive or successful brand can be defined as follows: *A successful brand is a name, symbol, design, or some combination, which identifies the 'product' of a particular organization as having a sustainable differential advantage.*

'Differential advantage' means simply that customers have a reason for preferring that brand to competitors' brands. 'Sustainable' means an advantage that is not easily copied by competitors. That is, the business creates barriers to entry, for example by developing an outstanding reputation or image for quality, service or reliability (for a useful study of the issues surrounding the concept of a differential advantage see Day and Wensley (1988)). Brands like IBM, Coca-Cola, Sony and Marks and Spencer are successful brands because they have such sustainable differential advantages, which, as shown below, invariably results in superior profit and market performance. Successful brands are *always* brand leaders in their segments.

Two implications of this definition can be noted. First, brands are only assets if they have sustainable differential advantages. If they are negative or neutral brands like BT, Woolworth, or the Austin Maestro, they should not appear on the balance sheet, however much is spent on advertising. Any profit these brands achieve is through their property or distribution investments rather than through the brand's differential advantage.

Similarly, if the differential advantage is not sustainable, it should not appear on the balance sheet. In some markets such as games or children's toys, a successful brand often has a life expectancy of only six months and thereafter has no value.

Second, like most other assets, brands depreciate without further investment. If management fails to re-invest in enhancing quality, service and brand image then the brand will decline. Hoover, Singer, Fridgidaire, and MG are examples of brands which were once so successful as to be almost generic names for the product, but which have since declined or disappeared due to lack of investment.

This is often underestimated. Most models suggest that brands tend to decay logarithmically (e.g., Parsons and Schultz, 1984). This means that in the short term, managers can increase profits without damaging the brand's market share, by cutting back brand support. However, the mistake is thinking that brand disinvestment can be continued. Without adequate support, typically after around a year (Clarke, 1976), the brand enters a period of spiralling decline.

How brands work

Brands work by facilitating and making more effective the consumer's choice process. Every day an individual makes hundreds of decisions. He/she is besieged by countless products and messages competing for attention. To make life bearable and to simplify this decision-making process, the individual looks for short-cuts. The most important of these short-cuts is to rely on *habit* – buy brands that have proved satisfactory in the past. This is particularly the case for low involvement purchases, which make up most of the things people buy. This does not mean that people are totally brand loyal, of course, since most of them know that many brands will satisfy their needs. Most people ask for Coca-Cola but they are not too disappointed when they are offered Pepsi.

But this habit rule is not just based upon experience of use, it can also be based upon longstanding *perceptions*. People can have quite strong brand preferences even though they have never bought the products. This is especially true for aspirational products. My son has long had a preference for a Porsche, even though he has still to wait another five years before he is old enough for a driving licence. Such preferences or brand images are based upon cultural, social and personality factors, as well as commercial stimuli like advertising, public relations and prominence of distribution.

Even with non-routine, supposedly highly rational purchasing situations in the industrial sector, where decisions are taken by technical personnel, it is remarkable how important brand image is in the choice process. Even industrial buyers tend to rely on experience and long-held attitudes about the brand, rather than undertake a zero-based approach to the wide range of alternative options (Levitt, 1983). As the cynical IBM salesperson is supposed to have said to a purchasing manager, 'Nobody's ever been fired for buying IBM'.

Successful brands are those which create this image or 'personality'. They do it by encouraging customers to perceive the attributes they aspire to as being strongly associated with the brand. These attributes may be real and objective (e.g. quality, value for money), or abstract and emotional (e.g. status, youthfulness). The personality of the brand is a function of its rational characteristics but this has to be augmented and communicated to consumers through advertising, design, packaging and effective distribution and display. These position the brand's personality in the consumer's mind, generate confidence, and create the purchasing environment. A more complete description of consumer behaviour and its implications for brands can be found in a number of excellent texts including Bettman (1979); Engel *et al.* (1978); Howard and Sheth (1969).

The value of a successful brand

Successful brands are valuable because they can create a stream of future earnings. It is useful to dissect the mechanisms by which brands generate these income streams.

Brands, market share and profits

A successful brand is one which customers want to buy and retailers want to stock – it achieves a high market share. Brands with a high market share are much more profitable. The well-known PIMS findings (Buzzell and Gale, 1987), based on detailed studies of 2600 businesses, showed that on average,

products with a market share of 40 per cent generate three times the return on investment of those with a market share of only 10 per cent (Figure 18.1). Weak brands mean weak profits. A UK study shows that for grocery brands the relationship is even stronger. The number one brand generates over six times the return on sales of the number two brand, while the number three and four brands are totally unprofitable (Figure 18.2). The pattern is similar in the US, where a recent survey of American consumer goods showed that the number one brand earned 20 per cent return, the number two around 5 per cent and the rest lost money (*The Economist*, 1988).

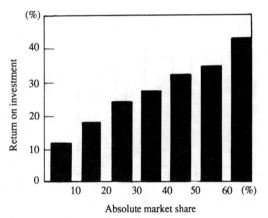

Figure 18.1 *The relationship between market share and profitability*
Source: Buzzell and Gale, 1987.

Rank	Net margin (%)
1	17.9
2	2.8
3	–0.9
4	–5.9

Figure 18.2 *Market share rank and average net margins for UK grocery brands*

The value of niche brands

The above findings do not mean that the brand has to be large in absolute terms. It is normally much more profitable to be number one in a small niche market than to be number three in a huge market. It is market share which is the key to performance, not absolute sales. In fact, Clifford and Cavanagh (1985) provide convincing evidence that a strong brand in a niche market earns a higher percentage return than a strong brand in a big market (Figure 18.3). In large markets, competitive threats and retailer pressure can hold back profits even for the top brand.

Four year average return on investment

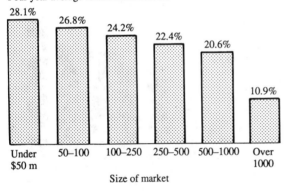

Figure 18.3 *Size of market and business performance*
Source: Clifford and Cavanagh, 1985

Brand values and prices

Because successful brands have differential advantages, they are normally able to obtain higher prices than less successful brands. Sometimes this occurs at the customer level but more frequently it is earned at the retailer level. Strong brands can resist pressure from the trade for discounts. This, in turn, generates superior earnings. Clifford and Cavanagh (1985) found that, on average, premium price products earned 20 per cent more than discount brands (Figure 18.4).

Four year average return on investment

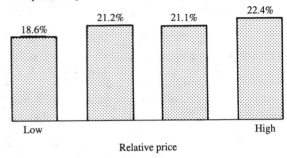

Figure 18.4 *Relative price of products and business performance*
Source: Clifford and Cavanagh, 1985

Brand loyalty and beliefs

Successful brands achieve higher customer loyalty. Unsuccessful brands or new brands have to attract customers. This hits the net margin because it is much more expensive in advertising, promotion and selling to win new customers than to hold existing satisfied ones. One study suggested that it cost six times as much to win new customers as to retain current users (Peters, 1988).

Strong brands can also override the occasional hitches and even disasters which can destroy weaker brands. After terrorists poisoned samples of the leading analgesic, Tylenol, in 1987, US retailers had to remove entirely the brand from their shelves for several months. Once the scare was over, however, customers went back to the brand they trusted, leading to a remarkably complete recovery for Tylenol. Tom Peters tells a revealing story about Federal Express (FEX), which has a superb reputation for service. He telephoned FEX twenty-seven times over a six-month period to request service. Twenty-six times a FEX employee answered before the first ring of the telephone. On the twenty-seventh time the telephone ran repeatedly without any response. After repeated rings, he put the phone down because he assumed that *he* had made the mistake of calling the wrong number! Of course, if this had been a neutral or negative brand it would have simply reinforced one's current image of the brand.

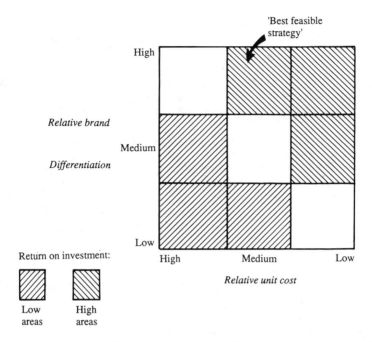

Figure 18.5 *Brand differentiation, unit cost and business performance*
Source: Adapted by author from Hall, 1980

Common products, unique brands

Today, competition can quickly emulate advances in technology or product formulation. Competitors can quickly copy a cigarette, a soft drink formula or PC specification. But what cannot be copied is the Silk Cut, Coca-Cola or IBM brand personalities. Studies show overwhelmingly that the best feasible strategy is to focus on brand differentiation (Figure 18.5), rather than cost and price, as a way of building profitability and growth. While the best strategy in theory is both low cost and high differentiation, in practice it is worth paying some cost penalty to achieve strong differentiation (Hall, 1980).

The brand growth direction matrix

The product life-cycle is a well-known phenomenon. The product peaks and eventually dies as its markets mature and new technologies replace it. But this life-cycle refers to products, not to brands.

There is no reason why a brand cannot adapt to new technologies and move from mature into new growth markets. The brand growth direction matrix (Figure 18.6) indicates the main growth opportunities available. Initially brand share is the strategic focus. But most of the successful brands which have lasted the decades have shifted to

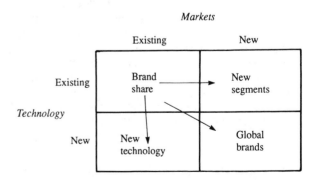

Figure 18.6 *Brand growth direction matrix*

incorporate *new technology*, ingredients and packaging developments to circumvent the product life-cycle. Similarly, Johnson and Johnson's Baby Shampoo is only one of the many examples of brands which have moved into *new market segments* to continue growth. The fourth growth direction is towards *global branding*, which appears to offer increasing opportunities to today's multinationals (Levitt, 1983). Growth based upon continuously developing successful brands appears to provide a more secure foundation than that based upon unrelated acquisitions or new untried products where failure rates are as high as 95 per cent (Booz *et al.*, 1982).

Competitive depositioning

The brand leader is in an enormously strong position to fend off attacks. First, it has financial strength – almost invariably it will have the highest market share and the higher profit margins. This should enable it to outgun competitors in terms of aggressive promotion and innovation. Second, the trade is always reluctant to add new brands if the existing brand leader satisfies the customers and themselves. Third, the brand leader can exploit its superiority, as Coca-Cola does with its 'real thing' advertising. Without a major strategic window (Abell, 1978), only a substantial underinvestment in quality and brand support is likely to dethrone a successful brand.

Motivates stakeholders

Companies with strong brands find recruitment easier. People want to work with companies that exhibit success. Strong brands also widen share ownership by increasing awareness and understanding of the company. Finally, successful brands elicit local authority and governmental support. Western countries, for example, compete with inducements to attract the better known Japanese companies to build their brands with them.

The creation of successful brands

Brands are rarely created by advertising. This is often misunderstood because the advertising is generally much more visible than the factor which creates the differential advantage. For example, Singapore Airlines is a strong brand and does some attractive advertising. But the advertising is not the basis of the brand – rather the advertising communicates and positions it. The basis of the brand is the superior customer service provided by the cabin staff. This, in turn, is largely achieved by Singapore Airlines putting in more cabin staff per plane than other airlines. Equally striking is the fact that Britain's strongest brand – Marks and Spencer – has historically done little or no advertising at all. There is little correlation between the amount spent on advertising and the strength of the brand.

The other common mistake is to think that brand loyalty is irrational. A recent survey on branding by *The Economist* reflected this view, 'people all over the world form irrational attachments to different products. Humans like to take sides. . . . By most 'tangible' measures, BMW cars and IBM computers are not significantly better than rivals, but customers will pay significantly more for them' (*The Economist*, 1988). Levitt (1983) provides a framework for understanding how successful brands are created and why customers are not 'irrational' to choose them (Figure 18.7).

At the core of every brand there is a *tangible* product – the commodity which meets the basic customer need. For the thirsty customer, there is water. For the production manager with a data storage problem, there is the computer. This tangible product is what economists believe rational consumers should base their choices on.

But to generate sales in a competitive environment, this tangible core has to be put in the form of a *basic* brand. It has to be packaged conveniently, the customer needs to know the features of the product and its quality. It should be designed to facilitate ease of use. But there are further ways to *augment* the brand to enhance its value by guaranteeing its performance, providing credit, delivery, and effective after-sales service. Finally, there is the *potential* brand, which consists of anything that conceivably could be done to build customer preference and loyalty. Which of these dimensions appear to be most important in practice?

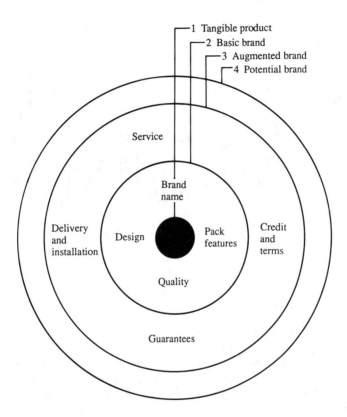

1 Tangible product
2 Basic brand
3 Augmented brand
4 Potential brand

Service

Brand name

Delivery and installation

Design

Pack features

Credit and terms

Quality

Guarantees

Figure 18.7   *What is a brand?*
Source: Adapted by author from Levitt, 1983

1   *Quality is number one.* Overwhelmingly the most important determinant of brand strength is its perceived quality. Britain's top ten brands (Figure 18.8) are all quality brands. The PIMS analysis showed that brands with high perceived quality earned double the return on investment and return and sales of low quality brands (Figure 18.9).

Quality generates higher margins in either or both of two ways. First, quality boosts market share, which results in lower unit costs through economies of scale. Second, by creating a differential advantage, quality permits higher relative price.

2   *Build superior service.* Service is perhaps the most sustainable differential advantage. While products are easily copied by competitors, service, because it depends on the culture of the organization and the training and attitudes of its employees, is much more difficult. McDonald's, IBM, Singapore Airlines and Federal Express are all brands built on service.

A recent study (Albrecht and Zemke, 1985) showed the importance of service: In their sample survey, 67 per cent of customers changed brands because of poor service. Of these cus-

1 Marks and Spencer	6 Boots
2 Cadbury	7 Nescafé
3 Kellogg	8 BBC
4 Heinz	9 Rowntree
5 Rolls-Royce	10 Sainsbury

Figure 18.8   *Britain's top ten brands*
Source: Landor Imagepower Survey, 1989

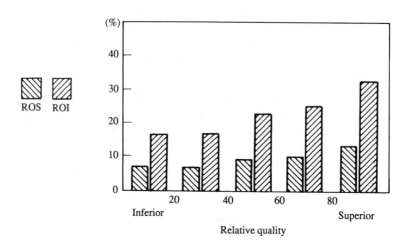

Figure 18.9 *Quality and profitability*
Source: Buzzell and Gale, 1987

tomers who did feel unhappy with the service provided by the bank, hotel or supplier, only 4 per cent bothered to complain – they just did not expect any satisfaction. Of these that did complain, 91 per cent dropped the brand permanently. But, interestingly, suppliers which dealt with complaints fast and generously held on to the vast majority of dissatisfied customers. In fact, there was some evidence that really effective responses to complaints actually increased brand loyalty.

3 *Get there first*. Perhaps the most common means of building an outstanding brand is being first into a market. This does not mean being technologically first, but rather being first into the mind of the consumer. IBM, Kleenex, Casio and McDonalds did not invent their respective products, but they were first to build major brands out of them and bring them into the mass market. It is much easier to build a strong brand in the customer's mind and in the market when the brand has no established competitors. This is why Clifford and Cavanagh (1985) found that pioneering brands earned on average more than one-third higher returns on investment than late entrants (Figure 18.10).

There are five ways of 'getting there first':

(a) Exploiting new technology (e.g. Xerox, IBM);

(b) New positioning concepts (Body Shop, Fosters lager);
(c) New distribution channels (e.g. Argos);
(d) New market segments (e.g. Amstrad);
(e) Exploiting gaps created by sudden environmental changes (e.g. egg substitutes).

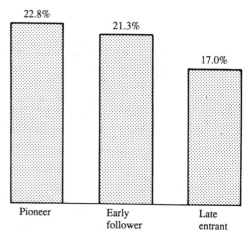

Figure 18.10 *Timing of market entry and business performance*
Source: Clifford and Cavanagh, 1985

4   *Look for differentiation.* In building brands the principle is to invest in markets which are highly differentiated or where such differentiation can be created, as for example the Body Shop or Levi jeans have done in recent years. Where markets are strongly differentiated, i.e., different segments are looking for different bundles of attributes, then both niche brands and big power brands can potentially earn very high returns on investment. Power brands like IBM, Marks and Spencer and Coca-Cola can earn high returns because they are perceived of as high-quality brands in most of the segments. Niche brands like Top Shop or Irn Bru can earn high profits by being preferred in one segment even though their overall rating in the broad market is not great. In markets which are undifferentiated, however, i.e. where customers do not see much difference between the brands, none typically earns exceptional returns.

To summarize, building successful brands is about quality, service, innovation and differentiation. What then is the role of advertising? Advertising has two functions in building successful brands. First, successful advertising accelerates the communications process. Marks and Spencer built a great brand without advertising. They relied primarily on their high street presence, customer experience with the brand, and word of mouth. But it took them thirty years to build the strong brand of today. Now, one cannot wait that long – competition would pre-empt the brand before it had positioned itself in the customer's mind. Advertising speeds up the process of generating awareness and interest in the brand. The second function of advertising is to position the brand's values in a manner which appeals to the target customers and increases confidence in the choice process. The creative messages of the Levi or the Nescafé advertisements, for example, present the brand as having a set of values which match the aspirations of target customers.

Buying brands versus building brands

Today there are two routes a company can follow to obtain brands: it can build and develop them; or it can acquire them, or rather acquire companies which possess them. The former is obviously a high risk, slow and expensive route. Studies have shown clearly that a very high proportion of new brands tested and introduced into the market fail (e.g. Booz *et al.*, 1982). It takes time and investment to build a brand and position it in the minds of consumers. In contrast, acquisitions are a deceptively quick route to obtaining a brand portfolio and it is a route which is increasingly followed today, especially by British companies. It also appears a cheap alternative, especially if the acquirer is exchanging high-valued shares in buying a company operating on a lower-price earnings ratio. Unfortunately, there is comprehensive evidence that most such acquisitions fail to generate long-term value for the acquiror's shareholders or build lasting brand portfolios (e.g. Porter, 1987). How can this dilemma be explained and resolved?

Previous studies (Doyle,1987, Doyle *et al.*, 1986) suggest the approach companies adopt depends upon what their primary objectives are. Some companies have objectives which are primarily about marketing and market share. Others are primarily orientated to return on investment and financial objectives (Figure 18.11). Generally, companies which have objectives that are mainly marketing ones ('right-hand companies'), choose to build brands. Companies whose objectives are primarily financial, ('left-hand companies'), are orientated towards buying brands or companies with brands.

Japanese companies, for example, tend to be overwhelmingly right-hand orientated. The objective is market share. They believe that the most appropriate way to achieve market share is the development of strong brands which offer customers differential advantages. So they adopt a classical marketing approach – understand the expectations of customers in the target market segments and seek to match them. They seek to build brands that provide the customers with value and which beat the competition. Japanese companies rarely acquire because they believe that they have the skills to do it better. It is not surprising that most of the great new global brands in the last decade have been Japanese – Sony, Toyota, National Panasonic, Honda, Canon, Casio, etc.

British companies, on the other hand, have been more left-hand or financially orientated. Stock

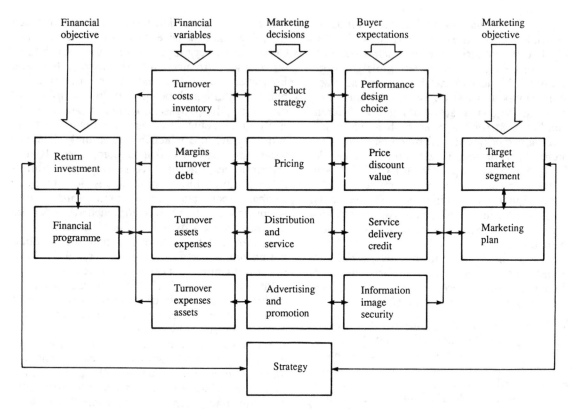

Figure 18.11 *Marketing and financial objectives of the business*

market pressures have made return on investment the primary goal and financial budgets rather than marketing plans the main planning mechanisms. In these companies, products, pricing and promotional decisions are dictated mainly by financial constraints rather than marketing requirements. One result is that while there have been very few major global brands developed by British companies in the last ten years, they have led the world in acquisitions.

During the past twelve months, for example, British companies have acquired four times the amount of all Japanese companies, five times American companies and twenty times as much as German businesses.

The recent debate about brands in the balance sheet in Britain is essentially about acquisition strategy rather than about building customer value.

Acquisition orientated managers have observed that if brands are put in the balance sheet, then balance sheet gearing can be reduced, retained earning enhanced and so further acquisitions are facilitated. Paradoxically, companies that put brands in the balance sheet are likely to put *less* emphasis on brand building and brand development than those that do not follow this practice.

Of course, acquiring brands sometimes makes sense. The problems with acquisitions are, first, that in the long run the evidence suggests they rarely work. Second, they do not create coherent brand strategies, especially at the international level. In general, the company ends up with a rag-bag of brands with different brand names in different countries, different positioning strategies and no synergy with the existing business. Figure 18.12 suggests a checklist which appraises those

	Build	Buy
Market attractiveness		
Market growth	High	Low
Strength of competitors	Weak	Strong
Retailer power	Weak	Strong
Relative cost of acquisitions		
Industry attractiveness	High	Low
Valuation of company	Full	Undervalued
Restructuring potential	Low	High
Brand's potential	Realized	Unrealized
Acquisitions potential synergy		
Cost reduction potential	Low	High
Marketing competence	Unchanged	Increased
Complementarity	Low	High
Relevant management expertise	Low	Transfers
Brand's strategic opportunity		
Product performance	Breakthrough	Me-too
Positioning concept	New	Mature
Market opportunity	High	Low
Corporate situation		
Growth potential	High	Low
Cash situation	Average	Abundant
Marketing/R&D capability	Strong	Weak

Figure 18.12 *Building versus buying brands*

conditions when acquiring companies with brands makes sense.

If it is a low-growth unattractive market, building a brand costs too much. It is generally cheaper to buy competition and competitors' retail space than to beat out well-entrenched brands. This is why companies like Hanson and BTR have focused their acquisition strategies on these dull mature markets. The other advantage of these types of markets is that the relative cost of acquisitions may be low. Often the stock market undervalues these apparently dull companies and there is substantial restructuring potential in selling off parts after the acquisition.

Acquisitions work when there is real potential synergy – when the acquiror can reduce the joint costs or improve marketing competence by coming together. Finally, the strategic opportunities offered by the acquiror's existing brand portfolio and its corporate cash situation, play a major role. If the company's current products are me-too, if it has limited skills but abundant cash spun-off from its portfolio of mature products, then acquisitions appear attractive. By contrast, it is generally better to develop and build on the company's own brands if these are operating in growth markets, if the company possesses potentially strong brands and if inside the company there are strong marketing and development skills. These five sets of factors are the key criteria in making judgements about the balance between building and purchasing brands.

Brand extension strategies

Brand extension strategies are another controversial area in branding. Brand extension means transferring the name of a successful brand to additional products possessed by the company. The advantages of such extensions may be three:

1 It encourages customer confidence in a new product;
2 It may create scale economies in advertising and promotion;
3 It opens distribution and retail channels.

The dangers are that it confuses the brand identity and can degrade the reputation of a successful brand.

What are the principles in striking a balance? The right approach depends on the similarity of the position strategies of the brands. Four brand extension options can be identified (Figure 18.13).

1 If the brands appeal to the same target segment and have the same differential advantage, then they can safely share the same company name or range. Here, there is consistency in the positioning strategies – examples of this type of extension would include IBM, Tomotei (from

Unilever), Dunhill and Sony – the same name applied to different products.
2 If the differential advantage is the same but the target market differs, then the company name can be extended because the benefit is similar. However, it is important to identify the 'grade'. For example, both the Mercedes Benz 200 and 500 series offer differential advantages based upon quality, but the more expensive 500 series appeals to a much more prestige segment of the market. The supplemental number acts to preserve the prestige positioning of the latter mark.
3 If a company has different differential advantages, then it should use separate brand names. It can find some synergy if the brands are appealing to the same target market, by using the same company name with separate brand names. For example, different brands of Kellogg's may well be selected within the same family unit.
4 But if both the target customers and the differential advantages are different then using unique brand names is logically the most appropriate strategy. So Procter and Gamble believe that it is worth losing out on the advantages of a common corporate name in order to separately position the brands in the market – to give each brand a distinct positioning appeal to a separate benefit segment. Similarly, Honda has recently separately positioned its Acura brand because it wishes to position it uniquely away from its existing models.

Brand Positioning Grid

	Differential advantage	
	Similar	Different
Similar	Company or range name (IBM, Timotei)	Company plus brands (Kelloggs Cornflakes, Kellogs Rice Krispies)
Target market segment		
Different	Company plus grade ID (Mercedes 200 Mercedes 500)	Unique brand names (P&G: Tide, Bold, Dreft, Ariel . . .)

Figure 18.13 *Brand extension strategies*

Conclusion

Successful brands are built upon the principle of seeking to build sustainable differential advantages for the customer. The levers for developing such brands are four: quality; service; innovation; and differentiation. Strategies based upon acquiring brands generally fail to work because they are more usually geared to satisfying the interest of the stock market rather than the long-term interests of customers. The danger of the 'brand in the balance sheet' argument is that it leads to weaker rather than stronger branding strategies. Finally, on brand extension strategies, there are real advantages in brands sharing a corporate logo, but care is required in not eroding a successful brand's unique positioning.

References

Abell, D. F., 'Strategic Windows', *Journal of Marketing*, 42(3), May, 1978.

Albrecht, K. and Zenke, R., *Service America*, IEE Dow Jones Irwin, 1985.

Bettman, J. R., *An Information Processing Theory of Consumer Choice*, Addison-Wesley, 1979.

Booz, Allen and Hamilton, *New Products Management for the 1980s*, Booz, Allen and Hamilton, 1982.

Buzzell, R. D. and Gale, B. T., *The PIMS Principles: linking strategy to performance*, Collier Macmillan, 1987.

Clarke, D. G., 'Econometric measurement of the duration of advertising effect on sales', *Journal of Marketing Research*, 13(3), Fall, 1976.

Clifford, D. K. and Cavanagh, R. E., *The Winning Performance: How America's high growth midsize companies succeed*, Sidgwick and Jackson, 1985.

Day, G. S. and Wensley, R., 'Assessing advantage: A framework for diagnosing competitive superiority', *Journal of Marketing* 52(1), April, 1988.

Doyle, P., 'Marketing and the British chief executive', *Journal of Marketing Management*, 3(2), Winter, 1987.

Doyle, P., Saunders, J. and Wong, V., 'A comparative study of Japanese marketing strategies in the British market', *Journal of International Business Studies*, 17(1), Spring, 1986.

The Economist, 'The year of the brand', December 24, 1988.

Engel, J. F., Blackwell, R. D. and Kollat, D. T., *Consumer Behavior*, Holt, Rinehart and Winston, 1978.

Hall, W. K., 'Survival strategies in a hostile environment', *Harvard Business Review*, 58(5), September, 1980.

Howard, J. A. and Sheth, J. M., *The Theory of Consumer Behavior*, Wiley, 1969.

Landor Associates, *The World's Leading Brands: A survey*, Landor Associates, 1989.

Levitt, T., *The Marketing Imagination*, Collier Macmillan, 1983.

Levitt, T., 'The globalisation of markets', *Harvard Business Review*, 83(3), May, 1983.

Parsons, L. J. and Schultz, R. L., *Marketing Models and Econometric Research*, North-Holland, 1984.

Peters, T., *Thriving on Chaos*, Macmillan, 1988.

Porter, M. E., 'From competitive advantage to corporate strategy', *Harvard Business Review*, 65(3), May, 1987.

Rodgers B., *The IBM Way*, Harper and Row, 1986.

19
Promotion
KEITH CROSIER

Introduction

The idea that you can merchandise candidates for high office, like breakfast cereal, is the ultimate indignity of the democratic process.

Adlai Stevenson

Advertisements contain the only truths to be relied on in a newspaper.

Thomas Jefferson

In this chapter, we turn to the question of *promoting* a product or service that has already been developed (Chapter 15) and priced (Chapter 16), and will concurrently be sold (Chapter 17) and distributed (Chapter 20). What exactly is involved in the management of this particular element of the marketing mix?

Defining terms

As Figure 19.1 shows, using McCarthy's useful four Ps terminology, we are here concerned with deploying and controlling a mix within a mix. Let us agree to call this subset the *promotional mix*, though other authors may use 'marketing communications mix' to describe the same set of activities, explicitly recognizing their common communicative nature and intent.

It will not be possible to deal with the management of all five ingredients within the confines of a single chapter. Instead, the following working definitions have been constructed to emphasize two characteristics simultaneously: the close family similarities among them and the fundamentally important points of difference.

- *Advertising* is a promotion via recognizable advertisements placed in definable advertising media at a published rate for the space or time used and directed at a target audience.

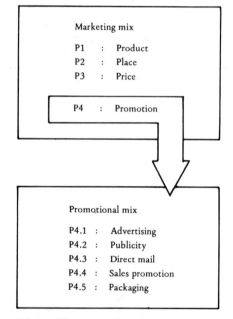

Figure 19.1 *The promotional mix*

- *Publicity* is promotion via news releases (or press releases) distributed to news media in anticipation that they will earn editorial mention at no charge and be noticed by a target audience.
- *Direct mail* is promotion via mailings distributed

by post (mail shots) or door-to-door (mail drops) to specific target consumers.

- *Packaging* is promotion via design and display, intended to be seen at the point of sale by potential consumers.
- *Sales promotion* is a portmanteau term describing promotion by means other than those so far defined. *Economic-incentive* sales promotions comprise such devices as price deals, premium offers, gifts and prize draws; *Communication-initiative* sales promotions are such means of promotion as product literature, sponsorship and competitions.

Unfortunately, terminology is carelessly used in practice and our tidy scheme must be subject to several caveats.

First, note that marketing practitioners often say 'promotions' when they mean 'sales promotions', directly contradicting the broader meaning advocated here, but sometimes use the term in the same sense as ours. Context should make it clear which meaning is intended.

Second, many activities routinely described as 'sales promotion' or 'promotions' actually belong logically within another of McCarthy's four Ps: price. That is why they are distinguished here as *economic-incentive* sales promotions. The separation is not intellectual but practical, for the two subcategories are typically the responsibility of different functional executives: the advertising manager on the one hand and the sales manager on the other. Only where a firm operates a brand management system (see Chapter 14) will the same person coordinate both kinds of sales promotion.

Third, it is very common practice to use the descriptive term 'direct mail advertising'. Yet our working definitions make it abundantly clear that direct mail is *not* a form of advertising but an entirely distinct means to a common end. Quite apart from the obvious procedural variation, manuals written for direct mail users always stress the radical differences between the literary and graphical styles appropriate to the two techniques. Personal experience as a recipient of mailings from *Reader's Digest*, or the AA will readily confirm how different they indeed are from press advertising.

When the aim of a direct mail campaign is to secure an order immediately, it is correctly de-

scribed as a mail order or direct marketing initiative. The word 'advertising' is frequently tacked on to the end of 'mail order' too, again erroneously.

Neither direct mail nor mail order should be confused with direct-response advertising, which describes the kind of advertisements intended to 'sell the product off the page' and therefore including such incentives as reply coupons or Freefone and Linkline telephone numbers. The style is often very similar to a direct mail shot, but the vehicle is very clearly advertising in the strict sense of the word.

Finally, the distinction carefully drawn between advertising and publicity is not always observed in practitioners' everyday usage, even though the two are obviously quite separate and often complementary tactics directed towards a common strategic goal.

In the case of advertising, firms buy the right to fill a block of air time or print space with messages and graphics exactly to their own specification, as long as they do not violate the law or various codes of standards. The advertising media have a duty to make sure that no variations or distortions occur. The price of this control is high, as we shall see later. In the case of publicity, the only costs are the production of news releases, photographs and so on, and postage and telephone calls: there is no equivalent of the charge for advertising space and time. The penalty, however, is weak control, in that the news media have a perfect right to use the information to suit their own purposes rather than the firm's, or not to use it at all. In practice, publicity managers are constantly frustrated by what they see as wilful misrepresentation or devious rejection.

Sceptics often assume that favourable editorial comment can be bought at the cost of a modest purchase of advertising space. While personal experience teaches that this certainly happens in the case of lesser print media (though the editorial plugs are usually pretty mechanistic and transparent), it would be prudent not to make this assertion within the earshot of a television news editor or a newspaper advertising sales manager. The historically rigid boundaries between the editorial and sales functions are still scrupulously observed by the reputable media. There is one exception to this rule, but an overt and institutionalized one: the 'advertisement features' which appear regularly in regional newspapers, and some magazines, less frequently in the serious press and not at all in the case of television, radio or cinema advertising.

Two terms commonly encountered in other textbook treatments of the promotional mix are deliberately omitted from Figure 19.1: *personal selling* and *public relations*.

The first of these has been excluded for three pragmatic reasons: it uniquely involves face-to-face communication; it has its own, large literature; the associated function is in practice very clearly separated from those which attend to the other elements of the promotional mix. To do justice to personal selling within the same framework would demand a chapter at least twice its present length.

Public relations has been excluded, by contrast, for conceptual reasons. The Institute of Public Relations defines its discipline as 'the planned and sustained effort to establish and maintain goodwill and mutual understanding between an organization and its publics'. This definition clearly identifies a corporate and strategic focus, in contrast to the more tactical nature of the promotional mix ingredients. Indeed, public relations programmes regularly make use of two of those in particular: advertising, of the corporate variety, and publicity. Public relations is thus bigger than the promotional mix, not part of it.

In practice, this fundamental distinction can be obscured by careless usage. For instance, one might hear 'the advertising isn't working hard enough – we need a bit of PR to support it'. The speaker will almost certainly have meant 'publicity', not 'public relations'.

Vital statistics

Promotion is a significant economic activity. Table 19.1 shows total annual UK expenditures in 1989. The absence of a figure for the publicity element of the promotional mix does not seriously distort the grand total since, as already explained, the cost of publicity initiatives is low and certainly of a different order altogether from that of corresponding sales promotion, advertising or packaging budgets. Table 19.2 provides a frame of reference for such huge sums of money by comparing the 1988 total figure with other items of national expenditure for that year, the most recent figures available as this edition went to press.

The promotion of goods and services has been big business ever since the age of bold enterprise in the 1890s, when 'Professor' Thomas Holloway spent £30,000 a year in contemporary currency to advertise his Universal Ointment & Pill, Lever Brothers and Pears' slogged it out for dominance of the soap market in every available promotional medium and Coca-Cola was promoted as a 'brain tonic' at an annual budget of $120,000. Plus ça change.

To look at £21.8 billion in another way, it corresponds to £383 per capita per year or £1,005 per household. It represents 4.3 per cent of our gross national product or 6.7 per cent of total consumers' expenditure.

And yet, at the level of the firm, promotion is not as significant a proportion of total selling cost as might perhaps be expected. In a submission to the Secretary of State for Prices and Consumer Protection in 1974, the Advertising Association presented the typical cost data in Table 19.3. The combination of sales promotion with sales is a feature of the original document.

Nevertheless, the promotional budgets of the nation's major marketers can be very large indeed. For lack of reliable data on other ingredients of the marketing mix, *advertising* figures are used as a surrogate for total promotional expenditure in Table 19.4. The half-dozen largest advertisers in the UK collectively accounted for 3.5 per cent of total advertising expenditure in 1989.

So those are the big spenders. Let us now see how they allocate their budgets among the five major *advertising media*, as shown in Table 19.5. Notice that television does not dominate, as many outsiders expect it to. The explanation is, of course, that 'press' embraces an enormous variety of separate

Table 19.1 *UK annual expenditures on promotion 1988*

	£ million
Advertising	7,555
Sales promotion	5,000 (estimate)
Packaging	8,500 (estimate)
Direct mail	758
Publicity	na
	21,813

Sources: Advertising Association, Institute of Packaging Marketing Week, RNIA Limited.

Table 19.2 *Selected UK national expenditures, 1988*

	£ million
Social security	51.6
Defence	26.0
Health	25.8
Promotion	*19.3*
Education	14.7

Source: Central Statistical Office.

Table 19.3 *Breakdown of total selling cost*

Production	70%
Distribution	9%
Sales and *sales promotion*	7%
R & D and administration	5%
Interest and profit	5%
Advertising	4%

Source: Advertising in Perspective, Advertising Association, 1977.

Table 19.4 *Largest UK advertising budgets 1989*

	£ million
Procter & Gamble	53.9
British Telecom	47.5
Kelloggs	45.1
Lever Bros	40.9
Ford	40.8
Nestlé	37.9

Source: Marketing Week.

Table 19.5 *Advertising media's shares of total UK advertising revenue, 1989*

	%
Press	63.6
Independent television	30.3
Posters	3.6
Independent local radio	2.1
Cinema	0.5

Source: Advertising Association

publications whereas, for the present, 'television' comprises only the fourteen non-overlapping regional ITV companies, national TV-am and networked Channel 4.

As we shall shortly see, firms typically delegate the planning and execution of promotional campaigns to independent companies. Table 19.6 lists the half-dozen largest *advertising agencies* in the UK, in terms of 'billings': the amount of their clients' money they spend on buying media space and time. These six collectively accounted for 21.6 per cent of total advertising expenditure in 1989.

Table 19.6 *Largest UK advertising agencies, 1989*

	Billings £ million
Saatchi & Saatchi	373.0
J Walter Thompson	308.0
BSB Dorland	285.0
Young & Rubicam	238.0
BMP DDB Needham	216.0
D'Arcy Masius Benton & Bowles	208.0

Source: Advertising Association.

Numbers, one two and three are wholly British, the American agencies J Walter Thompson and Ogilvy & Mather having been bought by the WPP Group in 1987 and 1989 respectively. Numbers four and six are the British offices of American multinationals. Number five is a merger of one British and two American agencies. This domestic presence is a recent phenomenon. In 1975, there was no home-grown agency in the top ten. By 1986 Saatchi & Saatchi, probably best known for its work for the Conservative Party, had become the largest advertising agency group in the world after only sixteen years in existence. Its success was a symptom of newly found confidence and international horizons among native UK agencies, though it has shown clear signs of losing its way recently. The WPP Group has perhaps replaced it as the home-grown success story of the 1990s.

Focus on advertising

It was noted earlier that space will not allow us to consider the management of all five ingredients of the promotional mix separately. Equally, the variations of practice within the mix defeat any attempt at a generalized treatment of 'promotional management'. By default, the remainder of this chapter will focus on *advertising*.

This particular strategic option accounts for neither the most expenditure nor the greatest volume of output, but it is undoubtedly the most complex and sophisticated of the five to plan, implement, control and evaluate: that is the rationale for selecting it.

The advertising system

The advertising transaction typically involves four parties: *advertisers; advertising agencies; media owners;* and audiences. In this section, we are concerned with the business relationships among the first three, who produce the advertising and direct it at the fourth party. Figure 19.2 represents them graphically.

Though one normally thinks of advertisers as sellers of a product, using advertising to facilitate the selling effort, they are buyers in this particular transaction. They buy a product from the media owners, *advertising space* or time, which will eventually contain their advertisements. Typically, they also buy a service from advertising agencies: expertise in the devising of effective *media selection* and *creative strategy*.

Arrows 1, 2, and 3 in Figure 19.2 summarize this part of the total system. An advertiser may buy space or time direct from media owners (1) and devise its own advertisements, but will more usually direct an advertising agency to select media options that can most effectively reach a specified target audience and to devise advertisements that will convert that audience into customers (2). The agency buys the time and space from the media owners and places the advertising with them (3). The advertiser does not pay the media bills itself in this case because of a longstanding tradition that agencies make their livelihood from commission on the purchase of space and time, a process which will be explained fully in due course.

The media owners are clearly the *sellers* in the transaction, as arrows 4 and 5 symbolize in Figure 19.2. Because of advertising agencies' dependence on media commission for their livelihood, a convention has long been established in the business that media owners' sales representatives do not make pitches to advertisers which have agencies, but to the agencies instead. Of course, they do both in practice – demand-pull to supplement supply-push – but are careful to observe the correct priority to ensure that the agencies know their clients have been solicited and to avoid closing the sale themselves.

The role of the media owners in the system is actually slightly more complex than this, for they have two functions. The first, their editorial function, is to deliver news and entertainment to readers, viewers and listeners: their second function, *advertisement sales,* is to deliver a certain portion of their total space or time to advertisers, who subsidize the price of news and entertainment by paying for the opportunity to address those readers, viewers and listeners.

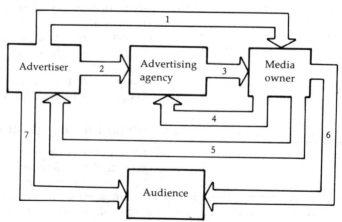

Figure 19.2 *The four parties to the advertising transaction*

Thus, as arrow 6 symbolizes, advertisements come to the audience from the media owners, strictly speaking. Arrow 7 acknowledges that advertisers expect their potential customers to perceive them as the source of the message all the same, and that they do in practice.

Not surprisingly, it is usual to describe the advertising agency's position in the system as *intermediary*. This is not technically correct. Though they do buy a product from one party and resell it to another, and do offer professional services to what they describe as their 'clients', the law defines them neither as wholesalers nor as agents. History provides the explanation.

Advertising agencies have their ultimate origin in the 'space brokers' of the early nineteenth century. By buying blocks of advertising space from newspapers and magazines and reselling it in smaller units to individual advertisers, they performed the classic function of both intermediary and professional service. The sellers of space could deal with one agent instead of many separate advertisers: the buyers could consult and instruct one expert intermediary instead of dealing with many separate sellers.

In 1841, one such agent persuaded media owners to allow him a standard commission discount of 15 per cent off the price they would charge an advertiser who dealt direct, in recognition of his prepaid bulk-buying on behalf of many advertisers. An insurance broker is a close analogy. He thus formalized the present day 'media commission system' of advertising agency remuneration, which will be explained in more detail shortly. It is overwhelmingly commoner than the alternative fee system, in practice.

His initiative radically affected the legal position of these 'agents', which would have to be regularized sooner or later. The case of *Tranter v Astor* (Lord Astor the publisher), tried at the Queen's Bench in 1917, established the precedent that advertising agencies are not in fact agents acting on behalf of principals at all but rather *principals* themselves – because it is they who make the buyer's contract with the media owners. This ruling was re-affirmed by *Emmett v DeWitt* 1957 and has never been challenged since. It has profound implications for the way in which advertising agencies must conduct their business, as we shall see shortly.

The three business partners in Figure 19.2 should strictly be five. By the 1880s space brokers had begun to offer a creative service to advertisers, paid for out of their mark-up, to gain the competitive edge over their rivals. In the 1960s, this full-service ideal came under fire from advertisers, who apparently suspected that jack-of-all-trades can be master of none. *Creative specialists*, called boutiques or hot shops ('shop' being trade jargon for an agency) burgeoned, offering no media buying or other kinds of client service, only design and writing. Not having access to media commission, they were paid by fee from the outset.

A decade later, the full-service ideal was challenged again, for the same reason, as *media specialists* proliferated. They took commission, if granted eligibility by the media. Since they had smaller overheads than full-service agencies and no other services to provide, they typically 'rebated' varying proportions of the commission to their clients, who were thereby effectively paid by the media rather than vice versa. They are today known as 'media independents'.

A trend of the 1980s has been for advisers not to establish long-term working relationships with one or more agencies, but to issue ad hoc piecework according to circumstances – as indeed, they always have done to direct mail houses and market research agencies. This solution to the problem-solving need, usually dubbed *à la carte*, is a considerable departure from historical precedent.

To sum up the last few paragraphs, we see that five different working arrangements are open to contemporary advertisers:

1 Do-it-yourself, or 'in-house advertising'.
2 Use a full-service advertising agency.
3 Use a creative shop,
4 Use a media independent.
5 Go à la carte.

The most recent industry statistics available, published jointly by the Advertising Association and the Institute of Practitioners in Advertising (IPA) in 1978 show that just less than a quarter of total advertising expenditure is paid direct to media owners by do-it-yourself advertisers. Further, just over three-quarters is transacted via IPA member-agencies, almost all of the conventional full-service type. Since no large-scale change in advertisers' choice of working arrangements has been reported since the late 1970s, we may conclude that the conventional full-service advertising agency remains the overwhelming norm despite the range of options available today.

The agency–client working relationship

Of the interrelationships depicted in Figure 19.2, that between advertiser and advertising agency is undoubtedly the most crucial.

The Institute of Practitioners in Advertising conducted a field survey of the state of relations between two parties in 1972. Of the 433 brand managers and 164 chief executives questioned, exactly three-quarters said they enjoyed 'happy' relations with their agencies. The IPA reports that a survey they had conducted in 1963 found this degree of satisfaction in exactly two-thirds of all respondents, so the trend is clearly upwards over the decade.

Two unpublished surveys of Scottish advertisers have since confirmed a high level of general satisfaction on the client side. In 1977 just less than 100 executives with responsibility for advertising were questioned. Almost half answered that they were 'completely satisfied' and a further 40 per cent felt 'fairly satisfied'. In 1985, identical questions were put by the same researchers to fifty executives with responsibility for advertising. This time only a third professed themselves 'completely satisfied' but nearly 60 per cent were 'fairly satisfied'.

It appears that no surveys have investigated agencies' feelings about their relationship with their clients, the other side of the same coin.

These survey findings imply a remarkably high level of client satisfaction and yet the trade press has reported rifts between famous clients and agencies with apparently increasing regularity.

The recent history of Guinness is probably the most notorious example. After forty years with the S.H. Benson advertising agency, it moved to J. Walter Thompson, then the biggest in Britain and the world. After twelve years, the business suddenly moved to a young British agency, Allen Brady & Marsh, the chief executive of the deserted partners learning what had happened from the trade press, not the client. Two years later, it moved again to the multinational Ogilvy & Mather, where it is today. The Guinness executive who left J. Walter Thomson and then Allen Brady & Marsh in the lurch was Ernest Saunders, tried and convicted in 1990 of conspiracy, theft and false accounting in an infamous case of illegal share dealing in support of a takeover bid. We live in remarkable times.

All this seems to suggest that the pace of change is quickening, that clients are perhaps less likely to be satisfied than the survey findings.

In that case, what reasons are given by clients willing to admit to dissatisfaction and those who have fired their agencies? Generally they are bland generalizations that leave us none the wiser. When *Marketing* magazine surveyed 100 advertisers involved in agency changes during 1984, the only reasons offered by more than a quarter of all respondents were 'in a rut', 'results fell short of expectations', 'did not understand our problems' and 'could not develop the right chemistry'.

The role of the agency account executive

Client–agency working relations boil down to a person-to-person relationship, for it is a convention of the business that contact is managed by individuals with specific responsibility.

For the advertiser, this will be either an *advertising manager* or a *brand manager*. The former is more typical of business-to-business advertisers and consumer-durables producers, the latter of fast-moving consumer-goods companies. The distinction is that advertising managers have responsibility for all their companies' advertising (and most other forms of promotion too) but for no other element of the marketing mix, while brand managers deploy the whole marketing mix but are responsible for only part of their firms' product range.

At the advertising agency, the responsible person is the *account executive*. In this context, 'account' means customer or client. For example, the *Marketing* magazine article just cited refers to 'J. Walter Thompson's loss of the Guinness account'. A few agencies use the more accurate and self-explanatory description *client service executive*, but 'account executive' is certainly the generic term, just as 'brand manager' is for what may in fact be called marketing managers or product managers.

As we have already seen, an advertising agency's main product is in fact a service. As in any other kind of service organization, the quality of after-sales customer-service is a critical factor in the winning of repeat business, and it is the account executive's job to deliver it. In particular, his or her role is to minimize the potential for *culture clash* between agency and client. This is crucial because the atmosphere and ethos of typical examples of the former and the latter could hardly be more different. Agency creative types do not sit opposite client R & D people at briefing meetings: instead advertising managers report client priorities to account executives, and account executives propose agency creative or media solutions to advertising managers.

It follows that two skills in particular are essential attributes of effective account executives: *negotiation* and *coordination*. The latter is vital because one person is dealing on behalf of a whole organization. Without it, advertising campaigns will resemble horses designed by committees, deadlines will be missed, opportunities lost and much more besides.

Negotiation is not simply a matter of standing between the two parties keeping their respective specialists apart. An essential aspect of the job is to be advocate for the point of view of each side when with the other: somewhat akin to the role of industrial relations negotiators. Although clearly employed by the agency, account executives have to live somewhat in no-man's-land between agency and client. Certainly, if the relationship is to endure, they must be as conscientious in explaining the client's needs and attitudes to the agency people as they are in advocating the agency's solutions and attitudes to the client – however irritating and petty a client's tinkering with creative treatments of media plans may seem.

As one account executive vividly explained in a presentation to a class of university students: 'Whenever I'm at the client's office, I must be the agency's man; back at the agency, I must be the client's man'. Divided loyalty is part of the modus operandi – and a positive one, given that the job remit is after-sales service.

Advertising agency remuneration

The conventional *media commission system* for the remuneration of advertising agencies – not by their clients but by the media owners – has already been introduced.

The arithmetic of remuneration by commission is simple enough but widely misunderstood. Suppose that the total 'ratecard cost' of media bookings, as published in the media owners' *rate cards* and in *British Rate and Data (Brad)*, is £123,456. A *recognized* advertising agency is automatically invoiced at a fixed discount whereas any other buyer, including large advertisers dealing direct, would be charged the full rate. The normal commission discount is 15 per cent; smaller-circulation newspapers and magazines may allow only 10 per cent.

Assuming a standard rate of commission, then:

Rate card cost	£123,456
Less media commission at 15%	18,518
Price to recognized agency	104,938

The agency in due course invoices its client £123,456 – the full cost which is readily verifiable in *Brad* – and thereby 'earns' £18,518 on the transaction from the media owners, not from the client that has ostensibly employed it.

Ever since agencies began to offer creative services to their clients, it has been obvious that the conventional 15 per cent media commission could not cover all the production costs of a professionally executed advertising campaign. The norm has therefore been established that all 'production charges' and certain creative costs are invoiced direct to the advertiser by the agency.

Furthermore, full-service agencies offer their clients services over and above the planning and executing of media and creative strategies, and a second norm has emerged that the agency is entitled to mark up the real cost of such items by the equivalent of 15 per cent off the list price. The question is, what does the agency add to its buying price to arrive at the correct figure?

Consider a rate card cost of £1,000. Mental arithmetic quickly establishes that the media commission discount amounts to £150 and that a recognized agency's buying price would be £850. Now consider a non-media service costing the agency £850. They are entitled to charge the client £1,000 for it, a mark-up of £150. So the question can be rephrased as 'what percentage is £150 of £850?' Your calculator will show you 17.65 to the second place of decimals. Hence, an agency's formula for arriving at its selling price in these circumstances is to add a *17.65% mark up* to its buying price – not 17.7 or a round 18, but exactly that figure. Improbable, but true.

Returning to our previous example, the same question would be 'what percentage is £18,518 or £104,938?' The answer is 17.65 to two decimal places, despite rounding off to whole pounds in the example. Quod erat demonstrandum.

In recent years, *commission rebating* has been regularly in the news as recessionary pressures force advertising agencies to compete on more fronts than just the quality of their service and technical skills. Reports normally speak of agencies 'cutting their commission' or 'rebating some of their commission to the client', but this is inaccurate. Commission is a discount on their buying price, received automatically. What agencies in fact do is to discount their invoices to their clients in turn, which has the *effect* of reducing their commission: hence the description 'rebating'.

If advertising agencies do rebate, it is normally promised in order to win a new client or done to retain one which has threatened that it may be going to 'review the account'. Suppose, then, that a powerful client talks an insecure agency into rebating 'only' 2 per cent or, as commentators reports are likely to report it inaccurately, 'cutting its commission to 13 per cent'. The consequence would be to erode the agency's revenue by roughly an eighth, rather than 2 per cent, since two is 13.3 per cent of fifteen.

In 1982, Allen Brady & Marsh (ABM), inheritors of the Guinness account from J. Walter Thompson as we saw earlier, took a three-page advertisement in the trade newspaper, *Campaign*, to put the case against commission rebating. The main thrust of its argument was that the 15 per cent yields 2 per cent net profit after tax for the typical full-service agency, according to an IPA survey of 1981; that if the margin is eroded by rebating, the quality of service must suffer commensurately. The advertisement was adamant that ABM would refuse point blank to work with a client who expected a rebate. Almost exactly a year later, it resigned the £3.5 million B & Q account because it was already barely profitable and the client had nevertheless demanded a rebate.

Extending ABM's argument further, one can also surmise that smaller advertisers would suffer most; if a large client puts the pressure on an agency to rebate,

standards will be maintained on their account at the expense of the less significant accounts in the agency's portfolio.

The anti-rebaters clearly have logic on their side. What ABM's forcefully-stated position conveniently overlooks, however, is that the commission system could alternatively be replaced entirely by a negotiated *fee*, adequate for the maintenance of standards.

The operational environment of promotional practice

Promotion does not take place in a vacuum. Advertising, publicity and sales promotion campaigns are public acts; they invite scrutiny of the originator's motives, values and sense of social responsibility. That is an operational constraint for promotional strategists.

Criticisms of advertising

In this section, we will look first at the attitudes of policy-formers and opinion-leaders towards promotion and then at public opinion on the subject. Inevitably, we will find that most commentators focus their attention on *advertising* rather than the other ingredients of the promotional mix. To place these external views in a proper context, it will help to bear in mind these relevant characteristics of the social and economic environment in which contemporary advertising takes place:

1 A highly developed consumer economy, in which advertising bridges the gap between producers and consumers;
2 Well-educated and fairly sophisticated consumers;
3 Articulate consumer pressure-groups;
4 A highly sophisticated advertising business;
5 Consumer-protection legislation;
6 Formal statutory control over broadcast advertising;
7 A formal system of self-regulatory controls over non-broadcast advertising.

Economists are prolific commentators on the subject of advertising. Given that the media typically employ 'economics correspondents' for business news and that our policy formers' higher education typically consists of degrees involving the study of classical economics, their views must be counted highly influential. It is fair to say that the conventional wisdom among professional economists is to accept the role of promotion in shifting the demand curve upwards in theory but to disapprove of advertising in practice. This contradiction may be due in large part to that comtempt for 'trade' which has bedevilled British commercial attitudes for so long.

We can extract from the economics literature three dominant pairs of argument and counter-argument, as follows:

Proposition 1:   A *cost* that drives up prices.
Counter 1:   Stimulates *demand*, holds prices in
                    check.
Proposition 2:   Sets up *barriers to entry* and thereby
                    reduces consumer choice.
Counter 2:   Facilitates *competition* and there-
                    by creates choice.
Proposition 3:   Appeals are *emotional not rational.*
Counter 3:   Delivers welcome *added values.*

With respect to propositions 1 and 2, it is highly arbitrary to single out advertising as the culprit. As White (1980) puts it: 'When economists say that customers are paying for the advertising when they buy the product, they are guilty of a false analysis – unless they also say that the customer is paying for the sales forces, the delivery vans, the warehouses and the order clerks'. We have already seen data from Cadbury-Schweppes (Table 19.3) which show that selling and distribution both contribute more heavily to the cost equation than advertising does.

Likewise, it is not typically advertising that monopolists use to erect barriers against competitors but rather price wars and saturation of distribution channels. Furthermore, effective advertising is not a matter of simple quantity: quality counts heavily when consumers are sophisticated and know how to play the game. An entrenched oligopolist might actually decrease the appeal of its product by heavy advertising, badly executed: on the other hand, a lively new entrant might steal enough customers for its own satisfaction by nimble and original promotion.

White puts it well again: 'In fact, the possibility open to new challengers of using media advertising, with its rapid coverage of mass audiences, tends to make monopolies more rather than less vulnerable to attack'. The recent cola wars bear this out. In 1982, PepsiCo used heavy advertising to attack Coke's market dominance and succeeded in increasing its share by 20 per cent. Coca-Cola retaliated not by counter-advertising but by starting a price war.

Research studies have also cast doubt on the validity of the first proposition, for all its logical appeal. An academic economist investigated price movements in sixty-five heavily-advertised food brands in 1978 and came to the conclusion that advertising had helped to keep price rises in check during a period of strong inflation rather than driving them up (Reekie, 1979). Earlier, he had found the relationship between advertising and competitive advantage to vary so much from market to market that he warned against 'the danger of making broad generalizations' (Reekie, 1975).

Proposition 3 presupposes that consumers ought to want reasons and hard facts, not emotional involvement or intangible satisfactions. It is a reflection of the long-standing economic model of 'rational man'. Yet it was an economist who remarked almost thirty years ago: 'There is tremendous spiritual satisfaction in buying a trusted brand of cocoa – not a shovelful of brown powder of uncertain origin' (Robertson, 1958). Note the word trusted: it expresses the concept of an intangible added value. The danger of the economists' line of argument is that it denies legitimate subjective satisfactions. Shoppers do not need to buy 'the best' if the second or third best pleases them more. Nor must they always buy the most 'economical' if they trust the promoted brand more. That is why supermarket shoppers often buy Cadbury's drinking chocolate instead of Safeway's own brand, of course.

Not only economists have strong views about promotion; it is regularly subject to cultural and ethical criticism. Such commentators are generally journalists, politicians, consumerists and academics. Three main strands are discernible in their objections:

Proposition 1:   Can control consumption
                    behaviour.
Proposition 2:   Can debase cultural values.
Proposition 3:   Can control the media.

The first of these rests on the implicit belief that relatively powerful advertisers can manipulate relatively powerless audiences, which in turn hinges on the 'mad scientist' view of advertising people. Those who take this view generally cite the immensely influential American book, *The Hidden Persuaders*, by Vance Packard (1975). They do not always mention that the author was a journalist who knew how to write good copy or that his book, one of a series in the expose genre, was first written thirty years ago when times were distinctly different, though republished more recently.

If advertising people do have special powers, whether based on psychological principles as Packard suggests or derived from whatever else, these remain the most closely guarded of secrets. Even those who work in the business cannot explain what they are. As two British journalists, Pearson and Turner (1965), remarked after visiting the J. Walter Thompson advertising agency:

> Instead of the steely-minded manipulators of public taste which some critics seem to be concerned about, we found a surprisingly high proportion of muddled, worried men who seemed disturbingly out of touch with the people they were paid high salaries to convince.

It is furthermore an uncomfortably contradictory fact that, on average, four in every five new products fail in the marketplace despite introductory advertising. Either the hidden persuaders are very bad at making use of their special powers or modern audiences are better than the critics think at resisting the promotional 'hype'.

The second proposition, debasement of our cultural values, is widespread among academic commentators, some politicians and specialist media commentators.

Inglis (1972) of the University of Bristol provides a typical example: 'Advertising is a main voice in our culture, and what it says is largely malignant'. Equally uncompromising statements can be found in a BBC Publications paperback by Berger (1972) a general textbook by Halloran (1963), an academic text, *Decoding Advertisements* (Williamson, 1978), and the populist paperback *Understains* by an academic author (Myers, 1985).

Politicians hostile to advertising are normally of the Left. This is a fact of political life, not a value judgement, and there is little sense in shying away from the issue when advertising practitioners need to be vitally interested in it. In the early 1970s, an opposition Green Paper propounded the ideological thesis that 'advertising tends to encourage gross materialism and dissatisfaction' (Labour Party, 1972). By the end of the decade, the Secretary of State for Prices and Consumer Protection had entered the lion's den at an Advertising Association annual conference to announce the Labour Government's plans for strongly increased formal regulation of advertising. In March 1986, the Party's 'consumer charter' confirmed the aim of a future government to introduce a statutory code of advertising practice. From the practitioners' point of view, this is alarming sabre-rattling.

It is noteworthy that criticism from these two quarters and media commentators tends to concentrate on 'advertising' rather than 'advertisements': they seem often to detect an organized conspiracy to corrupt the culture, masterminded on Madison Avenue or in Mayfair. Supporters of advertising respond that advertisements in fact hold a mirror up to our culture, rather than shaping it, and that the audiences concerned are fully capable of 'decoding' them in their own way and forming their own value judgements. They argue that the critics' view of popular culture, including contemporary advertising, is condescending to the populace.

The third proposition, potential control of the media, is of course based on the fact that the press, ITV and Independent Local Radio are all subsidized to a greater or lesser extent by advertising revenue. It is therefore presumed that they will be unwilling to bite the hand that feeds them if it deserves to be bitten in the public interest. This line of argument is summed up in the standard disclaimer to be found in *Consumers' Association* sales promotion mailings: 'We accept no advertising . . . so no one can influence us'.

There is some justification in the fear that *sponsorship* of programmes on television or radio might buy the power to insist on desensitizing of editorial comment. Picture, for instance, a documentary on environmenal conservation sponsored by a multinational chemical company. In the same way, a dozen consecutive pages of advertising in a magazine might buy the temporary suspension of editorial impartiality. However, sponsorship and multiple-page press advertising happen to a very limited and formally controlled extent in Britian; the scenario is imported from America.

Media owners themselves counter-argue that advertising revenue guarantees editorial freedom. Without it, they would need either to charge prices for the product that would guarantee its demise or to ask for a government subsidy. The latter solution raises, they point out, the equally dangerous possibility of political control, a familiar obstacle to reporting matters of public concern in too many other countries.

What is not clear about the non-economic criticisms of advertising described is why the critics should assume the worst possible case. There is a strong hint of the polemic in their approach to the issues, which seems unnecessary in the face of a typically British middle-of-the-road approach to the business of producing advertisements. This is not to deny that advertisers occasionally mislead and misrepresent, by accident or on purpose, and that their output can be tawdry, vulgar, full of innuendo and aesthetically disastrous. However, a system of controls exists to prevent attempts at dishonesty, as we

shall shortly see. As for manipulation: if the average Western consumer is not in fact sophisticated enough to cope with advertising, then the right counter-measure is *consumer education* rather than more constraints. If we believe people can be taught to recognize and resist political indoctrination, there is no reason to suppose education cannot do the same where advertising is concerned.

Public opinion

What, then, about the opinions of the people themselves? The *Advertising Association* has carried out nine field surveys in Britain over three decades, asking representative samples questions about both the abstract concept, 'advertising' and the concrete manifestation, 'advertisements'.

Figure 19.3 presents their answers with respect to advertising, given by means of a five-point scale of possible responses: approve a lot or a little, disapprove a lot or a little, don't know. We see clearly

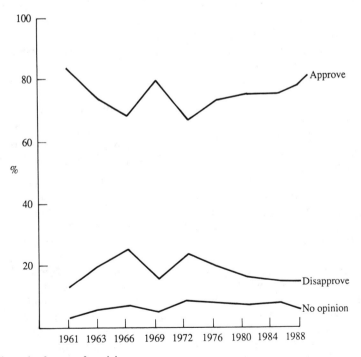

Figure 19.3 *Public attitudes to advertising*
Source: Advertising Association.

that public opinion became steadily more unfavourable through the 1960s and into the early 1970s, except for the puzzling anomaly of 1969. That was very much the time of consumer enlightenment. Over the last decade, the trend has equally clearly been for approval to increase while disapproval declines.

Asked why they approved or disapproved, the same respondents gave the pattern of main reasons shown in Figure 19.4. It is clear that generalized approval of advertising as handmaiden of the free-market system is declining while specific concerns about its effect on prices or its potential to mislead are on the increase. The rather patronizing belief that advertising makes (other) people buy things they do not really need and should not therefore want holds constant over the sixteen-year period. This question was not asked since the 1976 survey.

So, only about an eighth of the British populace expresses disapproval of advertising when invited to do so, while four out of every five say they approve. And yet there is increasing concern, albeit among a minority, about some of its possible effects.

An obvious potential reason for disapproval missing from the AA's findings is that there is too much advertising altogether. In 1983, *Which?* magazine surveyed 1300 readers, presumably more likely than average to have critical opinions, and found:

About right	53%
Should be less	36%
Should be none	11%

Figure 19.5 summarizes the Advertising Association (AA) survey respondents' attitudes to press advertisements and television commercials, given on a five point internal scale offering the option to like or quite like, dislike or not really like, or have no opinion. Immediately noticeable is the much higher 'don't know' proportion than when the question concerned the abstract concept.

It is instructive to note that ordinary people these days do not dislike television commercials, as is often supposed. The decline in those who say they do from almost a third of the sample to about a seventh is steady and unarguable, while the proportion admitting to liking them rises equally steadily and passes the declining figure for press advertisements in the mid-1970s. The two parts of the figure together demonstrate clearly that the British public

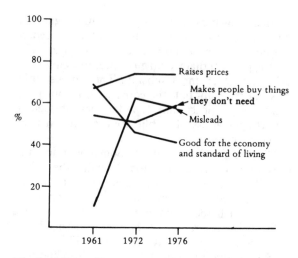

Figure 19.4. *Reasons for approving or disapproving of advertising*
Source: Advertising Association.

is at worst undecided about advertisements and at best positively enjoys them.

The findings so far demonstrate attitudes and opinions of respondents who have had their thoughts concentrated on advertising and advertisements. How likely are people to think about the topic or talk about it, left to their own devices?

The AA surveys investigated this question of *salience* by presenting a list of potential topics for conversation and debate to respondents and asking:

1 Which do you and your friends talk most about?
2 Which do you have the strongest opinions about?
3 Which are most in need of attention and change?

'Advertising' has been one of the three least mentioned topics in response to all three questions in each of the years that they were included in the survey: 1972, 1976, 1980, 1984 and 1988. In the most recent survey, exactly 10 per cent of the 496 respondents said it was something 'talked most about' while (for example) almost 60 per cent cited family life and roughly a third mentioned the government, fashion and sport. This shows very clearly that, although advertising affects almost everybody's lives daily and very directly, it is not a topic that most find at all salient. One could perhaps say that they ought to; but the fact is that they do not.

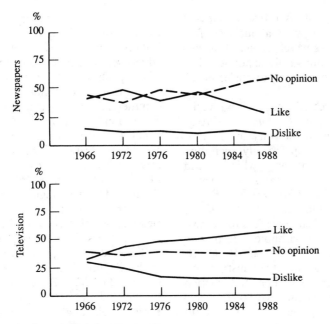

Figure 19.5. *Public attitudes to advertisements*
Source: Advertising Association.

The regulation of promotion

Despite the low level of manifest public concern about advertising just noted, promotion is formally regulated in three ways in Britain:

1 By legislation,
2 By statutory authority,
3 By self regulation.

No major laws relate directly and only to advertising, but some eighty regulate it as a *by-product* of more general control of marketing (in the lawyers' quaint jargon, 'consumer trade practices'). The most significant of those are the Trade Descriptions Acts of 1968 and 1972, and the 1973 Fair Trading Act, passed during the heyday of 'consumer consciousness'.

The *Trade Descriptions Act* requires the Department of Trade and Industry to make rulings about the meaning of *descriptions* and *claims* in promotional material, among other things, and to require that the product or service in question matches up to them in use. It also established the national network of *Consumer Advice Centres*, to which

aggrieved consumers may take their complaint. Before 1968, they would have had to raise a personal civil action against the producer or provider, a prospect which understandably deterred the very people most likely to be victims of sharp marketing practice. Since the Act, Consumer Advice Centres refer cases they consider worthy of further action to statutory agencies on the consumer's behalf. That can result in a criminal action, brought by the Crown rather than the individual.

When the Act had been in force for six months, the National Consumer Council analysed approximately 11,000 complaints by then received at Consumer Advice Centres and found that:

55.0% concerned claims and descriptions on labels, or packaging;
 0.5% concerned claims and descriptions in advertisements;
44.5% concerned other kinds of claims and descriptions.

An advertising agency director furthermore commented recently: 'Legend has it that in the first year of the Trade Descriptions Act, over 90 per cent of the complaints upheld were about classified advertising. The offenders were not heartless corporations trying to hoodwink a gullible public. They were members of the public trying to mislead each other' (Wilkins, 1985).

The *Fair Trading Act* created a statutory body, the *Consumer Protection Advisory Committee* (CPAC), charged by Parliament with the duty to 'monitor consumer trade practices', specifically including promotion, and to prevent any which could 'adversely affect the economic interest of consumers'. It also set up the *Office of Fair Trading* (OFT), which has a statutory right to refer to the CPAC any promotional material which it considers to be misleading or confusing, or to withhold information essential to an informed decision. If the CPAC agrees, it will draw up a 'statutory instrument' requiring the originator to desist. The OFT's action may be precipitated by a consumer complaint, as in the case of the Trade Descriptions Act, or may result from its own monitoring activities.

For the detail of both Acts, refer to the specialist text on advertising law by Woolley (1974) or Lawson (1978). Nothing more recent appears to be available.

At the time of writing, control by statutory authority is exercised by the *Independent Broadcasting Authority* (IBA). During 1990 and 1991, the IBA are to be replaced by *The Radio Authority* and the *Independent Television Commission*, both of which have already signalled their intention to bring a 'lighter touch' to the regulation of advertising.

The IBA's predecessor was charged by the 1964 Television Act with the duty to draw up a mandatory code of standards governing the content of television commercials and a mechanism for enforcing it. The result was what is now called the *IBA Code of Advertising Standards and Practice*, stating: 'The general principle which will govern all broadcast advertising is that it should be legal, decent, honest and truthful'. That basic requirement is elaborated in thirty-six clauses and three appendices.

The most important feature of the IBA control mechanism is that it demands *pre-clearance* of proposed commercials. Figure 19.6 summarizes the process diagrammatically. Arrow 1 symbolizes the transmission of the control criteria and advice in the form of the Code and a large number of advisory leaflets. This process is efficient enough that no advertiser or agency could credibly claim ignorance of the prohibitions and guidelines. Arrow 2 represents mandatory submission of proposed television commercials for pre-clearance to the Independent Television Companies' Association (ITCA), to which the IBA delegates responsibility for day-to-day administration of the system. Arrow 3 symbolizes notification of clearance, or embargo, to the ITV stations scheduled for the eventual campaign. Because of the very high cost of modifying a finished commercial, material is normally submitted for clearance-in-principle, indicated by arrow 4, at several stages in its development.

Radio advertising is controlled slightly less rigorously. Responsibility for pre-clearance is normally delegated to the ILR companies themselves, guided by the Code, as arrow 5 symbolizes. In the case of commercials for alcoholic beverages, medicines and treatments, veterinary products and 'highly technical' goods, arrow 6 represents pre-clearance in the television manner.

Despite these control mechanisms, viewers could still find television or radio commercials offensive, misleading or dishonest. In that event, they can complain to the IBA, which then has the statutory duty to respond by setting the whole process in motion again. It is questionable, however, that the public knows of its right to complain or of the IBA's duty to act, for the facts are only occasionally advertised by the IBA itself.

The ITCA pre-clears several thousand television and radio commercials per year, with the outcome that:

85%   confirm to the Code and are otherwise acceptable;
15%   require revision;
 5%   are rejected outright.

The IBA received 2000 complaints in 1988–89, 20 per cent fewer than in the previous year. About a dozen commercials were withdrawn as a result.

The third element of Britain's tripartite system for the control of promotion is self-regulation, exercised by the *Advertising Standards Authority* (ASA). It affects all forms except broadcast advertising, regulated by the mechanism just described.

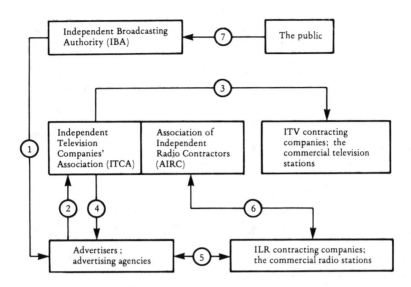

Figure 19.6 *Regulation of broadcast advertising*

The ASA was set up in 1962 by the Advertising Association, with the remit to receive and investigate complaints from business and public and to publicize the existence of its control system and the mechanism for using it. It was to judge complaints according to the criteria of acceptability contained in the *British Code of Advertising Standards* drawn up by the AA a year earlier. Like the IBA's Code, this articulates the general principle that 'all advertisements should be legal, decent, honest and truthful', elaborated in eighty pages supplemented by appendices relating to tobacco products and alcoholic beverages. In 1980, the ASA published a separate *British Code of Sales Promotion Practice*.

Financing of the Authority's activities and its own advertising campaigns, to discharge the second part of its remit, is achieved by a 0.1 per cent levy on the cost of advertising space, routinely added by media owners to the invoices sent to advertising agencies or direct advertisers.

The most important characteristic of the ASA control mechanism is that it does not demand pre-clearance but requires a complaint to set it in motion. Indeed, it would hardly be practical to pre-clear all non-broadcast advertising, let alone other forms of promotion, for the ASA has estimated that about 25,000,000 distinct and separate examples appear in Britain each year.

Figure 19.7 summarizes the advertising control process diagrammatically. Arrow 1 symbolizes the transmission of guidelines about acceptability to advertisers and advertising agencies in the form of the 'BCAP'. The process is efficient enough that it would not be credible to claim ignorance of the contents of the Code. Arrow 2 reflects the fact that the ASA would like advertisers to submit proposed advertisements for pre-clearance, but cannot oblige them to. By default, the mechanism is set in motion by complaints from the public to the ASA or commercial organizations to the CAP Committee: arrows 4 and 5.

If the ASA upholds a complaint, it first asks the advertiser to withdraw and amend the advertisement, in the name of collective responsibility. If that fails, it will issue a *Media Notice* calling upon media owners to take action against the offending advertiser, as arrow 6 symbolizes, by:

- Denying advertising space in future,
- Denying media commission in future,
- Refusing future advertisements from the same source unless pre-cleared.

It simultaneously informs the news media and consumer-interest organizations by means of periodic *Case Reports*. The evidence is that most advertisers give in when this happens, so the ASA

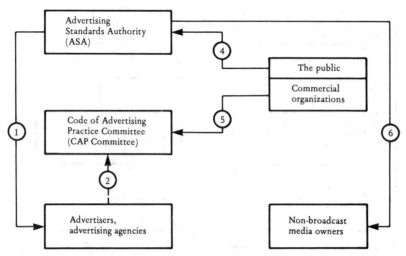

Figure 19.7   *Regulation of non-broadcast advertising*

very seldom has to resort to referral of a case to other elements of the control system. After the event, regular post-checks guard against surreptitious attempts to reinstate the banned material

25,000,000 non-broadcast advertisements per year currently generate about 8000 complaints, which fare as follows:

50%   not pursued;
10%   no case to answer, in the ASA's judgement;
30%   case to answer, but not upheld;
10%   upheld.

Complaints are not pursued for such reasons as a lack of sufficient information, that they have already been dealt with or that they concern broadcast advertising.

In 1978, the Advertising Association, the Office of Fair Trading and the Consumers' Association jointly commissioned an independent assessment of 3000 press advertisements, which found that 93 per cent 'conformed to the spirit and letter of the British Code of Advertising Practice'.

The advertising media mix

We have already briefly encountered *media shares* in the section of this chapter devoted to the 'vital statistics' of promotion. Table 19.7 presents a five-year trend in the shares of the five *major media* with a breakdown of the portmanteau category, 'press', into its constituent parts. Several noteworthy facts are immediately apparent.

First, Table 19.7 reminds us that *independent television* is not the dominant advertising medium that popular opinion typically supposes, unless each subcategory of the *press* is treated as an individual medium in its own right. Only in two years has total expenditure on television advertising ever exceeded half the amount allocated to press advertising. We have already noted that the reason is the enormous variety of media vehicles embraced in the description 'press' compared with the relatively limited television network.

The first edition of *The Marketing Book* observed, on the basis of media share figures up to 1985, that the press category as a whole was 'losing share steadily and comparatively rapidly' in a virtual mirror image of the increase enjoyed by ITV. Both trends have since very clearly reversed, still mirroring one another with uncanny accuracy. The explanation is not a simple matter of funds being transferred from one to the other, however. Media share is measured by money spent, and the fact is that the cost of television airtime had for several years been increasing faster than the general index of media rates computed by the Advertising Association, whereas the cost of press space had not. The first edition also remarked that 'there must sooner or later come a point at which

Table 19.7 *Trend in advertising media's shares of total UK advertising revenue*

	1985 %	1986 %	1987 %	1988 %	1989 %
Press total:	63.2	61.5	61.9	62.9	63.6
regional newspapers	22.5	21.4	22.0	22.6	22.6
national newspapers	16.8	16.4	16.5	16.1	16.1
business and professional magazines	7.7	7.3	7.0	7.4	8.0
consumer magazines	6.0	5.8	5.9	6.2	5.9
directories	4.7	5.2	5.3	5.4	5.8
production costs*	5.5	5.4	5.2	5.2	5.2
Independent Television	30.9	32.6	32.2	31.1	30.3
Posters	3.7	3.8	3.7	3.6	3.6
Independent Local Radio	1.8	1.8	1.9	2.0	2.1
Cinema	0.4	0.4	0.4	0.4	0.5

* Included in figures for other media.
Source: Advertising Association.

advertisers will doubt the cost-effectiveness of a medium which raises its prices every year by more than the general rate of inflation'. With a recession on the horizon, deregulation round the corner and a new Television Authority about to come into being, that point seems to have been reached.

Within the press, it is worth noting that the often maligned *regional newspapers* actually hold a larger share than the national press. Part of the explanation is again the greater variety of vehicles available to advertisers, but it is clear from Table 19.7 that the regionals' share is steadily increasing while the nationals' declines. The other subcategory to enjoy a steadily growing slice of the total pie is *directories*. Both categories of *magazine* exhibit a level trend over the period, their respective rankings being perhaps the opposite of what an outsider might expect.

It is worth noting that none of the remaining three 'major' media can in fact command a share as high as any of the press subcategories alone. They are in truth major by name rather than by performance. *Posters*, which includes transport advertising, and *cinema* potter along on level or slowly declining trends, despite the clear advantages of impact and creative scope each offers to advertisers. Both were once much more significant media: their decline is

undoubtedly the result of inept marketing management, which has alienated potential users by permitting the buying process to become inordinately complicated and singularly failing until very recently to conduct convincing audience research.

Recent improvements in the quality of the cinema product, most noticeably the purpose-built 'multiplex' developments with their associated restaurants and crèches, have spectacularly reversed the apparently inexorable decline in audience numbers. Total admissions in 1989 were back at the 90 million mark last achieved in 1980, having climbed out of a 50 million trough in 1984. In response, the number of screens available to advertisers increased sharply in 1988, having been decreasing throughout the 1980s. These two factors have combined to produce a hint that the media share may in the 1990s be able to rise from the floor it has been occupying since 1984.

In the first edition, *independent local radio* was said to be 'a striking case of a short-term product life cycle entering the decline phase'. Its media share had risen to just over 2 per cent in the first decade after the introduction of commercial radio in 1973, but had then fallen back below 2 per cent for the next five years. A modest rejuvenation of the PLC seems to have been in progress since, but the share remains well below that in most other countries with organized commercial radio networks.

The explanation of radio's unexpectedly weak performance as an advertising medium seem to be that British advertisers, especially national brands, simply do not take this upstart in the media mix as seriously as their counterparts in other countries where it is much longer established. The Independent Local Radio network belatedly responded by setting up the Radio Marketing Bureau in early 1983, but the damage would seem to have been done. Development of its potential was furthermore hamstrung by disputes about the validity of the syndicated audience-research system, JICRAR, not resolved until mid-1983.

As well as these five, an extremely wide variety of 'minor media' offers advertisers further opportunities for reaching particular target audiences. There are, for example, perimeter advertising at sports venues, videotext, parking meters, matchbooks, spaces on other companies' delivery trucks. Others come and go, such as all-over painted Minis and large-screen videos in pubs. Remember, too, the vast array of sales promotion vehicles on which £6 billion was spent in 1988, and the direct mail medium.

Media selection

The confines of a single chapter scarcely permit us to examine in detail the performance characteristics of a media mix as broad as that just described. Therefore, this section will:

1 Explain the essential vocabulary of media specialists,
2 Propose a framework for making valid comparisons among media and hence for media selection,
3 Specify sources of information on the quantitative characteristics of media options,
4 Summarize the qualitative characteristics of the major media,
5 Recommend specialist further reading.

Vocabulary

The vocabulary of media planning and buying is esoteric to say the least. 'Bleeding into the gutter' is the notorious and genuine example. More prosaically, *above-the-line* and *below-the-line* are terms used to distinguish media which allow commission to recognized advertising agencies (above) from those which do not (below). 'Above-the-line' therefore roughly corresponds to the 'major media'; 'below-the-line' by itself is often used as a synonym for sales promotion activities.

Where the *press* is concerned, the basic unit of charge for space, quoted in the publishers' rate cards and in *Brad* is the single column centimetre (s.c.c.). It is a purely notional space one column wide by one centimetre deep. Space is bought in multiples of it, except for half-page, full-page and double-page spread (d.p.s.) sizes.

Press media vehicles offer the advertiser a *circulation*, the size of which is also published in *Brad*. It corresponds to the number of copies actually sold and will be independently authenticated in the case of the most significant titles by the Audit Bureau of Circulations (ABC) or Verified Free

Distribution (VFD) systems, the latter relating to free-distribution local newspapers, more usually called freesheets.

Magazines and newspapers are typically read by more than one person before being discarded, however, so *readership* defines the number of readers rather than the number of sales. It is independently measured by the Joint Industry committee for National Readership Surveys (JICNARS), through the medium of the National Readership Survey (NRS). This continuous research operation yields not only numbers but also demographic descriptions of readers, information about their buying habits and data on their exposure to other media: a readership profile.

In the case of commercial *television* and *radio*, the basic unit of charge for time is the spot. *Brad* and the contracting companies' rate cards quote the price of spots in multiples of ten seconds. A set of consecutive spots between or within programmes is a commercial break. The pricing structure for time buying can be very complex indeed, especially in the case of some television stations. As a result, it is common for advertisers to buy packages, which guarantee to deliver an agreed number of television rating points, called TVRs, or radio ratings. One rating point is 1 per cent of the total potential audience for the station in question, called its universe. The price of buying packages is, confusingly, quoted as a cost per thousand viewers or listeners.

Television audiences are measured numerically and demographically by the Broadcasters' Audience Research Board (BARB), which also counts the BBC's competitive figures. For radio, a similar kind of presence and attention survey is carried out periodically by the Joint Industry Committee for Radio Audience Research (JICRAR).

The size of *poster* sites is measured in sheets. A purely notional unit, no longer corresponding to one piece of paper except in the case of the smallest sites, these are 30 in by 40 in, still unmetricated. Four-sheet, sixteen-sheet and forty-eight sheet have traditionally been the commonest sizes, but the Continental thirty-two sheet roadside format is gaining ground at the expense of the forty-eight sheet. Some poster sites are constructed differently, however; these are always ten feet high, while their length is a multiple of three feet, the width of the vertical panels which make them up. Twenty-seven foot and thirty-six foot sites are the commonest, known respectively as 270 and 360 supersites.

Advertisers almost always buy poster campaigns in preselected packages of sites offered by the outdoor advertising contractors. Until very recently, the poster medium was generally criticized for its inability to deliver any creditable measure of the audience delivered by such packages. The reason for this comparative disadvantage was partly inertia but also the undoubted difficulty of actually measuring a mobile audience. In 1985, the contractors finally instituted Outdoor Site Classification and Audience Research (OSCAR), which promises to offer vital data hitherto unavailable to media planners.

Cinema advertising 'space' (oddly) is also bought by spots, commonly thirty or sixty seconds or two minutes. Advertisers can buy the whole national network of 1264 screens in 677 cinemas, ITV Regions, metropolitan conurbations, single screens from individual cinema screen advertising contractors or 'audience delivery plan' (ADP) packages from the Cinema Advertising Association. Until very recently, this medium was also bedevilled by a lack of reputable or reliable audience research, but CAVIAR now exists, the Cinema and Video Industry Audience Research consortium.

In very general terms, media buyers seek to achieve *coverage* of an audience or readership. The Media Research Group says:

> Coverage is probably the most important concept in the planning of media . . . To try to put is simply, the net coverage of a schedule is the proportion of a target group who will have at least one opportunity of seeing the advertisement.

'Gross cover' is a television term expressing the total number of TVRs achieved by separate spots in a schedule, without taking account of repeat exposure. Thus, if three spots score 15, 25 and 10 TVRs respectively, gross cover is fifty TVRs. Gross OTS is a press term expressing the total number of opportunities-to-see achieved by each advertisement in a schedule and expressed in thousands. As a rule of thumb, a press campaign would expect a figure of at least five OTS (whereas a television campaign might be deemed acceptable at the TVR equivalent of about half that).

Media planners also talk of the *reach* and *penetra-tion* of media vehicles. This is a measure of the actual audience for a given television or radio commercial as opposed to the 'universe' of the station (reach) or of the proportion of a target audience which reads a publication regularly (penetration). Thus, one might read that Radio Clyde has an 'average reach' of 66 per cent or that *Ideal Home* achieves a similar average penetration of the DIY market segment. A key consideration with respect to these measure is the avoidance of *wastage*: that is, the proportion of a readership or audience that is of no practical use to the advertiser because it consists of people other than the target market. It is inevitably high in national campaigns using television or mass-circulation newspapers.

Before leaving the matter of definitions, let us return briefly to the cost per thousand (CPT) criterion of cost-effectiveness: the price of achieving a certain coverage. Although seductive because it is a quantifiable ratio, this measure is very limited. It tells us how many people were potentially reached by the advertising at what cost, but not what sort of people they probably were. As the advertising trade magazine, *Campaign* (1986) put it: 'More sensitive buyers nowadays are interested in position, environment and reach, rather than cost per thousands'. Position refers to the location of a press advertisement in the publication, some being undeniably better than others, and environment on the company an advertisement or commercial keeps.

Media buyers and planners daily use dozens of highly precise technical terms, by no means self-explanatory to outsiders, which have not been mentioned here. Over two hundred of them are defined in the *Macmillan Dictionary of Marketing and Advertising* (Baker *et al.*, 2nd ed., 1990).

Quantitative characteristics of the five major media

Media have both *quantitative* and *qualitative* characteristics. Each must enter into the media planner's decision making. There is no sense, for instance, in buying a vehicle which delivers the right audience at an extremely favourable cost if it happens not to offer the creative scope demanded by the creative strategy. Conversely, it would be equally counter-productive to devise a creative strategy which could not be executed in the media vehicles capable of delivering the prime target audience.

The basic quantitative characteristics are, as we have seen, cost and coverage. The British media mix is so diverse, as we have also seen, that it would be quite impossible within the confines of this chapter even to summarize the unit costs, readerships and audiences of the five major media and the media options they collectively comprise. In any case, both quantities are subject to quite considerable change in the lifetime of one edition of a textbook. Moreover, new options appear (*The Independent* and *The Sunday Correspondent*, reaching circulations of approximately 406,000 and 280,000 respectively and acquiring readership profiles of considerable interest to advertisers) while others disappear (Centre Radio, Leicester and the *News on Sunday*).

Therefore, interested readers must check these facts for themselves. The fundamental source book is *British Rate and Data*, published monthly and containing over 500 pages of densely packed basic information on virtually every available media option in Britain. More complete profiles of the vehicles and their readers or audiences are to be found in the periodic publications of BARB, JICNARS, JICRAR, OSCAR and CAVIAR.

The price of time or space is not the only cost to be considered, however; there is also the matter of *production*. Because of very wide variation according to circumstances, it is impossible to generalize about the cost of *print* production – except to note that press production charges totalled £5.3 million in 1988, which is about 8 per cent of the corresponding cost of space bought, according to the Advertising Association.

Television production is expensive; one can safely generalize about that. Even without the much-reported predilection of advertising agencies and production houses for exotic locations or state-of-the-art computer graphics, few forty-second commercials will cost less than £50,000 to produce these days. A much applied rule of thumb is £1,000 per second of eventual running time.

Cinema commercials cost the same amount as television commercials to make, except that they are often longer in the first place. Thereafter, the cost of production escalates alarmingly. The cinema advertising contractors demand two 70 mm colour prints per screen and the soundtrack must be capable of producing the kind of quality normal in cinemas, as distinct from that tolerated by television viewers.

These prints cost several hundred pounds each. The price of *radio* production can be summarized in one word: low.

So much for the quantitative characteristics of media.

Qualitative characteristics of the five major media

Qualitative characteristics may be conveniently categorized under four headings: usage; creative scope; vehicle effect; and user-friendliness. 'Usage' relates to the way in which readers or audiences make use of a media vehicle, the circumstances in which they consume it. 'Creative scope' describes the range of opportunity to achieve particular verbal or visual effects. 'Vehicle effect' is concerned with the fact that the media vehicle itself may exercise a mediating influence on readers' or audiences' perceptions of the advertiser and the message. 'User-friendliness' describes the degree to which media buyers find the vehicle easy or difficult to buy, schedule, control and post-evaluate.

1 The press: daily, evening and Sunday newspapers

Usage: Deliberately read, not treated as background noise or visual wallpaper, as radio and television may be. Should be possible to convey quite detailed information and arguments. But daily and evening papers have transitory life, are not generally kept for reference; Sundays may be better in that respect. Furthermore, ads must compete for attention with editorial and other ads on same page whereas television, radio and cinema present commercials serially and free from competition for attention, except for totally extraneous distractions.

Creative scope: Detailed messages possible. But product demonstration virtually impossible because movement and sound not available. Mainly monochrome medium or at best two-colour, except colour supplements. Full colour costs a lot if available and quality can be poor.

Vehicle effect: Evening papers usually thought to be 'urgent'; Sunday papers claimed to be read in especially relaxed and receptive frame of mind. Daily newspapers have wide variety of images that might 'rub off' on to the advertising: respectability and authority of *The Financial Times*, strident tone of *The Sun*, and so on.

User-friendliness: Fact that most people read papers every day permits high frequency of repetition, at a cost.

Insertions can be booked, changed and withdrawn at fairly short notice, without cost penalty. Short lead-times permit topicality. Newspaper production techniques long-established and well-understood, and comparatively inexpensive. Readership research plentiful and reliable.

2 The press: regional newspapers

Usage: Local newspapers do seem to be kept and repeatedly referred to.

Creative scope: More limited than national dailies or Sundays because of advertising clutter and difficult layout for anything approaching special positions – evening papers are a bit similar, perhaps. Very regular 'advertisement features' offer good opportunity to tie ads to particular market segment.

Vehicle effect: More sophisticated advertisers could be harmed by rub-off from relatively unsophisticated company.

User-friendliness: Less frequency of repetition, though re-exposure per issue may well be higher than in dailies. Not a difficult sub-medium to use. Research figures less plentiful, but one role of the Newspaper Society, formerly discharged by the Regional Newspaper Advertising Bureau, is to provide data and ease complexity of buying coordinated national schedules that could cover several hundred different titles.

3 The press: magazines

Usage: Readers generally quite involved with their chosen magazine, and can be expected to be receptive. Thus should be possible to convey very detailed information and messages. Magazines typically kept and referred to. Some have very high 'pass-on readership' – among families, in offices or in waiting rooms, for example. But ads must compete for attention on equal terms with editorial and other advertising, whereas television and radio present commercials serially without competition, except for totally extraneous distractions. Advertising clutter often considerable. Advertisers can overcome problems to some extent by buying whole pages or double-page spreads, but at heavy cost penalty.

Vehicle effect: Huge variety of images and standards of content; impossible to generalize. Some specialist magazines may transfer 'authoritative' atmosphere from editorial to advertising. Readers thought to be generally involved and attentive.

User-friendliness: Fact that publication frequency varies from weekly through monthly to quarterly greatly reduced opportunity for repetition of exposure – only slightly counteracted by the fact that magazines typically kept and re-read, because re-reading is probably selective and ad may well be missed second and third times. Long lead-times prevent truly topical advertising. Production in four colours expensive, and very high quality originals needed for best reproduction in glossiest magazines.

4 Television: Independent Television

Usage: Viewers see commercials serially, not in competition with programme material or other advertising, as on the printed page. Viewers relaxed and receptive, at home, but may stop paying attention during commercial breaks: this is regularly claimed but has never been conclusively proved. At very least, some suspicion that viewers use television as visual wallpaper rather than for reception of detailed messages. In any case, highly transitory medium; ads cannot be clipped and kept, or deliberately rescrutinized. This drawback mitigated to some extent by possibility of scheduling spots, but at high cost penalty. Videorecording may increase re-exposure.

Creative scope: Pictures, colour, movement, sound. Scope equalled only by cinema. Product can be demonstrated in use. But time constraint imposed by fixed-duration spots and cost of longer ones means message cannot be detailed. Production technology much more complicated than print media and cost typically very high if full creative scope exercised. Picture small, reducing impact. Sound quality poor.

Vehicle effect: Television is *the* mass medium, so vehicle effect pretty well neutral.

User-friendliness: Long notice required for booking and cancellation, except for off-peak spots and special packages. Pre-empt price structures complicated and puzzling to non-experts. Long lead-times, exacerbated by need for ITCA pre-clearance, so topicality difficult. Timing and spacing of TV schedules complicated by lack of knowledge about optimum frequency for maximum impact and excessively complicated structure of most rate cards. TV buying a job for experts only. Production costs very high, usually. Vast amount of reliable audience data easily available, at a cost.

5 Posters

Usage: Exceptional potential for re-exposure time and time again in favourable locations. Big 'solus' sites can have substantial impact and some smaller ones may benefit from shortage of anything else to look at, especially in transport subdivision. But posters in general may be treated as part of landscape and not really noticed. Some sites suffer considerable clutter, especially transport subdivision again, so advertiser has to fight for attention.

Always various extraneous distractions competing for attention of passer-by, particularly drivers.

Vehicle effect: Difficult to say. Big poster sites may have certain contemporary, vaguely alternative-culture feel, which could be transferred to advertiser.

Creative scope: Huge images and high-quality colour; potential impact very high indeed in case of bigger sites. Nevertheless, scope limited by need to make point very quickly because audience is moving – except in case of some parts of transport subdivision. This restricts typical creative treatment to short headlines and simple graphics. For this reason, posters often dismissed as 'back-up medium'.

User-friendliness: Severe problems of coordination and control if national campaign required, especially because of recent history of flux and confusion among poster contractors. Highly fragmented medium to deal with. Advertisers and agencies normally avoid tailor-made campaigns and buy contractors' packages instead. Problem then is that not really sure exactly what bought. Long booking and cancellation notice demanded by contractors. Topicality very difficult, except at stiff cost. Notorious 'till countermanded' (TC) booking procedure results in prime sites being monopolized over long periods by regular advertisers, to exclusion of others. Advertisers voice concern about contractors' conscientiousness in ensuring that campaigns do run as booked. Audience research recently significantly improved by 'Oscar' (Outdoor Site Classification and Audience Research), but still not really user-friendly medium.

6 Radio: Independent Local Radio

Usage: Commercials aired serially, so do not vie for listeners' attention with programme material or other advertising, as in print media. Some concern that radio used as audio wallpaper, but equally can be claimed that it has unique 'immediacy' and 'urgency'. Transitory medium: listeners cannot clip and keep ads, or deliberately rescrutinize them. This drawback counteracted to some extent by possibility of scheduling many spots, at some cost penalty. Radio is as portable as newspaper or magazine, unlike TV, and is 24-hour medium in prime broadcasting areas.

Creative scope: Limited by restriction to audio only. Least effective of all for demonstrating product in use. But sound quality much better than TV, so creatives can make the most of sound effects. Despite conventional wisdom, outstandingly creative and attention-winning radio commercials have been made. Some research evidence that listeners mentally transfer visual element of television commercials to radio commercials with same sound track.

Vehicle effect: Some observers believe authority and immediacy of radio news transfers to advertising. Otherwise, probably seen as a not-quite-serious medium, especially by major national brand manufacturers.

User-friendliness: Campaigns can be booked and cancelled at short notice. Ultra-short lead-times permit high degree of topicality. IBA pre-clearance handled locally in most cases, and therefore fast. Timing and spacing of schedules somewhat complicated by lack of knowledge about optimum frequency for maximum impact. Effective ILR buying best left to experts, of whom not yet many even after fourteen years. Agency media planners still treating ILR as new and unproven medium, especially for national campaigns. Easiest and least complicated production technology of all. Audience research of dubious value so far, although rigorous.

7 Cinema

Usage: Audiences view commercials serially, not in competition with programme or other advertising, as on printed page. Have chosen to watch, and usually do so in atmosphere of relaxation, attention and willing suspension of disbelief: ideal conditions for impact. But little or no repeat exposure, since commercials only screened once per programme. Transitory medium: audience cannot clip and keep commercials, or deliberately rescrutinize them. But research evidence that they recall cinema commercials better than TV commercials.

Creative scope: Pictures, colour, movement, sound. Big screen, high-quality colour, high-fidelity sound. Viewed in dark with minimum distraction. Therefore highest creative scope of all media. Vivid product demonstration possible.

Vehicle effect: High-quality atmosphere should rub off on advertising, but media planners continue to ignore cinema so ads can often suffer by poor standards of the company they keep in commercial break. Quality of film, good or bad, can also rub off on advertising.

User-friendliness: Complicated to schedule national campaigns: over a thousand screens nationwide, despite decline, and contractors not noted for helpfulness. Few package deals and no centralized buying facilities. Long campaigns needed to build up coverage and frequency to useful levels. Production costs higher even than television, and techniques very sophisticated. Audience research data virtually non-existent. Second-least user-friendly of media. Standardized advertising films can be hired and local advertisers' details superimposed, rather like slide-plus-voice-over TV commercials that occupy least favoured time slots; results are distinctly unsophisticated.

Computers in media planning

In recent years, computer power and the widespread availability of desk-top data handling have increased the sophistication of the media selection very considerably. While the programs and software packages now at media planners' and buyers' disposal can greatly improve the effectiveness of their choices in the quantitative terms, no one has yet built the qualitative characteristics into them to any significant degree. Media planning therefore remains part science and part art. The most effective practitioners are those not seduced by the apparent rigorousness of numbers and ratios, but prepared to take carefully into account the much 'softer' and infinitely more time-consuming qualitative criteria.

Further reading

These thumbnail have necessarily been short on detail which can be found in three British specialist texts: Adams (1977), Broadbent and Jacobs (1984) and Davis (1981). *Admap* is the trade journal of advertising agency media planners in Britain. It is the source par excellence of technical detail and news of innovations in an extremely sophisticated and often fast changing discipline within the advertising business. *Media World* is pitched at a more popular level but is no less useful.

Planning and controlling the promotional campaign

In this final section, we turn to a necessarily brief consideration of key elements of the planning and controlling process:

1 The promotional budget.
2 Selecting an advertising agency or other collaborator.
3 Briefing it.
4 Measuring the effectiveness of the campaign.

The promotional budget

Most of the material in this chapter can be of only academic interest until it has been established how much money is available for allocation to the purchase of a media space or time, to production charges, to the cost of sales promotion initiatives, to direct-mail postage, and so on. In short, what is the *promotional budget*?

The advertising sub-budget is often called an appropriation, rather than a budget. This term usefully reminds us that advertising managers do not enjoy the luxury of setting it in isolation, but must in practice compete with other functional heads for their share of a larger *marketing* budget, which will in turn represent a hard-won fraction of the total operating budget. This imposes a ceiling on the promotional appropriation which may actually bear little relationship to specific promotion objectives or the firm's situation relative to the competition.

There is a universal tendency in the established literature to discuss the promotional budget exclusively in terms of procedures for deciding its size. This is dangerous because (quite apart from the point just made) it fails to acknowledge the true purpose of budgeting. As the sole exception to the rule puts it (McGann and Russell, 1981):

> The budgetary process is not a matter of allocating funds prior to the start of the campaign and then forgetting about them. Instead, the budgetary process of planning, expenditure and control should be viewed as an integral part of the campaign and one which must continue throughout its duration.

In short a budget is a *plan*, describing sources and uses of funds over a given future period, normally a year.

The four key benefits of budgeting for promotion in this full sense of the word is that it will:

1 Demand forward planning.
2 Provide an integrative focus for operational decisions.
3 Furnish standards of cost-effective performance.
4 Offer a financial control mechanism.

The second pair merit further discussion.

The task of the promotional appropriation is to buy media options and pay production charges, mainly. But it is not enough to decide an amount to discharge the task. That leaves scope for considerable waste of scarce money if an implied general responsibility for cost control fills the vacuum left by the absence of an explicit statement about criteria of cost-effectiveness. An obvious example of such a criterion is the cost per thousand measure described earlier, except that it reveals itself as a very crude and limited test on close inspection. It should be accompanied by criteria of communicative effectiveness derived from specific objectives – something which is very rare in practice, as we shall shortly see. To be an effective planning and control mechanism, the promotional budget must incorporate such explicit and preferably quantified standards of performance.

As an instrument of financial control, a budget must furthermore specify procedures for the management of current commitments, future commitments and contingencies. In the context of promotion, the first of these is a straightforward matter of verifying that invoices received do correspond to the media orders issued or the production work delivered, that applicable series or volume discounts have been subtracted, that the advertising did appear as scheduled and that extra chargeable items are invoiced at the conventional 17.65% mark-up explained previously. The second acknowledges the important fact that future cost benefits can commonly be achieved by placing orders and committing expenditure now.

As for the notion of contingency funds, it is always prudent to set aside some reserve, not for such negative reasons as that some activity has been carelessly allowed to exceed its allocation but rather for such positive ones as correcting hitherto unsuspected campaign weaknesses, countering unpredicted competitive reaction or taking advantage of fortuitous happenings in the marketplace.

Turning finally to the popular preoccupation with deciding the size of the appropriation and remembering that this decision is not normally within the authority of a line manager with responsibility for promotion, we find a substantial inventory of methods proposed in the standard textbooks, as follows:

Group 1: *Executive judgement*
 'All you can afford'
 'Notional sum'
 'Arbitrary method'
 'Affordable approach'

Group 2: *Ratios*
 (a) External

   Competitive parity
   'Share of voice'
 (b) Internal
   Historical parity
   Advertising-to-sales (A/S) ratio

Group 3: *Marginal costing*
 Marginal method
 Per-unit method

Group 4: *Computer solutions*
 Incremental models
 Simulation models
 Econometric models

Group 5: *Costing the campaign objective*
 Objective-and-task

Such an apparent diversity clearly prohibits full explanations of all available options. However, six field surveys in Britain and America since 1970, the most recent reported in 1985, have consistently shown that only three procedures are in genuinely common use. Aggregating the six sets of results, we find:

A/S ratio: 44% of all responses
Executive judgement: 21%
Objective-and-task: 18%
All others: 17%

As *A/S ratio* method sets the promotional budget at a figure corresponding to a particular percentage of sales revenue or, much less often, profit. Conceptually, appropriations should be determined for individual brands by reference to the revenue or profit attributable to each. In practice, even sophisticated multi-brand companies tend to fix one figure on the basis of total sales. Beecham Products, for instance, set its 1978 worldwide advertising budget at 10 per cent of worldwide sales. A serious flaw in the A/S ratio logic is that the ratio itself must be decided before the method can be used. In practice, this is generally done by reference to a set of perceived industry norms: 10 per cent for fast-moving consumer goods, about 5 per cent of durables and 1 per cent or less for business-to-business and service advertising. The A/S ratio is therefore really no more than collective executive judgement.

It is tempting to dismiss *executive judgement* as an unacceptably unsophisticated 'method'. Yet the intuition of experienced managers can be a viable proposition in practice, particularly when the apparently more scientific procedures can be disturbingly illogical, as further reading in any standard advertising textbook will reveal, and almost totally inflexible. If this approach is used regularly, it is bound to acquire historical and competitive dimensions and thereby shade into the group 2 methods.

Objective-and-task reverses the logic of the others by first defining the task to be achieved and then costing the means of achieving it, whereas they produce an amount of money and leave unanswered the question of what to do with it. But there are two severe practical objections to this apparently exemplary solution. First, there is ample evidence that advertisers find it difficult in practice to articulate the kind of clear, unequivocal, measurable, actionable objectives that could define the task. Second, the method does not specify how the cost of achieving it will be calculated. It is easy enough to tot up the figures for a vaguely suitable campaign, but quite another to devise one capable of meeting precise objectives. The temptation to revert to a more mechanistic procedure is very strong.

Though individual available procedures are conceptually dubious, suffer practical drawbacks or are unpopular, there is the obvious possibility that a mix of methods could lead to a better-informed decision based on a variety of inputs and range of answers. The conservative firm might go for the low end of the range to minimize cost, while an entrepreneurial advertiser could decide even to move outside the top bound of the range and invest in the future. Alas, reworking the results of the six surveys referred to earlier reveals that the average number of methods per respondent was exactly two. Evidently the use of a real mix is not in fact common practice.

We can conclude this discussion of promotional budgeting with a pessimistic but apposite remark made by a media planner from a top London advertising agency at a conference in 1978: 'The topic of budget setting has attracted almost a disproportionate number of contributions from home and abroad in recent years (but) the subject is as remote today from a conclusion as it has always been'. There is no readily detectably evidence of improvement since then.

Selecting a professional collaborator

Since it is widespread practice among British advertisers to call upon the problem-solving expertise of advertising agencies, media shops, creative shops, sales promotion agencies, direct mail houses or package design consultancies, a major planning and control task in promotional management will sooner or later be to select one for the first time or to replace an unsatisfactory incumbent. Too many texts offer vague analogies with courtship and marriage when discussing these decisions, which scarcely help to explain how it should be done. How many of us, after all, followed a strictly benefit-maximization approach to our own courtships? Figure 19.8 offers a flowchart alternative, strongly based on personal experience.

The very first step is a truism, of course, but something that is too often not done in practice. Without an explicit, written-down statement of requirements, there will be no commonly-agreed criteria at later stages when they are urgently needed.

At step 2, the trade press is invaluable as a source of general opinion-forming information about what is available; *Marketing Week* and *Campaign* are especially useful, if one bears in mind that newsworthy outfits are not necessarily the most competent and vice versa. *Campaign Portfolio* lists the salient facts about some 150 advertising agencies, with specimens of their work and their own philosophy statement. The *Advertising Agency Register* is a commercial service which will show standard-format video presentations by its client agencies on neutral territory, so that the interest remains for the time being undisclosed. The relevant professional associations can also provide valuable information at this stage. Given a simple statement about the potential client and its expectations, they will supply a list of members judged competent to handle the business and not prevented from doing so by any conflict of interest.

At step 4, it is vital to distinguish a 'credentials presentation' from a 'formal presentation', or a full-scale sales pitch is likely to ensue. When it does come to soliciting that deliberately from the short-listed candidates at step 6, it is important that all should be given exactly the same formal brief and indication of the eventual budget. Ideally, some way should be

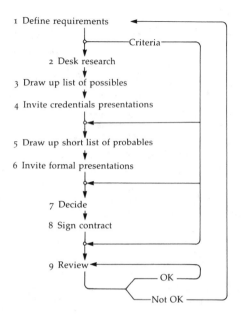

Figure 19.8 *Selecting an advertising agency or other collaborator*

found to ensure that they all spend roughly the same amount on production of their presentations. Without these precautions, comparability is impossible.

If requirements were never defined and formal criteria are therefore unavailable at step 7, the Incorporated Society of British Advertisers will provide a thirteen-item checklist and a ranking matrix of ten criteria and six-point scales. Flowcharts and matrices tend to emphasize strict rationality, but intuition has a place in the process. As the ISBA puts it, 'a clinical and relatively simplistic approach should not be followed too slavishly'. Gut reaction has a place in the making of decisions about long-term human working relationships.

Step 8 emphasizes a vital step surprisingly often absent in practice. Handshakes and gentlemen's agreements are apt to substitute. This may work at the Stock Exchange, but is a risky way to set up a business relationship as complex as that between, for instance, advertising agency and client. Step 9 draws attention to the desirability of periodically reviewing the state of health of the relationship, preferably by reference to explicit criteria. This seldom happens either – overtly, at least. The lack of formal contracts and formal reviews explains the number of argumentative relationships and messy

partings so regularly reported in the pages of *Campaign*.

Briefing a professional collaborator

Once a collaborator has been selected it must be formally briefed, if the eventual campaign is to stand a chance of bearing any resemblance at all to the client's expectations. 'Briefing' of some sort inevitably happens every time advertising managers (for instance) speak to account executives, but we are here concerned with organized, purposeful transmission of information as the basis for planning a new initiative or revising a current one.

The role of the advertising manager or brand manager is crucial: it is interpreter, not originator. The raw material of the brief originates with in-house production and marketing specialists, and needs to be subtly translated into the right form for passing on to another set of specialists outside. Otherwise, misunderstanding will abound and the recipients's own view of the client's needs will fill the vacuum left by the failure of real communication.

Table 19.8 proposes a list of ingredients of an ideal promotional brief, again drawn mostly from personal experience. In practice, numbers one and nine are regularly absent from even the best of briefs, being much harder to get to grips with than the others. In providing such guidance, clients should nevertheless beware of dogmatism, which can have a stultifying effect on the agency's response.

Table 19.8 *Ingredients of the promotional brief*

1 Precise, actionable and measurable promotional objectives.
2 Budget.
3 Product profile, consisting of:
   (a) Technical specifications,
   (b) Customer satisfactions deliverable.
4 Company profile.
5 Market analysis.
6 Production plans.
7 Price structure and pricing policy.
8 Distribution plans.
9 Criteria for evaluation of campaign effectiveness.

Otherwise, the ingredients are self-explanatory and collectively furnish enough information about other elements of the marketing mix to avoid the common pitfall of producing a promotional campaign seriously out of step with the perceptions formed by the target audience on the strength of product, place or price.

How much detail should be included under each heading? The only possible answer is that classically given about the length of a piece of string. As the ISBA says, 'a good brief should be as short as possible but as long as necessary'. This implies that brevity is the key aim, as the very name 'brief' suggests. The recipient can always ask follow-up questions.

Assessing campaign effectiveness

The final aspect of planning and controlling is measurement of the effectiveness of a promotional campaign. This should be a straightforward matter of comparing actual *performance* with explicit *criteria* derived from predetermined *objectives*. The fact is that practitioners typically experience substantial difficulty in articulating objectives that are either achievable or measurable.

Some examples will illustrate the problem. All the quoted statements have appeared in trade publications. First, consider 'to position Black Magic as the ultimate'. This clearly demonstrates two common tendencies: to mistake aspirations, often grandiose, for realistically achievable objectives; to charge promotion with the attainment of objectives it could hardly achieve in isolation from other elements of the marketing mix. A highly respectable American textbook lists sixteen specimen advertising objectives, of which five at most are capable of being achieved by promotional initiatives alone. One of the others is 'increase the number or quality of retail outlets'. To pass or fail a promotion campaign by that criterion would be reckless indeed.

Next, for Wall's Viennetta: 'to very quickly establish awareness of a product known to be very interesting to the customer and thereby maximize consumer trial'. Here, we clearly see another common failing: lack of precision and quantification. Awareness of *what* about the product? Among *which* target audience? *How much* awareness, and by *when*? *What* constitutes 'maximized' trial and by *when* is it to be achieved? Precisely *who* are 'customers'?

If criteria are thus unspecified, the tendency is for ready-made tests to substitute for purpose-designed measures. It certainly happens when, as is common, no objectives have even been stated. This is not semantic quibbling. Consider the normal British driving test, for instance. It is a legitimate test of something, to be sure, but not a specific measure of driving performance in any rigorous sense. Its objective is to identify potentially dangerous drivers (counter-productive promotional campaigns) rather than to measure degree of ability at the wheel. The Viennetta case example illustrates this point. Whereas the objective spoke of awareness and trial the report of 'campaign results' begins: 'achieved sales of over £8 million at rsp in 1983. . .within 18 months, had become the company's largest-selling ice cream line'. It continues in this vein, never mentioning any measure of awareness or trial at all.

A case history from the Boase Massimi Pollitt advertising agency contains the bold assertion that a campaign 'is performing consistently with the defined objectives'. Those were defined as: 'to provide advertising that is interesting/amusing to children; to communicate to children that Sugar Puffs are the most exciting/best tasting breakfast cereal; to reassure mothers that Sugar Puffs are a nourishing breakfast for their children'. The tests applied to the campaign in fact refer to none of them, but are the same standby and false friend as in the Viennetta case: sales changes.

The most usual surrogate tests are in fact based on a popular but very unsophisticated explanation of how advertising is presumed to work: the 'hierarchy of effects model'. AIDA is a very early but still much encountered example. Proposed by E K Strong in 1925 it simply says *attention→interest→desire→action*. There is no explanation of how one state leads to the next, or what measures are appropriate to test for each one.

A handful of variations on the theme have appeared since, using different vocabulary and varying the number of stages but all enshrining the same principle of stepwise progression. Table 19.9 summarizes them, proposing two distinct ways of looking at what the models claim to be describing. The question relevant to our present discussion now becomes: what 'standard tests' are available to measure either performance or response at each level in the hierarchy? The answer is that in practice cognitive response is overwhelmingly likely to be tested

Table 19.9 *The hierarchical model of advertising effect*

Level	Performance characteristic of the advertisement	Expected response by the audience	Mental 'realm'
6	Motivation	Action	Conative
5	Persuasion	Conviction	Affective
4	Empathy	Sympathy	
3	Communication	Comprehension	
2	Involvement	Interest	Cognitive
1	Impact	Attention	

by measures of *attention* or *recall*, affective response by *attitude* scaling and conative response by *sales*.

Yet there is no evidence in psychological experimentation that attention necessarily leads to higher level responses nor, perhaps more surprisingly, that attitude change necessarily leads to new patterns of behaviour. So the whole basis for these surrogate tests is very much open to criticism. Indeed, the hierarchical principle has been subject to more or less continous attack from influential quarters for thirty years. It nevertheless remains the pragmatic choice of the advertising business.

A full explanation and discussion of hierarchical models of advertising effect can be found in Chapter 6 of a companion text to this (Baker, 1983). Provided that the caveats noted here are borne in mind, Lovell and Potter (1975) is an authoritative review of the actual methods used to test advertising effectiveness, with case examples.

Before we leave the question of measurement – and, indeed, this whole chapter – there is one fact to be reported which even further blackens the picture painted. In practice, advertisers can prove reluctant to test their advertising at all. This is hardly what an intelligent observer would expect to find. Possible reasons for failure to pre-test are:

- The cost of making any modifications which might be indicated, at so late a stage.
- Reluctance to risk a bad evaluation of their skills on the part of agencies.

As for post-testing, they may be:

1 The over-and-done-with syndrome.
2 Clients' reluctance to discover an unwelcome truth.
3 Strong signals from clients that the campaign had better work, convincing the agency that

discretion is the better part of valour.
4 Reluctance on the agency's part to risk a bad evaluation of their skills, whatever the client may or may not have implied about testing.
5 Other vested interests on both sides.

If these factors do not lead to a total neglect of evaluation, they are at least likely to cause a subliminally premeditated decision to substitute a surrogate test such as recall (easy to pass if the campaign is built around reiteration of a main proposition and frequency of repetition) for a more probing evaluation via more meaningful criteria. Television commercials for detergents spring to mind.

Conclusion

'Promotion' is a mix of activities: advertising, publicity, direct mail, packaging and sales promotion. Terminology is often carelessly used in practice and important strategic differences among the five thereby blurred. Very considerable sums of money are transacted in the process of conducting promotional campaigns, especially on sales promotion, advertising and packaging.

The advertising system (which is the focus of much of the chapter, by default) consists of advertisers, advertising agencies, media owners and potential consumers. The text examines working relationships among the first three in fair detail. Advertising agencies are not agents at all, but principals. A historical anomaly explains this contradiction and also why they are normally remunerated by receiving a commission discount from the media rather than a fee from their clients. The 'account executive' plays a key role in managing the advertiser-agency relationship. Surveys show that advertisers are mostly very satisfied with the service they receive from agencies, but there is a puzzlingly contradictory tendency to regular changing of partners, according to press reports.

Promotion management cannot operate in a vacuum and must take account of perceptions of its activity held in the world outside. Economic, sociological and cultural attitudes to advertising have therefore been examined and discussed in enough detail to demonstrate the prevailing view of opinion-formers and other influentials. Public opinion, as described by a series of field surveys, is significantly different. Ordinary people do not spontaneously think about advertising very often. When their attention is directed, they are overwhelmingly likely to approve of advertising and enjoy advertisements, including television commercials. Promotion is controlled in Britain by a tripartite system comprising legislation, regulation by statutory authority and self-regulation.

The press remains the largest of the five 'major' advertising media, despite steadily losing share of total UK advertising expenditure over the last ten years, and still attracts almost exactly twice as much revenue as the second-placed medium, television, which is simultaneously increasing its share. Together, these two account for 94 per cent of the whole. The remaining three are therefore major in name only.

Media planning vocabulary is esoteric, but the key quantitative concepts explained in the text are coverage, reach, wastage, cost per thousand, and production cost. Such criteria must be counterbalanced by qualitative characteristics of media if informed decisions are to be made. These can be summarized as usage, creative scope, vehicle effect and user-friendliness.

Planning and control of promotional campaigns involves budgeting, choosing an advertising agency or other collaborator, briefing it and measuring effectiveness. Budgeting is usually discussed in terms of deciding the size of an appropriation, but a budget should be an important planning and control tool in its own right. Both choice and briefing are typically conducted in a disappointingly haphazard manner. More rigorous frameworks have therefore been proposed here. Measurement of effectiveness typically founders on a chronic inability in the business to articulate properly usable objectives which

yield valid criteria of performance. The resulting vacuum is filled by a set of barely satisfactory surrogate tests based on an elderly and questionable conceptual model of advertising effect. Case examples corroborate this view of the state of the art in a crucial aspect of promotional management.

References

Adams, J.R. *Media Planning*, 2nd ed., Business Books, 1977.

Baker, M.J. *Marketing: Theory and Practice*, 2nd ed., Macmillan, 1983.

Baker, M. J. *et al.*, *Macmillan Dictionary of Marketing and Advertising*, 2nd ed., Macmillan, 1990.

Broadbent, S. and Jacobs, B., *Spending Advertising Money*, 4th ed., Business Books, 1984.

Berger, J., *Ways of Seeing*, BBC and Penguin, 1978.

Campaign, 'Why it is time the Sunday colour titles came of age', 30 May 1986, p. 43.

Halloran, J.D. *Control or Consent?* Sheed & Ward, 1963, pp. 60–1.

Inglis, F., *The Imagery of Power*, Heinemann, 1972.

Labour Party, *Opposition Green Paper: Advertising*, The Labour Party, 1972, p. 55.

Lawson, R.G. 1979 *Advertising Law*, Macdonald & Evans, 1979.

Lovell, M. and Potter, J. *Assessing the Effectiveness of Advertising*, Business Books 1975.

McGann, A.F., and Russell, J.T., *Advertising Media*, Irwin, 1981, Chapter 3.

Myers, K., *Understains: Sense and Seduction in Advertising*, Comedia, 1985.

Packard, V. *The Hidden Persuaders*, 2nd ed., Penguin, 1975.

Pearson, J. and Turner, G. *The Persuasion Industry*, Eyre & Spottiswoode, 1965.

Reekie, W.D. *Advertising and the Competition which Counts*. The Advertising Assocation (Research Studies in Advertising, no.8;) 1975.

Reekie, W.D. *Advertising and Price*, The Advertising Association, 1979.

Robertson, D.H. *Lectures on Economic Principles*, Staples, 1958, p. 169.

White, R. *Advertising: What it is and how to do it*, 2nd ed., McGraw-Hill, 1988, p. 196.

Wilkins, C., 'Chris Wilkins assesses the amateur art of the classified ad', *Design & Art Direction*, No.40, 9 August 1985, p. 20.

Woolley, D., *Advertising Law Handbook*, 2nd ed. (with supplement dated 1979), Business Books, 1976.

20
Distribution and customer service

MARTIN CHRISTOPHER

Introduction

The recent upsurge of interest in corporate 'excell-ence' has heightened management's consciousness and awareness of the importance of customer ser-vice. We have come to recognize that a crucial source of competitive advantage can be achieved through superior marketplace service. This in turn has served to remind us that distribution is the major vehicle within the business for the generation of service. As such it is imperative for any organization seeking to improve its overall marketing perform-ance to integrate distribution fully into the develop-ment of marketing strategy.

Traditionally, distribution has been viewed by many as a source of cost – admittedly a necessary cost, but a cost nevertheless. Inevitably such a viewpoint leads to a search for improvement in operating efficiency and a focus on cost reduction. Thus improving vehicle utilization, warehouse throughput times, materials handling methods and so on are the constant concern of many distribution managers.

While not wishing to diminish the importance of cost containment, it can be argued that such a concern with *efficiency* can on occasion lead to a failure to recognize the real issue in distribution – that is how *effective* is our distribution strategy?

This distinction between efficiency and effective-ness was most clearly defined by Peter Drucker who argued that efficiency was a concern with 'doing things right', while effectiveness placed the emph-asis on 'doing the right things'.

Such a statement could easily be dismissed as purely a clever play on words and yet it has a crucial significance for management. So often much of what we do is akin to rearranging the deck chairs on the Titanic – we make the ship look tidier but neglect its overall direction. In other words operating efficien-cy takes precedence over strategy. On the other hand the successful companies – those who have developed leadership position in their markets – tend to be those that have recognized that competi-tive advantage comes first from their strategic posi-tion and second from their operating efficiency. Clearly a combination of the two is better still.

How then does this philosophy relate to the man-agement of the distribution task?

First it must be recognised that logistics costs account for a large proportion of the sales value of many products. Thus it will follow that in a competi-tive market, particularly where substitutes are available and acceptable to the customer, a major advantage can be gained if logistics costs can be reduced while still maintaining the required service levels. A recent report (*Guardian*, 26 March 1986) stated that car industry experts are forecasting that each car made in Nissan UK's new Tyneside plant will be produced for about £600 less than it costs a British manufacturer to make. The report went on to state that the reason for this Japanese cost advantage is no longer primarily cheaper labour costs but is due to superior logistics management. Nissan will be managing the total material flow, from component source to final user, as an entity. As a result its inventory of materials, work in progress, goods in transit and finished goods will be kept to a minimum: throughput times will be reduced; transport costs will be low – yet its ability to service the end market will not be diminished.

Such an advantage will be difficult for competitors to overcome without the adoption of similar methods.

However, it must be recognized that the advantage in the marketplace does not always go to the lowest cost producer. In the same industry as Nissan, Jaguar has achieved substantial success not so much by cutting costs but by adding value. Much has been said about the new approach to quality at Jaguar and how it has led to major improvements in the final product. Just as important however in its success has been its concentration on improving customer service, specifically in North America. A radical overhaul of its US dealer network plus a major emphasis on improving the logistics of spares support has transformed its market position.

Other examples of value added strategies based around superior service could be cited; companies like DEC and IBM, for example, dominate the segments in which they compete as much through their service package as through their technology.

Evidence such as this suggests that it may be advisable for British companies to shift their emphasis towards the adoption of value added strategies instead of struggling in vain to become the lowest cost producers. The relationship between market share and unit costs are well known but in so many markets UK companies have little chance of regaining lost volume except through offering the customer something over and above that provided by competitors.

If this is true what contribution can distribution and logistics management make in the search for value added?

Marketing and logistics converge

Most marketing executives probably have never considered the very real contribution to success in the marketplace that can be made by more effective logistics management. While many would acknowledge the sense of the old adage 'the right product in the right place at the right time', how many actually factor it explicitly into their marketing strategy?

On the other hand, some of the more innovative companies recognize that if developing a position of sustainable competitive advantage is the name of the game, then a major source of that advantage is superior logistics performance.

Thus it can be argued that instead of viewing distribution, marketing and manufacturing as largely separate activities within the business, they need to be unified – particularly at the strategic level. One might be tempted to describe such an integrated approach to strategy and planning as 'Marketing logistics'. Whatever we call it, the important requirement is to understand that any business can only compete and survive through one or other of two options: by winning a cost advantage or by providing superior values and benefits to the customer.

Certain changes in the marketing environment make such a revised orientation even more appropriate. One such change has been the steady transition to 'commodity' type markets. By this is meant that increasingly the power of the 'brand' is diminishing as technologies of competing products converge, thus making product differences less apparent. Faced with such situations the customer may be influenced by price or by 'image' perceptions, but overriding these aspects may well be 'availability' – in other words – is the product in stock. Nor is it only in consumer markets that we are encountering the force of customer service as a determinant of purchase; there is much evidence from industrial markets of the same phenomenon.

A second change is that customer expectations of service have increased, thus in almost every market the customer is now more demanding, more 'sophisticated' than he/she was, say, thirty years ago. Industrial buyers are more professional, too, increasing use is made of formal 'vendor appraisal' systems and suppliers are now confronted with the need to provide 'just-in-time' delivery performance.

The third change that has had a particularly

severe impact in many industries is the trend for product life cycles to become shorter. The product life cycle represents the period of time that a brand or specific product model is an effective player in the market. There are many implications for management of shorter product life cycles but one in particular is worthy of note.

What we have witnessed in many markets is the effect of changes in technology and consumer demand combining to produce more volatile markets. There are many current examples of shortening life cycles but perhaps the personal computer symbolizes them all.

In this particular case we have seen rapid developments in technology which have firstly created markets where none existed before and then almost as quickly have rendered them obsolete as the next generation of product is announced.

Such shortening life cycles create substantial problems for logistics management. In particular shorter life cycles demand shorter lead times – indeed our definition of lead time may well need to change. Lead times are traditionally defined as the elapsed period from receipt of customer order to delivery. However in today's environment there is a second aspect to lead time: how long does it take from the procurement of raw materials, subassemblies, etc. through to the delivery of the final product to the customer.

That same personal computer referred to earlier may have a total procurement-to-delivery lead time of twelve months! In other words, some of the components may remain in stock for several weeks before being incorporated in a subassembly or module. Those subassemblies may then be in transit to another location, possibly overseas, for another couple of weeks where they then, say, are held up pending customs clearance, then further delays in storage and manufacturing and so on.

What we are now witnessing is a situation where the product life cycle, in some cases, is in danger of becoming shorter than the procurement-to-delivery lead time with all the consequent problems for planning and operations that such a situation will create.

The answer to this problem must lie in greater attempts to manage the total lead time throughout the entire system. So often it is found that a substantial proportion of this total lead time is created through lack of insight and clearly defined managerial responsibilities at the interfaces between adjacent functions.

We have also identified a further trend in that because *production* lead times are shortening through the use of new technology, this in effect means that a greater proportion of the total procurement-to-delivery lead time is accounted for by transport and storage. Thus we see greater pressure for integrated distribution/logistics management arising as a result.

The customer service dimension

These changes in the environment, previously described, have served to move logistics to centre stage and, in turn, to focus the spotlight on customer service.

Customer service is the thread that links the logistics and marketing processes, because, in the end, the output of the logistics system *is* customer service. The skill lies in managing the two arms of marketing and logistics in such a way as to maximize the value added through customer service while still seeking a cost advantage. It can be done, and perhaps one of the most intriguing examples of recent years has come from the world of high fashion – the Italian company Benetton.

Benetton has become a world leader in the production and retailing of high fashion casual wear – particularly knitwear. As Montgomery and Hausman's (1985) description of its approach indicates, Benetton has found a way to gain a marketing edge through superior logistics management:

Benetton's order system is 'just-in-time' as production runs are not started until orders have been received. A key aspect of its system is the dyeing of knitted goods after production rather than dyeing yarn prior to knitting. This allows Benetton outlets to delay commitment to particular colours until later in the production cycle. Since each selling season typically begins with about ten alternative colours with only about three usually resulting in high demand, the delay in colour choice affords Benetton an opportunity to respond directly to market demand. The retail system itself provides valuable information to Benetton for production planning via daily orders. These feed production with current demand, on which replenishment schedules for designs and colours may be based. The timeliness of this order data is crucial since popular colours will often sell out in the first ten days of a new season. This rapid response system gives Benetton retailers a competitive edge over their less responsive competitors. The order information is digested and fed back to those customers whose orders appear to be out of line with others in their area. Further, Benetton uses CAD for design and cutting in order to respond to dynamic demand as rapidly as possible. Finally, the company's marketing strategy promotes simple colour fashion with heavy advertising support, which in turn maximises the benefits from the delayed dyeing production process.

Examples such as this demonstrate the opportunities that exist for using a closely integrated logistics and marketing system in order to provide high levels of service at lowest cost. The competitive edge that Benetton has achieved through this means is considerable – it has both added value and achieved a cost advantage.

Given that the evidence to support the case for customer service driven strategies is so strong, where should those businesses that wish to travel down that road begin?

Defining and measuring customer service

It is sometimes suggested that the role of customer service is to provide 'time and place utility' in the transfer of goods and services between buyer and seller. Put another way, there is no value in a product or service until it is in the hands of the customer or consumer. It follows that making the product or service 'available' is what, in essence, the distribution function of the business is all about. 'Availability' is in itself a complex concept, impacted upon by a galaxy of factors which together constitute customer service. These factors might include, for example, delivery frequency and reliability, stock levels and order cycle time, as they impact upon availability. Indeed, it could be said that ultimately customer service is determined by the interaction of all those factors that affect the process of making products and services available to the buyer.

Many commentators have defined various ele-ments of customer service, the most commonly occurring seem to be:

- Order cycle time.
- Consistency and reliability of delivery.
- Inventory availability.
- Order-size constraints.
- Ordering convenience.
- Delivery time and flexibility.
- Invoicing procedures and accuracy.
- Claims procedure.
- Condition of goods.
- Salesperson's visits.
- Order status information.
- After sales support.

In any particular product/market situation, some of these elements will be more important than others and there may be factors other than those listed above which have a significance in a specific market. Indeed, the argument that will be developed in this chapter is that it is essential to understand customer service in terms of differing requirements of different market segments and that no universally appropriate list of elements exists; each market that the company services will attach different importance to different service elements.

Customer service is perceptual

It is a common fault in marketing to fail to realize that customers do not always attach the same importance to product attributes as the vendor. Thus, it sometimes happens that products are promoted on attributes or features that are less important to the customer in reality than other aspects. A floor cleaner that is sold on its ease of application, for example, will not succeed unless 'ease of application' is a salient benefit sought by the customer. If 'shine' or the need for less frequent cleaning are important to the customer then we might be better advised to feature those aspects in our promotion. The same principle applies in customer service: which aspects of service are rated most highly by the customer? If a company places its emphasis upon stock availablity but the customer regards delivery reliability more highly, it may not be allocating its resources in a way likely to maximize sales. Alternatively, a company that realizes that its customers place a higher value on completeness of orders than they do on say, regular scheduled deliveries could develop this to its advantage.

There is, thus, a great premium to be placed on gaining an insight into the factors that influence buyer behaviour and, in the context of customer service, which particular elements are seen by the customer to be the most important. The use of market research techniques in customer service has lagged behind their application in such areas as product testing and advertising research, yet the importance of researching the service needs of customers is just as great as, say, the need to understand the market reaction to price. In fact, it is possible to apply standard, proven market research methods to gain considerable insight into the ways that customers will react to customer service.

The first step in research of this type is to identify the relative source of influence on the purchase decision. If we are selling components to a manufacturer, for example, who will make the decision on the source of supply? This is not always an easy question to answer as, in many cases, there will be several people involved. The purchasing manager of the company to whom we are selling may only be acting as an agent for others within the firm. In other cases, his/her influence will be much greater. Alternatively, if we are manufacturing products for sale through retail outlets, is the decision to stock made centrally or by individual store managers? The answers to these questions can often be supplied by the sales force. The sales representative should know from experience who the decision makers are.

Given that a clear indication of the source of decision-making power can be gained, the customer service researcher at least knows who to research. The question still remains however – which elements of the vendor's total marketing offering have what effect on the purchase decision? Ideally, once the decision-making unit in a specific market has been identified, an initial, small-scale research programme should be initiated which would be based on personal interviews with a representative sample of buyers. The purpose of these interviews is to elicit, *in the language of the customers*, first, the importance they attach to customer service vis-à-vis the other marketing mix elements such as price, product quality, promotion and so on and second, the specific importance they attach to the individual components of customer service.

Assessing the customer service climate

In our eagerness to develop a customer service strategy it would be a mistake to focus exclusively on the 'external' dimension of service, i.e. customer perceptions. Of equal importance is the 'internal' dimension, i.e. how do our own people, our managers and work force, view service? What is their attitude to customers? Do they share the same concept and definition of service as our customers?

It would be a truism to suggest that ultimately a company's performance is limited more by the vision and the quality of its people than it is by market factors or competitive forces. However it is perhaps only belatedly that we have come to recognize this.

Much has been written and spoken about 'corporate culture'. We have come to recognize that the shared values that are held throughout the organization can provide a powerful driving force and focus for all its actions. More often than not though we have to admit that most organizations lack a cohesive and communicated culture – even if there is a defined philosophy of the business, it may be little understood.

This lack of shared values can impact the company in many ways and particularly its approach to customer service.

One viable way to assess the customer service 'climate' within the firm is to take the temperature by means of an employee survey. One such approach that has been developed begins with identifying all those personnel who have a direct or indirect impact upon customer service. A useful device here is to consider the complete 'order to cash' cycle and to ensure that we have identified all those people involved in all the different departments that influence the order flow. The focus of the survey should be upon these key people's perceptions of service: what do *they* think is important to the customers and how do they think we perform service-wise?

What quite often emerges from these internal surveys is that employees hold quite different views as to what constitutes customer service. Similarly, they may often over rate the company's actual performance compared with the customers' own rating. Making such comparisons between customers' perceptions and the employees' perceptions can provide a powerful means of identifying customer service problems and their sources.

This 'audit' of internal perceptions and attitudes towards service can form the basis of a programme of action aimed at developing a customer service culture. However such a process, which almost inevitably will involve a major re-orientation within the firm, cannot work without the total commitment of top management. The service culture must grow outwards from the board room and the chief executive must be its greatest champion.

Within the logistics function one very practical step is to set up the equivalent of a 'quality circle'. Such a scheme might involve looking at the total order processing and invoicing cycle and selecting individuals from all the departments or sections involved. This group would meet at least once a week with the expressed objective of seeking improvements to customer service from whatever source they might come. A further task that might usefully be given to this group is to handle all customer complaints that relate to service.

Underpinning all of these initiatives should be a company-wide education programme. Increasingly, more and more organizations have come to recognize the key role that in-company education can have in developing a sense of shared values. Furthermore, because it is a basic tenet of psychology that attitude change must precede behaviour change, education can lead to measurably improved performance. One of the best examples recently has come from British Airways whose 'putting people first' campaign has resulted in a significant change in employee behaviour and thus in the company's marketplace performance.

Using service to sell

Earlier it was stressed that it is important to establish those components of the total customer service mix which have the greatest impact on the buyer's perceptions of us as a supplier. This thinking needs to be carried right through into the design of the customer service offering. This offering can best be described as the customer service 'package', for it will most likely contain more than one component.

The design of the package will need to take account of the differing needs of different market segments so that the resources allocated to customer service can be used in the most cost-effective way. Too often, a uniform, blanket approach to service is adopted by companies which does not distinguish between the real requirements of different customer types. This can lead to customers being offered too little service or too much.

The precise composition of the customer service package for any market segment will depend on the results of the analysis described earlier. It will also be determined by budgetary and cost constraints. If alternative packages can be identified which seem to be equally acceptable to the buyer, it makes sense to choose the least cost alternative.

For example, it may be possible to identify a customer service package with high acceptability which enables the emphasis to be switched away from a high level of inventory availability towards, say, improved customer communications. Once a cost-effective package has been identified in this way, it should become a major part of the company's marketing mix – 'using service to sell' is the message here. If the market segments we serve are sensitive to service, then the service package must be actively promoted. One way in which this can be achieved with great effect is by stressing the impact on *customers'* costs of the improved service package, for example, what improved reliability will do for their own stock planning; what shorter lead times will do for their inventory levels; how improved ordering and invoicing systems will lead to fewer errors; and so on. All too often, customers will not appreciate the impact that improved service offered by the supplier can have on their bottom line.

Conclusion

The main theme of this chapter has been that logistics and marketing can combine together to provide a powerful means of achieving a sustainable competitive advantage. The combination of added value through service and cost advantage through greater efficiency make a winning team wherever they are tried.

There are probably more opportunities for profit improvement through superior marketing logistics than from any other source.

Reference

Montgomery, D. and Hausman, W., 'Managing the Marketing/Manufacturing Interface', *Journal of Management*, vol. 2, no. 2, 1985.

21
Controlling marketing

JAMES R. BUREAU

Introduction

The development in the last fifty years of the concept of marketing has turned out to be as revolutionary in its impact on the attitudes and practices of the business organization as has the impact of the technological revolution which has accompanied it.

In order to accommodate the new discipline of marketing, and to ensure that its growing power base within the enterprise is properly managed and controlled, radically new systems of operation have had to be developed, new priorities have emerged; new structures have had to be created. Inevitably such changes to traditional customs and routines have caused frictions, aroused antagonisms, set off alarm bells among those given the responsibility of running the enterprise with efficiency. The introduction of marketing, both as a concept and as a new department within the organization, has often been initially greeted with severe scepticism, hostility and general resistance.

The anxiety aroused by the function of marketing is not surprising. Properly and fully organized, the marketing function's tentacles reach into most corners of the enterprise; exerting some controlling influence in many areas of the organization. The acceptance of the logical credo that satisfying the customer is the primary concern of the whole organization leads inevitably to the intrusion of the

marketing function into virtually every area of business operation. The psychological dominance of this belief comes to be accepted very quickly in the organization that has recognized the immense benefits it confers. Yet there remains the need to control the new power centre that this belief has created, in order to ensure that the marketing department's activities are properly enmeshed and coordinated with those of the older functions of the enterprise.

But, the need to control marketing activity within the organization is *not* only founded on administrative good sense. There are very special reasons specific to the marketing discipline which will always ensure that the beady eye of top management is sharply focused on marketing plans, decisions and recommendations:

1 *Most alarmingly, many – if not most – of the recommendations made by marketers in establishing marketing policy are founded on informed speculation*, rarely on incontrovertible facts, put forward on the basis of tenable but tenuous forecasts of their likely effects in the marketplace and recommended in the fair certainty that convincing proof of the subsequent effects of their recommendations will probably never be clearly demonstrated. Such a view is not to be considered unduly cynical: it is simply the nature of the beast that certainty and provability are very

infrequent companions of marketing forecasts.

If, at the same time, marketing policy recommendations lie at the heart of future success, good sense dictates a need for a very careful watch over the function that is charged with the creation of the organization's life-blood – its revenue.

2 *Because of the speculative nature of marketing decision making, failure is normal.* Put less pessimistically, marketing recommendations are subject to considerably greater levels of risk than is normal in virtually every other function within the business enterprise. The new product failure rate normal in marketing would be an astonishing percentage to apply to failures in machinery or materials acquisition, personnel turnover or any other aspect of business operation. Even in the 'best' companies the failure rate is probably as high as 50 per cent. Yet the uncertainties of the marketplace have innured the organization to the shock of marketing failure: it is par for the course. And an activity as here the failure rate is high must inevitably come under the closest scrutiny and control.

3 *Good marketing is expensive.* Typically, the organization seriously embarking on marketing activity will find it to be expensive. It is the fearful paradox confronting all new business ventures that you have to be rich to enable you to afford the marketing expenditure required to become rich. Thus the scale of expenditure required to market effectively must inevitably place marketing under the closest scrutiny, and require of it a most disciplined control in all its expensive activities.

4 *Marketing activity has high public visibility.* Any major mistake in marketing decision-making has the frequent side effect of being a mistake that is very visible to those groups of individuals who, in the short or long term, may most affect the success of the enterprise: customers, the buying public, the media owners, even the government. Every product failure, every poor advertising campaign, every unacceptable change in price, every unsuccessful redesign of existing products or their packaging will have some effect on the revenue earning potential of the enterprise. Poor decisions made in other areas – personnel, production, purchasing, R & D – may affect the competence and profitability of the organization without having any impact on the outside world on which the organization depends.

5 *Marketing mistakes are more difficult to reverse* than errors made in other areas of the operation of the enterprise. Being more visible, marketing decisions may be more difficult to change without damage to the organizational image. Poor pricing, design and product performance may be too fundamental to reverse in the marketplace. While Clive Sinclair's C5 electric car could be continuously modified inside the research laboratories and the manufacturing plant, once the product was committed to the marketplace serious modifications were unlikely to resolve either the product or the reputation of the organization to the extent of retrieving lost ground.

6 *Because the marketing function is a cross-functional trespasser* it must attract greater scrutiny and management control. In an organization that has fully accepted the planning implications of the marketing function; that is, that the marketing department is held responsible for managing all aspects of the organization's products in the marketplace and is thus expected to help to plan *all* aspects of the product, the marketing function will inevitably trespass into the territory of production, purchasing, quality control and any other department whose performance directly affects the competence of the product in the marketplace. The trespassing is undertaken, of course, with senior management's approval, but it remains trespassing. As such, much care is taken to ensure that the coordinative, planning role of the marketing department comes under the closest scrutiny.

Such a list of factors, marking out marketing as the special target for scrutiny and control within the organization, results in the development of routines, procedures and systems which make such control effective as well as comprehensive. Three sets of routines may be separately identified:

1 Corporate control systems.
2 Marketing department control systems.
3 External control systems.

Corporate control systems

While the boardroom of the organization will be

concerned with the marketing function's own control systems, it will develop separate – though interlocked – systems which may serve as the basis of the authority it gives marketing to enact marketing policy, and which serves to monitor progress against agreed plans. The principal corporate systems of control over marketing are those of the management accountant's discipline, and the primary review time is the monthly board meeting.

Marketing department control systems

In common with every other organizational discipline, the marketing function measures, monitors, analyses and controls its effectiveness on a continuous basis in order to ensure it is meeting its short-term financial responsibilities and its long-term administrative competences: in other words, it ensures that it is meeting its revenue and profit goals as agreed in the annual budget, while it monitors and continuously assesses the systems it employs to achieve those short-term goals – planning, selling, promoting, pricing, product evaluation, distribution and other systems.

External control systems

Many business organizations make use of services external to the organization which provide systems to monitor the competence of the marketing function, either on an occasional basis (for example the formal marketing audit undertaken by consultants) or on a continuous basis (for example Nielsen audits of retail sales).

These three groupings of control routines will form the basis of the remainder of this chapter.

Before detailing with these procedures, however, it is necessary to outline some principles which lie behind control systems:

Formality

Control systems require to be formalized into firm rituals, for fear any looseness in their application will result in their discontinuance through the pressures of more immediate problem-solving. The discipline of formalizing routines is often the only way of ensuring that the thing is done at all.

Necessity

From the above, it follows that any such formal systems – of documentation, report writing, meetings – should be clearly useful to the organization and not simply the ritual necessities of obsessionals. Any excess in such systems leads quickly to more time being spent on documenting and planning the solving of problems than on solving problems.

Priority

Control systems should be concerned with those elements which it is important to control and not with controlling *everything*. Such systems should be developed for key profit earners, key trouble spots, key future profit earners. Control systems, once in operation, can seem sufficiently elegant and attractive to senior management for them, mistakenly, to insist on their availability to control every element of marketing operations.

Veracity

Control systems require to be data based. The control system which is based on speculation and intuition is unlikely to provide any true picture of the real situation. It is important that such systems report the truth (or at least an approximation to it), providing confidence, if not certainty, that solutions to problems are at least logically based on fact.

Regularity

To be in control of the marketing environment requires that measurements of effectiveness – financial, marketing research or selling – happen as regularly as is affordable. But the regularity of the application of control systems is clearly dependent on the volatility of the market, the problem being monitored, and the organization's wealth. Formal routines of strategic market planning may be sufficient once every two years, whereas measuring the achievements of sales orders against targets may be required every four weeks.

Finally, all such systems are time-consuming in that they generate much activity in the marketing department and, additionally, in the other corporate functions which are frequently involved (most obviously the management accountants called on to supply much of the data and analysis required for good control). In common with other routines newly introduced to a company, an organization embarking on routines of marketing control will need to find the extra staff to cope with the extra work generated.

Corporate control systems

In practice there are no clear divisions between control procedures developed by the organization to ensure that top management retains control over the marketing function, and those procedures developed by the marketing function itself to retain firm control over its activities. For example, sales order analysis – common as a means of effecting control of the sales force by sales management – is frequently copied to top management personnel, who then use it as *their* means of monitoring progress of the whole marketing operation. In many organizations daily, weekly and monthly sales analyses are widely circulated.

It is probably true to say that virtually all control routines demanded by senior management as a means of controlling marketing would be continued by the marketing function even if the boardroom no longer required them, simply because they powerfully serve the long-term best interests in monitoring its competence.

While different organizations vary widely in the systems they adopt, there are certain common denominators among all companies concerned to review and control marketing effectiveness. The key corporate control mechanisms of the marketing function are:

- Corporate strategic plan.
- Annual marketing plan ('the budget').
- Marketing progress reviews.
- Price-cost-profit reviews.
- New product development reviews.

Corporate strategic plan

It is good business practice for the enterprise to undertake long-term strategic planning, in which it reviews the fundamental philosophies and the primary goals of the organization. Clearly stated and with

clear, numerical and unequivocal financial targets, such a plan lays down the essential rules to which the marketing department will adhere, and the goals which the marketing department will be expected to meet in its annual activities in the marketplace. As such, the annual reiteration of the organization's strategic goals provides the marketing function with an essential template from which it can work.

In practice, the marketing function will have been heavily involved in such strategic planning, by providing many of the inputs to the plan. It will have been the marketing department to which the strategic planners will have turned to obtain data about past sales, past data concerning each of the company's markets, data about other prospective markets the company may be considering entering and so on, in order that the boardroom may have a clear understanding of the realities of the market-place when they come to set their strategic goals.

In addition, it will be the marketing function for which the strategic goals are frequently created: strategic requirements for growth in revenue, profits and market share must ultimately devolve on marketing. The strategic requirement for new product growth – a frequent target of strategic plans – will also generally devolve on the marketing function: it is they who will coordinate, develop and plan new product development activity to achieve such growth requirements.

In order to retain the most rigorous control over the marketing function in the area of new business development, corporate bodies do well to ordain the constraints under which they require marketing to function in their search for new products and markets with which to 'close the gap' between what can be achieved by current products in current markets, and what needs to be sought additionally to meet the new targets of the strategists. Quite simply this requires that the organization's top managers outline for marketing what is acceptable and what is unacceptable in their search for new business:

- *Technological constraints*: what the company considers to be the limits of any new technology required in the process of making new products.
- *Marketing constraints*: the extent to which the company feels limited in the areas of selling, distribution, promotion and other marketing mix

elements in its expansion into new markets.

- *Financial constraints*: what the organization considers as the essential financial ground rules for new product development, marketing or acquisition. Rules are needed here to guide the marketing function as to return on investment, payback, capital investment maxima (or minima), profit requirements from new business ventures and so on.
- *Managerial constraints:* guidance as to the acceptability of new ventures in their demands on current management skills and numbers, or in their need for new skills and additional managers.
- *Social constraints:* the extent, if any, of any control on new business development arising from, for example, ecological or consumerist constraints.

Annual marketing plan

The strategic plan, with its broad brush strokes painted on a big canvas with a distant horizon, provides only a broad control over the direction marketing activities may take in the organization. However useful, strategy does not determine the reality of the day-to-day activity of solving short-term marketing problems. Such solutions lie in the domain of operational, or short-term, marketing planning.

The extent to which it is possible to plan short-term marketing activity in detail (three to eighteen months ahead) is dependent on many factors: the ability to identify separate markets, separate products; the amount of data available on which to forecast the probable outcomes of alternative activities and the data availability in measuring such effects; the number of personnel available to undertake such planning, and so on. Such planning takes place routinely under the brand management system employed by all the major fast moving consumer goods companies, where it is clearly effective and profitable, and is increasingly being adopted elsewhere. However, if you build power stations or battleships, every product is tailor-made, and 'product planning' happens in the boardroom.

An acceptance of the importance of the marketing concept, the continued sharpening of competition

in all markets, the increasing scale of the penalties associated with failure in the marketplace, and the growing realization of the benefits that accrue to organizations which plan their short-term marketing tactics, market by market and product by product, is pushing all organizations inexorably into setting up sound product/market planning systems – and, more latterly, planning for major customers in the marketplace – in order to maximize the probability of marketing success. For all the years in which 'business' has existed there had always been an acceptance of the importance of the most careful planning of expenditure. The time has now arrived for the equally careful planning of revenue. Gone are the days when a simple forecast of next year's sales by the sales force, based on sales for the last few years, is considered an adequate substitute for the positive planning of all the elements of the marketing mix. Every product is now required to be the subject of a dynamic response to the marketplace: passive extrapolation – essentially what the old fashioned 'sales forecast' was about – will no longer drive the marketing ship.

The modern, marketing orientated boardroom now requires a detailed marketing plan annually for each of the major products or markets in which it operates, in order to be convinced that the full panoply of marketing opportunities, alternatives and tactics have been investigated and the recommended course is the one most likely to sustain the company's offering in the competitive marketplace. This philosophy recognizes, above all, that the diverse offerings each company makes available in the marketplace most often operate in markets which are significantly different one from the other, with significantly different problems of product, price, promotion and place. Such differences require individual attention and cannot be readily catered for in a single marketing plan. The Ford Motor Company does not earn Ford profits: it earns Fiesta profits, Granada profits, Sierra and Orion profits. And they all experience different problems which require detailed and separate investigation.

Hence the organization's top mangement will require from the marketing function a detailed explanation of its intended activities for the year ahead, annually. As a control mechanism such a procedure has many benefits:

Synchronizes corporate activity

An annual establishment of corporate marketing policy results from an annual review of the organization's marketing tactics and recommendations for the future, product by product. It provides top management with a chance to change or endorse policy in the ideal circumstances of a complete review of all elements of the marketing of each product. Marketing policy becomes an integrated response to a complex set of problems, and stops being a piecemeal response to short-term panics (the level and frequency of panics is much reduced!)

Marketing policy approval

A once-a-year formal presentation and approval of product policy maximizes the level of delegation through the remaining year. Simply as an administrative system, the annual review and approval is thus only subject to routine monitoring – to estabish that the promises made at the annual review are being met. In a multinational, or multidivisional organization with centralized approval systems, such a system maximizes divisional freedom of operation.

Marketing expenditure justification

Bearing in mind the frequently considerable sums of expenditure involved promotionally in a marketing plan, the annual review formally presented will make out a detailed case for all such expenditure. In this area in particular the boardroom requires to be satisfied that all approved expenditures are necessary.

Review of marketing assumptions and of the market

An annual review allows for a full examination of changes in the marketplace 'since the last annual review'. Such a procedure makes for a well informed company. For the multinational operation it will also be valuable in bringing the company's controllers up to date on their multinational markets.

Review of marketing competence

Finally, the full presentation of marketing recommendations for the following year puts a severe spotlight on the general competence of the marketing function overall. Such a review may well throw light on the strengths or weaknesses of the selling, distribution, data gathering and marketing planning functions, quite separately from the performance of the organization's products.

Thus the annual process which results in a very thorough review of the products yields the detailed blueprint for marketing action both for the organization itself and for the marketing function within it.

The end result of this frantic activity is, ultimately, the same as the old fashioned sales forecast: a detailed month-by-month forecast of unit sales, product by product, with estimated selling prices enabling the financial department to calculate a monthly budgeted revenue account which will serve the organization as *the budget*: the core target for the enterprise for the year to come. But the approach taken will have served a more demanding purpose, and the final outcome will provide for a more certain future.

Marketing progress reviews

The budgeted targets for each product – both by value and by volume – may now serve as the measuring device, month by month, of the marketing function's effectiveness through the year to come.

To maintain the constant watch on the planned progress of corporate revenue, expenditure and subsequent profits that are central to the boardroom's responsibilities, a regular system needs to be set up to review such progress, and the accounting function of the organization is required to provide the data essential to such an examination.

Whatever meeting is convened to enable this monitoring to take place – most companies will do this at monthly board meetings – it will control the efficiency of marketing operations if it observes some key rules:

1 Management accounting data must be available at the level which is the *realistic diagnostic level of information* – not at the 'Ford' level only, but at the 'Fiesta' level.

   Marketing can be made most accountable if they can be asked to explain revenue variances at the product (brand, or – in some cases – market) level. Clearly this requires detailed analysis to enable discrimination between sales volume variances against budgeted volumes, as against selling-price variances against standards agreed in the budget.

2   It will help the marketing function's efficiency if it has a recognized profit contribution responsibility and that it is considered as an organizational profit centre.

The marketing function can then be called upon to explain shortfalls against budgeted targets, product by product, and is expected to recommend short-term remedies to these problem areas, should this be necessary.

3   Continued shortfalls versus budget targets may call for drastic reviews of marketing policy. The monthly review of marketing progress will crystallize such an event and may be the right place for the presentation of a revised marketing plan for the ailing product/market sector.

4   Such meetings are also good for the dissemination of marketing research data as it becomes available. Where an organization uses a barometer survey – one which (like a Nielsen audit) provides a continuous measure of marketing effectiveness – a synopsis of its recent findings may well illuminate the review of the market.

Price-cost-profit reviews

Fundamental to the revenue earning competence of the marketing function are the Siamese twins of volume and price. To achieve the targeted volume of sales at the targeted price is to achieve the essential corporate goals, subject only to the housekeeping disciplines of controlling costs. In a buoyant market, under economic circumstances of low inflation,

no undue problems may exist to make such a goal difficult to achieve. During an economic recession or under periods of marked inflation the organization may be hard pressed to control its capacity to meet the right volume at the right price, associated with the right level of costs.

Clearly two out of the three elements in this formula – sales volume achievement and selling price – are in the direct control of the marketing function, and its clear responsibility. While the third element, the variable cost of goods, is equally clearly *not* the direct responsibility of marketing, marketing should be given the responsibility of reacting swiftly to changes in variable costs by calling for changes to the selling price. As such the marketing department will require a continuous flow of data to ensure that it can monitor the price-cost-gross margin relationship for all of the products it is selling. Monitoring such changes can then become a regularized routine which naturally triggers action through reviewing profitability and changing the selling prices as becomes necessary. What is necessary in the first place – routine in many companies – is the establishment of norms or 'standards' for the three elements.

Marketing is required to forecast an average selling price for each product (net of discounts), cost accountancy to forecast average variable cost-of-goods for each product. The result produces a forecasted gross profit margin for all products. Subsequent monitoring requires only that the order processing function produces actual average selling prices achieved as the financial year progresses, and the cost accountants produce regular estimates of changes in material, labour and other processing and overhead costs to provide new variable costs through the year. (The word 'only' will seem offensive to those who are charged with producing this very considerable volume of information!). Set up

Table 21.1   *Price-cost-profit control*

| | 1987 standard | 1987 actual achieved in sales period: | | | | Total |
		1	2	3	4	
Per unit:	£	£	£	£	£	£
Average selling price	14.63	14.28	14.84	14.19	14.57	14.48
Cost of goods	8.27	7.98	8.14	8.14	8.21	8.07
Gross margin	6.36	6.30	6.70	6.05	6.36	6.41
Margin as % of selling	43.5	44.1	45.1	42.6	43.7	44.3

on a regular basis, such routines provide the organization's top management with a powerful control for effective marketing. One line from such a control document might look like Table 21.1.

New product development reviews

While a regular examination of marketing progress against budgeted targets and a firm system monitoring the essential price-cost-profit ratios on all products provides a powerful set of control systems for corporate management, one final area – controlling new business development – remains.

Managing the organization's new business ventures is among the most difficult of the organization's administrative problems. Few organizations have solved the problem to their total satisfaction. Administratively the central problem lies in the fact that:

- *Specialist new venture executives*, devoting all their energies to bringing new business into the world, are very liable to the frustrations inevitable from as uncertain a risk area as the one in which they are operating. High failure rates – the norm within new products – are made worse by even greater frustrations in the constant screening out (usually after much work) of new ventures that founder at one or other of the preliminary stages of development. And when a new venture is successful, it must then be handed over to those who handle established products.
- *Non-specialist new venture executives*. The other way new business may be handled is to give executives who handle established products responsibility for developing new business as well. In these circumstances it is normal to find either that the new business takes up too much of the executives' time, to the detriment of current business, or that current business, being clearly more urgent and tangible, continuously prevails over the need to develop new business.

While the administrative problem may never be fully resolved, corporate monitoring systems introduced to ensure progress in new business development may serve as a strong stimulus to the marketing function to meet its new business development obligations.

The simplest system is a reporting/meeting system at regular intervals which monitors progress on nominated projects. Such meetings will pull together those functions within the organization charged most closely with new business development: marketing and research-and-development – who always form the core participants – together with other functions (manufacturing, purchasing, finance) as are dictated by the status of individual projects to be discussed. While such meetings have the task of reviewing every aspect of the new business development programme, they have the overriding, crucial function of ensuring that scarce resources are never allocated to projects which are either technically incapable of achievement within reasonable marketing parameters, or are of little marketing interest whether they can be made or not: both such types of project are the bane of new venture development activity and must be prevented from eating up organizational resources.

Corporate control systems: summary

The systems and procedures discussed do not, of course, encompass all corporate control activities normal in the business world. The systems that have been covered may well serve as the major elements of control, to be added to by the dictates of the macroenvironment in which the organization operates, the products which it sells, and the organizational structure within which it operates. The systems will also be powerfully affected by the managerial ethos which prevails in the corporate body. Some organizations work through domination from the centre, others through direct delegation to each divisional function. Corporate control systems will clearly be more elaborate, formalized and inflexible in organizations tightly controlled at the centre. In some organizations virtually no delegation of responsibility is given to marketing decision making: every advertising campaign, package change, price alteration requires central corporate authority. In that event, systems for controlling these things must be set up and made to work. Every marketing department, and every marketing director, however, has to learn to live with the fact that the nature of marketing inevitably ensures top management's closest involvement in all the key areas of decision making. Experience shows that these systems provide more freedom of operation rather than less, by reducing the level of arbitrary and whimsical corporate interference in the day-to-day decision making of the marketers.

Marketing department control systems

The control mechanisms instituted by the marketing function of the business organization may be broadly divided into two areas: those mechanisms which administratively ensure that the function is managed as a department; and those which ensure that activities in the marketplace are sufficiently efficient to maximize the volume of sales at the greatest possible long-term profit to the organization. The control systems to be discussed here concern the latter, without any belittlement of the importance attached to proper departmental administration. Marketing department control systems will be discussed under five activity headings which dominate the marketing year:

1 Planning.
2 Promoting.
3 Selling.
4 Distributing.
5 Monitoring.

It is, of course, recognized that each activity is interlocked with all the other activities and no real chronology can be established, nor an order of importance. Controlling all these elements is a continous responsibility for the marketing function's managers, each of whom will be a specialist (brand manager, salesperson, advertiser, distribution, export, marketing researcher) having to learn to understand all the other specialisms to produce concerted departmental activity.

Planning

Borden's enumeration of the various tools which may be employed by marketing in the quest for market share and corporate profits – his 'mix' ingredients – underlines two important facts. First, the considerable diversity and complexity of the marketing discipline. Second, the need which thereby arises for a tool which will bring together all the others in order to manage the market successfully in a coherent and controlled manner: that tool is the one which takes precedence in Borden's list – planning.

By 'planning' two quite separate – if connected – activities are envisaged:

1 *Macroplanning:* the marketing planning activity concerned to ensure that the sum of market offerings – the product portfolio – maximizes the organizational potential for market power and profits.
2 *Microplanning:* the marketing planning activity that takes care to nurture each element of the portfolio in the market to the maximum long-term advantage of that element – whether it be product or service.

Macroplanning is more generally referred to as strategic marketing planning. Microplanning is called brand or product management or, where these are not relevant to the organization, market/marketing management.

While strategic marketing planning is crucial to control within the marketing department, its essential controls already exist through the corporate controls exerted, over marketing, in creating corporate strategy and relating such strategy to products and markets.

Planning controls can, thus, be restricted here to controls over microplanning.

Annual planning and marketing progress reports

The control systems that have been developed in order to give corporate management the wherewithal to control marketing will, of course, serve internally within the marketing function as their own control system. However, the marketing function will find these systems to have departmental benefits over and above their clear corporate benefits:

Cooordination

While the marketing function may usefully be considered a single entity within the business enterprise, those who have inhabited such an entity know it to consist of quite separate – and sometimes disparate – groups of specialists, each with their special needs, targets, cares and problems. The salesperson, the planner, the market researcher and the media experts may all know they serve the same departmental goals, but the subset of goals they have to meet make it very easy for each to be little concerned with the others, unconcerned to communicate except through necessity and, on occasion, happily fighting each other in order to serve their own specialist needs. The existence of annual planning as a formal departmental discipline requires each to contribute to the planners' function as a centralizing and coordinating influence within the marketing department.

The head of the marketing department will demand of all of their staff that the annual product plans presented by the planners will have the (broad) approval of the sales force, the researcher and any other specialist who may be involved. Failing such an agreement, the function itself – annual plan presentations – demands and gets a resolution to any differences of opinion that may exist between the different branches of the marketing discipline.

Reference points

The formal documentation produced by the marketing function for corporate control will be heavily used internally by the marketing department to brief, remind, reassess and reconsider the market-place and its problems. Prior to writing next year's product plans, the planners and others in the department will remind themselves of the basis of the current year's planned activities by looking up 'last year's' plan.

Authority

Once the product/brand/market plan has received official (boardroom) approval, the plan document becomes the template to authorize marketing department requests on other company functions: the marketing department plan becomes, in effect, the company marketing plan. It is this which provides the basis for the clout carried by product managers in marketing orientated organizations.

Subsequent regular reports recording marketing progress versus budgeted targets also form part of the department's control system. Such reports – financial reports emanating from the company's management accounting function, reporting progress against targets, product by product – will form the basis of reports by the planners to the head of marketing (see Table 21.2).

Table 21.2 *Financial monthly product report format*

| | May 1987 | | | 1987 to date | | |
	Actual	Plan	%	Actual	Plan	%
Unit sales (000)	220	200	100	1050	1000	105
£000						
Gross revenue	66	62	106	315	310	102
Cost of goods	31	28	111	142	140	101
Gross margin	35	34	103	173	170	102
Marketing expenditures						
Advertising	3	3		15	16	94
Sales promotion						
Off invoice	2	2		8	8	100
Other	2	2		9	8	113
Other	1	2		2	3	67
Total	8	9		34	35	97
Marketing contribution	27	25	108	139	135	103
Unit price (pence)	30	31		30	31	
Cost of goods as % of gross revenue	47	45		45	45	
Marketing contribution as % of gross revenue	41	40		44	44	

There is a clear-cut case for all detailed marketing planning to take place – in the first instance – at the product level. That is clearly the view of a person trained in the marketing of goods in the highly branded, product-specific area of fast-moving consumer goods. The principal remains, however, for virtually all business organizations: all businesses must identify the basic building brick of their marketing edifice and draw plans for each brick – or, if there are too many of them, those that generate the bulk of organizational profits. Such a basis is becoming increasingly recognized as the necessary foundation of good planning in banks, insurance companies and other service and individual goods operations.

For each product, service or other form of offering in the marketplace the marketing function will draw up a plan of action annually. While different markets and products may require plans with markedly different emphases, most, at their core, will present plans under the headings of product policy, promotional policy and selling policy and will, additionally, summarize their planning goals with a forecast of units of sale, and a profit-and-loss account summarizing the outcome of all marketing activity. Under these headings, then, the marketing function can be sure that all the marketing elements most central to the effectiveness of each market offering are thoroughly reviewed, changes are closely argued and examined, and new directions formally presented and subsequently approved.

Product policy

Inevitably the most fundamental questions in marketing concern those which are at the heart of its planning role – the product. Above all, the marketing function must make sure that the range of products the organization offers in the marketplace is reviewed, reassessed, re-examined and, if necessary, revitalized annually,

The annual product plan will review the product under its three constituent elements of:

1 *Performance:* What the product actually 'does', in the eyes of the laboratory technician who measures such performance characteristics that are relevant (if any) and, more importantly, in the eyes of the customer who is expected to buy the product.
2 *Packaging:* Here the word is used in a very wide sense to include all the design elements of the product – both the product and its associated 'wrappings' of name, packaging and the images triggered by these ephemeral but vital characteristics.
3 *Price:* The actual price of the product to the buyer and – if relevant – to the intermediaries in the distribution chain. Also the value of the product as perceived by buyers – which may not be the same thing at all.

While the marketing function is clearly *not* responsible for creating, designing or making the product, it is marketing's role to determine its marketing effectiveness and to call on creators, designers and makers to change the product, or create a new one, as they detect change in market requirements. The marketing planning system, supported by the data and analysis available through the marketing research function, ensures that such scrutiny and control is maintained over the product.

Promotional policy

The annual product plan is the primary vehicle for controlling expenditure and agreeing resource allocation policy, product by product, across the full spectrum of promotional tools. In many organizations such expenditure may run into millions of pounds: as such, considerable detailing of this activity will be required. For the purposes of discussion, promotional control should be split out into two groups:

1 Advertising.
2 Other promotional activity.

Advertising

In controlling all aspects of advertising, the marketing department is supported by the professionals in the advertising agency they will have recruited to undertake the work. Among those organizations who spend particularly large sums on advertising – principally those in fast-moving consumer goods, both manufacturers and distributors – there will often be a three-cornered control system consisting of

- *The marketing planning function* – perhaps a brand manager, reporting to a marketing manager. This group will be the principal managers and controllers of advertising activity, supported by
- *A media services specialist* – a member of the marketing department who, specializing in all aspects of advertising (and probably recruited from an advertising agency), may provide skilled advice and control, particularly necessary in a discipline of such unusual complexity and cost. If the organization spends very large sums on advertising, this function in the marketing department may also provide a skilled watch over all media buying, make recommendations about media schedules to be adopted, provide insights into new developments in the advertising world, check the accuracy of invoices received from the multitude of media owners (in support of the advertising agency's own invoice checking process), discretely compare the relative efficiencies of one advertising agency versus another (many advertisers use the services of more than one agency) and generally provide a full briefing service on advertising to the planning function of the marketing department.
- *The advertising agency*, with its combination of specialists skilled in media planning, buying and media research, specialists in creating advertising images and the copy that accompanies them, liaising with the advertiser through client contact personnel ('account executives'). Having an earnest and profitable desire to retain the advertiser's goodwill, agency personnel apply their own rigorous quality and expenditure control systems to add to those of their clients.

The routine of regular control over the advertising effort is supported by:

1 *The annual product plan* which will lay down, for the next twelve months:
  (a) *Creative platform* – the essence of *what* the advertising has been planned to communicate.
  (b) *Media strategy* – *where* that communication will take place (in what media).
  (c) *Media schedule* – the frequency and planned reach (*how many* people will it get to) of the advertising, precisely scheduled month by month.
  (d) *Appropriation* – the money involved, broken out by different media, and not forgetting the costs incurred in producing the advertisements.
2 *Formalized progress reports.* Traditionally the advertising agency writes formal reports of all its meetings with the advertiser ('call reports') and circulates them to the advertiser. Additionally, the accounts function within advertising agencies will provide regular billing details, giving advertisers the opportunity to double check that they get what has been paid for.
3 *External media research.* The major owners of advertising vehicles – the national newspapers, magazines, and television contractors, together with the advertising agencies, have a strongly vested interest in independent, reliable and frequent data on reading and viewing habits in Britain, to justify the rate card (the media owners' price list) and to provide details of audience composition to enable advertisers to pick the right medium for the right product. Such research is undertaken to control the competence of media buying.

In the matter of control over the creative element of advertising as against the control over media buying and scheduling, a new, different and more intractable problem arises: what criteria may be meaningfully applied? While certain elements of the creative process are amenable to logical research and analysis, many are not. One may measure a response to the content of advertising by testing it among audiences (live or laboratory) and discover that the message is, or is not, understood in the way it was meant to be understood – that simple communication of information has or has not occurred. But no reliable tests to date have been devised which clearly connect audience response from a single advertisement to its ability to sell products in the marketplace. The subtleties and nuances of creative form are no less complex for being a press advertisement or a forty-second TV commercial. True control mechanisms to give clear guidance to the creators as to what pictures and words they must use to sell products are (perhaps mercifully) not yet available.

The person in the organization who knows best what is a good ad and what is bad is, thus, the managing director – unless he/she chooses to delegate that responsibility to the marketing director.

Other promotional activities

Promotional activities below the line (other than advertising, that is) present a bewildering variety, and may not be individually treated except at great length. Trade promotions, consumer promotions, exhibitions, catalogues, point of sale materials, salespeople's selling aids, permanent and semi-permanent merchandisers to stock product at point of sale, brochures, service manuals, sales leaflets – the list is endless. And this is to ignore the activities of public relations and its associated events – sponsorship, for example. All these tools are available to the marketers and must be planned for and controlled as much as, and as effectively as the control of advertising.

Once again the annual product plan will outline both the case for, and the planned details of, such expenditure.

Control requirements demand that each promotional item incurring serious expenditure will need to be detailed as to:

1 *The objectives* in using that promotional tool.
2 *The precise format* of the promotional item.
3 *Details of any quantities of product* associated with the promotion.
4 *Other materials associated with* the promotional item, and their quantities; leaflets, point of sale materials, etc.
5 *Other promotional activity* to be tied to the promotional item: for example when a competition featured on the pack is publicized in a TV commercial.
6 *Details of costs* for each of these elements.
7 *Timing schedule* for the promotion.

In the field of fast-moving consumer goods, where such activity is widespread and frequently very costly, there will be a need for a calendar of such promotions across the range of products carried by the sales force, to be carefully planned such that the sales force can cope with the promotional activities demanded of them, and so that the distributors – retailers and wholesalers may themselves be happy to cope with the offerings presented.

Public relations

A programme of public relations activity is perhaps easier to control because it tends to be less fragmented and, second, prime responsibility for control and planning may be given to a public relations agency recruited to handle the work on behalf of the organization recruiting it. Where such work is on a large scale, or where an organization finds itself in a sensitive position relative to its many publics, a public relations officer may be recruited directly by the organization to give it additional support and expertise. Such an executive would sensibly be located within the marketing department, working closely with the product planners.

Selling

As the biggest employer of marketing personnel, the selling function will get particular benefits from tight administrative control: recruiting, training, sales planning, supervising, briefing, motivating, monitoring, providing support systems and materials. The administrative complexity of handling even a small sales force is considerable. Thus much effort is applied to this necessary chore within the total marketing control effort.

In restricting detailed discussion of control methods to those which monitor competence in achieving goals in the marketplace, control of the selling function can be examined under four headings:

1 Achieving sales orders.
2 Sales effectiveness ratios.
3 Cost benefit analysis.
4 Pricing and discount control.

Achieving sales orders

The salesperson shares in common with the machine operative the fact that – unlike other members of the marketing function – competence may be measured (and usually is) on a weekly, and sometimes even a daily basis.

The marketing planner's monthly forecast of unit sales will have been taken from the product plans by sales management, product by product, and broken down to individual targets for each salesperson. Measuring the competence of each individual now becomes a simple matter of whether – and how well

– the salesperson achieves sales orders versus their targets. With an efficient postal system to ferry daily sales orders from each salesperson to head office, and an equally efficient computerized order processing system to handle the incoming orders, the time span between achieving the orders and management's scrutiny of that achievement is now measured in hours.

Furthermore, increasingly sophisticated computer software makes possible very much more complex analysis than a simple actual-versus-target score for each salesperson and each product. It is simple to process this information in such a way as to provide a complex diagnostic analysis of selling competence – as well as the competence of the marketing plan which lies behind the salesperson's success or failure.

Thus the first line of control over selling, and those who do it, is in sales order analysis. Typically such information may be made to show (for example):

Daily/weekly/by sales-cycle-to-date/year-to-date/as a % of last year's comparable time period, actual orders or actual as % of target:

- *Orders achieved:*
    by salesperson.
    by sales region.
    by type of account.
    by size class of account.
- *Orders achieved:*
    at standard pricing terms or special discounts.
- *Sales territory analysis:*
    total volume/value of sales versus target.
    sales achievement versus previous sales cycle.

With a virtually endless list of selling analyses available, there is a clear danger of suffocation by information: care has to be taken to restrict data to what can most usefully be used; to a level of information which will encourage and not discourage usage.

Sales effectiveness ratios

While the achievement of sales orders is clearly the key measuring device of selling competence, such figures do not indicate what level of effort was involved, and whether the effort made the best use of an expensive resource – a salesperson. Keeping good records of selling activities makes available a set of competence ratios of selling efficiency:

1 *Call frequency:* fundamental to the cost of running the sales force is the forecast of the number of customers the salesperson will visit daily. Company forms – and distribution curves around this norm – are readily available from historical analysis of call frequencies, and may be improved by intercompany comparisons.
2 *Orders-to-calls ratio:* few salespeople will achieve an order from every selling call they make: 'norms' vary considerably from market to market. In the selling of industrial goods such norms are usually dramatically lower than in the selling of fast-moving consumer goods; wholesaler calls will normally generate a higher order-to-call success than calls on independent retailers. But every sales force is well aware of its own norms, and should be aware of its competitors' norms.
3 *Customer universe:* norms usually exist to establish the average workload – the number of 'live' customers the salesperson has to service.
4 *New-to-current customers:* if a salesforce is expected to canvas for new customers (most are), then the salesperson will be measured for the number of orders he/she obtains from new business, as against 'current' customers.
5 *Sales per customer:* while the level of sales revenue achieved per customer may vary dramatically from salesperson to salesperson through no fault of their own, and due to factors over which they can never have control, a historical analysis of the sales from the territory and customer lists they manage will show trends indicative of their effectiveness in generating revenue for their company, in comparison with such trends for the total corporate selling effort.

The competent salesperson will, in addition to maintaining high standards against these effectiveness criteria, also show other evidence of his/her ability. By maintaining up-to-date, full and usable customer record systems, returning daily sales orders promptly and correctly filled out, reporting effectively on the marketplace in weekly/monthly reports to head office, and getting the respect and confidence of the customers to whom he/she sells.

Cost benefit analysis

The basic building bricks of selling – salespeople – are valuable to the company that employs them not least because they are expensive. To the cost of their salary must be added the mandatory company car, travelling expenses and the full costs inevitable in running a group of people who do not work at head office. (Many organizations run regional sales offices; all sales forces have to pay very heavy telephone and postal bills, and so on). As a £30,000 to £40,000 unit of work, salespeople have to justify their costs not simply by generating targeted revenue, but by avoiding spending time on unprofitable activity. Calling regularly on customers who never place an order (it can easily happen with industrial accounts), calling regularly on customers who only ever place small and unprofitable orders, cold-canvassing for new business among unrewarding targets, excessive travelling time through poor journey planning, wasting too much time waiting in customer reception rooms for want of proper appointment booking systems, these and other signs are the hallmarks of poor planning and a weak profit-orientation. Good sales management requires a strict control over such procedures and an awareness that, even in the best managed sales teams, such profitless practices creep in year by year and require vigilance to prevent.

Pricing and discount control

The sales force is viewed by modern management as the front line of corporate profitability because it may often be in a position to 'make' both profitable and unprofitable deals with its customers. Many sales forces – or at least one or two senior salespeople in every sales force – are given some necessary discretionary power in the quotation of price. The careless application of such discretion can lead to serious inroads into planned profits. Hence the marketing function regards the control of sales pricing and sales discounts as crucial to successful selling competence. This problem is becoming daily a more serious one as market after market becomes dominated by fewer and fewer buyers. As the power of the buyer grows, so does the pressure on the seller to weaken price: if you are confronted by a buyer who accounts for 10 per cent or more of your total business, it is hard to say no to their demand for a 'better' price. Thus there is an increasing premium on competence in negotiation skills; an increasing importance in coping profitably with price flexibility. At a more mundane level, the sales force must

also be monitored in its application of scale pricing in those markets where quantity discounts are normally applied through a scale of prices – a normal practice when operating through distributors. Such monitoring becomes even more necessary when, to standard scale prices, the organization applies special promotional discounts as part of its marketing weaponry in the battle for market share. Controls in these areas are applied principally through the dual activities of careful pre-planning of all sales calls and of the discounts that will be offered, and of post-mortems which check out what has actually been agreed when the sales presentation has been made. A sophisticated selling operation may have a subunit of the sales administration function devoted exclusively to monitoring and recording all such promotional discounting activities.

Distributing

The distribution process – taking decisions about which channels will be used to carry the organization's products and then organizing their physical distribution through those channels is, for most organizations a very major undertaking, involving heavy expenditure both of capital and revenue. Certain departmental control procedures need to be outlined, as their implications are of central importance to the marketing effectiveness of the organization.

Decisions about channels of distribution and about the physical processeses of that distribution involve, at their heart, decisions about the quality of service to be given to the customer – both the end user and the distributors. Any reputable organization would *wish* to make its products available at all times in all outlets which the buyer might require, would *wish* to have finished goods always available to meet any order, no matter how large and how unexpected, for immediate ('inside twenty-four hours anywhere') delivery so as to eliminate the dreaded 'out-of-stock' problem. Such customer servicing standards are rarely achieved, indeed rarely planned to be achieved, in the face of the prohibitive costs they would incur. It is thus necessary for the marketing function to calculate how closely it can approximate to this ideal set of servicing conditions within the capital and revenue sums the organization will tolerate.

This issue raises in turn the whole subject –

in manufacturing organizations – of marketing's need for manufacturing flexibility in its production planning process, versus manufacturing's need for (inflexible) well-planned, long run production processes: 'if (say, the marketing people) we cannot have large stocks of finished goods ready for instant delivery to our customers – because it costs too much in tied-up capital, warehousing space and so on – then we must, at least, have a production process which is willing, at the drop of a hat, to change its production schedules to meet the stock-out emergencies created by having too little finished stock to meet unforecastable orders'.

Such a set of interlocked and intractable problems require much conscientious and effective coordination between the marketing planners, salesperson, production planners and distribution executives to make sure that the service that is made available to the customers is the best that the organization can afford. In an increasingly competitive environment the ability to deliver the product on time and in the right place has become increasingly important.

Additionally, decisions require to be made by the organization concerning the return of products to the organization – returned either because they are damaged or faulty, or returned because they have failed to sell. It is the distribution function of the organization that has to cope with 'returns' and handle a returns policy. Inevitably such policy considerations are at the heart of the service the organization is willing to provide customers through its distribution function.

Monitoring

Many of the control processes so far discussed are heavily intertwined with the marketing research function, whose offices will be called upon to undertake the fact finding essential to establish the existence and scale of the problems requiring control. The activity of monitoring and measuring the marketplace – and the impact of the organization's marketing activities on the marketplace – is pervasive in the marketing orientated enterprise. Marketing research budgets in such organizations may, thus, be considerable.

While *every* organizational problem and marketing activity is capable of some measurement, budgetary constraints apply limits to what may be

achieved, restricting such measuring to the most serious problems and those elements ignorance of which may lead to the greatest corporate danger. As a control mechanism within the marketing function marketing research has no substitute.

Typically, organizations will undertake monitoring in a number of key areas:

Consumer usage and attitudes

The marketing department needs to understand both what consumers do and why they do it. Analysis of activity and attitude is greatly enhanced if the data is obtained sufficiently regularly to yield clear patterns of changing trends. Hence organizations undertake annual or bi-annual surveys to provide the marketing planners with usage and attitude facts fundamental to marketing decision making.

Promotional activity monitoring

For those organizations who may spend millions on promotional activity, market research may help decide the value of such expenditure. Research into media audiences, for example, provides the basis for better media selection and buying. Advertising research is undertaken in order to improve the effectiveness of the communication process.

Product testing

Marketing has a need both for testing of existing products and for development testing of new products or new variants for existing products.

Modelling

Increasingly, organizations are experimenting with building models of the marketplace to help in predicting the possible outcomes of alternative marketing strategies. The advent of powerful computer capabilities has opened up experimentation that would otherwise have remained too expensive and too cumbersome to undertake.

External control systems

In the normal course of events, marketing makes

little direct use of outside consultants to maintain a monitoring eye on it. However, a number of scrutineers exist who serve a similar function:

Advertising agency

A mature and progressive advertising agency will have the wisdom to disagree with its client's marketing policies when such policies seem to it to be inappropriate to the market situation. The marketing planning branch of the organization's marketing department does well to bring the advertising agency into its confidence early in the discussion of next year's product plans in which the agency will inevitably be involved. That point of time gives the agency a perfect opportunity – *before* policy has congealed into bigotry – to state its reservations. The agency can thus be used as an independent marketing consultant, working on the marketing plan in tandem with the client.

Market research agency

Those fast-moving consumer goods companies who make use of one of the national sales audit operators (independent market research bodies providing a measure of consumer sales either over the counter or in-home) get the benefit of an independent view of the company's marketing success.

Marketing audit

Ultimately, the organization may wish to undertake a complete and serious re-appraisal of the efficiency of the marketing operation by calling in marketing experts to undertake a thorough review of the marketing strengths and weaknesses of the company. This may be handled either (in the case of a large or multidivisional or multinational corporation) by asking a marketing team from one of the other divisions to undertake the review, or by calling in independent – but very expensive – consultants.

Such a skills audit may provide great benefits to the organization, subject to certain provisos:

● *That such audits happen infrequently:* once every five years is psychologically about the minimum time span between audits. More frequent audits will not only demoralize marketing personnel, but would indicate that the organization's recruitment policies required serious review.

● That they take place *with the cooperation of marketing* personnel, to whom the audit results will be principally addressed.
● That they are *seen as part of routine skills auditing* of all the organizational skills vital to corporate success, that is, that other skills are also routinely audited.

Properly conducted, the annual marketing plan, while no substitute for an independent audit, nevertheless provides an annual re-appraisal of all marketing skills as well as product tactics, and the result of this plan should give top management clear guidance to indicate the health or otherwise of the organization's marketing function.

Conclusion

This chapter has examined systems and procedures of control over the marketing function at two levels: the corporate level and the functional, or departmental, level.

First those aspects of the marketing discipline which make close supervision of many of its activities especially necessary and important to the organization were established before outlining some of the fundamental principles which underpin control mechanisms – formality, necessity, priority, veracity and regularity.

From general principles of control procedures, control systems applied to the marketing function at the corporate boardroom level to ensure proper control over marketing strategic and operational activities were identified. This was reviewed under five headings: corporate strategic planning systems as they affect marketing; the annual marketing plan as a corporate control mechanism; formal corporate progress reviews of marketing competence; price-cost-profit review systems and, finally, systems which monitor new product development projects.

At the departmental level, procedures of operational control were examined under five functional levels of planning, promoting, selling, distributing and monitoring (marketing research). These activities were related back to the corporate control systems previously outlined.

Finally, the chapter took a very brief look at systems external to the enterprise which also act as control mechanisms on the effectiveness and general competence of the marketing function.

PART FOUR

The Application of Marketing

22
Industrial
marketing
PETER M. CHISNALL

Introduction

Before discussing in any detail the principles and practices of industrial marketing, it would be useful to clarify this term. Earlier chapters have defined the marketing concept and related it to consumer goods and services, but there are, of course, other areas in which marketing techniques can be applied with great effect.

In many cases, the products and services bought for industrial and commercial consumption will be similar, if not identical, to those purchased by consumers; for example, carpets, heating fuel, canteen supplies, paint, etc., but the *reasons* for these purchases will be different. In other words, the buying motivations and buying criteria of personal and organizational buyers are likely to be distinctly different.

Organizational buyers are influenced by the objectives and needs of their organizations; the supplies acquired by them will be expected to contribute to the overall success of their organizations which, in the case of businesses, is generally measured by overall profitability.

Apart from private sector industry and commerce, significant markets for many goods and services lie in the public sector; government departments, local authorities, energy boards, health authorities, etc.; all consume vast quantities of sup-

plies which need to be negotiated in increasingly competitive conditions.

Yet another sector of economic and social activities which offers marketing opportunities are the professions: banks and other financial institutions, legal practices, estate agents etc. In addition, there are several large-scale charity organizations which necessarily consume large volumes of goods and services in order to fulfil their missions.

The term 'industrial marketing' could, therefore, be viewed as having a very wide and diverse area of responsibility. Subsequent chapters in this book deal specifically with the marketing of services and marketing related to non-profit organizations, so this chapter will concentrate on *industrial* marketing, although there are clearly difficulties in, for example, discussing many industrial products in isolation from the services needed to render them useful.

Despite the lead given by the consumer goods industries, many industrial firms still seem reluctant to acknowledge that marketing is a legitimate function of management which is relevant to their needs. Even today, the view is often taken that marketing is all very well, and indeed admirable, for firms selling to supermarket chains and other types of consumer goods distributors, but that it has dubious value, if any, for companies producing technical and industrial products. This curiously biased perception was certainly not shared by the Machine Tools Economic Development Committee (MTEDC) which, following a two-year intensive study of the British machine tool industry at manufacturing and distribution levels, observed that successful firms were characterized by their dedication to their customers' needs. 'Every executive in these companies – from top management down through the entire management structure – was personally orientated towards the customer. Marketing attitudes generated the specific motivation of these successful companies.' (MTEDC, 1970).

The positive attitudes and successful marketing behaviour of these machine tool companies demonstrates the value of understanding the role of marketing in helping to make technical and industrial firms successful. Good products deserve professional marketing: the old adage about beating a path to the door of the inventor is now surely rather threadbare. Invention itself cannot make a company successful; the process of innovation – as noted in Chapter 15 – is complex and vital; it is concerned with applying the fruits of invention and developing successful new products and services, such as credit cards and cash-card pay systems.

Marketing in the firm

As discussed earlier, attitudes as well as activities are important in developing effective responses to competition in whatever market a company operates. 'Marketing covers the collective attitudes of management to markets as well as the operation itself' (NEDC, 1971). This emphasizes the need for everyone in a business – irrespective of their particular functional responsibilities – to be aware of the importance of customers by offering them products and services which are likely to benefit them. It has often been observed that customers buy the expectations of *benefits*, not just products or services. Astute business people make sure that the goods and services they market are packed full of 'customer benefits'. In some cases, technological marvels are not what customers really want; they seek solutions to their problems and should be offered products *relevant* to their needs. This is where the R & D people, the designers and the marketing team should work hand-in-hand to develop *effective* solutions for specific kinds of industrial customers.

Organizations are managed by people acting in their various roles; individual efforts should be coordinated into team performance. Sadly, some firms seem to exhibit more competitive behaviour *within* their organizations than in positive reactions (and proactivity) towards those who keep them in business, viz. customers.

Top management must accept responsibility for building a strong, well-resourced marketing management and encourage everyone in the firm to work together to achieve business growth.

Successful marketing managers act as catalysts in their firms; they should inform technical management about market trends and the nature and level of competitive activities; financial accountants should be advised of likely market opportunities and what these might mean in terms of capital investment, market development, etc. Personnel management should be kept in touch with changing patterns of consumption which might result in new ranges of products and require different kinds of employee skills.

The responsibilities of marketing managers are not, therefore, confined to customers; they have distinct roles to play in communicating effectively with the diverse functional areas of their firms.

Technically trained managers, provided they also have sound marketing training, are often outstandingly successful, largely because they can relate the needs of their customers to the resources of their firms. As Levitt (1974), with his customary vigour, has observed: 'Marketing is not just a business function. It is a consolidating view of the entire business process'.

Industrial product manufacturers can put a cutting edge on their businesses through adopting sound marketing practices. The corporate performance of a company depends on the successful combination of managerial inputs from all sections of the business. Indicated in Figure 22.1 are six principal areas of management expertise which make distinctive contributions to corporate performance. Together they form a coherent and balanced set of specialized skills; one weak performer in this 'circle of competences' can frustrate overall performance and even result in corporate losses being incurred (Chisnall, 1985).

The integration of marketing plans with all the other vital functions of a business must be ensured.

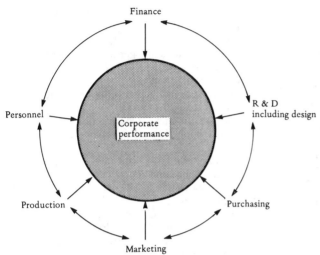

Figure 22.1 *Vital inputs to corporate performance*
Source: P. Chisnall, *Strategic Industrial Marketing*,
Prentice-Hall, 1985.

Adventurous sales campaigns can be totally destructive if production lines are not able to meet the resultant orders. To assume that all products have equal price sensitivities also reflects market ignorance (see Chapter 16).

Increasingly, managers work in complex organizations, often at great distance from their markets, and so there is always the danger that because of this isolation, their attitudes and behaviour become strangely 'artificial'. But they should always remember that industrial markets are made of firms and other organizations which are managed, like their own businesses, by people who make decisions, favourable or otherwise, affecting their suppliers. Markets are constructs of people, and these are influenced by many factors, technical, economic and also psychological, cultural etc. Drucker (1971) has drawn special attention, for example, to the role of cultural norms in industrial negotiation. When, for example, the Westerner and the Japanese talk of decision making, they mean different things. With Westerners, 'all the emphasis is on the answer to the question. . . . To the Japanese, however, the important element in decision making is defining the question. The important and crucial steps are to decide whether there is a need for a decision and what the decision is about'.

Characteristics of industrial markets

Economic activities

Traditionally, the economic activities of a country have been classified as: primary, secondary and tertiary. Primary or extractive industries cover the oldest forms of human working practices, such as agriculture, fishing, mining and forestry. The secondary or manufacturing sector refers to the manufacturing and construction industries which, as economies evolve, competes with and finally largely supplants the primary sector as the major source of economic wealth. The tertiary sector relates to the service industries; to what is sometimes termed 'incorporeal production'.

Advanced economies are characterized by a shift from growing to making products and, then, to providing increasingly sophisticated services such as those related to business and professional needs like computer analyses.

A service economy is now evident in most modern communities; technically advanced production demands sophisticated back-up services. 'Service industries will increasingly absorb more spending power, while being responsible for a greater proportion of the national economic progress' (Chisnall, 1985). The transition of labour and economic effort from primary to secondary and thence to the tertiary sector was first evident in the US and became apparent in the UK from the mid-1960s. (The marketing of services is covered in Chapter 25.)

As already mentioned, differentiating between products and services is not easy, and in some cases, is not even desirable because of the trends towards offering complete 'packages' to industrial (and sometimes personal) customers; this aspect of marketing will be discussed more fully later. The benefits derived from the ownership or use of a product are frequently so interrelated with their support services that it is important for suppliers to integrate their product and service operations to ensure customer satisfaction. Unfortunately, and certainly in past years, the service side of many firms seems to have been regarded as distinct from the overall marketing effort. The leasing of industrial equipment further illustrates the danger of divorcing the production and service activities of a business.

Nature and types of industrial products

The products and services used in industry, commerce, and the public sector, tend to be more complex and sophisticated than those used in personal consumption, for example power stations, automatic processing plants, oil drilling platforms, or operating theatres. Such capital equipment is bought fairly infrequently by any one organization; it has high durability; purchasing can often be postponed for fairly long periods of time (compared with personal purchases such as food); policy decisions may be affected by complex influences such as political factors, perhaps in overseas markets; buying decision making invariably involves several people, and may take prolonged negotiation (further aspects of organizational buying behaviour are given in Chapter 8).

Some industrial supplies may be limited, of course, to relatively simple low-cost products like small components or subassemblies.

It is difficult, therefore, to classify industrial supplies definitively; border-line cases inevitably occur, as in many other kinds of classification. 'One approach would be to start at the fundamental point of basic raw materials and then to proceed through to semi-processed products, components and eventually to completely finished equipment. This was the foundation of the classifications adopted by the Industrial Marketing Association' (Chisnall, 1985).

Other classificatory approaches have been used; Kotler (1980), for example, refers to 'the producer market (also called the industrial market)' as 'the market consisting of individuals and organisations who acquire goods and services to be used in the production of further products and services for sale or rental to others', and classifies these in three ways:

I *Goods entering the product completely – materials and parts*
  A Raw materials
    1 farm products (wheat, etc.)
    2 natural products (fish, crude petroleum, iron ore)
  B Manufactured materials and parts
    1 component materials (e.g. steel, cement, wire, textiles)
    2 component parts (small motors, tyres, castings)

II *Goods entering product partly – capital items*
  A Installations
    1 buildings and land rights (factories, offices)
    2 fixed equipment (generators, computers, elevators)
  B Accessory equipment
    1 portable or light factory equipment and tools (hand tools, lift trucks)
    2 office equipment (typewriters, desks)

III *Goods not entering the product – supplies and services*
  A Supplies
    1 operating supplies (lubricants, typing paper)
    2 maintenance and repair items (paint, nails, brooms)
  B Business services
    1 maintenance and repair services (window cleaning, typewriter repairs)
    2 business advisory service (legal, management consulting, advertising)

Another classification has been promoted by Stanton (1978) who stated that industrial goods are differentiated from consumer goods on account of their ultimate use. His five-part classification is as follows:

1 *Raw materials:* 'industrial goods which will become part of another physical product and which have received no processing at all, other than that necessary for economy or protection in physical handling', e.g. (a) minerals, land; (b) wheat, cotton, tobacco, fruit and vegetables, livestock, and animal products such as eggs and raw milk.

2 *Fabricating materials and parts:* become actual part of finished product: already processed to some extent. Fabricating *materials*, e.g., pig iron, yarn, will undergo further processing. Fabricating *parts* will be assembled with no further change in form, e.g. spark plugs, fan belts, buttons.

3 *Installations:* manufactured industrial products – the long-lived expensive major equipment of an industrial user, e.g. large generators, factory building, jet aeroplanes for airlines. 'The differentiation characteristic of installations is that they set the scale of operation in a firm.'

4 *Accessory equipment:* used to aid production operations of an industrial user, but it does not have a significant influence on the scale of operations in a firm; does not become actual part of finished product. Life is shorter than installations (3) and longer than operating supplies (5), e.g. office equipment, small power tools, forklift trucks.

5 *Operating supplies:* 'convenience goods' of

industrial field. Short-lived, low-priced items usually purchased with minimum of effort. Help firm's operations but do not become part of finished product, e.g. lubricating oils, stationery, heating fuel.

A British researcher (Marrian, 1968) described industrial goods as all those goods and services purchased, hired or leased for use either directly (in the production of) other goods and services destined for either the industrial or ultimate consumer markets (domestic and export) or for rendering services to organizations engaged in serving the industrial or ultimate consumer markets.

McCarthy's (1975) typology of industrial goods has six categories as follows:

Categories of industrial goods	cf Kotler
1 Installations	} II
2 Accessory equipment	
3 Raw materials	} I
4 Component parts and materials	
5 Supplies	} III
6 Services	

Compared with Kotler's system, a degree of compatability is seen to exist.

Finally, Hill *et al.* (1975) also have six categories which can be related to Kotler's and McCarthy's classifications:

	cf McCarthy	Kotler
1 Major equipment	1	II
2 Accessory equipment	2	
3 Fabricating or component parts	4	I
4 Process material	5	III
5 Operating supplies	6	
6 Raw materials	3	I

From this brief review it will readily be noted that industrial product classifications have much in common. Obviously, products are viewed in different ways according to their usage in diverse industries; original equipment products would attract a different classification from similar supplies offered as replacement sales to fleet-owners or distributors. Judgement is clearly called for and some degree of arbitrary allocation seems almost unavoidable.

Concentration factors

Apart from the sophistication of many industrial supplies, complexity of negotiations is also apparent and is frequently affected by concentration of buying power which is particularly present in some industries, such as petrochemicals, cement, computers, brewing, shipbuilding, electronic engineering etc. 'Industrial markets are often dominated by a relatively limited number of enterprises with aggregate sales accounting for the bulk of industry sales in specific markets, . . .' (Chisnall, 1985). In such firms, buyers exercise considerable power over their suppliers. The well-known 80/20 rule appears to have increasingly powerful effect in many markets, and suppliers need to be continually alert to avoid overdue dependence on one or two very large industrial customers.

Buying practices and marketing strategies represent the crucial inputs into the negotiation equation. Buying ranges from virtually monopsonistic (single buyer) power to multiple buying points, where no individual buyer is in a position to dictate terms. Price competition, and, indeed, the whole tenor of negotiation, is closely related to the degree of concentration of buying power, and the structure of the supply industry.

Hakansson's (1983) interaction model of industrial buying reflects the power-dependence relationship between industrial buyers and suppliers. Expectations are held by both parties; the business environment is dynamic, and buyer and seller interact and so establish distinctive patterns of behaviour. Provided the negotiations are skilfully conducted, mutually satisfactory trading relationships result. 'Supplier-bashing' is hardly likely to be a productive purchasing strategy in the long run. Marketers, on the other hand, should be prepared to work alongside their industrial customers, helping them, perhaps, in the early stages of product development and testing. Two-way benefits are then likely to accrue, because the whole process of successful negotiation is built on foundations of mutual trust and advantage.

Nature of demand

Derived demand is a significant factor in industrial marketing: this means that for many industrial products, demand is directly dependent on the rate of usage which may be several stages from the initial buyer. The demand for capital goods, for example, is largely dependent on the prospective demand for the goods (consumer or industrial) which particular

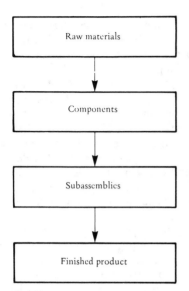

Figure 22.2 *Pattern of derived demand of industrial raw materials*

types of plant are capable of producing. Similarly, the levels of demand for the raw materials and components used in the manufacture of process plant will depend heavily on the rate of sales of that equipment. Derived demand is, therefore, widely applicable and industrial suppliers need to understand the factors which influence consumption of their particular product (basic materials, components or complete assemblies). The typical impact of derived demand is shown in Figure 22.2.

The dependency of derived-demand products on factors outside the control of, for example, basic materials suppliers, has led some suppliers to attempt to influence demand further down the demand chain; there is, in a way, a kind of 'knock-on effect' which can reverberate through several levels of suppliers. Different lead times are also likely to be experienced; new capital equipment, for example, may take many months and even years to develop and market, whereas raw materials such as sheet steel or timber are more readily available. In other cases, such as fashion clothing, lead times are comparatively short, consumer demand is dynamic, and the fashion cycle strongly influences sales. But suppliers of yarns, dyers, spinners, and weavers have to be able to deal with the vagaries of public taste which bring great uncertainty into their own markets.

Fibre manufacturers, like Courtaulds, undertake systematic market research at several levels of the fashion industry, and also advertise directly to consumers in order to gain insight into trends in demand and influence, to some degree, the derived demand for the synthetic yarns which they manufacture and market. This type of market intervention is termed 'back-pressure' selling or 'reverse' selling (Chisnall, 1985).

Technical advisory services are operated by several industrial marketing organizations in order to promote goodwill and secure a firm position in competitive markets.

End-use analysis is another significant factor, closely related to the phenomenon of derived demand. Many industrial goods – ranging from basic materials through to finished products – have multiple applications in industry and commerce: for some others, market opportunities may be very limited.

Effective marketing of industrial supplies takes note of the kinds of needs which specific products can satisfy. Experienced marketers research end-use markets, so that they are fully aware of trends in product design and other developments which may affect their own sales prospects. Technological development, such as printed circuits, have had strong impact on the design of many types of consumer and industrial products. Some years back, the introduction of radial tyres significantly affected dependent suppliers as well as radically changing the pattern of consumption because of the relatively longer life span of the new-style tyres compared with cross-ply tyres.

Some products experience *horizontal demand* and have many applications across several industries; for example, fork-lift trucks, weighing machines, steel or delivery vehicles. Other products may have only limited applications, experience *vertical demand*, and have virtually only one source of business, as with coal mining machinery in the UK, or specific types of equipment for the UK nuclear fuel industry. In general, the greater the concentration of demand for a particular type of product the more likely is the demand in that market to be vertical; such supplies are faced with parameters of risk which are likely to be substantially higher than those operating in horizontal demand markets.

There may also be 'vertical' segments occurring within horizontal markets, as happens with fire protection products which are bought by virtually every industry. However, some special fire protection products, like fire-engines, have a very limited numbers of buyers, mostly in the public sector in the UK and elsewhere.

Elasticity of demand

The interrelationship of price and demand variations has been termed the elasticity of demand, and occurs where, as price falls, demand tends to rise, and vice versa. In classical economic theory, certain assumptions are made about buying behaviour in order to support this theory.

The alternative model of demand, viz. inelastic, occurs when only relatively small changes in demand result from price alterations.

With many consumer products, price reductions are made in order to attract increased sales quickly, but industrial products do not usually experience such reaction if prices are reduced. This is largely because of the more complex decision making involved in industrial buying; buyers may also deliberately delay ordering, if they hold adequate stocks, in the expectation of further price reductions; where components, for example, represent only a relatively minor element in the total cost structure, a price reduction may largely be quite ineffective in stimulating orders; where, however, certain types of materials or components contribute significantly to the overall cost of the finished product, price reductions are likely to attract attention and may, in some cases, result in extended adoption of that particular material/component.

Elasticity of demand in industrial markets is not, therefore, as apparent as in consumer markets; different elasticities may be apparent in distinctive industrial market segments for a particular basic product such as aluminium which has many end-uses, ranging from airframes, kettles, cooking foil to packaging. The specific technical qualities of aluminium make it ideal for airframes, so that at even higher prices it would still enjoy high demand, whereas in the packaging market, for example, it is in direct competition with other types of wrapping, such as cellulose film, and the opportunities to raise prices without adversely affecting demand are likely to be limited.

In general, the freedom of individual suppliers to vary prices will be determined by their relationship with their customers, their degree of dependency upon them (perhaps for essential strategic supplies), the general level of competition, and the extent to which they can differentiate their product through 'added-values'. Industrial buyers are generally experienced, knowledgeable executives who are not easily persuaded to change well-tried and tested suppliers. Non-price factors such as reliability of delivery, efficient after-sales servicing, valuable technical advice, etc., will all be weighed in the balance when evaluating offers.

Trends in demand

Significant movements in demand may be attributable, in whole or part, to certain kinds of trends in specific markets. It may be possible to identify the prime causes of some changes in market demand, wholly or partly attributable, perhaps, to technological, fiscal, financial, economic, political, cultural or demographic factors.

Four general types of demand trend have been noted: secular (or 'normal'); seasonal; cyclical; and erratic. Precise identification is by no means a matter of certainty; classification systems tend to lend an air of tidiness, whereas, as experienced marketers know, the environments in which they transact business are often volatile most certainly far from neat and orderly.

Secular trend refers to the persistent, regular movement of a series of data recorded over a fairly long time period; this will be related to the type of product and the general nature of the industry concerned, and may extend to a decade or even longer. Upward, sustained curves are likely to be associated with innovative products which have now gained wide acceptability, for example microprocessors, central heating, etc. Downward trends are observable in cinema admissions, rail freight, etc.

Seasonal trend influences may be observable in some markets, particularly consumer fashion goods, but also active in certain industrial markets. Seasonal variation is not necessarily related to seasons of the year, but signifies any kind of variation of a recurrent nature where the period of time involved is no more than one year. Fertilizers, paint and heating fuels are typical examples of markets experiencing seasonal trends.

Cyclical variations of demand occur in certain industries subject to market changes in the levels of demand for their products and services. These wave-like movements involve periods of prosperity, recession, depression, and recovery, and are caused by factors other than the weather or cultural or social behaviour. Explanations of cyclical activity are diverse and sometimes contradictory. 'No simple explanation is really possible, there is not just *one* type of cycle' (Chisnall, 1985). Individual cyclical variations require distinct evaluations, although the degree of understanding of these phenomena remains uncertain. Cyclical variations affect capital investment goods in particular and make forecasting for the industries producing such products particularly difficult. Certain industries tend to 'lead' a general upswing in economic activity; they are also prone to be the first to undergo a downturn in demand.

Erratic movements in demand are obviously extremely problematic because they cannot be predicted from marketing or other types of research. However, experience and sensitive interpretation of market behaviour may suggest that some unusual trend is likely to occur fairly soon. Natural disasters like blizzards, droughts and famines may trigger off irregular market movements. Economic and political interference, such as experienced in the 1970s, resulting in energy crises for virtually the whole developed world, was certainly not expected in many quarters (including the US Cabinet Task Force on Oil which reported that it did not predict a substantial price rise in world oil markets over the next ten years).

Long-term trends in demand have been investigated by several notable economists, including Kondratieff (Chisnall, 1985), who, after some years of research into selected economic indicators, observed that fifty-year cycles existed. He identified several cycles of economic activity associated with historic inventions and developments. As Drucker (1984) commented: 'Typically, in the last decades of one of these cycles, old and mature industries seem to do exceptionally well, earning record profits and providing record employment. Actually, they are already in decline, for what looks like record profits is in fact under-investment and the distribution of no-longer-needed capital'. He went on to say that when rapid decline becomes apparent, a twenty-year long period of stagnation, low profits, and unem-

ployment results, because the rising industries cannot immediately absorb sufficient capital or generate employment to fuel the economic growth needed to start another period of expansion. However, new technologies expand so quickly that they are able to counter the down swing of the old and mature industries.

In turbulent economies, Drucker (1984) endorses Schumpeter's considered opinion that what distinguishes an atypical business cycle from a more conventional trough 'is not the play of abstract economic forces. It is entrepreneurial energy'.

Although the general applicability of Kondratieff's theory is disputed by Drucker and other leading writers, it is evident that during certain periods of time, inventions had profound effects on technologies and led to new industrial processes and products.

Nature of supply

Industrial products and services, as noted earlier, vary considerably in complexity, sophistication, and their applications or end-use.

Standard or basic commodity products are, generally, more exposed to competition, particularly when little differentiation exists between alternative sources of supply. Such marketers should consider carefully how they can get out of the dangerous rut into which undifferentiated products and services so readily lead them. Low added-value products offer marketers little market leverage, and, as discussed already, price competition becomes dominant.

The *extended product* is a particularly interesting concept for industrial suppliers. Simply stated, it is that a product or service is more than just a basic transaction: it provides not merely the physical benefits inherent in its use but can be designed to give a cluster of benefits that are attractive to specific kinds of buyers (Chisnall, 1985). By applying this concept, suppliers of basic commodity-type products can increase the attractiveness of their ranges and establish some degree of product differentiation.

Products can be extended through better design, improved technical services or higher standards of business behaviour in general: there are many added-values which can be used to great effect. One large chemical company takes special care to provide excellent technical data to support their field force in selling commodity-type products, and this has contributed to their marketing success.

The importance of service as an added value was shown to be effective in the valve and pump industry. Services were classified as *convenience* and *reliability*; these referred to what are usually described as before- and after-sales service. It was found that 'buyers were not only prepared to pay for a more reliable service but were also reluctant to change suppliers for a reduction in price of less the 5 per cent' (Cunningham and Roberts, 1974). This UK research inspired a similar study of Canadian pump and valve manufacturers, when it was found that delivery reliability, prompt quotations and provision of technical advice were the most important service features which suppliers of forgings and castings could offer pump and valve makers (Banting, 1976).

Product design

Product design is of paramount importance in all markets where buyers are more demanding and knowledgeable, and particularly where global competition is evident. A carefully developed marketing strategy integrates design policy with the other factors which help to make a business successful. The core contribution of design to adding value to products is unique.

The aesthetics of design have pragmatic influence, as was illustrated by a testing machine which was shown to a panel of highly experienced technical directors, one version of which had a front panel designed by the engineers who were responsible for the equipment; the alternative machine, intrinsically identical, was fitted with a control panel designed by professional industrial designers. It was this latter version which won twice the purchase intention compared with the engineers' designs. The appeal of good styling is by no means limited to consumer products.

Product design is, or should be, concerned with, not merely aesthetic appeals, but also to ensuring that products do what they are supposed to do, i.e. they work well and supply the benefits expected from them. Market-orientated design opens up vast new and profitable opportunities for industrial marketers. A NEDO report (Corfield, 1979),

concerned with manufacturing industry, described product design as 'both engineering design and aesthetic design. Both are important. Too often industrial design considerations predominate in consumer goods, to the detriment of engineering design, and the reverse is true of engineering capital goods.' Sadly, as the NEDO report noted, products tend to be designed 'in isolation from all the other key functions', and, as a result, product modifications have to be made after market introduction. Also, designs are changed later because of production problems or cost constraints that had not been identified during the development stages. The design function should be integrated fully into the management team, and, moreover, the talents of designers should be exercised within the disciplines of commercial behaviour. A report by the Department of Education and Science in association with the Design Council (1983) revealed that there was overall agreement in the UK, France, Germany, Italy, Scandinavia and the Netherlands that more emphasis on corporate skills in design education would improve company competitiveness.

Product liability

Closely associated with product design is the emerging phenomenon in the UK of product liability. This is inevitable, has already existed in the USA for nearly twenty years, and operates to some extent in France, Luxembourg and Belgium.

As far back as 1893, the Sale of Goods Act conferred extensive new rights on buyers who were, in general terms, entitled to goods of merchantable quality fit for the purpose for which they were sold. However, this protection was reduced by privity of contract and exclusion clauses. The latter were rendered illegal in the 1970s; the former will disappear under strict product liability legislation.

American product liability legislation is complicated because of varying interpretations of strict liability in different states. The European Commission has prepared a Draft Directive on product liability which has been under discussion for a long time, and the precise nature of product liability in the UK is still to be determined. Certainly, privity of contract, by which contracts under English law are normally only binding on the parties who made them, would disappear: the producer of goods would be liable for loss suffered by the ultimate user arising from some defect in their design or construction. Also, the user who suffers damage does not have to prove any negligence on the part of the producer. The monetary limits are still being hotly debated, as also is the period of time during which liability will exist for a product. Designers, development engineers, production managers, and marketing managers will have to work even more closely together to avoid exposing their companies to crippling losses and very unfavourable publicity.

Custom-built products

These specially designed products tend to be more evident in industrial than in consumer markets. Major processing plants, for example, require very extensive development time and involve costs before contracts are completed. Specialized machinery may be necessary in order to meet the production requirements of some user industries. In all these cases, industrial marketers are able to reinforce their bargaining position, because, perhaps, they are able to offer unique products.

The concept of systems selling refers to a complete package of products and/or services designed and offered to identified target customers (see page 410).

Distribution

Industrial products are generally sold direct to users, apart from such functions as steel stockholding, builders' merchants or agricultural machinery distributors. Orders are likely to be relatively substantial and entail long-term commitments, particularly in the case of capital investment goods. Products of all types must be readily available to customers, so it is important for industrial marketers to evaluate alternative methods of selling and distribution. Distribution systems are very costly to develop and maintain, and established firms enjoy cost advantages that are not available to potential competitors. On the other hand, traditional channels of distribution may become outmoded or wasteful to use, so it is advisable to monitor existing systems, and, at the same time, keep alert to new trends in distribution which may offer economies to both customers and suppliers. Telephone selling, for example, has been very effective in opening up new markets and in servicing existing customers, often involved in the repeat purchase of basic supplies. Marketing research can be very helpful in exploring alternative methods of selling and distributing industrial goods of many kinds.

Some years ago a British firm of crane makers sold pulley blocks, singly, through their sales engineers; high costs were entailed in salespeople's time; the cost of one call by a sales engineer wiped out completely the profit on a pulley block. Subsequently, these blocks were packaged and distributed through merchants. Economies in overseas markets were also effected by exporting crane kits which could be expertly constructed and thus save the very high costs entailed in despatching bulky products made substantially of structural steel.

Special trading practices

There are several special trading practices which can contribute to successful industrial marketing strategies.

Reciprocal trading

Reciprocal trading (reciprocity) is evident in some markets where buying and selling firms enter into reciprocal trading agreements, and agree, so far as practicable, to inter-trade in certain products. Reciprocity may inhibit buying freedom and render it difficult for new suppliers to enter some markets. Inter-group trading is practiced in some industrial organizations with diverse manufacturing activities, although this practice is tending to be less apparent because of board directives to buy in the best possible markets, and 'arms-length' trading replaces it.

Joint ventures

Joint ventures usually relate to large industrial and commercial organizations which pool their substantial combined corporate resources in order to attain certain contracts. For instance, R.M. Douglas Construction of Birmingham was reported (Gray, 1986) as going into a joint venture with the New York based Turner Corporation so that it could effectively handle the building of a £85 million Convention Centre which would supplement Birmingham's National Exhibition Centre which Douglas constructed in 1973.

The terms of joint ventures need to be specific and agreed by both parties, who will accept responsibility jointly for the contract and individually for certain aspects of the venture, such as providing technological or marketing advice.

Consortia

These types of voluntary industrial association are found typically in the construction industries, where a number of companies agree to pool their resources to attract significant contracts, such as overseas civil engineering projects involving the construction of new hospitals, universities, airports etc.

Project management ('turnkey operations')

Large capital investment projects, usually abroad, entail the application of many specialized skills over a period of some years. It is vital for all these activities to be expertly coordinated so that contracts are finished on time. Frequently, a 'turnkey contractor' is appointed who takes responsibility for both design and construction. Long-term planning skills are demanded of such managers.

Leasing

There is an increasing trend towards renting instead of buying machinery which may involve considerable capital cost. The construction industry, for instance, uses leased equipment fairly extensively. According to the conditions of individual contracts, customers may be allowed to exercise options to buy after certain time periods. Astute leasors often supply leased equipment on the understanding that supplies of materials or parts are ordered exclusively from them, and, sometimes, equipment is leased at nominal cost in order to stimulate sales of dependent materials.

Licensing

Many very successful marketing operations depend on licence deals through which new products can be introduced readily without the enormous high costs and risks associated with innovation. A classic example occurred some years ago when the General Foods Corporation purchased from Birds Eye the rights to its invention of deep freezing methods. An analysis (Banting, 1976) of the origins of twenty-five important process and product innovations by Du Pont revealed that only ten were based on discoveries attributable to Du Pont's own staff.

Lead time is so critical in innovation that a licensing strategy is particularly attractive, as was noted in a report of the Central Advisory Council for Science and Technology (1968).

Conclusion

Industrial marketing has tended to be neglected for several reasons, among them, perhaps, the arrogance of some technical management who believe that customers should buy what they make. This myopic perception of the market is by no means confined to industrial products and services, although it is certainly far less prevalent today in consumer markets which are often experiencing zero real growth.

To become efficient in marketing is not to debase in any way the qualities or technical efficiency of industrial products. Marketing has a role to play which should be viewed as strengthening and extending the technical attractions of products by targeting them at industrial firms where they are most likely to be successful.

Just as several distinct talents and skills go into the design, development and production of industrial goods, so there are specialized skills in marketing which should not be disregarded. No firm exists without customers, but today these are more difficult to please and to keep.

In this chapter, a review has been given of the principles and practices of industrial marketing; individual companies should assess their own business opportunities, weighing up their strengths and weaknesses, and then prepare carefully their production and marketing plans.

References

Banting, Peter M., 'Customer Service in Industrial Marketing', *European Journal of Marketing*, vol. 10, no. 3, 1976.

Chisnall, Peter M., *Strategic Industrial Marketing*, Prentice-Hall, 1985.

Report of the Central Advisory Council for Science and Technology, Technological Innovation in Britain, HMSO, 1968.

Corfield, K. G., 'Product Design', NEDU, March 1979.

Cunningham, M. T. and Roberts, D. A., 'The Role of Customer Service in Industrial Marketing', *European Journal of Marketing*, Spring 1974.

'The Industrial Design Requirements of Industry', Design Council, September, 1983.

Drucker, Peter F., 'What we can learn from Japanese management', *Harvard Business Review*, March-April 1971.

Drucker, Peter F., 'Our Entrepreneurial Economy', *Harvard Business Review*, January-February 1984.

Gray, Joan, 'Birmingham Convention Centre Complex', *The Financial Times*, 13 October 1986.

Hakansson, Hakan (ed.), *International Marketing and Purchasing of Industrial Goods: an Interaction Approach*, Wiley, 1983.

Hill, Richard, M., Alexander, Ralph S and Cross, James, *Industrial Marketing*, Richard D. Harris, 1975.

Kotler, Philip, *Marketing Management, Analysis and Control*, Prentice-Hall, 1980.

Langrish, J., Gibbons, M., Evans, W.G. and Jevons, F. R., *Wealth from Knowledge – Studies of Innovation in Industry*, Macmillan, 1972.

Levitt, Theodore, 'The Morality of Advertising', *Harvard Business Review*, July-August 1970.

Levitt, Theodore, *Marketing for Business Growth*, McGraw-Hill 1974.

Machine Tools Economic Development Committee, *A Handbook for Marketing Machinery*, HMSO, October 1970.

Marrian, Jacqueline, 'Marketing Characteristics of Industrial Goods and Buyers', in Aubrey Wilson, (ed.) *The Marketing of Industrial Products*, Hutchinson, 1968.

McCarthy, E. Jerome, *Basic Marketing*, Richard D. Irwin, 1975.

National Economic Development Office, 'The Plastics Industry and its Prospects', A Report of the Plastics Working Party of the Chemicals EDC, HMSO, July 1971.

23
International marketing – the main issues

SIMON MAJARO

Introduction

Students often ask me a simple question: 'What is the difference between marketing in a national market and so-called international or global marketing? Is it purely a matter of size and volume or does it entail something a lot more fundamental?' The general belief is that anybody who is fully versed with the basic concepts of marketing theory and practice can move from the domestic to the global scene with great ease.

The sad fact is that marketers who have gained their experience in a domestic market often find the transition to the international scene fraught with problems and complexities. Yet at the same time it is also true to say that moving from a multinational marketing environment to a national arena is also not an easy one. Many managers returning from a spell in a position entailing multinational responsibilities find that the tasks involved in marketing a product or a service in a single homogeneous marketplace are different from their earlier activities. Nevertheless it is true to say that the basic framework of conceptual knowledge and techniques is the same.

The difference appears to lie in individual outlook and personal attitudes. There is little doubt that the person who manages to excel in the field of international marketing, unlike his/her one-country coun-terpart, has acquired the ability to think, to analyse and to plan on a global scale. A very valuable survey conducted recently by the magazine *International Management* on the 'globalization of business' has highlighted among other important conclusions the fact that 30 per cent of the responding companies have trouble finding managers with a 'global outlook'. These two simple words encompass the basic differences between a person who is capable of operating in world markets as against the one who can only be effective in a single national marketplace.

It is worth exploring briefly the personal armoury of an effective manager and considering how the various components must be adapted to the needs of a career in international marketing.

Managers require three distinct albeit interrelated facets to their personal development. They fall into three groups: *knowledge; skills*, and *attitudes*. A company's training and management development efforts are normally structured towards instilling and/or developing one or more of these areas. It is important to remember that while the 'skills' required for carrying out marketing tasks in a single market or on a global scale are more or less the same it is in the area of 'knowledge' and 'attitudes' that significant variations exist between the one-country and the international marketers.

It is upon these two elements that attention must be focused in some detail.

The 'knowledge' needs for international marketing

Knowledge is an essential ingredient in a person's ability to plan and execute effective marketing activities. Very often a marketing failure is due to the fact that the 'marketing mix', determined by its planners, has been based on inadequate knowledge. The whole process of collecting information in the marketplace is nothing other than the acquisition of 'knowledge'. The amount of knowledge that a person can acquire about one market is much more detailed than one is expected to obtain about many countries. It is very rare for an individual to possess detailed knowledge of more than a very small number of markets.

One sometimes encounters managers who claim in their curriculum vitae that they possess a vast level of knowledge about dozens of countries. Such a claim invariably represents a poor understanding as to what 'knowledge' is required to be able to perform an effective marketing task on a transnational basis. Living and working in a country can provide an individual with an in-depth knowledge of the operational environment of such a country. However absence from such markets for any length of time makes such knowledge out of date very quickly. Inevitably this means that very few people can truthfully claim an intimate and up-to-date understanding of the marketing scene of more than a handful of markets.

The first area of 'knowledge' which distinguishes the domestic from the international marketer is knowing sources of international data and information. The marketer in a single country usually knows what sources of intelligence are available in his/her market. On the other hand and as suggested earlier, nobody can be expected to know all the sources which exist in all countries.

To take a simple example: when a marketer in the UK requires details of media availability he/she would know that the best source for information is *Brad British Rates and Data*). Obviously *Brad* is of no help to somebody who needs to plan an international campaign. The equivalent of *Brad* exists in many countries but it is too much to expect an international marketer to store in his/her mind details of such institutions in all countries. The inter-

national marketer would know of the existence of a very helpful publication called *Ulrich's International Periodicals Directory*. '*Ulrich's*' to the international marketer is what *Brad* or its counterpart is to the national marketer.

Another tale-tell signal that a person is fully familiar with the subtleties of international marketing is the ability to locate quickly and easily sources of information which have been prepared in accordance with the rules of comparability. Emphasis will be placed later on the importance of planning multinational market research projects on a comparable basis. Understanding the rules of comparability are fundamental to effective international research projects. The fully-fledged international marketer knows where to find sources which have been assembled and prepared in accordance with these rules.

Generally speaking international marketers know exactly what questions to ask when investigating and analysing a number of markets simultaneously. Moreover they know that it is important that a standard questionnaire is submitted to the various countries under investigation. If this is not done the eventual comparison of input will be extremely complicated.

In this connection the 'marketing mix' concept must be revisited and its international dimension explored.

Every experienced marketer understands what the term 'marketing mix' means. (If you do not refer to Chapter 14 – ed.) The components of the 'mix' may differ from company to company or from industry to industry, but it is generally recognized that it represents the assemblage of elements with which one is seeking to satisfy customer needs. It also represents the basis upon which the firm's marketing resources are allocated in order to attain the dual results of:

1 Satisfying the customers.
2 Achieving the firm's objectives.

Some companies talk about the four Ps (product, price, promotion and place). Others include an S for service. Yet others list the 'mix' to include product, price, promotion, selling and distribution. The subject has been covered in detail elsewhere in this book and it is not intended to plough through this very important concept again. Nevertheless it is essential that the international dimension is added here.

International marketers must understand fully the environmental, and to a great extent uncontrollable, factors which affect each ingredient of the 'mix' in a multi-country marketing effort. Not only must they acquire full knowledge of the differences which prevail in the various countries in their patch but they must also identify the environmental similarities. Unfortunately marketers often spend too much time highlighting the differences that exist between markets and forget to list the areas of similarity and congruence. As we shall see later it is the similarities which can help to determine whether a standardization or globalization of products and/or brands is possible.

A host of external and environmental factors and pressures impinge upon the freedom of a marketer to mix his/her 'mix'. Culture, local habits, stage of economic development, languages, law, existing institutions such as channels of distribution and media etc. are bound to have a significant impact upon the marketing programme that the firm can design for each market or for a cluster of markets. This means that a vast amount of relevant knowledge has to be assembled about each country. International marketers need a checklist of questions the answer to which will provide them with the relevant knowledge upon which a marketing programme can be designed and planned.

The external elements that affect marketing decisions normally fall into four distinct groups:

1 The customer's environment.
2 Competition.
3 Institutions.
4 Legal system.

It is difficult to think of any item which does not fall into one of those categories of factors. It is therefore possible to insert the traditional marketing mix which every marketer knows intimately into its external context as described in Figure 23.1.

The interaction between the external and internal ingredients of the 'mix' represents the inventory of knowledge that an international marketer must seek to obtain and analyse with the utmost thoroughness. One of the major challenges that people operating in multinational markets have to face nowadays is the question as to how far marketing programmes can be standardized across borders. Decisions pertain-

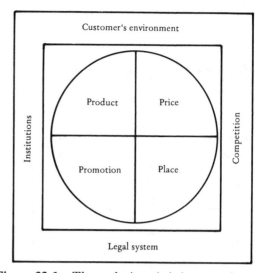

Figure 23.1 *The marketing mix in its external context*

ing to this vital issue cannot be reached without a comprehensive analysis of the 'knowledge' that stems from the interaction of the various elements of the model described in Figure 23.2.

A most valuable aid to determining 'what one needs to know' about multinational markets is what is often referred to as 'marketing profile analysis'. It is a schematic spread sheet that encompasses the two interrelated elements of the 'mix' on the two axes:

1 The horizontal axis depicts the elements which are within the control of the marketing company (e.g. the four Ps).
2 The vertical axis represents the various external factors that impinge upon each of the above.

The spreadsheet that emerges is illustrated in Figure 23.2. It consists of sixteen segments (or more, if one decides to break the internal 'mix' ingredients into additional components). Each segment provides an opportunity to ask and list a host of questions. It is a methodical aid to listing the most relevant areas of knowledge upon which a well-informed marketing programme can be designed. It is important to remember that the matrix described is not a questionnaire. It is an aide mémoire to ensuring that nothing of value is forgotten.

It is inappropriate to reproduce here a completed matrix in so far as it must, at all times, be related to specific products, markets and situations. Nevertheless a few segments have been filled in order to

Country	Product	Price	Promotion	'Place'
Environment				
Competition				— How do competitors distribute? — Strengths and weaknesses of their system
Institutions			— Are media of the type we are used to available? — Code of advertising practice?	
Legal system	— Details to be shown on labels? — Compulsory safeguards on product?			
General observations				

Figure 23.2 *Marketing profile analysis (only partially completed for illustrative purposes)*

provide the reader with a flavour of this valuable tool.

Great emphasis has been placed on the need to acquire 'knowledge' as a preamble to effective international marketing. Indeed this is the area in which the difference between a professional international marketer and an amateur lies. It is often said that the hardest thing about knowledge is 'knowing what one needs to know' . . . A diligent use of the 'marketing profile analysis' technique is one of the safest ways of ensuring that one's knowledge of world markets adheres to a structured and comparable format.

International marketing as a corporate attitude

It is not always appreciated by company strategists that in the competitive world we live in 'international marketing' is much more than just selling goods abroad.

A fundamental difference exists between 'export marketing' and 'international marketing'. Export marketing seeks to increase the sales of a company's products abroad as a way of maximizing volume and, hopefully, decreasing overall unit costs as a result. The main aim is to sell a product which has gained a market acceptance at home in foreign markets. Exporters often resent the fact that as a result of environmental and legal exigencies the product and/or other ingredients of the marketing mix have to be modified. It is almost seen as a

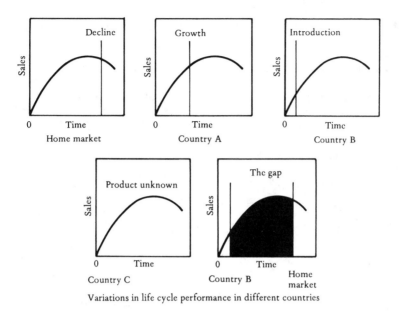

Variations in life cycle performance in different countries

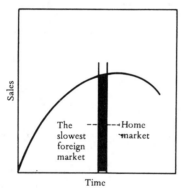

The narrowing gap between product life cycle extremities

Figure 23.3 *Global patterns of product life cycle*
Source: Simon Majaro, *International Marketing*, Allen & Unwin, 1986.

capricious imposition upon the firm's smooth operational productivity.

International marketing is a much more sophisticated process. It assumes that the world is one very large market consisting of a vast number of segments and seeks to develop a marketing plan which aims to meet the needs of the most profitable segments therein. Countries are no more than segments of a macro market which consists of three billion consumers. International marketers are prepared to gloss over differences when they are trivial but never fail to identify the similarities when they are significant. They constantly try to find common denominators which can help to reduce the need to modify the offering to heterogenous markets.

A motorcar manufacturer who resorts to export modifies its car, literature, promotion etc. in response to local demands. Inevitably it ends with many product variations and a myriad of promotional campaigns. The international marketer designs a car with all its panoply of marketing aids on the basis of providing the 'greatest happiness of the greatest number' on global scale. The marketer tries very hard to reduce unnecessary alterations although he/she recognizes that there are circumstances in which they are inevitable. An effective exporter is responsive to needs; the effective international marketer anticipates local needs with the view of avoiding unnecessary and costly changes.

The difference in the two approaches sounds subtle, yet it describes a very fundamental difference in corporate attitude.

The essence of this attitude can be summarized as follows:

1 The world is one large market which offers valuable opportunities to capitalize upon innovation and ever-shortening product life cycles.

2 Standardization or globalization of products, whenever possible, is highly desirable.

   On the other hand unnecessary differentiation can be a costly luxury.

3 No international marketing programme should be planned without an attempt at determining the level of globalization that can be achieved.

   Clearly there are many situations where such a strategy is impractical or even harmful. However to forego the opportunity to standardize when it is within one's grasp is certainly a waste.

All this requires a 'global outlook', a managerial attitude, which not every manager possesses. It takes a person with a long-standing exposure to a number of cultural, political and commercial environments. It calls for a personal sensitivity and empathy to multifarious national variations. A true internationalist does not develop overnight nor does he/she emerge from a purely domestic company even if it happens to be a subsidiary of a multinational giant. A person responsible for marketing margarine in the UK does not necessarily possess the attitudinal wherewithal for international marketing just because the company he/she works for is a subsidiary of Unilever.

The benefits of international marketing

Many companies enter the complex world of international marketing without fully reflecting upon the merits of doing so. It is not unusual for firms to embark upon the internationalization process simply through an accidental sale abroad or through a desire to visit foreign lands. Clearly neither of these reasons need be commercially viable.

A compelling message that is transmitted to us at frequent intervals from governmental and institutional bodies is the fact that 'selling abroad' is good for the national interest. Undoubtedly this is a valid argument. Britain is a country that needs to export a high proportion of its GNP in order to pay for everything it imports. To that extent it must devote a lot of effort to its international trade. Nevertheless no businessperson in his right mind would undertake international marketing activities if they are likely to weaken the overall performance of the company. International marketing must be right within the strategic context of the firm. In a free economy the national interest is an added bonus, an adjunct to a sound strategy, and not an end in itself.

On the other hand there are a few vital factors that provide a powerful rationale for the internationalization route:

Exploiting the product life cycle as fast as possible

The product life cycle has a major relevance to international marketing. Traditionally most firms tended to operate in their domestic markets as long as such markets yielded adequate commercial rewards. As soon as signs of sales and profit erosion manifested themselves the pressure to move into foreign markets increased. The result was that every product manifested different life cycle patterns in different markets. In some markets the product reached a 'decline' stage, in others it still enjoyed 'growth', yet in others it was starting its life cycle from scratch.

Unfortunately this kind of cosy pattern has virtually disappeared. The advent of the communication revolution and the enormous increase in international travel and tourism has meant that the gap between the point at which the product reaches saturation at home and abroad has narrowed. The life span of a product has gained global patterns. This change is illustrated in Figure 23.3. It helps to emphasize why it is so important to plan a product policy in relation to world markets simultaneously.

In this connection it is worth remembering that in strategic terms a product is only deemed to be successful when it has recovered the total investment that was incurred in its development. A product must be capable of earning sufficient funds to recover the full investment that the firm has sunk into it and clearly this must happen during the life of such a product. Profits per se are meaningless until full investment recovery has taken place. If the product reaches its decline stage and full recovery has not taken place the company faces a serious failure. Investment includes marketing, design, pre-launch R & D, production, etc.

Figure 23.4 illustrates the relationship between investment, sales, costs, margins over the life of a product including the pre-launch period. It can be argued that the role of an effective international marketing effort is to shorten the investment recovery period in such a way as to enable the firm to maximize the returns on product innovation. If the product life cycle is shortening it is important to recover the total investment therein as quickly as possible. This can be done much more effectively if the product is marketed on a global scale from the very beginning.

The benefits of volume and 'experience curve'

The so-called 'experience curve' has taught us that a strong relationship exists between costs of production over the life of a product and volume of units produced.

This concept started its life as the 'learning curve' as a result of the work carried out by the commander of the Wright-Patterson Air Force base. It was observed in 1925 that the number of direct labour hours required to assemble a plane decreased as the total number of aircraft assembled increased. In other words as experience is gained costs should go down in a predictable manner. Figure 23.5 illustrates a typical 'curve' and Figure 23.6 illustrates the same relationship between 'cost per unit' and 'experience' (based on a cumulative number of units of production) transcribed on to a log-log scale thus

coverting a curve into a straight line.

The various studies conducted by the Boston Consulting Group as far back as 1972 have highlighted the dramatic decline in costs that accumulated volume of production and experience can yield. While the true value of the experience theory to strategic decisions can be debated there is little doubt that the firm that has accumulated a large quantum of experience in a given product ought to benefit from low cost behaviour with a resultant cost advantage.

Internationalizing the marketing effort of the firm is a clear route that a firm can pursue if it wishes to derive cost leadership based on the full benefit of experience (learning, scale and technology). To a great extent the phenomenal success of some of the Japanese companies in the field of electronics, cars and motorcycles is based on a sound appreciation of the benefits of the experience curve concept.

Cushioning the firm against the vagaries of national economic cycles

Most countries go through economic cycles oscillating between periods of relative prosperity and stagnation. Companies that market their products in one domestic market often find that their performance is directly linked with the level of buoyancy that exists in their respective countries. It is rare for all countries especially among developed nations to undergo economic crises simultaneously.

Companies that operate in many countries normally find that they can enjoy a certain level of cushioning resulting from the fact that peaks and troughs of demand follow a staggered pattern. The benefits of exposure to a myriad of heterogeneous economies can be significant.

Many companies have internationalized their marketing effort without ever having reflected upon the strategic implications. It was simply deemed the fashionable thing to do. Internationalization is a very potent tool of corporate strategy and must not be embarked upon without a clear understanding of the implications. The rationale for total or selective international penetration must be based on a clearly-defined mission statement resulting from a thorough and conscientious analysis of both internal and external input pertaining to the firm's capabilities and opportunities.

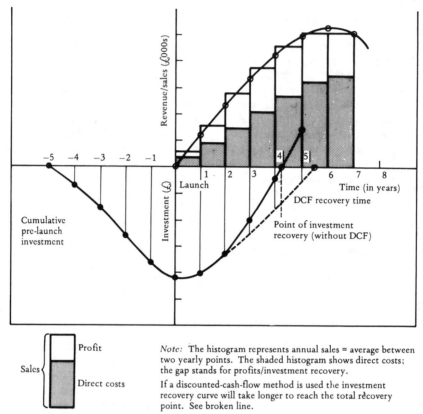

Figure 23.4 *The investment recovery process and the product life cycle*
Source: Simon Majaro, *ibid.*

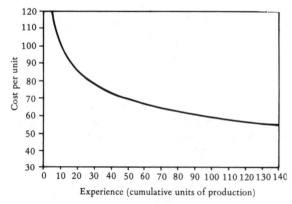

Figure 23.5 *The typical experience curve*

'Going international' is not an end in itself. Like most corporate strategies it is a chosen route for achieving company objectives.

International marketing and the organization

'Which comes first: the organization or a strategy?'

In theory an organization is set up to equip a company with the systems, resources and staff which it requires in order to meet its objectives and implement a selected strategic direction. If the firm's objectives and strategies are changed drastically the organization must, if appropriate, be changed as well.

In practice one finds that many companies operate within an organizational pattern which is semi-sacrosanct and which impinges heavily upon its freedom to develop strategies or respond to a new direction. In my consultancy practice I have encountered many firms where the boss expressed a *cri de coeur:* 'If we could only start life afresh we would

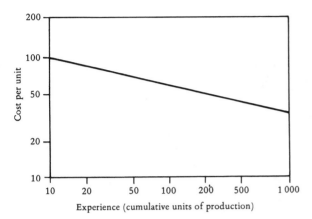

Figure 23.6 *Experience curve converted*

organise ourselves differently and life would be much simpler . . .'

This issue is of vital importance in international marketing. It needs very little imagination to recognize that a highly centralized firm is more likely to develop a global product and/or brand. On the other hand a firm which is structured in a decentralized fashion is unlikely to attain any measure of standardization in world markets. The structure is going to militate against such a strategy. For a full discussion of these issues see Chapter 4.

A brief exploration of the kind of structures that exist in multinational operations is appropriate at this point.

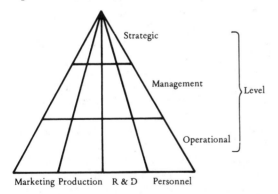

Figure 23.7 *The firm – a conceptual framework*

In purely conceptual terms a firm can be described as a pyramid as illustrated in Figure 23.7. It consists of an intricate conglomeration of decision and activity levels. It consists of three distinct levels:

1 Strategic.
2 Management.
3 Operational.

Briefly, the *strategic* level is responsible for formulating the firm's mission statement, determining objectives, identifying the resources that will be required if the firm is to attain its objectives and selecting the most appropriate corporate strategy for the firm to pursue.

The *management* level has the task of translating corporate objectives into functional and/or unit objectives and ensuring that resources placed at its disposal are used effectively in the pursuit of those which will make the achievement of the firm's goals possible.

The *operational* level is responsible for the effective performance of those tasks which underly the achievement of unit/functional objectives. The achievement of operational objectives is what enables the firm to achieve its management and strategic aims. All three levels are interdependent and clarity of purpose from the top enables everybody in the firm to work in an integrated fashion towards a common aim.

This simple concept of the firm can now be translated into the global scene. Three distinct types of structure exist:

1 The 'macropyramid' structure
2 The 'umbrella' structure
3 The 'international conglomerate' (also known as the 'interglomerate')

Let us explore the characteristics of each and the way they impact upon international marketing decisions.

The 'macropyramid' structure

This is a multinational firm with a well-defined 'nerve-centre' where all strategic decisions are taken. The affairs of the company are conducted in a centralized fashion and the central strategic organ is the unequivocal formulator of direction and policy for all the international operations. The firm's foreign activities, whether they include production or marketing or both, are structured from levels below the strategic level. They look like pyramids that have had their pinnacles chopped off. Figure 23.8 illustrates this structure in a diagrammatic form.

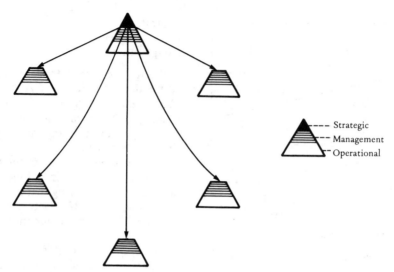

Figure 23.8 *The macropyramid model*
Source: Simon Majaro, *ibid.*

The following are the main results of such a structure in relation to international marketing decisions:

1   Strategic marketing planning tends to be carried out in a centralized fashion.
2   Major decisions pertaining to product policy and other 'mix' elements are taken at the centre.
3   The marketing effort is often directed towards a maximum standardization of the mix.
4   In human/social terms the firm can be rigid in its approach to world markets. It often lacks the empathy and sensitivity for dealing effectively with local/national needs and pressures.
5   In terms of productivity and use of resources the structure can be quite effective. However in terms of creativity the channels of communication of ideas are so long that the chance of ideas working their way through the system is fairly remote.
6   Because other functions such as production and R & D etc. also tend to be centrally planned (but quite often locally executed) communication problems in the field are rife.
7   Marketing talent tends to gravitate to the centre.

The 'umbrella' structure

This organizational pattern is based on the recognition that markets and countries differ and as such must be treated with local independence and some freedom of action. This means that subsidiaries around the world enjoy a measure of strategic, managerial and operational freedom. While a definitive nerve centre still exists – invariably at the location of the firm's major unit or where the firm started its dynamic growth – such a nerve centre has deliberately curbed its strategic jurisdiction in relation to the operating companies around the globe. It is basically a 'hands off' structure and management style. None the less the centre normally exercises a few major roles: a central planning function, the formulation of broad objectives for the total firm and the provision of assistance, advice and support to the various branches of the organization. The headquarters often develop a series of service departments which are available to all the units wherever they may be located. Hence the descriptive term 'umbrella' structure. Figure 23.9 describes the structure in a diagrammatic form.

The main impact of such a structure upon international marketing activities can be summarized as follows:

1   Local management enjoys so much strategic and operational freedom that significant changes often take place in the adaptation of products and other marketing mix elements to local needs and expectations.

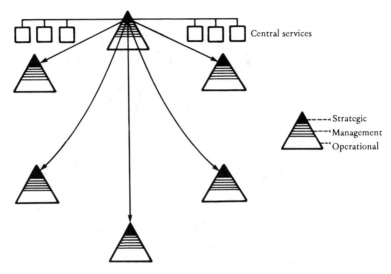

Figure 23.9 *The umbrella model*
Source: Simon Majaro, *ibid.*

2 Marketing strategies are formulated and decisions are taken in the operating companies. The result is that fully fledged marketing departments tend to develop in the branches.

This often leads to communication problems and even conflicts between the marketing personnel in the outposts and the central marketing services.

3 The firm is usually very responsive to local needs and acquires a great understanding of the marketing environment in which it operates.

4 In product development a strong pressure towards differentiation exists and inevitably impinges upon other functions such as R & D, production and personnel.

In other words the prospects of developing a global standardization strategy are remote.

5 Overall the structure tends towards profligacy and can be less cost-effective. At the same time it can be described as a much more market orientated structure than the macropyramid option.

The international conglomerate (the 'interglomerate') structure

Here we have a complex international organization embracing multinational, multimarket, multiproduct, multitechnology activities. The diversity is such that the only meaningful scope for synergy hinges around the financial dimension. In fact the 'centre' abdicates from the process of managing individual companies; it is only concerned with the 'bottom line'. Top management at the centre – and the location of the centre probably depends on financial considerations – expects each member of the organization to generate a given amount of profits and cash flow in accordance with pre-set criteria.

If the chief executive of an Australian subsidiary feels that there is more profit in property development than in dairy products, nobody will stand in his/her way provided the financial criteria of the parent board are met. The interglomerate encourages entrepreneurship of this kind. The strategic level at the centre manages money. The strategic level of the individual international subsidiaries manage businesses which in turn are expected to generate money. Figure 23.10 shows how such a firm is structured. The strategic level of the centre looks like a pinnacle without a body: it represents a small unit of thinkers/planners/deciders/controllers. It does not manage anything; it directs and controls a large number of semi-independent pyramids each with its own strategic level.

The implications for the marketing function in such a structure are:

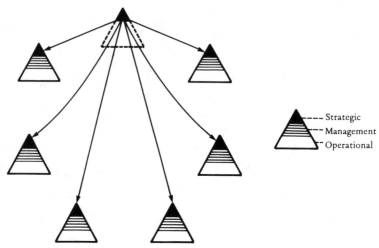

Figure 23.10 *The international conglomerate*
Source: Simon Majaro, *ibid.*

1 The obsession with financial controls means that marketing is often subjugated to control and accountancy effectiveness. In other words accountants are more important than marketers.
2 'Marketing' is seldom represented at the centre. To that extent the subject of globalization of brands, products or communication is not normally ventilated at top management level.
3 Social/cultural local needs are only responded to when omission to do so affects profitability.
4 Marketing strategies and decisions are normally delegated to the various subsidiaries. Some of those are organized as macropyramids, others as umbrella structures. Little cohesiveness and synergy exists among the constituent parts.

Few readers will need to concern themselves unduly with the marketing function of an interglomerate. As suggested earlier fully-fledged conglomerates do not get too excited about the marketing function of the constituent parts. It is the role of marketing in the other two structures that must be reflected upon with some care. Moreover it must be remembered that in some businesses the structure can be a vital source of strength while the opposite organizational pattern can be a debilitating factor for a competitor in the same business.

It took the US and European car industry a good few years to realize that centralization of the strategic marketing function was an essential factor in achieving a measure of globalization of their products. The Japanese had recognized the power of standardization and organized their marketing effort accordingly. Their enormous success was based, to a great extent, on this insight.

The main issues

It was suggested earlier that the transition from domestic to international marketing is not always as simple as one bargains for. Nevertheless it is useful to highlight the main issues which the person moving into a more internationally orientated environment must grapple with.

Researching world markets

The process of researching international markets is not very different from the one which is pursued in a purely domestic arrangement. The objectives, tasks and methodologies are very similar. However the scope, coverage, complexities and, inevitably, cost are very different. It is quite easy to spend vast amounts of cash on researching international markets with minimal pay-off.

Before indulging in a full-scale international marketing research two major issues should be borne in mind:

Assuming five countries are to be researched; three products and three market segments — possible projects for research 5 × 3 × 3 = 45

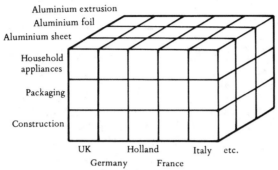

Assuming seventy countries are to be researched; five products, six market segments — possible number of projects: 70 × 5 × 6 = 2100

Figure 23.11 *Possible projects for market measurement activities of an aluminium company*

Selection of projects

An international firm that operates in a large number of countries (X) and markets a range of products (Y) in a number of segments (Z) can find that it has X × Y × Z number of areas that it can research. Logically some of these projects are more important than others and a pecking order of importance must be formulated.

Figure 23.11 illustrates the number of projects for research and/or market measurement that an aluminium company operating in five countries with three products and three market segments has to cope with. If one assumes that the company is operating in eighty countries with five products and six market segments the number increases to:

$$80 \times 5 \times 6 = 2400 \ldots$$

In a macropyramid type organization there is a fair chance that somebody will monitor how much is spent on researching markets worldwide. In an umbrella structure the total cost is likely to get lost in the individual companies although the aggregate cost is likely to be astronomical.

A useful device for ensuring that research projects are screened carefully and their potential 'pay-off' fully appraised is the *research project appraisal method*. It is similar in approach and content to the type of appraisal that most firms use in relation to normal capital investment approval. Figure 23.13 illustrates a simple form describing the type of information that should help to appraise and compare the value of each marketing research project. This may appear at first glance as a bureaucratic method. Yet if it can help a company to establish criteria of value and choice before spending resources on international research projects the procedure is worth adopting.

Coupled with the appraisal form one can also use an algorithm-type flow chart as described in Figure 23.12.

Comparability of results

This is a major problem in international marketing research. If one derives data from national sources which do not conform to the same benchmark there is a danger that one is not comparing 'like for like'.

For instance if one compares levels of unemployment in ten different countries one cannot assume that all ten countries calculate unemployment in an identical way. Some countries base their 'returns' on the number of people who collect benefits. Others calculate the number of people unemployed by simply deducting those at work from those who have ever worked and are still of working age (including women who left work to bring up a family). Clearly the two are not comparable.

In this connection it is important, at all times, to

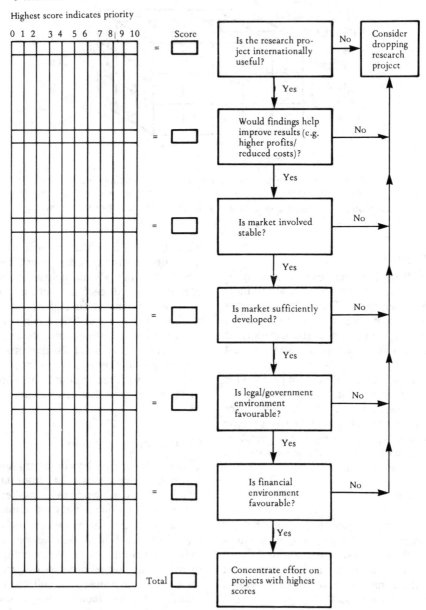

Figure 23.12 *Procedure for screening marketing research projects*
Source: Simon Majaro, *ibid*.

```
┌─────────────────────────────────────────────────────────────┐
│                              ┌──────────────────────────┐     │
│                              │ Reference no. _____  │     │
│                              └──────────────────────────┘     │
│        1  Project title_____    │
│           _____    │
│                                                               │
│        2  Project objectives_____    │
│           _____    │
│           _____    │
│           _____    │
│                                                               │
│        3  Tasks required to achieve objectives, their duration and cost │
│           (Note: Cost of internal resources to be included)   │
└─────────────────────────────────────────────────────────────┘
```

Objectives as defined in 2	Tasks	Resources*		Duration	Cost
		Internal	External		
Total:					

Additional costs_____

Give details_____   Total:

To be shown in man/days or other quantifiable standards

4 Pay off

(Explain how you feel that savings and/or added contribution could result from this project. Endeavour to quantify such 'pay off' in monetary terms. Attach supportive evidence.)

_____
_____
_____
_____
_____ Estimated pay off: [_____]

Proposal submitted by_____   Authorized by_____
Date_____   Date _____

Figure 23.13 *International marketing research authorization form*
Source: Simon Majaro, *ibid.*

ensure that sources of information used have been prepared in accordance with the rules of comparability. For general statistical data the United Nations and its various agencies is an excellent source of comparable and objective primary data. Its data is not always as detailed as information from national sources but in most instances one can rely on the fact that it has been assembled and tabulated in accordance with the rules of comparability.

It is strongly recommended that before one delves deeply into local governmental statistics or data collected by semi-official organizations, such as chambers of commerce and trade associations, one should study the material provided by such bodies as:

European Economic Community (EEC)
European Coal and Steel Community (ECSC)
Economic Commission for Africa (ECA)
Economic Commission for Asia and the Far East (ECAFE)
Economic Commission for Latin America (ECLA)
Organization for Economic Co-Operation and Development (OECD)
General Agreement on Tariffs and Trade (GATT)
Food and Agriculture Organization (FAO)
International Labor Organization (ILO)
International Civil Aviation Organization (ICAO)
International Bank for Reconstruction and Development (IBRD)
International Monetary Fund (IMF)
International Telecommunications Union (ITU)
International Union of Railways (UICF)
International Air Transport Association (IATA)
Universal Postal Union (UPU)
World Health Organization (WHO)

Other useful sources of international information

Business International
Informations Internationales
World Trade Information Service – The US Department of Commerce

Before leaving the question of comparability it is useful to alert the reader to a number of pitfalls:

Languages

International researchers must ensure that they understand the nuances of terms used in foreign countries. The most subtle difference in meaning may nullify the objective of comparability thus reducing the overall value of the study.

Target group and segments

When planning a multicountry project it is important to make sure that variations in segmentation patterns are brought into consideration. Thus, for instance, if a study of tyre consumption is under-taken in a number of countries it must be remembered that some countries manufacture cars and therefore have an 'OEM' segment as well as a 'replacement' segment while other countries only have a 'replacement' segment. Ignoring such an input can of course make a nonsense of the results.

Product variations

A few years ago research highlighted the fact that the per capita consumption of bananas (by weight) in Germany was double that of the UK. On closer analysis it was discovered that the reason for this enormous disparity in consumption was due to a simple phenomenon: for historical reasons the UK derived its bananas from the Caribbean while Germany's imports came mainly from central and Latin American sources. The Caribbean bananas were half the weight. In other words, consumption in numbers was almost identical but consumption in weight was double in Germany.

Needless to say that failure to identify such variations in product and recognizing the bases upon which data is compiled can create a hopeless misinterpretation of results.

Cultural values

This is particularly important when one is seeking to carry out consumer research on a multinational scale. When a Japanese has to respond to a scale ranging from 1 for 'poor' to 5 for 'excellent' he/she would tend to err upwards. They do not like to judge a situation too harshly in case the recipient feels hurt and loses face. By the same token in some cultures placing one's response at the half-way mark namely 3 is deemed to be a safe and fairly generous approbation. If one attempts to compare the results without a built-in correcting mechanism one may be led to absurd conclusions.

Socioeconomic conditions

In the UK we accept the AB, C1, C2, D and E stratification of the market as a basis upon which to segment marketing programmes. In the Scandinavian countries this classification is virtually meaningless in as much as the socioeconomic variations among classes has become blurred. One cannot undertake research projects in India and in Sweden without building into the comparability equation existing variables such as family size, family life cycle patterns, social classes, education, etc.

Monetary problems

This problem has increased during the last few years as a result of the large number of floating currencies. When the dollar drops 20 per cent in relation to the German mark it distorts overnight all previous attempts at comparability in levels of consumption. If the average German used to spend x marks per annum on milk do we now conclude that he has increased his consumption by 20 per cent since our last analysis?

Per capita income is measured in terms of dollars for ease of comparability. Do we jump to the conclusion that the PCI of the average Swiss has increased by 25% in one year simply because the dollar has dropped by 25% in relation to the Swiss francs?

Careful 'shopping basket' benchmarks with suitable 'multiplicants' must be formulated before one can derive sensible and meaningful comparisons.

Identifying the best markets for development

There are around 200 countries in the world. Very few companies can afford the luxury of marketing their products or service in all of them. The Pareto law usually applies to international marketing strategies with its full vigour. The most broadly-based and well-established multinational firms will probably find that 20 per cent of the countries they serve generate at least 80 per cent of the results. Obviously the 'star' countries must receive greater managerial attention and allocation of resources.

Moreover an international marketer who only has limited resources at his/her disposal must identify the few commercially attractive countries upon which to shower marketing and promotional efforts. Even if the resources which are available are more lavish one needs to establish a 'pecking order' of attractiveness. Common sense ordains that more money is invested in markets which promise to be 'star' performers than secondary or tertiary opportunities.

The common practice is to classify countries in distinct categories as follows (an example only):

A countries: These are the best opportunity mar-

kets both in the short term and for the longer term. Such countries are sometimes referred to as 'strategic markets'. The company aims to establish a permanent presence and invest the resources required to achieve significant penetration there.

B countries: These are the kind of countries which represent a medium level of attractiveness but either through size or due to economic or political constraints the company is reluctant to invest heavily therein. Such markets are often tackled in a more pragmatic fashion and one usually relies on local distributors and/or agents rather than on the company's own subsidiaries. The main objective is to capitalize upon such opportunity markets but not through expensive and irrevocable commitments.

C countries: Countries falling under this category are those that can be described as the 'catch what catch can' markets. Allocation of resources to such markets is minimal and at the slightest sign of trouble one desists from spending any further time or money on such markets.

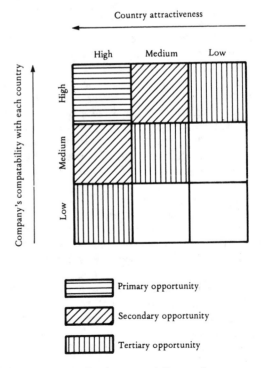

Figure 23.14 *Business portfolio matrix*

This is almost a segmentation system on a global scale. Other ways of dividing world markets have been used by various international marketers. However what one often forgets is that what is a 'best opportunity' for company X is not necessarily equally attractive to company Y. Each company has its specific inventory of strengths and weaknesses and these must be borne in mind before plunging into a short-list cluster of markets destined for exploitation. Company X may be much more compatible with a given market owing to a myriad of factors such as the nationality of the parent corporation, the historical connections between the firm and the government of the foreign country, the image that the firm has enjoyed in the market and so on.

In other words, the 'best opportunity' country is not only an objective and quantitative appraisal of each market per se. It must be congruent with the specific characteristics of the marketing company, its strengths and capabilities.

A powerful aid to the identification of the 'best opportunity' target countries is the application of the 'business portfolio' concept to the screening process. Figure 23.14 describes the kind of matrix that can be used. On the horizontal axis one evaluates the attractiveness of each market on objective and measurable criteria (e.g. size, stability, wealth, type and number of competitors, ease of entry, etc.). On the vertical axis one appraises the firm's compatibility with each country on a more subjective and judgemental basis (e.g. the firm's flag, presence in the country, empathy between the company's management and local population or institutions, language, historical links with the respective governments etc.) Undoubtedly the 'high/high's should be the prime markets upon which to concentrate one's attention and resources.

Another useful methodology which can be applied during the process of reducing the plethora of countries to a more manageable number is the so-called 'mapping' technique. If one can identify the two major parameters which underlie purchasing decisions one can experiment with a correlation exercise which sometimes can highlight valuable clusters of potential opportunity.

Let us take a short case study: Medi Systems International.

The company was charged with the task of

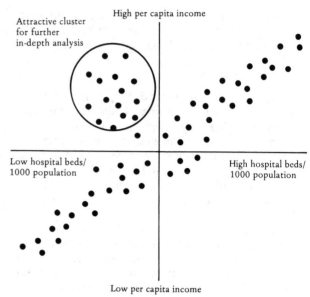

Figure 23.15 *Mapping exercise*

marketing 'turnkey' hospitals around the world. The company's marketing personnel were asked to identify quickly a short-list of countries for in-depth investigation. Clearly one could not afford to waste too much time looking at data about 200 countries.

In the circumstances it was decided that the two major dimensions that would qualify countries for the detailed analysis phase were: (i) ability to pay and (ii) need for hospitals. The former parameter can be expressed in 'per capita income'; the latter in 'hospital beds per 1000 people'. A simple albeit most valuable 'mapping' exercise can now take place as shown in Figure 23.15.

Standardizing the marketing mix – myth or reality?

We now come to the most difficult problem that the modern international marketer must grapple with: how far is it possible to standardize products for world markets? Or, an even more ambitious question: how far is it possible to standardize other ingredients of the 'mix'? Obviously if one could offer the same product, and the same price and with the same promotional mix and distribution practices to all markets life would be wonderful.

Unfortunately it does not seem to be that easy.

The controversy has been raging for years and will no doubt continue to do so for many years to come. Yet we know that an increasing number of firms have managed to achieve a measure of standardization in their global marketing strategy. Coca-Cola has achieved considerable standardization of its products and promotional activities on a worldwide scale. Kodak and Polaroid have both reached a high level of standardization. Many of the large manufacturers of motorcars are talking about 'world cars' and have come to recognize the benefits of such a strategy.

On the other hand, cigarette manufacturers would claim that standardization is virtually an impossible strategy because of the legal rules and regulations that appear to differ from country to country. It is not easy to design a pack which encompasses the health warnings prescribed by the legal systems of 200 countries! At the same time one can find in the market an anti-dandruff shampoo that describes how to cure dandruff in seven languages. In the absence of long-winded legal health warnings in the shampoo business some standardization, albeit for a cluster of countries only, is possible.

The fundamental rule which every international marketer must engrave on his/her heart is:

> If an opportunity to standardize exists do not differentiate!

Unnecessary differentiation is wasteful while purposeful standardization whenever it is possible can save resources and lower costs.

It is important to emphasize that when one is talking about non-differentiation one is not referring to the process of differentiating one's product vis-a-vis competitors. Changing one's products with the view of establishing a competitive advantage in the marketplace is a desirable strategy and should be considered at all times. What we are talking about here is the development of a product (however heavily differentiated it may be against competitive products) which is more or less the same for a selected cluster of countries or even for the whole world. The latter of course is a very tall order.

One can strive to have a product for EEC markets or a product for the Americas or for Far Eastern countries. These are 'clusters' of markets which, with careful and judicious planning, can be approached in a similar manner. The one thing which is impossible to do is to develop a product for the UK market and then hope that it will have full acceptance in all other markets. Either the brand will not 'travel' or the packaging will not be acceptable or the labelling will fail to meet legal requirements or the local testing institutions will have queer ideas as to what is sound and what is not in each respective country. Even experienced companies like General Motors can fall into traps that adequate planning could have helped to avoid. One of its 'world cars' which is known as 'Nova' in many parts of the world is marketed as 'Corsa' in Spain and a few other countries. 'Nova' in Spanish means 'does not go' which is rather inappropriate for a car.

The essential ingredient that one requires when one is investigating a standardization policy in a systematic way is 'knowledge' as described earlier. The preamble to the standardization analysis process is the accumulation of detailed 'marketing profiles' about each market under review. Once such documents are at hand it is possible to commence a 'paired comparison' exercise. Briefly it is a systematic attempt at comparing how the external/environmental factors of each market impinge on the internal elements of the marketing mix. It is an analysis of the similarities as well as the differences that exist in each market. Figure 23.16 describes a simple methodology that can help to determine how far the similarities and the differences are significant. When the differences are substantial one cannot ignore them but minor small adjustments to the products or the promotional mix can help to attain a certain amount of standardization. It is essentially a judgemental and qualitative method but designed to ensure that international marketing decisions are not taken without a thorough and intelligent endeavour to determine whether the standardization route is a holy grail or not.

Conclusion

I have attempted to emphasize how international marketing differs from marketing in a domestic or national environment. The two activities are similar in many respects but in order to internationalize one's perspective one must learn how to systematize one's knowledge-acquisition. In particular one must

	Similarities					Differences					Detailed remarks
	5	4	3	2	1	1	2	3	4	5	
Environment Culture Languages Attitudes											
Competition Local Foreign											
Institutions											
Legal systems											
Other factors											

5 = Almost identical   1 = Insignificant differences
4 = Very similar   2 = Surmountable differences
3 = Fairly similar   3 = Fairly significant differences
2 = Some similarity   4 = Major differences
1 = Poor   5 = Insurmountable major differences

Figure 23.16 *Pair comparison analysis*

learn how to collect information and analyse it in a comparable way. Comparability of information and intelligence is vital as a preamble to the important task of deciding how far one can unify and standardize the approach to as many countries as possible.

All the evidence is pointing at the fact that companies that have invested thought and resources towards the globalization of products and brands will become the winners of the 1990s.

24
International marketing – getting started
STAN PALIWODA

Introduction

International marketing is a term which is over-used and ill-defined. In essence, it concerns the maintenance of competitive advantage across international borders.

The exchange process, which forms the basis of international marketing, is different from that found in the domestic market and is more than just exporting. To export means simply to send or carry abroad, especially for trade or sale. Marketing goes beyond that in introducing the concept of the end-user, moving the orientation away from finding sales for a company's existing products to analysing the market and assessing whether the company is able to produce a product or service for which there is either current or potential demand given other factors can be controlled such as price, promotion and distribution.

International marketing can be very profitable but it is a serious business which requires the long-term commitment of resources. It will mean the outlay of a substantial investment in a foreign market often with a long projected payback. This issue of the planning time horizon is quite crucial. Table 24.1 outlines the essential differences between a short-term 'sales' approach and a longer-term entry strategy of three to four years.

Why go abroad?

Theoretically, the motivation to expand into foreign markets may arise through different means. Porter (1986) has explained this phenomenon of internationalization in terms of:

1 *Currents* which drive international competition:
   (a) Growing similarity of countries with universal features, large retail chains, TV advertising and credit cards.
   (b) Falling tariff barriers.
   (c) Technological revolutions which reshape industry and create shifts in leadership.
   (d) Integrating role of technology. Improved communication dismantles geographical barriers to trade and improves information in a world where buyers are increasingly aware of world markets.
   (e) New global competitors. The Pacific Basin countries have become fully-fledged competitors to well-established Western rivals.
2 *Cross-currents* which make the pattern of international competition different from earlier decades:
   (a) Slowing rates of economic growth.
   (b) Changes in the basis of competitive advan-

Table 24.1   *Entry strategy approach versus 'sales' approach to international markets*

	'Sales' approach	*Entry strategy approach*
Time horizons	Short-run	Long-run (say three to five years)
Target markets	No systematic selection	Selection based on analysis of market/ sales potential
Dominant objective	Immediate sales	Build permanent market position
Resource commitment	Only enough to get immediate sales	What is necessary to gain permanent market position
Entry mode	No systematic choice	Systematic choice of most appropriate mode
New-product development	Exclusively for home market	For both home and foreign markets
Product adaptation	Only mandatory adaptations (to meet legal/technical requirements) of domestic products	Adaptation of domestic products to foreign buyers' preferences, incomes and use conditions
Channels	No effort to control	Effort to control in support of market objectives/goals
Price	Determined by domestic full cost with some ad hoc adjustments to specific sales situations	Determined by demand, competition, objectives and other marketing policies, as well as cost
Promotion	Mainly confined to personal selling or left to middlemen	Advertising, sales promotion and personal selling mix to achieve market objective goals

Source: Franklin R. Root, *Entry Strategies for International Markets*, Lexington Books, 1987, p. 5.

tage. Labour cost, natural resources and technology access are less important than before.

(c) New forms of protectionism, e.g. requirements for local content and local ownership.

(d) New types of government inducement, working between governments to attract foreign direct investment.

(e) Joint ventures, proliferating coalitions among firms from different countries. Broader, deeper collaboration than the marketing joint venture and production licences of the past.

(f) Growing ability to tailor to local conditions. New technologies support globalization but does allow customized tailored product offerings. The need to standardize products worldwide is diminishing.

Other possible explanations for internationalization include:

1 *Product life cycle effects.* Where a product on the home market enters a mature phase, theory argues that the company concerned may be able to find new export markets abroad where product markets have not reached the same stage of development.

This argument, however, becomes increasingly less relevant with the passage of time as a result of two trends. First, competition today being international rather than domestic for all goods and services, consequently has reduced the time lag between product research, development and production leading to the simultaneous appearance of a standardized product in all major world markets. Second, it is not production in the highly labour intensive industries which is moving to the low labour cost countries with freeport advantages such as Taiwan, but the capital intensive industries such as electronics, creating the anomalous situation of basing production for high value, high technology goods in the countries least able to afford them.

2 *Competition* in a chosen target market may be less intense than at home or there may be the

promise of tariff barriers to exclude potential competitors in return for a substantial foreign investment in plant machinery and knowhow.

3 *Excess capacity utilization.* When the domestic market experiences a downturn or reaches saturation, companies may turn to export markets to make good the shortfall. For companies in industries requiring long production runs to ensure commercial viability, foreign orders may make the crucial difference between profit and loss. However, there is no commitment to exporting or to foreign markets at this stage.

Another feature which may also appear is that low prices are often quoted to ensure sales success in order to secure long production runs or to sell off high inventory levels. It is indeed possible for a company which has a mature product line to regard its original investment in product research and development to have been long since recouped and therefore to price on the basis of actual production costs plus overheads. This is profitable exporting, but means that a company will be charging a different price in foreign markets from that which it charges in its own domestic market. This invites charges of 'dumping' which in the case of the USA and also the EEC is assessed on two criteria: the basis of injury to local industry and whether the price being charged is lower than the price charged in the producer's own domestic market.

This strategy may succeed in the short term, solving the need for near capacity production runs. Finding foreign customers on whom to offload production means also that the company does not have to resort to discounting for established customers, thereby protecting its price structure on the home market and avoiding the setting of precedents for future price negotiations.

4 *Geographical diversification* arises where companies find it preferable to remain with the product line which they know and are successful with, to diversifying into new product lines or product technologies. This is a strategy of finding new markets for existing or modified products.

5 *Potential of population and purchasing power.* There are few untapped markets left, China representing the most populous of those remaining. However, the capacity to consume or to absorb the product has to be matched with the capacity to pay for it. High levels of indebtedness in the Third World have created financial innovations in the variants of countertrade now available, which in total are estimated by the US Department of Commerce to account for 30 per cent of world trade and 50 per cent of East-West trade.

6 *Strategic competitive advantage* which may also be interpreted as market 'spoiling'. The purpose here is less actively to pursue a market than to register a presence with a competitor particularly where this also concerns market entry into a rival's domestic market. Timing is on the side of the existing market player who draws revenue from sales while his/her competitors plan their response. In world markets, it is the case that multinationals view market segments for the presence of their multinational rivals. Narrowly defined segments in which there is little competition add to their total corporate power structure. A small but significant base in one part of the world may enable a multinational to access other markets in the same region and at the same time to discourage competitors, occasionally by taking competitive retaliation against a multinational rival into the rival's home market undercutting his/her home base and the market for his/her main product.

Market research of markets abroad

As an activity this attracts only a small percentage of a company's total market research budget. Many companies do not spend money on foreign market research or entrust an on-the-spot appraisal to one of the most junior members of the firm often entering into a particular target market for the first time and without any proper briefing or linguistic skills. What results is a 'go/no go' decision based on a poor understanding of the specific market characteristics. Figure 24.1 illustrates how this activity ought to be approached as part of the company's ongoing strategic planning and development.

A decision to enter a market should only be taken with proper understanding and appreciation of what is currently happening in that target market and what is likely to happen. Once the

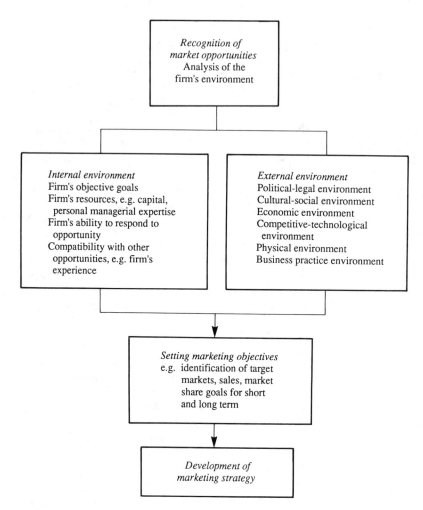

Figure 24.1   *An overview of the process of the marketing strategy development*
Source: Adapted from E. W. Cundiff and N. T. Hilger, *Marketing In The International Environment*, Prentice-Hall, 1984, p. 5.

decision is made to enter, a continual monitoring process has to be set in motion. However, there are differences existing between companies as to whether they perceive foreign market entry as:

1   A strategic or tactical option, i.e. whether they see entry into the target market as being of potential value in the medium to long term or whether it is a spoiling tactic undertaken by multinationals as they pursue their global quest for global market share.

2   Whether in terms of motivation and behaviour it is opportunity seeking or problem-solving behaviour that is being reflected. Foreign market entry may be motivated by a desire to reduce current excess capacity. Alternatively, there may be a genuine desire to continue to service the target market in question. The underlying motivation is an important factor as it determines the company's degree of commitment to foreign markets as well.

Market research is possible but less reliable in those markets where market research data is scarce or the data available is not directly comparable due to different statistical bases being used. This has often been cited by the United Nations' Economic Commission for Europe (UNECE) as a barrier to trade in their Consolidated Inventory of Barriers to Trade in the ECE Region which includes Western and Eastern Europe. All of Eastern Europe is guilty of poor statistical reporting, indicating usually either volume or value consumption figures, but not both.

To research country markets effectively, governmental sources should be used where they exist. Where these are deficient, there is a number of agencies including the US Central Intelligence Agency and many specialist companies such as Business International SA, EIU and others (see Table 24.2) which offer 'guesstimates' as to probable production and consumption figures. A company which then thinks it knows its market ought then to assess its state of preparation against the industrial marketer's checklist provided free by the Department of Trade and Industry. Identification of national personal disposable income levels may well be meaningless and one should seek to identify important affluent target segments within a national market with data on lifestyles, educational background, location and spending patterns, all of which are useful indicators for any company seriously considering market entry. Figure 24.2 depicts world GNP in two different forms. First, redrawing country sizes in proportion to GNP which reduces the continent of Africa to approximately the size of France; Ireland becomes a much smaller island relative to the British mainland and the United States is represented as many times the size of South America. The USSR, too, is much reduced while small countries such as the Netherlands and Belgium together appear equal to Spain.

The lower pie chart depicts percentage shares of gross world product. What should be explained is that the USSR and most of Comecon (or CMEA, Council for Mutual Economic Assistance, as it is also known) are excluded from this pie chart, but not the representation above. What is important to remember is that GNP per capita as a measure of national wealth is an arithmetic mean, which gives a value for national wealth when calculated on per capita basis.

Table 24.2 *Documentation on foreign markets*

1 Basic information

Advertiser's Annual, Thomas Skinner Directories, East Grinstead, Sussex RH 19 1HE.

ASLIB Directory of Information Sources in the UK (ed. E. M. Codlin), 3 Belgrave Square, London SW1X 8PL.

Benn's Press Directory, Tunbridge Wells, Kent.

British Institute of Management, 'Where to find it', Management House, Cottingham Road, Corby, Northants, NN17 1TT, 1986.

British Institute of Management, information sheets provided on a key-word basis.

BSI Buyers' Guide 1988/89 – listing of all British Standards Institute Kitemark and safety mark licences, registered forms and registered stockists, BSI Quarterly Assurance, PO Box, 375, Milton Keynes, MK14 6LL.

Companies Registration Office, Crown Way, Maindy, Cardiff, CF4 3UZ and London Search Rooms, 55 City Road, London EC1Y 1RB. Company records on microfilm. Microfilm index all live companies. Annual report published by HMSO.

Croner's Reference Book for Exporters, Croner Publications, Croner House, London Road, Kingston upon Thames, Surrey, KTZ 6SR, loose-leaf book with monthly supplements.

Croner's Reference Book for Importers. Commonwealth Secretariat, *Commonwealth Organizations: a handbook of official and unofficial organisations active in the Commonwealth*, 2nd edition, 1979.

Department of Trade and Industry, *Register of Quarterly Assessed United Kingdom Companies*, 3rd edition, London 1986.

Directory of British Associations, CBD Research, Beckenham, Kent.

Directory of Directors (pub. T. Skinner, Windsor Court, East Grinstead House, East Grinstead, West Sussex RH19 1XE.

European Directory of Non-official Statistical sources, 1988, Euromonitor Publications Limited, 87–88 Turnmill Street, London EC1M 5QU.

Table 24.2 *cont.*

Europa Yearbook, detailed information on every country in the world and international organizations, Europa Publications Ltd, 12 Bedford Square, London WC1B 3JN.

The Europe 1992 Directory: A research and information guide, ITCU/Coventry Polytechnic, 1989

Hollis Press and Public Relations Annual, Hollis Directories, Lower Hampton Road, Sunbury-on-Thames, Middlesex TW16 5HG.

Key Business Enterprises, The Top 20,000 British Companies, Dun and Bradstreet, 26–32 Clifton Street, London EC2P 2LY.

Kompass Register of British Industry & Commerce, 4 volumes. Windsor Court, East Grinstead House, East Grinstead, West Sussex RH19 1XD.

OECD Economic Surveys, for all member countries, HMSO London.

Sell's Directory of Products & Services, Sell's Publications, Epsom, Surrey KT17 1BQ.

London Chamber of Commerce and Industry, *Chambers of Commerce Worldwide – a selected list: 1989*, 68 Cannon Street, London EC4N 5AB.

Statesman's Yearbook, Macmillan Press, London.

Stock Exchange Official Yearbook, London (pub. T. Skinner, Windsor Court, East Grinstead House, East Grinstead, West Sussex RH19 1XE.

Telephone Directories Inc. *Yellow Pages*.

Trade Associations and Professional Bodies of the UK, ed. p. Millard, Pergamon Press, Oxford.

UN Statistical Yearbook, New York. Also IMF, UNIDO, GAT, UNECE, FAO and other UN organizations publish their own statistics.

Whitaker's Almanac, published by J. Whittaker & Sons, 12 Dyott Street, London WC1A 1DF.

Who Owns Whom, Dun and Bradstreet, London EC2A 4BU.

Willings Press Guide, Thomas Skinner Directories, East Grinstead, Sussex RH19 1HE.

Europages, European Business Directory (annual) 7th edition, Thomson Directories,

296 Farnborough Road, Farnborough, Hampstead, GU14 7NU.

Europe's 15,000 largest companies: 1989, ELC International, Sinclair House, The Avenue, London, W13 8NT.

Major Companies of Europe, *1989–90* Graham and Trotman, Sterling House, 66 Wilton Road, London SW1V 1DE.

2   Bank publications

Lloyds Bank personally judged to be the best overseas series of the main banks but banks with a strong regional or national base should not be overlooked

3   Financial data

ICC Directory of UK Stockbroker Reports

Extel Cards showing balance sheets, profit and loss accounts, dividends and activities, 37–45 Paul Street, London EC2A 4PB.

Annual Company Reports.

Stock Exchange Official Yearbook (as above).

FT (Financial Times) Publications.

EIU (Economist Intelligence Unit) Publications, various country, industry and product reports. 25 St James' Street, London SW1A 1HG.

Times 1000, Times Books, 16 Golden Square, London W1R 4BV, annually.

World Banking Abstracts World Banking Intelligence, Professional Publishing Ltd, 7 Swallow Place, London W1R 8AB.

4   Guides to British statistics

Central Statistical Office, *Guide to Official Statistics*, HMSO, London.

Central Statistical Office, *Government Statistics, a brief guide to sources*, HMSO, London.

Mort D. Siddall S., *Sources of Unofficial UK Statistics*, Gower, 1986.

5   Indexes and abstracts

Anbar. Published in collaboration with the Chartered Institute of Marketing. Five abstracting journals containing one paragraph abstract of articles surveyed. Anbar is a division of MCB University Press, 62 Toller Lane, Bradford, West Yorks.

Table 24.2 *cont.*

Business Periodicals Index, H. W. Wilson Ltd, 950 University Avenue, Bronx NY 10452, USA. American publication chiefly of American publications, some difficult to locate in the UK.

Contents Pages in Management. Monthly publication by Manchester Business School.

Predicasts Inc *F & S Index*, monthly reports on business, economics and industry, 11001 Cedar Avenue, Cleveland, Ohio, 44106 USA.

SCIMP European Index of Management Periodicals, European Business School Librarians Group, Helsinki School of Economics and Business Administration, Runebarginkaty 22–24, 00100 Helsinki, Finland.

Index to Business Reports, Quarry Press, Plantation Road, Harrogate, West Yorkshire, twice yearly.

Marketing Surveys Index (pub. in association with the Chartered Institute of Marketing), Marketing Strategies for Industry (UK) Ltd, Heathcourt House, Parsons Green, London SW6 4TJ.

6 International reports

Business International Corporation produces several regional business newsletters, e.g. Business Asia.

Directory of US and Canadian Marketing Surveys and Services, pub. Kline, Fairfield, New Jersey, USA.

European Company Information: EEC Countries, 3rd edition, London Business School Information Service, 1989.

Euromonitor, Market Research Europe.
Industrial Marketing Research Assoc, *European Guide to Industrial Market Research*, 11 Bird Street, Lichfield, Staffs.

Industrial Marketing Research Association, *European Sources of Industrial Market Research*.

Price Waterhouse – 2 series: *Tax in . . . and . . . Doing business in . . .*

Published data on Middle and Far East, Industrial Aids Ltd, 14 Buckingham Palace Road, London SW1.

US Dept. of Commerce, *Overseas Business Reports* (thanks to an Exchange of Information Act with the US, American foreign market research reports are to be found in the Dept. of Trade and Industry's SMIL. (Statistics and Market Intelligence Library, Victoria Street, London SW1.)

7 Market research survey reports

British Library, *British Reports, Translations and Theses*, monthly, Boston Spa, Wetherby, West Yorkshire.

Business International Corporation (International), 1 Dag Hammarskjold Plaza, New York, NY 10017, USA.

Euromonitor, *Market Research Great Britain*.

JICNARS, *National Readership Survey of UK*.

Top Companies (by local region) Jordan Information Services Ltd, Jordan House, 47 Brunswick Place, London N1 6EE.

Keynote Reports, a range of 220 industry sector reports monthly, UK, some European, Keynote Publications Ltd., Field House, 72 Oldfield Road, Hampton, Middlesex TW12 1BR.

Marketsearch (formerly International Directory of Published Market Research).

MEAL, Media Expenditure Analysis Ltd., 110 St Martin's Lane, London WC2N 4BH.

Mintel: *Market Intelligence*, monthly reports of consumer goods in Britain, Mintel Ltd, Bromley, Kent.

National Economic Development Office, occasional specific industry reports, Millbank, London.

8 Market sector reports

Business Monitor (aggregated sales, production, exports, etc. for specific industrial sectors), Dept. of Trade and Industry, London.

Predicasts, Overview of Markets and Technology (PROMPT) quarterly abstracts, PREDICASTS Inc., 11001 Cedar Avenue, Cleveland, Ohio, USA.

Worldcasts, abstracts of published international forecasts, for all countries, Predicast Inc., 200 University Circle Research Center, 11001 Cedar Avenue, Cleveland, Ohio, USA.

Table 24.2 *cont.*
9 Newspapers' indexes
Financial Times, Research Publishers Ltd, PO
   Box 45, Reading RG1 8HF. Monthly index.
Times Index, Newspaper Archive Develop-
   ments Ltd, Reading RG1 8HF.
Wall Street Journal Index, Dow Jones &
   Company Inc., 200 Liberty Street, New
   York, NY 10281, USA.
Research Index, pub. Business Surveys Ltd,
   PO Box 21, Dorking, Surrey RH4 2YU,
   Fortnightly index of newspapers and pro-
   ducts by keyword – also publish *Reports
   Index*.
McCarthy *Information Services*. Manor
   House, Ash Walk, Warminster, Wilts. BA12
   8PY. Company as well as subject indexes.

10   On-line information retrieval databases
A full listing is available in Angela Hodden,
*Management and Marketing Databases,
1988*, Aslib, London. Also, *On-line Busi-
ness Information*. Monthly. *On-Line Busi-
ness Sourcebook*, from Headland Press
Publications, 1 Henry Smith's Terrace,
Headland, Cleveland, TS24 0PD, Tel. 0429
231902. (Twice a year.)
Popular on-line services include:
Financial Times, *Profile*, Tel: 0932 761444.
   Offers McCarthy Information services as
   well as *Financial Times*.
Pergamon Financial Data Services, Tel. 071
   992 3456. Offers Dun and Bradstreet,
   European Marketing On-Line, Infomat, ICC.
Various on-line services offer on-line PROMT:
   ICC Business Information. Frost and
   Sullivan Market Research Reports includ-
   ing: *Datastar*. Tel. 071-930-5503; *Dialog*.
   Tel. 0101-415-858-3810; *ABI-Inform*. Tel.
   0883-844123.

It does not equate with disposable income actually available to citizens to spend, nor their willingness to spend. In communist countries where wages and prices are politically set, this statistic of per capita GNP offers no useful indicator whatsoever of market potential. For all other countries this statistic is equally meaningless as it offers no guidance as to the dispersion of wealth across the population or the possible identification of important affluent segments across a nation.

Risk

International marketing differs from domestic marketing in that when the company is dealing with its own domestic market, key variables can be taken as known such as:

Political risk;
Economic risk;
Commercial risk;
Taxes and legislation relating to company incorporation.

To a marketer in his/her own country these are background factors which influence the business climate, but in the international context become unknown factors which could assume important proportions particularly when combined with historical cultural and linguistic differences. Table 24.3 summarizes some sample indicators for assessing risks and opportunities.

Political risk

To illustrate this, the Middle East may perhaps popularly be perceived as an area of political uncertainty yet British companies can claim punctual payment for supplies and expropriation has not taken place in recent years. Instead the various oil states (previously only oil producers) have engaged in forward vertical integration to control refining, shipping and to some degree, retail distribution within Europe. On the other hand, a quite different form of political risk emerged in calm politically stable Europe when a socialist government administration under Mitterand started to create widespread uncertainty when it embarked on a nationalization policy.

Elsewhere there may be embargoes on strategic exports as in the case of the CoCom list of prohibited Western exports to the Soviet bloc. Also important in this context, is the use of voluntary import restrictions as applied by Italy and less effectively by Britain on Japanese cars.

The distribution of world GNP

Country shown in proportion to GNP

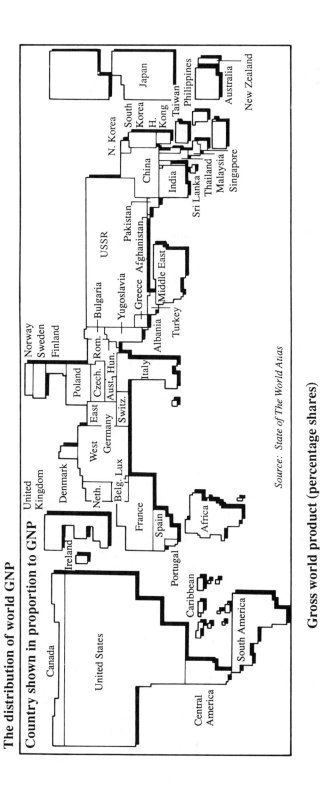

Source: State of The World Atlas

Gross world product (percentage shares)

World GNP does not include USSR and most of Comecon

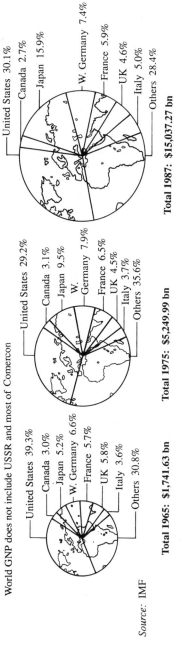

Total 1965: **$1,741.63 bn**

Total 1975: **$5,249.99 bn**

Total 1987: **$15,037.27 bn**

Source: IMF

Figure 24.2 *Distribution of World GNP*

Source: Financial Times, September 26, 1989

Table 24.3 *Sample indicators for assessing risks and opportunities*

Country entry decisions	Type of indicator	Sample indicator
Risks	Political risk	Number of expropriations/nationalizations export ratings of stability
	Economic financial risk	Rate of inflation; Foreign exchange rate; Restrictions on capital flow
	Commercial risk	Acceptability of goods in foreign market; Risks in transportation; Buyer payment; Supplier control
	Legal risk	Import–export restrictions; Restrictions on ownership
Opportunities	Macromarket potential	Growth of GNP, ratio of investments to GNP, population size, density, urbanization, educational level
Modes of entry decisions	Production and marketing costs	Electricity, energy costs, labour skills and costs, management training, capital and technology availability and costs, rates of interest
Product market decision	Product market size	Sales volume of product, ownership of product, sales of complementary and substitute products number, and size of competing firms

Source: Adapted from Susan P. Douglas and C. Samuel Craig, *International Market Research*, Prentice-Hall, 1983, p. 31.

Another quite different form of government intervention is through a countervailing duty. By introducing a countervailing duty, a government increases the selling price of the cheapest imported good to the level of the cheapest domestic competitor by means of a special tax. In this way governments may discriminate against cheap imports and effectively price them out of the market by instantly removing their price competitiveness.

While tariff barriers have continued to fall as a result of the GATT 'rounds', which have taken place among nations approximately every nine years since the end of the Second World War, there has been a corresponding increase in non-tariff barriers often illustrating ingenuity in the pursuit of excluding unwanted imports as when Japan instituted a new national standard for skiing equipment, claiming different skiing characteristics for the Japanese from those prevailing everywhere else.

Economic/financial risk

Similarly, there are economic risks where there are difficulties in repatriating capital due to government exchange controls, high taxation or a rapidly devaluing currency. However, this may be surmounted by resort to devices such as management fees, royalties, repayments on loans and/or interest, leasing, or intracorporate transfers, known also as 'transfer pricing'. As it is entirely the responsibility of the individual company to price final goods, intermediate goods, such as assemblies and components which are being transferred within the company, it provides also an opportunity to move money out of one country into another where levels of taxation may also be lower.

Transfer pricing then may become a political issue when foreign subsidiaries are seen to be exporting but are recording losses. The price at which goods are to be transferred remains at all times a company issue over which the national customs services have no control.

Given a situation where multinational corporations control more than one third of world trade, transfer pricing is viewed by politicians as an ever constant threat to the nation state. To counter this, many large companies such as Exxon take the trouble to publish a code of ethics in which they publish the basis on which they transfer goods between company subsidiaries. Most commonly, this is found to be 'arms length' pricing which means setting a market price as though to an outsider. However, this has not been fully defined.

Other possibilities include 'cost plus' pricing which means including a percentage such as 10 per cent for overheads, including administration. Transfer pricing could therefore provide a means for a company to close down a plant abroad by showing how unprofitable it was by simply sending imports with a high transfer price. Alternatively, a plant in a low labour cost country with a very favourable tax regime could be seen as even more profitable if benefiting from low transfer prices from the parent company organization. Taxation and politics are important factors in this highly sensitive area of operations.

Commercial risk

Commercial risk is:
1 The uncertainty of the ultimate acceptability of the goods to the final consumer. However, even small companies are aware today of prevailing international industrial standards for technical equipment as there are few national markets left. In the pursuit of critical mass and the need for economies of scale in production, domestic markets are rarely large enough to satisfy customers. Consequently, producers have sought every opportunity to standardize their products and make them available to an even larger number of markets.

The British Standards Institution THE (Technical Help for Exporters) scheme was created to provide British manufacturers with information on national product standards worldwide. However, even if manufactured to acceptable national standards, there is still the risk that the goods may yet be found unacceptable to consumers in the target market perhaps because of price, design, lack of state of the art technology, inappropriate brand name or inability to provide the package of benefits including service which customers, particularly in Western developed markets, have come to expect.

2 The risks of transportation, transshipment, pilferage, damage and loss are risks against which the supplier may obtain insurance but increasingly this is only available at a high price and against demands that the exporter gives the insurance company all of his/her export business and not just the risky part of the export portfolio, or alternatively accept perhaps only 30 per cent cover. Insurers are providing less of a service nowadays and are dictating terms pointing to the bad debt provisions of the major clearing banks and state export insurance agencies.

To some degree improved export packing and product packaging have reduced this risk but certain regions of the world are more risky in this sense than others.

3 The ability of the buyer to actually pay for the goods ordered. Again, there has been a mistaken assumption that it is less important to have insurance cover for an importer in North America as opposed to South America. This confuses the solvency of the nation with the solvency of an industrial buyer. Financial status reports on a buyer ought always to be obtained whenever there is a shadow of doubt. Insurance is available to an exporter, but the cost increases with the exposure to risk and so the exporter ought to decide whether to proceed knowing fully the risk and whether he or the buyer is to accept the costs of insurance cover.

4 Control and ownership are further points to consider given that in the most common form of going international, the use of an agent, the question of control usually concerns the conflict of interest where an agent is sharing his/her time over a portfolio of products for which he/she receives differential rates of commission. Control for the supplier must mean direction of the use of the company's name, product, representation and customer service offered.

Ownership may imply but does not mean control

in practice. It usually means only that large scale investment in a sales subsidiary and/or manufacturing plant has taken place and that there will be a payback period before this investment is able to achieve a significant return. More effective control may be achieved by other means which do not involve equity or ownership but may be a form of leverage over the foreign partner exercised via the flow of funds, components, technology knowhow by the Western partner. In longer-term agreements, the search for a continuing form of leveraged control over a foreign partner is difficult (Paliwoda, 1989).

Effect of culture

To understand culture, we have to realize that it is behavioural attitudes which we as members of a society learn and pass on to others. Whereas exporting is about sending products and services blindly into foreign markets for others to distribute, promote and sell to final customers, the intelligent international marketer recognizes the importance of maintaining control over his/her branded products to the point of sale. Culture for the international marketer is seen to operate at three levels:

1 *Habits and conventions*, where we may be able to most effectively change behaviour by influencing potential users possibly by demonstration of a better, more modern, more intelligent way of doing a certain frequently repeated daily task or chore. With habits which rely on automatic responses, if we demonstrate a better way of doing something and that product concept does not ask us to challenge our own beliefs, then we can usually rely on that idea being successfully adopted. For example, electronic calculators have been successfully taken up everywhere. No disquiet has been voiced over the demise of the abacus or sliderule.
2 *Mores* is a Latin word for 'morals' and is taken often to mean the established religion of a particular society and the norms which it observes. Attempts to challenge the established religion in a country will not meet with success. With regard to international advertising, scantily clad women must not appear in advertising

destined for Muslim countries or Muslim parts of countries.

Sometimes, it is not the fundamentalists or adherents who may raise the problem but those who do not practise the religion in question but nevertheless feel a certain unease.

The issue of Sunday opening of shops has yet to be resolved in England, although it has long since been resolved in Scotland with its own established Presbyterian church which in many respects is fundamentalist and less tolerant than the Church of England.

3 *Laws*. There is no such thing as international law, only domestic law which may have extra-territorial reach. This is primarily the case with US law which affects the operations not only of US multinationals but other Western companies represented in the USA as well. The lack of international law means there is a gap to be filled in case of international trading disputes.

In effect, this is often undertaken by the various industrial arbitration councils whose establishment is not formally recognized but whose judgements have always been accepted in subsequent actions in civil courts of law. Where existing law prohibits the sale of a product the only strategy may be to try to have that law rescinded. This means lobbying for a change in legislation or even new legislation to enable this new and proposed product or service to be offered to the buying public. This could range from a variation being required in planning permission to allow out-of-hours shopping centres; Sunday opening of shops; or settle the ethical questions raised by medical science such as in-vitro fertilization of women or human embryo experimentation. As laws reflect a society's attitude towards a certain issue at a given moment in time and society changes there is always scope and argument for legal revision.

In the USA and Britain increasingly now that the EEC is being seen as an effective legislative agency in its own right, lobbying is becoming more intense, while in a corresponding, separate movement markets slowly become more similar. New services, such as satellite television, are not national but international in character and require special legal attention for their effective regulation.

Psychic or psychological distance

This affects both supplier and buyer. For a supplier, knowledge of a market takes away fear and lessens risks both actual and perceived. For marketers, unlike sociologists or social anthropologists, the aim is to identify that which is similar, that which unites people as a common characteristic or feature which is to be found with the same degree of frequency across national boundaries. The more we know of a target market and the degree to which it approximates with our own, the better placed we are to design an acceptable offering.

In numerous studies, newcomers to exporting have been found to export first to those markets which were more like extended domestic markets than foreign markets because of similarities of language, customs and institutions. British exporters for long were able to find the psychological distance between themselves and Australian, Nigerian or Ganaian buyers much less than that existing with French or another continental European buyer. Language, history, institutions, currency and familiar standards of size, weight or volume influence greatly the perceived degree of foreignness. The lack of a previous British Empire within Europe has been at the root of the dismal British effort in the extended European Community of the twelve as it heads towards the single market. This attitude gives rise to the multidomestic approach to international marketing.

Segmentation

Having identified a sufficient number of people who could be at least potential customers of a product, it is necessary to find out more about their market characteristics in terms of personal disposable income and the degree to which this target segment is either dispersed throughout the length and breadth of the country or the degree to which they are found to be concentrated in the main conurbations.

Before proceeding further with considerations on product distribution we have to establish that the product is legal in the country in which it is to be sold and that the resources exist to target the chosen target segment effectively. Some companies

seek to promote their highly standardized product to essentially the same segment, i.e., a buying public with very similar profiles across national boundaries as in the case of the major credit cards such as Diners Club and American Express.

In addition to appealing to the same segment across national boundaries it may also be possible to sell the same products to different segments in foreign markets. However, to do this successfully may require product or communication strategy modifications. Small companies with a niche product may be able to do this as successfully as their multinational counterpart.

Modes of market entry

This ties in with the degree of commitment which the company has to export business generally as well as company policy which may rule out certain types of association, e.g. joint equity ventures abroad or trading with a certain country or political bloc. Beyond that, there is no single 'best' strategy which may be adopted for market entry. There is no correct answer only to say that this must be examined within an exclusive situation context. For each market this may throw up new and exciting but untried alternatives leading an experienced international marketing firm to be able to boast of a portfolio of actual market entry modes currently in operation internationally. Situational 'fit' is the answer. Table 24.4 describes the essential characteristics of the various possible market entry methods. While the choice of market entry mode is wide, the costs of making a mistake may be heavy. Selection is best made against a number of criteria such as the company's estimation of the perceived value of this particular market and their total commitment to it whether short or long term as per Table 24.1.

Corporate competitive response

Traditional marketing theory dictates that it is by adjusting the four Ps for the correct marketing mix that companies are able to communicate effectively with their buying public. This, however, does not take into consideration the marketing environment as this can differ quite markedly; two examples of

Table 24.4 *A possible portfolio of modes of foreign market entry*

Market entry method (alphabetically)	Characteristics
Agents	Paid on commission usually with exclusivity of sales territory but handling more than one company and/or product line
Consortium exporting	Encourages small companies to engage in joint representation in foreign markets. Assisted by government schemes in US and UK to encourage more small companies to participate in exporting
Distributors	Differ in that they take title to the goods. This lessens risk and improves cashflow but weakens control as less is known about the final end-user or price charged
Export houses	Approximately 700–800 of these in UK, accounting for 20 per cent of UK exports. Export house represent a buyer abroad. Trading company buying and selling on own account following a particular Japanese strength
Franchising	High growth of 10 per cent p.a. in UK. Estimated 230 active franchises in UK employing 71,000 people, with total turnover in excess of a billion pounds. Expected to employ 230,000 and have five billion pound turnover in UK by 1990. Transfers the rights to use the company's name, logo and all that may be identifiable with the company. Examples abound in the fast-food industry. May also include a management contract
Freight forwarder	Documentation and delivery service to foreign destination
Joint ventures	Two distinct types: industrial cooperation (contractual) and joint-equity. Contractual is of fixed duration; responsibilities and duties defined. Joint-equity involves investment, no fixed duration, and is continually evolving
Licensing	Often regarded as second-best to exporting. It confers a right to utilise a company-specific process in manufacturing a proprietary product and may also include a management contract and continuing exports of components embodying advanced technology
Management contracts	Transfer know-how and company-specific management control systems, and are widely evidenced in the services sector, e.g. hotel industry, private hospital management
Piggybacking	Originated and still remains strong among one-third of US companies. Uses the distribution channel of another company. Returns achieved by means of commission or outright sale.

Source: S. Paliwoda, *International Marketing*, Heinemann, 1986.

quite different environmental changes follow later. Only the interaction model devised by the IMP Group places emphasis on the importance of the company interfacing within its environment. The marketing mix, reduced to only four Ps, assumes passive markets while the interaction approach accepts that there are dynamic relationships between buyers and sellers involving product and process adjustments, logistical coordination, knowledge about the counterpart, personal confidence and liking, special credit agreements and long-term contracts. Getting established in a new market involves creating a network new to the firm. It has to build relationships new to itself and its counterparts. This may lead to the breaking of old existing relationships sometimes adding a new relationship to an existing one. Initiatives may be taken by either the buyer or the seller. Markets then are only seen as networks of relationships between firms. This environment is not static but dynamic. The internationalization of the firm is affected by the internationalization of its markets (Johanson and Gunnar-Mattsson, 1986).

Figure 24.3 has four cells, each of which depicts a company and its environment at different developmental stages of internationalization:

1   *The early starter* is the company who has few rather unimportant relationships abroad but is no different in this respect from his/her competitors, so this kind of situation is a developmental one which faced Europe at the start of this century.
2   *The lonely international.* The firm is highly internationalized while its market environment is not.
3   *Late starter.* Indirectly involved with foreign markets. This is a specialized company who has to decide either to adapt or to get customers to adapt.
4   *International among others.* Both firm and its environment are highly internationalized.

The marketing mix for international marketing is still the same four Ps of product, price, promotion and place of sale but each P introduces new variables now that it has been transposed from a purely domestic setting to an international marketing environment.

Price

This has a strategic role from export contract pricing to final sale to the ultimate customer.

1   Marginal pricing is tantamount to dumping which can take three forms being sporadic; predatory; or persistent. Each implies a different competitive threat from an aggressive foreign supplier.
2   Countertrade (CT) is a new generic term for barter which has many possible variants. CT incurs costs to the buyer and to the seller, yet is estimated by the US Department of Commerce to account for 30 per cent of world trade (Paliwoda, 1989).
3   Transfer pricing as referred to above.
4   Price harmonization between country markets is impossible to achieve except within fixed bands but when this gap widens it opens up

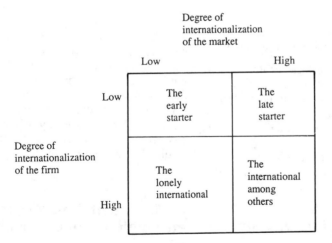

Figure 24.3   *Four cases of international marketing situations*

Source Jan Johanson, L. Gunnar-Mattsson, 'International Marketing and Internationalisation Processes – a network approach' in Peter W. Turnbull, and Stanley J. Paliwoda, *Research in International Marketing*, Croom-Helm, 1986, p. 252.

opportunities for parallel exports and parallel imports whereby domestic wholesalers effectively disrupt a manufacturer's official channels of distribution in a foreign market with exports of goods thought to be for the home market designed to take advantage of a price differential.

This trade is not illegal and is encouraged by the European Community in the interest of free trade. This trade may have been brought about by a particularly favourable foreign rate of exchange, but given the volatility of exchange markets this can change suddenly in the opposite direction.

For the manufacturer concerned who is facing hostile distributors abroad he/she can either take the product off the market at home, increase the price on the home market or do nothing and wait for exchange rates to change against the domestic wholesalers who are exporting.

5   Levels of personal disposable income vary across markets. There are differences in inflation rates, access to personal credit, product prices, specifications and sizes. All this serves to make direct comparisons very difficult.

Product

Market research answers the question as to what sort of product or brand is required in terms of:

1   Branding and the degree of local protection.
2   Patent and trademark issues, and again the degree of protection for these intellectual and industrial property rights.
3   Conflicting pressures to standardize or modify for local markets.
4   Packaging for various export markets.
5   Certification of origin, which allows imports right of access.

Place of sale or channels of distribution to be employed

1   Length of distribution channel may be less a function of economic activity than of history, e.g. the Japanese have the longest distribution channels from producer to consumer.

2   Black markets which illegally distribute illicit or rationed goods at high prices.
3   Grey markets, where the incidence of parallel export/imports referred to above is ever increasing, and threatening manufacturers but still being endorsed by the EC in the name of free trade. This is increasing in pharmaceuticals. (See below for price differentials still existing on certain equipment sold across the European Community.)
4   Freeports account now for more than 9 per cent of world trade. Those freeports of the Pacific Basin which encourage manufacture, assembly and transshipment of goods for export are particularly important. Located mainly within the Third World it is difficult to compete with these freeports on price as their governments have in many cases exempted the freeports not only from taxes and duties, which would otherwise be payable, but also minimum wage controls and health and safety at work legislation which might apply outside of the freeport area. Freeports now exist in all parts of the world but their operating regulations vary widely.

Promotion

There are a number of questions here starting with the degree of similarity with the domestic market and the availability of suitable advertising media: personal selling; sales promotion; direct mail; trade exhibitions; sampling; merchandising displays and public relations. If this proves to be the case then the question arises of the applicability of transferring abroad a successful domestic advertising campaign. A further possibility then exists of the use of cooperative joint advertising with distributors, wholesalers or major retailers.

Environmental market change case 1: the single European market

The true trading potential of the European Community as a single market of 320 million people as opposed to a trading bloc of twelve member states has yet to be realized, hence the moves to create a single market by 1993.

The costs of doing business at present within the European Community appear to be 30 to 45 per cent higher for small firms with less than 250 employees than for larger companies. There presently also appear to be anomalies in the costs of entering the different market states in that importing into Italy bears a cost five times that of importing into Belgium, which is difficult to explain.

The potential significance of such unification or harmonization cannot be overemphasized. The benefits of integration are highly significant, estimated at being worth 4.5–6.5 per cent of the Community's GDP. It involves:

1   The creation of European-wide industrial standards.
2   The opening up of public procurement markets to Community-wide competition.
3   Harmonization of company law and the creation of European law to facilitate joint ventures, mergers and acquisitions.
4   Liberalization of the service sector: air; transport; banking; securities; investment.
5   Freeing of capital movements, access to the money markets and freedom to invest in any EEC country or currency.
6   A community-wide law on intellectual property, covering patents, trademarks and copyright now extended to computer software and services.
7   The approximation of indirect taxes such as value added tax which presently ranges across the member states from 0–37 per cent. Car tax rates vary between 12 per cent in Luxembourg to 200 per cent in Denmark and Greece.
8   Customs formalities were revolutionized in the movement which in Britain was known as 'Customs 88', meaning that on 1 January 1988, Britain implemented the Single Administrative Document (SAD) and new community tariff code known as TARIC. This had the effect of removing 150 different forms across Europe and was a preliminary stage to the abolition of customs frontiers by the end of 1992.

The single market promises economic gains in that:

(a)   It will increase the variety of goods available.

(b)   Encourage price equalization.
(c)   Free trade will allow the relocation of production to areas with lower costs.
(d)   Concentration of the production of each good in fewer locations will bring in currently unexploited economies of scale.
(e)   Competition generates both technical and dynamic efficiency.

The only estimates of the possible benefit in cost savings of the new single market are contained in the Cecchini Report (1988) which was funded by the European Commission and has been criticized for its overoptimistic approach. Cecchini points to the price differential existing within different product categories and refers to them as potential price savings, for example:

Pharmaceuticals	52% (FRG)	40% (UK)
Office equipment	12% (Fr)	27% (It)
Telephone switching	60% (Bel)	40% (Fr)
	70% (FRG)	50% (It, UK)
Telephones	20% (Bel)	43% (Fr);
		39% (FRG)
Coal	50% (FRG)	25% (UK)

Again Cecchini makes his assumptions on the costs of administrative formalities and border controls (1 ECU (European currency unit) is approximately equal to 1 US dollar) reporting estimates such as:

Administration	7500 m ECUs
Delays	415–830 m ECUs
Business foregone	4500–15,000 m ECUs
Government spending on six internal EEC customs controls	500–1000 m ECUs

Aside from the arbitrariness of these figures it also has to be realized that because of the problem of terrorism which is a common problem to all, but particularly UK, France, Germany and Spain, it will not be possible to abolish all frontier controls so the projected figures remain no more than a theoretical saving impossible of being achieved. The company reality of the single market is very real, although here, too, information is scant. The Confederation of British Industry estimates that 50 per cent of European firms trading in 1989 will be out of business by 1995 because of the greater competition resulting from the creation of a single market. The other side of the coin was reported in

Management Today, July 1988 which carried an article on how Ford had created their Ford of Europe structure in 1967 in anticipation of this single market which now capturing so much of our attention. If other multinationals were as equally well prepared, this may then explain dis-interest. However, for the small- to medium-sized company there remains still the reality of nine different official languages; the need for technical and cultural skills; legal and taxation advice; exchange rate strategies; and a knowledge of the administrative practices in each of the countries concerned. These costs have not been calculated by Cecchini or anyone else. The further irony must be that the companies best placed to take advantage of a single market offering ease of access to all internal markets and economies of scale to present-day large producers are the Japanese multinational corporations.

Environmental market change case 2: East European changes and East-West trade

Political change is new

The political risks have lessened in many respects. Post-war communism was Stalinist and adopted a fundamentalist ideological non-market strategy approach. Stalinism created a socialist bureaucracy responsible for all areas of state activity and created the following:

1   Extension of state ownership to all economic activities.
2   A highly centralized command economy.
3   State control over arts, religion etc.
4   Fusion of administrative institutions into one complex: a 'mono-organization' society where ministries were more important than the party.
5   Suppression of consumer demand.
6   A gradual increase in the coercive power of the state.
7   A professional bureaucratic administration.

In the limited reforms effected in the 1960s there was little to do with political reform. Only those current reforms taking place in USSR, Poland and Hungary have been accompanied by political

reform. This has been shown as heavily pragmatic, displaying:

● Commitment to realistic recovery.
● Reform to wages, removing limits to wage differentials.
● Shareholdings by companies and by workers.
● Phasing out of subsidies and payments for what was previously free.
● Facing up to bankruptcy in the case of certain enterprises.
● Facing up to higher levels of unemployment once overmanning has been eliminated.

Export under-performance

40 per cent of CMEA exports go to Western markets but a study by the WIIF Institute in Vienna in 1985 indicated that only seven out of fifty-five major goods exported by CMEA to OECD in 1970–83 maintained, or slightly increased their share attained in export markets. These included fish and metal ores at 0.7 per cent and 0.8 per cent respectively, pulp and paper (a rise from 0.5 to 0.8) petroleum producers from 0.6 to 1.1, electricity from 2.1 to 4.4, fertilizers 4.5 to 6.0 and wood and coke from 1.7 to 1.8. None of these goods has any high-technology components and given the supply-side barriers on the Eastern side they do not represent a substantial basis for East-West trade expansion.

Weak export levels, high debt levels

Eastern Europe in 1986 had 9.2 per cent of world trade, down from 10 per cent in 1963. The USSR had 3 per cent of world trade as against 11.9 per cent for West Germany; 11.6 per cent for USA and 9 per cent for Japan. Through choice, Eastern Europe has persisted in isolating itself from the rest of the world, conducting most of its trade within the member states of the CMEA. In the attached Table 24.5 of indebtedness it has to be stated that Romania has since repaid its total foreign debt but at a high social cost to the domestic economy.

Eastern European changes required

● Improving and motivating a management used to be driven by directives only and given negative

Table 24.5 *East European hard currency debt 1981–87 ($ billion)*

	1981	1982	1983	1984	1985	1986	1987
Bulgaria							
gross	3.16	2.98	2.48	2.17	3.64	5.08	6.00
net	2.35	2.02	1.31	0.74	1.55	3.69	4.60
Czechoslovakia*							
gross	4.60	4.00	3.61	3.14	3.51	4.25	5.30
net	3.53	3.27	2.67	2.13	2.50	3.04	4.00
GDR†							
gross	15.42	13.00	12.19	11.33	13.56	15.76	18.50
net	13.27	11.19	8.80	6.80	7.04	8.31	10.50
Hungary							
gross	8.70	7.95	8.25	8.84	11.75	15.09	17.50
net	7.80	7.22	6.93	7.30	9.47	12.90	15.80
Poland							
gross	25.47	24.70	26.44	26.80	29.70	33.53	37.60
net	24.71	23.73	25.17	25.25	28.11	31.81	35.30
Romania							
gross	10.16	9.77	8.88	7.20	6.63	6.40	5.70
net	9.86	9.47	8.37	6.56	6.27	5.76	4.75
USSR							
gross	26.53	26.74	23.59	22.51	28.47	33.06	38.00
net	18.08	16.71	12.55	11.17	15.40	18.29	24.50

Source: OECD, *Financial Market Trend*, 1988.
* Now CSFR, Czech and Slovak Federated Republic.
† Merged with West Germany, October 1990 but inter-German credits from West Germany have always made it difficult to assess exactly the extent of GDR indebtedness.

disincentives to perform such a criminal offence of 'mismanagement' which was misuse of state funds, a charge applied for trying to exceed stated published targets and failing in the process.
- More flexible organizational response to market needs and costs.
- Understanding the consumer.
- Introducing quality into production.
- Improving distribution systems.
- Understanding how to compete with competition.
- Becoming acquainted with the use of interest on borrowed capital.
- Seeking higher value-added from exports by means of quality and branding which should allow for higher margins on units sold.
- Improving packaging.
- Improving availablity of finance for industry.

Eastern Europe and the West

Changes are welcome as they make Eastern Society more open – an effect of 'Glasnost'. Yet in this new restructuring known as 'perestroika', although democratic institutions have been introduced, the means of doing business changes little. The possibilities for doing business are multiplied, new forms now exist such as allowing General Electric of the USA to buy out Tungsram Electric Light Bulb Factory of Hungary. The foreign trade administration continues, although with some devolution of power to the enterprise level but with a significant shortage of staff to man all the possible openings now being created by the enterprises. The result is that opportunities for trade and investment increase at a time when Western goodwill runs high but little changes with regard to the time that it takes to do business so the delays will continue to remain and the costs of doing business remain high.

Conclusion

International marketing is not to be seen as an esoteric interest. It is increasingly becoming a vital commercial activity for companies of all sizes. With increasing moves towards political and commercial harmonization worldwide, the potential market that a company can reach correspondingly increases. Small companies in high-technology sectors of industry have increasingly to turn not to the domestic market but to international or even global markets for their specialized products.

International marketing is different from marketing simply within one's own domestic economy. Variables which can be assessed in the domestic context, for example political change, inflation, pending product legislation etc., are unknown when one starts to consider the international marketing arena.

Markets are not passive but active even if you happen to treat your domestic market as passive. Do not assume that your standard marketing mix will work, the examples of truly global products are few. Coca-Cola and Pepsi-Cola are seen as the archetypal global products which satisfy a global need, i.e., thirst. There is also the IBM PC personal computer which satisfies a global need for information technology yet beyond these examples it becomes difficult to identify many more.

1 *Markets are changing.* Demographically, West Germany is becoming older while economically it remains affluent. This gives rise to new opportunities perhaps marketing leisure to the middle-aged and senior citizens within that society. Again, politically, the unification of East and West Germany creates the largest single market in Europe. Again, looking at a psychographic segmentation, there are many new product opportunities. Coca-Cola and Pepsi-Cola have left behind the days when they were simply one-product companies. Responding to societal changes, new products have included diet, low calorie, sugar-free, caffeine free and other additional non-traditional flavours as well.

Elsewhere, environmental concern has given rise to new product formulations for detergents and cleaning materials; new packaging requirements avoiding the use of chlorofluorocarbons (CFCs) as an aerosol propellant: maximizing the use of recycled materials in paper and card: and emphasizing the degradability of plastics used in carrier bags or disposable nappies which might otherwise have been around for another 500 years.

2 *Techniques are changing.* Money has not gone out of fashion and never will, but there are a number of markets where there is consumer potential but a shortage of convertible currency. Financial innovation is therefore required unless you are prepared to walk away from a sale. This has given rise to countertrade in all of its many forms basically allowing for partial payment in goods as well as convertible currency. Concurrent with this increase in countertrade has been the internationalization of product standards adding to slow economic growth and high interest rates as further incentives to internationalize. The acceptance of common product standards can only fuel further global competition.

As global competition increases, certain countries and regions may be expected to increase their market share. Given the return to free market forces of the previously centrally-planned economies of Eastern Europe and the USSR we can expect to see them acquire a more realistic share of world trade, more in keeping with their economic and industrial potential.

Conditions are therefore going to become tougher. Success, though, will come from well-directed effort, based on finding out as much as possible in advance of market entry about the target market in question. Advice to the executive is to read, look and, listen.

Internationalization is the means by which companies will exist in the future. The single European market allows manufacturers in eleven other countries to manufacture to standards which are accepted in your country. To exist in this new competitive environment will require an attitude forged of a realization of this new reality. The gains of a new enlarged domestic market are immense but so too are the risks. The CBI prediction is that half of the companies presently trading will not exist by 1995 because of failure, merger or acquisition.

Be proactive rather than reactive. Constant monitoring of company success as opposed to effort expended may rightfully question the use of resource allocation. Market entry is not a 'once-only' decision but requires constant monitoring and evaluation.

References

Cecchini, Paolo, *1992: The European Challenge*, Wild-wood House, 1988.

Johanson, Jan, Gunnar-Mattsson, L., 'International Marketing and Internationalisation Processes – A Network Approach', in Turnbull, Peter W., Paliwoda, Stanley J., *Research in International Marketing*, Croom-Helm, 1986.

Paliwoda, Stanley J., 'Countertrade' in Thomas, Michael J., *The Marketing Handbook*, Gower, 1989.

Paliwoda, Stanley J., Liebrenz, Marilyn, 'Expectations and Results of Commercial Joint Ventures by US and UK MNCs in Eastern Europe', *European Journal of Marketing*, vol. 18, no. 3, 19xx, pp. 51–66.

Porter, Michael E., *Competition in Global Industries*, Harvard Business School Press, pp. 3–6.

25
Marketing services

DONALD W. COWELL

Introduction

Britain is a service economy. That is, in terms of employment, more people now work in the service sector than in all other sectors of the economy. Also, in terms of output, the major contributor to national output is the service sector (public and private). In export trade, too, Britain's service earnings from abroad, labelled 'invisibles', make a significant contribution to international transactions.

The service sector in Britain is large and varied. The government, for example, is a major provider of services. They range across legal, educational, health, military, employment, credit, communications, transportation and information services. Many are provided on a non-profit basis but others may operate for profit. The private non-profit sector with art and music groups, leisure facilities, charities, churches, foundations and colleges is also part of the service economy. So, too, are the business and professional services provided by airlines, banks, hotels, insurance companies, management consultants, solicitors, architects, advertising agencies and marketing research companies.

Underlying this varied range of service sector activities there is a problem of defining what is a service. There is no single, universally accepted definition of the term. In marketing there is still much debate about what services are and whether the distinctions between goods and services are of significance.

Coupled with the definitional problem of what is a service is the evidence on the status of marketing practice in many parts of the service sector is patchy and fragmentary. It is impossible to generalize across such a large sector and range of situations whether organizations generally considered to be part of it have or have not embraced the marketing concept. There are clearly many service organizations that are highly market orientated like some well-known retail, transport hire, cleaning and hotel groups. Equally there are many organizations in the service sector that have only begun to adopt marketing ideas and practices in recent years, like professional and financial services, and have some way to go yet along the road to a true market orientation. What it is possible to generalize about, however, is:

1   That many managers operating in various kinds of service organizations have shown great interest in the relevance and applicability of marketing ideas to their particular fields.

2   That as competition intensifies in many parts of the service sector; as managers with marketing experience from outside the service sector switch jobs into it; as attempts are made by many hard pressed service organizations to maintain and

improve quality under resource constraints; as ethical and legal barriers are eroded; as these and other influences take effect, they will encourage the extension of marketing ideas and practices much more in the service sector.

Approaches to defining services

Marketing scholars have taken a number of different approaches to clarify what are services. Some of these approaches are:

1 Definitions of services.
2 Characteristics of services.
3 Functional differences.
4 Classifications of services.

Definitions of services

The American Marketing Association definition of services describes them as 'activities, benefits or satisfactions which are offered for sale or are provided in connection with the sale of goods'. This definition has been used for a number of years though its chief weakness is that it does not discriminate sufficiently between goods and services. Goods, too, are presumably offered for sale because they provide 'benefits' and 'satisfactions'.

Various refinements have been suggested. Thus Kotler (1982) defines a service as:

> . . . any activity or benefit that one party can offer to another that is essentially intangible and does not result in the ownership of anything. Its production may or may not be tied to a physical product.

What many of the current definitions share in common is their emphasis, directly or indirectly, upon the essentially intangible nature of a service. This quality of intangibility is central to another approach to service definition which focuses on their distinctive characteristics.

Characteristics of services

A number of characteristics have been proposed to help distinguish goods and services. The more commonly used ones are:

1 Intangibility.
2 Inseparability.
3 Heterogeneity.
4 Perishability.
5 Ownership.

Intangibility

Services are essentially intangible. It is often not possible to taste, feel, see, hear or smell services before they are purchased. Opinions and attitudes may be sought beforehand, a repeat purchase may rely upon previous experience, the customer may be given something tangible to represent the service, but ultimately the purchase of a service is the purchase of something intangible.

Refinements of the notion of intangibility have been suggested by Wilson (1972), Bateson (1977), Rathmell (1966) and others. These largely suggest that the goods–service continuum can be represented as a tangible–intangible dominant continuum. Illustrated in the work of Shostack (1977),

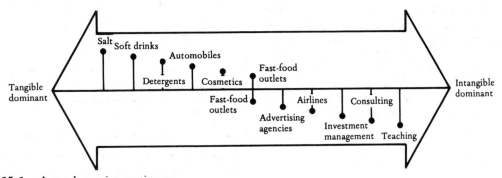

Figure 25.1 *A goods-service continuum*
Source: G.L. Shostack, 'Breaking Free from Product Marketing', *Journal of Marketing*, vol. 41, no. 2, April 1977, p. 77.

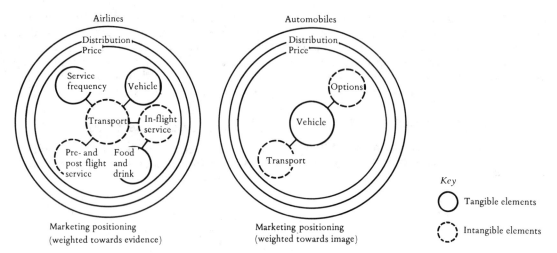

Figure 25.2 *The molecular model*
Source: G.L. Shostack, *ibid.*, p. 76.

the continuum idea emphasizes that most 'products' are combinations of elements or attributes which are linked and which consist of tangibles and intangibles. There are few 'pure' products and 'pure' services. See Figure 25.1.

Shostack suggests that marketing 'entities' are combinations of discrete elements, tangible and intangible. Her molecular model provides a way of visualizing and of managing a total market entity. It can show the elements making up a product, the interrelationships between them and the dominance of goods or services, tangibles or intangibles in an offer. Figure 25.2 is a simplified example to demonstrate her notion of a product entity.

Here airlines and motor cars are divided according to some of their major attributes. The two products have different nuclei and they also differ in dominance. Airlines are more intangible dominant – there is no ownership of a tangible good. Airline travel cannot be physically possessed, only experienced. The inherent benefit is a service. On the other hand a car is more tangible dominant. A car can be physically possessed, though the benefit it yields is a service too.

Inseparability

Services often cannot be separated from the person of the seller. A corollary of this is that creating or

performing the service may occur at the same time as full or partial consumption of it. Goods are usually purchased, sold and consumed whereas services are usually sold and then produced and consumed. The inseparability of the creation and the performance of certain kinds of services applies particularly to some personal services (for example, dental or medical treatment; professional services). Figure 25.3 shows the relationship between production, marketing and consumption for goods and services.

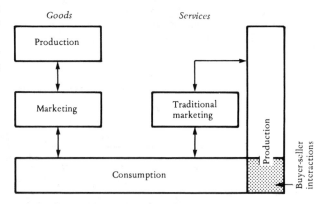

Figure 25.3 *The relationship between production, marketing and consumption*
Source: J.M. Rathmell, *Marketing in the Service Sector*, Winthrop, 1974, p. 7.

Table 25.1 *Some constraints on the management of services and ways of overcoming them*

Characteristics of service	Some implications	Some means of overcoming characteristics
Intangibility	Sampling difficult. Places strain on promotional element of marketing mix. No patents possible. Difficult to judge price and quality in advance.	Focus on benefits. Increase tangibility of service (e.g. physical representations of it). Use brand names. Use personalities to personalize service. Develop reputation.
Inseparability	Requires presence of producer. Direct sale. Limited scale of operations.	Learn to work in larger groups. Work faster. Train more competent service providers.
Heterogeneity	Standard depends upon who and when provided. Difficult to assure quality.	Careful personnel selection and training. Ensure standards are monitored. Pre-package service. Mechanise and industrialize for quality control. Emphasize bespoke features.
Perishability	Cannot be stored. Problems with demand fluctuation.	Better match between supply and demand (e.g. price reductions off peak).
Ownership	Customer has access to but not ownership of activity or facility.	Stress advantages of non-ownership (e.g. easier payment systems).

Heterogeneity

It is often difficult to achieve standardization in the output of certain services. The standard of a service in terms of its conformity to what may be prescribed by the seller may depend on who provides the service or when it is provided. So even though standard systems may be used to handle a flight reservation, book in a car for service or quote for life insurance, each 'unit' of service may differ from other 'units'. Franchise operations attempt to ensure standards of conformity but ultimately with services it is difficult to ensure the same level of quality of output as it may be with goods. From the customer's viewpoint too, it is often difficult to judge quality in advance of purchase.

Perishability

Services are perishable and cannot be stored. Spare seats on a package tour or an empty hotel room represent capacity lost forever if they are not 'consumed' when they are available at any point in time. In addition considerable fluctuating demand patterns may apply to some services which aggravate this perishability feature further. Key marketing decisions in service organizations relate to what service levels they will provide and how they will respond in times of low and excessive usage (for example through differential pricing; special promotions).

Ownership

Lack of ownership is a basic difference between a service and a good. With a service a customer may only have access to or use of a facility (for example hotel room). Payment is usually for the use of, access to or hire of items.

With the sale of a good, barring restrictions imposed by, say, a hire purchase scheme, the buyer has full use of the product.

A summary of these characteristics of services is shown in Table 25.1. Also shown are some implications of these characteristics and suggested means of overcoming the problems posed.

There is, though, still some difference of opinion on whether some of these characteristics do help

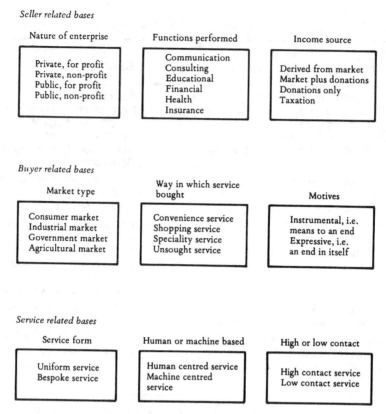

Figure 25.4 *Some current ways of classifying services*

to discriminate between goods and services. For example, Wyckham *et al.* (1975) provide cogent arguments why intangibility, heterogeneity and perishability at least are not of themselves sufficiently discriminating characteristics. They believe there are too many exceptions to their use for services alone and believe that what is required is not a simple product/service scheme differentiating on the basis of the characteristics of the offer itself but a more complex taxonomy of offerings which differentiates on the basis of product/service characteristics and market characteristics. Their criticism is valid for another approach used to define services, that based on functional diferences.

Functional differences

This approach contrasts services marketing with goods marketing. Typical generalizations made about services marketing are that:

- Services cannot be stocked.
- Services cannot be patented.
- Service channels are usually short.
- Services cannot be sampled.
- Services standards cannot be precise.

The difficulty with this approach is that some of the functional features do not apply to all services (however defined). Like the characteristics of services approach a number of exceptions to the general principles exist.

Classifications of services

The elusiveness of a widely accepted definition of services has not prevented the development of a variety of schemes which classify services. Many of the classification schemes used in services marketing are derived from those used in goods marketing. Also many services classification schemes are based on assumptions about what is or is not a service. Some common ways of classifying services are shown in Figure 25.4.

Seller related bases of classification include whether the enterprise is private or public; profit motivated or non-profit motivated. The functions the enterprise performs may also be a basis for classification as may how income is derived. Buyer related bases of classification include market typologies, ways the service is bought and motives for purchase. Service related bases of classification include the form of service provided, whether based on people or equipment use and the levels of personal contact involved.

Obviously there is no one classification which applies in all cases for a particular service. Thus, for example, a hotel may serve different markets (for example consumer and industrial) may offer highly personal as well as highly standardized services and consumer motives for purchase and use may be varied.

The benefits of classification schemes are that they act as a first step in obtaining an understanding of the ways in which markets operate. Certainly when undertaken from a consumer viewpoint, valuable insights may be gained into consumers' reasons for making a purchase and the ways in which products are bought. This kind of information is in turn helpful in developing marketing strategies for services and in evaluating current strategies and tactics in use.

What all the above schemes reflect, however, is the attempt which has been made to delimit the boundaries of services marketing as a separately identifiable field for marketing theory and practice. It is only in recent years that much attention has been given to marketing services as a separate and distinctive area. To date it would seem to be erroneous to suggest that marketing services is somehow fundamentally different from marketing products. As Levitt (1972) suggested:

> . . . there is no such thing as service industries. There are only industries where service components are greater or less than those of other industries. Everybody is in service.

This goes to the heart of the matter. From a marketing viewpoint both goods and services provide benefits and satisfactions: both goods and services are products. The same principles and concepts of marketing are of relevance to both fields. As Baker (1976) says:

> . . . the same sequence of market research, product/ service planning and development, pricing, promotion, distribution, sale and after-sales service would seem to be equally appropriate to all marketing situations.

What is significant about services, where they are the objects being marketed, is the relative dominance of intangible attributes in the make up of the service product. Services are a special kind of product. So the differences are not fundamental, they are classificatory and no one classification suits all ends. What differences there are, are differences of degree and of emphasis. Just as there are differences of degree and of emphasis between consumer marketing and marketing to organizations. What is required in service marketing is more attention to the adaptations which may be required to general marketing principles and practices when core products being marketed are essentially intangible rather than tangible. Examples of some areas of marketing where adaptations for services may be required and where further work is necessary are given in the rest of this chapter. They are intended to be illustrative rather than comprehensive.

Marketing strategy and services

It has been suggested by Thomas (1978) that the strategic management of a service business is different from a non-service business and that marketing strategy planning and marketing strategies themselves are different for service organizations. Of course any particular marketing strategy is unique anyway because it is specific to a particular organization whether marketing services or not. Having said that marketing strategies of service businesses may contain significant differences to those of other organizations. Some of these differences, for example, may arise in the analytical stages which precede the development of a marketing strategy. Examples of these are when service managers pose questions like:

- Who are our customers and how do they discriminate between organizations?
- How do we defend our business from competitors?
- How do we develop more cost-effective operations?
- How does marketing strategy influence other areas of the business?

Who are our customers and how do they discriminate between organizations?

An important step in strategy development is the identification of target markets, understanding the needs of customers and the bases they use in the choices they make. Clearly these problems are common to all market orientated organizations. Service organizations' problems though may often be different. For example, there are many theoretical models of consumer behaviour but few of these models are adequate to explain the basis of consumer decision making and choice for services, though some important insights have been given for specific kinds of services. For example, the purchaser of a professional service buys the capabilities of the seller and he/she can be expected to evaluate the behaviour and characteristics of the manager of the service firm or its representative when making a purchase decision. The purchaser will also evaluate the firm itself, its location, reputation and appearance (Wilson, 1972). But service marketers as yet have an incomplete understanding of this complex and under-researched area. Limited evidence so far available does suggest:

1 That consumers do seem able to perceive differences between goods and services across many dimensions proposed in the service marketing literature (for example intangibility).
2 That consumers do seem able to distinguish between different kinds of services when applying a range of factors to those services in making choices between them (for example customers control over the situation; total time required) (Langeard et al., 1981).

But further work is required in the area to contribute greater insight into service marketing strategy formulation.

How do we defend our business from competitors?

Every business organization has to consider how to enter a market and then build and protect its competitive position. There are a number of ways in which such distinctive positions can be developed and maintained. They are, however, often more difficult to accomplish in service businesses because of the absence of a strong tangible core to the service offer. Witness, for example, the range of strategies adopted by UK building societies at the beginning of 1987 with the greater freedom given to them as a result of changes in the law regulating their activities. The absence of a strong tangible core to a service offer and the greater ease of copying service ideas can lead to more corporate 'me-tooism' in service strategies. This poses substantial problems in both differentiating one service business from another and in building barriers to competitive action.

How do we develop more cost-effective operations?

Many labour intensive service operations have tried to improve their efficiency by substituting capital for labour. This kind of solution to service operating cost escalation and more effective service delivery can only be effective in certain situations. It is inappropriate in those service organizations where the human element of service is central to what is provided. The strategic challenges in such situations are different from those faced by producers of more tangible outputs. There may also be limitations on the practical scale of operations where a particular individual or group of people are essential to service provision as is the case with many people-based services and where economies of scale may not be possible.

How does marketing strategy influence other areas of the business?

In service businesses marketing strategies, production strategies and personnel strategies cannot be separated from each other. The trade-offs between decisions made in the different parts of the organization and their interactive effects are crucial. For example, attempts to improve production efficiency using equipment in place of people may have harmful effects upon marketing efficiency. Customers may interpret such changes with the consequent decrease in the amount of personal service given, as a reflection of a general decline in service standards. The effects though may go deeper. Customers may interpret the changes as changes in the nature of the service itself. They may re-assess the extent to which the service now meets their needs. So functional strategies in service organizations, including marketing strategies, are often more closely enmeshed than in other kinds of business.

The marketing mix and services

Adaptation of marketing principles for services may also be required in the formulation of the marketing mix.

An essential element of any marketing strategy is the marketing mix. The process of mix formulation and balancing is unique to each organization and product. As in marketing planning there is nothing distinctive about the process, as such, for services. Where there does appear to be a difference though is in the elements that make up the marketing mix. The utility of the marketing mix framework for service businesses has been subjected to criticism in recent years by a number of writers on service businesses (Booms and Bitner, 1981).

For example, one marketing mix element of great importance in many service marketing situations is 'people'. Neil Borden (1965) accommodated people in his original idea of the marketing mix (which also incidentally was based upon research in manufacturing organizations). However such people were part of the personal selling element of the mix. What was not included were:

1   People who perform production or operational roles in service organizations (for example bank clerks, steakhouse cooks) who from the customer's viewpoint are a visible and important component of any service received. A critical feature of any service organization – which

market orientated service business already recognize – is that operations staff occupy the dual role of both performing or producing a service and selling a service. In service organizations the distinction between service delivery and service selling is blurred. All functions visible (and sometimes invisible) to the customer are part of the service offering. In that sense marketing management has to be involved in the operational aspects of performance and in influencing and controlling certain dimensions of the relationship between customers and staff; something more indeed than are currently and fashionably labelled 'customer care programmes'.

2   An associated aspect is the relationship between customers. That is a customer's perception of the quality of a service product may be formed and influenced by other customers. Thus marketing managers are often concerned in service businesses with 'quality controlling' and 'engineering' the nature of the interactions between customers and in managing such relationships (for example, the composition of a group on a tour; the seating arrangements at a dinner; queuing systems in a restaurant).

Human beings play a key role in the production and marketing of many services and certainly to a much greater extent than is suggested by the conventional marketing mix concept. The kinds of people employed in customer contact roles by service businesses will be influenced by whether the business involves high or low levels of contact (i.e. the extent of customer contact involved in the creation of a service) and the discretion implicit in such customer contact roles. This means that service businesses may have to focus attention on a wider range of 'people issues' than other businesses which have clear impacts upon marketing effectiveness and efficiency. For example, the kinds of people employed by one service business may be different to those employed by another service business operating in the same market (for example food retailing) because of the differing marketing strategies being pursued. In a service business where operational personnel are expected to exercise relatively low levels of discretion and initiative in undertaking their jobs and to accord with prescribed practices and rules, then service businesses are likely to operate highly prescriptive practices with regard to:

1 Selection and training.
2 Internal marketing (i.e. marketing the service to employees as well as to customers).
3 Ensuring conformity of behaviour.
4 Emphasizing the importance of consistent appearance (e.g. formal uniforms and standards of dress).
5 Mechanising certain aspects of service performance where possible and acceptable to the marketplace.
6 Auditing personnel performance to ensure standards set are being maintained.

Other elements of the marketing mix may require different levels of attention in service industries (for example atmosphere and image) than in other kinds of industries.

Consumer behaviour and services

A major gap in our knowledge of marketing services is in the field of consumer behaviour. Most texts on marketing deal, at some stage, with the topic of consumer behaviour. It is central to the marketing concept that they should do so for an understanding of what factors influence choice and how consumers behave is clearly of vital importance to marketing success. However, two factors are important about the status of knowledge of consumer behaviour for marketers in service organizations.

1 No model of consumer behaviour has yet provided anything other than a partial explanation of consumer behaviour. The mechanisms implicit in the various models available are not wholly understood.
2 Few models focus explicitly on the behaviour of customers for services rather than for goods.

There is therefore growing interest in and an urgent need to develop models of consumer behaviour which are explicitly based upon service choice and evaluation. Such models should incorporate two elements not contained in most conventional models of consumer behaviour. These are:

1 Incorporation of the consumer's role as a party in the production of services – or at least in some elements of them – as well as a consumer of services.
2 Incorporation of the relationships and interactions between customers during the service performance and consumption process and not just in the pre-consumption or post-consumption stages of purchase or use.

What is different about many services is that customers are active in producing services (for example, self-service; performing tasks for the producer) and in influencing the quality of the service production and consumption experience of other service customers. More systematic, empirical work is required to further our understanding of these dimensions of consumer behaviour before satisfactory models are available for many service contexts.

Another neglected area for attention is the linkage between marketing and other functions. An example of this is the linkage with operations management.

Operations management and services

In service marketing cooperation between marketing management and operations management is vital. Indeed the two functions are often inextricably intertwined. This is because a significant component of any service product from the customer's point of view is how the process of service delivery functions. Customers of service organizations obtain benefits and satisfactions from the services themselves and from how these services are delivered. The way in which service systems operate then is crucial. Service systems which operate efficiently and effectively can give marketing management considerable marketing leverage and promotional advantage. A smooth running service process offers competitive advantages particularly where differentiation between service systems is minimal. Those service systems which make it easier for a customer to leave and collect a car for service; to hire industrial plant; which ensure prompt and efficient service in a restaurant; which allow customers to book a hairdressing or dental appointment or book a holiday with minimal effort; all will have advantages over competitive systems which do not run on time, impose excessive demands upon customers, break down while operating or simply do not deliver what they promise. Ensuring that service systems work efficiently and effectively is traditionally an operations management task. In services marketing, however, operations management is too important to be left to operations managers. Marketers must be just as involved with the operational aspects of service performance as operations managers; that is with the 'how' and the 'process' of service delivery. Thus how well the overall system works; its procedures and policies; customer involvement in the process; the degree of standardization in the system; the capacity of the system to cope with workload fluctuations; these are marketing concerns as well as operations concerns.

Operations management specialists have begun to give greater attention to service systems in recent years and to how their skills and experience can be transferred to service systems (Sasser *et al.*, 1981). This is welcome as clear marketing benefits accrue from efficient and effective service processes.

Conclusion

There is now common agreement that the broad principles of marketing are applicable to marketing services and products. There is less agreement about how readily broad marketing principles are of value in specific service contexts. Nevertheless marketing ideas and practices are being more widely used and are likely to be more intensively used in the future (for example, in financial services).

The field of marketing services though is still in its growth phase. It offers great scope for further academic research and innovative marketing practice. This chapter has touched briefly on just four areas where further development is possible, i.e., marketing strategy and services; the marketing mix and services; consumer behaviour and services, and operations management and services.

Two factors should guide academics and practitioners as they attempt to extend knowledge of and apply broad marketing principles to services. First, care should be taken before making generalizations about marketing in all service situations based upon evidence drawn from particular service situations and in assuming that marketing tools and techniques are equally applicable across all services The sheer size of the service sector and the problems of defining what is a service anyway – touched on earlier in this chapter – demand that caution is exercised when generalizations are made. Second, the key to the successful marketing of services is people. Most services are provided by people (they may be performed by equipment) but all services are provided for people. It is vital then that service organizations extend their understanding of their customers and consumers, why they behave as they do and how they make their decisions and choices. The centrality of the customer reminds us that in one sense marketing services is no different to any other kind of marketing.

References

Baker, M. J. (ed.), *Marketing: Theory and Practice*, Macmillan, 1976.

Bateson, J., 'Do we need service marketing?' *Marketing Consumer Services: New Insights*, report no. 75–115, Marketing Science Institute, 1977.

Booms, B. H. and Bitner, M. J., 'Marketing strategies and organization structures for service firms' in J. Donnelly and W. R. George (ed.), *Marketing of Services*, American Marketing Association, 1981, pp. 47–51.

Borden, N. H., 'The concept of the marketing mix' in G. Schwartz, *Science in Marketing*, J. Wiley & Sons, 1965, pp. 386–97.

Buffa, E.S., *Elements of Production/Operations Management*, J. Wiley & Sons, 1981.

Gronroos, C., 'A Service Orientated Approach to Marketing of Services', *European Journal of Marketing*, vol. 12, no. 8, 1978, p. 589.

Kotler, P., *Principles of Marketing*, Prentice-Hall, 1982, p. 624.

Langeard, E., Bateson, J. E. G., Lovelock, C. H. and Eiglier, P., *Service Marketing: New Insights from Consumers and Managers*, report no. 81–104, Marketing Science Institute, August 1981.

Levitt, T., 'Production line approach to service', *Harvard Business Review*, September-October 1972, pp. 41–52.

Rathmell, J. M., 'What is meant by services?', *Journal of Marketing*, vol. 30, no. 4, October 1966, pp. 32–6.

Sasser, W. E., Olsen, R. P. and Wyckoff, D. D., *Management of Service Operations*, Allyn and Bacon, Boston, Mass. 1978.

Shostack, G. Lynn., 'Breaking free from product market-
ing', *Journal of Marketing*, vol. 41, no. 2, April 1977,
pp. 73–80.
Stanton, W. J., *Fundamentals of Marketing*, McGraw-
Hill, 1981, p. 441.
Thomas, D. R. E., 'Strategy is different in service
businesses', *Harvard Business Review*, July-August
1978, pp. 158–65.
Wilson, A., *The Marketing of Professional Services*,
McGraw-Hill, 1972.
Wyckham, R. G., Fitzroy, P. T. and Mandry, S. D.,
'Marketing of Services', *European Journal of Marketing*,
vol. 9, no. 1, 1975, pp. 59–67.

26
Marketing for small businesses

TOM CANNON

Introduction

Changing attitudes to small firms

The last twenty years has seen a change in attitudes to small business and entrepreneurship among policy makers and managers. As recently as 1965 the UK government's White Paper setting up the Industrial Reorganization Corporation argued that:

> The need for more concentration and rationalization to promote the greater efficiency and international competitiveness of British industry . . . is now widely recognized.

Twenty years later the White Paper 'Lifting The Burden' asserted that:

> It is the growth of enterprise . . . that is the real driving force of the economy . . . it is the small and new businesses which are precisely those we need to encourage.

This shift in views goes far beyond the rhetoric of politics. It reflects:

- An increased emphasis on economics 'as if people mattered' with the human dimension to decisions and policies coming to the fore.
- A stress on those aspects of commercial activity notably innovation and communication in which

the advantages of scale might be outweighed by the strengths of smaller enterprises.
- An acknowledgement of the continuing importance of the sector in terms of number of enterprises, job creation and proportion of the GNP.

Both the emphasis on people and the stress on innovation and communication are central to modern marketing thinking.

The classical definitions of marketing place enormous emphasis on the human side to decision making in terms of both the supplier and the buyer. The amendments to the definition (Baker, 1985) below indicate the degree to which this aspect of marketing is central to thinking:

> We are claiming that marketing is concerned with the establishment of mutually satisfying exchange relationships (between people) in which the judgements (by people) of what is satisfying depend upon the perception of the parties to the exchange.

At the same time much marketing practice revolves around innovative responses to changing internal and external forces. In 1986 the 'State of Small-Business' report by the US President noted that:

> Small businesses contribute a disproportionately greater share of product innovations and bring these products to market faster than large businesses.

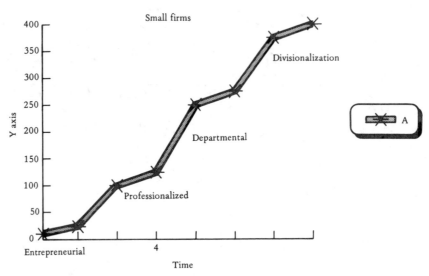

Figure 26.1   *Stages of development of firms*

The combination of these circumstances would suggest that the emphasis on enterprise and small business would be reflected in an extensive and relevant literature on marketing and the small firm. This is not the case, Davis *et al.* (1985) found that there was not a single article in the *Journal of Marketing* specifically addressing the theme of marketing and firm size. The literature which exists is largely descriptive or pedagogical. Only recently has there been a move to more analytical and research related material.

There are several possible explanations for this apparent neglect. Perhaps the most likely is that the dramatic growth in interest in marketing itself has forced researchers to make choices which have tended to focus their attention on the more researchable or accessible areas of the subject. The large and heterogeneous small firm sector does not easily fit that description. At the same time, small firm activity tends to be concentrated in those sectors of commerce which have been relatively low down the research agenda. These include industrial markets, services and retailing. A potentially more satisfying explanation for this seeming neglect lies in the argument that there is no significant difference in marketing for enterprises of different sizes. This approach suggests that the main propositions underlying work in this area remain true, with some relatively minor adjustments of the kind that

would be true in any changing context. This notion of the *universality* of marketing has much to commend it especially when the concept is stripped down to its essential core of customer and need orientation. The difficulties emerge when issues of implementation or management are raised.

Generally, there are two types of question introduced when this topic is raised. There are conceptual problems in wedding aspects of the behaviour of entrepreneurial firm to the demands of marketing management. These revolve around the nature of the entrepreneur and his/her enterprise. Most accepted models of entrepreneurial behaviour emphasize the notion of the proprietor as a generalist whose strength lies in the ability to integrate the different aspects of his/her businesses activities. This poses some difficulties to the notion of marketing management as an increasingly professionalized pursuit. Many models of corporate evolution place the entrepreneurial phase prior to the professionalized. See Figure 26.1.

A related problem exists in the examination of time horizons and planning processes. Much of the research undertaken into small firms suggests that proprietors operate to very short-term horizons (Chell, 1985). Speed and responsiveness is sometime seen as the key strength of the smaller firm (Cannon, 1985). But, a great deal of marketing thinking places considerable emphasis on long-term perspectives and strategic vision (Weitz and Wensley, 1985):

> During the last five years (this) emphasis on tactical decisions has been supplanted by a growing involvement in strategic decisions . . .
> Strategies last for long periods of time, while tactics have short durations.

This challenge to marketing is seen most clearly when the issue of planning is explored. There is considerable data to suggest that smaller firms either avoid planning or undertake implicit rather than explicit planning. The current emphasis on marketing planning in the literature would suggest a clear dilemma (Kotler, 1985):

> Management is recognizing that intuition alone is no longer enough for succeeding in today's environment. More and more companies are turning to formal planning systems to guide their courses.

This contrasts starkly with the notion of entrepreneurs as opportunists capable of spotting gaps in the market before the larger enterprise can adjust its sights and act.

Davis *et al.* (1985) suggest that the nature of the goals sought by small firms poses problems for the successful introduction of marketing as generally defined within the literature.

> Large companies strive toward maximizing sales, market share, and/or profit. Although small enterprises may have growth maxmization goals, they are more likely to have satisficing objectives to ensure a controlled growth level or, in some cases, to even limit growth and maintain the current character of the enterprise.

Besides these broad and largely conceptual difficulties in introducing the marketing approach into the smaller firm there are a number of practical difficulties. Most smaller enterprises operate within very severe resource constraints. Access to certain types of media or forms of communication and distribution are very restricted. At the same time the nature of the relationship between the buyer and the supplier can often be close to monopsony. A very small number of buyers can dominate the small firm's market. Even in those cases in which the buyer has a high reputation for its dealing, for example Marks and Spencer, its dominance allied to its expertise can shape the smaller firm's view of the market. A small firm can find:

1   A single dominant customer can easily absorb all its output.
2   A consequent lack of pressure to seek new opportunities.
3   A tendency on the part of this client to direct and shape production, design, development and research.
4   This dependence grows as the supplier reduces his/her investment in these areas as it seems increasingly unnecessary.

The highly concentrated nature of UK retailing and other sectors of UK commerce would seem to reinforce this pattern.

Several possible mechanisms exist for dealing with the issues raised in this review of the fit between small businesses and marketing. The simplest approach lies in suggesting that smaller firms might adapt or fail. The critical importance of marketing to commercial success has been vividly demonstrated. At the other extreme it can be argued that marketing thinkers should be exploring ways in which ideas and practices may be adapted to fit with the needs of smaller enterprises, especially those which are entrepreneurially based. The following discussion suggests that a combination of these is needed. The small business sector is too large and important to be ignored by marketing thinkers while key features of marketing need to be appreciated by entrepreneurs if their enterprises are to prosper. A contingency model of marketing is suggested which may have a rather wider relevance.

Current thinking

The small firm

The creation of the Committee of Enquiry into Small Firms under the Chairmanship of John Bolton (1971) marked a turning point in appreciation in the UK of:

1   The role of the small firm in the economy.
2   The nature of small business management in Britain today and the constraints under which it operates.

These twin themes continue to dominate thinking and research into the sector. The changing economic landscape of the late 1970s and 1980s focused attention on the former. The problems of converting the goals of new business formation and growth into success and development has directed increasing attention towards the latter.

The interest in job creation was spurred by the dramatic results of the Birch Report (1979) which seemed to indicate that small firms were major new generators of jobs in the USA. Evidence has been presented (President's Report to Congress 1986) which would suggest that:

> Employment growth in small business-dominated industries, at 5.1%, far outpaced that of large business-dominated industries, at 0.7% . . . employment increased by 2 million during the period 1979–83, as small firms generated most of the jobs.

Although there has been considerable debate in the US about the magnitude of these moves in job creation there is a widespread consensus on the shape and direction of change. Outside the USA there is far wider disagreement about the role of smaller firms in job creation in domestic economies.

Early research (Hamilton, 1983; Scott, 1980; Fothergill and Gudgin, 1979) in the UK tended to support the notion that small firms were net creators of jobs but at a far less significant scale than in North America. These studies tended to be relatively localized and concentrated on manufacturing industries. The dangers of building a national picture from a series of local studies were emphasized by Storey (1982).

However, recent work by Gallagher and Stewart (1984) indicated that for the period 1971 to 1981 over 50 per cent of the new jobs in the UK were created in firms employing less than 100 workers. The smallest size band appeared to be generating new employment at roughly three times the rate that would be predicted given their share of total employment. The debate which has followed the publication of these results has tended to confirm the balance of job generation but raised questions about scale. It would seem that the overall pattern of small firms providing most of the new jobs has been confirmed. Early fears about the nature of these jobs – were they purely in non-exportable services – has not been supported. Against this background the efficient management of these companies is a matter of considerable importance.

The scale of entrepreneurial activity

Number of enterprises

An accurate picture of the scale and pattern of small business activity is hard to establish. The data bases such as VAT registrations or Dunn and Bradstreet have flaws which most researchers and observers recognize. Many of the weaknesses reflect the reluctance of the very smallest firms to invest scarce resources in accurate record keeping. Definitional problems make the situation especially complex as most of the data is gathered for other purposes. Although there are some counter-acting factors, for example non-active registrations, most of these factors would tend to imply an underrecording of numbers and scale. Despite this, the small firm universe is large and growing.

The vast majority of firms fall into the small or very small category. The table below categorizes them on the most commonly employed basis –

Table 26.1 *The scale of small firm activity in the UK*

Year	Stock at start of year	Births %	Deaths %
1974	1,158,156	12.8	8.9
1975	1,202,697	13.4	11.5
1976	1,225,417	13.8	11.9
1977	1,248,401	12.6	12.7
1978	1,247,394	12.0	12.4
1979	1,241,325	13.8	10.0
1980	1,303,660	12.1	10.9
1981	1,335,412	11.3	8.9
1982	1,357,041	12.1	10.5
1983	1,399,605	12.4	9.4
1984	1,441,598		

Source: P. Ganguly, *UK Small Business Statistics and International Comparisons*, Harper & Row, 1985.

Table 26.2 *The size structure by employees of firms*

Number of employees	% of total firms	
	Actual	Cumulative
<5	65	65
5–10	20	85
11–20	10	95
>20	5	100

Source: S. Johnson, 'What sort of Jobs Do Small Firms Create – Some Recent Evidence', UK Small Business Policy and Research Conference, 1986.

employees. Although this is not a perfect measure it is useful in giving some picture of the overall structure of business activity by scale.

This data is broadly in line with the patterns elsewhere, i.e. a vast small business sector heavily weighted towards the smaller sectors. In North America, the recent upsurge in new business formations has added to an already large pool of companies.

Table 26.3   *The scale of small business in the USA in 1983*

Non-farm sole	Partner-ships	Corpora-tions	Total
10,704,000	1,542,000	2,999,000	15,245,000

Source: President's report to Congress, 'State of Small Business', US Government Printing Office, 1986.

The overall distribution by size is broadly in line with the UK although the size categories are a little different.

Table 26.4   *The size structure by employees of firms*

Number of employees	% of total firms	
	Actual	Cumulative
<20	88	88
20–99	10.5	98.5
100–499	1.3	99.8
>500	0.2	100

Areas of activity

Sectoral

Although, in terms of numbers, it is largely inevitable that small firms will 'dominate' most sectors of commerce in specific fields, this might be linked with market power and an especially important role in the market. The latter tend to be characterized by one or more of the following features:

1 Relatively low entry costs.
2 High service content in offering.
3 Novelty or high rates of change.

This would lead to industries such as mining, chemical processing and telecommunications being dominated by larger firms with personal and business services ranging from interior design to software development, retailing and distribution being more supportive of smaller units.

During periods of turbulence, traditional large firm sectors will show an upsurge of small business activity. This was observed in the synthetic organic chemicals sector during the mid to late 1970s. An extended period of stability can increase the market power of larger enterprises. The rubber processing industry has seen a rapid reduction in the number of operating units over the last decade.

Geographical

A particular strength of the smaller firm lies in its ability to satisfy the requirements of a local market. The classical illustration of this is the local retailer who survives despite larger competition. A similar pattern can be seen in many industrial markets. Large producers depend on the ability of processors and component suppliers to meet their needs promptly and efficiently. Many actively seek out or support local plastics processors, foundries, electronic component producers, designers etc. The proximity of their operation to those of their suppliers minimizes the risks of disruption. At the same time the personal commitment of the smaller firm is seen as a major asset in building trading links.

Some larger firms have adopted policies of positive discrimination towards smaller local business. IBM sees this as an important aspect of its local, corporate responsibility as well as good business. It reflects a pattern of *local* discrimination which influences trade in many areas and parts of the world. In the USA policies of *affirmative action* have been adopted to help small companies win a larger share of government procurement. This has been extended to minority-owned smaller businesses and those with women as proprietors. In some cases this creates submarkets such as the *Women's Yellow Pages*, much of whose success derives from the need to find woman-owned businesses to buy from to satisfy affirmative action programmes.

Marketing issues

Consistency of approach?

The scale, inner dynamics and changing nature of the small firm sector suggests that marketing must meet the needs of the firms in this sector or adapt to their requirements. There is some evidence that there are problems of fit at present. The extent of apparent need for improved marketing has been highlighted in numerous surveys of small business activity. At the same time there is little evidence that communicating the importance of marketing or the identification of ways to develop skills are having a significant impact on behaviour. Small firms seem willing to acknowledge its importance but are unable or unwilling to adopt the lessons of marketing. A marketing approach to marketing would suggest that the notion of a contingency model of marketing is worth considering.

The notion of a contingency approach to marketing, notably in its application to small and medium-sized enterprises, raises issues for both the practitioner and the teacher/researcher. In particular it focuses attention on the ways in which the approach to marketing should be reshaped to the different conditions. These might be seen to exist at different levels. Prior to examining these in detail it is worth looking at the strengths and weaknesses of small firms in applying the marketing concept.

Central to the marketing approach to business is the notion of keeping close to customers, understanding needs and responding to them as they exist today and as they shift over time. The proprietor or chief executive of the smaller firm has many advantages over his/her colleague in the larger enterprise. Many small firms serve the needs of a local community. Others have emerged to satisfy specialist niches or the requirements of particular groups. This means the chief executive can be physically closer to his/her customers if they are located close to the factory, shop or office or can build up a wide ranging rapport. The firm's customer base is inevitably smaller hence more manageable. The chief executive may know the clients personally. He/she will assume that his/her senior executives have this knowledge even if they do not. This personal knowledge may be far richer and more detailed than anything available to the chief executive officer or top management of the larger firm.

However, it can be misleading and its quality can be distorted by subjectivity or selectivity. It is an asset but may not be exploited. The problems of access to buyers forces marketing orientated top managers of large firms to organize the gathering of information. The implicit discipline influences the way the data is used. In many small firms it is too easy to become complacent and confuse access with insight.

In marketing the ability, effectively to mobilize the firm's resources behind the company's efforts can mean that opportunities can be grasped and gaps in the market exploited (Pride and Ferrell, 1985):

> Since the marketing concept affects all types of business activities, not only marketing activities, the top management of an organization must adopt it wholeheartedly.

For smaller firms, short lines of communication allied to the pervasive involvement of the proprietor can facilitate the production of this effect. The commitment of top management allied to its ability to directly influence staff at all levels cannot easily be matched in the large firm. The scale of operations means that senior executives must work through others. This can produce the type of bureaucratization which can be inimical to creative marketing. This is especially true in innovation where it would seem that those firms which adopt a loose, flexible and informal structure are more likely to identify and develop successful new products and processes. These firms appear to be equally adept at coping with rapid external change (Burns and Stalker, 1961). In 1983 the 'State of Small Business' report by the US President noted that:

> Small firms produce 2.5 times as many innovations as large firms, relative to the number of people employed.
> The time necessary to bring an innovation to market averaged 2.22 years for small firms, compared with 3.05 years for large firms.

Table 22.5 gives some indication of the results of a range of studies into this issue.

The type of open and organic structure which is often seen as especially effective at coping with change is illustrated in Figure 26.2. Lines of authority and communication flow in terms of needs and expertise rather than form or position. The salesperson with an idea can contact the researcher with the

Table 26.5 *Selected research on the frequency of major innovations by small firms or independent inventors*

	Innovations	
Author	*Type of innovation*	*By small firms or inventors*
Jewkes *et al.* (1958)	61 important inventions and innovations	<50%
Hamberg (1963)	Major inventions (1946–55)	<67%
Peck (1962)	149 inventions in aluminium welding, fabricating techniques and finishing	86%
Hamberg (1963)	7 major innovations in the US steel industry	100%
Enos (1962)	7 major inventions in the refining and cracking of petroleum	100%
Gellman (1976)	319 product innovations by US industries (1953–73)	24%
Gellman (1982)	635 product innovations (1970–78)	40%
Mueller (1982)	246 award-winning process innovations in food processing and manufacturing industries	45%

Source: 'The State of Small Business', President's report to Congress, US Government Printing Office, 1983.

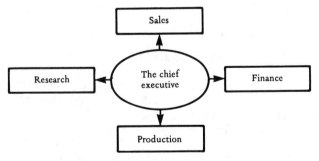

Figure 26.2 *The open organization*

skill directly without going though an elaborate and potentially negative hierarchy.

The creation of multidiscipline teams to tackle complex problems is technically easier. These frequently show a high level of cohesion and commitment to company goals.

However, it is highly dependent on the commitment of the owner or proprietor. He/she has immense power to encourage or stifle innovation. Many chief executives in this situation fail to recognize this opportunity. They may show the type of closed mind which when allied to an autocratic management style precludes any new ideas from junior staff.

The tendency for communication and authority to flow directly from the owner-manager is frequently associated with clarity of vision and decisiveness. The cross-referencing and clearances needed for decisions in larger enterprises may not be needed. The proprietor has all the authority required to make decisions. In areas such as negotiations, experimentation and the overall process of exploiting opportunities this may mean that the smaller firm can exploit opportunities very effectively.

Many of these openings in the market can only be successfully realized if a firm has the resources to satisfy customer needs. The weaknesses of smaller firms often centre on their lack of access to the resources to realize fully the potential of the gaps in the market they identify. It is not unusual for large firms to wait for smaller enterprises to open up markets and make the mistakes before they use their resource base to capitalize on the opportunity. This version of *poisoned apple marketing* can take three basic forms with the larger firm:

1 Attempting to take over the market.
2 Trying to take over or absorb the smaller rival.
3 Striving to identify or exploit new opportunities for the innovation.

In the US recently, the move by Warner Communications into the home shopping market developed by Home Shopping Network clearly illustrates the attraction of new markets pioneered by smaller enterprises to industrial giants. The link up between IBM and Rölm illustrates the appeal of an innovative smaller firm to a major corporation striving to move into a new market. The success of *Women's Yellow Pages* has prompted numerous large firms to attempt to emulate this in other fields, markets and sectors. In Europe similar patterns of behaviour can be observed. Peter Powell's kites provided a model which numerous larger manufacturers successfully emulated. More recently the acquisition by Olivetti of Acorn computers gave it access to new markets and technologies. The success of Cambridge Electronics has prompted many major firms to seek ways of wedding academic expertise to commercial power. *Time Out* magazine's success has led to a wide range of similar developments in other locations and fields.

This pattern of apparent, entrepreneurial success in innovation has stimulated a wider interest in the phenomenon. The notion of intrapreneuring, i.e. acting entrepreneurially while within the large corporation has been popularized by Pinchot (1985). It reflects two parallel developments. The first is the wish to stimulate more positive attitudes towards risk in the traditionally conservative world of the corporation. Beside this there is a recognition that there is a tendency for many newer technologies to provide opportunities for enterprises operating on a smaller scale. This can be described as the *creative disintegration of the larger firm*. Under this model, the corporation is deliberately broken down into smaller, semi-autonomous, operating units. It can be seen in firms such as Olivetti, Hanson Trust, Ferranti, Cadbury-Schweppes and United Biscuits. The head office functions are kept to a minimum and the subsidiaries are encouraged to act independently.

This combination of enterprise and scale helps to overcome a persistent problem of marketing by the smaller firm – risk aversion among buyers. Many observations by sales and marketing staff confirm the findings that purchasers feel greater reassurance when they deal with longer established, larger firms. This is especially true in industrial or commercial markets where a saving on price can easily be offset by any problems with supply. Buyers may fear that small firms:

1 Cannot cope with the quantities involved.
2 Lack the managerial expertise to deal with major contracts.
3 Will find resource shortages impede supplies.
4 Cannot call on back-up from the parent enterprise to overcome problems.

These reservations are compounded by the failure of many small firms to use the tools of marketing to counteract these impressions. In turn it reflects a general failure in many smaller firms to use marketing to realize their true potential. This is true for both the newly formed and the established enterprise. Reassurance becomes a major aspect of marketing.

Contexts

Marketing and the newly formed business

There are many parallels between the creation of a new business and the launch of a new product. The prospective entrepreneur will need to determine

1 The viability of his/her project.
2 The overall marketing strategy.
3 The market or customer groups.
4 The optimal marketing mix.
5 The approach adopted to each mix element.
6 The criteria for assessing success, failure and any modifications.

There are important differences especially in terms of attitude, involvement and skills. The degree of involvement is typically very high. This is both a strength and a weakness. There is evidence that the existence of a product champion is vitally important to success in new product success. However the extent of this commitment needs to be carefully managed. The central questions:

- Who is going to buy it from me?
- Why will they?

must be answered with as much objectivity as possible. The temptation to say:

- Everyone!
- Because it is better.

is very common among those involved in forming a business. This type of faith may be an integral part of the psychological process of accepting the risks of enterprise creation. A disciplined approach to marketing at this stage requires a greater degree of objectivity. The nature of the need which will be met has to be fully understood. The alternative ways of meeting this requirement should be appreciated.

At its most basic, this may mean a reappraisal of customer needs and the ways of satisfying them. Product myopia is common among entrepreneurs. They develop a fixation on a particular product or service which they believe should be offered to the market. One of the most vivid and best publicized illustrations of this in recent years has been the development of the pocket television by Sir Clive

Sinclair. It was first introduced to the market at the Radio and TV Exhibition in 1966. It took at least ten more years of development before a technically robust version was produced in significant quantities. A decade later, the market remains small and relatively static. The returns for over twenty years of work are very limited. This type of product myopia reflects the development of a symbiosis which can make it hard for the entrepreneurial originator to step back from his/her creation and objectively appraise it. Overcoming this calls for a willingness to undertake a form of idea generation. This is designed to highlight alternatives while introducing a degree of objectivity into the development process.

This process of appraisal requires early exposure of the idea, concept or project to potential buyers. Small firms have particular problems and opportunities with this. The entrepreneur may be reluctant to expose the idea because of fears over imitation as this type of enterprise may lack the resources to protect the innovation or defend it from competition in the early stages. At the same time, prospective buyers may be willing to invest time and energy to support a newly formed business. Companies such as Marks and Spencer, United Biscuits and Pilkington Glass have positive programmes to assist this type of enterprise. Despite the reservations of many of those involved in new businesses, the risks of failing to explore the market, far outweigh the risks associated with lack of investigation. Research in Britain (Storey, 1982) and the US (President's Report, 1986) cites lack of preliminary research into the project as the most common cause of failure among new businesses. This is wholly consistent with similar research into innovation.

Undertaking research into the potential for the business is not sufficient in itself. It must take place among the right people with the correct issues raised. There is a tendency for those involved in business formation to restrict their inquiry among those likely to give 'supportive' answers. This can occur because the interviewees appreciate how important the project is to the originator or because they are directly involved in its development. Decisions about who to research and the issues to arise can only have value if based on a desire to receive negative as well as supportive feedback. In most advanced countries networks of advisory agencies have been set up which seek to provide this type of guidance. In Britain the Department of Trade and Industry's Small Firms Service is complemented by the work of Enterprise Agencies and other similar bodies. In the USA the Small Business Administration provides a wide range of advice. Similar organizations exist in most countries with a small firms sector.

An especially important aspect of this process for the prospective entrepreneur is the discipline of looking beyond the product to the range of other aspects of the total product proposition which are important in achieving and sustaining customer satisfaction.

The tunnel vision which can occur from too close a focus on the initial project frequently extends to a reluctance to think beyond the short term and reservations about investments in further product development, promotional policies, distribution and service policies and a marketing approach to pricing. These may reflect a passive approach to market development. This is commonly seen in the smaller firm which sees itself as too small or too weak to manage the development of its markets.

Strategies

Strategy and the smaller firm

Many smaller firms survive despite taking a relatively passive approach to their market. They have developed an expertise, a facility or some other asset. Their overall approach to their prospective customers involved building upon established purchase patterns or simply waiting for the potential client to find them. Many small manufacturers, service companies or retailers adopt this approach. In favourable conditions it is possible for firms to survive, even prosper, with this type of approach. Once circumstances change because demand declines, the pattern changes or rivals enter the market this approach becomes very dangerous. Illustrations of these changes can be seen in many parts of Britain.

A study of the shipbuilding industry in the north-east of England (Gibb and Ritchie, 1984) indicated the problems associated with declining demand and lack of market orientated business development by suppliers. Shipbuilding was one of the major industries of Britain. However, changing needs and increased competition have led to a dramatic decline in output from yards in the north of England. This decline is long established and is unlikely to be reversed in the short to medium term. The impact of this type of change goes far beyond the large shipbuilders. In fact more people were employed in small suppliers than in the large companies. Examination of the response of these firms to the decline in their customer base indicated the likely consequence of a passive approach. Management became fatalistic. In most firms there was a belief that they could do nothing to shape their future. Competition became increasingly price orientated. The surviving small firms struggled to get an increasing share of a rapidly declining cake.

There was virtually no search for new applications for their skills or technologies. Business prospecting disappeared with many firms cutting back on their limited promotional effort. The long-term consequence was a dramatic decline in the number of businesses in this sector.

A different type of change has faced small retailers in virtually all parts of Britain. The growth of the major multiples has been associated with changing consumer buying patterns. Out-of-town shopping in giant supermarkets has become the norm for many households. Small shopkeepers have seen their customer base disappears. In the vast majority of cases despair and failure have been the only response. Few have tried to examine the assets which they retain. All too seldom have they responded by exploring with their customers the type of survival and growth strategy to be adopted to meet needs and build their business.

The impact of new competition has been even more dramatic in its impact on the UK furniture trade. In sectors as diverse as fitted kitchens and reproduction furniture, small British firms have allowed business to be won by market orientated rivals often from Europe. In the fitted kitchen market, this coincided with a major change in customer buying patterns. The shift from veneered to solid wood products meant that customers were spending far more per unit. Under these circumstances, there was a need for greater reassurance about design and quality. Continental firms were relatively quick to recognize this and the role that advertising and effective channel management could play in this.

The result was that they thrived while many home firms declined. In the reproduction furniture market the pattern of change was equally marked. The European market was primarily for English reproduction furniture. Until recently the market in Europe was supplied largely by English companies. However, their lack of market knowledge meant that they failed to recognize that their market was increasingly developing into a generic grouping. Customers were willing to buy English reproduction furniture from non-English suppliers. A major share of the market had been won by Italian and other producers before there was any positive response in terms of promotion or image building from the UK.

Establishing an active approach to marketing management is an integral part of overcoming these problems. An important aspect of this is the formulation of relevant and implementable marketing strategies. In smaller firms *penetration* strategies are likely to prove both the most practical and the most likely to achieve returns in the short to medium term. This approach involves building business through products the firm is familiar with in markets which the company knows. A steel stockholder in the London area established his firm on a growth pattern by keeping his staff in selling stainless steels fully informed of the opportunities produced from new developments in cutting and shaping. This meant that clients who had not been able to use this material before could be converted to better quality, higher added-value lines. A similar pattern of development occurred with a small plastics firm in the north-east of England. It had established considerable expertise in self-skinned foam in work with British Rail. It successfully transferred this technology to certain of its established customers in the auto industry. Although it was a more expensive product, it reduced production and maintenance costs for the customer.

This approach is useful for increasing market share especially in growth sectors. Elsewhere a *market development* strategy may be more effective. It means taking the company's existing offering, perhaps marginally adapted, to new markets, areas or countries. Two interesting illustrations of this have been widely reported recently. Job Creation Limited was set up in the UK to help firms forced to reduce their work force to find alternative opportunities for ex-employees notably through self-employment. As noted in *Fortune*, 7 July 1986, it now:

> Operates across Europe . . . When synthetic-fibre producer ENKA shut its plant in Kassel, West Germany, Job Creation helped convert the old facility into a home for more than 50 businesses.

In the field of training, MDE Services has converted its programmes into a range of areas while winning successful export orders. The move into new markets will require the firm to develop new skills and knowledge.

Market development tends to be less capital or resource intensive than *product or service development*. This involves the introduction of new products to existing customer groups. It can mean new technologies to help clients remain competitive or new offerings to satisfy changing needs. In the boating field a combination of these was illustrated by Piranha Mouldings. This specialist producer of white water kayaks reached the peak of its initial stage of development in the early 1980s when twelve out of the sixteen teams competing in the world championships used their boats. They dominated their niche in the market with relatively sophisticated and expensive products. The scope for growth was limited. Its research into the market identified an important opportunity within its existing customer base. Many buyers were associated with sports centres. They could not pay the high prices charged by Piranha for their more workday products, i.e. those used by visitors. The firm responded by investing in the technology which allowed them to produce higher volume, good quality canoes for this market. Sales and customer loyalty for both products grew.

There is little doubt that *diversification* is the most difficult strategic alternative for smaller firms. The risks are high as the firm knows little about the market or the product involved. The opportunity can seem very attractive but unforeseen difficulties can pose potentially insuperable difficulties for the smaller enterprise. Cleaver Marine was a very successful leisure firm which confronted this when they adopted a diversification strategy to maintain growth. The firm's core business was a canal hire operation in the midlands. When growth in this tailed off in the early 1970s the company successfully moved into the chandlery trade. It provided a wide range of products and services to those using the canals for holidays and leisure. This form of service development stimulated a new era of growth. By the mid to late 1970s new opportunities were needed for growth. The firm's researchers had noted the frequency with which former customers were taking holidays in continental Europe. At the same time the firm noted that the French canals were undergoing the type of change in use seen in Britain in the early 1950s, i.e. a shift from commercial to leisure use. The firm used its expertise in the canal boat leisure market to establish a very successful hire operation in France. Its problems occurred when it sought to diversify into flotilla yachting. This activity had grown rapidly in popularity in the late 1970s. Cleaver saw this as a major growth opportunity. However, lack of knowledge of the market and the different products involved created serious difficulties which the firm was fortunate to survive.

Identification of the strategic alternatives is only the first step in the creation of effective marketing strategies for smaller firms. A comprehensive appraisal of the challenges faced by the enterprise is needed. However, the sense of close identity between the firm and the owner makes this especially important. At the same time the lack of resources specially in terms of specialist, senior management means that the chief executive needs to go outside the company for much of the support in this process. The groups involved are charged with the task of highlighting;

- The challenges in some form of rank order.
- The business decisions related to these.
- The strategies open for tackling these.
- The implications for other aspects of the firm.
- Costs, risks and likely returns.

In many smaller firms the enthusiasm and commitment of the owner provides a drive which can ensure the successful implementation of policies. Often, this is linked with a reluctance to consider alternatives or different scenarios. At this stage in the formation of strategies a rigorous assessment is needed of potential negatives and the ability of the strategy to sustain the firm if the anticipated outcomes do not occur. The ultimate value of the strategy will be shown in the market. This means that it must be fully costed and the implications for action at all levels appreciated.

The mix and advertising

The marketing mix

Traditional models of entrepreneurs have tended to emphasize the opportunism, the ability to spot 'gaps' and the relatively short term perspective shown by this type of individual (Schumpeter 1934). These characteristics suggest that the type of enterprise directed by them will be more effective at developing and implementing tactics than strategies. In a similar way, it would seem that small firms will be more effective in those areas of marketing with high personal inputs and closely linked with short-term purchase behaviour than impersonal, longer-term activities.

Research into the sector would tend to support this proposition (Longenecker and Moore, 1980). Small firms tend to concentrate their effort on those aspects of the marketing mix which are linked with relatively short-term benefits. In promotional activity it means emphasizing sales or merchandising based activity probably at the expense of image orientated, display advertising. In distribution, it leads to an emphasis on high levels of availability and broadly based, relatively unselective channels. Prices tend to be negotiated, usually on the basis of costs instead of fixed with a high market orientation. Product development tends to be responsive to specific needs not geared to building ranges or portfolios.

These aspects of the smaller firm's approach to marketing reflect an inward looking rather than a market orientated approach to business development. In many cases they fail to realize the true potential of the enterprise in its market. These dangers can be seen in many aspects of the marketing mix.

Promotion

Many small firms struggle to convince larger clients that they have the resources to successfully meet their needs. In industrial markets, buyers are wary of purchasing components if breakdowns in deliveries or quality problems will interrupt large scale production processes. Reassurance about the strength, quality and viability of the producer is very important to this. A well developed image built through successful advertising can play a major part in this. It will do much to overcome the classic 'I don't know you . . . I don't know your company' barrier put up by purchasers. The efforts of sales staff will be assisted if the buyer feels there are no greater risks in this transaction than in buying from a larger rival. Media advertising can help reinforce the advantages of using small firms as suppliers. Building confidence continues after the purchase has been made. This is most clearly seen in the period following the placing of an order with a smaller, relatively unknown supplier. Buyers tend to contact them far more frequently, largely for reassurance.

Many small firms fail to achieve their potential because potential customers are ignorant of their existence or range of products or services. Media advertising may provide the primary means of reaching this market. The resource shortage of smaller firms make them reluctant to explore this aspect of promotion. Often, a well targeted and carefully prepared advertising effort can easily repay the investment. Smaller companies can generally expect to win increasing returns to scale in this area.

The mix and distribution

It is common for smaller firms and those writing about their role in the market to highlight the importance of service in business development in this sector. It is clear that smaller enterprises can use short lines of communication, flexibility and responsiveness to provide a high level of service for their customers. This can be seen in the retailer who knows customers so well that deliveries can be made to the housebound, with opening hours built around local work patterns and a personal rapport established with individuals. In manufacturing, small component suppliers will deliver in small order sizes and at short notice. In catering and other services similar patterns of high quality customer support can be seen.

Despite this, few smaller companies fully exploit the marketing potential of their strengths in distribution and channel management. It is unusual to see these companies consciously develop strategies which wed their investment in high levels of services to some notion of the returns sought. It is not unusual to find small firms who made little attempt to consciously manage these costs. At the same time, the proportion of all costs tied up in distribution is generally far larger for small companies than for larger companies. A study of the UK furniture industry found that distribution costs were typically 10 per cent more for firms employing more than 50 workers, i.e. as a percentage of all costs.

Building a clearly defined differential advantage in this sector can mean significant returns at relatively low cost. At its most basic level it means understanding the link between the provision of services to customers in terms of:

- Availability.
- Delivery.
- Back-Up.
- Materials handling.
- Order quantities.
- Order processing.
- Inventory.
- Packaging.
- Warehousing.
- Location.

with the benefit sought by customers in terms of service. Once the company appreciates this relationship it can start linking the costs of provision with the returns from clients from benefits. This can be especially important during periods of economic contraction when large rivals might respond to adversity by reducing customer support in these areas thus providing an opportunity for the entrepreneur to cash in.

This is likely to call for considerable insight into the workings of the distribution channel and their position and role in it. Many small firms underestimate their potential influence and the alternatives which exist for developing different approaches and capitalizing on these. There is a strong temptation for small businesses to adopt, instinctively an *intensive* distribution approach to channels. In essence this means accepting virtually every opportunity offered to get their products stocked. Although this may be the right approach under certain conditions there are alternatives which may generate better returns.

This has been clearly illustrated by the success of Church's, the footwear manufacturer. The firm was one of a relatively large number of producers of extremely high quality shoes in Britain. In the 1960s these old established companies faced increasing competiton at home and overseas from foreign competition. Church's responded by carefully developing its distribution through a highly exclusive distribution strategy. This meant making a very careful selection of the outlets that could stock its product and working hard to establish and maintain standards. Customers knew that the quality of the shoe was reflected in the quality of the outlet. Over the next twenty years many of the first old established rivals at the top end of the market declined or failed. In contrast, Church's went from strength to strength.

There are other strategic options open to the smaller firm in channel policy. The approach adopted should reflect wider company or marketing objectives. Effectiveness in this area depends on the company deciding to manage its marketing rather than merely respond to external pressures.

The mix and pricing

This challenge of converting a response into a managed action poses most problems to smaller firms in the field of pricing. A number of investigations have indicated that cost plus methods dominate (Hakansson, 1986). Often, this is the area in which companies feel most vulnerable to external pressures. This is partly a function of the nature of small business especially in manufacturing. Small businesses tend to predominate in component supply, in servicing industrial or commercial clients or in business or personal services as well as retailing. In the manufacturing sector it generally means that their customers are typically much larger and they frequently specify the products to produce. It is not unusual for a small metals, plastics or timber company to make many products but say they have no product. In this they mean that they are providing a manufacturing service to someone else's specification.

A typical illustration of this is the situation in the plastics processing industry. There are likely to be very large numbers of firms with the equipment and skills to manufacture components for the car industry. A situation akin to perfect competition may exist:

- There are large numbers of suppliers.
- The output is specified by the client (hence it is homogeneous).

● The professional buyers of the firms are likely to have almost perfect information.

A smaller firm which fails to build a degree of differentiation will find that its freedom in pricing soon disappears. The first step in this process will involve a full appreciation of the nature and components of price. The price of a product reflects promptness of payment and credit terms as much as the amount charged. There is growing evidence that ensuring that the terms and conditions of payment are met is a major problem for smaller companies. A much publicized aspect of this is the practice of certain larger firms to delay payment to smaller suppliers. Less well known but accounting for more days *lost* through slow payment is late invoicing.

Small firms are likely to find that the best way to maximize their benefits lies in managing the non-core aspects of price. This extends to such areas as:

● Terms and conditions of payment.
● Credit.
● Discount structure.
● Allowances or trade-in.
● Form of payment.

Price bundling is especially important in industrial markets. The supplier of a part or component is likely to be responsible for an element of design, tooling, production of sample quantities and volume manufacture. Prices can vary between full payment of each element separately, part payment for certain items, for example tools, or amortization of all costs against volume orders. Each has a different impact on the relationship between the buyer and supplier. The nature of this requires to be determined on the basis of its impact on the firm's position in the market. This approach calls for a greater recognition of the scope for market orientated pricing.

Davis *et al.* (1985) suggest that smaller firms are likely to be especially successful in their pricing strategies under four specific conditions:

When price is de-emphasized as a strategic element . . . (they) are unlikely to fare well in significant price competition, much less price wars, with larger competitors.

When a flexible or 'negotiable' pricing strategy is followed.

If following 'suggested' prices from other channel members.

If they enter 'comfortable margin' industries.

These suggest that these companies have some latitude in the products or services they produce and the markets within which they trade. This process of directing the firm is closely linked with the product or service policies of the firms.

The view that small companies have particular assets in the field of innovation has been expressed by many commentators. Schumpeter (1934) described the entrepreneur, primarily through the process of company formation, as the driving force of industrial innovation. A proper understanding of the marketing implication of the association between the small firm and product or service development requires an attempt to understand how this works in smaller companies.

Traditional approaches to innovation in marketing tend to assume that new product development takes place through fairly discrete stages. Models such as those presented by Booz, Allen and Hamilton describe a start (idea generation), follow-up stages and an end (launch). In most smaller firms especially in industrial markets or services this does not take place. Innovation is a continuous process of adaptation and response. It may be possible in retrospect to describe these steps but not in advance. This is partly a reflection of the type of interactive, network-based relationship described by Cunningham and Ford. The component supplier is likely to be interacting constantly with his client with adjustments and adaptation taking place continuously. At the same time a novel item is likely to be specified by the customer not the supplier, eliminating stages such as *business analysis* and *market testing*.

These features of innovation in the smaller firm reflect the main strengths of the existing small firm in product development. This tends to take the form of problem solving within externally defined parameters. Customers or suppliers often provide these besides the technical back-up to develop or test proposed solutions. Many chief executives play a vital role as technological gatekeepers in this. He/she provides access to many of the external sources while being the person most frequently referred to in overcoming any barriers. Although this approach has many advantages for small firms its long-term costs in marketing can be very high. Firms are reluctant to take positive action to protect their innovations through patents or licences. This reflects worries about the nature of ownership and concerns about the costs of protection. It results in poor exploitation of the benefits of new product development (Cannon, 1985).

Many companies adopting this problem-solving approach to innovation become overdependent on their larger partners for ideas or technologies. They fail to use the alternative sources listed below in any systematic way.

- Market research
- Foreign search
- Gap analysis
- Usage studies
- Technology search
- Brainstorming
- Internal R & D
- Design development
- Individual insight

The exception to this tends to be the first generation, new technology based firm. Here, the innovations tend to be internally directed. However their use of market intelligence and programmed marketing can be poor and undermine their business.

Marketing research

Research into the ways in which small business owners have developed their enterprises has tended to emphasize the subjective and personal nature of their management practice. Some models of entrepreneurial behaviour explain the decision to follow this life style largely in terms of personal or social factors not commercial. Researchers such as Babson saw the entrepreneur as; born not made, prompted to start a business by an *inner* drive to achieve. De Vries (1977) takes this notion further by suggesting that they are driven by ambition which may be *viewed as a need to contradict strong feelings of inferiority or helplessness*. Although many commentators would reject this type of view as an explanation of all entrepreneurial behaviour most would accept that there is a strong subjective, individual or social element in the decision to start or operate a small business.

This approach to management runs counter to much of the thinking behind marketing research as a discipline. This is often described in terms of its objectivity, its systems and its professionalism. Some authors (Green and Tull, 1978) suggest that it is the attempt to introduce a degree of science into the marketing system.

This clash of values is reflected in the reluctance of many managers of small firms to accept the discipline of marketing research in the gathering of information to assist them in tackling their problems. It is not a problem confined to marketing. Lewis (1986) highlights the poor quality of the financial information systems used by small firms. In Belgium, Donkels (1985) noted that:

> There is a significant lack of information awareness with more than two thirds of the respondents (in one group) never using information on the surrounding socio-economic environment.

Against this background the attempt to improve the use of marketing intelligence by smaller firms must wed awareness of need with an understanding of the likely response.

Successful small firm marketing intelligence systems are likely to combine the personal information held by individuals in the firm with more systematically gathered 'objective' information. In the small firm the former tends to be highly regarded while the latter is treated with scant respect. There is a tendency to view data which is published or gathered by some formal process as 'too general', 'too widely available' or generally suspect because the sources are not 'known'. There is some truth in these reservations. The small, highly specialized producer is unlikely to find information from any external source which directly meets his/her needs. A firm such as Rubberastic which provides rubber cones for coal hoppers at pit-heads in the north of England will not find published data on its market. The highly individual and specialized nature of many small firms precludes this type of information provision.

In large firms the difficulty is overcome by a combination of extrapolation and expertise. Overall shifts in larger markets will have a direct effect on sales of many of United Biscuits' products. Debbie Harrington's sales of cookies to health food shops in central Scotland may be independent of these shifts. At the same time the 'dedicated' nature of managers makes it hard for them to transfer lessons from an external situation to their particular circumstances. The extent of identification with the enterprise means that information which is not clear and specific may be rejected as irrelevant. This means that the process of building a marketing research and information system will normally start with internally held personal data. Small firms may not be good users of information but they are typically assiduous storers of information.

Large amounts of unused data, some of it with considerable marketing value, lies fallow in many small companies. The first step may be a data reduction exercise designed to reduce the material to manageable proportions. This is likely to start from an information inventory in which the proprietor and the appropriate marketing staff are invited to classify information, on the classical, nice to know/need to know basis. This will tend to highlight the material which exists and is worth using and the gaps in provision. This process of examination is useful in heightening awareness of the potential role and contribution of information in decision making. It may be useful to set up some form of information centre as part of this. This model is likely to reflect the centralized nature of decision making in smaller firms.

Attitudes to information can be changed in smaller companies within relatively short time scales. Greater difficulties occur in building up the level of specialist expertise required to establish a definable marketing research or intelligence function. Resistance tends to emerge from two sources. The 'generalist' nature of small business management can stimulate opposition to the kind of professionalism linked with this area. This generally requires a high level of commitment to active communication by staff in this field. Barriers are frequently built up by established sales staff who see this process as a threat to their personal, decentralized stocks of information. Communication allied to an attempt to generate some relatively short-term benefits seems to be effective at dissolving this type of oppostition.

Once the groundwork has been done the traditional stages of marketing information gathering and organizing can be undertaken. The basis of this lies in the organization of 'internal secondary in-

formation'. This includes all the data collected by the firm for a different purpose which might cast light on marketing issues. It encompasses such routine but potentially valuable material as; inquiries, complaints, deliveries, stocks, damage rates, returns, tender documents (and performance) as well as customer lists and leads from suppliers etc.

This type of material can seldom fully resolve a complex marketing question. Often it provides clues or plays some light on a topic. 'Internal primary information' is likely to be needed to take the matter further. This involves inquiries within the firm to answer questions about an issue. It can involve quizzing staff about material they already hold or looking to them to gather new material. In some aspects of this the small firm can gain benefits not open to the larger company. A plastics company in the west of England found that its delivery staff were invaluable sources of information about developments at clients and rivals. The chief executive found that time spent with his drivers more than repaid his effort in leads and contacts.

This type of information may prove to be adequate for most of the time. Changing conditions or new developments are likely to demand a wider information base. The exploitation of 'external secondary data' gives the company the benefit of the material which has been gathered by a range of agencies which can be obtained. Development agencies such as Scottish Enterprise and Enterprise Trusts are likely to provide guidance on the source and quality of this. Many universities and colleges are invaluable sources of the data and have the expertise to analyse and use the material.

Often, the steps outlined above will still leave key issues unresolved, important questions unanswered. It may require 'external primary research' to tackle these. This means going outside the firm to answer the specific questions raised in an inquiry. The principles of sound market research are relatively simple. It seeks to answer questions about the market in a disciplined, objective and systematic way. The basic principle is that the standards are sufficiently clear and consistent that the same answer would be produced if the study was repeated. Achieving this is not easy. It is very hard without the training undertaken by the professionals of the Market Research Society.

In using researchers it is important to ensure that they match up to the standards of the Market Research Society. A useful checklist against which to measure the reports provided by a company is produced by the Society.

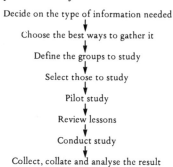

Decide on the type of information needed

Choose the best ways to gather it

Define the groups to study

Select those to study

Pilot study

Review lessons

Conduct study

Collect, collate and analyse the result

Figure 26.3   *The research process*

Where to from here?

Does marketing need to change?

The effective implementation of marketing in smaller firms requires both a creative synthesis of ideas about the way management in smaller firms operates and thinking about marketing. At the same time, it will be important to recognize that there is a gap between appreciation of a concept and the ability to use it. Argyris describes this as the *double loop of learning*. It highlights the difference between building up knowledge and establishing a basis for action using it.

Training will play an important part in this. Conventional models of management development seem to lack the reinforcement through supportive action which is called for when significant behavioural changes are sought. Action learning approaches provide this but demand a high resource input. Committed chief executives seem willing to undertake this especially when relatively quick returns can be identified. Building the right marketing attitudes throughout the firm is especially important. This calls for determined efforts at communication and feedback.

Conclusion

These broad principles outlined above should not disguise the paucity of established knowledge in the field. Research is still embryonic with major areas largely untapped. Perhaps the most critical is the role of the entrepreneur in the development of marketing. The traditional role ascribed to this individual within economic theory gave considerable emphasis to market opportunity spotting (Domar, 1968; Baumol, 1968). The mechanisms by which this is done, the skills and aptitudes which underpin it have received little attention. Other aspects of the marketing/small business interface reflect this. An especially significant feature today is the international dimension to small business management and its evolution. There is increasing attention paid to the role of smaller firms in economic development. The skills in marketing which are applied to this process are likely to have a material effect on the competitiveness of the enterprises developed.

Throughout this area of research and practice there is a combination of insight into opportunities and awareness of limitations. Many of the most clearly identified commercial successes of recent years have grown from the effective combination of entrepreneurship and marketing insight. The combination has shown remarkable power to shape and reshape markets. Theories and research are lagging but there is sufficient progress to suggest that considerable promise exists for lessons to be learnt to translate the good practice of the few to the lessons for the many.

References

Baker, M.J., *Marketing: An Introductory Text*, 4th ed. Macmillan, 1985.

Baumol, W. J., 'Entrepreneurship in Economic Theory', *American Economic Review*, 58, 1968.

Birch, D. L. *The Job Generation Process*, MIT Press, 1979.

Bolton, J., *Small Firms*, Cmnd 4811, HMSO, 1971.

Burns, T. and Stalker, G. M., *The Management of Innovation*, Tavistock, 1961.

Chell, E., 'The Entrepreneurial Personality: A Few Ghosts Laid To Rest', *International Small Business Journal*, Spring 1985.

Cannon, T., 'Innovation Creativity and Small Firm Organization', *International Small Business Journal*, Autumn 1985.

Davis, C.D., Hills, G.E. and La Forge, R.W., 'The Marketing/Small Enterprise Paradox', *International Small Business Journal*, Spring 1985.

Domar, E., 'Entrepreneurship in Economic Theory', *American Economic Review*, 58, 1968.

Donkels, R., 'SMEs and Public Authorities: On the Information and Communication Gap', *International Small Business Journal*, Spring 1985.

Fothergill, S. and Gudgin, G., *The Job Generation Process*, Centre For Environmental Studies, 1979.

Gallagher, C.C. and Stewart, H., 'Jobs and the Business Cycle in the UK', Newcastle Research Report No.2, Department of Industrial Management, 1984.

Ganguly, P., *UK Small Business Statistics and International Comparisons*, Harper & Row, 1985.

Gibb, A. and Ritchie, J., 'Influences on entrepreneurship', UK Policy and Research Conference, 1984.

Green P.E. and Tull D.S., *Research for Marketing Decisions*, Prentice-Hall, 1978.

Hakansson, A. 'The Marketing Attitudes of Small Engineering Companies', UK Policy and Research Conference, Stirling, 1986.

Hamilton, R. 'Job Generation in Scotland', unpublished Ph.D, Stirling, 1983.

Johnson, S., 'What Sort of Jobs Do Small Firms Create: Some Recent Evidence', UK Policy and Research Conference, Stirling 1986.

Kotler, P., *Marketing Management*, Prentice-Hall, 1985.

Lewis, J., Toon, K. and Bird, I., 'Accounting Support For The Small Firm', UK Policy and Research Conference, Stirling, 1986.

Longenecker, J. and Moore, C., 'Marketing and Small Business Entrepreneurship' in G.E. Hill, D. Barnaby, and L. Dufus, (eds) *Marketing and Small Business Entrepreneurship; Conceptual Research and Directions*, International Council For Small Business, 1980.

Pinchot, G., *Intrapreneuring*, Harper & Row, 1985.

President's report to Congress, 'The State Of Small Business', US Government Printing Office, 1986.

Pride, W. and Ferrell, O.C. *Marketing*, Houghton Mifflin, 1985.

Scott, M., 'Mythology and Misplaced Pessimism', paper presented at Manchester Business School 1980.

Schumpeter, J.A., *The Theory of Economic Development*, Harvard University Press, 1934.

Storey, D., *Entrepreneurship and the New Firm*, Croom Helm, 1982.

de Vries, K., 'The Entrepreneurial Personality', *Journal of Management Studies*, February 1977.

Weitz, B.A. and Wensley, R., *Strategic Marketing*, Belmont, 1985.

27
Non-profit organizations and marketing

KEITH J. BLOIS

Introduction

Is it a product you sell or a service you provide? J. Williams, 'Water carriers face the deep end', *The Sunday Times*, 8 June 1986.

The above question encapsulates a number of the issues which concern many people about the appropriateness of non-profit organizations using marketing. As the following discussion will establish, the formulation of this question indicates a lack of understanding of what marketing is and of its role in modern society. However, the discussion will necessarily lack precision, though hopefully not clarity, in places due to the lack of agreed definitions of many of the terms used. Furthermore, the fact that there is not a dichotomy between non-profit organizations and 'for profit' organizations with regard to their attainment of a profit creates difficulties. The aim of the discussion will therefore be to identify categories of behaviour which are generally observable in non-profit organizations.

What is a non-profit organization?

Within the UK there is no agreed definition of what a non-profit organization is (Octon, 1983). Indeed, the term remains one, though often used,

which most people find difficult to delineate. However, people will state that they consider certain types of organizations, such as charities, to be 'non-profit making' organizations. Unfortunately such definitions take the search for clarity little further because the definition of 'a charity' is far from clear – though most people would claim 'to recognize one when they see one'!

The problem is further complicated because, as most members of the public recognize, many non-profit making organizations need to make profits in the sense of having an income in excess of expenditure. Indeed, such organizations often undertake some activities with a clear intention of making a profit – a process described as 'piggy-backing' (Nielsen, 1982). Oxfam, for example, runs more shops in Britain than any other commercial organization and they are run at a profit and the Royal Society for the Protection of Birds has a mail-order trading company with a turnover of £4 million which provides a 25 per cent return on capital (Maclaughlin, 1986).

The recognition that some organizations, commonly considered to be classified as 'non-profit', do at least need to cover their costs and may therefore maintain activities designed to create profits perhaps indicates a way of moving towards a definition of a non-profit organization. Essentially, the aim of such an organization is to be 'a non-loss organization' in that continued expenditure in excess of revenue will inevitably produce problems. However, the term 'a not-for-profit organization' actually encaptures the non-loss aspect and also the idea of profits being made but only as a means to an end. What the term 'not-for-profit' points to is that some organizations:

1 Do not have as their prime goal the creation of profits, *but* do need to cover their costs.
2 May pursue profit-making activities *but* only in support of their prime goal.

Thus, an organization may have as its prime goal the alleviation of poverty among some groups in the population. To enable it to achieve this objective it will, over a period of time, incur some costs and will therefore need funds both to cover these costs and also to distribute among its target group. It may raise these funds in a variety of ways including seeking out donations, but also possibly including running a shop, holding a jumble sale, etc. The clear intent of these latter activities being to make a profit which can then be used to finance the organization's pursuit of its prime goal.

The definition of a non-profit organization used in this chapter will therefore be as follows:

A non-profit organization is an organization whose attainment of its prime goal is not assessed by economic measures. However, in pursuit of that goal it may undertake profit-making activities.

It will be noted that this definition does not refer to the legal status of the organization. Indeed, an organization conforming to this definition might have any one of several legal statuses, such as that of a charity, a statutory water company or whatever. Indeed, it is possible, though relatively unusual, to find an organization with the status of a public limited company which under the above definition could be considered to be a non-profit organization. (It is, of course, important to distinguish between public limited companies, which do not make profits and those which are non-profit under this definition. Some public limited companies do not make profits for periods of time even though that was not their intention!)

That this definition does not mention the organization's legal status in no way implies that the matter is unimportant. In fact, the most effec-

tive way for a non-profit organization to achieve its prime goal is often through a legal status other than that of a public limited company. In the particular case of charities, there can be substantial advantages in obtaining charitable status – though such a status also imposes certain limitations on the organization's activities and its development.

The managerial implications of being 'non-profit'

If non-profit organizations can be defined in this way what, if any, is the implication for their use of marketing? The best way of determining this is by considering the organizational characteristics of such bodies. There are five commonly recognized characteristics (Hofstede, 1981) which apply to most non-profit organizations. However, as was indicated earlier, there will be some non-profit organizations to which not all (or even none) of these apply and there will be some 'for profit' organizations to which some (or even all) of them apply.

1 *Ambiguous goals*. Voluntary, charitable and professional bodies are often the scene of conflicts over specific goals and objectives. Thus, when seeking to plan an organization's activities the goals and objectives need to be set down and placed in order of priority. At such a time conflicts may arise within the management team and/or governing body. Given that either because of its constitution or the value system of the members there is also a right or assumed right for members to have a 'say' in the running of the organization then the setting of priorities may be complex, time-consuming and subject to frequent reappraisal (*The Times*, 1986)

Where such organizations employ some full-time staff a further form of conflict may arise in that the personal objectives of the full-time staff may, understandably, differ from those of the voluntary members. Thus career objectives, the desire for job security, etc., may lead full-time employees to seek to change the goal of a non-profit organization. This was observed when polio was effectively conquered and the full-time employees of the American Foundation for Infantile Paralysis sought to find new goals for the

Foundation, so as to ensure their future employment (Perrow, 1970).

2 *Lack of agreement on means-ends relationship*. Even where there is a consensus among an organization's members as to its goals, there may be lack of agreement as to how they should be achieved. This may be based on either a lack of knowledge as to how to achieve the goal, lack of agreement as to which method most effectively leads to the goal's attainment or the refusal by some members to accept some methods which others believe will lead to achieving the goal. The fact that some inputs, particularly labour, may have either a large direct financial cost or, if volunteers are substituted for paid employees, a zero or near zero direct financial cost making both measurement of costs and projections of costs very difficult.

3 *Environmental turbulence*. All organizations face some environmental turbulence but many non-profit organizations seem to face even greater difficulties in this regard than 'for profit' organizations. Part of the problem being that their goals, although often ambiguous, are usually more specific than those of 'for-profit' organizations.

Thus a 'for-profit' organization will usually be prepared to move into any area of activity which enables it to achieve its economic goals, but a non-profit organization is often tied by its goals to define areas of concern or activity. Furthermore, if an organization holds the legal status of a charity it is possible for a very small proportion of its trustees to block any move to change its specified goals and/or its legal status. If these areas are totally dealt with or even only affected by, say, legislation, technological development, social change, etc., then the organization may need either to accept new goals or substantial adaptions to existing ones. (The polio case, above, illustrates this.)

4 *Unmeasurable outputs*. Even where an organization's goals are clearly specified and agreed upon, it may be impossible for a non-profit organization to quantify its level of achievement. Where this is the case, then difficulties in measuring both efficiency and effectiveness arise. Furthermore, there is the danger that measures will be evolved which, while originally recognized to be very poor proxies, ultimately become prime objectives. For example, assessing the output of a counselling organization is clearly difficult (particularly in those cases where the anonymity of the client is guaranteed and it is therefore very difficult to follow a client's progress without their agreement and cooperation). Proxy measures of an organization's output such as the number of clients, average time spent with each client, etc., are potentially misleading as indicators of goal achievement and can be mischievous in their effect on the counsellors' attitudes and behaviour.

What happens in many non-profit organizations is that inputs can be measured and outputs cannot. The danger is that input measures are then used to measure outputs. Furthermore, much management time is spent on resource allocation but this use of time has little direct effect on the organization's efficiency or effectiveness because nobody knows which allocation of measures corresponds to maximum effectiveness.

5 *The effects of management intervention are unknown*. Obviously, management of any organization is difficult where any or all of characteristics 1 to 4 apply. However, even where they do not apply, it does seem that in non-profit organizations the links between management actions and their results are little understood. Very often this is because the prime goals of both the organizations and the individual members are not economic. This makes the assessment of the effects of a management decision much more difficult because it makes the use of monetary value as a uniform unit of measurement inappropriate.

In summary, these are five characteristics of non-profit organizations which distinguish them from 'for-profit' organizations.

Many non-profit organizations, such as those concerned with drug addiction, clearly illustrate those characteristics. What are their goals? Even within individual organizations once discussion of goals becomes more specific than 'dealing with the problems of drug addiction' great disagreement is observed – to stop all drug taking; concentrate on hard drugs only, etc. Even where a goal is reasonably specific and agreed, how can it be achieved? Unfortunately nobody knows though many experiments are tried. What of environmental turbulence? How does the arrival of 'crack'; increased police activity; more public awareness; etc., affect such organization's goals and activities? What measures would such organizations use to measure their effectiveness – a particularly difficult issue where their clients are often very concerned about confidentiality.

Implications for marketing

If these are the characteristics of non-profit organizations, what implications do they have for the use of marketing in support of their pursuit of their prime goals?

It has been suggested by Hofstede (1981) that there are several types of management decision making:

1 Routine.
2 Expert.
3 Trial and error.
4 Intuitive.
5 Judgemental.
6 Political.

Hofstede also says that the decision-making style is more likely to be judgmental or political where an organization displays those characteristics, described above, as applying to non-profit organizations.

What is important about both these categories, but particularly 'political', is that significant decisions can only result from negotiations between groups and/or individuals within the organization. Such groups may support particular interests and hold conflicting value positions. In addition, non-profit organizations' governing bodies are often elected annually from and by the whole membership. (They may include a small number of representatives of any full-time employees though these are often ex-officio members with only 'observer' status.) The membership of such bodies may change reasonably often as the time demands on non-employees become heavy and the chairman of such bodies usually need to be re-elected each year. Together, these factors can create a relatively

unstable leadership situation and make it easier for 'politically' active groups within the membership to achieve changes to the ruling body.

Furthermore, many non-profit organizations do not possess a hierarchy with sufficient power to impose a solution upon conflicting parties – such power in profit-making organizations usually ultimately devolving from ownership rights. It follows that decisions are often composed of a rational element heavily laced with values which differ between groups in the organizations, and norms which change over time. Indeed, it has been suggested that those decisions which cannot be derived from clear goals and result from a process of negotiation are almost unpredictable!

Such a situation has significant implications for the application of marketing in non-profit organizations. First, as most definitions of marketing point out (Rodger, 1971), marketing is a purposive activity whose aim is to enable the organization to achieve its goals by providing consumer satisfaction. Clearly, therefore, if goal ambiguity exists, it is very difficult for marketing action to be effective. Second, the political mode of decision making creates the probability that goals and objectives will be changed over quite short periods of time as the political process evolves and different groups or individuals become dominant. As much marketing activity is concerned with activities which require a consistent policy over a period of time, say establishing an organizational image, this creates a substantial problem.

Third, the unmeasurable nature of many non-profit organizations' output means that there are difficulties in determining the effectiveness of some critical marketing activities – for example creating consumer satisfaction. Thus brand managers in fast-moving consumer goods companies will not only have very clear goals and good measures of the level of their achievement, but also a good idea of how to react if the measures indicate an unsatisfactory level of achievement. However, managers of, say, a museum may not only have an ambiguous set of goals, but also have difficulty in measuring their attainment of any of them and little detailed knowledge of how the available marketing tactics will relate to the desired level of outputs. One result of this is that learning from marketing experiences in non-profit organizations is less easy.

A final and very critical issue regarding marketing's role in non-profit organizations is that the very appropriateness of marketing, with its various connotations and associations, to these organizations' needs is questioned by many people. To be precise, some members of such organizations while willing to use marketing in relation to their for-profit support activities, are often resolutely opposed to the use of it in support of their prime goal. This opposition may be based upon one of a wide range of positions ranging from the feeling that 'being commercial is not nice' through to a belief that capitalism is exploitive and that marketing is a tool of capitalism. It is not appropriate to argue with such positions here but common to this range of views is the assumption that the use of marketing would in some way adversely affect the nature of the organization's core product. Such an assumption does need examination as it underlies the aversion to marketing which exists among significant groups of the non-profit sector of the economy and arises from a view that 'the customer is not always right'.

'The customer is not always right'

There are a significant number of non-profit organizations which basically hold the view that they know what is best for their consumers. As a consequence of this, they are instinctively ill at ease with marketing for it appears to make the consumer dominant (Andreasen, 1982) and place the customer in a position to challenge their view of what the product should be.

The 'knowing best' may be based upon a belief (for example, a religion), a conviction (for example, vegetarianism), training (for example, a profession such as medicine), or a law (for example, treatment of animals). The effect of this may be two-fold. First, an organization whose primary goal is based upon such a certainty is likely to regard the characteristics of its product as fixed and only to be changed when the organization's members determine that a change is necessary. Second, even where clear evidence becomes available that actual or potential consumers would like some change there will be a refusal to make such a change if it relates to what is perceived as the primary goal of the organization.

However, this situation is not unknown among for-profit organizations, many of which are unable to adjust elements of their product (and some who could but will not) regardless of consumer reaction. For example, many products have some aspects of their physical specifications which are legally determined. Such legally imposed standards are often made by Parliament with little evidence that individual members of the public want the legislation. Car manufacturers, for example, now incorporate safety features in their vehicles which are legally required, but were 'unsaleable' prior to the introduction of the legislation.

Cases do arise though where for-profit organizations impose on themselves certain limitations which arise not from legal requirements but from the organization's value system. The owners of Lego, for example, are reputed to refuse to allow sets of their bricks to be sold in colours which are militaristic or in sets which depict military activity.

It would appear, therefore, that 'knowing best' does not of itself create difficulties in accepting marketing as 'for-profit' organizations can also find themselves either unable or unwilling to alter aspects of their product and yet accept marketing and can be very profitable. What seems to be the problem is that members of non-profit organizations, due to their non-economic prime goals plus their legal status, which is usually not that of a public limited company, can extend their certainty about the rightness of their core product to every aspect of the service that they offer. Indeed, a failure to distinguish between the essential core product, and the peripheral elements can often be observed with, on occasions the peripheral elements becoming if not dominant then given almost as much emphasis as the core product. This is observable among some Christian groups when an issue which, while important (or important at a given point in time) but not fundamental to their belief, may be given a degree of prominence, which is unwarranted. For example, some Methodists still behave as if they regard teetotalism as a central tenet of their faith – which it has never been (though it was certainly in the eighteenth century a valued contribution to the improvement of the health of the British population).

It must be emphasized that the members of such organizations are usually fundamentally committed to the well-being of their customers. However, their belief in the prime importance of their activity, the characteristics of non-profit organizations and their insulation, often as a result of their organization's legal status, from market pressures allow them to become insensitive to aspects of their market's needs.

If you are sure that you know what customers require and are either isolated from market forces or are prepared to accept the consequences of ignoring them (as the true idealist will or those sheltered from market forces can) then logically there is no need for market research, the concept of the marketing mix is irrelevant and marketing planning is only of interest as a way of determining future resource needs not as a way of planning the provision of consumer satisfaction.

However, there are two reasons why acceptance of a marketing approach may be of value to a non-profit organization as it pursues its primary goal. First it will, through providing an insight into the consumers' (actual and potential) view, enable the organization to understand how it can present its core product in as effective a manner as possible – effective in the sense of bringing the results of the organization's activities close to its goals. Second, it will increase the organization's efficiency by identifying those ways of relating to consumers which provide the best response within the constraints it imposes on itself.

As will be seen below it is important that these two reasons are communicated to and understood by members of non-profit organizations seeking to use marketing for the first time. Only if the members can be convinced that these reasons are applicable to their organization are they likely to accept a marketing approach.

Marketing information, the marketing mix and marketing planning in non-profit organizations

Within for-profit organizations, information is gathered and analysed with the intent of narrowing the gap between what is known about the customers and what needs to be known if effective marketing is to be undertaken. Although many non-profit orga-

nizations do have access to some market information, it is noticeable that much of it is actually of the type traditionally viewed as market research rather than marketing research. In other words, it is primarily quantitative, descriptive information such as

- Number of donors.
- Number of customers.
- Location of clients, etc.

In particular, there is commonly a lack of information regarding:

- Customers' evaluation of competitive activities.
- Evaluation of clients' changing policies.
- Evaluation of new offerings, etc.

However, examination of the situation shows that the reason why there is a failure to collect marketing information has little or nothing to do with whether or not it is a non-profit organization. Rather, the reason lies with the organization's view of its own activities. Thus, if those running an organization believe that they know what is best for their customers then there is little point in asking how people evaluate the product. There may, of course, be a need to know how many customers there are and the volume of their requirements. For example, the Water Companies in Britain have their main activities prescribed by law. They also are restricted in their price setting by legislation which requires them to be able to provide a cost justification for any differential pricing. In such circumstances, given their monopoly position, it could be argued that the only market research needed is with regard to the demand for water. In the case of non-metered households (the great majority) this demand information is independent of price and is therefore a relatively simple piece of information. However, even in the case of those users who are metered and thus pay a price per gallon, there is little attempt to measure price elasticity because of the legislation which precludes differential pricing except where based on cost differentials.

Consideration of the problems faced by at least some water companies would indicate that, had they collected marketing information over a period of years it would enable them to respond more effectively to their current problems. For example, in some districts there are bottlenecks in the regular supply of water and also clearance of sewage. It seems that often nothing is known about how consumers in these areas will react to the various alternative solutions which the local water board can legally propose. In such circumstances, a solution will be implemented which best meets the need to make technoeconomic trade-offs within the company. Only by luck will the solution so chosen be the one most satisfying to the consumers affected. Indeed, any assessment of consumer preference is likely to come, at best from discussions with Consumer Consultative Committees, or from the views of the Authority's employees. It is, therefore, quite feasible for the solution chosen to be more expensive than the solution acceptable to the consumers. Even worse, it could be that the solution selected may not be the least expensive, and may also cause consumer dissatisfaction.

The lack of marketing information, rather than market information, can lead to both inefficiency and ineffectiveness.

The marketing mix

Much of the discussion of the problems of applying marketing to non-profit organizations has essentially revolved around the concept of the marketing mix. A greater part of these discussions has been almost vacuous based as they have been on a naive or simplistic view of the marketing mix which equates it with 'the four Ps' (McCarthy, 1975). That this is an inadequate representation of the concept is less important than the fact that it actually appears to create difficulties in the minds of those considering applying marketing to non-profit organizations.

The formulation of a marketing mix requires:

1   A list of the organization's product features and controllable variables.
2   A list of the market forces to which the organization must respond.

Borden (1965) who is an early and authorative exponent of this concept, provides illustrative lists but stresses that other people and other situations will require different lists. It follows, therefore, that the absence of, say, price from the list of

product features is quite feasible in certain circumstances (Fox, 1986).

In spite of this, some writers do seem to find it difficult to accept that not all marketing mixes must have some representation of each of the four Ps and go to great lengths to demonstrate that, for example, there is a non-economic price involved in dealing with some non-profit organizations (Shapiro, 1973). Doing this, apparently for no other reason than that they have thus filled four boxes, each labelled 'P'! This preoccupation with the four Ps distracts from the essential problem which marketing managers face which is to identify:

1   The organization's product features and controllable variables and, separately, those features which they can alter.
2   Those market forces which influence demand and, separately, those forces which they can modify.

With this information, they must assemble using their available resources a mix of variables which both responds to the unalterable market forces; modifies those market forces which can be altered; and, is coherent in itself. In this process certain product features will be identified as being of greater importance than others, while some will be recognized to be of little significance (even though those within the organization may find this to contradict their beliefs, convictions or perceptions!)

Consider the problems of marketing universities (clearly non-profit organizations!) to potential undergraduates. There is a large number of product features which can be listed but some are unalterable by the university itself (for example, tuition fees). Examination of the factors which influence student choice will indicate that some of the product features have very limited impact – for example, the academic reputation of the faculty (much as this may annoy the more academically eminent members of the faculty and confirm them in their view that students are Philistines!) However, other features affecting student choice will be beyond the influence of the university – for example, the low cost of public transport in the locality (a feature which is reputed to have strongly influenced student demand for places in one city's university). Of course, identification of such a factor enables those universities not in such a beneficial position to respond by emphasizing, say, the high proportion of students living on campus and thus not needing much public transport.

Marketing managers thus assemble a marketing mix which responds to those factors which they identify as influencing student demand. Some of the response being direct, such as stressing the social facilities available, and other parts of the response being indirect, as in the case of the cost of public transport. Some of the response omitting or giving little influence to those features of the product which the organization's members consider to be important but which in the short-term either do not influence market forces or may have a negative effect. Thus, while the academic excellence and reputation of the staff of a university may have a strong influence on its long-term viability, if it is found to have little short-term influence on the demand for student places, then emphasizing it in the marketing mix would be inappropriate.

The problem in using the marketing mix in non-profit organizations is not that the concept is inapplicable but:

1 Such organizations, as was pointed out earlier, lack the information needed to effectively formulate a marketing mix.
2 Where such information becomes available it may challenge the views of members of an organization as to what is important and may thus be unacceptable.

What is observable in the activities of some non-profit organizations is not that they do not have a marketing mix (indeed, unless an organization lives in a vacuum it is arguable that it cannot avoid having a marketing mix), but that it has not been formulated in the above manner. In particular, there seems to be a lack of appreciation or understanding of market forces and the need for a coherent set of variables. However, this situation is not unique to non-profit organizations.

It does seem, though, that some criticisms of non-profit organizations' lack of an appropriate marketing mix is superficial and that the marketing undertaken is more sophisticated than is often suggested. For example, criticisms have been made of some non-profit organizations' failure to make full use of the range of available communication variables. However, many organizations have investigated this matter and have found that:

1 Certain types of communication may be self-defeating. This is illustrated by the anticipated reactions to some suggestions on how to advertise the Church of England (Jones, 1987) and by the reaction of some organizations to 'cause-related marketing' (Caesar, 1986). A more subtle issue which illustrates the importance of segmentation in communications policies, is the need to present official documents in a style which, while not too lavish, is at least business-like (Burnett, 1986).
2 That excessive expenditure on advertising can raise questions in the minds of donors of time and/or money as to whether funds are being currently spent wisely (McEwan, 1982).

Again, consider the possibility of the use of price as a variable. Certainly, in the case of the Blood Transfusion Service, there is evidence that offering to pay people for their blood has several negative effects:

1 Many non-economic blood donors withdraw if others sell their blood thus possibly reducing the total supply of blood.
2 The number of people willing to sell their blood is not high.
3 The costs of administering the service and checking the quality of the blood rise when blood is bought from donors.

Indeed, this service faces substantial problems in creating a marketing mix given the nature of its physical product. One area of this service once experimented in informing donors as to what use their blood had been put, the aim being to make the donor feel involved. However, the effects on the appetites of donors who received their post during breakfast did not increase donor commitment!

Marketing planning

The process of marketing planning is aimed at producing a market plan which can be described as 'a statement that specifies a systematic and integrated programme for achieving certain marketing goals within a prescribed period of time'. Such a plan once implemented will, it is claimed, help an organization to achieve its goals.

The fact that most non-profit organizations do not undertake marketing planning activities does not distinguish them from large numbers of 'for-profit' organizations (Greenley, 1985). Indeed most commentators agree that relatively few organizations of any type undertake any form of marketing planning. The issues which therefore have to be considered are first, whether or not there are reasons why a non-profit organization cannot undertake marketing planning. The second question is, even if such an organization can undertake such planning, could it be of any benefit?

Examination of the activities which are typically listed as consituting the marketing planning process (see Table 27.1 for an example) indicate some problems (Blois and Octon, 1982) when related to the characteristics of non-profit organizations identified above. In particular, there are the evident difficulties in establishing specific goals and also the lack of knowlege concerning linkages between inputs and outputs. Obviously, if goals cannot be specified then planning becomes pointless except in the sense that the stages in Table 27.1 emphasize the problem of resources. So, working through the stages in the table, forces recognition of the need to consider the organization's resource base, its use and its need for periodic renewal. Such a process *might* cause an organization to query 'renewal for what purpose'?

However, it must be stressed that this lack of goal clarity, while typical of most non-profit organizations, is also frequently observed in 'for-profit' organizations and is one of the reasons why marketing planning is so often not undertaken. There are, nevertheless, some non-profit organizations which have been able to define their goals with sufficient clarity to enable them to attempt the planning process (Medley, 1984). Although it is difficult to produce evidence to support this contention, it does appear that where such clarity of goals has been achieved it is because of strong leadership developing within the organization. Leadership which has been able to 'handle' the complex political processes within such organizations.Unfortunately, it must be noted that such leaders are not infrequently removed from office after a period of time as new coalitions and groupings evolve within the organization.

Table 27.1 *Distinguishable planning phases*

1   State the firm's marketing objectives.

2   Assess the firm's marketing resources.

3   Review recent developments that are relevant to marketing the firm's products.

4   Forecast future developments that are relevant to the firm's products.

5   Identify the feasible courses of action suitable for the expected circumstances.

6   Select the most promising alternatives.

7   Establish a programme to carry out the selected alternatives.

8   Periodically review progress of a plan.

9   Revise the plan.

Note: These phases may not be followed in sequence. Indeed many of the phases interact with each other as a decision in one may cause a reappraisal of decisions made in another phase.

The second issue concerns the value of marketing planning to non-profit organizations. Again, a comparison with for-profit organizations is relevant and here the fact is that it is difficult to find concrete evidence that marketing planning is beneficial. However, many firms which have implemented systems for creating marketing planning procedures claim that they are of value. Fundamentally, whether or not any organization undertakes marketing planning reflects their view as to whether they will just react to a changing environment or make planned responses to such changes and commit resources in anticipation of changes in the environment (McCorkey, 1981).

It has been argued above that for a variety of reasons, many non-profit organizations simply do not perceive a need to respond to environmental change. This view deriving either from the organization's primary goal and/or their organizational status which shields them, particularly from the economic environment.

Conclusion

The above discussion has sought to indicate that marketing can be used by non-profit organizations in support of their goals (Yorke, 1984). The fact that such organizations often do not use marketing is, it is suggested, less to do with their 'non-profitness' than with their members' views and values. Whilst any organization which is legal has a right to exist, no organization has a right to the support which is required if it is to exist. What members of non-profit organizations need to understand is the role that marketing can play in obtaining that support. In other words, there is a need to market 'marketing' to the members of these non-profit organizations.

As was outlined above, members of non-profit organizations often have a core product which is unchangeable because of their beliefs, convictions, training or the law. Often their commitment to supply this product is based upon a genuine desire to serve the public.

However, without marketing, two things can and do happen which lessen the value of what they do. First, their pre-occupation with their core product (and its importance to them) can blinker them to the overall needs of their customers and ways in which their product can be augmented to increase consumer satisfaction. Second, when additions and alterations are made they sometimes, over time, become rigidly associated with the core products even though they are not essential to the achievement of the organization's prime goal. The consequence of this being both the deflection of resources from the achievement of the prime goal and consumer dissatisfaction, if the preoccupation with the extended product distracts from considering consumers' current needs.

The question 'Is it a product you sell or a service you give?' was asked by Maurice Lowther, managing director of a water company (Williams, 1986). He asked it in the context of a discussion as to whether or not the Water Authorities should be privatized. Mr Lowther was opposed to privatization, believing that one of the results of privatization will be to make the high standards which his (and other) Water Authorities have set and attained more difficult to maintain.

His views are diametrically opposed to those of Roy Watts, Chairman of Thames Water, (Williams, 1986) who wanted his organization to be privatized but, in any case, was intent on making Thames Water more consumer orientated.

Lowther's comments are typical of many of those who manage non-profit organizations. They believe that they are serving the public well – Lowther, for

example, further stated 'we've always put the community first' – and indeed there may be little evidence of consumer dissatisfaction (Thames Water Report, 1984–5). However, given such organizations' lack of marketing information, their organizational structures and the commitment of their employees there is a constant danger of them becoming paternalistic. Such paternalism often developing into complacency and also possibly dictatorial attitudes. Marketing's role is to stop this happening for as McKitterick (1957) stated over thirty years ago:

> The principal task of the marketing function in a management concept is not so much to be skilful in making the customer do what suits the interest of the business, as to be skilful in conceiving and then making the business do what suits the interest of the customer.

References

Andreasen, Alan, R., 'Non-Profits: Check your Attention to Customers, *Harvard Business Review*, vol. 60, no. 3, May-June 1982. pp. 105–10.

Blois, Keith J. and Octon, Carol M, 'Marketing Planning in Local Authority Leisure Centres' *Quarterly Review of Marketing*, vol. 8, no. 1, Autumn 1982, pp. 19–25.

Borden, N.H., 'The Concept of the Marketing Mix', in George Schwartz, *Science in Marketing*, John Wiley & Sons, 1965, p. 386–97.

Burnett, K., 'Does your Annual Report Deserve to win any prizes?', *Accountancy*, February 1986, pp. 76–9.

Caesar, P., 'Cause-Related Marketing: the new face of corporate philanthropy', *Business and Society Review*, no. 59, Fall 1986, pp. 15–19.

Fox, Mike, 'What Price Petrol?', *Marketing*, 4 September 1986, p. 12.

Greenley, Gordon G., 'Marketing Plan Utilisation', *The Quarterly Review of Marketing*, vol. 10, no. 4, July 1985, pp. 12–19.

Hofstede, Geert, 'Management Control of Public and Not-For-Profit Activities', *Accounting, Organisations and Society*, vol. 6, no. 3, 1981, pp. 193–211.

Jones, M., 'The gospel according to the admen', *Campaign*, July, 1987, pp. 32, 33 and 35.

MacLaughlin Nicola, 'Tendering for a Touch', *Marketing*, 24 April 1986, pp. 26–9.

McCarthy, E. Jerome, *Basic Marketing*, 5th ed., Richard D Irwin Inc, 1975, pp. 75–81.

McCorkey, Dale D., 'Strategic Planning in Non-Profit Organizations', *Business Quarterly*, Summer 1981, pp. 24–33.

McEwan, Fiona, 'Why Charity Now Begins With an Advertisement', *The Financial Times*, 30 September 1982, p. 18.

McKitterick, J.B., 'What is the Marketing Management Concept?', in Frank M. Bass, (ed.), *The Frontiers of Marketing Thought and Science*. American Marketing Association, 1957, pp. 71–81.

Medley, G. J., 'Strategic Planning for the World Wild Life Fund', *Journal of Long Range Planning*, 1988, vol. 21, no. 1, pp. 46–54.

Nielsen, R. P., 'Strategic Piggybacking – Self-subsidization strategy for non-profit organizations', *Sloan Management Review*, Summer 1982, pp. 65–70.

Octon, C.M., 'A Re-Examination of Marketing for British Non-profit Organizations', *European Journal of Marketing*, vol. 17, no. 5, 1983, pp. 33–43.

Perrow, Charles, *Organizational Analysis*, Tavistock Publications, 1970, pp. 136–7.

Rodger, L.W. *Marketing in a Competitive Economy*, 3rd ed., Halstead Press, 1971.

Shapiro, Benson, P., 'Marketing for Non-Profit Organizations', *Harvard Business Review*, vol. 51, no. 5, October-September 1973.

Annual Report and Accounts 1984–5, Thames Water.

'Charity Head in Expenses Dispute'; 'Galloway at Bay' The Times Diary, *The Times*, 29 October 1986, p. 5 and 16.

Yorke, D.A. (ed.), 'The Marketing of Local Authortity Leisure Services', *European Journal of Marketing*, vol. 18, No. 2, 1984.

Williams, J., 'Water Carriers Face the Deep End', *The Sunday Times*, 8 June 1986, p. 58.

28
The pursuit of quality

MICHAEL J. BAKER

Introduction

In recent years it has become increasingly fashionable to speak of change. Of course change has always been with us but, like marketing, events have conspired to throw it into even sharper focus in the second half of this century. In the case of marketing a concern for satisfying demand through the optimum use of scarce resources has been the driving force behind all economic development. However, it is only in the twentieth century that the possibility of achieving this goal on a large scale has become apparent – albeit only in the rich and advanced countries – and precipitated a radical revision of our view of the world.

On the other hand, there is extensive evidence to suggest that our present preoccupation with the nature and consequences of change is but a phase in an evolutionary cycle and that the same concern has been experienced a number of times in the past. While it is sound counsel not to live in the past, there is every reason why we should seek to learn from it for, by doing so, we may improve our future. To suggest that in years to come the second half of the twentieth century will be seen as a major watershed in man's evolution may seem a little far fetched. But if one wishes to promote such a proposition where better than as the epilogue to a state of the art book on marketing?

Evolutionary cycles

In Chapter 1 we introduced the concept of life cycles and evolution. There is an extensive and pervasive body of evidence that unmistakably points to the evolutionary nature of progress and change. Indeed the evidence is so universal that it leads to the inescapable conclusion that the advance of civilization – economic, political and social – is the consequence of a series of cycles of flourishing growth, complacent maturity, of decadence and decay and regeneration giving rise to a new wave of optimism and growth.

Some years ago I put forward a simple example to demonstrate why the diffusion of innovation – which is the well spring of all change – should be an exponential process subject to limiting or boundary conditions which prevent it continuing to infinity. This example was based upon the well-documented field of biological growth and ran as follows:

Assume that we possess a simple organism that reproduces itself by cell division then, *ceteris paribus*, we may anticipate that the rate of increase of the population will follow the series 1, 2, 4, 8, 16, 32, 64. . . . Unfortunately for our simple cell it is not immortal, but can only reproduce itself twice before dying so that the population will in fact expand in a series which starts 1, 2, 3, 5, 8, 13, 21 . . . . Further, it is also apparent that there must be a finite limit to the resources on which the organism depends for its existence so that growth cannot continue indefinitely. The validity of this contention may easily be demonstrated by placing a simple cell which reproduces itself by division into a restricted environment such as a sealed test-tube. Growth may well continue to the point where the test-tube is visibly filled with cells which are invisible by themselves but, ultimately, the lack of space and neccessary nutrients will stabilise growth at some upper limit. In fact, if some factors are in fixed supply then their consumption will eventually lead to the decline and extinction of our population of cells.

However, one must be careful not to assume that decline and extinction will automatically occur for, as Price points out, the existence of a ceiling to exponential growth frequently gives rise to a strong reaction as that ceiling is approached.

Price describes a number of ways in which an exponentially growing phenomenon will seek to avoid a reduction in growth as it nears its ceiling. Two of these, 'escalation' and 'loss of definition' are viewed as particularly important for they occur more frequently than the '. . . plain S-shaped ogive'.

In the case of escalation, minor modification of the original phenomenon takes place at or near the point of inflection and '. . . a new logistic curve rises phoenixlike on the ashes of the old . . .' (Price). In a marketing context a close analogy of this is provided by the 'product rejuvenation strategy' whereby further modification of a product is undertaken to revitalise stagnant demand for it.

In many cases, however, it is not possible to raise the ceiling through modification and the phenomenon will fluctuate wildly in an attempt to avoid the inevitable. As a result of these oscillations the phenomenon may become so changed as to be unrecognizable (loss of definition), for example the cell described in our earlier example may mutate into a new species of cell suited to the conditions which were limiting to continued growth of the original cell. Alternatively, the phenomenon may accept the inevitable, smoothing out the oscillations and settling in equilibrium at a stable limit, or under different circumstances, slowly decline to nothing.

Figure 28.1 depicts this process.

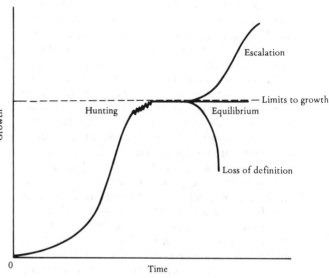

Figure 28.1   *Growth cycles*

A second renaissance

As I indicated earlier, while it may appear fanciful to suggest that in years to come our times will be seen as a major watershed in the evolution of civilization, this would seem to be as appropriate a place as any to suggest that we could be facing a similar opportunity today. The turbulence of the past twenty five years resembles strongly to me the wild oscillations of our cell as it seeks to avoid the apparently inevitable 'limits to growth', so eloquently described by the Club of Rome, or the 'Silent Spring' of Rachel Carson.

Of course turbulence is a relative state and it may be in years to come that people will look back and see that twentieth century man achieved a smooth transition from industrial to post-industrial society just as some historians see the Renaissance as a discontinuity with the Dark Ages which preceded it (for example Burckhardt's *The Civilisation of the Renaissance in Italy* (1860) while others see it as an escalation of a trend. On balance the latter view seems the more plausible.

Following the loss of definition of the Roman Empire which led to its decline and fall there was a period of comparative obscurity in the development of Western civilization – hence the Dark Ages. But this period of inconspicuous growth suddenly escalated with the economic revolution pre-cipitated by the Crusaders and breathed new life into the trading ports of both Northern Europe and the Mediterranean. As a consequence a new middle class of merchants, traders and bankers emerged and it was they who were to lay the foundations on which the Renaissance was created. It is a moot point whether political forces act as the catalyst for economic change or vice versa but it does seem that political stability and economic wealth are neces-sary preconditions for revolutions in thought and culture. Certainly the origins of the Renaissance owe much to the renewal of civic liberty and inter-nal order in the Italian city states of the fourteenth and fifteenth century and the patronage and protec-tion of the rich and powerful, like the Medicis. It is also appropriate to point out that the wealth of the Medicis was based upon capital accumulation and, in the case of Florence, its investment in manufac-turing industry (textiles).

But the real breakthrough of the Renaissance came in 1564 with the birth of Galileo Galilei the Florentine physicist, philosopher and inventor whose name has become the cardinal emblem of Renaissance science and the ensuing technological revolution in which we are still engaged. Again, Galileo appears to represent a discontinuity but, in the long view, should be regarded as the catalyst which initiated new momentum and escalation to the evolutionary process. Thus Galileo is both a symbol of the revolt of reason against the blind forces of ignorance and authority and of the clarity of science contrasted with the obscurity of medieval philosophy and theology. He must also be acclaimed for developing new instruments like the telescope, thermometer and pendulum clock which gave a new reach and accuracy to science so neces-sary for its further development.

Today we continue to face changes which seem revolutionary to us but with the passage of time will show up as only minor oscillations in our evolution-ary cycle. If we believe there are limits to growth it is likely that we do so only because we cannot conceive of the developments which will free us from our present understanding. However, it is not my purpose to speculate upon where mankind will be in a thousand years from now but to address the much more specific question of whether we are entering upon a new *phase* in the evolutionary cycle and, if so, what are its implications for, say the year 2000?

Synthesis and progress

It is unfortunate that *synthetic* has the connotations of 'artificial, ersatz, fake and mock' when it is a consequence of the process of *synthesis* which has the meaning of 'amalgamation, coalescence, combina-tion, integration, unification and welding' (*Collins New Thesaurus*). Of course synthetic also means manmade or manufactured and therefore represents something not available in nature which, in turn, must mean an extension in the choice available to mankind.

The discipline of marketing, and even more so that of management, is a synthetic one. Because it is synthetic I believe it to be superior to the core or single disciplines which it seeks to combine into a more powerful interpretation and analysis of the complexity of the real world. Of course marketing and management being new disciplines are seen as threatening to those which they appear to subsume or displace. They are assailed on all sides. Academics criticize them for their lack of rigour (and antiquity) while practitioners without formal qualifications dismiss academic theorizing as unnecessary to practice or even irrelevant.

Such attitudes and pronouncements are as ignor-ant and authoritarian as those of the medieval philosophers and theologians whom Galileo sought to overthrow. They would return our understand-ing of economic behaviour to the state of astronomy prior to Copernicus, of medicine before Harvey's discovery of the circulation of the blood, and en-gineering to a pre-Newtonian simplicity. Thus, un-fettered by the constraints of a single discipline, and fully recognizing that medicine, engineering and management add value through their *practice*, I would like to review a number of concepts or ideas which collectively can be integrated to provide the coalescence which represents true synthesis.

Maslow's hierarchy of needs

In that the whole is the sum of its parts so society is the sum of the individuals which comprise it. It would seem sensible, therefore, to commence my synthesis with a simple model which seeks to classify motives. Motives have been described by Engel *et al.*, (1986) as 'enduring dispositions that direct be-haviour towards certain goals' – in other words motives act as both a catalyst for and drive towards behaviour. Although the subject of much study and debate among psychologists and others there is general support for the simple classification proposed by Maslow (1954) in which he argues that motives are organized in a hierarchy which establish both priority and importance ('prepotency'). His model recognises five stages which, in ascending order of importance, may be defined as follows:

1 *Physiological*: the fundamentals of survival, including hunger and thirst.
2 *Safety*: concern over physical survival and safety which might be overcome in satisfying physiological needs.
3 *Belongingness and love*: the need to be accepted by one's immediate family and to be important to them.
4 *Esteem and status*: the need to achieve a high standing relative to others outside the immediate family; the desire for mastery, reputation and prestige.
5 *Self-actualization*: desire to know, understand, systematize and construct a system of values.

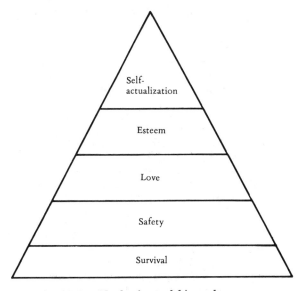

Figure 28.2 *Maslow's need hierarchy*

Symbolically this hierarchy is usually depicted as a pyramid as in Figure 28.2.

In essence then, Maslow is proposing three levels of (1) survival, (2) human interaction and involvement and (3) competency and the self with each

higher order motive usually lying dormant until lower levels are satisfied. Of course there are exceptions to this generalization and ample evidence that individuals at the highest level can sublimate lower order motives, for example Gandhi and hunger strikes. That said the model does reflect that throughout history mankind has aspired to higher levels of satisfaction than prompted by purely temporal, physical and material needs. To a significant degree their success in doing so has been constrained by their productivity which, in turn, has depended upon organizational and technological development.

Socioeconomic evolution

To a large extent the ability of individuals to progress to the pinnacle of their personal need hierarchy is conditioned by social and economic factors. Social in terms of the way in which people organize their collective activity, and economic in terms of the success which they achieve in addressing the central economic problem of maximizing satisfaction through the utilization of scarce resources. A synoptic and eclectic review of economic history may help serve to establish the proposition that while some individuals have always been able to achieve the higher levels of the need hierarchy, it is only in recent times that a significant porportion of the total population have been able to aspire to the top two levels.

While physiological needs are intensely personal, groups are virtually an essential prerequisite for the achievement of safety and love needs! Once groups are established it becomes clear that collective action and social organization will lead to increased productivity and welfare; first through task specilization, and second through the divison of labour. The first is admirably exemplified by the medieval craft guilds and the second by Adam Smith's classic example of the pin making industry.

Smith noted that where men were engaged in all processes involved in the manufacture of pins their average output was twenty pins per day; when the manufacture of pins was broken down into separate processes output for the group rose to 4000 pins per man per day. Two points are of particular significance in this step forward. First, organization or 'management' is required to bring together the men, provide a place of work and supply raw materials. Second, the enormous increase in output reduces the price of the commodity, necessitates the development of channels of distribution to make the article available to those with a demand for it, and leads to a significant increase in consumer welfare.

However, the real potential of task specialization and the division of labour can only be realized when harnessed to technological innovation of a kind initiated by the scientific breakthroughs of the Renaissance and translated into commercial products by the craftsmen and artisans of the period. In turn, new materials, methods and machines greatly increase the scope for further discovery and so lend further impetus to the accelerating rate of change with which we are now so familiar. But, while the spirit of inquiry may have lent force to the enormous rate of economic development experienced in the past 200 years, there can be no doubt that the real catalyst was the existence of market opportunities, for it is these which transform speculative inventions into profitable innovations.

In turn, market opportunities reflected both the growth of population (itself a consequence of improved standards of living resulting from greater productivity) and the aspirations of individuals to move up their own personal need hierarchies. But, what happens if, for whatever reason, supply exceeds demand? Until comparatively recently such a question would have been viewed as hypothetical and probably absurd. Yet much of our recent economic (and managerial) history has been dominated by this issue as the perception of a levelling off of demand (growth) has lead to the strong reactions described earlier.

At the national level this possibility was experienced by a number of countries towards the end of the last century and is epitomized by Robert Reich's (1984) analysis and description of what he calls 'The era of management' as a response to this problem characterized as 'overproduction'.

> The explosion in productive capacity that marked the first decades of America's industrialisation soon outpaced the nation's ability to distribute, market, and consume all the new output. Firms had energetically built up capacity, despite the fact that their rivals were doing the same. As supply burgeoned, producers anxious to sell enough to recover the cost of their new factories turned to cut throat competi-

tion. Prices declined. The wholesale price index, which had stood at 193 in 1864, had dropped to 82 by 1890. A major depression jolted the economy in 1893, improverishing entire agricultural areas, closing thousands of banks, and throwing more than one-fourth of the unskilled urban labour force out of jobs.

Shades of the 1970s!

The immediate reaction in the USA was to follow the German example and form cartels. But, lacking the existence of a large public bureaucracy able to exercise control over cartels, as in Germany, American's viewed cartelization as illegitimate and passed the Sherman Anti-Trust legislation which prohibited them. Mergers and acquisition followed (shades of the 1980s) and, where they led to economies of scale, such as in US Steel, General Electric and Standard Oil, resulted in survival and then success.

However, the emergence of the mega-corporation exaggerated a problem which had already begun to be felt in the earlier stages of industrialization – the management of people. It was this which resulted in the twentieth century becoming 'the era of management' (Reich, 1984):

> Management emerged around 1920 as a philosophy, a science, and a pervasive metaphor which would dominate the way Americans viewed themselves and their institutions for the next fifty years. Management was America's own creation. No other industrialised nation so fully embraced it or experienced its spectacular capacity to generate new wealth. The paradigm of management served to dominate its time.
>
> Many of the problems that emerged in America before World War I – within its factories, among its enterprises, and in society at large – had been rooted in bottlenecks, inefficiencies, poor coordination, and inadequate controls. The managerial ideas and institutions that arose after the war solved many of these problems. They bore for America the fruits of high-volume, standardised production. The managed organisation replicated itself across the country – in business, government agencies, and labour unions – promising stability, order, and prosperity. For fifty years it faithfully delivered.

Reich's review of the era of management deserves careful consideration, particularly in terms of the three cardinal principles of scientific management – specialization through simplification, predetermined rules and the detailed monitoring of performance. Task specialization has already been referred to but its full potential was only realized with 'the birth of a new race of time and motion specialists. Of course once the job has been broken down in the minutest detail few, if any workers, had much conception of how their own contribution meshed with that of adjacent tasks, let alone the overall operation. To ensure the necessary coordination explicit rules and close supervision through a managerial hierarchy became essential. To ensure it was being exercised both efficiently and effectively management information was a necessity.

Managerial orientations

While Reich's concern is largely with the nature of the managerial task and its execution my own concern lies more with the underlying motivation or orientation of management. While facing the risk of gross over-simplification it seems to me that one can distinguish three or possibly four basic orientations which have dominated the organization of production and distribution.

The first and least apparent approach to management I have labelled 'collection' which is typical of the nomadic or traditional society eking out a survival existence. The limitations on such societies are painfully obvious to us all in the famines which have blighted Africa in recent years. To improve welfare and exercise a degree of control over the environment one needs a more sophisticated approach and this I have characterized as a 'production' orientation, which as we have seen, is made possible by task specialization, the division of labour and industrialization. Its zenith is represented by Taylor's scientific management and it is clearly the most appropriate response when demand exceeds supply. Under such conditions the nature of demand tends to be fairly self-evident and the ultimate objective of maximizing satisfaction is best realized by producing the 'mostest for the leastest'. But, consider again what happens if the capacity to produce exceeds the ability to consume?

As we have seen, such conditions developed in the USA (and elsewhere) towards the end of the last century and lead to recession. They also occurred in the 1920s and again in the 1970s. The immediate response to the recession of the 1890s was a reorga-

nization of production which both reduced direct competition of the kind which economists misguidedly term 'perfect' and enhanced the efficiency of those who survived the shake-out. In the 1920s (and the 1970s) similar responses are apparent, as is the emergence of a switch in emphasis from a production to a sales orientation. Under a sales orientation producers are still concerned to sell what they can make but under the pressures of competition they realize they must take an active rather than a passive interest in their potential customer and so invest considerable effort in seeking to secure their patronage. It is this pressure to encourage us to consume more which has attracted such adverse criticism of high pressure selling and 'the age of high mass consumption'.

Selling has and always will be an essential management function. It is not a sound basis for orientating a business in the long run because its essence is to *push* products at customers when the preferred status is to have customers *pull* products through channels of production and distribution. It was recognition of this which led to the emergence of the marketing concept and its attendant marketing orientation. Of course marketing is not new – every successful entrepreneur since time immemorial has been good at marketing even if he/she didn't know of its existence. The problem is that with increasing competition and stagnating demand success does not come as easily. Products are infinitely more complex, consumers are better educated and informed, and the production and consumption functions in society have become separated by elaborate channels of distribution. Clearly to succeed nowadays producers need to re-establish contact with their markets and take the trouble to find out what consumers really want – an orientation to the market rather than a preoccupation with the factory.

Coalescing trends

While potentially misleading to represent managerial orientations as a hierarchy like Maslow's it will help substantiate my point about coalescing trends if they are represented symbolically as in Figure 28.3. Similarly, it will be useful to represent the stages of economic and technological evolution touched on earlier in a similar fashion. In the case of the stages of economic growth we already possess

Rostow's well-known model reproduced in Figure 28.4, while the organizational cum technological stages of development might appear as in Figure 28.5.

Figure 28.3 *Managerial orientations*

If these models are combined as in Figure 28.6 we can see that the age of high mass consumption made possible by high technology, stimulated by selling and epitomized by esteem – keeping up with the Jones' – has arrived in the post Second World War era. Maslow tells us that the stage beyond esteem is self-actualization and I have argued that if consumers became more individualistic we shall need a marketing orientation. But what about the stages of economic growth – 'beyond high mass consumption' like 'post industrial society' is not a particularly helpful descriptor.

Rostow himself recognized this and in a revision of his model labelled the 'pinnacle' – 'the search for quality' and it is this which provides the theme of this chapter.

But we still have one space unfilled. What comes after 'high technology'? In fact it is not so much what comes after high technology for all the indications are that it will continue to evolve. As Alvin Toffler has pointed out it is the progress of high technology which has brought us to the stage where self-actualization, customization and quality are all within our grasp.

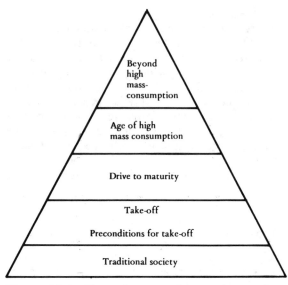

Figure 28.4 *Rostow's stages of economic growth*

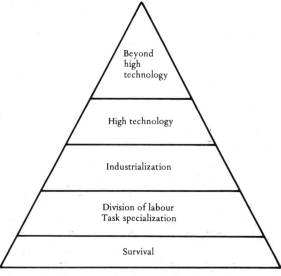

Figure 28.5 *Organizational/technological stages of development*

Take mass production. Nothing was more characteristic of the industrial era. Yet we're already moving from a mass production, mass consumption economy to what I've called a 'de-massified' economy.

In traditional mass manufacturing, factories pour out a stream of identical objects, by the million. In

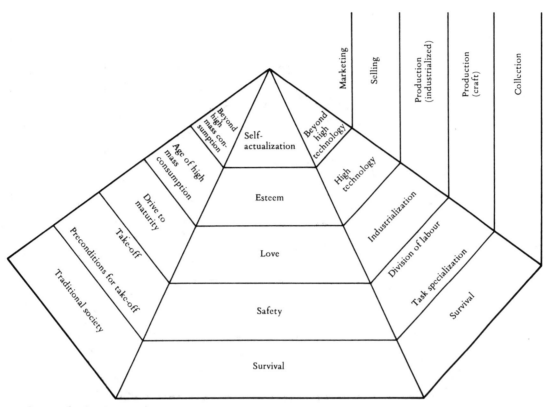

Figure 28.6 *Coalescing trends 1*

the Third Wave sector, mass production is replaced by its opposite: de-massified production – short runs, even customized, one-by-one production, based on computers and numerical controls. Even where we turn out millions of identical components, they are frequently configured into more and more customized end products.

The significance of this can't be overestimated. It's not simply that products are now more varied. The processes of production are themselves transformed. The smokestack – that symbol of the industrial assembly-line society – is becoming a relic.

We still think of ourselves as a mass production society, yet in the advanced sectors of the economy, mass production is already an outmoded technique. And the idea that we can keep our old mass manufacturing industries competitive indefinitely is based on ignorance of what is actually happening on the factory floor.

The new techniques make diversity as cheap as uniformity. In fact, in many industries, it's customize or die. This is exactly the opposite of what was required in the Second Wave economy.

In fact, it is almost a dialectical return to pre-industrial, one-of-a-kind production, but now on a high technology basis.

And exactly the same trends are visible in the distribution system, too, where we see more and more market segmentation, direct mail targeting, speciality stores, and even individualized delivery systems based on home computers and teleshopping. People are increasingly diverse, and, as a result, the mass market is breaking into small, continually changing sectors.

The real challenge is whether we will be able to respond to the opportunity which burgeoning technology offers to us. This is the question addressed by Reich (1984) in which he proposes that the next step in our socioeconomic and political evolution has to be 'the era of human capital'.

As Citizens we must transcend the old categories of civic culture and business culture and recognize the relationship between the nation's social and economic development. Americans concerned with so-

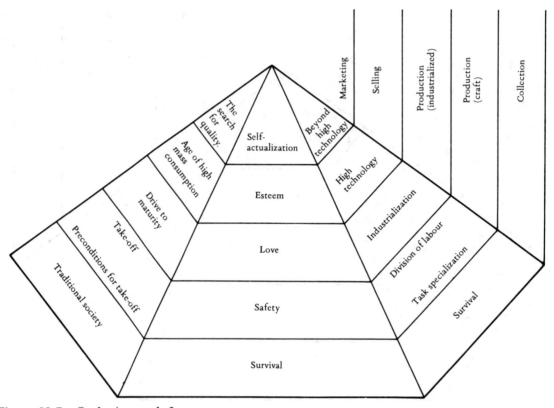

Figure 28.7 *Coalescing trends 2*

cial justice must become familiar with the subtleties of American business and recognise the importance of profit seeking and investment in economic growth. American businessmen must accept that claims for participation and fairness are not obstacles to their mission, but ultimately its very substance.

For American read 'World'.

If we are to break through the constraints which appear to inhibit our progress we must see quality as our aspiration. In pursuit of quality we must recognize that it is the needs of the individual which are paramount. It is entirely fitting, therefore, that as marketers with a primary concern for the consumer we can move into the era of human capital and complete the model by adding to it 'human resource development'.

References

Engel, J.F., Blackwell, R.D. and Miniard, P.W., *Consumer Behaviour*, 5th ed., Dryden, 1986.

Maslow, Abraham, *Motivation and Personality*, Harper & Row, 1954.

Reich, Robert, *The Next American Frontier*, Penguin, 1984.

A version of this chapter was given as M.J. Baker's (Chairman) keynote address to the 1986 Annual Conference of the European Foundation for management Development held in Florence.

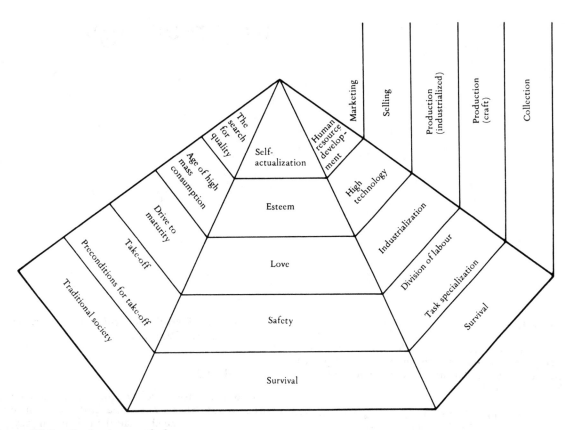

Figure 28.8   *Coalescing trends 3*

Key readings

Chapter 1

These references represent a cross section of articles tracing the development of the marketing concept up to present day state-of-the art. They are therefore listed in chronological order.

McKitterick, John B., 'What is the Marketing Management Concept?' The Frontiers of Marketing Thought and Action, US Marketing Association, 1957, pp. 71–82.

Keith, Robert J., 'The Marketing Revolution', *Journal of Marketing*, January, 1960, pp. 35–8.

Levitt, Theodore, 'Marketing Myopia', *Harvard Business Review*, July-August 1960, pp. 45–56.

Ames, Charles, 'Trappings versus substance in industrial marketing', *Harvard Business Review*, July-August 1970, pp. 93–103.

Kotler, P. and Zaltman, G. 'Social marketing, an approach to planned social change', *Journal of Marketing*, July 1971, pp. 3–12.

Bell, M.L. and Emory, C.W. 'The faltering marketing concept', *Journal of Marketing*, October 1971, pp. 37–42.

Crosier, Keith, 'What exactly is marketing', *Quarterly Review of Marketing*, vol. 1, no. 2, Winter 1975, pp. 21–5.

Hunt, Shelby D., 'The nature and scope of marketing', *Journal of Marketing*, July 1976, pp. 17–28.

Arndt, Johan, 'How broad should the marketing concept be?' *Journal of Marketing*, January 1978, pp. 101–4.

King, Stephen, 'Has marketing failed or was it never really tried?' *Journal of Marketing Management*, vol. 1, no. 1, Summer 1985, pp. 1–19.

Chapter 2

For obvious reasons, most of the key readings are the major works that are referenced in the text. These fall into four groups: the classical; the military analogy; the oriental; and Porter.

Classical

Clausewitz, C. von, *On War*, Hodder and Stoughton, 1981.

Liddell-Hart, B. H., *Strategy*, Praeger, 1967.

Sun Tzu, *The Art of War*, Hodder and Stoughton, 1981.

To appreciate these the reader needs the mental agility to transfer ideas from military strategy to business. Not easy, but it is the sort of forced fit that can provide creative insights. Like most of the oriental classics, Sun Tzu is brief and easy to read; Liddell-Hart is harder going but modern and thorough; in contrast, Clausewitz is heavy going. The books may not fit competitive strategy perfectly but they will be around and quoted long after the rest of the readings are forgotten.

Military analogy

The military analogies widely quote the classical texts but they only capture part of the story:

Ayal, I. and Zif, J., 'Competitive Market Choice

Strategies in Multinational Marketing', *Columbia Journal of World Business*, Fall 1978.

Kotler, P. and Singh, R., 'Marketing Warfare in the 1980's, *Journal of Business Strategy*, Fall 1980.

Oriental

The orientals are largely concerned with explaining how the Japanese have done it. They are quite different but all valuable to read. Ohmae is particularly interesting since it is written by a Japanese national working for McKinsey:

Ohmae, K. *The Art of Japanese Business*, McGraw-Hill, 1982.

Tsurumi, Y. *Multinational Management*, Ballinger, 1983.

Porter

The final books are the influential works by Porter:

Porter, M.E., *Competitive Strategy: Techniques for Analyzing Industries and Competitors*, Free Press, 1980.

Porter, M.E., *Competitive Advantage: Creating and Sustaining Superior Perfomance*, Free Press, 1985.

They take a managerial economics view of competition but are spoilt by their complete lack of evidence. Nevertheless, many of the conclusions are well founded and occur elsewhere in business literature. Of the two books, the latter one is the most readable although it does not have the scope of *Competitive Strategy*.

Chapter 3

Aaker, D. A., *Strategic Market Management*, Wiley, 1984.

A good advanced textbook on the various approaches to strategic marketing although it tends to overlap into issues which are more appropriately seen as pure business policy.

Boxer, P.J. and Wensley, R., 'The Need for Middle Out Development of Marketing Strategy', *Journal of Management Studies*, 23(2), March 1986, pp. 189–204.

A discussion of some of the problems and implications that arise because of the limitations of strategic analysis and the over-use of the marketing mix notion as a means of controlling and directing marketing activity.

Day, George S., *Strategic Market Planning: The Pursuit of Competitive Advantage*, West Publishing Co., 1984; and *Analysis for Strategic Market Decisions*, West Publishing Co., 1986.

Two excellent books that summarize most of the analytical techniques available within market strategy. The discussion on process and procedure of strategy development is also rather analysis inclined but generally well presented.

Day, George S., and Wensley, Robin, 'Marketing Theory with a Strategic Orientation', *Journal of Marketing*, 47, Fall 1983, pp. 79–89.

A rather theoretical article which attempts to summarize the developments in marketing theory and practice and the problems in relating these to emerging issues in strategic marketing.

Jacobson, Robert, and Aaker, David A., 'Is Market Share All That It's Cracked Up To Be', *Journal of Marketing*, vol. 49, no. 4, Fall 1985, pp. 11–22.

A good summary article on the nature of the debates so far on the issue of the significance of the 'market share effect'. Unfortunately the article is better as a summary than as the final item of research in the area because there are important limitations in the actual estimation model that they use.

Oliver, Gordon, 'Developing Marketing Strategy' *Marketing Today*, Prentice Hall, 1986, Chapter 9.

A sound basic introduction to the issues in marketing strategy which is well referenced and covers the main practical concerns.

Simmonds, Kenneth, 'Marketing as Innovation: The Eighth Paradigm', *Journal of Management Studies*, 23 (5), September 1986, pp. 479–500.

A broad review of the role of marketing within the enterprise, which covers a number of areas which are not strictly within marketing strategy. The article does, however, provide an excellent context in which to discuss the possible roles for marketing strategy.

Weitz, B. A., and Wensley, R., *Strategic Marketing: Planning, Implementation and Control*, Kent Publishing Co., 1984.

A resonably comprehensive selection of the key articles in the area of strategic marketing. There is an introduction to each section but the main part of the book is the readings themselves.

Wensley, Robin, 'Teaching Marketing Strategy: Pretentious or Practical', *The Quarterly Review of Marketing*, Autumn 1983, pp. 9–14.

An attempt to summarize the basic content of a course in marketing strategy and the role of the various forms of analysis in the formulation of strategy for the firm.

Chapter 4

Frost, P. J., Moore, L. F., Louis, M. R., Lundberg, C. C. and Martin, J., *Organizational Culture*, Sage, 1985.

A challenging series of essays on the general theme of organizational culture: what it is, how it is formed, whether it can be managed and the processes by which it is linked to the wider social context.

Galbraith, J. R. and Nathanson, D. A., *Strategy Implementation: The Role of Structure and Process*, West Publishing, 1978.

A resumé of recent work investigating links between strategy and structure. Excellent reviews of the differing perspectives.

Handy, C. B., *Understanding Organizations*, 3rd ed., Penguin, 1985.

A coherent introduction to the general field of organization theory with a particular slant towards managerial practice.

Strategy Alternatives for the British Motorcycle Industry, HMSO, 1975.

An excellent case study summarizing the reason for the decline of the UK motorcycle industry and a statement of possible future strategies for survival. The links between organizational structure and past and possible future strategies are implicit, however, rather than explicit. Nevertheless, the relationships are strong and are best brought out in Appendix 10 where the consequences of organizational failure are highlighted.

Kidder, T., *The Soul of a New Machine*, Penguin, 1981.

A work of 'faction' which highlights very well the kind of culture needed for innovative development work on a new product. Obviously based on reality the book makes excellent bedtime reading as long as one is in a learning mode at such a time!

Morgan, G., *Images of Organization*, Sage, 1986.

A refreshingly new approach to the study of organizations through the drawing of metaphors. Organizations are studied as machines, organisms, brains, cultures, political systems, prisons and instruments of domination.

Not a lot of marketing, but plenty of ideas for reflection when your organization starts to look ineffective.

Porter, M. E., *Competitive Advantage*, Free Press, 1985.

One of the seminal works on links between specific strategies for creating sustainable competitive advantage and the structural matters that need to be considered in order to bring it about.

Rogers, K., *Managers – Personality and Performance*, Tavistock, 1963.

Not a new book, but one of the best which looks at links between marketing performance and individual personality and company culture. Case-based, the work is a challenging and stimulating view from an organizational psychologist's perspective.

Ruebert, R. W., Walker, D. C. and Roering, K. J., 'The Organization of Marketing Activities: A contingency theory of structure and performance', *Journal of Marketing*, vol. 49, 1985, pp. 13–25.

A useful overview of organizational considerations and their impact upon the performance of marketing tasks. The article takes a contingency viewpoint and attempts a synthesis of the structural, systems and transactional approaches to studying marketing organizations.

Spillard, P., *Organization and Marketing*, Croom Helm, 1985.

A view of the practical and theoretical links between organizational structures and marketing performance. The book introduces concepts not covered in depth in the present chapter (the notion of organizational logic, for instance and the set of contingency factors that determine the shape of an organization) and treats the topics of conflict and integration from a marketing perspective.

Finally, two textbooks for those who want to study the whole area in more depth:

Khandwalla, P. N., *The Design of Organizations*, Harcourt Brace, 1977.

A compendium of thought and work in the area of organizational structure.

Thompson, J. D., *Organizations in Action*, McGraw-Hill, 1967.

Another seminal piece of work; a little 'heavy' but if the style can be forgiven a generator of much thought.

Chapter 5

Abell, D. F., *Defining the Business: the starting point for strategic planning*, Prentice Hall, 1980.

A useful book for widening the student's understanding of the nature of business.

Ansoff, I., *Corporate Strategy*, McGraw-Hill, 1965.

Probably the best book ever written on corporate planning. It will provide a wider contextual framework.

Day, G., 'Analytical Appproaches to Strategic Market Planning' in *Review of Marketing* (ed.), Enis B. and Roering, K., Chicago, A.M.A., 1981.

For students interested in a more quantitative approach to marketing planning.

Giles, W., 'Marketing Planning for Maximum Growth' *Marketing Intelligence and Planning*, vol. 3, no. 3, 1985.

This is a piece for very quick reading. It will provide quite a useful insight into the relationship between planning and growth.

Greenley, G. E., 'Marketing Plan Utilisation', *Quarterly Review of Marketing*, Summer 1985.

A really useful comparison between three independent studies into marketing planning practices. A must for serious students.

Greenley, G. E., *The Strategic and Operational Planning of Marketing*, McGraw Hill, 1986.

This book deals with the total marketing planning process in considerable detail. Very useful alongside McDonald's book.

Hopkins, D. S., 'The Marketing Plan', the Conference Board Report no. 801, 1981.

A useful set of examples of marketing planning in practice in the USA. It defines how certain companies do it.

McDonald, M. H. B., 'Theory and Practice of Marketing Planning for Industrial Goods in International Markets, Cranfield Institute of Technology PhD, 1982.

This is a very detailed study for serious students of marketing planning. It explains and summarizes research into the marketing planning practices of 200 UK industrial companies.

McDonald, M. H. B., *Marketing Plans: how to prepare them; how to use them*, Heinemann, 1984.

One of the UK's best selling textbooks which is used by many companies as the actual basis for the preparation of marketing plans.

Steiner, G. A., 'Formal Strategic Planning in the United States Today', *Long Range Planning*, 16 (3), 1983, pp. 12–17.

A review of the state of the art in strategic planning. It examines several schools of thought.

Chapter 6

Aguilar, F. J. *Scanning the Business Environment*, Macmillan, 1967.

Discusses the results of Aguilar's pioneering study of environmental scanning in American and European chemical companies. It has become established as a standard reference text on the subject and has withstood the passage of time.

Ansoff, H. I. *Implanting Strategic Management*, Prentice Hall, 1984, chapters 1, 2, 5.2, 5.3, 5.4.

A comprehensive treatment of the author's eclectic ideas on the subject of strategic management. The chapters on weak signal analysis and strategic issues management are particularly apposite.

Brownlie, D. T., Saren, M. A. 'A review of technology forecasting techniques and their application', *Management Bibliographies and Reviews*, vol. 9, 4, 1983.

An up-to-date review of the major forecasting methodologies as they find application in the context of technology forecasting.

Diffenbach, J., 'Corporate Environmental Analysis in large US Corporations', *Long Range Planning*, June 1983, pp. 107–16.

Addresses the questions of the usefulness, implementation and payoffs of organized environmental analysis. Identifies three phases in its evolution: appreciation, analysis and application.

Fahey, L., King, W. R. and Narayanan, V. K., 'Environmental Scanning and Forecasting in Strategic Planning – The State of the Art', *Long Range Planning*, February 1981, pp. 32–9.

Reports the results of an empirical study which revealed that environmental scanning was not a well established corporate activity and that it faced serious conceptual and organizational difficulties.

Godiwalla, Y.M., Meinhart, W. A. and Warde, W. D., 'Environmental Scanning – Does it help the Chief Executive?' *Long Range Planning*, October 1980, pp. 87–99.

Discusses an empirical study that concludes that if environmental scanning is to have any impact on company strategy, a close liaison is needed between the CEO and the operating managers facing change.

King, W. R. and Cleland, D. I. 'Environmental Information Systems for Strategic Marketing Planning', *Journal of Marketing*, October 1974, pp. 35–40.

Argues for a continuous approach to environmental scanning. Identifies six areas in which environmental information systems should operate: company image; customers; potential customers; regulatory bodies; intelligence; and competitors. Deals with the product-market domain.

Segev, E., 'How to use environmental analysis in strategy making', *Management Review*, March 1972, pp. 4–13.

Discusses the results of a longitudinal study of environmental analysis. Develops a model of how such analysis is best conducted in a formal and systematic manner.

Thomas, P.S., 'Environmental Scanning – The state of the Art', *Long Range Planning*, February 1980, pp. 20–8.

Reports what firms were doing in the way of environmental scanning. Found the trend towards increasingly sophisticated and systematic efforts. Disputed some of Fahey *et al.*'s findings.

Stubbart, C. 'Are Environmental Scanning Units Effective?' *Long Range Planning*, June 1982, pp. 139–45.

Updates and replicates the work of Fahey *et al.* and Thomas. Reports some discrepancies which were observed and criticizes the then prevailing normative work.

Chapter 7

Drayton, J. L., 'Consumer Behaviour', in M. J. Baker (ed.), *Marketing: Theory and Practice*, 2nd ed., Macmillan, 1983.

While among texts, provide a detailed, comprehensive view of the state of consumer research, many researchers require a more succinct, yet informed, treatment. Here it is.

Driver, J. C. and Foxall, G.R., *Advertising Policy and Practice*, Holt, Rinehart and Winston; St Martin's Press, 1984.

An interdisciplinary discussion of the policy aspects of advertising, including a critical analysis of the nature of consumer behaviour and its relevance to marketing communications.

Ehrenberg, A. S. C., *Repeat Buying: Theory and Applications*, North Holland, 1972.

A thorough exposition of the method and results of the analysis of market behaviour at the aggregate level and its managerial implications.

Ehrenberg, A. S. C. and Goodhardt, G. J. (with G. R. Foxall), *Understanding Buyer Behaviour*, John Wiley, 1988.

An account written specially for managers, researchers and students of the descriptive approach to the investigation of consumer choice, with applications to areas of managerial decision making such as new product development.

Engel, J. F., Blackwell, R. D. and Miniard, P. W., *Consumer Behavior*, 5th ed., Dryden Press, 1986.

This has become the standard text and provides a useful starting point for anyone who wishes to obtain an overview of thought and research. The book represents current trends well and is evaluative as well as descriptive of recent research.

Consumer Behaviour in Theory and in Practice. Special Issue of the *European Journal of Marketing*, vol. 20, no. 3/4, 1986.

Recent research on: behavioural aspects of consumer choice; attitudes and behaviour; learning models; personality and consumer behaviour; consumer innovativeness; consumer loyalty; and negative marketing communication.

Foxall, G. R., *Consumer Choice*, St Martin's Press, 1983.

A thorough and rigorous examination of the problem of attitude-behaviour consistency in marketing and its implications for the study of consumer behaviour.

Foxall, G. R., *Corporate Innovation: Marketing and Strategy*, Croom Helm; St Martin's Press, 1984.

Contains a critical review of the contribution of consumer research to understanding the process of innovation and new product development.

Foxall, G. R., *Consumer Behaviour*, Croom Helm, 1980.

An introductory text for students at all levels, including those preparing for professional examinations.

Wilkie, W. L., *Consumer Behaviour*, John Wiley, 1986.

This comparatively recent text also covers the spectrum of consumer research in the marketing context. It contains useful chapters on the various perspectives from which consumer behaviour is approached: including those of the marketer, the consumer, and the public policy-maker. There is also a considered discussion of situational and behavioural influences on consumer choice.

Chapter 8

Ames, B. C. and Hlavacek, J. D., *Managerial Marketing for Industrial Firms*, Random House, 1984.

Shows how modern marketing management concepts and methods can be applied in the realm of industrial marketing.

Chisnall, P. M. *Strategic Industrial Marketing*, Prentice-Hall International, 1985.

A clearly written and practical book by a respected British author. It provides a systematic discussion of the principal strategic factors in the marketing of industrial and organizational goods and services.

Hakansson, H. (ed.), *International Marketing & Purchasing of Industrial Goods: An Interaction Approach*, John Wiley, 1982.

The theoretical base of the interaction approach to industrial marketing is described in detail and then a series of international case studies are presented which shows the application potential of the theorectical model.

Hutt, M. D. and Speh, T.W., *Industrial Marketing Management*, (2nd ed.), Dryden Press, 1985.

Integrates the growing body of literature into an operational treatment of industrial marketing management.

La Placa, P. J. *Industrial Marketing Management: Cases and Readings*, Random House, 1984.

An excellent collection of major articles supplemented by a comprehensive selection of case studies. The material is, however, all American based.

McDonald, M., *European Insights in Industrial Marketing*, MCB Publications, 1979.

Another collection of interesting articles but in this case mainly from Western Europe.

Parkinson, S.T. and Baker, M.J., *Organizational Buying Behaviour*, Macmillan, 1986.

A concise and readable text which uses European case material to develop and enhance the theoretical material.

Robinson, P. J., Faris, C. W. and Wind, Y., *Industrial Buying and Creative Marketing*, Allyn & Bacon, 1967.

Still worth reading as one of the early 'classics' in the field of industrial marketing.

Turnbull, P. W. and Valla, J. P. (eds.), *Strategies for International Industrial Marketing*, 1986.

From the same group of authors as Hakansson this book provides interesting and unusual insights into industrial marketing strategies.

Webster, F. E. and Wind, Y., *Organizational Buying Behaviour*, Prentice-Hall, 1972.

One of the milestones in published texts on organizational buying behaviour.

Chapter 9

Alt, M. and Brighton, M., Analysing data: or telling stories? *Journal of the Market Research Society*, vol. 23, no. 4, October 1981, pp. 209–19.

This paper examines the question of what constitutes good evidence in survey research.

Anderson, R. J., Hughes, J. A. and Sharrock, W. W., *Philosophy and the Human Sciences*, Croom-Helm, 1986.

A good overview of the major philosophical arguments that underpin the debate on the utility of quantitative and qualitative research methods.

Andreason, A. R., 'Backward market research', *Harvard Business Review*, May–June 1985, pp. 176–86.

Andreason advocates the best way to design usable research is to start where the process usually ends and then work backwards.

Boyd, Jr, H. W. Westfall, R. and Stasch, S. F., *Marketing Research: Text and Cases*, 7th ed, Irwin, 1989.

First published in 1956. A text from the USA, weak on qualitative research but clearly puts research into a managerial context and describes the process and techniques of market research well.

Bradley, U. (ed.) *Applied Marketing and Social Research*, 2nd ed, Wiley, 1987.

A series of cases of marketing and research problems with good explanations of how research was planned and executed to help solve the set problems.

Deshpande, R., 'The organizational context of market research use'. *Journal of Marketing*, vol. 46, Fall 1982, pp. 91–101.

A study that examines the types of organization in which research is more likely to be used.

Goldman, A. E. and McDonald, S. S., *The Group Depth Interview: Principles and Practice*, Prentice Hall, 1987.

A book that covers the practical problems of planning, conducting, analysing and reporting depth interviews and group interviews.

Greenhalgh, C., 'How should we initiate effective research?', *Annual Conference of the Market Research Society*, 1983.

A good guide to the structure and presentation of a formal market research brief.

Krum, J. R., Rau, P. A. and Keiser, S. K., 'The marketing research process: role perceptions of researchers and users', *Journal of Advertising Research*, December 1987/January 1988, pp. 9–21.

The results of an interesting study of how researchers and users perceive the role of marketing research at each step in the marketing research process.

Worcester, R. and Downham, J. (eds.) *Consumer Market Research Handbook*, 3rd ed., McGraw-Hill, 1986.

A text written by practitioners in the UK with detailed descriptions of the techniques of market research and the uses of consumer market research.

Chapter 10

Green, P. E. and Tull, D. S., *Research for Marketing Decisions*, 4th ed., Prentice-Hall International, 1978.

A classical text offering a comprehensive survey of the quantitative methods and their marketing applications.

Jain, A., Pinson, C. and Ratchford, B., *Marketing Research: Applications and Problems*, John Wiley, 1982.

A text focusing on the applications of the various methods in marketing.

Quantitative Application in the Social Sciences, Sage University Papers, London 1986.

This is a series of sixty short booklets suitable for students of marketing interested in a thorough and methodological understanding of the various quantitative methods, and their application.

Chapter 11

Readings in the area of information technology tend to be very diverse, encompassing writings on computing, telecommunications, office automation, information systems, expert systems, etc. The following are key articles which relate specifically to the area covered by the chapter. A broader view of the impact of information technology on marketing management can be found in my book: *Marketing Management and Information Technology*, Prentice Hall, 1990.

Articles

Porter, M. and Miller, V., 'How information gives you competitive advantage', *Harvard Business Review*, July/August 1985, pp. 149–60.

Porter's ideas on the value chain are explained and the ways in which information technology permeates the value chain discussed. Excellent paper.

Parsons, G. L., 'Information Technology: A competitive weapon', *Sloan Management Review*, vol. 25, no. 1, 1983, pp. 3–14.

Porter's overall framework is used to consider the impact of IT at industry and firm level, and the effect of IT on a firm's potential strategic responses. As such it gives a good framework for reviewing the more general impact of IT.

Wiseman, C. and MacMillan, I., 'Creating a competitive weapon from information systems', *Journal of Business Strategy*, vol. 5, no. 2, 1984, pp. 42–9.

The authors use the differentiation, cost, innovation framework to analyse the competitive advantage possible from using information strategically. Suppliers, customers and competitors are considered as strategic targets, forming a matrix with differentiation, cost and innovation. The authors suggest a sequence of structured questions which they call an option generator.

McFarlan, F. W., 'Information technology changes the way you compete', *Harvard Business Review*, May/June 1984, no. 3, pp. 98–193.

The article builds upon Porter's ideas and discusses how information systems can be used to build barriers to entry, increase switching costs, or change the nature of competition and balance of power.

Moriarty, R. T., and Swartz, G. S., 'Automation to boost sales and marketing', *Harvard Business Review*, January/February 1989, pp. 100–109.

Looks at how marketing and sales productivity can be increased by the use of IT, particularly sales productivity through direct marketing techniques harnessed to IT.

Chapter 12

Information technology and management

Peltu, M., *The Electronic Office*, Ariel Books, BBC, 1984.

A readable account of how developments in information technology will affect the office environment of the future. Useful for those readers planning office systems in the sales and marketing area.

Zorkoczy, P., *Information Technology: An Introduction*, Pitman, 1985.

An introduction to broader aspects of information technology and their impact on the organization.

The computer and marketing

Derrick, J. and Oppenheim, (eds), '*What to Buy for Business*' What to Buy Ltd.

Provides a regular update on rapidly changing technologies in computer applications and software. Useful as a source to monitor developments. Also regularly includes reviews of specific topics. Useful as a briefing source.

Foster, A., and Smith, G. (eds), *On-line Business Source Book*, Headline Press, 1987.

Provides a regularly updated guide to on-line data bases, reveiwing new data bases as they appear. Contains de-tailed information on costs of accessing each data base, and contacts.

Parkinson, L. K., and Parkinson, S. T., *Using the Microcomputer in Marketing*, McGraw-Hill, 1987.

Shows how the computer can be applied to a wide range of different marketing tasks. Contains examples of commercial software written for marketing applications, and applications developed on standard software packages which the reader can produce on a microcomputer.

Chapter 13

Information systems and competitive advantage

King W. R., 'Developing strategic business advantage from informational technology', in N. Piercy (ed.), *Management Information Systems: The Technology Challenge*, Croom Helm, 1986.

Porter, M. E. and Millar, V. E., 'How information gives you competitive advantage', *Harvard Business Review*, July–August 1985, pp. 149–60.

These readings provide insight into how developing information systems is about changing competitive stances, not simply internal systems.

The marketing information system

Piercy, N. and Evans, M. *Managing Marketing Information*, Croom Helm, 1983.

This is a treatment of the development process involved in developing a marketing information system, and extends the summary of that process provided in this chapter.

The components of the marketing information system

Barrett, T. F., 'Issues in the design of marketing accounting systems', in N. Piercy (ed.) *Management Information Systems: The Technology Challenge*, Croom Helm, 1986.

Crimp, M., *The Marketing Research Process*, 2nd ed., Prentice-Hall International, 1986.

Martell, D., 'Marketing information and new technology', in N. Piercy (ed.) *Management Information Systems: The Technology Challenge*, Croom Helm, 1986.

de Vasconcellos Filho, P., 'Environmental analysis for strategic planning, *Managerial Planning*, January February 1985, pp. 23–30.

These readings give coverage of the current issues and techniques related to the major components of the MIS, with the exception of model-building and management science techniques which are considered elsewhere in the book.

Information strategy

Earl, M., 'Formulating information strategies' in N. Piercy (ed.), *Management Information Systems: The Technology Challenge*, Croom Helm, 1986.
Keen, P. G. W. and Morton, M. S. S., *Decision Support Systems: An Organizational Perspective*, Addison-Wesley, 1978.

Keen and Morton give one of the best-informed analyses of the need to develop a strategy for decision support systems development, which is rooted in the organization's functioning, while Earl provides an up-to-date perspective on the impact of new technology on strategic thought in developing information systems.

Information and organization

Piercy, N., *Marketing Organisation: An Analysis of Information Processing, Power and Politics*, Allen & Unwin, 1985.

This book provides a link between informational and organizational issues in marketing by focusing on information processing as a key to organizational design, and through making a case for both information and organizational strategies in marketing.

Chapter 14

Abell, D. F., 'Strategic Windows', *Journal of Marketing*, April, 1978.
Kotler, P., Fahey, L. and Jatuscripitak, S., *The New Competition*, Prentice-Hall, 1985.
Levitt, T., 'The Globalization of markets', *Harvard Business Review*, June, 1983.
Tull, D. S. and Hawkins, D. T., *Marketing Research*, Macmillan, 1980.

These references discuss the changing environment of marketing today, how to analyse it and its effects on marketing mix decisions.

Kotler, P., *Marketing Management*, Prentice-Hall, 1984.
Bonoma, T. V., *Marketing Management*, Macmillan, 1984.

These are two excellent textbooks which deal very comprehensively with marketing mix decisions.

Lilien, G. L. and Kotler, P., *Marketing Decision Making: A Model-Building Approach*, Harper & Row, 1983.

This book provides a full treatment of the modelling approach to marketing.

Drucker, P. F., *Management*, Pan, 1973.
Handy, C. B., *Understanding Organizations*, Pelican, 1985.
Kantner, R. M., *The Change Masters*, Unwin, 1985.

These books focus on the broader issue of how to change organizations in order to make them more decisive and marketing orientated.

Chapter 15

Bonoma, Thomas, V., *The Marketing Edge: Making Strategies Work*, The Free Press, Macmillan, 1985.

A new and very insightful book by the latest marketing star in the Harvard Business School firmament. Very strong emphasis on execution, showing how to implement strategy.

Baker, Michael, J., *Market Development*, Penguin, 1983.

A stimulating, case-orientated book, showing how to enter and successfully exploit market opportunities.

Baker, Michael, J., *Market Strategy and Management*, Macmillan, 1985.

This should become the standard British textbook. I commend its treatment of market segmentation, marketing planning, and product policy and management.

Hisrich, R. D. and Peters, M. P. *Marketing Decisions for New and Mature Products: Planning Development and Control*, Charles Merrill 1984.

A recent and comprehensive American textbook which is particularly strong on new product development.

Kraushar, Peter, *Practical Business Development*, Holt, Rinehart & Winston, 1986.

Written by a very successful practitioner in the new product development field.

Midgley, David F., *Innovation and New Product Development*, 2nd ed., Croom Helm, 1986.

A lively and original contribution to the new product development literature.

O'Shaughnessy, John, *Competitive Marketing: A strategic approach*, Allen & Unwin, 1984.

Quite the best American textbook, written by an Englishman who is a professor in the Graduate Business School at Columbia University.

Pessemier, Edgar, A., *Product Management: Strategy and Organization*, John Wiley, 1977.

Somewhat dated but still an excellent book.

Porter, M. E., *Competitive Strategy: Techniques for analysing industries and competitors* The Free Press, 1980.

A book that has changed the way many have been thinking about marketing management, the nature of the competitive environment, and the management of product policy.

Wind, Yoram, T., *Product Policy: Concepts, Methods and Strategies*, Addison-Wesley, 1982.

An excellent textbook covering all aspects of product policy by an outstanding American marketing scholar.

Chapter 16

The following readings represent a cross-section of relatively recent theoretical and empirical contributions relating to the pricing of consumer and industrial products as well as services.

Christopher, M., 'Value-in-Use Pricing', *European Journal of Marketing*, vol. 16, no. 5, 1982, pp. 35–47.
Foxall, G. R., 'The Logic of Price Decision-Making', *Management Decision*, vol. 18, no. 5, 1980, pp. 235–45.
Gabor, A., *Pricing Principles and Practices*, Heinemann, 1977.
Monroe, K. B., *Pricing: Making Profitable Decisions*, McGraw-Hill, 1978.
Winkler, J., *Pricing for Results*, Heinemann, 1983.

Pricing of industrial products

Barback, R.H., 'The pricing of Industrial Products', *European Journal of Marketing*, vol. 13, no. 4, 1979, pp. 160–7.
Jain, S. C. and Laric, M. V., 'A Framework for Strategic Industrial Pricing', *Industrial Marketing Management*, vol. 8, January 1979, pp. 75–81.
Laric, M. V., 'Pricing Strategies in Industrial Markets', *European Journal of Marketing*, vol. 14, no. 5/6, 1980, pp. 303–21.

Pricing of services

Goetz, J. G., 'The Pricing Decision in Service Industries', *Journal of Small Business Management*, vol. 23, April 1985, pp. 61–8.
Schissel, A., 'Pricing in a Service Industry', *MSU Business Topics*, vol. 25, Spring 1977, pp. 37–48.

Chapter 17

Lidstone, J. B. J., *Negotiating Profitable Sales*, Gower, 1977.
Lidstone, J. B. J., *Training Salesmen on the Job*, 2nd ed., Gower, 1986.
Lidstone, J. B. J. and Kirkby, P. B., *The Sales Presentation*, Gower, 1985.
Melkman, A. V., *How to Handle Major Customers Profitably*, Gower, 1979.
McMurry, Robert, N., 'The Mystique of Super-Salesmanship', *Harvard Business Review*, March-April 1961.
Shapiro, Benson, P. and Posner, Ronald S., 'Making the Major Sale', *Harvard Business Review*, March-April 1976, pp. 68–78.
Thompson, J. W., and Evans, W. W., 'Behavioural Approach to Industrial Selling', *Harvard Business Review*, March-April, 1969.
Wilson, M. T., *Managing a Sales Force*, 2nd ed., Gower, 1983.
Wittreich, J. Warren, 'How to Buy/Sell Professional Services', *Harvard Business Review*, March-April 1966, pp. 127–38.
Young, James, R. and Mondy, Robert W., *Personal Selling, Function, Theory*, The Dryden Press, 1978.

Chapter 18

Levitt, T., *The Marketing Imagination*, Collier Macmillan, 1988.

A brilliant collection of essays around the theme of branding. Includes Levitt's famous 1983 *Harvard Business Review* article 'The globalisation of markets'.

Porter, M. E., *Competitive Advantage: Creating and Sustaining Superior Performance*, Free Press, 1985.

A fundamental look at how differential advantages are built by companies and brands.

Engel, J. F., Blackwell, R. D., and Miniard, P. W., *Consumer Behaviour*, Holt, Rinehart and Winston, 1986.

This is an excellent review of the theory of how consumers make choices, which is crucial background for
understanding how brands succeed.

Quelch, J. A., Buzzell, R. D., and Salama, E. R., *The
Marketing Challenge of 1992*, Addison-Wesley, 1990.

A timely book on branding and marketing issues in the
changing European and global marketplace.

Chapter 19

Aaker, D. A., and Myers, J. G., *Advertising Management*,
2nd ed., Englewood Cliffs, Prentice-Hall, 1982.

An American text, so British readers should beware that
conditions and practice in the US are different in certain
key respects, despite general close similarities. Otherwise, well organized and focuses on the management of
the advertising function.

Broadbent, S., *Twenty Advertising Case Histories*, Holt,
Rinehart & Winston, 1984.

These case histories of British advertising campaigns are
chosen by the editor, a highly regarded practitioner with
strong academic credentials, from among the best papers
submitted for the Institute of Practitioners in Advertising's Advertising Effectiveness Awards competitions in
1980 and 1982. Invaluable to anyone who agrees that we
can learn from the experience of others.

Broadbent. S., and Jacobs, B., *Spending Advertising
Money*, Business Books, 1984.

Emphatically the best and most complete text dealing
with the cost-effective selection of advertising media, by
the editor of *Twenty Advertising Case Histories* and the
Media Director of the multinational Leo Burnett advertising agency in London.

Dyer, G., *Advertising as Communication*, Methuen, 1982.

A slim paperback which tackles the normally much over-
simplified question of how advertisements 'work' in a
thoroughly readable way, clearly explaining such advanced theoretical frames of reference as semiotics and
content analysis, especially in chapters 4 to 8.

Gable, J., *The Tuppenny Punch and Judy Show: 25 Years
of TV Commercials*, Michael Joseph, 1980.

Authoritative and absorbing review of the first quarter
century of the ITV network in Britain, with plenty of
background material in addition to the commercials
promised by the title.

Nevett, T. R., *Advertising in Britain: A History*, Heinemann, 1982.

Sponsored by the History of Advertising Trust. Though
sometimes heavy going, this 225-page textbook meticu-
lously explains the antecedents of present-day idiosyncracies of the advertising business and sets its development
in the broader context of social and economic history.

Ogilvy, D., *Ogilvy on Advertising*, Pan Books, 1983.

Occasionally dogmatic, smug, glib, and irritating but
always stimulating. Written by one of the living legends
of advertising, a Scot who founded what is today the
second biggest advertising agency in the world and wrote
immortal advertisements for Rolls Royce cars and Hath-
away shirts. Unusually for an advertising textbook, includes a strong advocacy of direct mail.

Spillard, P., *Sales Promotion: Its Place in Marketing
Strategy*, 2nd ed., Business Books, 1975.

Out of print but still available from libraries, this is the
only British textbook dealing exclusively with sales
promotion, on which advertisers actually spend more per
year than on advertising. By the Head of the Lancaster
University Department of Marketing.

White, R., *Advertising: What is it and how to do it*, McGraw-
Hill, 1980.

Authoritative and vigorous text directed at inexperienced
practitioners and managers from other disciplines who
need to work productively with advertising people, by an
experienced practitioner. Strong on examples but comparatively weak on detail. Not structured as a conventional textbook and consequently very readable.

Wilmshurst, J., *The Fundamentals of Advertising*, Heinemann, 1985.

Most recent of the standard British student textbooks,
endorsed by the Institute of Marketing. Full coverage,
though unavoidably short on detail in only 260 pages.
Organization of the chapters makes it an easy reference
book for basic explanations of most aspects of advertising
practice, as the title suggests.

Chapter 20

Ballou, R. H., *Business Logistics Management*, Prentice-
Hall 1985.
Christopher, M. G., *The Strategy of Distribution Manage-
ment*, Heinemann, 1986.
Lambert, D. M., and Stock, J. R., *Strategic Logistics Man-
agement*, Irwin, 1987.

Schary, P. B., *Logistics Decisions: Text and Cases*, Dryden Press, 1984.

Shapiro, R. D. and Heskett, J. L., *Logistics Strategy – Cases and Concepts*, West Publishing Company, 1985.

Stern, L.W. and El-Ansary, A., *Marketing Channels*, Prentice-Hall, 1982

These books between them will provide the fullest possible coverage of the interface between marketing and distribution. In particular they focus on the role played by logistics management in achieving marketing success.

Chapter 21

Strategic planning and control tools

Brownlie, Douglas, in *Marketing: Theory and Practice*, 2nd ed., edited by M. J. Baker, Macmillan, 1983, Chapter 11.

General area of planning control

Wilson, R. M. S., *Management controls and Marketing Planning*, Heinemann, 1979.

Bureau, J. R., *Brand Management: Planning and Control*, Macmillan, 1981.

Financial management and control

Eiler, Robert G., Goletz, Walter K., and Keegan, Daniel P., 'Is Your Cost Accounting Up To Date?' *Harvard Business Review*, July-August, 1982.

Sizer, John, *An Insight into Management Accounting*, 3rd ed Penguin, 1985, particularly the chapters on Budgetary planning control systems and 'Accounting information for marketing managers.'

Wilson, R. M. S. 'Financial Control of the Marketing Function' in N. Hart (ed.), *The Marketing of Industrial Products*, McGraw-Hill, 1984, Chapter 12.

Marketing research control systems

Crimp, Margaret, 'Evaluating Performance and Prediction', *The Marketing Research Process*, 2nd ed., Prentice-Hall, 1985.

Takeuchi, Hirotaka, and Quelch, John A., 'Quality is more than making a good product' *Harvard Business Review*, July-August, 1983.

New product development

Quinn, James Brian, 'Managing innovation: Controlled Chaos', *Harvard Business Review*, May-June 1985.

Advertising control and monitoring

Jones, John Philip, *What's In A Name?*, Gower 1986, chapters 10, 11, and 12.

Chapter 22

Chisnall, Peter M., *Strategic Industrial Marketing*, Prentice-Hall, 1985.

Widely adopted British text which systematically and clearly discusses the principal strategic factors affecting the marketing of industrial and organizational goods and services.

Chisnall, Peter M., *Marketing: a Behavioural Analysis*, 2nd ed., McGraw-Hill, 1985.

First published in 1975, this award-winning book was the first British comprehensive text which described and analysed the many behavioural factors that influence the buying of goods and services. Chapter 10 of the second edition, published in 1985, relates to industrial markets.

Chisnall, Peter M., *Marketing Research*, 3rd ed. McGraw-Hill, 1986.

Third edition of this standard British text dealing with the principles and practices of marketing research; chapter 12 specifically covers industrial marketing research.

Hakansson, H. (ed.), *International Marketing and Purchasing of Industrial Goods: an Interaction Approach*, John Wiley, 1981.

Research-based text on industrial marketing and purchasing practices in five European countries which emphasizes the need to understand the nature of the relationships built up during business transactions. Buyers and sellers become interdependent and forge links which stabilise negotiating behaviour.

Hart, Norman A. (ed.), *The Marketing of Industrial Products*, 2nd ed., McGraw-Hill, 1984.

Very useful set of management readings covering salient aspects of industrial marketing.

Levitt, Theodore, *Marketing for Business Growth*, McGraw-Hill, 1974.

A senior Harvard Business School professor comments with wit and wisdom on marketing theory and practice.

Chapter 23

Atac, Osman A. 'International Experience – Theory and Global Strategy', *International Marketing Review*, vol. 3, no. 4, Winter 1986.

Bartlett, Christopher A. and Ghoshal, Sumantra, 'Tap Your Subsidiaries for Global Reach', *Harvard Business Review*, Vol. 64(6), November-December 1986.

Britt, S. H., 'Standardizing Marketing for the International Market', *Columbia Journal of World Business*, Winter 1974, pp. 39–45.

Cannon, T., 'Managing International and Export Marketing', *European Journal of Marketing*, 14 (1), 1980, pp. 34–49.

Cateora, Philip R., *International Marketing*, 5th ed., Irwin, 1983.

Green, Robert T., Cunningham, W. H. and Cunningham, I. C. M., 'The Effectiveness of Standardized Global Advertising', *Journal of Advertising*, 4, 3, Summer 1975, pp. 25–30.

Levitt, Theodore, 'The Globalization of Markets', *Harvard Business Review*, May–June 1983, pp. 92–102.

Majaro, Simon, 'Standardization for International Markets', *Marketing (United Kingdom)*, May 1977, pp. 19–24.

Majaro, Simon, *Marketing in Perspective*, Allen & Unwin, 1982.

Majaro, Simon, *International Marketing – A Strategic Approach to World Markets*, 4th ed., Allen & Unwin, 1986.

Terpstra, Vern, *The Cultural Environment of International Business*, South-Western, 1985.

de la Torre, Jose, 'Product Life Cycle as a Determinant of Global Marketing Strategies', *Atlanta Economic Review*, September–October 1977, pp. 9–14.

Chapter 24

ACECO, *Practical Guide to Countertrade*, Metal Bulletin Inc., 1985.

Branch, Alan E., *Elements of Export Marketing and Management*, Chapman and Hall, 1984.

Branch, Alan E., *Elements of Export Practice*, Chapman and Hall, 1985.

BOTB, *Industrial Marketing Researcher's Check List*, BOTB, 1979.

Business International Corporation, *Competitive Alliances – How to Succeed at Cross-Regional Collaboration*, 1987.

Business International Corporation, *Decision-Making in International Operations: 151 Checklists*, 1974.

Business International Corporation, *161 More Checklists*: Decision Making in International Operations, 1985.

Butler, Jack, *The Importer's Handbook*, Woodhead Faulkner Ltd/British Importer's Confederation, 1988.

Cannon, Tom and Willis, Mike, *How to Buy and Sell Overseas*, Business Books, 1986.

Cecchini, Paolo, *1992: the European Challenge; the benefits of a single market*, Gower Press, 1988.

Commission of the European Communities, *Europe 1992*, Whurr Publishers, 19xx.

Contractor, Farok J., Laronge, Peter, *Competitive Strategies in International Business*, Lexington Books, 1988.

Czinkota, M. R. and Ronkainen, I.A., *International Marketing*, Dryden Press, 1988.

Dahrendorf, Ralf, *et al.*, *Whose Europe? Competing visions for 1992*, Institute of Economic Affairs, 1989.

Daily Telegraph, How to Export, Daily Telegraph Business Enterprise Book, 1988.

Davies, Gary, *Managing Export Distribution*, Heinemann, 1984.

Douglas, Susan P., and Craig, C. Samuel, *International Marketing Research*, Prentice-Hall, 1983.

Department of Trade and Industry, *Joint Ventures in Eastern Europe*, HMSO, 1989.

Department of Trade and Industry, *The Single Market – the Facts*, 2nd edn, HMSO, 1988.

Dudley, James, W., *Exporting*, Pitman/Natwest Small Business Bookshelf, 1989.

Dudley, James W., *1992: Strategies for the Single Market*, Kogan Page, 1989.

Economist, The, *Surveys of Europe's Internal Market*, 1989.

Forsgren, Mats, *Managing the Internationalisation Process*, Routledge, 1989.

Galbraith, J. K., and Menshikov, S., *Capitalism, Communism and Coexistence*, Hamish Hamilton, 1988.

Hamilton, Geoffrey, *Red Multinationals or Red Herrings*, Frances Pinter, 1984.

Hearn, Patrick, *International Business Agreements*, Gower, 1987.

Hibbert, E. P., *Marketing Strategy in International Business*, McGraw-Hill, 1989.

Jain, Subhash, *International Marketing Management*, 3rd edn, PWS-Kent Publishing Group, 1990.

Keegan, Warren J., *Global Marketing Management*, 4th edn, Prentice-Hall, 1989.

Keynote Guides, *1992: The Single European Market*, Hampton, 1989.

Kinsey, Joanna, *Marketing in Developing Countries*, Macmillan, 1988.

Lindsay, Margie, *International Business in Gorbachev's Soviet Union*, Pinter Publishers, 1989.

Liston, David, Reeves, Nigel, *The Invisible Economy – A Profile of Britain's Invisible Exports*, Pitman/Institute of Export, 1988.

Moutinho, Luiz, *Cases in Marketing Management*, Addison-Wesley, 1989.

NEDO, *International Marketing Performance – UK Process Plant Industry*, Millbank, 1986.

Paliwoda, S. J., *International Marketing*, Heinemann, 1986.

Paliwoda, S. J., 'Countertrade', in M. J. Thomas, *Marketing Handbook*, 3rd edn, Gower, 1989.

Paliwoda, S. J., *Advances in International Marketing*, Routledge, 1990.

Paliwoda, S. J., *New Perspectives in International Marketing*, Routledge, 1991.

  MNCs in Eastern Europe', *European Journal of Marketing*, vol. 18, no. 3, 1987, pp. 51–66.

Palmer, John, *Trading Places*, Radins Press/Century-Hutchinson, 1988.

Pelkmans, Jacques and Winters, Alan, *Europe's Domestic Market*, Royal Institute of International Affairs, Chatham House Paper 43, Routledge, 1988.

Porter, Michael E., *Competition in Global Industries*, Harvard Business School Press, 1986, pp. 3–6.

Quelch, John A., Buzzell, Robert D., *The Marketing Challenge of 1992*, Addison-Wesley, 1990.

Rijkens, Rein, Miracle, Gordon E., *European Regulation of Advertising*, North-Holland, 1986.

Rines, S. Melvin, Bogdanowicz, Christine A., *The Supranationals*, Euromoney Publications, 1986.

Root, Franklin, R., *Entry Strategies for International Markets*, Lexington Books, 1987.

Stapleton, John, *Elements of Export Marketing*, Woodhead Faulkner, 1984.

Turnbull, P. W. and Paliwoda, S. J., *Research in International Marketing*, Croom-Helm, 1986.

Turnbull, P. W. and Valla, J. P., *Strategies for International Industrial Marketing*, Croom-Helm, 1986.

Verzariu, Pompiliu, *Countertrade, Barter, Offsets – New Strategies for Profit in International Trade*, McGraw-Hill, 1985.

Walmsley, John, *The Development of International Markets*, Graham and Trotman, 1989.

West, A., *Marketing Overseas*, M & E Handbooks, 1987.

Whitehead, Geoffrey, *Elements of International Trade and Payments*, Woodhead Faulkner, 1983.

Chapter 25

Selecting a key reading list in the area of services marketing is difficult. It implies that there is a limited number of elite, influential readings that encapsulate the current status, breadth and depth of the subject.

In the first edition of *The Marketing Book* I selected ten articles which influenced some of my own thinking on the marketing of services. For this edition I have selected

key readings of a different kind which will allow the interested reader to explore the subject in more depth. The readings consist of books and conference papers. They are:

1   Marketing texts of services

Cowell, D. W., *The Marketing of Services*, Heinemann, 1984.

Johnson, E. M., Scheuing E. E. and Gaida, K. A., *Profitable Service Marketing*, Dow Jones-Irwin, 1986.

Lovelock C. H., *Services Marketing*, Prentice-Hall, 1984.

A book of text cases and readings.

2   More general books on managing service operations

Heskett, J. L., *Managing in the Service Economy*, Harvard Business School Press, 1986.

Lovelock, C. H., *Managing Services*, Prentice-Hall, 1988.

A book of readings and cases.

3   Conference papers

The American Marketing Association, Chicago, publishes the *Annual Services Marketing Conference Proceedings* which reflect something of the chiefly academic developments of the subject.

The Annual Marketing Education Group Conference in the UK and the Annual European Marketing Academy conference now have regular tracks on marketing services which reflect something of the development of the subject in the UK and Europe.

The above list ignore the work of some major contributors to the area. It also ignores works which deal with particular subsectors of the services area like leisure, transport and tourism. This is not, therefore, a comprehensive list but its contents do reflect the way in which the area has developed during the 1980s and some current concerns in service marketing for the 1990s.

Chapter 26

Birch, D.L., *The Job Generation Process*, MIT Press, 1979.

Bolton, J. Chr., *Small Firms*, HMSO. Cmnd 4811, 1971.

Cannon, T. *How to Win Profitable Business*, Business Books, 1984.

Drucker, P.F., 'Innovation and Entrepreneurship', Heinemann, 1984.

Hill, G.E., Barnaby, D. and Dufus, L. (eds), 'Marketing and Small Business Entrepreneurship; Conceptual Research and Directions', Washington D.C. International Council For Small Business.

Pinchot, G., *Intrapreneuring*, Harper & Row, 1985.

President's report to Congress' The State Of Small Business', US Government Printing Office, 1983, 1984, 1985, 1986.

Proceedings of UK Small Firms Policy and Research Conference published annual by Gower Publications.

Schumacher, E.F., *Small is Beautiful*, Harper & Row, 1973.

Vesper, K.H., *New Venture Strategies*, Prentice-Hall, 1980.

Chapter 27

Andreason, A. R., 'Marketing for Non-profit Organisations', *Harvard Business Review*, vol. 60, no. 3, May–June 1982, pp. 105–10.

Using anonymous examples this paper demonstrates how non-profit organizations which appear to be commercially orientated are in fact 'selling' rather than 'marketing'. It suggests some ways in which such organizations can re-orientate themselves.

Crozier, K. 'How Effective is the Contribution of Market Research to Social Marketing', *Journal of Market Research Society*, vol. 21, no. 1, January 1979, pp. 3–16.

Argues that the research input to most social marketing initiatives is less than optimum and also that too little research is undertaken during the review of policies which are implemented. Stresses the need, for social responsiveness as well as commercial effectiveness.

Foxall, G, 'Can the Public Sector Provision of Leisure Services be Customer-Orientated?', *The Services Industries Journal*, vol. 3, no. 3 November 1983, pp. 279–95.

This paper examines the applicability of marketing to areas other than those of commercial businesses. It reviews evidence that indicates that local authority leisure centres are far from customer-orientated in practice and suggests that, given their organizational structure, it is unlikely that they can be.

Kotler, P., *Marketing for Non-Profit Organisations*, 2nd ed., Prentice-Hall 1982.

The second edition is a major improvement on the first edition (1975) in a variety of ways. For example, the chapter on pricing no longer discusses 'profit maximization' (an oddity in a book on non-profit organizations!). However, it is a pity that the cases presented in the first edition are now omitted. In particular, Case 12 (pages 418–21) 'A Public Official Comments on Marketing' is a delightful illustration of the way in which many public officials think about marketing and the appropriateness of using it in their organizations.

McCorkey, D.D., 'Strategic Planning in Non-Profit Organisations', *Business Quarterly*, Summer 1981, pp. 24–33.

Suggests that there are differences between strategic and long-term planning which are important for non-profit organizations. Suggests a framework for helping to define the priority of the components of strategy and how such components should be handled.

Rodos, D. Z., *Marketing for Non-Profit Organisations*, Auburn House Publishing Co, 1981.

A useful book which has a differing style and emphasis than Kotler's. At its simplest the difference lies in its accepting more evidently that non-profit organizations often do not and sometimes cannot, accept values current in commercial organizations.

Yorke, D. A. (ed.), 'The Marketing of Local Authority Leisure Services', *European Journal of Marketing* (special ed.), vol. 18, no. 2, 1984.

This edition of the Journal contains fourteen papers which describe and explore the application of marketing to a range of local authority services including libraries, museums and leisure services. Some of the papers are purely descriptive of actual activity while others explore the concepts involved.

Index